Justice to Be Accorded to the Indians

Agent Peter Ronan Reports on the Flathead Indian Reservation, Montana, 1888 – 1893

Peter Ronan
1839 – 1893

Justice to Be Accorded to the Indians

Agent Peter Ronan Reports on the Flathead Indian Reservation, Montana, 1888 – 1893

Peter Ronan

edited by Robert J. Bigart

published by
Salish Kootenai College Press
Pablo, Montana

distributed by
University of Nebraska Press
Lincoln, Nebraska

Cover illustrations. *Top:* Chief Eneas. Archives and Special Collections, Mansfield Library, University of Montana, Missoula, Mont. (photograph number 81-284). *Bottom left:* Louison. Photograph by F. A. Rinehart, National Anthropological Archives, Smithsonian Institution, Washington, D.C., negative number 03545500. *Bottom right:* Flathead Indian Agent Peter Ronan. Montana Historical Society Photograph Archives, Helena, negative MMM900-004. *Back cover:* Ronan family and residence. Photograph by F. Jay Haynes, Flathead Indian Agency, Jocko, Montana, 1884. Montana Historical Society Photograph Archives, Helena, negative H-1271.

Frontpiece. Flathead Indian Agent Peter Ronan. Montana Historical Society Photograph Archives, Helena, negative MMM900-004.

Library of Congress Cataloging-in-Publication Data:
Ronan, Peter, 1839-1893.
Justice to be accorded to the Indians : agent Peter Ronan reports on the Flathead Indian Reservation, Montana, 1888-1893 / Peter Ronan ; edited by Robert J. Bigart.
p. cm.
Includes bibliographical references and index.
ISBN 978-1-934594-11-7
1. Salish Indians. 2. Kootenai Indians. 3. Flathead Indian Reservation (Mont.)--History--19th century--Sources. I. Bigart, Robert, editor. II. Title.
E99.S2R73 2014
978.6'82--dc23

2013051324

Distributed by University of Nebraska Press, 1111 Lincoln Mall, Lincoln, NE 68588-0630, order 1-800-755-1105, www.nebraskapress.unl.edu.

Editor's Dedication

Chuck and Eldena Hunter

with many thanks for their friendship and hospitality

Preface

This is the second volume of a two volume edition of Agent Peter Ronan's letters from the Flathead Indian Reservation in western Montana between 1877 and 1893. The first volume containing Ronan's 1877-1887 letters was published under the title: *"A Great Many of Us Have Good Farms."* The Flathead Reservation is the home to the Bitterroot Salish, Upper Pend d'Oreille, and Ksanka Kootenai Indian people.

The first volume has the full introduction, a biographical sketch of Peter Ronan, and a map. References to other Ronan letters give the dates under which those letters can be located in this collection. Some of the cross references to biographical information and other letters that appear in this volume refer to material in the first volume of the set.

The 1888 through 1893 time period on the Flathead Reservation was a critical time in reservation history as the tribes fought to protect their economic independence and to have control over the political decisions affecting them. The tribes were successful in developing their farming and ranching economy to the point that they were self-supporting despite the loss of the buffalo and other big game. The government gave temporary rations to some of the newly relocated bands such as the Bitterroot Salish, but most tribal members received only incidental help from the agency in exchange for hauling freight, providing firewood, or other labor. Tribal leaders worked hard to keep the peace with the aggressive white settlers just outside of the reservation boundaries. Trying to get justice from the white law officials and courts was also a challenge.

I have tried to limit the use of [sic] to places where the original document is particularly confusing. If I used it to describe every misspelled word in the originals, the published letters would be much harder to read.

Hopefully the reader will find these reports an interesting and informative trip into Flathead Indian Reservation history.

Sincerely,
Bob Bigart
Salish Kootenai College
Pablo, Montana

Special Thanks

Very special thanks are due two people who played critical roles in making these volumes possible:

Mary Frances Ronan, Reference Librarian, Natural Resources Division, National Archives, Washington, D.C.

Ms. Ronan [no relation to Peter Ronan] gave above and beyond the call of duty in tracking down the references I had compiled in the 1970s to locate Ronan letters in Record Group 75 or Records of the Commissioner of Indian Affairs. During the 1970s I did not have funds enough to make xerox copies of all the Ronan letters that were of interest, so I took notes and file information from many of the letters. To publish the letters, however, I needed to work from xerox copies to increase the accuracy of the transcriptions. Mary Frances patiently and graciously made it possible for me to order copies without having to travel to Washington, D.C. Thank you again for your personal interest and assistance that made this publication possible.

Bill Bennington, Salish Kootenai College, Pablo, Montana.

Carefully proofing the transcription of 800 single space pages of manuscript typed from xeroxes of original letters required two people. Bill kindly donated several hundred hours over several years to listen to me drone on reading the letters while checking the typed version. He helped find many typos and transcription errors which greatly improved the accuracy of the finished publication. Thank you again for your interest and invaluable help with the Ronan letters project.

Table of Contents

1888

January 2, 1888
LR 765/1888, enclosure in 2,379/888, RG 75, National Archives, Washington, D.C.

On February 24, 1888, the Commissioner instructed Ronan to send a more detailed report about the timber trespass by Kenneth Ross and to sell the cut timber for the best price possible.[1] Ronan replied on March 22, 1888. In his January 2, 1888, letter, Ronan claimed Chief Arlee attempted to sell the timber Ross had already cut, but Ronan stopped the sale. According to the second letter, Ross was willing to pay $1.25 per thousand board feet for the cut yellow pine logs. Ronan reported that Ross' offer was higher than the going price in Missoula County. On July 3, 1888, Ronan was given official permission to sell the down timber to Ross for the price offered, with the proceeds to go to the U.S. Treasury to be used for the benefit of the tribes.[2]

Kenneth F. Ross, of Nova Scotia, came to Missoula in 1883 and worked on various jobs in the western Montana lumber business of A. B. Hammond. Ross also helped erect the Marent trestle on the Northern Pacific Railroad at Evaro.[3]

> United States Indian Service,
> Flathead Agency,
> January 2, 1888.

Hon. Commissioner Indian Affairs
Washington, D.C.

Sir:

In the last week of December last, it was reported to me that a steam saw mill and a logging camp had been established near the southern boundary of the Flathead Reservation, by one Kenneth Ross. Upon investigation I found that the mill and the buildings for accommodation of loggers and workmen were located on the Reservation; and also that some three hundred thousand feet of logs had been cut on the reserve and were skidded and ready to haul to the mill to be sawed into lumber for the Anaconda mine. I ordered all work stopped and the mill and buildings moved off the Reservation at once. The reputed owner of the mill said he would act promptly in obeying my order although protesting his innocence of any intention to trespass upon the Indian Reservation, and that he was misled by wrong information in regard to the southern boundary line. Subsequently I learned that Arlee, the Chief of Flatheads appointed by Garfield, attempted to negotiate a sale of the logs already cut to the mill owner. This business I immediately put a stop to, informing Arlee that he nor any other Indian have no right to sell timber growing on the reservation. However, if I may be permitted to suggest, I would add that the logs cut will be of no use to any person except to the owner of said mill and if not disposed of will rot where they lay. He is willing to pay a fair price for them to the Indians, which would probably be of more practical benefit than to instigate a suit, especially as he acknowledges his error, obeys the order to move off and pleads ignorance as an excuse. I would be thankful for an early reply and orders in regard to this business.

> I am very respectfully
> Your obedient Servant,

Peter Ronan
United States Indian Agent.

January 22, 1888
LR 1,883/1888, telegram, RG 75, National Archives, Washington, D.C.

On January 25, 1888, Ronan received authority to make an open market purchase of up to $1400 for subsistence supplies for the Lower Kalispel Indians under Chief Michel who removed to the Flathead Reservation in 1887.[4] See Ronan's September 25, 1887, and August 7, 1888, letters.

Jan 22, 1888
Missoula Mont

Commr Indian Affairs
Washn, D.C.

Reply to letter fourteenth Inst Kalispels without subsistence unless taken from Reservation Indians there supplies Will fall short & suffering follow if this done an immediate open market purchase necessary to prevent suffering among Kalispels delay advertising & authority Will leave Kalispels With subsistence during Winter months.

Ronan Agt.

January 23, 1888
LR 2,877/1888, RG 75, National Archives, Washington, D.C.

This letter was marked "File," so the Commissioner did not authorize Ronan to give aid to the Bitterroot Salish families who were willing to removed to the Jocko Reservation in 1888. At about this same time Congress was considering a bill to allow the sale of the Salish allotments in the Bitterroot Valley. In 1889 the proposal resulted in General Henry B. Carrington's appointment to negotiate with Charlo and his band about removing to the Flathead Reservation.[5]

United States Indian Service,
Flathead Agency,
January 23d, 1888.

Hon. Commissioner Indian Affairs
Washington, D.C.

Sir:

Under promise made by me to Charlot's band of Bitter Root Indians, and approved of by the Indian Department, thirty-two families removed from that valley and have settled upon this reservation. The promises were as follows: To each head of family: 1st. A choice of 160 acres of unoccupied land on the Jocko reservation. 2d. Assistance in the erection of a substantial house. 3d. Assistance in fencing and breaking up of a field of at least ten acres. 4th. The following gifts: Two cows; a wagon and harness; a plow, with other necessary agricultural implements. Seed for the first year and provisions until the first crop was harvested. Relying upon the fulfilment [sic] of the promises above enumerated, seventeen families left all their belongings in the Bitter Root Valley and removed to this reservation. The promises were fulfilled to them and they are now comfortably located with fenced fields where they produced last year a good yield of grain and vegetables — in fact some of the families had a surplus for sale.

Fifteen additional families have since removed to this reservation relying upon the hope that they will be provided for by the government as were the original families who removed from the Bitter Root Valley. Other families still living in the Bitter Root Valley have signified their willingness to remove soon as I guarantee that the same privileges will be granted them as were extended to the first families who removed. As attention has so often been called to the advisability of removing Charlots band from the Bitter Root Valley to this reservation, and to settle this long-standing and vexed question, which at some time in the near future may lead to trouble among the white settlers and Indians of the Bitter Root Valley, I would respectfully recommend that a renewal of the promises cited be made to these Indians and that means be made available to fulfil [sic] such promises.

Trusting that I may soon be advised upon this matter, in order to make definite statements to the Indians of Charlot's band who often come to the Agency to enquire what the Government will do for them if they give up their lands in the Bitter Root Valley and remove to this reservation.

> I am very respectfully,
> Your obedient servant
> Peter Ronan
> United States Indian Agent.

March 15, 1888
LR 7,709/1888, RG 75, National Archives, Washington, D.C.

> The fourth judge for the Flathead Agency Court of Indian Offences was recommended by the Commissioner of Indian Affairs on May 18, 1888, but was denied by the First Assistant Secretary of the Interior on May 19, 1888.[6] But see Ronan's July 26, 1888, letter.
>
> Joseph Koo-too-lay-uch served as judge on the Flathead Reservation Indian court from 1888 until his death in 1894. Joseph was eulogized by then Flathead Agent Joseph T. Carter as "wise, just, and strict — almost Draconian."[7]

> United States Indian Service,
> Flathead Agency, M.T.
> March 15th, 1888.

The Hon. Commissioner of Indian Affairs,
Washington, D.C.
   Sir:
   As each judge of the court of Indian offences, in the district in which he lives, exercises a good influence over the well-being of the Indians of his neighborhood, I respectfully recommend that Joseph Ka-too-layuch be appointed as an additional judge to act with the other judges already commissioned for this reservation.

   The agricultural settlements of the Indians are widely separated, and as Joseph lives in a settled locality, remote from the other Judges, I recommend his appointment as beneficial to the service on this reservation.

> Very respectfully
> Your ob'd't serv't.
> Peter Ronan
> U.S. Indian Agent.

March 22, 1888
LR 8,268/1888, RG 75, National Archives, Washington, D.C.

See Ronan's January 2, 1888, letter and annotation for more information about this timber depredation on the southern boundary of the reservation.

> United States Indian Service,
> Flathead Agency, M.T.
> March 22d, 1888.

Hon. Commissioner Indian Affairs
Washington, D.C.

Sir:

Referring to your letter of the 24th ultimo L. 2379–1888, relative to timber depredations on the Flathead reservation, by one Kenneth Ross, and enclosing a letter from the Hon. Secretary of the Interior, dated January 22d, 1888, directing me to secure the best offer possible for the logs, and report it at your office, with a clear and full statement as to the location of the mill; the character of the timber, etc. I have the honor to report:

That I found the mill referred to located inside of the Southern boundary of the reservation thus described in the Stevens treaty: "Commencing at the source of the main branch of the Jocko River; thence along the divide separating the waters flowing into the Bitter Root River from those flowing into the Jocko etc." The mill was set up on a small tributary flowing into the Jocko and the logs referred to were cut on the water shed of the Jocko near the Southern limit of the reservation. As stated in my letter to you bearing date of January 2d, 1888, the reputed owner promised to remove his mill and buildings promptly, which he did; and the mill is now located some two miles from its former site on the reservation outside of the boundary of the same and on the water flowing into the Bitter Root River. The timber cut on the reservation is of Yellow pine, and would measure up some three hundred thousand feet of logs.

On the 21st of March, 1888, an Agent or owner of the mill proposed to pay one dollar and a quarter per thousand for the logs, and hawl [sic] them from where they are cut on the reservation to his mill. I have been informed, but cannot now state as a fact, that timber of the same description cut on the reserve is being bought by lumber men, in Missoula County, Montana from owners, at the rate of one dollar per thousand in the tree. The Indians are desirous to have the logs sold if the Hon. Commissioner is of opinion the price offered is sufficient. As before stated the logs will rot where they are, and the person responsible for the cutting disclaims all intention to trespass, and as before stated promptly removed his mill from the reservation when ordered.

> I have the honor to be
> Your obedient servant,
> Peter Ronan,
> United States Indian Agent.

April 17, 1888
LR 10,741/1888, RG 75, National Archives, Washington, D.C.

The 1887 murder of two white prospectors on Wolf Creek and the 1888 lynching of the Flathead Reservation Kootenai accused of the crime introduced a troubled period of Kootenai-white relations in the Upper Flathead Valley. Ralph Ramsdell was one of the leaders of the white vigilantes who lynched the suspected murderers.[8] In the face of the hostile provocations by Ramsdell and the white posse, Chief Eneas' restraint and adroit diplomacy in avoiding open hostilities was remarkable. Eneas obviously disapproved of the murder of the white miners, but he and Ronan objected to lynch justice. Ramsdell's racist version of the lynching and confrontation with Eneas was published in "Horrible Massacre," *The Weekly Missoulian*.[9]

United States Indian Service,
Flathead Agency,
April 17th, 1888.

Hon. Commissioner of Indian Affairs
Washington, D.C.
    Sir:
    Herewith I have the honor to forward copy of report which I mad[e] at the request of Brigadier Gen. Thos N. Ruger, and which will explain itself.

I have the honor to be
Your obedient servant
Peter Ronan
United States Indian Agt.

Enclosure:

United States Indian Service
Flathead Agency, M.T.
April 17th, 1888.

Thos. H. Ruger
Brigadier General,
Commanding Department of Dakota,
St. Paul, Minn.
    Sir:
    In reply to your letter of April 12th, 1888, calling attention to the newspaper reports of trouble about Ashley, at the Head of the Flathead Lake, and asking for such information as I may be able to furnish, I would respectfully state that it is a fact that the citizens of that vicinity did execute two Kootenai Indians some time last month, and that a third one made his escape or he would also follow the fate of the other two.
    From diligent inquiries among the Indians of this reservation, I am afraid that the reported murder of the whitemen is true, and that no mistake was made by the citizens as to the identity of the Indian murderers. As near as I can ascertain the whitemen were Killed about the 17th of last June, at a place called Woolf Creek beyond Pleasant Valley, on the trail leading to Horse Plains. The Indians who committed the crime, and who were lynched, are said to belong to the band of Chief Eneas, who have their homes on this reservation, and live about sixty miles north of the Agency, at Dayton Creek. One of the murderers, who is still at large, confessed the crime to reliable Indians of this reserve, who gave the information, which I give to you as furnished to me: It seems that a party of some ten Kootenai Indians while passing along the trail noticed three whitemen encamped and cooking their meal. One Indian proposed to two others to go to the camp and intimidate the whites. On nearing them the Indians fired over their heads; but the whitemen only laughed at it as a joke, whereupon one of the Indians proposed to kill them and the others agreed. Two of the white party being seated eating, in range, a bullet fired by

an Indian passed through both men Killing them instantly. The third was fired upon and wounded and was killed by the blows of an axe or hatchet. No motive was given for the crime when the story was told of the bloody work.

I sent for Chief Eneas, of the reservation Kootenais, and he stated in the interview that while on his way to St. Ignatius Mission, a few days before Easter Sunday, he was overtaken by an Indian who informed him that a party of armed whitemen, from the Head of the Lake, were at Dayton Creek looking for him. The chief stated that he turned back and met the whitemen and asked why they were there searching for him with arms. The leader of the whites talked the Kootenai language — his name is Ramsdale, and last summer he Kept a trading post near the British line, some six miles south on the American side. This man replied that they had hung two of his Indians and were there to find out what he was going to do about it. It was explained to Eneas, that a white traveller [sic] who camped near Dayton Creek, on hearing of the hanging of the Indians, mounted a horse and rode into Ashley, and stated that the band of Eneas were in Arms — that they had attacked him and he made his escape while the Indians were plundering his wagon. This was easily refuted by Eneas, who told the whites that the wagon was standing where the man encamped; that no Indian molested him or his property, and it was easy to ascertain that fact by examination, which was made by the whites and nothing was found disturbed. The action of the whiteman who caused the excitement on the reservation is inexcusable and might have caused a fight but for the fact that the matter was so quickly and satisfactorily explained on both sides.

Chief Eneas in his statement to me, while he was reticent in regard to having heard of any confession from his people in regard to the murder, stated that if murder had been committed by the Indians it was nothing more than justice to hang the guilty ones; but was sorry that the Lake settlers took the law into their own hands and lynched the prisoners, as a trial, conviction and execution by due process of law would have a more salutory effect upon the Indians and prevent recourse to revenge.

In regard to the state of things relative to security of the white settlers in the region north of the Flathead Lake, I think there is no cause to fear. To my knowledge there has been no change since last year, and the handful of North Kootenai Indians south of the border, in the Tobacco Plains region have not increased since last Summer and fall and have no such idea of making war on the whites.

As it appears the Indians who were lynched did not belong to the Tobacco Plains band, but to that of Chief Eneas, of this reservation, I repeat I cannot see what cause the settlers can have for excitement, especially as the Chief of the band to which the culprits belonged states that no trouble will come from him or his people, as it is a conceded fact they were unjustifiable murderers of whitemen and deserved their fate whether by lynch law or otherwise.

The suppression of the sale of whisky to Indians on the border would prevent lawlessness and the settlers should make an effort to that end.

I hope for the establishment of a military post in that region has a great tendency, I think, to Keep up excitement and to Exagerate [sic] the real state of affairs.

I am, very respectfully,
Your ob'd't servant,

[blank]
United States Indian Agent.

June 14, 1888
LR 15,665/1888, RG 75, National Archives, Washington, D.C.

On July 2, 1888, the Commissioner approved Ronan's actions forcing W. H. Noll, the Arlee Station Agent for the Northern Pacific Railroad, off the reservation.[10] Noll worked as station master for the Northern Pacific Railroad and his wife worked as a telegraph operator for the railroad.[11] Dr. John Dade, from Missouri, was Flathead Agency Physician between 1886 and his death in 1898. A veteran of the Mexican American War, he had been a physician in the Confederate Army during the Civil War.[12]

United States Indian Service,
Flathead Agency,
Montana, June 14, 1888.

Hon. Commissioner Indian Affairs
Washington, D.C.
　　Sir:
　　Upon investigation, I found that the charges contained in attached letters were true; and that the person mentioned also carried on an illegal trade with the Indians, and had purchased from them a small band of cattle and was having them herded upon the reservation. I laid the facts before the Division Superintendent of the Northern Pacific Railroad, and this man is no longer in the employment of the Company. I learn that he is now at a Northern portion of the Reservation looking after and attending to his cattle interests on the reserve. Should this prove a fact I shall issue an order for his removal from the Indian country, and trust that my action will be approved by the Indian Office. The presence of this man among the English speaking hal[f]breeds and Indians, with his slanders against religion — the government school, and its teachers; the Agency physician — an aged gentleman — the Agent, and others connected with the Indian Service, in addition to his illegal dealings with the Indians warrant prompt action for the good government and well being of this Indian Reservation.

I am very respectfully
Your obed't Servt.
Peter Ronan
U.S. Ind. Agt.

First enclosure:

United States Indian Service,
Flathead Agency,
June 4th, 1888.

Peter Ronan
U.S. Indian Agent
Flathead Agency, M.T.
　　D' Sir:
　　I have to report that on June 4th 1888, during your absence at St. Ignatius Mission school — I went to Arlee, in Company with Dr. Dade — to receive the mail and bring the Same to the agency for distribution — Just as I had received the mail — W. H. Noll; station ag't. at Arlee, asked me, if there was a

letter addressed to a certain member of your family — and, asked to look at
the envelope — Saying at the Same time, that he thought the letter was from
his wife — I showed him the letter. When he immediately proceeded to Pocket
it; Saying he would would [sic] Keep, it untill his wifes return (some weeks
hence). I informed Mr. Noll, that the letter was addressed to a member of your
family; and must be delivered intact — during the discussion, he indulged in
a series of profanity and vulgarity — to [sic] obscene to be placed upon this
paper: — he eventually Made an attack upon me; and as a matter of protection I was Compelled to throw him; but refrained from inflicting bodily injury;
— considering it more compatible with the dignity of the Public Service, that
this man should be delt [sic] with through official Channels; rather than personal violence: I would further state that I returned to the agency leaving the
letter in the hands of the above named individual.

In conclusion, I would say — that I understand, from other parties — that
this man has been in the habit of using injurious language to the Indians and
others; Thereby — tending to influence them against the Public Institutions of
this reservation — especially the Schools and those conducting the Same.

Should you desire any further information upon the Subject, I would respectfully refer you to Dr. John Dade, Agency Physician, Who was present, as a
disinterested Witness, during the altercation.

Very sincerely
Thos E. Adams
(Agency clerk).

Second enclosure:

United States Indian Service,
Flathead Agency,
June 4th, 1888.

Maj P Ronan, Agent
Sir
I wish to inform you that Wm. Nolls Agent for the North P. R. R. has been
talking in a way that is causing a great deal of trouble, he is talking about the
Priests and Sisters of Charity saying that the Fathers are cheating and wrong-
ing the Indians and that they with the Sisters of Charity were Keeping nothing
more than house of prostitution, when we and all that Know them Know that
they are doing all in their power to educate and Christianize the Indians. He is
also slandering you and trying to injure your influence among the Indians by
saying that you are cheating them, we all Know that this is false and that you
are doing all that you possibly can for their good. He is also trying to injure my
influence among them, indeed he seems to be trying to cause all the trouble
he can.

Your Friend
Jno Dade
Physician to Agency.

June 23, 1888
Missoula Gazette *(weekly), June 23, 1888, page 2, col. 5.*

> Notice that Ronan called on the chiefs and other tribal members to endorse the removal
> of white-owned cattle from the Flathead Reservation. The Commissioner of Indian Affairs
> had approved the removal on April 6, 1888, in reply to Ronan's monthly report of March 1,

1888, which has not survived in the National Archives.[13] *The Missoula Gazette* newspaper welcomed the removal because it would allow Missoula County to tax the white-owned stock which had been kept on the reservation.[14]

The Cattle Must Go.

The Indian police of the Flathead reservation are around serving notices upon all white persons herding cattle on the reserve illegally. The following is a copy: At a meeting of the chiefs and Indians of this reservation, held at the Agency on the 12th day of June, 1888, it was concluded that all white men having cattle on the reserve should drive them off before the 18th day of July, 1888, in compliance with the following instructions from the Indian office, and that should any owner of cattle illegally on the reserve, not conform with the wishes of the Indians, the cattle will be rounded up by the Indian police and driven beyond the limits of the reservation, and each owner may expect that a sufficient number of cattle from his herd will be taken up by the Indians to pay for the trouble and expense incurred in such round-up and drive.

Respectfully,
Peter Ronan,
U.S. Indian Agent.

* * * * *

Dep't of Interior,
Office of Indian Affairs,
Washington, April 16, 1888.

Peter Ronan, Esq.,
U.S. Indian Agent,
Flathead, Montana.

Sir: — As relates to cattle trespassers on your reservation, until the boundary lines thereof, as has been recommended by this office to the department, are surveyed and permanently fixed, the following plan be adopted: The brands and marks of cattle so herded to be ascertained and a list of the owners secured; the said owners to be given a certain time to round up their cattle and drive them off the reservation. If they fail to do so within the time allowed, the Indian agent to order the Indian police to make the round-up and drive the stock off the reserve, and thereafter to exercise the utmost vigilance in seeing that all stock illegally grazing on the said reservation is driven beyond the limits of the same. You are directed to put the same into operation.

Very respectfully,
(Signed) J. D. C. Atkins,
Commissioner.

July 13, 1888
LR 17,525/1888, telegram, RG 75, National Archives, Washington, D.C.

On August 14, 1888, the Commissioner denied Ronan's request for travel assistance for Victor and his band of Lower Kalispel Indians to remove to the Jocko Reservation. No funds were available because the 1887 agreement between the Lower Kalispel and the Northwest Indian Commission had not been ratified by Congress.[15] See also Ronan telegram of July 16, 1888. See biographical sketch of Victor in annotation to Ronan's December 10, 1877, letter.

July 13th, 1888
Flathead Agy Mont, Arlee Mont.

Commer Indian Affairs

Victor, head chief of Kalispels desires to remove to this reservation from Idaho with several families to join Kalispels already removed here under agreement with northwest Indian Commission May I arrang[e] for their transportation.

Ronan, Agent.

July 16, 1888
LR 17,834/1888, telegram, RG 75, National Archives, Washington, D.C.

July 16th, 1888
Flathead Agy Mont.

Comm'r Ind Affairs

There are in the neighborhood of one hundred & fifty indians under Victor. Cost of transportation by railroad Sandpoint to Arlee, will amount to one thousand & fifty dollars, which includes all Expenses.

Rohan [sic], Agt.

July 18, 1888
Missoula Gazette *(weekly)*, *July 21, 1888, page 2, col. 3.*
Timber on Indian Reservations.
Flathead Agency, July 18, 1888.

Editor Gazette:

We wish to call public attention through the columns of the Gazette to an act of congress approved June 4th, 1888, entitled, "An act to amend section fifty-three hundred and eighty-eight of the Revised Statutes of the United States, in relation to timber depredations," in which, it will be perceived, the provisions of said section are modified, and extended to Indian reservations or lands belonging to or occupied by any tribe of Indians under authority of the United States.

Peter Ronan,
U.S. Indian Agent.

The following is the act referred to by Major Ronan:

That section fifty-three hundred and eighty-eight of the Revised Statutes of the United States be amended to read as follows: "Every person who unlawfully cuts, or aids or is employed in unlawfully cutting, or wantonly destroys or procures to be wantonly destroyed, any timber standing upon the land of the United States, which, in pursuance of law, may be reserved or purchased for military or other purposes, or upon any Indian reservation, or lands belonging to or occupied by any tribe of Indians under authority of the United States, shall pay a fine of not more than five hundred dollars or be imprisoned not more than twelve months, or both, in the discretion of the court."

July 25, 1888
LR 19,078/1888, RG 75, National Archives, Washington, D.C.

In 1888 treatment for victims of mental illness was rudimentary at best, but Ronan was able to arrange for 18-year-old Francois Matt to become a patient in the territorial asylum at Warm Springs. See also Ronan letters of August 25, November 21, and December 12, 1888, on the same subject.[16] See Ronan's letter of June 20, 1885, for an earlier case who was not admitted to Warm Springs. Francois was the son of John Baptiste and Teresa Mary Finley Matt. He was born in 1869.[17]

United States Indian Service,
Flathead Agency, M.T.
July 25th, 1888.

The Hon. Commissioner of Indian Affairs
Washington, D.C.
Sir:

I have the honor to forward herewith copy of communication from me to the Governor of this Territory and his reply thereto, relative to the care of an insane Indian youth of this reservation. This case has been previously reported by me to the Indian Office, at the time the demented was but a boy. He is now a strong, large youth, and, in his unfortunate condition, is dangerous to the members of his family as well as to the community at large. I would respectfully request to be advised as to what I shall do in the premises for the care of this person and for the protection of his family and others who may at any time be attacked by him.

Your obedt. servt.
Peter Ronan
U.S. Indian Agent.

First enclosure:

United States Indian Service,
Flathead Agency, M.T.
July 17th, 1888.

To His Excellency
P. H. Leslie,
Governor of Montana
Sir:

I desire to call your attention to a case at this Indian reservation which appeals to charity and humanity. It is that of an Indian boy, now eighteen years of age, who has been demented from childhood. He has grown to be a strong able-bodied youth, and is growing dangerous. There are several children in the same family and it is feared, unless he is taken care of, that he will do bodily injury. I appeal to you, as Governor of the Territory, for assistance in this case. I believe he should be taken at once to the asylum and the matter reported to the Hon. Secretary of the Interior and the Commissioner of Indian Affairs, who should provide for the expense and care of this unfortunate youth.

Please notify me if he will be received at the asylum, pending a report to the Indian Office. The Case is urgent, and I would act immediately if you will authorize his removal and reception at the asylum.

Very respectfully,
(Signed) Peter Ronan,
U.S. Indian Agent.

Second enclosure:

Territory of Montana
Executive Office,
Helena, Montana.
21 July, 1888

Peter Ronan
US Indian Agent
Flathead Agency.

I am in receipt of your letter advising me of an Insane Indian Boy at your agency and of his dangerous tendencies to violence and asking if the Territory of Montana can take charge of him, support & hold him till further orders, or provisions by the US Govt.

I have examined the Territorial Statutes & find no provision under which I can have him cared for. If his Condition demands that for the Safety of others: that he be Confined or Separated from them and Guarded it Should be done at once & the Commissioner of Indian Affairs, or the Secty of the Interior advised of the facts so arrangements can be made by the US Govt for his treatment.

Yr Frd,
P. H. Leslie.

July 26, 1888
LR 19,079/1888, RG 75, National Archives, Washington, D.C.

> Ronan's request for a fourth judge for the government sponsored Court of Indian Offenses had been denied in May 1888 but was approved for the 1888-1889 fiscal year. The new Indian Appropriation Act included funds to pay the judges. Previously the work had not been compensated.[18]
>
> The conflict between the traditional chiefs and the agency courts and police would continue for the balance of the nineteenth century.[19] Ronan followed the government policy of undermining traditional tribal social controls but also complained about the law and order problems resulting from the policy.

United States Indian Service,
Flathead Agency, M.T.
July 26th, 1888.

The Hon. Commissioner of Indian Affairs
Washington, D.C.

Sir:

Reply in [sic] to your letter "L," dated July 18th, 1888, in reference to the Indian Appropriation Act for the current fiscal year, which provides for compensation of Judges of Indian Courts. I would respectfully report: that since the establishment of this tribunal on the reservation there has been a marked change. Before its inauguration the chiefs were head and front and their decision and action went unchallenged among the tribes. A small bribe from a cattle owner secured the right from the chief, without consulting anybody, to drive cattle and herd them on the reservation. Questionable characters, in the same way introduced themselves among the Indians in various occupations. Gambling and the introduction of whisky with all their attendant excesses and crimes was the rule. But after the Court of Indian offences became established, and the induction into office of Indians of character, with the elevation and advancement of the tribes in view, a curb was put upon the action of the chiefs, who at first opposed the rulings of the court of Indian offences, and the action of the Indian police. But by prompt action and by firmness, the court was sustained, and the Chiefs, as well as the Indians, were brought under its rulings.

It gives me great pleasure to learn that provisions have been made to allow the Judges compensation for their service, as their duties entail a loss of time which should be compensated as each of them are tillers of the soil and stock raisers.

[Here Ronan quotes his letter of March 15, 1888, reproduced above, requesting a fourth judge for the Flathead Reservation.]

Very respectfully submitted,
Peter Ronan
U.S. Indian Agent.

Enclosure:

"Descriptive Statement of proposed changes in Employés," provided for $12 per month compensation for the Flathead judges and the selection of Joseph Kootoolayuch as the fourth judge. All the judges were married, male tribal members. Joseph, 52 years old, lived at St. Ignatius; Parti, 46 years old, lived at St. Ignatius; Louison, 52 years old, lived at the Agency; and Joseph Kootoolayuch, 55 years old, lived on the Jocko River.

August 6, 1888
LR 20,406/1888, RG 75, National Archives, Washington, D.C.

The government bureaucracy managed to make compensating Bitterroot Salish farmers for lands taken by the Northern Pacific Railroad a very complicated affair. The officials finally decided that since the patents under the 1872 law were inalienable, the lands could legally only be transferred to the railroad by Congressional action. In September 1890 the railroad made an offer for the lands, but the Commissioner of Indian Affairs decided to ask for Congressional authority to accept the money and pay the Salish landowners.[20] In 1901 the land had not been paid for, but the Commissioner decided a recent right-of-way law would authorize the railroad to purchase the land from the allottees.[21] In 1905 the allottees still had not been paid and the railroad claimed it did not need to pay because Congress had granted the railroad a charter in 1875.[22] See also Ronan's letters of February 4, 1889, and September 15, 1890.

Thomas C. Marshall, of Kentucky, came to Missoula in 1883. He was a prominent lawyer, member of the 1889 Montana Constitutional Convention, legislator, judge, and even mayor of Missoula.[23]

United States Indian Service,
Flathead Agency, M.T.
August 6th, 188[8].

The Hon. Commissioner of Indian Affairs,
Washington, D.C.

Sir:

I would respectfully report that a branch from the Northern Pacific Railroad has been built from the town of Missoula through the Bitter Root Valley, in Montana Territory. This branch railroad runs through several farms, patented to said Indians, without power of alienation, by act of Congress approved June 5th 1872, entitled "An act to provide for the removal of the Flatheads and other Indians from the Bitter Root Valley in the Territory of Montana."

It appears that the Company adjusted the right of way with white settlers, but made no settlement with Indians holding patents under Act, and otherwise occupying land in the Bitter Root Valley. Under date of June 16th, I called attention of the branch railroad company to this fact and herewith annex replies.

I would thank you to inform me if I have any further duties to perform in this case.

The Indians through whose farms the railroad has been constructed think that they are not justly dealt with, in not being paid for the right of way, as was done by the Company when the railroad was constructed through the lands of whitemen.

I am, very respectfully
Your ob'd't serv't
Peter Ronan
U.S. Indian Agent.

First enclosure:

Missoula Mercantile Co.
Missoula, M.T. June 19th 1888

Maj. P. Ronan,
U.S. Indian Agt.
Arlee, Mont.
Dear Sir:
Replying to your letter of the 16th inst. concerning the right of way through the Indian lands in the Bitter Root Valley I will state, that I have referred your letter to the attorneys of the Company for such action as they may deem proper in the matter, and also requested them to communicate with you concerning same at as early date as possible.

Yours truly
A. B. Hammond

Second enclosure:

Thos. C. Marshall,
Attorney at Law.
Missoula, Montana, June 22nd, 1888

Maj. Peter Ronan
Flathead Indian Agent
Arlee Mont
Dear Sir
Your favor of some days since addressed to Mr. A. B. Hammond was handed me for reply and will say regarding right of way over indian lands that the company through myself as agent is ready to treat with any one having authority to adjust the matter for the indians over whose lands the road runs. Taking it that this would perhaps come within the perview of your duties as indian agent would be glad to see and confer with you in relation to the matter.

Awaiting your reply I remain with much respect
Your obt Servt
Thos C. Marshall.

August 7, 1888
LR 20,220/1888, RG 75, National Archives, Washington, D.C.

On August 17, 1888, Ronan was instructed to use the general funds appropriated to assist the Flathead Reservation tribes to provide subsistence for those Lower Kalispel who had already removed to Flathead. As noted above in the annotation to Ronan's July 13, 1888, letter, on August 14, 1888, he was informed there were no funds available to pay the transportation costs for removing additional Kalispel to the reservation.[24]

> United States Indian Service,
> Flathead Agency, M.T.
> August 7th, 1888.

The Hon. Commissioner of Indian Affairs
Washington, D.C.

Sir:

I would respectfully report that last year some seventeen families consisting of sixty-two people, of the Lower Kalispel tribe were removed by me, under your instruction from the Kalispel valley to this reservation. I was also authorized to purchase certain supplies for the maintenance of these people until the end of the fiscal year, 1888. Said supplies are now exhausted and I respectfully refer the matter to you for consideration and action. The families belong to the tribe of Kalispels who negotiated with the Northwest Indian Commission in April 1887, to remove to this Agency, and begged to come here last fall before their agreement was ratified by Congress as they were perfectly destitute. The remainder of the tribe now living in the Kalispel valley, in Idaho, under head-chief Victor, asked for transportation to remove here, last month and I reported the matter the matter [sic] to your office at the time, but am not yet apprised if the proposition received favorable consideration. I would respectfully recommend that immediate action be taken for the care and support of the families already here until they can be placed on farms and furnished with assistance to commence the cultivation of the soil and obtain a living thereby.

> Your ob'd't serv't
> Peter Ronan
> U.S. Indian Agent.

August 16, 1888

U.S. Commissioner of Indian Affairs, Annual Report of the Commissioner of Indian Affairs *(Washington, D.C.: U.S. Government Printing Office, 1888), pages 155-158.*

Ronan's twelfth annual report brought together many topics already covered in his correspondence with the Commissioner. His discussion of the economic development on the reservation treated the change from hunting and gathering to farming and ranching as a moral rather than an economic choice. Ronan's prejudices were especially obvious in his discussion of the economic status of the Kootenai.

The account of developments relating to the Salish in the Bitterroot Valley ignored the government's failure to fulfill its promise in the 1855 Hellgate Treaty to protect Salish interests. By 1888 Ronan was having trouble getting funds to assist those Salish who had moved. In early 1888 some Bitterroot whites petitioned J. K. Toole, the Montana Territorial Delegate to Congress, for legislation to end Salish title to unoccupied allotments in the valley and to allow Salish farmers to sell their land.[25] In 1889 the request had morphed into the appointment of General Henry B. Carrington to negotiate the removal of the Bitterroot Salish to the Jocko Valley.

The failure of Congress to approve the 1887 agreements between the Northwest Indian Commission and the Lower Kalispel Indians and the Flathead Reservation tribes, continued to cause problems long after Ronan died in 1893. Ronan's account of his role in the origins of the Flathead Reservation buffalo herd was not supported by other sources. His account could represent a story that grew as he retold it over the years.[26] His account of the conflict over the Court of Indian Offenses summarized several earlier letters in 1888. According to Ronan, despite a slow start, the Northern Pacific Railroad was settling damage claims to the satisfaction of tribal members.

Report of Flathead Agency.

Flathead Agency, Montana,
August 16, 1888.

Sir: In accordance with instructions, I herewith submit my twelfth annual report, with census and accompanying statistics.

The confederated tribes of this reservation consist of the Pend d'Oreilles, the Flatheads, and the Kootenais, Charlot's band of Bitter Root Flatheads, and Michel's band of Lower Kalispels, who removed here last year, making a total in all of Indians under my charge 2,018, under the following

Recapitulations.

Confederated tribes: Total number	1,767
Males over eighteen years	535
Females over fourteen years	628
School children between six and sixteen years	428
Charlot's band of Bitter Root Flatheads: Total number	189
Males over eighteen years	56
Females over fourteen years	68
Children between six and sixteen years	42
Lower Kalispels: Total number	62
Males over eighteen years	21
Females over fourteen years	22
Children between six and sixteen years	14

The Pend d'Oreilles

Are the most numerous tribe of the confederation, and are, as a rule, well behaved and industrious. They are fast advancing in the various paths of civilization, education, and industrial habits. Their homes are principally in the vicinity of the Mission Valley. They have well-cultivated farms, comfortable dwellings, herds of cattle, and a number of them take great pride in cultivation of orchards and gardens. Their chief is an old man, of good character, who cultivates the soil and leads a quiet and unobtrusive life among his people.

The Kootenai Indians.

Of the Kootenai Indians who reside on the reservation and who are of the confederated tribes of the reserve, very little can be said in the way of advancement, either in civilizing pursuits, morality, or religion. They live on Dayton Creek, on the border of the Flathead Lake, and are, as a rule, inveterate loafers and gamblers. It is a distance of about 70 miles from the agency to where the Kootenai tribe make their home. They have some land under cultivation, but are so far from the agency that their efforts at improvement can not be well seconded by the employés or the agent.

The missionaries at Saint Ignatius are building a church at the Kootenai settlement, and through them and the efforts of the chief, who is himself a progressive Indian, I hope to report an improvement this year. A resident farmer should be sent to Dayton Creek to aid, direct, and encourage the efforts which are already being made to elevate this tribe from their present condition.

Chief Arlee.

This is the Flathead chief who entered into an agreement with General Garfield on the 27th of August, 1872, to remove from the Bitter Root Valley to the Jocko Reservation, which he did, and was followed by about twenty-two families. The head chief, Charlot, refuses to sign the agreement and also refused to remove from the Bitter Root Valley. Arlee is now an old man, and respected by the families who followed him from the Bitter Root Valley to this reservation. Those said families are settled around in the vicinity of the agency, and although they have farms and houses and cultivate the soil and raise cattle, are not as well off as they should be. Arlee was second chief when the Garfield agreement was signed, and upon his removal to this reservation was recognized by the Government as the head of the tribe and with his people received all its bounty. This is the great cause of Charlot's bitterness and his refusal to remove to the reservation.

Charlot's Band of Bitter Root Flatheads.

On the 12th of August, 1884, under orders from the Secretary of the Interior, I met Charlot's band of Bitter Root Indians at Saint Mary's Mission, in the Bitter Root Valley, and after a careful census found the following result:

Married men	79
Unmarried males above 16 years	25
Boys under 16	68
Total number of males	172
Married women	100
Marriageable girls	9
Girls under the age of puberty	61
Total number of females	170

In all, 342 individuals, of whom 101 were heads of families.

At this date, August 12, 1888, there remains of Charlot's band living in the Bitter Root Valley:

Total number of Indians	189
Males above 18 years	56
Females above 14 years	68
Children between 6 and 16 years	42

By above figures it will be seen that the band of Charlot's are gradually removing from the Bitter Root Valley and are settling on the Jocko Reservation.

In January, 1884, Chief Charlot and four of his head-men, accompanied by the agent and an interpreter, visited Washington under orders from the Indian Department. Nearly a month was spent at the National Capital, and during that time several interviews were held with the Secretary of the Interior, but no offer of pecuniary reward or persuasion of the Secretary could shake Charlot's resolution to remain in the Bitter Root Valley. An offer to build him a house, fence in and plow a sufficiency of land for a farm; give him cattle, horses, seed, agricultural implements, and to do likewise for each head of a family in his band; also a yearly pension to Charlot of $500, and be recognized as the heir of Victor, his deceased father, and to take his place as head chief of the confederated tribes of Flatheads, Pend d'Oreilles, and Kootenais Indians living on the Jocko Reservation, had no effect.

After returning to the reservation the agent was instructed to use his best judgment in regard to inducing the removal of the tribe. Under the following offer seventeen families removed and settled on the reservation:

First. Choice of 160 acres of unoccupied land.

Second. Assistance in the erection of a substantial house.

Third. Assistance in fencing and breaking up a field of 10 acres.

Fourth. The following gift: Two cows, a wagon and harness, plows, with other necessary implements, seed for the first year, and provisions until the first crop was harvested.

Having taken advantage of the opportunity, they removed and were settled as agreed, and most of them are now selling a surplus of the productions of the soil. Other families followed afterwards, but authority has not yet been granted to extend to them the same facilities as were given the original families who took advantage of the offer.

If Congress would give the Indians the right of alienation and to sell and dispose of their possessions in the Bitter Root Valley for their own benefit or to let the land revert back to the Government, and let it be sold for the benefit of the rightful owners and heirs, with a view of expending the money in giving them homes on the reservation the question would soon be settled and the Flatheads would remove to the Jocko reservation, including Chief Charlot, who has lived to regret his refusal of the generous offer made to him by the Government.

The Lower Kalispels.

On the 27th day of April, 1887, the Northwest Indian Commission on the part of the United States and the chiefs and head-men and other adult Indians of the confederated bands of Flatheads, Pend d'Oreilles, and Kootenai Indians entered into a certain agreement at this reservation. It was there and then announced that it was the policy of the United States Government to remove to and settle upon Indian reservations scattered bands of non-reservation Indians, so as to bring them under the care and protection of the United States. As the Lower Pend d'Oreilles or Kalispel Indians expressed a desire and entered into an agreement under certain promises of assistance to be guarantied by the agreement to remove to the Flathead Reservation, the said confederate bands of Flatheads, Pend d'Oreilles, and Kootenais agreed with the commission to allow the Kalispels to remove to and settle upon their lands. It seems, up to present date, the United States Congress has not confirmed or passed upon said agreement and it leaves the Indians in question in a very undecided and unsatisfactory condition.

On the 25th of September 1887, I reported to the honorable Commissioner of Indian Affairs that Michael, one of the chiefs of the wandering bands of Lower Kalispels, who met the northwest Indian commission at Sand Point, in Idaho Territory, and who signed the agreement to remove to this reservation with the families who acknowledged him as chief, was at the Flathead Agency; that he came to request transportation by railroad or otherwise, for fifteen families from Idaho to the Flathead Reservation. The chief at the time fully understood that the agreement with the northwest commission, which he signed should be ratified by Congress before it could go into effect, and that there was no means at the disposal of the Indian Office to pay for transportation or to take care of those families until such provisions were made by Congress. But he appealed to the honorable Secretary of the Interior and the Commissioner of Indian Affairs, through my office, to grant them the aid and facilities he desired to remove his band while they were anxious and willing to come to the Flathead Reservation, where it was expected they would cultivate the soil for a living and abandon their wandering and vagabond life. The appeal was listened to, and the Indian Office furnished means to bring the band to this reservation, and also provided means of support until the close of the fiscal year, which ended June 30, 1888. During the year this band, with whatever aid could be afforded them from the agency, commenced farming in a small way, and gave ample evidence that with proper attention and the assistance promised in the agreement in which they entered with the northwest commission, they would soon become tillers of the soil and placed on the highway to civilization and self-support. The number of Michael's band removed from the Kalispel Valley to this reservation under such circumstances are as follows:

Total number	62
Males over 18 years	21
Females over 14 years	22
Children between 6 and 16 years	14

Victor, Head Chief

of this band, after the commission left talked to his people against removal to the reservation, but, as events show, is now solicitous and urgent in his appeal to the Government to carry out the provisions of the agreement with the northwest Indian commission, and to remove his people at once to the Flathead Reservation. In fact, he has asked, and I have made the request from the Indian Office to provide the means of transportation for himself and his band from the Kalispel Valley, in Idaho Territory, to this reservation.

Buffalo on the Reservation.

In 1878, one year after I took charge of the Flathead Reservation, believing that in the manner in which buffalo were being slaughtered by white hunters for their hides, and by travelers and would-be sportsmen, who shot the animals down and left their carcasses to taint the atmosphere where they fell, I conceived the idea that this noble beast, which is now almost extinct on the American plains, might be saved from total annihilation by getting some of them on an Indian reservation, where they could be bred, herded, and cared for by the Indians. There were no buffaloes west of the Rocky Mountains, and the nearest herd was on the eastern plains in the vicinity of Fort Shaw, in the Territory of Montana. At my suggestion, Indians undertook and succeeded in driving two young buffalo cows and a bull from a wild herd, near Fort Shaw, through Cadotte's Pass, and across the main divide of the Rocky Mountain range into the Flathead Reservation, on the Pacific slope. The buffalo have increased from three to twenty-seven head. Besides, several males were slaughtered by the Indians for their feast, as it was deemed better for propagation not to have too many bulls running in the herd. The buffalo are now owned by two individual half-breed cattle owners of this reservation. Tempting offers have been made to them to sell the herd, but I advise a continuation of ownership. It seems to me that the Government should take steps to secure these buffalo, which are among the last remnants of the millions that roamed the great American plains in former days. They could be herded, cared for, and the number increased in proportion to that of similar herd of stock cattle.

Agricultural and Pastoral Pursuits.

The average of planting has vastly increased this year, and every agricultural valley on the reservation is dotted with Indian homes, well-fenced farms, comfortable houses, cultivated fields and gardens. A majority of the Indians also have herds of cattle, for which they have individual brands, and herd and care for them with the same ambition for increase and profit as the white farmer and stock-raiser.

The Court of Indian Offenses.

Since the establishment of this tribunal on the reservation there has been a marked change. Before its inauguration the chiefs were head and front, and their decision and action went unquestioned among the tribes. A small bribe from a cattle-owner secured the right from the chief, without consulting anybody, to drive cattle and herd them on the reservation. Questionable characters in the same way introduced themselves among the Indians in various occupations; gambling and the introduction of whisky with all their attendant excesses and crimes was the rule. But after the court of Indian offenses became established and the induction into office of Indians of character with the elevation and advancement of the tribes in view, a curb was put upon the action of the chiefs, who at first opposed the rulings of the court of Indian offenses and the action of the Indian police. But by promptness and firmness the court was sustained and the chiefs as well as the Indians were brought under its rulings.

It gives me great pleasure to learn that provisions have been made to allow the judges compensation for their service, as their duties entail a loss of time which should be rewarded, as each of them at this agency are tillers of the soil and stock-raisers.

Stock Killed and Injured on the Railroad.

Since the opening of the Northern Pacific Railroad through this reservation a great number of Indian stock has been killed or injured. I kept a careful list of the stock so killed or injured, with the names of owners, their residence, the date of killing, the value thereof, etc., and on the 11th of November, 1884, D. K. Ford, the general claim agent of the railroad, visited the agency and allowed sixty claims to individual Indians for the killing and injuring of stock, amounting to the sum of $3,155. Since that date, including the sum allowed for the first sixty claims, the sum paid to the Indians on this reservation for killing and injury to stock to July 1, 1888, is $11,469.50. The company have made arrangements to put up a wire fence along the most dangerous part of their line running through the reserve. The settlements with the Indians by the Northern Pacific Railroad Company have been most honorable and the Indians were satisfied, as they received the full market value of their animals killed or maimed; but it will be a great benefit to the Indians to fence the railroad, as the money paid to them for the killing of cattle or horses is generally spent in frivolous ways instead of replacing the stock killed.

Very respectfully, your obedient servant,

Peter Ronan,
United States Indian Agent.

The Commissioner of Indian Affairs.

August 17, 1888
LR 21,158/1888, RG 75, National Archives, Washington, D.C.

This case illustrated some of the legal confusion surrounding Bitterroot Salish land claims after almost thirty-five years of encroachment by Montana whites and temporizing by the United States government. On November 24, 1888, the Commissioner of Indian Affairs decided no further action was needed in the matter.[27]

On January 2, 1889, the Commissioner of the General Land Office forwarded to the Commissioner of Indian Affairs a November 3, 1888, report by M. J. Haley, a Special Timber Agent. Haley felt the timber trespass had been intentional and the Missoula Mercantile Company, which purchased the timber, shared legal responsibility. Haley recommended prosecution in the case, but there was no indication in the file that any further action was taken.[28]

For biographical information on Chief Adolph see the annotation to Ronan's January 10, 1878, letter. No further information was found about Steven James, who sold the timber to Slocum, or Robert C. Smith, the United States Attorney. John B. De Nayer operated a sawmill at Stevensville.[29] Thomas M. Slocum was listed as a farmer in the Bitterroot Valley in the 1880 census. In 1890 Slocum operated a restaurant and hotel in Stevensville.[30]

> United States Indian Service,
> Flathead Agency, M.T.
> August 17th, 1888.

The Hon. Commissioner of Indian Affairs
Washington, D.C.
  Sir:
  Complaint having been made to me by one John B. De Nayer, of Stevensville, Montana, that timber depredations were being committed by one Thomas M. Slocum on the Indian patent right of Chief Adolph, in Bitter Root valley, viz: the South East qr. of Sec. twenty-nine; in township nine North of Range twenty, West, in Montana Territory.
  Chief Adolph removed to his reservation, and died here. The land is not alienable, and Steven James, who is an Indian, had no title to it nor the right of alienation. If he had, however, I am of opinion that Slocum, in the purchase, sworn to in his affidavit herewith attached, was in ignorance of the law. I have put a stop to timber depredations on the Indian land in Bitter Root valley, and herewith submit papers in the case of Slocum, and respectfully ask if I have any further duty to perform in the matter.

> Your ob'd't serv't
> Peter Ronan
> U.S. Indian Agent.

First enclosure:

> Butte City May 9, 1888

Thomas M. Slocum Esq.
Stevensville
  Dear Sir:
  I have reced a letter from agent Ronan & a Mr John B. DeNayer Concerning your Cutting timber on land belonging to heirs of Chief Adolph. to save

trouble you would best go at once to agent Ronan and settle for Damage you have done or I shall take steps to compel you to settle.

Yours truly
Robt B. Smith
U.S. Atty.

Second enclosure. The handwriting in this letter was very hard to read and the transcription below represents the editor's best interpretation:

Stevensville Hotel
Stevensville, Mont.,
May 14th, 1888.

Mr. Smith

Dear Sir

I Received your leter of The 9 inst Concerning the Indian timber I have bought of [Sane?] and indian Some timber for five hundred dolars. I have paid 368^1/_{100}$ now I owe him 148 dolars, to be paid The fourth of july, he is living on his land and he wants the timber taken of[f] it. I ast several lawyers if I had a right to buy it and they told me they thought they had a right to Sell it. I ast the Preast and he thought it was all right. I will Send the Indian to the Major to morow to see about it. I think that the Major has been wrongly in formed.

Now in regard to the Major information the Doctor Lanear he has a bout two hundred acrs of timber to Sell and is mad be caus he Cant get his price. he has ben & trying to Stop the mill & make them buy his timber. I think if the Major was to come up and here the Strate of it ther woldnd be any trobel if the Indian hant no right to Sell his wood or logs I dont want to buy it but if he dose and I buy it and pay him the money for it I think I have as good a right as any body. I will tell you the tribel [trouble] a bout this there is a few that is mad be caus I give the Indian to mutch for his timber. they wanted it for les. I wood like to know whether the Indian has a right to Sell his improvements on his land or posts or wood or logs. I wood be very much obliged to know.

The Indian is very mad a bout peopel inter fearing with his trade. I wood like to have it Seleled [settled]. there is lots of Indians traded of[f] ther im-provements, her and make farming them all over the valey if you will pleas in forme me how the thing Stanss it wood save us all lots of trubel for re [cen?] here any thing a bout the Indian land.

Yours Truley
T. M. Slocum.

Third enclosure:

Robert B. Smith,
Attorney and Counselor at Law,
Dillon, Montana, May 18, 1888.

Col. Ronan
Flathead M.T.

Dear Sir:

I have written to Slocum to walk up and settle with you or he would be prosecuted and I have rece'd from him a letter which I inclose to you. please have investigation Made and find out what truth there is in this letter and if not Correct give me the true status of the matter.

Yours Respecfully
Robt B. Smith
U.S. Atty.

Fourth enclosure:

Thos. C. Marshall,
Attorney at Law.
Missoula, Montana, July 21st, 1888

Maj Peter Ronan
Arlee Montana
   Dear Sir

   Herewith I hand you paper in regard to indian timber handed me by Mort Slocum with request that I send to you. He also told me to say that he had send a statement sometime which he had understood did not reach you. That he has not been indifferent in regard to the matter but has rested upon the idea that the paper was in your hands.

Respectfully
Thos C. Marshall.

Fifth enclosure:
Territory of Montana
County of Missoula.

   Thomas M Slocum being duly sworn on his oath deposes and say that he on or about the 5th day of October 1887 bought from an indian whos name is Stephen Jane a certain piece of land situated in the Bitter Root vally and Known as the Adolph land the said Stephen Jane was at the time in possession of said land and living on it claiming it as his own having purchased from one John Hill an indian who at the time lived upon and farmed a small portion of the land. I agreed to pay him $500.00 for it and did pay him in cash $365.00 and was to pay balance July 4th, 1888. After I purchased the land and not before I cut from the timber on it 29000 feet of lumber and hauled off of the land about 21000 feet of the logs cut by me and left about 8000 feet. That all the timber cut on said land by this affiant is not worth more than $29.00 and that affiant has largely more than paid for it in the $365.00 paid to the said indian Stephen Jane.

   Affiant further says that the said indian is still anxious and willing to carry out his agreement to sell said land to this affiant if permitted to do.

Thomas M. Slocum

Subscribed and sworn to before me on this 20 day of July 1888.

T. C. Marshall
Notary Public.

August 25, 1888
LR 21,860/1888, RG 75, National Archives, Washington, D.C.

United States Indian Service,
Flathead Agency, M.T.
August 25th, 1888.

The Hon. Commissioner of Indian Affairs,
Washington, D.C.
   Sir:

   I have the honor to report that accordin[g] to instructions contained in your letter "L 19078 – 1888" dated August 10th, I wrote to the Superintendent of the Territorial Insane Asylum of this Territory relative to the care and maintenance of an insane Indian youth of this reservation and inclose his reply herewith.

The name of the youth referred to is Francois Matte, age 18 years and he belongs to Charlo's Band of Bitter Root Flatheads, removed to the Jocko reservation. I deem it best that he be sent to the Montana Territorial Asylum for the Insane for the reason that he will then be nearer to his parents, (who would object to having him sent so far away from them as Idaho or Washington territories) — The charges are reasonable and by having him committed by the authorities of Missoula County arrangements might be made with the territory by which the charges could be collected from the Indian Department. I would respectfully request to be instructed as to what further proceedings to take in the matter.

Your ob'd't serv't
Peter Ronan
U.S. Indian Agent.

Enclosure:

Warm Springs,
Deer Lodge County, Mont.
Mitchell & Mussigbrod, Propr's.
Warm Springs, Montana, August 22d, 1888.

Peter Ronan Esq.
United States Indian Agent,
Flathead Agency, Mont.

Dear Sir:

In answer to yours of the 20th instant, will say that we don't take any private patients. In case you want to send that Indian to this institution, he will have to be adjudged insane by the Probate Judge of your county, after examination by a physician and a jury of three citizens, before the Probate Judge. After that, the Sheriff of the County will take him in his charge, bring him to the Asylum and the Territory will pay the expenses of keeping him here. We receive from the Territory $8. pr week and for said amount we have to furnish everything, including medication.

Hoping to hear from you what you intend to do, we are

Very respectfully,
Mitchell & Mussigbrod
by Erich S. Mussigbrod.

October 26, 1888
LR 27,158/1888, RG 75, National Archives, Washington, D.C.

This report resulted from a complaint by C. A. Stillinger to the Commissioner of Indian Affairs about competition for landing space for his ship at Polson on the Foot of Flathead Lake.[31] The Commissioner agreed with Ronan's assessment of the situation and instructed Ronan to have Stillinger apply for landing rights for his boat.[32]

In 1886, James Kerr purchased the steamer, U. S. Grant, and ran it on Flathead Lake. In 1891, he began running a stern-wheel steamer named, State of Montana, on the lake.[33] C. A. Stillinger came to the Flathead Reservation in about 1885 and worked for Charles Allard and Duncan McDonald. His first Flathead lake steamer was operated in conjunction with Duncan McDonald. In 1892 he bought out Allard's stage line and Duncan McDonald's store at Ravalli. In 1901 he sold his business interests on the reservation and moved to Superior, Montana.[34]

United States Indian Service,
Flathead Agency, M.T.
October 26th, 1888.

The Hon. Commissioner of Indian Affairs
Washington, D.C.

Sir:

Replying to your letter "L." 21408 – 1888 I would respectfully report, that I made proper investigation into the complaint of C. A. Stillinger, of Ravalli, Montana Territory, who represents that he is in charge of a boat (conjointly with an Indian) plying on Flathead Lake, and engaged in the transportation of freight; that he has been interfered with in the landing of his boat, at the usual landing place for boats on the Flathead reservation, by Captain James Kerr, owner of the boat, U. S. Grant, who, it is alleged, claims the exclusive right to said landing. I herewith attach statement of Captain Kerr, which I believe to be true. At the request of Mr. Kerr, Stillinger and associates removed their landing a short distance from the landing established by the former, and I know of no reason why he should be disturbed in the occupation of the same, as Stillinger and Company have equally as good a landing place, but did not display equal courtesy in first obtaining permission to occupy the same from the Indian Department. Captain Kerr is a respectable citizen, has the confidence of Indians as well as the traveling public and I respectfully recommend that he be not disturbed in the right already granted him to land his boat and erect suitable wharves and buildings for accomodation of the traveling public.

Very respectfully,
Your obdt servt,
Peter Ronan
U.S. Indian Agent.

Enclosure:

Clifford Sept 23, 1888

To Peter Ronan
U.S. Indian Agent
Arlee

Dear Sir

Hearing that C. A. Stillinger has entered Complaint to the Hon Commissioner of Indian Affairs Washington, Will State that I originally established the landing at the Foot of Flathead Lake on the Reservation and was in full ocupation of same when they started their Boat, and Had Made application to Interior Department for the nessisary [sic] permit previous to their putting Boat on in opposition to me. Received permission to fence in Said Landing, from the Indians and have never heard of any Complaints, except from Mr C. A. Stillinger. Hoping this will meet your approval I remain

Yours Very Resply
Jas Kerr.

November 17, 1888
LR 28,917/1888, RG 75, National Archives, Washington, D.C.

The Commissioner of Indian Affairs decided no action was needed on this affair and the letter was filed.

The woman who found the remains of the murdered man in the Jocko River was Emily Brown Couture Irvine who in 1888 was married to Maxime or Mack Couture. See the annotation for Ronan's August 25, 1891a letter. Dr. Frank S. Hedger came to Missoula in 1883. He served two terms as Missoula County Coroner and several years as Missoula County Physician. In 1894, he sold his Missoula practice and moved to the Pacific Coast.[35]

United States Indian Service,
Flathead Agency, M.T.
November 17th, 1888.

The Hon. Commissioner of Indian Affairs
Washington, D.C.
Sir:
I have the honor to enclose herewith copy of correspondence between myself and Hon. John Costigan, Minister of Land Revenue, Ottawa, Ont., relative to the supposed murder of one Henry William Keays, in the Flathead Country.

Very respectfully,
Your obdt ser't,
Peter Ronan
U.S. Indian Agent.

Enclosure:
(Copy)

United States Indian Service,
Flathead Agency, M.T.
November 17th, 1888.

Hon. John Costigan,
Minister of Land Revenue,
Ottawa, Ont.
Sir:
A telegram dated at Washington September 25th, 1888, addressed to Hon. P. H. Leslie, Governor of Montana, asked the following question: "Can you give this department any particulars concerning the alleged murder of Henry William Keays, at Flathead Montana

(Sgd) G. L. Reaves,
Acting Secretary of State"

The telegram above quoted was referred to me by Governor Leslie, and I reported to him that the body of a supposed murdered whiteman had been found on the bank of the Jocko river, on this Indian reservation.

Through this information I held considerable correspondence with yourself in regard to the matter, and received a letter, also, from the father and the bother of William Henry Keays, whose body it was supposed was found as stated above.

It appears from the correspondence that William Henry Keays deserted from the North-West Mounted Police on May 19th, 1888. On the 26th of July, 1888, I notified the coroner of Missoula County of the finding of the remains in question and I herewith attach coroner's report, which shows conclusively that the body could not be that of William Henry Keays, as indications were, according to the coroner's report, that the body had lain where found long previous to the disappearance of Keays from the North West Territory:

(Copy)

"Missoula, Montana, Nov. 13th, 1888.

On the 26th day of July, 1888, was notified of the finding of the remains of an unknown person, below Ravalli on the N. P. R. R. The report was that the man had been murdered and that an unsuccessful effort had been made to burn the body. I visited the place in company with Deputy Sheriff Harry Logan, found that the body had been discovered by a woman, in the brush about a hundred yards from the Jocko river. The woman was not in the country, but her husband Michael [****] accompanied us to find the body. After some search we found part of the bones of a human skeleton. The body had evidently been covered with earth and brush and the brush then set on fire. The bones of one side of the body were entirely consumed, the rest were there still in the clothes he wore. These showed him to have been a white man and a laborer. The skull was lying exposed and was fractured over the left eye. The bones were of those of a medium sized man. The body had been there for at least a year. As there was nothing to be gained and as there were no men to compose a coroner's Jury within many miles, I held no inquest and think that nothing would have been found out.

(Sgd) F. S. Hedger,
Coroner Missoula County"

I would respectfully state that another case came under my notice for investigation and report in which it was stated that three whitemen were killed by Kootenai Indians, about the 17th of June, 1887, at a place called Woolf Creek, near Tobacco Plains and close to the British boundary. As those two cases are the only ones of the murder of whitemen brought to my notice, or of which I have any knowledge of within the past few years it is safe to pronounce the murder of William Henry Keays, in the Flathead Country, a rumour without any foundation of truth.

I am respectfully,
Your obedient servant,
Peter Ronan
U.S. Indian Agent.

November 21, 1888
LR 29,237/1888, RG 75, National Archives, Washington, D.C.

United States Indian Service,
Flathead Agency, M.T.
November 21st, 1888.

Hon. Commissioner of Indian Affairs,
Washington, D.C.

Sir:

Replying to your letter L – 21860 – 88 relating to Francis Matte, An insane Indian youth, of this Agency, I would respectfully report, that Said demented Indian became unmanageable and dangerous, and I therefore Made prisoner of him — Took him before the probate Judge of the county of Missoula, Montana Territory. A Jury was empanelled by the Sheriff of Said county, consisting of two citizens and one physician. The prisoner was adjudged insane, and I was deputized, by the Sheriff to convey him to the Insane Asylum, at Warm Spring Creek, in the County of Deer Lodge, Montana Territory, Where the Territorial insane are cared for. Francis Matte is now confined at that institution, at the expense of the Territory of Montana.

Very respectfully
Your obt. svt.
Peter Ronan
U.S. Indian Agent.

December 12, 1888
LR 30,962/1888, RG 75, National Archives, Washington, D.C.

United States Indian Service,
Flathead Agency, M.T.
December 12th, 1888.

The Hon. Commissioner of Indian Affairs
Washington, D.C.
    Sir:
    I have the honor to enclose herewith a clipping from the Deer Lodge Northwest in which reference is made to the Insane youth recently incarcerated in the Territorial Insane Asylum, from this reservation.

Very respectfully
Your ob'd't. serv't
Peter Ronan
U.S. Ind. Agent.

Enclosed undated newspaper clipping:
    Dr. C. E. Mussigbrod, when in town the other day, informed us that there were 152 inmates in the insane asylum. There were several discharged last month, but so many are coming in just now the number is not diminished. The China woman recently sent from Helena is quite obstreperous, and an Indian, a half breed, who has been "off" ever since he was born, recently brought from the Flathead reservation to Missoula and sent up for insanity, makes the atmosphere fairly jingle with his whoops. — New Northwest.

December 18, 1888
LR 31,472/1888, RG 75, National Archives, Washington, D.C.

> See editor's annotation to Ronan's August 6, 1887, letter for more information about the efforts of Pierre Busha and the Cree Metis to settle on the Flathead Reservation. According to a note attached to this letter, the Office of Indian Affairs was providing $1500 to "keep these people through the winter — must shift for themselves after that." The action notation on this letter was "File," so no instructions were sent to Ronan.

United States Indian Service
Flathead Agency, M.T.
December 18, 1888.

The Hon. Commissioner of Indian Affairs
Washington, D.C.

Sir:

On the 6th day of August, 1887, I had occasion to report by letter to the Hon. Commissioner of Indian Affairs the presence on this reservation, of Pierre Busha, the Cree halfbreed associated with Louis Riel in the halfbreed rebellion in British Northwest Territory, who was executed by the British authorities in Regina. The executed chief had as his seconds in command, Gabriel Dumont, and the person in question, Pierre Busha. By reference to said report it will be seen that Busha came from the Cree halfbreed camp of refugees, then encamped on Depouire Creek, near Sun river, in Montana, to negotiate with the Indians of this reservation to be allowed to remove said encampment of halfbreed Crees, consisting of sixty families to this reservation. A council of the Confederated tribes was held at the time and the request of Busha was refused. At the request of Busha I sent the following dispatch to the Indian Office:

Arlee, Oct. 29th 1887

Commissioner of Indian Affairs
Washington, D.C.

Pierre Busha of Cree refugees is at this Agency and will leave for Cree encampment in three days from date — is desirous to learn if encouragement will be given to the Crees by the Government to either settle upon public lands or give them homes on some Indian reservation — Blackfoot reservation would suit if they can't remove here. Awaits answer if he can encourage his people to this effect.

(Sgd.) Ronan, Agent

To the above I received the following reply:

Washington, D. C.
October 31st, 1887

Tell Pierre Busha, Indian Department can make him no promise in regard to lands for British Cree refugees.

(Sgd) J. D. C. Atkins
Commissioner

Upon receipt of this I read it to Busha, and requested him to depart and not to return here with his followers as the Indians of this reservation would not permit of their settlement among them.

He departed but returned again and is now here with at least fifty of his followers, and several families, and the statement is said to be made by him that the Cree halfbreeds have resolved to settle on this reserve with or without the consent of the Indians who belong here. The Cree young men are not desirable associates for these Indians; most of them are gamblers who have nothing to lose but all to gain in their games; many are disolute [sic] in their habits and none have sympathy with the Indians of this reserve either in blood or religion.

The Chiefs and head-men of this reservation request that I ask the Indian Department to rid them of these people, whom they claim if not checked at once, will soon over run their country, not only by the sixty families from Sun river, Montana, but a threatened influx from the British Possessions.

I would respectfully call your attention to this matter and ask how to proceed under the circumstances.

1st If to be gathered into one encampment, I am of the opinion it will require the aid of the military to do so, as they will hardly obey the mandates of the Indian police.

2d The Crees have nothing upon which to live and depend for food upon the generosity of the Indians of this reservation. When gathered into camp rations should be provided for them until they are taken to some refuge and off of this reservation.

3d If escorted off of this reserve and back to their encampment on Depouire Creek, they will have to be provided for as they would be destitute of provisions and clothing.

I have ordered the Clerk and Farmer to go over the reservation and locate the whereabouts of the Crees, and ascertain as near as possible their exact numbers.

I am very respectfully
Your ob'dt serv't
Peter Ronan
U.S. Indian Agent.

1889

January 15, 1889
LR 1,894/1889, RG 75, National Archives, Washington, D.C.

Frank Decker had operated sawmills at Frenchtown and Missoula with various partners during the early 1870s before coming to work for the Flathead Agency.[1] On April 5, 1874, he married Louise LaFontaine at the Jocko Agency.[2] At the agency he operated the flour mill and sawmill. During 1878 Decker reported having ground 8,000 bushels of grain for tribal members.[3] Louise drowned in Missoula in 1894 under mysterious circumstances.[4] For information on Peter Finley see the annotation to Ronan's February 14, 1885, letter.

United States Indian Service,
Flathead Agency,
Jan. 15th, 1889.

Hon. Commissioner of Indian Affairs
Washington, D.C.
　　Sir:
　　I[n] reply to office A – 138 – 89, I would state, that Frank Decker's widow is living = but as she is of bad moral repute — being, at present, an inmate of a house of prostitution at Missoula — Mr Decker desired, that She have nothing to do either with children or any property he might leave.
　　None of his children are of age — the oldest being about twelve years.
　　By a will, dated, Just prior to his death, Mr Decker left one Peter Finley, a halfbreed of this reserve, in charge of his three children and whatever property he might die possessed of. Said Finley has not taken out letters of administration — What little property there is, being upon the reservation. I would, therefore, respectfully request, that Peter Finley be Authorized to sign for the pay of Frank Decker, during the month of October, without taking letters of Administration — As the cost of taking out same and appointing of appraisers would consume nearly, if not all of the Small possessions left by Decker for the benefit of his orphan Children.

Very respectfully
Your obt. Svt.
Peter Ronan
U.S. Indian Agent.

February 4, 1889
LR 3,882/1889, RG 75, National Archives, Washington, D.C.

Legal complications surrounding paying Salish Indians for the railroad right-of-way through Bitterroot Valley allotments dragged on for years. For more information see annotation for Ronan's August 6, 1888, letter.

United States Indian Service,
Flathead Agency, M. T.
February 4th, 1889.

The Hon. Commissioner of Indian Affairs,
Washington, D.C.

Sir:

Referring to your letter "L 20406 – 1888 – 28902,["] dated January 7th, 1889, with enclosure from the Hon. Secretary of the Interior, I would respectfully report that I referred the matter under discussion to W. F. Sanders, Attorney for Montana for the Northern Pacific Railroad Company and enclosed to his address a copy of said letter, and also a copy of the letter from the Secretary of the Interior. I herewith forward copy of Attorney's reply, and have the honor to be

Your ob'd't. serv't.
Peter Ronan
U.S. Indian Agent.

Enclosure:

(Copy)

Helena, Montana
Feb. 1st, 1889

Peter Ronan, Esq.,
Indian Agent,
Arlee, Mont.

Dear Sir:

I have received your letter, with enclosures; copies of letters from the Commissioner of Indian Affairs and the Secretary of the Interior, with reference to the non-payment by the Missoula and Bitter Root Valley Railroad Co. of damages occasioned by the construction of that company's road across certain farms belonging to individual Indians of the Flathead tribe in that Valley.

You were assured by Mr Marshall that the Company had no disposition to evade payment for those lands. I gave you the same assurance in a conversation I had with you, and I shall forward your communication to the General Counsel of the Company in New York for instructions, when I will advise you further.

Yours etc.
(Sgd) W. F. Sanders.

March 4, 1889
LR 5,921/1889, telegram, RG 75, National Archives, Washington, D.C.

John E. Clifford was the son-in-law of T. J. Demers, the Frenchtown merchant. Clifford's wife, Delima, was part Pend d'Oreille and educated in Montreal. In 1887 Demers put Clifford in charge of his store and other business enterprises in Demersville at the head of Flathead Lake. Clifford was flamboyant and popular among the white population in western Montana. In addition to his prominent business activities, Clifford was also a drinker and years later was arrested in Butte and sent to the Montana State Prison for grand larceny.[5] After the killing of an unnamed Kootenai Indian by Clifford, reports of an "Indian uprising" appeared in newspapers around the nation, including the *New York Times* and *Washington Post*.[6] A Dr. Cunningham was charged as complicit in the crime. Clifford and Cunningham were brought before the grand jury for murder and discharged.[7] Later Clifford returned to operate Demers' store at Demersville.[8] Chief Eneas' threat of revenge referred to by Ronan seemed to have been an example of Eneas' efforts to avoid general conflict with the whites while still seeking justice for his people. No biographical information was located on Dr. Cunningham.

3/4, 1889
Flat Head Agency Arlee Mont

To Indian Commissioner,
Washn D.C.

News reached me that an indian who was struck on the head with a revolver by one J. E. Clifford at head of Flathead Lake has since died from wound. It is stated that Chief Eneas and the father of the victim say that while they will not trouble innocent people they will Kill Clifford at all hazards. I start at once to Allay excitement among indians & to have arrests made.

Ronald [sic], Agent.

April 1, 1889
LR 9,008/1889, RG 75, National Archives, Washington, D.C.

On June 18, 1889, the Commissioner of Indian Affairs agreed to permit the trail through the southwest corner of the Flathead Reservation provided no buildings or stopping places were constructed on the reservation portion of the trail.[9]

United States Indian Service,
Flathead Agency,
April 1st, 1889.

Hon. Commissioner Indian Affairs,
Washington, D.C.

Sir:

Herewith I have the honor to forward communication from the Secretary of the "Iron Mountain Company," a corporation owning mines that border upon the Flathead reservation, asking the privilege — in the construction of a trail from the mines to the Northern Pacific Railroad — to cross with the said trail, a very small corner of the Southwest portion of this Reservation. In as much as the Third Article of the Treaty between the United States and the Flathead, Kootenai and Upper Pend 'd Oreilles Indians, concluded at Hell Gate, in the Bitter Root Valley, July 16th, 1855, and ratified by the Senate, March 8th, 1859: "*Provided* that if necessary for the public convenience, roads may be run through the said reservation." The trail through the Southwest corner of the reserve will not interfere with the Indians in any way, as its route lies through a Mountainous region unoccupied by said Indians. I have consulted with the chiefs and head men of the tribe and they offer no objection to the construction of the trail. I would respectfully recommend that the "Iron Mountain Company" be granted the privilege of opening said trail to the Northern Pacific Railroad through said portion of the Flathead reservation as a matter of public convenience.

I am very respectfully
Your obedient Servant,
Peter Ronan
U.S. Indian Agent.

Enclosure:

Office of
The Iron Mountain Company,
Helena, Mont., March 31st, 1889

Major Peter Ronan, U.S. Indian Agent, Flathead Indians,
Flathead Agency, Montana

Dear Sir:

The "Iron Mountain Company" of Montana, a corporation owning Mines that border upon the Reservation of the Flathead Indians, find that in the construction of a Trail from the mines to the Northern Pacific Railroad, that it will materially assist them if they can obtain permission from the proper authorities to cross with said trail a very small portion of the Southwest corner of said reservation; and I write to you to make application for such permission, from the proper authorities; and if you will kindly advise this office of the necessary formalities, we will carry out same according to the established precedents in your service.

I am very respectfully yours,
Chas. K. Wells
Secretary of the
"Iron Mountain Company"

N.B. The purpose of the Trail we desire to construct, is to ship our Ores from the mines, and to bring in our supplies.

May 1, 1889
LR 12,500/1889, RG 75, National Archives, Washington, D.C.

Chief Arlee carried on a running battle with the Flathead Agency sponsored Court of Indian Offenses and tribal police force. See the annotation to Ronan's January 1, 1887, letter. Twice during 1889, Arlee traveled to *The Weekly Missoulian* office to complain about whippings and other punishments ordered by the judges of the Court of Indian Offenses.[10] Agent Ronan and Arlee were able to work together on some things, but continually fought over other topics. On May 20, 1889, Henry M. Marchant, Special Agent for the Department of Justice, interviewed Chief Arlee and the Indian court judges about Arlee's complaints. Marchant found Arlee evasive, but ordered the whippings stopped because they offended white sensibilities.[11]

United States Indian Service,
Flathead Agency, M. T.
May 1st, 1889.

The Hon. Commissioner of Indian Affairs
Washington, D.C.

Sir:

It is my pleasant duty to report from this Agency, that during the month of April, the Indians have been very busy planting their crops and have, already, got in a very much larger acreage of wheat and oats, potatoes and all Kinds of garden seeds, than ever before. Extensive meadows of timothy have also been seeded. The orchards already planted by the Indians show vigorous thrift, and some of the trees are in blossom, greatly to their delight, as they expect to gather this season their first apples, plums, cherries, etc.

Snow fell very lightly in the mountains last winter which will cause low water and a scarcity for irrigation. The irrigation ditch is being put in the best possible condition to catch the water flow, and, I trust, with spring rains the crops will not suffer. Very few of the Indians are away from the reservation, and they constitute an element of young loafers, gamblers and drunkards, who cannot be restrained outside of prison walls. This is the class, who, backed by Arlee, Chief of Flatheads, make all the annoyance and disturbance on this reservation. Arlee has always bitterly opposed the Court of Indian Offences, the Judges and the Indian police, because he imagines it takes away from him full swing of arbitrary power. The vicious and the law-breakers are his only adherents now, and they are doing all in their power to break up the force of police, who do the best they can to suppress the vice of illegal cohabitation, drunkeness and gambling.

Soon as crops are planted attention will be turned to the whitewashing of fences and buildings at the Agency, and also the painting of roofs. The new matching and planing machine has arrived and soon as time will permit, will be put into place and in full running order.

I have the honor herewith to forward sanitary report and report of funds and indebtedness for the month of April, also report of Farmer and have the honor to be

Your obedient servant,
Peter Ronan
U.S. Indian Agent.

June 1, 1889
LR 15,058/1889, RG 75, National Archives, Washington, D.C.

Lawrence Finley was a thorn in Ronan's side for many years. See the annotation to Ronan's August 21, 1887, letter for more information about his run-ins with the law and time in Montana State Prison.

Ronan hired Al Sloan, a mixed blood living on the Flathead Reservation, to apprehend Finley. Sloan tracked Finley and captured him in the Sun River Country.[12] After he was jailed in Missoula, Finley stated that he had witnessed two Pend d'Oreilles Indians, Pierre Paul and Lalasee, kill two white men at the mouth of the Jocko River in fall 1888.[13] The Missoula County Sheriff immediately began trying to capture the two alleged murderers. Ronan told more about the circumstances surrounding the hiring of Al Sloan to capture Finley in his letter of July 8, 1889.

Allen Sloan was a mixed blood Chippewa Indian who had married a part Kootenai lady, Cecilia Morigeau, settled on the Flathead Reservation, and was adopted into the tribe. For many years he operated a ferry, stage line, and other businesses on the Flathead River between the towns of Ronan and Hot Springs.[14]

United States Indian Service,
Flathead Agency,
June 1st, 1889.

Hon. Commissioner Indian Affairs
Washington, D.C.
Sir:
In submitting my report for the month of May, I would respectfully state that all matters pertaining to the Indian Service on this reservation are in good condition. The Indians have given attention to their fields and farms and the flourishing appearance of their crops at this date give hope for a bountiful yield. Since the planting of their crops several have delivered pine logs at the Agency saw mill, to be cut into dimention [sic] lumber for building purposes. At least three hundred thousand feet of logs were delivered at the mill during

the month by Indians of the reserve to make lumber for their own use. This will involve considerable labor in the saw mill during the month of June.

A surplus of last year's wheat left over from seeding has also been hawled to the grist mill by Indians to be ground into flour.

The roofs of the Agency buildings have been painted, and the fences and buildings are now being whitewashed.

I have just returned from a prolonged pursuit of a halfbreed outlaw and murderer, whom I was successful in capturing, and placed in the Missoula county jail. On Saturday evening the 3d day of May, Larra Finlay, a mixed breed, accompanied by a Kootenai Indian called Jocko, went to the lodge of some Indians of that tribe, at the head of Flathead, off the reservation and near the store and saloon of one Ramsdell. They had several bottles of whisky with them, and all of the Indians commenced drinking. The result was the murder of Jocko, the Kootenai Indian, by Finlay.

This mixed breed, Finlay, is a noted outlaw who has given me more trouble than any [other] Indian or halfbreed on the reservation, for twelve years, or ever since his boyhood. In 1887, he committed a rape upon an Indian woman, and from his brutal treatment she died. He was arrested by the Indian Police and put in jail an [sic] the reservation. From there he escaped, and attempted to kill me, but I succeeded in his capture and turned him over to the military authorities at Fort Missoula. Under date of September 26, 1887, record will be found in your office that Finlay was released from his military imprisonment for want of evidence to make a conviction before the Territorial Courts. He has ever since been a terror to all respectable Indians, and has committed a number of crimes. He is now in jail and confessed to me his knowledge, and probable assistance in the murder of two whitemen about two years ago. He gave the names of two Indians who killed them. The Indian Police are now in pursuit of them and soon as arrested I shall report in detail. The expense in the pursuit and capture of this murderer is considerable. An account in detail will be forwarded to your office.

I herewith enclose Sanitary report and report of funds and indebtedness for the month of May, and also report of Farmer, and have the honor to be

Very respectfully
Your obedient servant
Peter Ronan
United States Indian Ag't.

June 3, 1889
Ronan, Peter, Charges file, RG 48, National Archives, Washington, D.C.

> William and Ralph Ramsdell were traders, law officers, and liquor dealers in Tobacco Plains and the Upper Flathead Valley. They were involved in a long running battle with Ronan over alleged crimes committed by Kootenai Indians in the Upper Flathead Valley. They seem to have antagonized the situation and committed crimes against Chief Eneas and other Kootenai Indians including the lynching of two accused murderers in 1888. See the annotation to Ronan's February 2, 1887, letter for more information about the Ramsdells.
>
> The article by Ramsdell attacking Ronan and Ronan's reply were enclosed with this letter to the Commissioner and are reproduced below.[15] Ramsdell's complaints against Ronan involved some cultural differences over fences, private property, and hospitality. Ramsdell

wanted tribal members confined to the reservation. Some of the murders of white people he referred to were committed by Nez Perce and other non-Flathead Reservation Indians. Ramsdell accused Ronan of being "an eager champion of the aborigines" motivated "by a prejudice towards those of his own color." Ronan replied that he had already submitted evidence in the criminal cases to the U.S. Marshall for prosecution. He also charged Ramsdell with selling liquor to Indians at his trading post.

An earlier Ramsdell rant against the Kootenais was published in "The Kootenai Indians," *Missoula Gazette*.[16]

Sophie Morigeau, the mixed blood Tobacco Plains trader, was a remarkable woman. She traded and ranched in northwest Montana for many years in the late nineteenth century. She was related to the Flathead Reservation tribes through both the Morigeau and Finley families.[17]

> United States Indian Service,
> Flathead Agency,
> June 3d, 1889.

Hon. Commissioner Indian Affairs,
Washington, D.C.
    Sir:

I am informed that one Ramsdell, has in circulation a petition to the President of the United States, for which he is obtaining signatures asking for my removal as Agent of the Flathead Indian Agency. In order that your office may be thoroughly informed of the character and motives of said Ramsdell, I herewith attach certain papers which will explain themselves. In conclusion I would respectfully state that Captain Henry M. Marchant Special Agent of the Department of Justice is now at this Agency, upon my request, through your office, and among other affairs pertaining to the good of the Indian Service, I have requested him to investigate and report to his department the charges contained in attached papers, presuming that copies of said reports may reach the Indian office through the proper channel.

> I am very respectfully,
> Your obedient servant,
> Peter Ronan
> United States Indian Agent.

First enclosure. Note that this letter was unsigned:
Major Peter Ronan.

The following information or "pointers" may be of use to you. Ramsdell Bros. are circulating a petition at the Head of the Lake asking the President to remove you and getting lots of signers. In fact Wm. Ramsdell boasts that he has started in to down you. As the Ramsdells would hesitate at nothing this letter for several reasons must be anonymous. They probably would not have engineered that lynching last year if they had not had a grudge against at least (believe it was something about some horses) one of the Indians. Knowing the way a letter of this kind is looked on, it is perhaps un-necessary to ask you say nothing about receiving it, but if you care to look up the persons and pointers you ought to find enough about them to show them up in their true light.

The Missoula Merc. Co. has sold them goods and whiskey for four or five years and they have sold it at Tobacco Plains to white-men or indians, without any license, most of the time. It was not long before they had what cattle the indians had and a good many of their horses.

Of parties now at Tobacco Plains who could give you information about the Ramsdells, as they know themselves got whiskey from them and know the Indians did. Colin Sinclair, Tom Quirk, John Campbell, Sophia Mosure [Morigeau]. Then there is S. Butler used to be at Tobacco Plains — believe he is now at Ashley, and McGregor, who bought old man Sullivan's cattle, and now has a ranch somewhere near Little Bitter Root. A. S. Lanneau of Ashley claims to have been swindled by Wm. Ramsdell and could give you the particulars and Hon. Wm. Ramsdell was a common tin-horn gambler and rounder at Golden and other Camps on the Canadian Pacific during 1885 until he was run out. Chris. Finnelson formerly of As[h]ley and Tobacco Plains, who is now at Demersville temporarily but whose family is at Butte City used to be a right hand man of Ramsdells but they quarreled and Finnelson has since said he knew things about the Ramsdells that they didn't want him to tell.

Some of the Indians at Tobacco Plains could tell you things if they wanted to, how the Ramsdells used to gamble with and rob them with marked cards and how they debauched the indian women, both the Ram[s]dell Bros, became diseased and Wm. Ramsdell went to the Deer Lodge Hot Springs for that reason last summer or fall. McGowen of Horse Plains knows something of their reputation and Oscar McMillan of the same place claimed to have a horse stealing case against them two or three years ago.

From some of the parties here given you should be able to find out all, that I have here touched on and much more. They have started in to try and down you and you had better show what kind of an outfit are fighting you as soon as possible. But you will have to be careful in speaking to these parties, some of them might be willing to tell all they knew, whether you mentioned their names or not and then again they may not. Finnelson, Lanneau and McGregor can give you plenty of information if they want to. I would advsie [sic] you to try and see Finnelson. He might tell you all he knew if he knew you were defendind [sic] yourself from Ramsdell and that he Finnelson would not be injured by it. In fact Finnelson has no use for them now.

I was present at the agency when agent Ronan received the original of which this is a true copy.

Henry M. Marchant
Special Agent Dept Justice

Second enclosure:

Copy.

British Columbia.
Indian Office.
Victoria, Jany. 14th. 1887.

Sir: —

I am informed on credible authority that messers Ramsdell Bros., traders on tobacco Plains, about six miles south of the Boundary Line, are in the habit of selling Indians from Kootenay spirituous liquors, in quantities, and many of the Natives of that place have lately been intoxicated.

I should be glad if you would take immediate steps tp [sic] put a stop to the traffic referred to, or, if out of your power, that you may kindly acquaint me accordingly.

I have the honor to be,
Sir,
Your obedient servant,
sg. S. W. Powell [i.e., I. W. Powell],
Indian Commissioner.

P. Ronan, Esq.,
U.S. Indian Agent.

Third enclosure. Clipping from The Helena Journal *(daily), April 27, 1889, page 1, col. 8:*

Flathead Fears.
The Aboriginal Nuisance Bereft of Poetic Primp.
Merciless Miscreants of Misery.

The Indian Agent of the Flathead Reservation Scored for Incompetency
— White Settlers Adjoining the Line Greatly Annoyed.
A List of Unpunished Crimes.

Egan, Mont., April 22. — [Correspondence to the Journal.] — The lawless attitude of the Indians both on the Flathead reservation and in the adjoining territory of the whites naturally arouses the query as to the efficiency of the Indian agent in charge. According to the annual reports of this individual, the Indians are fast overtaking their caucasian neighbors in the great march of civilization; crime has almost disappeared and those peculiar characteristics of the aborigines which have been opposed to progressive influences have been totally eradicated.

Such rosy-lined words paintings of this subject are, no doubt, gratifying to eastern missionaries and the Indian bureau, but to people acquainted with the facts, it is a caricature that is read with a feeling not unmixed with indignation.

Without reflecting on the personal character of the present Indian agent of the Flatheads, too strong language cannot be used in condemnation of his weak, purile, and apparantly [sic] indifferent policy in allowing the worst element of the reservation Indians free access to white men's homes. This unrestrained intercourse on the part of the Indians has been the production of a growing state of lawlessness and crime in the territory so invaded by these desperadoes, until at the present time humanity and justice demand that it cease.

For the information of the public the writer will submit a few of the principal crimes committed by these progressive wards of the indulgent major, who according to his reports divide their time scrupously [sic] between religious devotions and the elevating influences of agricultural pursuits.

In June, 1887, three white men were murdered at Wolf Prairie, within sixty miles of this place, as they sat around their camp fire, unconscious of the approach of the savage murderers. The crime was planned and executed with a callousness peculiarly characteristic of the savage, and in the subsequent burning of the bodies they exhibited emotions in their wild orgies around the funeral pile worthy of fiends incarnate.

The following summer the decayed remains of a white man, with the skull fractured, were found at the mouth of the Jocko river on the reservation. In connection with this tragedy, of which no survivor tells the sad tale, it is perhaps fitting to say that despite the strong suspicions attaching to certain Indians on the reservation nothing has been done in the matter and the murderers are still at large.

Aside from the suspicions referred to, pointing to the murderers, the woman first discovering the body being threatened with death if she disclosed the fact, places their guilt in the region of moral certainty. About the same time a renegade band wandered as far north as Tobacco Plains, where they killed several cattle for the settlers there, and were openly defiant and insulting in their demeanor towards the whites.

Only a few weeks ago the tragedy occurring at Dunersville [Demersville], so familiar to the public, was brought about by the lawless and defiant conduct of the deceased, who was one of the most notorious whisky rustlers in the whole tribe.

Not ten days ago a circumstance of the same kind happened near Camas prairie, which terminated in the death of the whiskey crazed, frenzied savage who was pursuing his white victim with murderous intent.

It is far from pleasant to contemplate such scenes in a peaceable community, where innocent women and children are at the mercy of these lawless Indian ruffians.

The minor offences which have been committed during the time mentioned would fill a volume. It is sufficient to remark in enumerating some of them that horses have been repeatedly stolen, cabins broken open and rifled of their contents, fences torn down to allow of unrestricted passage, and the privacy of homes and firesides invaded by these lawless, drunken savages, who use their reservation as a rendezvous from which to sally forth on their deviltry.

It is bad enough to have society torn and convulsed by the criminal acts of its own members, which cannot be extirpated by intelligently operating law; but when whole communities are to be constantly menaced with the invasion of a savage foe, whom the Indian agent allows unrestricted access to their territory, it is time a long-suffering people demanded the retirement of this incompetent and indifferent individual. What right have these Indians wandering through white mens' territory off from public highways? Is not the agent supposed to keep them at home?

These are pertinent questions and a great many people in this vicinity would like to have them answered authoritatively.

Had-Nack remained where he belonged at Dayton Creek on the reservation, Missoula tax-payers would be some $2,000 better off and Major Ronan still enjoy the benign influence of one of his warmest advocates, who when off the reservation was a daring horse thief, an impudent rascal, a skillful liar and a dangerous medicine-man, always ready to stir up race prejudices. It was his boast nearly the last coherent words he every uttered that in case he survived white blood would run like water in Flathead.

This matter should receive the public attention especially in places like Missoula county and vicinity where all the public highways are traversed by Indians.

Indeed it is alarming the number of murders that have been committed in the last few years by so-called peaceable Indians living under the protection of reservation laws. Not less than twenty-five murders have been committed by these savages in the last three years in a country with an area scarcely larger than Missoula county.

With the Wolf Creek murders mentioned in this article, the Sand Point and Spokane Falls murders, and the Rombaugh murder, so familiar to Missoula county people, it is no wonder that prospectors and miners alone in the mountains are becoming timid.

Did the Indian agent of the Flathead reservation manifest the same supreme indifference when the rights of Indians against whites were in question it might be urged as an extenuating circumstance in his official conduct towards his own race, but in this direction he is not only an eager champion of the aborigines but seems to be activated by a prejudice towards those of his own color, which early association and memories should still hold with some lingering regard.

There are some things that cannot be done easy, as there are acts that cannot be changed by changing their name and, although this article may seem to reflect severely on the present agent of the Flatheads, it is written in a spirit of due consideration, candor and truth, and things have been called by their proper names.

The rights of the masses are superior to the individual when they meet on the same level, and in justice to the people of this vicinity who have been long terrorized by drunken and vicious Indians, these charges have been preferred against the party responsible — the agent in charge of them.

It is hoped that the new administration will take hold of the matter and relieve the present incumbent, and, so far from feeling doubtful of better results in case of a change, it is the universal feeling here that blind chance could do no worse.

R.

Fourth enclosure. Clipping from The Helena Journal *(daily), May 12, 1889, page 1, col. 8:*

A Word in Return.
Major Peter Ronan of the Flathead Reservation Pays His Respects to Mr. Ramsdale.

Flathead Indian Agency, Mont., May 11, — [To the editor Helena Journal.] — Under date of April 27, 1889, you gave publication to a letter from one Ramsdale, dated at Egan, Montana, in which, as stated in your head lines, he scores the Indian agent of the Flathead reservation for incompetency, and in the article he gives a list of "unpunished Indians crimes," but failed to cite his own case, which as yet has gone unpunished and comes under the head of "unpunished crimes," as I shall try to show simply by official correspondence, without stultifying myself by taking notice of this fellow who seeks through public print to bring himself into notice, as he probably thinks his own case has been overlooked.

Under date of January 14, 1887, I received a letter from Hon. J. W. Powell [i.e., I. W. Powell], Indian Commissioner, Victoria, British Columbia, which being official I am not at liberty to publish without the consent of that gentleman. However I see no reason why I should not publish my reply, which is as follows:

[Here Ronan copied his February 2, 1887, letter to Powell regarding sales of whiskey to Indians by the Ramsdell Brothers store in Tobacco Plains, which is reproduced as an enclosure to Ronan letter to the Commissioner of Indian Affairs, February 2, 1887.]

United States Marshal's Office, District of Montana, Deer Lodge, Montana, Feb. 22, 1887: Hon. Peter Ronan, U.S. Indian Agent, Flathead Agency: Dear Sir: — I have the honor to inclose herewith original letter received from Hon. Robert B. Smith, U.S. attorney, in answer to my letter to him submitting the complaint of Major J. W. Powell [i.e., I. W. Powell], British Indian commissioner, against the Ramsdale Brothers. If the suggestions of Attorney Smith are adopted, and at any time the service of the marshal is required, I will promptly do anything in my power to correct the illegal traffic mentioned in Major Powell's letter.

Very respectfully yours,
R. S. Kelly, U.S. Marshal.

I would simply inform the public that the papers in the case of "this unpunished crime" have been turned over to Mr. Kelly's successor, Mr. Geo. W. Irvine.

I have only to say that there is another "unpunished crime" hanging over the author of the Journal's article, which will be sifted thoroughly by the next grand jury. In conclusion, I shall only add that the good people of Missoula county will probably see that no person upon whom a suspicion rests of an "unpunished crime" will be elected to the constitutional convention which meets on the 4th of July, 1889, at Helena.

Peter Ronan.

June 12, 1889
LR 16,035/1889, RG 75, National Archives, Washington, D.C.

This account of a June 8, 1889, council with Ronan, Special Agent of the Department of Justice H. M. Marchant, Chief Eneas, and Chief Michelle emphasized Eneas' efforts to maintain peace with the white settlers in the Upper Flathead Valley. In 1888 a mob of white men had lynched two Kootenai Indians accused of murder and then surrounded the Kootenai camp at Dayton and threatened Eneas. Eneas kept calm and defused the situation so it did not lead to more bloodshed. As he said in this council, he worked hard to keep his young men out of trouble, but local whites sold them whiskey. While Eneas asked for justice and government support to keep the peace, Marchant was primarily worried about the use of whipping for punishment. Since public whippings offended late nineteenth century white sensibilities, the Commissioner of Indian Affairs ordered them stopped. Without whippings to punish misbehavior, the reservation needed a new jail.[18]

United States Indian Service,
Flathead Agency,
June 12, 1889.

Hon. Commissioner of Indian Affairs
Washington, D.C.
   Sir:
In compliance with the request of Captain Henry M. Marchant, Special Agent of the Department of Justice, I accompanied that gentleman to the Foot of Flathead Lake, on this reservation, where I called an Indian Council, for the purpose of obtaining Indian evidence against whisky trading whitemen, who make a business of selling whisky to Indians. Also to inquire into and get evidence against a mob of white men who took the law into their own hands and

hung two Kootenai Indians of this reservation, and who after the hanging, with arms in their hands, surrounded the camp of Chief Eaneas, on this reservation, for the purpose of intimidation etc.

On the 8th of June the Indian Council met, and I herewith have the honor to submit a synopsis of the proceedings:

After the usual hand shaking and greeting were over Agent Ronan addressed his interpreter:

Tell Chief Eneas I agreed to meet him and his head men here two weeks ago, but one of his men was killed at the Head of the Lake, and I followed and captured the murderer at Great Falls, on the Missouri river, and that is the reason I did not get here on time.

Now tell Eneas that I have very little to say — only what I am here for and what Captain Marchant is here for. Tell him that for the last two years the drunkeness has been much worse then at any time since I came here — twelve years ago; also the debauchery of women by the young men of the tribes. It is my opinion that the beginning of all Indian trouble is whisky. When whisky comes on the reserve then commences all other crimes. I have asked from Washington the Great Fathers assistance to put a stop to this whisky selling to Indians. The Great Father ordered the Judge or Chief Justice to send some one here to put a stop to it, and he has sent this gentleman, Captain Henry M. Marchant, Special Agent from the Department of Justice, at Washington, to assist me in this effort to suppress the sale of whisky to the Indians.

Now tell Eneas, that something over a year ago two of his people were hung by a mob at the Head of the Lake; that though the Indians may have been guilty, no mob had a right to hang them. That is what the law is for — to punish crime; that is why taxes are paid — why we have Judges, Courts, Sheriffs and jails — why we have law! In the eyes of the law a croud [sic] of men who take a man and hang him are looked upon as criminals. It is the duty of Eneas or any of his men present, if they know the names of any of the men who did this hanging to give their names to Captain Marchant. It is also the duty of Chief Eneas and his men, and also of the Pend 'd Oreille Chief Michel, who is present, and his men, if they know, to give the names of any white men who are or have been guilty of selling whisky to Indians. If any present have bought whisky, it is their duty to give names, time and place to Captain Marchant.

Now I have only to add that there is a big steer in the corrall, and some sugar, coffee, flour etc., at my camp, and to send men after them and others to butcher the beef, and while the women are preparing the feast, Captain Marchant, through my interpreter will talk with Eaneas and Michel, and he and Mr. [Henry] Lambert will take what evidence they may have to present.

Captain Marchant to the Interpreter:

Say to Eneas that the Agent, Major Ronan has fully explained to them my mission here. I came from Washington to put a stop to selling whisky to Indians by whitemen, and that I need their assistance, and without it it will be almost impossible for me to do it; but if they will give me their aid I will do my utmost to stop it. I am here for their good and if they will put confidence in me I will help them. Important business calls the Major back to the Agency. I shall go to the Head of the Lake and make investigation as to who is selling whisky to Indians, and other matters connected with the good of the Indians. Say to Eneas that I want to ask him a few questions now.

Chief Eneas: Before answering you I desire to say a few words:

Michel [Revais, the interpreter], tell the Agent when the Great Father first sent him to us, he was a much younger man than he is to-day. His children have grown up around him on our reservation and I see one of his boys with him who was born in our country.

I was also young and strong — I looked like a Chief — I felt like a Chief. In my youth our Nation was at war with a great many tribes, and the last of our enemies that we made peace with were the Blackfeet. I was the War Chief of my tribe and was called Big Knife. To-day we are at peace with all of our enemies. The Blackfeet are our friends, and some of their children are at school with our children at the Mission. Until within a few years, there were few white people near our reservation. Now they surround us on all sides, thick almost as the leaves of the forest. When you came here there was only one white family living at Horse Plains. No white people at all at Thompson Falls; no miners in the Coer'd Alenes; and where the big city of Spokane Falls now stands I remember of but two white families living there. At the Head of the Flathead Lake where you are now going there was but one or two white men and no white families. Missoula had a small settlement of whites, but now it is a great big town — full of white people. In the days I speak of my young men could get but very little whisky — none knew the taste of it but those who hung around your settlement. It is different to-day! They have acquired the habit and love the influence of whisky, and in spite of your laws can procure all they can pay for. In old times I would take my whip in my hand and chastise any of my Indians that broke the law either by getting drunk or committing audultry [sic] or any other crime, and they feared me and my authority the same as your children fear your authority and chastisement as a father when they do wrong. I could controll my children then — I call all my tribe my children. Take the whip from my hand I have no controll. We have no good jails like the white people — no other mode of punishment in our camp, and the wild and desolute young men laugh at talk when it is not followed by punishment. The heart of a white man must be very small if he cannot see the necessity of authority by a chief in an Indian camp; and when I loose the use of the whip I loose all power to controll my people. I hope the Chief who has come here from Washington will help us. I am now ready to answer his questions.

Here the investigation and taking of evidence commenced, which I trust will soon lead to the arrest of guilty parties.

In reference to the remarks of Eneas about the use of the whip among the Indians, for the punishment of certain transgressions I would respectfully state that it has always been the rule of the tribes to use it. Captain Marchant made some objection to this as one of their modes of punishment; when the Judges and the policemen notified me that they would resign if they could not continue their own methods of punishment for crime. They claimed, with truth, that they had no good jail, and no other punishment to substitute that would strike terror where young men were guilty of drunkeness, running off with the wives of industrious Indians, debauching young girls of the tribes etc., etc. They also claim that they use the whip with moderation and practice no cruelty, and that the mere disgrace of being publicly flogged, however lightly, has more effect in keeping the young people straight than any other mode of punishment. I must say that I know of no act of cruelty practiced by the Indian Chiefs, Judges or Policemen, and all stories to that effect are mere exagerations. I have promised the Indians to submit the matter to the Hon. Commissioner of Indian

Affairs, and if, after Captain Marchants report is received, by his Department, he decides to order the abolishment of the whip altogether I shall so notify the Indians.

I herewith have the honor to enclose vouchers for expenses incurred in calling and feeding the Indians during the council, and have the honor to be

Your obedient servant
Peter Ronan
United States Indian Agent.

June 17, 1889
LR 16,722/1889, RG 75, National Archives, Washington, D.C.

> For more information on the accusations against Lawrence Finley and events surrounding his capture see Ronan's letters of August 21, 1887, and June 1, 1889, and their annotations. See also Ronan's July 8, 1889, letter. According to Ronan, Finley accused two other Indians, Pierre Paul and Lalasee, of murdering two white men in 1888. Baptiste Pierre Finley and his wife Sophie could not be found in the 1888 Flathead Reservation census.[19] For more information on Al Sloan, see Ronan's July 8, 1889, letter and annotation.

United States Indian Service,
Flathead Agency,
June 17th, 1889.

Hon. Commissioner Indian Affairs,
Washington, D.C.
Sir:

In my report for the month of May, I had the honor to state that I had returned from a prolonged pursuit of a half breed outlaw and murderer, whom I was successful in capturing and placing in the Missoula County Jail.

I also stated that on Saturday evening, the 3d day of May, Larra Finley, a mixed breed accompanied by a Kootenai Indian called Jocko went to the lodge of some Indians of that tribe at the head of Flathead Lake, off the reservation, and near the store and saloon of one Ramsdell. They had several bottles of whisky with them, and all of the Indians commenced drinking. The result was the murder of Jocko, the Kootenai Indian, by Finley.

This mixed breed Finley is a noted outlaw who has given me more trouble than any Indian or halfbreed on the reservation — for twelve years or ever since his boyhood. In 1887, he committed a rape upon a married Indian woman and from his brutal treatment she died. He was arrested by the Indian police and put in jail on the reservation. From there he escaped and attmped [sic] taking my life, but I succeeded in his capture and turned him over to the military authorities at Fort Missoula. Under date of September 26th, 1887, record will be found in your office that Finley was released from his military confinement for want of evidence to make a conviction before the Territorial Court. He has ever since been a terror to all respectable Indians, and has committed a number of crimes; among which was the murder of two white men who were encamped on this reservation something over a year ago. Finley confessed his knowledge and complicity in this terrible deed to me, in presence of the Sheriff of Missoula County, his deputy and H. A. Lambert, Agency farmer. He also gave the names of the Indian murderers who were accomplices and I am now making every effort in my power to place them under arrest and bring them to Justice. An accomplishment of these arrests and prompt and lawful punishment for the crime will accomplish untold good for the well being and good government of the Indians of this reserve. A small class of Indians and half-breeds, by their lawless acts, are a terror to the law abiding and industrious Indians and also a menace to the settlers outside of the reservation. I herewith attach some newspaper clippings from the Territorial press of Montana in regard to this arrest; and also have the honor to forward a bill of actual expenses in the running down of this notorious criminal and trust that my action will be approved and the expenses incurred by me allowed.

I have the honor to be
Very respectfully
Your obedient servant
Peter Ronan
United States Indian Agent.

First enclosure. Ronan attached three newspaper clippings to this letter. Only two of them are reproduced here. The first clipping was from The Helena Independent *(daily), May 14, 1889, page 1, col. 7:*

A Red Desperado.
Missoula Authorities on the Trail of a Half-Breed Murderer From the Flathead Reserve.

Some of the Crimes of Larra Finlay, Who Once Threatened Major Ronan's Life.

Imprisoned Several Times. But Each Time Released for Want of Evidence — The Cause of Arlee's Complaint.

Missoula, May 13. — [Special to the Independent.] — On Friday, the 9th inst. the following was wired to the sheriff of this county, and also to the sheriff of Choteau county:

Arlee, May 9th. — Arrest Larra Finlay, a half-breed murderer from this reservation. Will probably now be found with Peter Finlay, who is now on his way to Sun River and Fort Benton, over the trail by Haystack Butte, with a band of horses. Peter Finlay is all right, but get Larra. His upper lip is split. He talks English.

Ronan, U.S. Indian Agent.

Baptist Piere Finlay and his wife Sophie came to the agency and made the following statement to Maj. Ronan:

Several days ago I started with my wife to go to Tobacco plains, from the Jocko reservation. On my way up from the head of the lake I met two Indians with their wives coming fram [sic] Tobacco plains. They asked myself and wife to turn back with them, which we did. We camped near Demarsville, and a short distance from Egan, on Friday, the 3d of May. It rained all day Saturday, and we remained in our lodge. In the evening Larra Finlay, a mixed-breed, accompanied by a Kootenai Indian called Jock[o], came into the lodge and brought two bottles of whisky, and all commenced drinking. Tom, one of the Indians who camped with us, was outside of the lodge. When he came in Larra commenced to talk to him, when Jocko put his hand on Larra's mouth and told him to shut up — that he, Jocko, would do the talking. Then all got to their feet and I took hold of Jocko to prevent a fight. I threw Jocko down, when Larra jumped outside of the lodge and picked up a club with which he hit Jocko over the head while I had him down. The stick broke, I said, "don't hit him again

— you will kill him," and let go of Jocko to prevent Larra from repeating the blow, but he struck Jocko twice with the piece of stick he held in his hand, and killed him."

Larry Finley is a noted outlaw. In 1887 he committed a rape upon an Indian woman, and from his brutal treatment she died. He was arrested by the Indian police and put in jail at the reservation. From there he escaped, and meeting Major Ronan, who was on his way to Flathead lake, with his family, he followed him into the station at Arlee and demanded if he, the agent was looking for him. Ronan made an evasive reply until he was enabled to grab a gun, when he leveled it upon Larra and made him throw up his hands. Larra was then securely tied with a rope and Ronan got on a freight train and delivered him up to Col. Horace Jewett of the Third infantry then in command at Fort Missoula. Ronan reported his action to the Indian office and was ordered to turn Larra over to the civil authorities for trial. Upon date of September 26, 1887, Agent Ronan wrote to the authorities in Washington as follows: "I would respectfully report that I ordered the release of Larra Finlay from confinement at Fort Missoula. The woman he abused has since died, and as I can not obtain evidence upon which he would be probably be convicted I had the prisoner released. I arrested and conveyed the outlaw to Fort Missoula for safe keeping, because after he escaped from the Indian jail he made a personal attack upon me and threatened to take my life for having insisted upon his arrest by the Indian police for committing rape upon an Indian woman and from the effects of his brutal treatment asted [sic] above the woman has since died."

Having been released from the military jail, Larra came back to the reservation, a terror to all respectable Indians. From the reserve he went to Chewela, in Washington territory, stole two horses and eloped with wife of an Indian of that place. He returned to the reservation where he was arrested by the Indian police and compelled to give up horses in place of the ones he stole in Washington territory. In the mean time the festering body of a murdered white man was found on the Jocko river, and Larra was suspected of the crime. In order to prevent his escape until evidence could be procured against him he was put in jail and his hands were tied in the absence of a guard. This is the villain whom Arlee recently complained of being brutally treated by the police, and took to Missoula to make the complaint a half-breed who was in jail last winter for killing a Kootenai Indian, but released by the Indians on the plea of self-defense. Having been released he brought a supply of whisky to the reserve and for that offense was jailed by the Indian police, escaped and accompanied Arlee to Missoula to make sensational and lying complaints against the cruelty of the Indian police, particularly in the case of the murderer Sam Finlay, who got away from the Indian jail only to commit the crime of another murder, and for which he is now being hunted down.

Second enclosure. The source of this clipping has not been identified:

Finley Caged.
The Half-Breed Murderer Safely Lodged In the Missoula Jail.

Major Ronan, the Flathead Indian agent, went through last night on his return from Great Falls, where he had gone to bring back the half-breed murderer, Larra Finley, recently arrested for the murder of another Indian. He turned his prisoner over to Officer Keim, at the depot, who delivered him to the sheriff.

Major Ronan has taken a great deal of interest in this case, and has spared no expense to capture Finley, it costing him $250 for Al. Sloane's expenses, alone, which he paid out of his own pocket. Of the pursuit and capture of the murderer, the Great Falls Leader has this to say:

The crime with which Finley is charged was committed about a month ago. Finley, two Indians and a "tin-horn" gambler were together on the Flathead agency when a quarrel arose, followed by a fight. In the encounter it is alleged that Finley killed an Indian and fled. Major Ronan promptly issued a circular to sheriffs and Al. Sloane set out in quest of Finley. Sloane knows all about Indian habits. This aided him in tracking Finley, whom he found in the country north of Sun River. Sloane, who is a powerful man of determined look, took steps to secure his prisoner and accompanied him to town where he was safely jailed.

The story of the pursuit and capture of Finley reads like a romance.

At the instance of Major Ronan, Sloane set out in quest of Finley. He provided himself with horses and hired some half-breeds to go with him. He crossed the range and pushed forward to the Piegan agency, enduring much hardship on the way and incurring considerable expense, for the half-breeds knew that he needed them and they became costly companions. At length Sloane got a clue to the whereabouts of the fugitive. He kept on the trail until the other day he found himself near an Indian camp. On going nearer he saw about thirty Indians assembled. Among them was one whom his sharp eyes saw was Finley, although he was disguised in Indian clothes. Sloane resolved to loose no time. Accompanied by two half-breeds, he dashed boldly into the crowd and seized Finley. The Indians were amazed and were about to defend Finley when Sloane hustled him to a horse, compelling him to mount and then rode off. Sloane hired two more trusty half-breeds, placed them in charge of Finley, and then set out for this city. Resolving to keep clear of Indians he made a long circuit and came here by way of St. Peter's Mission. Here he informed Sheriff Downing of his success and asked him to go back with him and arrest Finley. The sheriff sent his efficient deputy, Joe Hamilton, who returned last evening with his prisoner.

June 24, 1889

LR 16,744/1889, telegram, RG 75, National Archives, Washington, D.C.

> See Ronan's full report on July 1, 1889, and the War Department correspondence at July 15, 1889, for further information on this fiasco. The Missoula Sheriff was hunting two Pend d'Oreilles accused of murdering white men but shot an innocent Indian instead.

June 24, 1889
Ravalli Mont.

Commissioner of Indian Affairs Washn DC

Sheriff has Killed one Indian. Shall I call for troops if prospect of an uprising.

Ronan
Agt.

July 1, 1889

LR 18,147/1889, RG 75, National Archives, Washington, D.C. The enclosed Ronan letter of June 27, 1889, to Gen. Thos. H. Ruger is now filed as LR 18,149/1889 in the National Archives.

Missoula County Sheriff D. J. Heyfron led a trigger-happy white posse onto the reservation in an effort to capture Pierre Paul and Lalasee, Pend d'Oreilles Indians accused by Lawrence Finley of having murdered two white men in 1888. The posse failed to capture the two fugitives, but managed to murder an innocent Indian in the process. The armed posse did not recognize the Indian but approached him with weapons drawn and then shot him because he ran. The sheriff and posse then fled west on the railroad to the safety of Horse Plains. The sheriff and the railroad employees at Ravalli spread alarmist reports of imminent Indian-white conflict which even reached East Coast newspapers.[20] According to the St. Ignatius Mission "Liber Defunctorum," the Indian killed by the posse was named Louis, husband of Justine: "He was killed by the Americans without any cause."[21]

Fearing further conflict, Ronan requested army troops from Fort Missoula to try to keep the situation from escalating.[22] Details of the deployment can be seen in the War Department correspondence reproduced at July 15, 1889, below.

Tribal members were upset about the murder of the innocent Indian but wanted justice, not expanded conflict. The situation quieted down, but no one was ever prosecuted for the murder of Louis by the posse.[23] The Indian version of these events was not recorded.

One newspaper account alleged that the Indian killed by the posse was guilty of a separate murder of a white miner near Horse Plains. No evidence was included to back up this claim, however, which could easily have been fabricated to exculpate the white posse members.[24]

Daniel J. Heyfron was a Civil War veteran, butcher, and prospector before coming to Missoula in 1882. In Missoula he operated a stone quarry and constructed irrigation ditches. In 1886 he was elected to the first of two terms as sheriff of Missoula County. A new jail was built during his term as sheriff.[25] Col. George Lippitt Andrews, commander of Fort Missoula in 1889, was born in Rhode Island. A Civil War veteran, he became a colonel on January 1, 1871, when assigned to the Twenty-Fifth Infantry Regiment. He retired in 1892.[26]

Almost no information has been found about Pierre Paul's and Lalasee's lives before the murders. They could not be identified in the 1889 Flathead Reservation census.[27] According to Duncan McDonald, Lalasee was a family man with children and "a good Indian" before his brother was killed by white men a few years earlier. In contrast, Duncan said, Pierre Paul was "a rowdy and a ruffian, a desperate man with a desire to kill. The Indians were afraid of him. He was in the habit of bullying and terrorizing all with whom he came in contact, but is at heart a coward."[28]

United States Indian Service,
Flathead Agency, M.T.
July 1st, 1889.

The Hon. Commissioner of Indian Affairs,
Washington, D.C.

Sir:

In submitting my report for the month of June, I am free to state, notwithstanding the sensational reports of war and insubordination among the Indians of this reservation, that the close of the present fiscal year finds the Indians of this reservation in a contented state and quietly attending their agricultural, pastoral and other pursuits. It is true that for the past week or ten days great excitement was caused, not only on the reservation but throughout the Territory, from the fact that a sheriff's posse came here from Missoula to arrest two Indians who are supposed to have been the murderers of two whitemen. I do not consider it necessary here to enter into details as to the cause of the presence of a sheriff's posse on this reservation, and the circumstances which led to the calling for troops, as it is fully stated in my report to Brigadier General Ruger, commanding the Department of Dakota, a copy of which I herewith enclose.

From exaggerated press reports, furnished principally from Ravalli Station, on the Northern Pacific Railroad, by excited and irresponsible persons, the troops are still retained here, although there is no necessity for their presence, and that fact has been communicated by me to the military authorities and also to the Governor of the Territory. United States Inspector, Marcum, who has been at this Agency for several days and who is here now, drove over the scene of the supposed excitement in my company, and wired to the Secretary of the Interior the fact that there was not any necessity for the retention of the troops, and that the Indians were quietly pursuing their various avocations and attending to their own business.

There was no excitement or suspension of work at this agency. The grist mill has been for some time and at this date is running on wheat belonging to Indians — a surplus from last years crop — while other employees are at work in the hay field and other necessary duties.

Owing to the unprecedented drought of the present season, there will be almost a total failure of crops, except where irrigation was attainable. Hay is very scarce and but little can be cut. I am doing the best I can to procure enough for Agency use, but fear I shall fall far short of a sufficient supply.

I herewith have the honor to enclose Sanitary report and reports of funds and indebtedness for the month of June, also report of farmer and quarterly report of schools, and have the honor to be,

Very respectfully,
Your obedient servant,
Peter Ronan
U.S. Indian Agent.

Enclosure:

United States Indian Service,
Flathead Agency, M.T.
June 27th, 1889.

Thos. H. Ruger
Brigadier General
Commanding Dept. Dakota
St. Paul, Minn.

Sir:

Under date of June 25th, 1889, I received a telegram from you in which it was stated you would be glad to have full statement of facts, including in addition to what was referred to in your telegram of the morning of the same date the facts as to the murder, when it took place, and the circumstances and to wire you at St. Paul. I replied briefly by telegraph but now will give you particulars by letter.

Under date of September 26th, 1888, P. H. Leslie, then Governor of Montana, received the following telegram from Washington:

"Can you give this Department any particulars concerning the alleged murder of Henry William Keys at Flathead, Montana?

(Signed) G. L. Rives
Acting Secretary of State."

Governor Leslie turned the matter over to me and I communicated with the authorities at Ottawa, and was informed by Hon. John Costigan, Minister of Inland Revenue, under the Dominion Government that the man who was reported to have been murdered and whose body was found near the mouth of the Jocko river, Flathead reservation, in July 1887, was reported to be William Henry Keys, of Ottawa. From the description and with the aid of Dr. Hedger, County Corner, I was enabled to report conclusively that the body found was not that of the person sought after by the Canadian authorities.

Recently a desperado, of mixed blood, named Lara Finley, murdered an Indian at the Head of the Flathead Lake, and I succeeded in having him arrested after a chase of several hundred miles and placed him in jail at Missoula.

Here Finley made the following confession which led to the issuance of warrants for the arrest of two Indians, who Killed the man who was supposed to be Keys, and also another man who was encamped with him:

Missoula, Montana,
May 27th, 1889.

Copy of
Statement of Lawrence Finlay relative to
Killing of two whitemen at Jocko river. My true name is Lawrence Finlay. I am 23 years of Age. One year ago last fall, July or later, below Duncan McDonalds, at mouth of Jocko river, I saw three full blood Indians shoot and Kill two whitemen who were in camp there. The whitemen were strangers. The Indians were Pierre Paul and La La See, the name of the other Indian I don't Know. I heard that he was some relative of Pierre Paul; the one whose name I don't Know did not do anything, although he was present. I was walking and heard 5 or 6 shots and when I got there the white men were dead. The Indians made me swear I would Keep it secret. They were going to Kill me at first. They made me swear 5 or 6 times. The Indians wanted me to shoot at the whitemen too so they could say I had a hand in it. The Indians told me they Killed the whitemen for revenge for the Killing of the Indian that Coombs Killed at Arlee. Would have told Maj. Ronan, but they said they would Kill one of my brothers if I did. I went and told the Chiefs about it but they told me to Keep quiet as it would make trouble for the Indians. Koo-too-lay-uch, a young chief, said stay quiet and only tell it when questioned by proper authorities and then tell a Straight story. I can show spot where whitemen were camped. The Indians said afterwards that they threw the whitemen in the river, that they did not float far so they took them out and buried them (I did not see them). It was just dark when the Killing was done. I understand another Indian by the name of Peter saw Killing. He dresses like a half-breed and lives with a squaw

near Horse Plains. He talks good English. I talked with him afterward. He stated that the Indian made him swear too. I did not see him there, I was only about 100 feet away when shooting was done, I only staid a few minutes.

Lawrence (his x mark) Finlay

On Sunday the 23d of June, a large gathering of Indians was expected to be at St. Ignatius to celebrate the feast of Corpus Christi and supposing that the murderers would be there, I informed the sheriff of Missoula County that it would be a good time to arrest the two Indians, that by locating their camps they could be surprised and taken into custody and hustled out of Camp without any trouble providing the plan was properly carried out. The result will show that the Indian culprits and their friends became aware of the sheriff's presence and armed and fixed themselves for a desperate resistance. More men were called for by the sheriff and they boarded a freight train and ran down from Ravalli Station, on the reserve, with the view of heading off the prisoners and some of their backers who had just before proceeded down the wagon road which leads along the railroad track. Overtaking an armed Indian, according to the story of pursuers, the train stopped; A demand was made upon the Indian to surrender and upon showing resistance he was shot and Killed. The posse did not wait to capture the men they were in pursuit of but boarded the train and ran down to Horse Plains which is off of the reservation. I was at Ravalli Station and an Indian runner came flying by on horseback going towards the Mission for a Priest to come down as an Indian had been shot and wounded by the sheriff's posse. Supposing the freight train went on and that the sheriff was making a fight to capture his men, I manned a hand Car with railroad section men and sent them down the road to do what they could to assist the sheriff, but they had hardly got out of sight when I received a telegram that the sheriff and his men were safe at Horse Plains and off of the reservation, but would come back again. Knowing that the Killing of an Indian who was not the one looked for by the posse, and owing to the great excitement among the Indians, I deemed it best to call for troops to overawe any attempt of the murderers and their friends to seize upon the exciting opportunity of attacking the sheriff's posse in force and thus involve the whole nation in war. By your orders Col. Andrews, commanding Fort Missoula, sent three companies of the 25th Infantry to Ravalli, on this reservation where they are now encamped. I held a consultation with the chiefs and head men on the 25 and 26th and all deplored the unfortunate circumstances which brought the sheriff's posse and the military upon the reservation. They claimed that they would be more than pleased to have the murderers arrested by the white authorities, but that they were not able to accomplish the arrest themselves, as they feared a conflict with their brethern [sic] which might result in blood shed and a never ending conflict among the relatives on each side.

This is the way the matter stands to-day. I apprehend not the slightest fear of any uprising among the people but the two Indians who have caused the trouble and who are now on the reservation defiant and blood thirsty should be taken at any cost, dead or alive.

I am,

Very respectfully,
(Sgd) Peter Ronan
U.S. Indian Agent.

July 7, 1889
LR 17,845/1889, telegram, RG 75, National Archives, Washington, D.C.

According to testimony in a Missoula probate court, only one of the Indians died, Seven Pipes or Benoit. Seven Pipes had assaulted Alex Matt and was shot by Alex's brother, Baptiste Matt. The court decided Baptiste and Joe Finley, who was also involved, had killed Seven Pipes in self-defense.[29]

July 7, 1889
Arlee Mont.

Indian Commissioner Washn DC

Indians brought Whiskey from Missoula. a drunken fight among Themselves resulted in the Shooting of two Indians who will probably Die. I arrested the Shooters and sent them to Jail anticipate no more trouble.

Ronan
Agt.

July 8, 1889
LR 18,823/1889, RG 75, National Archives, Washington, D.C.

See Ronan's letters of June 1, June 17, and July 1, 1889, for more information on Al Sloan's capture of accused murder Lawrence Finley in the Sun River country.

United States Indian Service,
Flathead Agency, M.T.
July 8th, 1889.

The Hon. Commissioner of Indian Affairs,
Washington, D.C.

Sir:

Replying to your favor F – Letter 16721 – '89 – Letter 16722 – '89, in reference to my report dated, 18th of June, regarding the arrest of Laurent Finlay and the voucher for $312⁵⁵/₁₀₀, covering the expense incurred in making the arrest, you desire to be informed more fully than was set forth in my report, the nature of the service rendered by Al. Slone [sic], for which I paid him $250.00.

You desire to be exactly informed what the services were and why the sheriff could not have been called upon to make the arrest.

Finlay, upon the commission of his last crime, namely the murder of a Kootenai Indian, escaped from this reservation by way of Cadotte pass, with intention of getting across the British line and joining the Cree Half-breeds to whom, I am informed he is related. It would have been useless to call upon the sheriff of Missoula county or any other county sheriff in Montana to follow upon his trail, as his arrest could not be accomplished for lack of knowledge of the country, nor of the Indians with whom he was seeking a refuge and protection. I therefore put Al. Sloan, who is a mixed-breed and a reliable and honest man, upon the trail of the outlaw, with a posse of half-breed Indians, with instructions to run him down. On the Teton river, on the Atlantic slope, and a long distance from this reservation, Sloan and his companions learned that Finlay was encamped with a party of Piegan Indians, who boasted of their ability to protect him from arrest. He thereupon armed and employed several other half-breeds, surrounded the camp, arrested Finlay and telegraphed to me to come to his assistance which I did and succeeded in placing the outlaw in the jail of

Missoula county, where he now awaits trial. Sloan is an illiterate man and unable to Keep accounts. I reimbursed him to the extent of his outlay of money, which was stated to be a very moderate sum by the sheriff of Cascade county. Should you so desire, I will get a statement to that effect from that officer. The distance to his county is so great that I cannot communicate and receive an answer in reasonable time to enclose in this letter.

Very respectfully,
Your obedient servant,
Peter Ronan
U.S. Indian Agent.

July 15, 1889
LR 19,439/1889, RG 75, National Archives, Washington, D.C. Typed copies of War Department telegram correspondence relative to "situation of affairs at Flathead Agency and means taken to prevent trouble between Indians and sheriff's posse."

> See Ronan's report of July 1, 1889, for more information on the murder of an innocent Indian by a Missoula County Sheriff's posse and the hysteria that resulted among western Montana whites.

Page 1

Copy.

Missoula, Montana, June 24, 1889.

General Ruger,
Commanding Department of Dakota,
Fort Snelling, Minn.

Indians on Flathead reservation in arms and in conflict with Sheriff's posse, one Indian killed. Please instruct Commanding Officer at Fort Missoula to act as posse comitatus at call of Sheriff or to furnish arms for volunteer force of citizens, which are raised, but unarmed. Situation imminent and prompt action required.

J. L. Sloan,
Mayor of Missoula.
Received 11:55 P.M., June 24.

Page 2

Telegram.

Headquarters Dept. of Dakota,
Saint Paul, Minn. June 25, 1889.

To Commanding Officer,
Fort Missoula, Montana.

The Mayor of Missoula telegraphs that Indians on Flathead Reservation have had conflict with Sheriff's posse, one Indian killed and situation critical and asks assistance of troops as a posse. Ascertain the condition of affairs and report as soon as may be. If state of affairs require presence of troops to prevent outbreak of Indians act in concert with Indian Agent to prevent trouble. Telegraph to Agent and communicate with Mayor.

Acknowledge receipt.

Ruger,
Brigadier General,
Commanding.

Page 3

Arlee, Montana, June 25, 1889.

General Ruger,
Fort Snelling, Minn.

Sheriff's posse killed one Indian and are determined to take two prisoners supposed murderer. Friends of criminals and dead Indian will probably resist arrest. This will cause bloodshed and probably Indian war. I go to-night to hold council with chiefs and try to induce them to deliver up Indians. Should I fail and attempt made to arrest Indians, life and property along the Northern Pacific may be jeopardized. Wire if I can have troops if my judgment requires them.

Ronan,
Agent.

Page 4

Telegram.

Headquarters Department of Dakota,
St. Paul, Minn., June 25th, 1889.

To United States Indian Agent Ronan,
Arlee, Montana.

The Commanding Officer Fort Missoula has been directed to communicate with you and to act in case of necessity in concert with you. Please telegraph me result of your conference with chiefs and any further facts.

Ruger,
Brigadier General,
Commanding.

Page 5

Missoula, Montana, June 25, 1889.

Adjutant General
Department of Dakota,
St. Paul, Minn.

Telegram of twenty-fifth received. Three companies ready to answer Indian Agent's call.

Andrews,
Colonel.

Page 6

Telegram.

Headquarters Department of Dakota,
St. Paul, Minn., June 25th, 1889.

To United States Indian Agent Peter Ronan,
Arlee, Montana Territory.

I will be glad to have full statement of facts, including, in addition to what was referred to in my telegram of this morning, the facts as to the murder, where it took place and the circumstances? Send telegrams to me at St. Paul, not to Fort Snelling.

Ruger,
Brigadier General,
Commanding Dept.

Page 7

Missoula, Montana, June 25, 1889.

Adjutant General
Department of Dakota,
St. Paul, Minn.

Lawson commanding one hundred thirty men left at two afternoon per rail to report to Indian Agent at his request.

Andrews,
Colonel.

Page 8

Ravalli, Montana, June 25, 1889.

Assistant Adjutant General
Department of Dakota,
St. Paul, Minn.

Arrived here with three companies at 5 p.m. Everything quiet. Sheriff's posse returns to Missoula to-night. Agent Ronan has demanded murderers and chiefs are now considering the matter. Agent hopes to know to-morrow. Will keep you advised.

Lawson,
Captain Commanding.

Page 9

Ravalli, Montana, June 26, 1889.

Adjutant General
Department of Dakota,
St. Paul, Minn.

Everything quiet. Chiefs have not and (in) my opinion cannot or will not deliver murderers. Sheriff and posse has returned to Missoula. Agent Ronan returns to Agency to-day. He informs me that troops are no longer required.

Lawson,
Capt. Comdg.

Page 10

Ravalli, Montana, June 27, 1889

General Ruger,
St. Paul, Minn.

Everything quiet. I do not think the Indians can or will comply with my demand to give up the murderers. I believe they have not over twelve backers but they are well armed and the Indians fear to take them. The presence of the troops quieted all excitement, but as the Indians cannot be found by them I believe they might be ordered home. The offering of a reward might effect arrest of mureders [sic] by half-breeds. I go to Agency to-day.

Ronan,
Agent.

Page 11

Ravalli, Montana, June 26, 1889

General Ruger,
Saint Paul, Minn.

Received the following from G. W. Dickinson, Division Superintendent N. P. R. R.:

"Missoula, 26. Ronan. Sheriff Heyfron has telegraphed Governor White for troops to remain at Ravalli till further orders, believing that our buildings, trains and the lives of our employes demand protection from Indians under your charge. Will you hold troops until answer is received. G. W. Dickinson."

I answered as follows:

"G. W. Dickinson. I do not coincide with Sheriff Heyfron in his opinion that troops are needed now to protect life and property on this reservation. Colonel Lawson of same opinion. A reward for the arrest of the supposed Indian murderers is all I deem necessary. No more necessity for troops at Ravalli than at any other station on the reservation."

Ronan,
Agent.

Page 12

Ravalli, Montana, June 26, 1889.

General Ruger,
Saint Paul, Minn.

The murderer of two white men, one of whose bodies was found over a year ago, was confessed to by Sara [Lara] Finley, a half-breed now in jail at Minnesota [i.e., Missoula]. Finley witnessed the killing by Pierce [Pierre] Paul and La La See, while four or five other Indians were mixed in affair whose identity I have not yet learned. Criminals are yet at large. The chiefs and headmen state they would be glad to see them arrested, but are afraid to capture them. A full report will be sent by letter as soon as I go to Agency. I apprehend no outbreak.

Ronan,
Agent.

Page 13

Helena, Montana, June 26, 1889.

General Ruger,
St. Paul, Minn.

Following is just received by wire from Missoula:

"I am credibly informed that party of Indians were intent on wrecking the Northern Pacific trains last night, between Ravalli and Joko. Indians are now in the hills and will remain there until the troops are withdrawn which will be some time to-day. Reliable half-breeds say that Indians swear vengeance on the railroad company as they claim that the Indians who were killed were shot from the train. Indians have sent their women and children to the hills, which is fair indication that trouble is not over. Indians have fired the woods in vicinity of Joko. Dickinson, Superintendent, N. P. R. R. asks for protection for his main tracks and buildings. Would request that troops be ordered to remain. D. J. Heyfron, Sheriff."

In view of the situation I ask that troops be left on the ground until I can personally investigate the situation.

Z. F. White [i.e, B. F. White],
Governor.

Page 14

Headquarters Department of Dakota,
St. Paul, Minn. June 26, 1889.

To Governor White,
Helena, Mont.

The troops at Ravalli have not been withdrawn. Captain Lawson in command, and Agent Ronan both report that the presence of the troops is no longer required.

Agent Ronan also says, a reward for the arrest of the supposed Indian murderers is all he deems necessary.

Judging from the reports I have received, there does not appear reason to apprehend danger to railroad property, as stated in the despatch of Sheriff Heyfron to you.

I have directed Captain Lawson to remain until further orders.

Ruger,
Brigadier General,
Comdg. Dept.

July 31, 1889
LR 22,118/1889, RG 75, National Archives, Washington, D.C.

The white justice system in Montana Territory vigorously pursued Indian people who murdered — or were accused of murdering — white people, but failed to prosecute with similar energy white men accused of murdering Indians. These murders of Chief Michelle's relatives were reported in both the *Washington Post* and the *New York Times*.[30] The Commissioner of Indians Affairs wrote the Secretary of the Interior requesting that the Montana Territorial Governor be instructed to take "appropriate action" to solve the case. The Commissioner also instructed Ronan to "urge upon" the Montana Territorial officials "the importance of the matter and the necessity, in the interest of harmony and good will between the Indians and the whites, for some earnest endeavor on their part to apprehend and convict the parties guilty of the murder complained of."[31] In February 1893 new evidence suggested that some British Cree Indians might have been responsible for the murders.[32] No records have been located indicating anyone was ever tried or punished for these murders. No biographical information was located for Anthony La Course, Cree, or Jake Wagoner, white.

United States Indian Service,
Flathead Agency, M.T.
July 31st, 1889.

Hon. Commissioner of Indian Affairs,
Washington, D.C.

Sir:

I have the honor to report that great Excitement Prevails among the Indians of this reservation on account of the discovery of the charred remains of the bodies of some of their missing people.

Last Summer a very respectable Indian, a nephew to Michel, the Head Chief of the Pend. d'Oreille Indians of this reserve, accompanied by his wife and his daughter, aged about sixteen years, and another Indian of the Flathead tribe, went out hunting and promised to return before winter. They did not come home at the promised time and no news was heard from them during the winter and spring, which caused great uneasiness among the reservation Indians as the missing ones were popular among all of the tribes.

A half-breed Cree, named Anthony La Course arrived at this Agency some times ago from the Blackfoot country, and brought a horse with him which belonged to the missing Indians. When questioned by myself and the Indians, as to how he got the horse, he told what I considered a straight story: He said that he traded his horse with a white man last fall for the one he rode to the reserve, receiving five dollars to boot. He gave a description of the whiteman and his place of residence, whose named he stated to be Jake Wagoner, and is Chopping wood and making fence rails on Deep Creek, in the Sun River valley, Chouteau County, Montana. Wagoner stated that he got the horse from a party of trappers.

A son and a brother of the missing Indian and other Indian companions started about six weeks ago in search of their missing relatives, and surely enough they found by the Warm Springs, between Sun River and Willow Creek, a mould [sic] of thoroughly buried matter and dirt. Digging a little they found the remains of burned bones; the two stone pipes which they recognized as those of the two missing men, and iron used by the women to dress hides and two pair of rosary beads. The mould and remains found was between the place where some whites had a camp, which the Indians recognized as the camp of whitemen by the signs: namely the Kind of stakes used and the pieces of news- paper scattered around the place.

The searchers came to the conclusion that their Indian relatives were mur- dered and the bodies carefully burned by some white people. Four days ago the Indian searchers brought in the few remains of the Charred bones, and the few objects found in the mould. They have already come to me and asked for an investigation into this terrible crime, and demand justice for all. If nothing is done in this case it will contribute to embitter more and more the feeling between the whites and Indians, and expose the lives of innocent white people for the future, as the unwritten law among the Indians is life for life from the race they consider guilty of the murder of their Kinsmen.

I have a full description of the horses the murdered Indians had with them, I have one horse that belonged to the murdered Indians, I have the half-breed Cree, Anthony La Course, who traded his horse to a whiteman for a horse which belonged to the murdered party; and La Course is willing to lead me to the camp of said whiteman, whom if not guilty could perhaps give a clue to the perpetrators of the crime. The Indians are greatly in earnest about this matter. They quote the fact that two of their people were hung at the head of Flathead Lake, by a mob of whitemen, on suspicion of having Killed three white pros- pectors, they also quote that two of their Indians were shot by whitemen, one at Arlee station, and another on the hunting grounds down the Mullan road leading through the Coeur D'Alene mountains. They say that the two outlaw Indians whose arrest was recently sought for by the sheriff of Missoula County, and which caused the trouble last month by which a call was made for troops, shot two innocent white travellers in revenge for the two last mentioned In- dians Killed by whitemen. They claim that if there is no effort made to ferrit out and punish the perpetrators of this last murder, that the Kinsmen of the murdered ones will be hard to restrain and might try to be avenged according to the traditions of the Indians, that is to take revenge by Killing any person, however innocent, if he belongs to the race suspected of the crime.

This matter might be placed in the the hands of the Sheriff of Choteau County, but the Indians claim and ask that their Agent be instructed to look into this matter, and if necessary go to the country where the bodies were found and there to institute a thorough investigation. I am ready to undertake the investigation for the sake of harmony and good will between the whites and Indians, but shall await instructions and authority before acting. It will require travel on horseback on an unfrequented trail save by Indians, of about one hundred and fifty miles over the Cadotte pass and towards the country

of the Sun River. I earnestly desire communication from your office in regard
to my duties in this case soon as possible as the Indians will await with impa-
tience my orders in this unfortunate affair.

Very respectfully,
Your obd't serv't
Peter Ronan
U.S. Indian Agent.

Enclosed newspaper clipping from unidentified source:
Another Indian Murder.

News has reached Helena of a ghastly discovery made last week on Sun
River. From the meagre particulars at hand it seems that a few months ago a
family of Flathead Indians left their reservation, crossed the mountains and
went into the Sun River country to hunt. They were seen by one of their relatives, a half-breed living on Sun River, when they first arrived. Last week the
half-breed found one of their ponies in the possession of a white man, who
claimed that he purchased the pony at Sun River. The half-baeed [sic] was satisfied that something was wrong and at once began a search for his relatives.
After hunting two or three days he found their camp, which had been burned
up and in it, the charred remains of his relatives, a family of three or four.
There is no doubt that they were robbed of their horses and outfit and then
murdered. The half-breed at once notified the law officers, who at last accounts
were still looking for the perpetrators of the fiendish act.

August 1, 1889
LR 22,434/1889, RG 75, National Archives, Washington, D.C.

The 1889 drought Ronan described was record breaking and wiped out many Indian and
white farmers in western Montana.[33]

The 1889 St. Ignatius day celebration that Ronan described here was a major social
and political event for the tribal community. In addition to the church services there were
horse races and outdoor sports.[34]

United States Indian Service,
Flathead Agency,
August 1st, 1889.

Hon. Commissioner Indian Affairs,
Washington, D.C.
    Sir:
    In submitting my report for the month of July, I would respectfully state
that the outlook for the Indians on this reservation for the coming fall and winter is gloomy and dismal in the extreme. The drought of this summer has been
unknown even to the oldest of the Indians. The face of the country is simply
parched and the usually luxuriant bunch grass is burned to the roots on prairie
and uplands. Nothing green remains save along the banks of the rivers and the
line of the irrigation ditch. The hay crop is almost a total failure; the grain and
vegetable crop has suffered in the same way, and not a quarter of the usual
amount can be harvested this season. To add to this, the forest is on fire all
around us, in every direction. The pra[i]ries, where any grass grew this season,
was fired also. The smoke covers the country, obscuring the sun, and causing
business houses in the town of Missoula to be lit up early in the afternoons.

These conditions will necessitate a call upon the Department for a larger supply of flour as breadstuff will certainly go beyond the reach of the Indians unless assisted. The failure of the crop this year is very discouraging as unusual efforts were made by the Indians to exceed the seeding of last year which rendered so bountifully a harvest, and encouraged them to future efforts.

One of the largest gatherings of Indians which I have known on the reservation took place at St. Ignatius Mission on the 31st of July. There was gathered there in the neighborhood of fourteen hundred Indians and halfbreeds, who came to celebrate, as is the custom every year, the feast of St. Ignatius, by religious exercises. The Catholic Bishop [John] Brondell of Montana, was present and confirmed about sixty children and grown Indians. The meeting of the tribes was not marred by a single case of drunkeness. The day passed off in an enterchange [sic] of greeting by the Indians and powerful appeals by the missionaries, in the Indian language, exhorting them to peaceful pursuits, the obeyance of the laws; the necessity of insisting upon the attendance of their children at school; a strict attention to their religious duties, and the necessity of labor in their fields, and a care to their pastorial [sic] pursuits, and other habits of industry in order to put them upon the highway of independence, manhood, and decent support for their families and themselves.

A surplus of wheat from last years crop remained in the granaries of some of the Indians, and the Gristmill was employed in turning the same into flour during a portion of the month.

Strenious [sic] efforts are being made by Indian cattle owners to cut hay in some of the marshy spots on the reservation, to feed their cattle during the winter; but a very small crop will be put up, as such favored places are few this season.

A special report of my recent visit to the Kootenai Indians of Northern Idaho, under instructions of June 21st, 1889 — office letter law and land — 12930 – 1889, will be prepared and forwarded to you in a day or two.

All industries connected with the service on this reservation have received proper attention during the month of July, and peace and good order prevails.

I herewith have the honor to enclose sanitary report, and report of funds and indebtedness for the month of July, and also report of farmer, and have the honor to be

Very respectfully, your obedient servant
Peter Ronan
U.S. Indian Agent.

August 6, 1889
LR 22,436/1889, RG 75, National Archives, Washington, D.C.

> Federal Indian policy during the late 1880s attempted to consolidate scattered bands of Indians onto reservations or provide off-reservation allotments under the Dawes Act of 1887. The Bonners Ferry Kootenai land claims along the Kootenai River in Idaho provided continuing problems for Ronan until his death in 1893. Between 1889 and 1892 more conflict arose between the Kootenai and invading white settlers. On May 19, 1892, Ronan reported on a trip to Bonners Ferry where some of the band chose to move to Canada, others agreed to remove to Dayton Creek on the Flathead Reservation, and eight families requested off-reservation allotments in the Kootenai Valley. On July 20, 1891, Catherine [i.e., Justine] Fry had

made preliminary allotment applications for her mixed blood family at the Coeur d'Alene Land Office.[35] Claims, counterclaims, and lawsuits over the lands began during Ronan's life and continued for many years after he died. The harassment extended into the twentieth century until the Bonners Ferry Kootenai had no land base remaining.[36]

Ronan's August 6, 1889, report was a result of instructions from the Commissioner of Indian Affairs on June 21, 1889, for Ronan to investigate the situation at Bonners Ferry.[37] On August 28, 1889, Ronan was instructed to gather the information that would be needed to make off-reservation allotments to the Kootenai who wanted to remain at Bonners Ferry.[38] Ronan provided the Commissioner with geographic and population information about the land claims of the Bonners Ferry Kootenai band on October 16, 1889. The Commissioner of Indian Affairs reported to the Secretary of the Interior on November 25, 1889, and asked that the Commissioner of the General Land Office be instructed to make the surveys for the allotments.[39]

George Fry's parents were Richard Fry, a white man, and Justine Fry, a Colville Indian. In 1876, Richard and Martin Fry had settled at Bonners Ferry on the Kootenai River in Idaho and operated a ferry, hotel, and trading post. George worked at the trading post and learned Kootenai. His first wife was Kootenai. According to Simon Francis, a Bonners Ferry Kootenai elder, Isaac was the assistant chief of the Bonners Ferry band during much of the late nineteenth century.[40] No biographical information was located on J. I. Anthony, the spokesman for the Kootenai River whites in 1889.

> United States Indian Service,
> Flathead Agency,
> August 6th, 1889.

Hon. Commissioner Indian Affairs
Washington, D.C.
    Sir:
    I have the honor to report that pursuant to instructions of June 21st 1889, office letter Law and Land 12930–1889, I called a council of Indians at the office of the Flathead Agency at which was present Michel, head Chief of the Pend 'd Oreilles, several of his head men, and also representative Indians from the Flathead and Kootenai, constituting the Confederated tribes of Flatheads, Pend 'd Oreilles and Kootenai Indians, living upon and occupying the Jocko or Flathead reservation. I stated to the Council that I had orders from Washington to go to Northern Idaho and there to look into the wants and necessities of a detached band of Kootenai Indians, who were represented to be in a wretched condition; that it was the policy of the Government and the Indian Department to persuade this class of Indians to remove to and take allotments of land upon some reservation; if they cannot be induced to do so then to encourage them to take allotments under the 4th section of the Act of Congress approved February 8th, 1887. Chief Michel, speaking for all of the Indians present, said that the Flathead reservation had ample room and lands to accomodate their friends the Kootenai of Northern Idaho, although they had no right to the land; that I might give them a cordial invitation to share their country with them, if they should see fit to avail themselves of the offer of the Government to remove them to a reservation.

Having settled that point I took my departure for the Kootenai river in Northern Idaho, where the Indians in question make their camping ground. Taking conveyance from Kootenai Station, on the Northern Pacific Railroad, I drove thrugh a dense forest of over thirty miles and arrived at Fry's Landing on the Kootenai river on the night of the 23d of July, 1889. Here I engaged the services of George Fry, a half breed Kootenai Indian, to act as interpreter, and then sent his father out to gather the Indians together. While this was being done I took the steamer Galena and sailed down the river for about one hundred and twenty miles, where it opened out into the Kootenai Lake, for the purpose of examining the extent and quality of the land along the river, suitable for Indian occupancy. After a run of five hours in which we made sixty miles, we arrived at the International Boundary Line — 49th parralell. Here a British custom house has been established, and a custom house officer came on board and examined the steamers manifest. I found a vast extent of bottom land along the river for the full extent of sixty miles, below Bonner's Ferry, or Fry's Landing, on the American side of the boundary line. The river bottom which has an average width of from three to five miles, is fringed along the banks by a heavy growth of timber, but slopes back to the base of the mountains in green and open meadows covered by a heavy growth of wild hay. The only draw back to this vast tract of country, which contains an area of about two hundred thousand acres of rich alluveum and vegetable deposits, is the fact that in some years the Kootenai river overflows its banks from the 15th of June until about the 4th of July, according to the quantity of snow fall in the Rocky Mountains. This, however, is the principal cause of the heavy hay crop, which follows the natural irrigation and inundation of the land. A few white settlers who have taken up land along the river, for the sake of the crop of hay on which to feed their cattle in the winter, claim that the production of potatoes and other vegetables cannot be surpassed in any country, where planted on the foothills and above the rise of the overflow. No attempt has yet been made to cultivate grain, but it occurs to me that grain will thrive and flourish as well as hay after the natural irrigation, providing it is not flooded too late in the season.

Above Fry's Landing, or Bonner Ferry, the Kootenai river is not supposed to be navigable, but there are several good plateaus that would answer well, and would suit these Indians better for farming purposes because the plateaus are clear of wood and never inundated by the water rise in spring. There, at present the Indians would be away from the high road of the whites. New mines have been discovered in the region of the Kootenai Lake, and are drawing thither settlers and adventurers, and but a short time will elapse ere the country will be settled up, and the Indians forced and driven from their hunting and camping ground. Therefore, no time should be lost in giving them titles to their lands and settling them down to work for their subsistance. It will be seen from the report of the council which I held with the Indians, that they prefer to occupy and settle on this soil which they claim to be their birth place and the home of their ancestory.

On my return from examination of the land, I met the Indians in council, and stated that it was the wish of the Indian Department that they should remove to and take up land in severalty upon some reservation, where they could be looked after and their necessities and wants supplied in order to give them a start in the way of agricultural pursuits, stock raising, education for their children; a start upon the road to civilization and decent support for themselves and their families. The Indians listened attentively and respectfully to all I had to say. After some hours consultation and council among themselves, it was announced that they were ready to talk again. Isaac, the head Chief announced that after full and free consultation with his people, that it was their unanimous desire to remain in their own country, and to take up land under the 4th Section of the Act of Congress, approved February 8th, 1887, as explained to them by me. He was grateful for the interest the Government had taken in them, and trusted that it would not be forgotten that it would be useless for the Indians to acquire title to land unless they were given a start in the way of cattle, agricultural implements; food and clothing for at least a year or two, or until the first crop could be raised. He also stated that the Indians were ready as soon as the Council adjourned to commence locating the land, and this business was actually commenced that day, so eager were they to remain in the Kootenai valley, and ten or twelve heads of families staked off their land near as they could understand 160 acres, and got notices written which were nailed on trees, notifying the public that the land was located by them. This action on the part of the Indians showed to me their eagerness to acquire title and to secure legal possession against the location of the land they claim by the whites.

If the Department should see fit to allot these lands to the Indians, I would respectfully suggest that a copy of rules and regulations for systematic [sic] procedure in making these allotments, and printed forms for the use of applicants for allotments should be forwarded at once, so that these Indians who so earnestly desire to avail themselves of the provisions of the said fourth section can have every facility for making their desires Known. If it be the wish of the Department to order me to attend to this work I desire full instructions.

These Indians are like children. They must have a guardian over them — a farmer in charge or some other authority, otherwise they will not do anything for themselves. They are experts in fishing and hunting, but when it comes to daily toil on the farm they will be found wanting except encouraged by gentle authority. They should at once be provided with provisions and clothing; implements of labor, and set to work to build themselves houses and improve the land they desire to settle upon. In summing up, I would state that if the Indians could be induced to remove to a reserve it would be far better for their future welfare; but they will never willingly consent to leave the Kootenai valley, and the best should be made of their desire to settle upon the land they claim as their inheritance.

Herewith I attach the census of the Kootenai Indians, giving names of the head of families and number of children in each family which I obtained on this visit.

I also have the honor to attach a remonstrance against the settlement of the Indians upon the lands in the Kootenai Bottom, which will explain itself, and have the honor to be most respectfully

Your obedient Servant
Peter Ronan
United States Indian Agent.

First enclosure. Format has been adjusted to save space:

List of Kootenai Indians in Northern Idaho.

Isaac, Head Chief (4 in family); Malice, 2d Chief (2 in family); Agel (7 in family); Tanish (8 in family); Milteas (7 in family); Ecetoll (6 in family); Joseph (old man) (5 in family); Cancaso (2 in family); Alexander (6 in family); Temo (5 in family); Antoine (5 in family); Trompaddle (3 in family); Lackard (3 in family); Cow (4 in family); Julian (3 in family); Lewictenci (4 in family); David Canid (3 in family); Abraham (3 in family); Abraham (orphan) (1 in family); Euasta (old) (4 in family); Franswall (3 in family); Moshell Isaac (4 in family); Serome (old) (5 in family); Nicholey (5 in family); Joseph Thef (2 in family); Eneas (5 in family); David (8 in family); Stanish (3 in family); Michel Teno (3 in family); Pierre an Wa (2 in family); Francois (3 in family); Pernipa (8 in family); Charley (3 in family); Cerome (3 in family); Enepy (1 in family); Custan (1 in family); Tiley (6 in family); Pierre Big Head (6 in family); Succell (5 in family); Malacoose (2 in family); Antoine Jug (2 in family); Malta (3 in family); Isaac (Little) (2 in family); Tamea (7 in family); Neo Pierre (2 in family); Nicholay (4 in family); Caslo (3 in family); Caprean (2 in family); Eusta (Big) (3 in family); Francois (2 in family); Tepaw (6 in family); Amoose (2 in family); Thomis (3 in family); Endesta (young) (1 in family); Family of Richard Fry (whiteman) (8 in family); Family of David McLaughlin (5 in family).

Total number of Indians —— 218.

Second enclosure. This handwriting is very hard to read and has been transcribed as accurately as possible:

Kootenai River, July 24th, 1889

Magor Peter Ronan,

Sir:

Understanding that You are here, for the perpose of removing, the few Indians, on a reservation, or give them land in Severalty, the Would be Settlers of this Valey, Would rather have them put on a reservation, than to let them Settel upon the land. there is Quite a Number of Settelers that Would Now take up land, but where ever they go, they find an Indian's Notice, Claiming 160 acres of land, With a white Mans Name, as Witness, on the Notice. So the White Man gets the benefit of this land, Rather-for-hay, or range, and to Cover-it-up, the Indian Will put in a few potatoes, Now if this land is given to them, they Will use it. Just the Same as Now. these few Whites will be benifited. take these Indians out and there Will be homes for Hundreds Nay thousands, and there Will be a [return?] to the Country, in the Way of improvements, Which the Indian, Will never-do, then again it has been reported, that these Indians belong to the Agency of the upper Kootenai in B. C. but have Strayed away to this Section and dont belong here at all, how true that is We dont Know, but the Miners that are out propsecting, every Summer in the Mountains, Know What they are to their Sorrow, hardly a Season passes, but there is Murder-or-Robbin of Camp, or Stock, if they take my Land they Will bring in Indians enough, to take up the Entire Country, and then this Beutifull Valey, Will be Just the Same as [lost?], Controled by Whites that Speak the language. this Section has a great future, before it; Mineral Mountains below, above and on eaither Sides of it. that are Now opened and others to be Sill opened, Open this up to the White Settelers and it Will be a glorious Country, but give it to the Indians, and it Will be a rendeveus for all of the renegade Indians in the Country, Mrs. [*****] will give You a Small Idea of what is Wanted, and You Know by Experience, how it is, and Know Just What is Wanted, the White Setteler With his family, Wants this Country, and when they take up Land, they dont Want to Come in Contact With Indians or ther Allys, for then troble Will Come, and to Save all troble, the best, is to place them on a Reservation, Where they belong, then they are out of the Way, and the Country Will be healther for-it-all around. again magor — if You think these few Witing Will help You. in Your report, all right, for-it-is hard Work, to get true facts, from those that are interested. in a large Way, the Miner and Prospector, Will one and all Concer, With the Setteler, in haveing a general round up and put the Indian, on a Reservation, where they belong, and where they Will be out of the Way.

hoping these few lines Will Meet With Consideration,

Respectfully
J. I. Anthony
and others.

August 13, 1889
LR 23,047/1889, RG 75, National Archives, Washington, D.C.

Government attempts to proscribe whippings as punishments were meant to impose late nineteenth century white American sensibilities on the Flathead Reservation tribes. If whippings were discontinued, however, there needed to be an alternative punishment available to the judges and chiefs: a secure jail. The federal government was anxious to end whipping but unwilling to pay for building and operating a jail.[41] See also Ronan letters of September 17, September 21, and October 28, 1889. The officials in Washington, D.C., also could not understand why the jail should be located at St. Ignatius rather than the agency at Jocko.[42] Ronan had encouraged the St. Ignatius Mission to construct the jail with the expectation that the Indian Office would reimburse their expenses. The jail building was not completed and the government balked at paying for the work that was done.[43]

The need for an alternative punishment for whipping was discussed by Pend d'Oreilles Chief Andre in 1878,[44] and Kootenai Chief Eneas in 1889.[45] On September 11, 1889, Inspector Wm. W. Junkin submitted a report recommending the government pay for a secure jail at St. Ignatius.[46] A May 23, 1889, report by Henry M. Marchant, Special Agent of the Department of Justice, included the transcript of his interviews with Chief Arlee and the tribal judges about the prohibition of whipping and the need for a tribal jail.[47]

United States Indian Service,
Flathead Agency, M.T.
August 13th, 1889.

The Hon. Commissioner of Indian Affairs,
Washington, D.C.

Sir:

Under date of Washington, November 29th, 1886, Letter 31022 – 86, was received at this Agency, and was in the following language:

"In a recent report on the affairs at the Flathead Agency, M.T., Inspector Pearsons recommended that a jail be built and that the Indian police be furnished with arms and ammunition. You are authorized to submit a detailed estimate for materials and labor required in the construction of a suitable building for a jail, and for the revolvers, holsters and belts required for the police for the consideration of this office.

Very respectfully,
(Sgd) A. B. Upshaw
Acting Commissioner."

My requisition for arms and ammunition for the policemen was granted, and under the impression that the absolute necessity for a good jail on the reservation would be favorably considered, I submitted a detailed estimate for material and labor required for the same, but did not receive authority to construct the jail. Meantime the necessity for such a structure became so great that I authorized the Missionaries at St. Ignatius Mission to erect a jail, as I felt sure that they would be reimbursed by the Department for their outlay.

The jail built by the missionaries over three years ago is a log building 64 feet long; 22 feet wide and nine feet high, with a gable 7 feet high. There are in it 10 cells 7 x 6 each with a floor of plank 3 inches thick and some of the cells were lined with 2 inch plank. Each cell has a door of plank 3 inches thick 6 x 2½. There are 2 rooms — a central one 22 x 10 where the prisoners take their meals and where there is a stove; the other room 22 x 18 intended for the jailor, with 2 windows 3 x 2½, 12 lights each, and one door. A central hall 6 feet wide on either side of central room.

The cost to the Missionaries to put up this building and repair it from time to time has been as follows:

Hewed logs, sawed planks and lumber for lining and floor, shingles and carpenters' work; doors and sashes $500.00

Nails, bolts, locks, spikes and blacksmith work $100.00

As no notice was taken of my requisition for means to construct the jail, the work was not completed, and the prisoners who were in its uncompleted state having Cut, sawed and burned some of the logs, joists and floors; and all of the locks having been broken the jail at present is in a delapidated condition and entirely unfit to hold prisoners.

Now, according to orders contained in letter "Law and Land — 16830 – 1889" viz: "The public whipping of an offender is not the proper way to reform him, and this mode of punishment must be superseded by some milder system, such as confinement and the prisoner be compelled to work if practicable." It is added: "You will therefore have the practice of whipping discontinued and if the Agency guard house is not sufficient for the confinement of prisoners, you will at once forward an estimate of the amount necessary to repair and put it in proper order."

The confinement of outlaw Indians being the only means of punishment left to the Judges and police, there is an urgent necessity to immediately repair the prison, and put it in condition to safely hold the prisoners. To this end the following improvements should be made:

The three inch plank floor should be renewed in the cells and hall, and all the cells should be lined inside with two inch boards. A small window with an iron grate should be opened in each cell. The central room where the prisoners take their meals should also be floored and lined with two inch plank.

The jailor's room has no floor nor, either is it lined, nor in any way provided for cooking or heating. All of the outer walls should be weather-boarded. Ten iron grates are needed for the ten cells. The ten doors of the cells and the door of the central room should be covered on both sides with sheet iron. Two grate-iron doors should be placed at the end of either portion of the central hall communicating with the central room. To do this work it will cost for

Lumber	$110.00
Carpenters' work	252.00
Nails, iron, locks, bolts, sheet iron and blacksmith's work	350.00
Altogether the expenses should be	
For work already done	$600.00
To work estimated to be done	712.00
Total	$1312.00

Material and labor is based on the very lowest scale procurable in this vicinity. The good of the Indians and the best interests of the Indian service demand at once the means to punish crime on this reservation and without a good jail the Agent, the Chiefs, the Judges and the police; in fact, the law abiding community of the Flathead reservation, will be powerless to preserve order against outlawry caused principally by the sale of intoxicants to the Indians, who, when drunk, relapse into savagery.

I am, very respectfully,
Your obedient servant,
Peter Ronan
U.S. Indian Agent.

Enclosed estimate for material to complete Indian jail for lumber, nails, spikes, iron, locks, bolts, and sheet iron, and carpenter and blacksmith work totaling $712.00.

August 20, 1889

U.S. Commissioner of Indian Affairs, Annual Report of the Commissioner of Indian Affairs *(Washington, D.C.: U.S. Government Printing Office, 1889), pages 227-231.*

Ronan's 1889 annual report touched on many topics which were also discussed in other Ronan letters to the Commissioner of Indian Affairs in this collection. The devastating drought during 1889, the irrigation ditches on the reservation, tribal opposition to allotment, Larra Finley's arrest, Finley's testimony against two other Indians accused of murdering two white men, a white justice system that failed to protect Indian people, and the conflict between the chiefs and the judges were all covered in other letters to the Commissioner of Indian Affairs.

One new topic in the report was Ronan's firing of Partee or Baptist Kakashee, one of the Indian judges, and seven policemen. Ronan accused them of insubordination and neglect of duty for failing to help the Missoula Sheriff capture two Indian murderers on the reservation.[48]

Report of Flathead Agency.

Flathead Agency, August 20, 1889.

Sir: In compliance with instructions from your office I have the honor to transmit herewith my thirteenth annual report.

The Flathead Indian Agency is situated on a small tributary of the Jocko River and distant about 1 mile from that stream, at the head of the Jocko Valley. A little distance back of the agency buildings a chain of lofty mountains rise abruptly above the valley. The mountains are covered with a dense forest of fir, pine, and tamarack or larch, which grow very large and furnish excellent lumber. In the lofty range and in close proximity to the agency are several clear mountain lakes abounding with trout, and from those lakes two waterfalls or cataracts thousands of feet high plunge down the mountain sides. The valley is formed in almost a triangular square about 5 miles in breadth and 12 miles in length. Along the river and tributaries there is some very fine farming land, cultivated mostly by Flatheads and half-breeds, but a good portion of it is rocky and gravelly. Following down the Jocko to its confluence with the Pend d'Oreille River the valley closes, and for a few miles the Jocko winds through a narrow gorge, but before joining its waters with the Pend d'Oreille River the valley again opens into a rich and fertile plain where a number of Indians are located.

Leaving the Jocko Valley to the left and passing through a narrow cañon and over a low divide of hills which form the south side of that valley, the road leads to St. Ignatius mission, some 20 miles from the agency, where the reservation schools are located. A large church, college for boys, academy buildings for girls, dwellings for the missionaries and the Sisters of Providence who teach the schools, are surrounded by some seventy log houses where principally Pend d'Oreille Indians dwell and cultivate the soil in the surrounding valley. The Mission Valley is broad and fertile, well watered by streams that flow from the range of mountains that rise on both sides of the valley from the Mission to the Flathead Lake, and around its borders there is farming land sufficient for a large settlement. Along the plain and skirting the mountains from the Mission to the foot of the Flathead Lake, a distance of some 30 miles, are scattered Indian farms, well fenced, and cultivated fields and gardens.

Flathead Lake.

This fine sheet of water is some 28 miles in length, and has an average width of 10 miles. Around the foot of the lake is grouped another Indian settlement, with thrifty looking farms and comfortable dwellings. Two steam-boats ply upon the lake, carrying freight and passengers to the settlers on Government land at the head of the lake. Crossing the lake and following a northerly direction to Dayton Creek will be found the home of the Kootenai Indians, who live about 60 miles from the agency. The Kootenais are a very improvident tribe, and spend most of their time gambling and wandering about. They live chiefly by hunting and fishing. They have a few houses, and fenced in some land, and with proper assistance and encouragement by a resident farmer among them might soon be brought to the civilizing habits which mark in contrast the Pend d'Oreille and Flatheads, who occupy jointly the Flathead Reserve.

The confederated tribes of this reservation consist of the Pend d'Oreilles, the Flatheads, the Kootenais, Charlot's band of Bitter Root Flatheads, and Michel's band of Lower Kalispels, making a total under my charge of 1,914, showing a decrease since my last annual report of 104. The deaths of the past year principally occurred among children and young people. The following is the

Recapitulation.

Confederated tribes:

Total number Indians	1,680
Males over eighteen years	469
Females over fourteen years	605
School children between six and sixteen	427

Charlot's band in Bitter Root:

Total	176
Males over eighteen	49

Females over fourteen	58
Children between six and sixteen	43
Lower Kalispels:	
Total	58
Males over eighteen	22
Females over fourteen	22
Children between six and sixteen	10

Schools.

There are two industrial school establishments, one for boys and one for girls, situated about 20 miles from the agency, at St. Ignatius Mission. They are conducted, under contract with the Government, by the missionaries of St. Ignatius and the Sisters of Providence. Last year the contract was for $150 for each of 75 children in each school. For this year, Congress doubled the appropriation, and provided for the education of 150 children in each school. There is a partial vacation in the month of August, but it extends only to a suspension of certain studies. The pupils are tractable and give good satisfaction in their application. Their health has been remarkably good; their quarters are comfortable, roomy, clean, and well ventilated. Though the school seems better appreciated by the tribes, still the full-bloods do not sufficiently realize the great advantages in store for their children by a good education and training. The progress in studies of the boys of the school has been very satisfactory. They take great interest in their various works and trades, and many prefer the workshop to the school room.

As the appropriation for educational purposes has been increased for this fiscal year on this reservation, and as I am forcibly impressed that education and agricultural pursuits with knowledge of such trades as are taught here, namely, carpentering, blacksmithing, shoemaking, harness making, tinsmithing, printing business, painting, sawing, milling, etc., are the great factors in civilizing these people, therefore it is necessary that the children should attend the schools despite the wishes of some of the Indian parents who would sacrifice the children to ignorance, idleness, and vice rather than send them to school. Their education should be compulsory, but in the absence of such law I shall use every suasion to induce parents who heretofore have used no effort to send their children to school to take a greater interest in this matter, which is of vital importance.

One of the great difficulties to be contended with in the boys' school is the fact that the parents are not willing to leave their sons long enough under instructions to give them a proper training. For the sake of the assistance they can give in herding stock or working about home the boys are taken away from school. Thus encouraged to leave their studies and having little prospect of comfortably settling themselves, the teachers have great difficulty to keep them when they attain a certain age. The inconveniences in the way of the proper training and civilization of the young Indians could be remedied by the establishment of a small fund directed to the end of aiding the new families formed by the marriage of the boys and girls of the school when of age. The prospect of this future aid might keep them longer at school.

The girls under the care and training of the Sisters of Providence have improved remarkably in their studies. Indeed, this is a model school and would reflect credit upon its managers and teachers in any country. Besides the ordinary education, they are taught music, vocal and instrumental, drawing, needle-work, knitting, crocheting, cooking, washing, mending, and making of their own clothing. The dairy and the garden work added to the various other work and studies leave them but very few leisure moments.

New and commodious buildings have been erected for the pupils, both boys and girls, [a]nd containing class-room, large dining-rooms, additional dormitories, bath-rooms, chapel, and other conveniences. I did not obtain the expense incurred in the erection of those fine buildings devoted to the educational work among the Indians of this reservation, but they are ample for the accommodation and a much larger number than the contract calls for. The management of these schools is excellent and the good work which is being done for the Indians by the Jesuit teachers and missionaries and the good Sisters of Providence can not be estimated.

Missionary Work.

The Indians and half-breeds are Catholic on this reservation. The missionary labors are in the hands of the Jesuit fathers, who are assisted by the Sisters of Providence as teachers and educators of the girls. The fathers devote their lives to this good work, and owing to their influence it may be said the Indians owe their present advancement in the civilizing pursuits as well as in their religious belief. The Catholic Bishop [John] Brondell, of Helena, on the 31st of July administered confirmation to 55 Indians, children and adults, at the Mission Chapel, and on the Sunday following consecrated a new church at the agency, which was erected by the missionaries of St. Ignatius. Those missionaries at their own expense last year erected a new church on Dayton Creek, near the Flathead Lake, in the village of the Kootenai Indians, where they are sparing no pains to teach religion and morality and a love of labor to this poor and degraded tribe.

Agricultural.

The outlook for the Indians this year is gloomy in the extreme. The drought of the summer has been unknown to the oldest Indians. The country is parched and the usually luxuriant bunch grass is burned to the roots on prairie and upland. Nothing green remains save along the banks of the rivers and the line of the irrigation ditch. The hay crop is almost a total failure; the grain and vegetable crops have suffered in the same way, and not one-quarter of the usual amount can be harvested this season. To add to this the forest is now and has been for weeks on fire all around us. The prairies where any grass grew this season was fired also. The smoke covers the country obscuring the sun and causing business houses in neighboring towns to be lit up at an early hour in the evenings. Breadstuff will certainly be scarce on the reservation, and unless assisted great want will prevail among the Indians until another crop can be harvested. The failure of crops this year is very discouraging to the Indians, as unusual efforts were made by them to exceed the planting of last year, which yielded so bountifully and encouraged them to greater efforts last spring to put in crops and fence and plow new and more extensive fields.

Irrigation.

Proper irrigation of this reservation is the most essential thing to be undertaken by the Department to give the Indians productive farms. During this season there has been a drought never before experienced. The grass crop is an assured failure, and where there are no irrigation facilities the hay, grain, and vegetable crops are also certain failures. The water in the rivers and brooks is lower than has ever been known before at this season of the year. Experience and observation have shown in this quarter that lands upon which water can be supplied by means of ditches are capable of being reduced to the highest state of cultivation without fear of failure from a season of drought. At present the system of irrigation here is primitive, but could it be a possibility to tap the various streams and natural mountain lakes and reservoirs, which only await the expenditure of a small amount of money to send water over the plains and plateaus freighted with the richest fertilizing materials, derived from decaying vegetation and the soils of the hills and the mountains, the result would be to enable the Indian tillers of the soil to gather home at the end of every season an abundant yield of grain, vegetables, and the products of meadows and orchards. The present irrigation facilities consist of only one ditch. A few years ago I succeeded in getting an appropriation from the Interior Department to divert a small portion of the waters of the Jocko River from its main channel to a vast plateau of rich agricultural land, which, if properly irrigated and cultivated, would furnish homes for hundreds of families. The amount appropriated was about $5,000, and was entirely too small to construct a large ditch, but with that much money I completed one of the following dimensions:

Two feet deep, 3 feet wide in the bottom, and 4 feet wide on top. The ditch was necessarily constructed until it reached the head of said plateau through a rough and rocky cañon for a distance of about 2 miles, and required a good deal of fluming and blasting. The flume, like the ditch, is 3 feet in the bottom, of 2-inch plank; 2 feet high, of inch and a half plank; bottom sills 4 by 6; side pieces 4 by 4; cap pieces 2 by 6; all mortised and tenoned, and, like the ditch, I gave it a fall of one-quarter of an inch to the rod. About 80,000 feet of lumber was used for the full completion of the flume and ditch, which was constructed along the foot-hills of the plateau for some 4 miles, and covering the fields and farms of the Indian settlers in that locality. The principal work of this undertaking was done by Indians, with the exception of one or two white men, who worked on the flume. The locating, laying off, and engineering of the ditch was done by myself and a placer miner, both having had former experience in laying off ditches to mines in a rude way. However, its construction was successful and water runs from end to end smooth and rippling. The raise from the river to the bench land was about 200 feet.

The ditch has been a source of water supply for irrigation purposes for the Indians along the line, and those who used it properly have good crops this year as well as every year since its construction. Unfortunately, its capacity was too small for all who needed it, and failure in crops is the result to many farmers along the line of the ditch, who could not be supplied with enough water. The Indians were willing and anxious to earn wages, and the construction of the ditch furnished them profitable employment and was a means of encouragement to labor; and also to keep them on the reservation and away from the towns where they obtain whisky, and also kept them from going to the hunting-grounds while the work lasted. The ditch and flume should be greatly enlarged, as there is a never-failing supply of water in the Jocko River, which could be turned into it all summer.

There are also numerous other streams and mountain lakes on this reservation which can be utilized for irrigation purposes at small expense and the immense valleys and bench lands made to yield, without any fear of failure, good crops that will sustain thousands of human beings in one of the most lovely and picturesque countries in the region of the Northwest.

Lands in Severalty.

The Indians are scattered over the full extent of the reservation and have their homes and farms in the various agricultural valleys. They fence in the quantity of land they desire to cultivate, and the boundary of each one is respected. Owing to the prejudices of the several chiefs and of the headmen of the tribes, a large majority of the Indians of the Flathead Reservation are yet adverse to taking of land in severalty under the act of Congress which became a law on the 8th of February, 1887. The older members of the tribes, and also the young men who have not received any of the advantages of education, go to swell the majority against land in severalty, because they are loath to give-up their savage customs. They say at councils and at their fireside talks that the residue of the land will be sold by the Government to white settlers, thus breaking up their reservation and mixing the Indians up promiscuously with the whites.

Crime.

In the month of May last, Larra Finley, a mixed-breed Kootenai Indian, while under the influence of liquor went to the lodge of some Indians of the same tribe at the head of Flathead Lake, and off the reservation, and engaged in a fight, in which he killed one of them. The murderer was a noted outlaw, who had given great trouble on the reserve on account of his many crimes, in which other previous murders were included. After much travel and expense I succeeded in his capture, and he is now in jail at Missoula.

Soon after his arrest he made a statement relative to the killing of two white men by Indians on the Jocko River, on this reservation. The charred remains of one of the unfortunate men were found before Finley's confession was made. Finley gave the names of the murderers, a warrant was issued, and the sheriff and his posse, on trying to capture the murderers unfortunately killed another Indian. Great excitement prevailed, and fearing that in any other attempt to make an arrest the sheriff and his posse would be attacked by the relatives of the man killed and the friends of the Indians he was seeking to arrest, I therefore telegraphed for troops, and they came upon the scene in time to save trouble. The Indian murderers escaped, but the governor of the Territory has offered a reward of $500 for the arrest of each of them.

Some two years ago a mob of white men at the head of Flathead Lake hung two Indians on suspicion that they murdered three white men who were prospecting. This hanging affair, the killing of an Indian by a white man at Arlee Station, and also the killing of another Indian by a storekeeper at Demarsville, head of Flathead Lake, are claimed by the Indians' murderers, now at large, to be the motives of the killing of the white men in revenge for their relatives.

Another cause of excitement occurred among the Indians. In July of this year a discovery was made of the charred remains of some missing Indians who went out from the reserve to hunt the year previous. The party consisted of the nephew of Head Chief Michell, of the Pend d'Oreilles, his wife, and daughter aged sixteen years, and another Indian of the Flathead tribe. A party of Indians who went out in search of the missing ones into the Sun River country found a mound of burned matter, and upon digging into it found the remains of burned bones, the stone pipes which they recognized as those of the two missing men, an iron used by the women to dress hides, and two pairs of rosary beads. The mound and the remains found were between the place where some whites had a camp, which the Indians recognized as the camp of white men by the signs, namely the kind of stakes used and pieces of newspapers scattered around the place. The searchers came to the conclusion that their Indian relatives were murdered and their bodies burned by some white people, to rob them of their furs and ponies. Other Indians hold that the signs indicate that the crime was committed by Cree half-breeds. The affair has caused no little excitement, and I have been requested by the Indians to give the matter a thorough investigation, as the killing and burning of the bodies of this party will probably lead to outrages by Indians upon innocent white people, unless efforts be made to find out and punish the perpetrators of this terrible deed.

One other case occurred this year in which a boy of Charlot's band of Bitter Root Flathead Indians was killed by a white man in Deer Lodge County. The trouble grew out of whisky drinking by the Indians at a saloon in an out-of-the-way camp.

The whisky-seller was arrested and killer of the Indian also, but he was discharged on the plea of self-defense. The sale of liquor to Indians is the head and front of all offending.

Court of Indian Offenses and Police.

This branch of the service did not give as good satisfaction this year as in time past. Ever since the establishment of the court of Indian offenses to present date its authority has been assailed by the head chiefs of the tribes, who used their influence to break up the power of the Judges to punish or to sentence Indians to penalties for crime. This was caused through jealousy, as the chiefs regarded the establishment of the court as an infringement upon their power. Before they exercised full sway over the police, who were mostly of their own choosing.

Such state of affairs naturally created two parties. The judges and policemen were able to hold control until the unfortunate circumstances occurred, under head of "Crime," which gave the chiefs an opportunity to point out that while an Indian was held to the full penalty of the law, and was hunted down by armed white men, and the wrong Indian shot in attempt to capture guilty ones, very little effort was made by the white officers to punish offenses against Indians. Their side of the case was strong, but I discharged the police and one of the judges, who seemed to shield culprits from arrest by the sheriff of Missoula County. Some dissatisfaction prevails, but careful management and an alacrity shown on the part of the Territorial officials to punish crime committed against Indians may restore that confidence and good-will which heretofore existed.

Very respectfully, your obedient servant,

Peter Ronan,
United States Indian Agent.

The Commissioner of Indian Affairs.

August 22, 1889
LR 23,500/1889, telegram, RG 75, National Archives, Washington, D.C.

> The alcohol saturated conflict in Demersville in late August 1889 resulted in the death of Kootenai Chief Eneas' son, Sam. Many versions of the events were recorded by white participants and witnesses over the years, so it was hard to sort out the facts. Chief Eneas' account in Ronan's September 9, 1889a, letter, below, seems reasonable. The Ramsdell brothers, who served as both whiskey dealers and law officers, had already been in conflict with

Ronan in the past.[49] The trouble was widely reported across the country.[50] The Commissioner of Indian Affairs immediately telegraphed Ronan to investigate.[51] See Ronan's September 9, 1889, letter for Chief Eneas' remarkable restraint in the affair.

Aug. 22, 1889
Arlee, Mont.

Comr Ind Affrs Washn DC

Demersville about one hundred miles from agency & off reservation trouble undoubtedly caused by whisky[.] Indians buy from people at head of flathead lake all the liquor they can pay for & Drunkeness is very frequent among them[.] I will investigate trouble. one Indian was Killed.

Ronan
Agent.

September 1, 1889

LR 25,223/1889, RG 75, National Archives, Washington, D.C. The attached clippings referred to in the letter were sent to D.C. on September 6 and are filed under 25,629/1889.

United States Indian Service,
Flathead Agency,
September 1st, 1889.

Hon. Commissioner Indian Affairs
Washington, D.C.

Sir:

I have the honor to submit my report for the month of August and in doing so sincerely regret to be compelled to notice the exaggerated press reports, and also the fanaticism and prejudice which is being inculcated by persons who have an interest to the prejudice of the Indians and the breaking up of their reservation could the same be accomplished by fair means or foul.

I herewith enclose copy of resolutions passed by some citizens at the Head of Flathead Lake, and submit my explanations. U.S. Inspector Junkin is now upon the reservation, and I believe that after an investigation, that his report if noticed will bear me out in its details. The Chairman W. R. Ramsdell has figured before in my communications to your office, as a suspected Indian whisky trader, but now a full fledged politician for Legislative honors in the Democratic ticket in Montana.

To illustrate the character of this man, I beg to submit copy of a letter I wrote to the Indian Commissioner of British Columbia in answer to inquiries about this same individual.

Flathead Agency, Montana Ter.
February 2nd, 1887

I. W. Powell
Indian Commissioner Victoria
British Columbia

Sir:

I am in receipt of your letter of January 14th 1887, and in reply thereto would state that the store or trading post of Ramsdell Brothers, on Tobacco Plains, is in the neighborhood of one hundred miles north of the Boundary Line of this Indian reservation, and embraced in the County of Missoula,

Territory of Montana. You complain that the above named firm are in the habit of selling liquors in quantities, and that many of the natives of that place have lately been intoxicated. I should be glad to put a stop to the traf[f]ic referred to if in my power, but I can only refer the matter to the authorities of Missoula County, and to the United States Marshal of Montana Territory.

As the store of Ramsdell Brothers is in the neighborhood of only about six miles from the British Border, if your information is correct in regard to the sale of intoxicating liquors to the natives, no doubt it affords an opportunity for the Indians of either side of the line to indulge in their habits of intoxication and should be looked after by the proper authorities, the trafic broken up and offenders punished.

I am respectfully your obedient ser'vt

(Signed) Peter Ronan
U.S. Ind. Agt.

Replying to a letter from W. H. Ruger, Brigadier General, Commanding the Department of Dakota, under date of April 17th, 1888 — his letter being dated April 12th of same month, in which he called attention of newspaper reports of trouble at the Head of Flathead Lake, and asking for such information as I might be able to furnish. I stated it was a fact that the citizens of that vicinity did unlawfully execute two Kootenai Indians, some time in the month of March of that year, and that a third one made his escape or he would follow the fate of the others. Leaving out the details as to the supposed murder of whitemen by the Indians who were unlawfully hung I wrote to the General that I sent for Chief Eneas, of the reservation Kootenais, and that he stated in the interview that while on his way to St. Ignatius Mission a few days before Easter Sunday, he was overtaken by an Indian who informed him that a party of armed whitemen from the Head of the Lake were on the reservation at Dayton Creek, looking for him. The Chief stated that he turned back and met the whitemen and asked by what authority they wer[e] on the reservation searching for him with arms.

The leader of the whites whose name was W. R. Ramsdell the same person who figures in the complaint of Major Powell talked the Kootenai language, and the summer before kept a trading post and whisky shop near the British line, some six miles south on the American side. This man Ramsdell replied (said the Chief) that he was the authority and they had hung two of his Indians and were there to find out what he was going to do about it. The action of Ramsdell and party for coming on the reservation in arms was inexcusable, and might have caused great bloodshed, but for the forbearance of the Indian Chief. Eneas stated to me that if murder had been committed by the Indians it was nothing more than justice to hang the guilty ones but was sorry that Ramsdell and party took the law into their own hands and lynched the Indians, as their trial and conviction and execution by due process of law would have a better effect upon the Indians and prevent recourse to revenge. Continuing this matter, I would respectfully refer the Hon. Commissioner of Indian Affairs to my monthly report dated March 1st 1889, and would take the liberty to here copy an extract which bears upon the history of the feeling existing between the Kootenai Indians, and the settlers at the Head of Flathead Lake.

"Considerable excitement prevailed throughout Montana recently and exagerated reports were telegraphed to the Associated press of a probably Indian uprising on this reservation. The rumored trouble grew out of the fact that one J. E. Clifford, who keeps a store in Demersville at the Head of the Flathead Lake, and North of the reservation, beat an Indian over the head with a pistol. It was first reported that the Indians in revenge killed Clifford, and a Doctor Cuningham. This was false. The Chief of the Kootenai tribe to whom the assaulted Indian belonged stated that while he could not blame the settlers at the Head of Flathead Lake, who were innocent of the doing of one or two men, that if the wounded Indian died Clifford would be killed at all hazzards. The Indian died. I procured the arrest of Clifford and Dr. Cuningham as accessory and had them brought to the town of Missoula. The case was examined, but the Grand jury failed to find indictments much to the disappointment of the Indians, who claimed that Clifford should at least be indicted and tried in open court, as they believe him to have committed an unjustifiable crime."

I now beg to refer the Hon. Commissioner to my report dated June 12th, 1889, in which I stated that Captain Henry M. Marchant Special Agent from the Department of Justice, was then on the reservation and I accompanied him to the Flathead Lake, and called an Indian Council for the purpose of obtaining Indian evidence against whisky trading whitemen, who make a business of selling whisky to Indians at the head of Flathead Lake, also to try to get evidence against a mob of whitemen who hung two Kootenai Indians at the same place taking the law into their own hands, thus imperiling the lives of innocent parties from revengeful feelings of the Indians, who saw two of their people taken from the hands of a deputy sheriff by a lawless mob and hung in handcuffs, without trial or investigation.

To add to all of this two weeks ago, the enclosed exciting press reports were furnished. Upon investigation on the reservation, and without going to Demersville something like one hundred miles from here, which requires travel by team or horseback, and also by steamboat, I found that the sale of whisky to the Indians was the cause of the trouble, and that the Indians admitted that one Indian had killed another, who was his brotherinlaw, and that no trouble would follow as the whites were not considered blameble. The Indian killed was the son of the Chief of the Kootenai tribe, and without my knowledge, he took some of his men to the scene of the murder, and claims without any hostile intent, but to ascertain for himself whether his son was killed by the whites or by his own soninlaw. If by whites, he would demand the arrest and punishment of the murderer of his son — and also stated that as the settlers hung two of his people for a murder, he thought it was no more than just that the slayer of his son if a whiteman should be tried and punished by whitemen. He also claimed that he wished to implore the white people not to sell whisky to the Indians, as that was the cause of all the unfriendeliness [sic] between the Indians and the settlers.

This visit of Chief Eneas to Demersville has been exagerated, and the resolutions published, I believe to excite public opinion against the investigation of the hanging of the Kootenai Indians by the next Grand Jury, also investigations into the sale of whisky to the Indians in that settlement, and to injure the influence and standing of your humble servant. In my last I reported the hay crop almost a total failure, and also that the grain and vegetable crop has suffered in the same way, and that not a quarter of the usual amount can be harvested this year.

I took accasion to cut several tons of coarse wild rye grass, which I had stacked. While not fit for horses, if the winter is hard it will do very well for the Indians to feed to cattle. Last week I sent the threshing machine out and the light crops are being threshed by the Indians. The sawmill has been in operation for the past week cutting lumber from logs delivered by Indians to be used by them in erecting shed and houses this fall.

All interests pertaining to the well fare of the Indians are in good shape, and I have the honor herewith to inclose sanitary report and report of funds and indebtedness for the month of August and also report of farmer, and am

Very respectfully your obedient servant

Peter Ronan

United States Indian Agent.

The following newspaper article from The Inter Lake *(Demersville, Mont.), August 30, 1889, page 4, col. 3 was supposed to be attached to Ronan's letter, but was actually sent to D.C. a few days later. The other articles Ronan sent repeat information in the above letter and are not reproduced here:*

Mass Meeting.

At a mass meeting held at Demersville Aug. 29, 1889. The fol- *[text missing in original]* above resolutions were unanimously adopted and a committee of three appointed to send the resolutions to the Department at Washington and in any other direction the committee might see fit.

A motion to ignore the Indian Agent, Peter Ronan in the matter was made and unanimously adopted. Judge John Lang, Wm. Penny and C. M. Shephard, were appointed a committee to send out resolutions.

After discussing some other matters relating to the intercourse of the whites and Indians the meeting adjourned without formulating an expression, except a unanimous desire of establishing friendly relations, and a settled determination to meet force with force.

We your committee on resolutions respectfully submit the following for your consideration:

Resolved, That we condemn in unmeasured terms, the sale of whiskey to the Indians, and we hold it to be every true citizens duty to aid in bringing the guilty parties to justice.

Resolved, That we condemn the hostile action, of the Kootenia [sic] Reservation Indians in coming into our midst, armed and with evident intention of intimidating our citizens.

Resolved, That hereafter we shall consider a similar armed invasion of our territory an open declaration of war, and all Indians in such invading force as lawful subjects of warfare.

Resolved, That the indifferent and careless action of the department in charge of these hostile Indians meets with our unqualified disaproval, and we deplore the tendency of our government in creating large Indian Reserves without a sufficient Military or Police force to guarantee protection to the property and lives of adjoining white settlers.

Resolved, That in view of the recent action of the Indian agent of the Flathead Reserve, in disregarding the threatening attitude of his wards, towards our people, we are forced through a common desire of self protection, to form ourselves into a self constituted Militia for the enforcement of the law, and the protection of our lives and homes against the ravages of a savage foe.

(Signed.)

W. R. Ramsdell, Chairman.

J. M. Price.

M. Therriault.

A. A. Schonfeldt.

Rupert Jordan.

Committee.

September 7, 1889
LR 25,727/1889, RG 75, National Archives, Washington, D.C.

Henry A. Lambert was born in Minnesota and came to Montana in 1871 where he held various clerical positions in Helena until 1877 when he became "head farmer," or agency clerk, for Ronan. He worked at Flathead Agency until 1881 when he left to become a bookkeeper for a mercantile firm. In 1882 he became a partner with Alex Demers in the store at St. Ignatius Mission. In 1884 he operated a store and hotel at the Foot of Flathead Lake (now Polson). He returned to the Flathead Agency in 1886 as farmer. Since in 1886 Ronan had an agency clerk, this time Lambert's duties were to assist tribal member farmers as well as help with the agency clerical work.[52]

United States Indian Service,
Flathead Agency, M.T.
Sept. 7th, 1889.

The Hon. Commissioner of Indian Affairs,
Washington, D.C.

Sir:

Referring to printed circular "A," dated August 14th, 1889, in which you call special attention to a paragraph in the Act of Congress making appropriations for the Indian service for the current fiscal year in reference to employment of farmers for the Indians, and quote the same.

I have but one farmer at this Agency, and, although I have earnestly applied on several occasions for an assistant farmer to be placed at the Kootenai Indian settlement, some sixty miles from this Agency, my appeals were not granted.

I consider the qualifications of the present farmer good, and the fact that he has so long held the position to my satisfaction, and also to the satisfaction of the Indians in general. Although he is a whiteman he talks the language of the Indians, and can make himself understood among them without the aid of an interpreter. He is married to an estimable lady and lives at the Agency with his family.

In answer to your questions:

1st. Name. Henry A. Lambert.

2d. Date of appointment June 14th, 1886.

3d. Not engaged in farming for immediate five years previous to appointment.

4th. Was employed in farming as a young man at White Bear Lake, in Minnesota, before coming to Montana.

5th. He has a full Knowledge of use and care of modern agricultural implements.

6th. It appears he has a proper understanding of selection of farm sites, seeds, time and manner of planting, cultivating, reaping, etc.

7th. He has since his appointment faithfully endeavored to discharge his duty as laid down in this paragraph.

8th. Married and has his family at the Agency.

9th. Yes; especially so, as already stated, he speaks their language and is popular among the Indians.

10th. Yes. He is in every way of good character.

11th. An answer fully to this question would require a trip of at least seventy-five miles in length on this reservation. At least sixty families were induced to begin farming during his appointments, who are cultivating from five to thirty acres, and some of them have planted orchards. The Indians realize that proper care of their implements of labor is necessary, and nearly all have provided themselves with sheds in which to store them. The slabs are hauled from the saw-mill for that purpose where the farms are located near the Agency. At other places poles and logs are used for construction. I am well satisfied with his administration of affairs in his line, and would recommend the appointment of an assistant farmer to reside among the Kootenai Indians at Dayton Creek, some sixty miles from this Agency. Farming on this reservation is not on a paying basis this season, on account of the drouth, and a more proper system of irrigation, which is necessary for successful cultivation of the soil on this reserve. I would recommend that the pay of the farmer be increased from his present compensation to seventy-five dollars per month, and, also, that I may be authorized to employ a competent Indian or half-breed, as assistant farmer, to reside at Dayton Creek, on this reservation, which is the home of the Kootenai Indians, under Chief Eneas.

> Very respectfully,
> Your obedient servant,
> Peter Ronan
> U.S. Indian Agent.

September 9, 1889a
LR 26,690/1889, RG 75, National Archives, Washington, D.C.

The killing of Chief Eneas' son, Samuel, in Demersville was a tragic affair and the historical records include many contradictory sources. The local whites seemed to be very anxious to blame an Indian for the killing, but this was possibly a self-serving falsehood.[53] Eneas' statement emphasized his diplomatic efforts to protect his tribe while also avoiding further bloodshed. He controlled his anger, despite the provocations from many of the Upper Flathead Valley whites. Ronan had Eneas' side of the story published in a Helena newspaper and his 1890 annual report to the Commissioner of Indian Affairs.[54] In response to this report, the Commissioner of Indian Affairs decided the killing may have been "totally without justification" and asked the Secretary of the Interior to have the United States Attorney for Montana investigate.[55] He also instructed Ronan to cooperate in the investigation.[56] The Commissioner of Indian Affairs then received various communications from white officials blaming the Indians for the conflict and asking for protection from the Kootenai. He requested that the U.S. Army investigate the conflicting claims.[57] A grand jury was convened but there was no record of anyone being punished for Sam's death.[58] The reminiscences of Claude R. Gregg, a white Kalispell resident, stated that his grandfather shot Sam and then the Demersville whites tried to blame a white vagrant who fled the area.[59] See also Ronan's letters of October 22, 1889, and November 29, 1889. A similar case of a Kootenai being shot in an alley made the newspapers in 1896. In that case Susan Kiona was murdered in a Kalispell alley, but no one was ever convicted.[60]

Joe Morant (or Morand) was a mixed blood Indian who lived on a farm six miles north of Bigfork. He was prominent in horse racing in the area. In 1886 his horse, Grand-Jo, beat a Frenchtown horse in a big race at Ashley. Morand was killed in Missoula in a fight over a card game.[61] According to Harry Turney-High, Louis Broken Leg was married to Eneas' daughter, Marian or "She Has Three Buckskin Dresses."[62] Jack Sheppard was a blacksmith at Demersville. In 1890 he was charged with cutting the throat of his father-in-law. In the subsequent divorce case he was accused of being a "habitual drunkard."[63] Eneas' statement mentioned that he sent a white man named Savia to recover his son's body. Savia was the nickname of Francois Gravelle, a Frenchman from Savoy in southeastern France, who had a ranch near the Kootenai village. He was married to Eneas' niece, Elizabeth or Little Eyes, and they had five children. According to the sources, he was goodhearted and respected by both whites and Indians in the area.[64] On his trip to Demersville, Eneas spent a night at the house of Baptist Le Bow or J. B. LeBeau, a French Canadian. During the 1870s LeBeau operated a flour mill in Frenchtown and also raised grain.[65] In the 1880s he raised cattle in the Flathead Valley, and in 1886 he was one of the larger taxpayers in Missoula County.[66] He died in 1907.[67]

To add to the tension, in August 1889 someone burned haystacks at Dayton belonging to Gravelle, LeBeau, and Chief Eneas.[68]

> United States Indian Service,
> Flathead Agency,
> September 9th, 1889.

Hon. Commissioner of Indian Affairs
Washington, D.C.
  Sir:
  With the hope of bringing certain criminals to justice, that live in the settlements at the Head of the Flathead Lake, I shall go to the County Seat of Missoula County, where the Grand Jury is now in session, and bring before them the following statement made to me by Eneas, Chief of the Kootenai Indians of this reservation. It refers to the events and cause of the last sensational reports published through the country of an Indian uprising in that region, and is as follows:

Chief Eneas:
Three Indian boys of my band were gambling near Oust Finley's place on Mud Creek on the reservation. They lost everything they had even to their blankets. They then started for the Head of the Lake going up the East side, and avoiding my home which is on the West side. On the way they passed a creek where there are some white settlers, about one mile from Demersville. At that

place a whiteman who was on foot took a horse away from another whiteman who was riding the same. The fellow who was set afoot begged of the Indians to loan him a horse to ride home, which they did and turned back with him. The Man's name is Joe Morant and he is a settler at the Head of the Lake. He gave the Indian boys whisky upon which they got drunk. When they got to Demersville they were drunk from the whisky obtained from Morant. At Demersville, they got into trouble and a whiteman drew a pistol on one of them but a fight was prevented by outsiders. I (Eneas) was camped near Chief Michel's place, and the day after the Indian boys mentioned started for Demersville, I moved my camp to go home. I camped for the night near the Steamboat landing at the Foot of the Lake. My son-in-law, Louie having loaned a horse to the Indian boys he took the steamer to Demersville to get him back. Before getting on the steamer Louie asked my son to take his horse and ride up to Demersville and meet him there. When I got to my home at Dayton Creek, my son and another Indian rode to Demersvill[e]. They had no arms when they left. They camped the first night with some Pend 'd Oreilles and Kootenais on this side of Demersville. In the morning they found the three Indian boys, the party altogether being six Indians. They sat around the store all day at Demersville. In the evening, two of the boys who previously got whisky from Morant were approached by a whiteman who came out of a saloon, and who is known to the Indians by the name of Jack Sheppard. He asked the boys if they wanted to buy whisky. The Indian boys replied that they had no money; they then reported to their companions that a whiteman offered to sell them whisky. My son-in-law Louie had money and he gave the boys four dollars to buy with. They found Jack and gave him the money. Jack pointed out a place on the bank of the river where he would deliver the whisky. True to agreement Jack returned with two bottles of whisky, which they carried to the other Indians. They all went away from the vicinity of the store to a more secluded spot and commenced drinking. One bottle was drank by six Indians, and my son after drinking said he was hungry and started to the hotel to get something to eat. My son in law Louie followed him. Louie heard a white man talking loud to my son through an upstairs window, ordering him to go away or he would shoot him. Lou[i]e took my son by the arm and tried to take him away. Louie said he heard some one come down stairs who came out the door and while he (Louie) held my son the white man shot him. When my son fell, Louie stated that the man who shot him told him to get away quick or he would be shot. Lou[i]e could not run as he is lame but he turned and saw two white men with guns who told him to get away, and followed him as he hobbled off, for about a hundred yards. Two of the Indian boys who got the whisky started that night after the shooting, for Tobacco Plains, and the other three Indians started back to my home on the reservation. They told me that white men killed my son at Demersville. I sent a whiteman called "Savia" [Francois Gravelle] who is married to a Kootenai woman to get the body of my son. When "Savia" returned with the dead body he told me that the white people at Demersville wanted me to go up there. The morning after the Killing a camp of British Kootenais arrived at Demersville from Tobacco Plains, and they recognized the body as being that of my son. The whitemen told them also to tell me to come to Demersville. I did not wish to go but was advised by a white man who lives in the Lake country to go. It was sixty miles from my home to the Agency and I started for Demersville without letting you (the Agent) know as the distance was so far. I took some of my people along, but sent word ahead that I was coming with no hostile intent, but simply to inquire if my son was killed by whitemen or not. If so to ask that the murder might be punished, and the men who sold the whisky might also be punished, as that was all the cause of the trouble between my Indians and whitemen. I camped on the night of my arrival at the house of Baptist Le Bow [J. B. LeBeau], who is a white settler and lives on this side of Demersville. In the morning I sent another man to let the people know I was coming to talk with them as a friend. When I got to Demersville the people seemed excited and afraid that I came there for revenge. I assured them through an interpreter as best I could my friendly intentions. I could not get any good council with them. I knew that not one of my Indians who had the trouble had a gun or a pistol with them when they left my camp for the Head of the Lake. I do not know where any of them could have borrowed or purchased a pistol or a gun. I told the people if they could tell me where any one of them got a gun or pistol then I might think my son was killed by an Indian. One of the Indians sold a horse to a white man. I asked that white man if he traded a gun or a pistol for the horse — he said no! I asked to see the ball which killed my son, and was answered that the ball was sent to the Agent (not so it was no[t] sent) and by him it would [be] sent to Missoula. Louie, my son-in-law told the whites at Demersville, in answer to a question that he saw the gun plainly in the hands of a white man which killed my son — that it was not a pistol but a gun which looked like a Winchester. Louie also claimed that he could recognize the man who held the gun, and was asked to do so if he was present. Louie pointed out the man but he was not arrested. That man lives in a house at Demersville, but Louie does not know his name, but can point out the house. Finding that I could not learn anything about who killed my son; whether it was a white man as claimed by the Indians; or by an Indian as claimed by the whitemen. I came home to my place at Dayton Creek. The whites wished me to stay one day longer but I felt it would be useless to do so.

I now leave it in the hands of the white men for investigation, and I trust they will do me the justice to investigate this killing. My Indians claim it was done by whitemen, the white men claim it was done by Indians. God Knows! I do not. I now throw myself upon your sense of justice to all.

A great many of my people have been killed by white men; two of them were hung by a mob. I know of no punishment or even a trial that was ever given to a white man for killing any of my Indians, and I now think it time to show that there is justice to be accorded to the Indians as well as to the whites. If this matter shall be brought before the Court at Missoula I am ready to be there and also to do all in my power to bring in witnesses who might be required.

Eneas Chief of Kootenais
his X mark

Respectfully submitted

Peter Ronan, U.S. Indian Agent.

September 9, 1889b
LR 25,995/1889, RG 75, National Archives, Washington, D.C.

> Congress had failed to approve the April 1887 agreement between the Northwest Indian Commission and the Lower Kalispel Indians. Federal policy during the late 1880s called for

moving small bands of Indian to reservations, but Congress was sometimes unwilling to pay for the consolidation. The long tragic failure of the government to honor the agreement with the Lower Kalispel was outlined in the annotation to Ronan's August 27, 1887, annual report.

On September 27, 1889, the Commissioner of Indian Affairs approved Ronan's request for subsistence supplies for the Lower Kalispel who had removed to Flathead.[69]

United States Indian Service,
Flathead Agency, M.T.
September 9th, 1889.

The Hon. Commissioner of Indian Affairs,
Washington, D.C.

Sir:

By reference to Annual report, page 157, it will be seen that on the 27th day of April, 1887, the Northwest Indian Commission entered into a certain agreement with the Indians at this reservation. It was announced at said meeting that it was the policy of the Government to remove to and settle upon Indian reservation, scattered bands of non-reservation Indians, so as to bring them under the care and protection of the United States. As the Lower Pend d'Oreilles, or Kalispel Indians, expressed a desire and entered into an agreement under certain promises of assistance to be granted by the agreement to remove to the Flathead reservation, the said confederated bands of Flatheads, Pend d'Oreilles and Kootenais agreed with the Commission to allow the Kalispels to remove to and Settle upon their lands. It seems, to present date, the United States Congress has not confirmed or passed upon said agreement and it leaves the Indians in question in a very undecided and unsatisfactory condition.

On the 25th of September, 1887, I reported to the Honorable Commissioner of Indian Affairs that Michel, one of the Chiefs of the wandering band of Lower Kalispels, who met the Northwest Indian Commission, at Sand Point, in Idaho Territory, and who signed the agreement to remove to this reservation with the families that acknowledged him as Chief, was at the Flathead Agency; that he came to request transportation for fifteen families from Idaho to the Flathead reservation. The Chief, at the time, fully understood that the agreement with the Northwest Commission which he signed, should be ratified by Congress before it could go into effect, and that there was not means at the disposal of the Indian Office to pay for transportation or to take care of those families until such provisions were made by Congress. But he appealed to the charity of the Honorable Secretary of the Interior and Commissioner of Indian Affairs, through my office, to grant him the aid and facilities he desired to remove his band while they were anxious and willing to come to the Flathead reservation, where it was expected they would cultivate the soil for a living and abandon their wandering and vagabond life. The appeal was listened to and the Indian Office furnished means to bring the band to this reservation, and also provided means of support to the close of the fiscal year which ended June 30th, 1888, and, also, for fiscal year of 1889. During the time since the removal of this band, with whatever aid could be afforded from the Agency, the families commenced fencing in, breaking up land and farming in a small way, and gave sufficient evidence that with proper attention and the assistance promised in the agreement in which they entered with the Northwest Commission, they would at once become tillers of the soil and placed on the highway to civilization and self-support.

From fifteen families that originally removed from Idaho, the number has been increased by subsequent removal to eighteen. I afforded every means at my limited disposal to assist those people with implements of labor, seeds, etc., and encouragement to put in crops this spring. In the early spring when vegetation appeared the crops were destroyed by crickets, which over ran their fields. Trusting to a good season, several of the families procured seeds at the Agency and made a second planting. The drouth of the Summer and the lack of proper irrigation facilities, again proved destructive to their crops and nothing to speak of was harvested by them.

In order that those Indians who removed here in the hope that their efforts might be assisted to obtain a livelihood by the promise and agreement of the Northwest Indian Commission, I respectfully request that enclosed estimate for their support be granted.

> I have the honor to be,
> Very respectfully,
> Your obedient servant,
> Peter Ronan
> U.S. Indian Agent.

Enclosed "Estimate for Supplies for Lower Kalispel Indians" for $1451.75 of bacon, baking powder, beans, coffee, flour, rice, sugar, soap, salt, and tea.

September 13, 1889

Exhibit "A" in William W. Junkin to Secretary of the Interior, September 14, 1889, U.S. Department of the Interior, "Reports of Inspection of the Field Jurisdictions of the Office of Indian Affairs, 1873-1900," National Archives Microfilm Publication M1070, reel 11, Flathead Agency, 5657/1889.

Missoula, Mont. Sept. 13th, 1889

Gen. Ruger
Commanding District of Dakota
St. Paul, Minn.

Sir:

The two Indian Murderers for whose arrest a reward of five hundred dollars each is offered, are yet at large on the reservation, terrorising the Indians to such extent that they are afraid of death to themselves and relatives, if they assist in arrest. The outlaws threaten to burn the Mission and the Indian Schools and Convent. They have followers, that back them against arrest by Indians and have succeeded in over awing the better class of the tribe. The arrest and punishment of the culprits and their backers will Settle all difficulty on this reserve, in present condition of affairs Indians will not accomplish this, a company of cavalry on the reserve with orders to arrest the two murderers and their backers, will settle matters and bring tranquility among the better Class of Indians. I ordered the Indians yesterday to bring in the outlaws or troops would come. They failed to do so.

I desire to Know from you, if I can have Military aid in this emergency. Answer at Arlee.

> (sgd) Peter Ronan
> U.S. Indian Agent.

Endorsed

(sg'd) William W. Junkin
U.S. Indian Inspector.

September 15, 1889
LR 25,929/1889, telegram, RG 75, National Archives, Washington, D.C.

The hunt for Pierre Paul and Lalasee, accused by Lawrence Finley of murdering two white men in 1888, continued through most of 1890. The white justice system in Montana was very motivated to arrest and punish Indians accused of murdering white men. To the disgust of tribal members and Ronan, the system was not as concerned about solving the murders of Chief Eneas' son or Chief Michelle's relatives. After the debacle of the Missoula Sheriff's posse who murdered an innocent Indian on the reservation during the summer of 1889, Ronan called on the U.S. Army to help with the pursuit. Ronan's request was endorsed by Inspector William Junkin, who was then at Flathead Agency.[70] On September 16, 1889, the Commissioner of Indian Affairs requested that the Secretary of the Interior recommend that the Secretary of War instruct the military authorities to "assist Agent Ronan in Arresting the two Indian outlaws."[71]

On November 27, 1889, charges of murder were filed in the Missoula District Court against Larra Finley, Lalasee, and Pierre Paul.[72]

See also Ronan's letters of September 21, October 1, and October 19, 1889, about efforts to get troops to arrest Pierre Paul and Lalasee. Much more information was in Ronan's 1890 correspondence.

Sept. 15, 1889
Flathead Agency, Arlee, Mont.
Commissioner Indian Affairs Washn DC

Two Indian Murderers are at large Enticing Sympathy of worse Class of Indians. Their Arrest by Indian police a failure. To Secure tranquility and for the best interests of the Service, A Company of Calvalry [sic] Should be Sent with orders to Arrest the outlaws and their backers. Have Wired Condition of affairs to General Ruger Commanding District. App[r]oved, William W. Jaunkin, U.S. Indian Inspector.

Ronan, Agent.

September 17, 1889
LR 27,114/1889, RG 75, National Archives, Washington, D.C.

There is a note on the original letter: "F It would seem to me that a jail should be near the agency & not 20 miles distant. B." See annotation for letter of August 13, 1889, for more about the need for a Flathead Reservation jail.

United States Indian Service,
Flathead Agency,
September 17th, 1889.
Hon. Commissioner Indian Affairs
Sir:

Replying to Letter 23047 '89 dated August 28, 1889, in which I referred to previous correspondence and enclosed an estimate for materials and labor required to repair and refit the Jail at this Agency.

You advise that it is out of the question to allow $1,312 for a jail, and that it is thought that it can be put in good condition with a smaller expenditure then the amount named.

The jail is located at the Mission twenty miles from this Agency.

It was so located because that point is more in the center of the Indian population than the Agency. It would cost as much if not more money to transport the lumber from the Agency mill than to obtain it from the saw mill belonging to the Missionaries at St. Ignatius.

I can reduce the estimate by supplying the labor of the carpenter and blacksmith, by sending those employes from the Agency to do the work required, but the material cannot be supplied at any less cost than stated. In answer to your question as to where the lumber used by the Missionaries in the construction of the jail was procured, I would state that the Missionaries have a saw mill of their own located at the Mission that they cut the logs and haul them to the mill from the timber in the locality on the reservation. That they have used this privilege of cutting timber on the reservation, for missionary, educational, residence, and church buildings for more than thirty years for the benefit of the Indians.

The price charged for the lumber would not more than cover the expense of its manufacture and delivery. Inspector Junkin was at the Agency this month, and his attention was especially called to the fact that law and order cannot be preserved on this reservation without a jail capable of holding prisoners. He made an inspection of the jail building and I trust his report on that subject will accord with the facts.

I am very respectfully
Your obedient Servant
Peter Ronan
U.S. Indian Agent.

September 21, 1889a
LR 27,143/1889, RG 75, National Archives, Washington, D.C.

United States Indian Service,
Flathead Agency,
Sept. 21st, 1889.

Hon. Commissioner Indian Affairs,
Washington, D.C.

Sir:

Referring to letter 23047 '89, and my report dated September 17th, 1889, relating to previous correspondence enclosing an estimate for material and labor required to repair and refit the jail at this Agency, I desire to submit the following as sup[p]lementary:

Under date of September 16th, 1889, I am in receipt of a letter from J. D'Aste, S.J., Superintendent of the Mission and School at St. Ignatius, on this reservation; the following is the language of the Reverend gentleman:

"In regard to statement of the expenses required to build and repair the jail, I have given for what was done on it, the statement from the carpenter who did the work. I am willing, however, in order to facilitate the greatly needed repairing of it, to charge only four hundred dollars for what has been done these last three years, to build and repair the jail. The government can make all the necessary repairing to make the jail safe, with little expense. I suggest, then, that the Mission will have nothing to do, any more, to keep the jail in repair, and that the government will do all the necessary work. The sooner the work be done, the better. Because the Indians have no means to punish their people but the jail, and this, as several Government Inspectors can and have testified, cannot safely hold the prisoners."

"In regard to the questions of the Acting Commissioner about the Missionaries, you can answer yourself. I cannot say whether there has ever been any formal demand to have a saw mill run by the Missionarie [sic] Fathers; but we had one before the Reservation was formally established, and the mill having been run for our own use, not to make money out of it, as all the buildings we put up at our own expense can testify. There was never a word said against it either by the Indians or by the numerous Government Inspectors, Commissioners and Agents. Having then done the work on the jail, with our hired hands, we thought, as all the Inspectors who came here and to the Agency during the past years, also thought, we were entitled to a compensation on the part of the Government."

Signed J. D. Aste, S.J."

Respectfully submitted.

I am very respectfully,
Your obedient Servant,
Peter Ronan
United States Indian Agent.

September 21, 1889b
LR 27,264/1889, RG 75, National Archives, Washington, D.C.

See the annotation to Ronan's September 15, 1889, telegram for a summary of his 1889 efforts to capture Pierre Paul and La La See.

United States Indian Service,
Flathead Agency, Mont.
Sept. 21st, 1889.

The Hon. Commissioner of Indian Affairs,
Washington, D.C.
   Sir:
   Herewith I have the honor to enclose copy of my report to Brig. General, Thos. H. Ruger, U.S.A., Commanding Dept. of Dakota, in relation to the necessity for troops to assist in capture of the two Indian outlaws Pierre Paul and La La See.

Very respectfully,
Your obd't servt,
Peter Ronan
U.S. Indian Agent.

Enclosure:

United States Indian Service,
Flathead Agency, Mont.
Sept. 19th, 1889.

Copy —
T. H. Ruger, U.S.A.
Brigadier General,
Commanding Dept. Dakota,
St. Paul, Minn.

Sir:

On the 13th of September, 1889, I wired you the situation of affairs at this Agency, and am in receipt of your courteous reply of the 15th.

In order that you may have an understanding of events which led to the necessity of asking for cavalry to assist in the capture of certain outlaw Indians, without going back to the commencement of this trouble which has been fully reported. I would respectfully state that on the 10th day of September, accompanied by H. A. Lambert, head farmer at this reservation, and three Indians of the police force, I arrived at St. Ignatius Mission for the purpose of arresting the murderous Indian outlaws Pierre Paul and La La See. The arrest of the former was accomplished by the Indians and it was arranged that evening to take him to the agency, a distance of about twenty miles, and from there to convey him to Missoula and deliver him to the proper authorities. The guard was formed by the two Indian judges, one riding on each side and a policeman riding behind; myself, farmer and interpreter riding in a spring wagon. On the way out of the Indian village a number of the outlaw's backers and followers were gathered. He begged the guard to let him bid his mother good-bye. I objected, but the guards said they arrested the prisoner, and in the interest of peace they would accord him that privilege, pledging themselves to a safe delivery of the prisoner at the Agency. There were but two whitemen among a throng of Indians and I saw no alternative but to consent. The Indian, watching an opportunity, sprang out of the lodge of his mother, leaped upon a horse, and went flying towards a neighboring creek fringed with brush. The guards gave chase and gained upon the outlaw. At the edge of the brush he threw himself from his horse and disappeared in the dense undergrowth. All night the Indians Continued the search for Pierre Paul and La La See, without success. Michel, the Chief of the Pend d'Oreilles, was present by my order and Early on the morning of the 11th a council with the Chiefs and Indians was held. I addressed the Indians through my interpreter. Relating the brutal murder of two innocent white travelers by those two Indians and the attempt of the Sheriff of Missoula County to capture them for the crime; the unfortunate Killing by the Sheriff's possée of an Indian who they were not seeking to arrest. The calling out of the military to prevent trouble on the reservation and the events which finally ended in the inducement of Governor [Benjamin] White to offer five hundred dollars reward for the arrest of each of the criminals. Of the way in which Pierre Paul and La La See terrorize the reservation, and of the criminal neglect of the Indians in not arresting them. Then stated how United States Inspector [Wm. W.] Junkin, and the Agency clerk were insulted by Pierre Paul on the Inspector's official visit to the Indian school at St. Ignatius Mission and concluded by saying that myself and Mr. Lambert were there to demand the prisoners. That if proper efforts were not made and the murders not given up in a reasonable time troops would be called for, the Indians surrounded and every suspicious man put under arrest until the criminals were found. The army officers did not Personally Know the murderers and it was presumed that this Plan would be adopted to secure them.

Chief Michel then made a speech to the Indians, deploring the events of the summer which brought his people into notoriety as criminals and law breakers. He said there were only two such Indians, but their friends shielded them from arrest. After a long harangue he Ended by ordering every Indian and half-breed out to search the country and arrest the murderers and turn them over to the Agent.

Believing that most of the Indians were trying to conceal the culprits, on the morning of the 12th, I called them together and said: I go back to the Agency to-day. I have observed that a few good men have tried to do their duty in trying to capture the murderers; but it is reported to me that a number of you instead of trying to make the arrests are doing what you can to conceal and befriend them. I leave Mr. Lambert here to act for me while I return to the Agency. I give you until to-morrow, at 9 o'clock to get the prisoners. You cannot deceive me — they were seen here last night and had you all tried they could be captured. The soldiers will be asked to come here. The officers of the Army not Knowing Pierre Paul and La La See, I suppose they will arrest, and put under guard every suspected Indian until they get the right ones. Your Chief has begged you to stop this my making the arrests yourselves, and your Agent, who has been with you for over thirteen years, and whom you Know has always been your friend, is here now as your friend and asks you to accomplish the arrests, or as sure as they sun goes down to-morrow night, and this [is] not done, the troops will be called for!

I can only add that it is my opinion that the arrests will not be made by the Indians as they seem to fear revenge from the backers and relations of the murderers. If one Company of Cavalry were sent here, Indians in a sense of Security, would assist in hunting them down; but without such force they fear the consequences.

I believe a lesson should be taught to those Indians, but showing that the government will not tolerate resistance to its laws, nor allow the escape of Indian murderers of innocent whitemen traveling through their reservation.

I am, very respectfully,
Your obedient servant,
Peter Ronan,
United States Indian Agent.

October 1, 1889
LR 28,411/1889, RG 75, National Archives, Washington, D.C.

> Ronan reported that despite the record-breaking drought of 1889, reservation farmers were able to harvest two-thirds of a crop.[73] For more information about the 1889 efforts of the Missoula County Sheriff and U.S. Army to arrest Pierre Paul and Lalasee, accused of murdering two white men, see annotation to Ronan's September 15, 1889, letter.

United States Indian Service,
Flathead Agency,
Oct. 1st, 1889.

The Hon. Commissioner of Indian Affairs,
Washington, D.C.

Sir:

At the close of the month of September, it is my pleasure to state that all matters pertaining to the service on this reservation are in a prosperous condition. The crops this season, owing to an unprecedented drought, were almost a failure. However, two threshing machines were sent out and the grain harvested was threshed for the Indians: the grist-mill is now grinding it into flour.

Less than two-thirds of a crop was raised this season and I fear the poorer class of Indians will want for bread-stuff. The saw-mill was in operation during a portion of the month, cutting pine logs delivered at the mill by Indians, for their own use in building and improving their premises. The shingle machine was also running and made several thousand shingles for the Indians.

I arranged matters to leave for Northern Idaho on the 3d of October, pursuant to your instructions of August 28th, "Law and Land 12930 – 1889 – 22436, 1889" and directed the Indians to meet me at Bonner's Ferry at that date. On account of the following communication, however, wired to me by Brigadier General Ruger, my trip will be postponed for, at least, one week:

"St. Paul, Oct. 1st 1889.

> Peter Ronan,
> Flathead Agency, Montana
> Referring to your letter of nineteenth ultimo, and prior telegram, I have been authorized to furnish you military assistance for the arrest of the two Indians charged with murder and will mail directions accordingly to the commanding officer, of Fort Missoula, who will be directed to communicate with you.
>
> Ruger,
> Brigadier General."

I shall try to locate the camp of the outlaws and their backers, and, if possible, secure their arrest. They are watchful but I hope to surprise them before they can escape into the mountains, which has often been accomplished before by them.

I herewith have the honor to enclose Sanitary report and reports of funds and indebtedness for the month of September, also report of farmer and quarterly report of schools and have the honor to be

Very respectfully,
Your ob'd't. serv't.
Peter Ronan
U.S. Indian Agent.

October 7, 1889
LR 29,211/1889, RG 75, National Archives, Washington, D.C.

In 1888 Republican Benjamin Harrison was elected President with the support of many anti-Catholic voters. Harrison appointed Thomas J. Morgan, a Baptist minister as Commissioner of Indian Affairs, who in turn appointed Daniel Dorchester, a Methodist clergyman, as Superintendent of Indian Schools. Morgan was considered hostile to the Catholic Church and had been opposed by the Bureau of Catholic Indian Missions in Washington, D.C.[74] Dorchester did not visit the Flathead Reservation until 1890 when he made a hurried one day visit.[75]

United States Indian Service,
Flathead Agency,
Oct. 7th, 1889.

Hon. Commissioner of Indian Affairs
Washington, D.C.

Sir:

I have the honor to report that school vacation ended with the month of August; and on the first Monday of September, the Children with renewed energy resumed their studies, they are eager to learn; and, heartily Set to work. The success they have obtained gives them courage to continue the work they have commenced.

During the month of September most of the boys have been promoted to higher classes and have resumed their Studies with more interest, being attracted by the novelty of the matter. The division of big and little boys alluded to in the last report, has proved beneficial to the school. The larger boys being now governed by a rule and system of discipline better adapted to their disposition, are willing to stay longer in school. Some older boys, who left the School have returned and but one left Since vacation.

Dr. Dorchester, Superintendent of Indian schools, has been expected here for the past two weeks, as his mail was sent to this agency, he has not yet arrived; and I do not expect to have the pleasure of meeting him, as I leave today for Northern Idaho, to attend to the Kootenais Indians, in obedience to instructions from your office.

I am very respectfully
Your obt. svt.
Peter Ronan
U.S. Indian Agent.

October 16, 1889
LR 29,817/1889, RG 75, National Archives, Washington, D.C.

See annotation for Ronan's August 6, 1889, letter, for more information about the Kootenai Valley allotments for the Bonners Ferry Kootenai.

United States Indian Service,
Flathead Agency,
October 16th, 1889.

Hon. Commissioner Indian Affairs
Washington, D.C.`

Sir:

In accordance with instructions contained in your letter "Law and Land 12930 – 1889 – 22436 – 1889,["] dated August 28, 1889, I visited the Kootenai Indians, located in the Kootenai river country, and found as upon my former visit there that they desire to remain in that country and to have the lands they occupy allotted to them under the 4th section of the General Allotment Act of February 8, 1887, (24 Stat. 388.)

While there I advised the Indians to so select and locate upon their claims that each person will receive, when allotments are made, the quantity to which he or she may be entitled to under the Act, and so that claims will not overlap or conflict with each other.

I herewith attach copy of description of the country, with such other information that I deemed useful which I forwarded to the Surveyor General of Idaho, as per your instructions.

I also attach an account in detail, giving the names and number of children of each head of family, and an estimate of the number of acres of land which will probably be asked for in allotments, and have the honor to be

Very respectfully,
Your obedient servant,
Peter Ronan,
U.S. Indian Agent.

First enclosure:

United States Indian Service,
Flathead Agency,
October 14th, 1889.

Joseph G. Straughan,
U.S. Surveyor General for Idaho,
Boise City, Idaho

Sir:

I would respectfully state that in accordance with instructions from the Honorable Commissioner of Indian Affairs, dated at Washington, D.C., August 28th, 1889, which directed me to proceed to Northern Idaho, as early as practicable and obtain an ac[c]urate description of the same, so that it might be identified, with other information as would be deemed useful, and forward the same to your office at Boise City, Idaho, in order that you might submit an estimate of the cost of the proposed survey to the Commissioner of the General Land Office.

The Indians of that country desire to remain there and to have the lands they occupy or claim allotted under the 4th Section of the General Allotment Act of February 8th, 1887 (24 Stat. 388).

While there I ascertained that the Indian locations would commence about five miles above Bonners Ferry, (the location of which you will find on H Amerine's map of the Northwest,) and follow down the meanderings of the Kootenai river to the British line, a distance following the winding of the river, of about sixty-five miles. On a straight course it would be about forty miles.

The standard (Boise) Meredian for Idaho has not been produced beyond Township No. 49 North. The proposed surveys will require its extension for about 95 or 98 miles.

The Kootenai Valley from Bonner's Ferry down to the British line is about three miles wide, including both sides of the river. Most of the land fit for cultivation is found along the banks of the river. The land near the Foothills is marshy and more subject to overflow than near the river banks. The marshy places are considered good hay lands, with strips of grazing land between the marshes. The water is at its highest about June 1st, and commences to receed [sic] from that date.

The Kootenai river is navigable up to Bonners Ferry at its lowest stages and has a width of about six hundred feet, and a depth of twenty feet in low water to that point. From the British line at the 49th parallel to the Kootenai Lake it is claimed the river has a depth of sixty feet. Two steamers make regular trips twice a week from Bonners Ferry to the quartz mines in the British possessions.

The quantity of land to which those Indians are entitled under the provisions of the Act are specified in the Sec one thereof.

After making a careful census, I should judge that it will take to supply them all, including heads of families and children about sixteen-thousand three hundred acres. However it may require more land as the section provides: "That where the lands allotted are only valuable for grazing purposes an additional allotment of such grazing lands, in quantities as above provided shall be made to each individual."

The land will be required to be surveyed in three detached blocks and subdivided into 160, 80 and 40 acre lots. It will be seen that the Kootenai river is of a size which will require meander lines. I trust that my report is full and satisfactory enough for you to make an estimate to the Department preliminary to an order for survey.

In connection I also have the honor to call your attention to circular issued September 17th, 1887, by the Honorable Secretary of the Interior, prescribing rules and regulations regarding the allotment of lands of the United States, not otherwise appropriated, to Indians, under Section 4 of the Act of February 8, 1887.

Please acknowledge receipt.

I am very respectfully
Your obedient Servant,
Peter Ronan
United States Indian Agent.

Second Enclosure:
Statement of number of Indians and amount of allotments.
Isaac, 160 acres, and 2 children over 18 years and 1 under 18 years 160 and 40. Total Acres: 360.

Malice, Head of Family. Total Acres: 160.

Agee, Head of Family, 160 and 5 children under 18 years @ 40 acres each – 200. Total Acres: 360.

Tanish, Head of Family 160 – 1 over 18 yrs, 80, and 3 under 18 yrs 120. Total Acres: 360.

Milteas, Head of Family 160 and 3 under 18 yrs. 120. Total Acres: 280.

Ecetoll, Head of Family 160 and 4 under 18 yrs 160. Total Acres: 320.

Joseph, Head of Family 160, 2 over 18 yrs and 1 under 40. Total Acres: 360.

Cancaso, Head of Family 160. Total Acres: 160.

Alexander, Head of Family 160 and 3 under 18 yrs 120. Total Acres: 280.

Temo, Head of Family 160, 3 under 120 and 1 over 18 yrs 80. Total Acres: 360.

Antoine, Head of Family 160, 1 under 40 and 1 over 18 yrs 80. Total Acres: 280.

Iron Paddle, Head of Family 160. Total Acres: 160.

Lacard, Widow, 160 and 2 under 18 yrs 80. Total Acres: 240.

Cow, Head of Family 160 and 1 over 18 years 80. Total Acres: 240.

Julian, Head of Family 160 and 2 under 18 years 80. Total Acres: 240.

Louie Tamia, Head of Family 160 and 2 under 18 yrs 80. Total Acres: 240.

David Camile, Head of Family 160 and 2 under 18 yrs 80. Total Acres: 240.

Abraham, Widower 160. Total Acres: 160.

Abraham, Hd of Family. Total Acres: 160.

Euasta, Hd of Family 160 and 2 under 18 yrs 80. Total Acres: 240.

Franswa, Hd of Family 160 and 3 under 18 yrs 120. Total Acres: 280.

Moshel Isaac, Hd of Family 160 and 4 under 18 yrs 160. Total Acres: 320.

Tabish, Hd of Family 160 and 1 over 18 yrs 80. Total Acres: 240.

Jerome, Hd of Family 160 and 2 over 18 – 160 and 1 under 40. Total Acres: 360.

Nicholey, Hd of Family 160 and 2 under 18 – 80. Total Acres: 240.

Joseph Thef, Hd of Family 160. Total Acres: 160.

Eneas, Hd of Family 160 – 1 over 18 yrs and 2 under 18 – 160. Total Acres: 320.

David, Hd of Family 160 – 1 over 18 yrs 80 and 6 under 18 – 240. Total Acres: 480.

Stanislaus, Hd of Family 160. Total Acres: 160.

Michel Teno, Hd of Family 160 and 2 under 18 yrs 80. Total Acres: 240.

Pierrenawa, Hd of Family. Total Acres: 160.

Francois, Hd of Family 160 and 1 under 18 yrs 40. Total Acres: 200.

Pernipe, Hd of Family 160 and 5 under 18 yrs 200 and 1 over 18 yrs 80. Total Acres: 440.

Charley, Hd of Family 160 and 1 under 18 yrs – 40. Total Acres: 200.

Cerome, Hd of Family 160 and 2 under 18 yrs 80. Total Acres: 240.

Enepy, Hd of Family 160. Total Acres: 160.

Custan, Hd of Family. Total Acres: 160.

Tiley, Hd of Family 160 and 4 under 18 – 160. Total Acres: 320.

Pierre Bighead, Hd family 160 and 4 under 18 – 160. Total Acres: 320.

Malacoose, Hd family. Total Acres: 160.

Antoine, Hd family. Total Acres: 160.

Malta, Hd family 160 and 2 under 18 – 80. Total Acres: 240.

Isaac Little, Hd family. Total Acres: 160.

Tamea, Hd family 160 and 4 under 18 yrs 160. Total Acres 320.

Caslo, Hd family 160 and 1 under 18 yrs 40. Total Acres: 200.

Caprean, Hd family. Total Acres: 160.

Custa, Big, Hd family 160 and 1 under 18 yrs 40. Total Acres: 200.

Francois Isaac, Hd family 160 and 1 under 18 yrs 40. Total Acres: 200.

Tepaw, Hd family 160 – 1 over 18 and 3 under 200. Total Acres: 360.

Amoose, Hd family. Total Acres: 160.

Thomas, Hd family 160 and 1 under 18 yrs 40. Total Acres: 200.

Endasta, Young, Hd family 160 and 1 under 18 yrs 40. Total Acres: 200.

Paul, Hd family 160 and 2 under 18 yrs 80. Total Acres: 240.

Kanacka, Hd family 160 and 2 under 18 yrs 80. Total Acres: 240.

Casmere, Hd family. Total Acres: 160.

Widow Sapine, Hd family. Total Acres: 160.

Ann Mary, Widow, Hd family. Total Acres: 160.

Mary Anne, Widow, Hd family 160 and 1 over 18 yrs 80. Total Acres: 240.

Susan, Widow, Hd family. Total Acre: 160.

Aluset, Widow, Hd family. Total Acres: 160.

Sustolee, Hd family 160 and 6 under 18 yrs 240. Total Acres: 400.

Jostile Fry, Hd family 160 and 4 under 18 – 160. Married to whiteman. Total Acres: 320.

Kate Manning, Hd family 160 and 1 under 18 yrs. Married to whiteman. Total Acres: 200.

George Fry, Hd family 160 and 2 under 18 yrs 80. Total Acres: 240.

Christine Bunting, Hd family 160. Married to whiteman. Total Acres: 160.

Julia Strong, Hd family 160. Married to whiteman. Total Acres: 160.

David McLaughlin, Hd family 160 and 5 under 18 yrs 200. Total Acres: 360.

Grand Total Acres: 16,280.

October 19, 1889
LR 30,152/1889, RG 75, National Archives, Washington, D.C.

United States Indian Service,
Flathead Agency,
October 19th, 1889.

Hon. Commissioner Indian Affairs
Washington, D.C.

Sir:

Referring to "L26943 – 1889 – 27264 – 1889," dated October 3d, relative to my request for military aid in arresting two Indian murderers on this reservation, I would respectfully state that I had a conference with the Commanding officer at Fort Missoula on the 17th, inst. I informed that officer that I located the murderers who were at that date encamped with a party of Indians consisting of some sixteen lodges, from this reserve, who are hunting at Pleasant Valley, North of the reservation. I informed the officer that, in my opinion, the arrests could be accomplished by sending a company or two of cavalry to a station called Horse Plains, on the Northern Pacific railroad. From there it would require a march, over a good trail, of about seventy miles, where the camp might be struck and surrounded and the outlaws arrested. By taking this trail a march through the reservation could be avoided and more secrecy maintained of the movements of the troops. Unfortunately there are no cavalry at Fort Missoula and should steps be taken to adopt this plan cavalry would have to be moved a long distance by rail. The military authorities have the affair under consideration.

It is the unanimous desire of all well disposed Indians on the reservation to have those desparados arrested, and a display of force would quiet all resistance, as the abettors of the culprits are only a few — perhaps not over six or eight, and it is thought they are implicated in the crime, either by witnessing or encouraging it, hence their friendship and protection from arrest.

As stated in former reports the Indian police have been terrorized by the few followers of the murderers and fear the threatened vengeance of the relatives and backers of the criminals.

I am very respectfully,
Your obedient Servant
Peter Ronan,
United States Indian Agent.

October 22, 1889a
LR 30,609/1889, RG 75, National Archives, Washington, D.C.

See annotation for Ronan's September 9, 1889, letter for more information about the murder of Chief Eneas' son, Samuel.

Elbert D. Weed, originally of New York state, came to Helena in 1883 where he practiced law. Between 1889 and 1894 he served as United States District Attorney for Montana. In 1894, he was elected mayor of Helena.[76]

General Henry B. Carrington came to the Bitterroot Valley to negotiate the sale of the Bitterroot Salish allotments following the failure of their crops during the 1889 drought. Carrington was able to convince Charlo to remove, but he made commitments the government did not honor. He left a legacy of bitterness and broken promises. The two year delay in the removal until 1891 further impoverished the Bitterroot Salish. They relied on Carrington's word that the removal would take place during spring 1890 and did not plant crops during 1890 or 1891.

Carrington had been a brigadier general of volunteers during the U.S. Civil War, in charge of raising, organizing, and training troops. He never served in combat, which limited his opportunities in the regular army after 1865. Carrington's military career effectively ended on December 21, 1866, near Fort Phil Kearny, Wyoming, when he ordered Lt. Col. William J. Fetterman to assist a wood train from the fort that was under attack by Sioux, Cheyenne, and Arapaho Indians. Fetterman and the eighty other men with him fell into an ambush and were annihilated that day. Fetterman's commander, Carrington was disgraced, and he spent the rest of his life explaining and defending his actions. After being removed as commander of Fort Phil Kearny, Carrington accidentally shot himself in the thigh. He retired from the army in 1870 and developed another career as a professor of military science and an author of books and articles on military history. Carrington also became involved with the Friends of the Indians, a white Protestant movement that worked to save Indians by protecting them from white military aggression, but that also wanted to coerce them into white American cultural patterns and values.[77]

United States Indian Service,
Flathead Agency, Mont.
October 22d, 1889.

The Hon. Commissioner of Indian Affairs
Washington, D.C.

Sir:

In replying to your letter dated October 14th, 1889, "L28659 – 1889" referring to my communication dated September 9th, 1889, submitting the statement of Eneas, Chief of the Kootenai Indians, relative to the killing of his son at Demersville, in this Territory, I have to say that I am also, in receipt of a letter from E. D. Weed, United States Attorney for Montana, upon this subject and I have the honor herewith to enclose copy of my reply to that officer, which will explain the situation to you.

I am, very respectfully,
Your obedient servant,
Peter Ronan
U.S. Indian Agent.

Enclosure:
(Copy)

United States Indian Service,
Flathead Agency, Montana
October 22d, 1889.

E. D. Weed, Esq.,
U.S. Attorney for Montana,
Helena, M.T.

Dear Sir:

I am in receipt of your favor of the 16th inst., with the information that you received a communication from the Attorney General, with enclosures from the Secretary of the Interior and the Commissioner of Indian Affairs, relating to the Killing of the son of Chief Eneas, of the Kootenai Indians, at Demersville, in this Territory, and that the Attorney General is very anxious that the matter be carefully investigated.

I am of the opinion that the statement of Chief Eneas, forwarded by me to the Commissioner of Indian Affairs, can be relied upon, as that chief has never deceived me to my Knowledge, and I regard him as a truthful man, or I would not have gone to the trouble to present his statement to the Indian Department.

As the Chief is now out in the mountains with his people on a fall hunt, I think it would not be well to proceed before the U.S. Commissioner at Missoula, pending the convening of the United States Grand Jury, as it would not give time to hunt up the Indian witnesses that Eneas promised to furnish, nor, indeed, to find the Chief himself.

I am in receipt of a letter from the Honorable Commissioner of Indian Affairs, under date of October 14th, in regard to this case, in which he requests that I extend to you all proper aid and facilities at my command in the prosecution of your investigation. I shall be happy to extend to you any assistance you may require of me.

As Eneas and his people are now away, I think it advisable to delay the matter until the meeting of the U.S. Grand Jury. In the meantime it would be well to issue subpoenas for witnesses with date and place where you may require their appearance. If you can leave a blank for names of witnesses, I shall insert their names, and give my personal attention to the procuring of their attendance at the proper time.

General Carrington, is now at this Agency, to settle the Bitter Root Indian land question, under authority of the Act approved June 15th, 1872 (17 Stat. 227) [sic, June 5, 1872 (17 Stat. 226)] also that of March 2d 1889 (25 Stat. 187) [sic, (25 Stat. 871)], and my time will necessarily be devoted to him for a few days, after which I shall be ready to take up this matter. Please communicate your suggestions, and command me.

I am,
Yours truly
Peter Ronan
U.S. Indian Agent.

October 22, 1889b

LR 30,812/1889, RG 75, National Archives, Washington, D.C.

For more about the St. Ignatius Mission schools in 1889, see Robert J. Bigart, editor, *A Pretty Village.*[78]

United States Indian Service,
Flathead Agency, Montana
October 22d, 1889.

The Hon. Commissioner of Indian Affairs
Washington, D.C.

Sir:

Replying to circular addressed to Indian Agents, (Education) dated at Washington, D.C. October 10th, 1889, I would respectfully report that the school of this reservation is situated at St. Ignatius Mission, about twenty miles North from the Agency. The school is conducted under contract with the government by the Missionary Fathers and Sisters of Providence. Last year the contract was for $150.00 for each, of seventy-five boys and the same number of girls. For this year Congress doubled the appropriation and provided for the education of three hundred boys and girls.

The pupils are tractable and give good satisfaction in their application. Their health has been remarkably good. Their quarters are comfortable, roomy, clean and well ventilated. The School will accomodate three hundred boys and girls very well, and are entirely separated. There are now in attendance seventy five boys and ninety-eight girls. Though the school now seems better appreciated by the tribes, still the full-bloods, especially the Kootenai tribe do not sufficiently realize the great advantage in store for their children by a good education and training. One disadvantage to be contended against is the selfishness of the parents who take their children from school, when they reach an age when they can be made useful at home in herding or other work. I visit the homes of Indians where there are children of school age and use every persuasion in my power to induce them to compel attendance at school. There will probably be an average attendance this year of two hundred. The school is a very efficient one. The progress in the studies of the pupils has been very satisfactory. The boys take great interest in the various works and trades and many prefer the workshops to the school-room. I am forcibly impressed that education and agricultural pursuits, with a knowledge of such trades as are taught here, namely, carpentering, blacksmithing, shoemaking, harness-making, tinsmithing, printing business, painting, sawyer, miller etc., are the great factors in civilizing those people; therefore it is necessary that the children attend the schools despite the wishes of some of the Indian parents who would sacrifice their children to ignorance, idleness and vice rather than send them to school. Their education should be compulsory but in the absence of that law, I shall use every suasion to induce parents who heretofore have used no effort to send their children to school to take a greater interest in the matter which is of vital importance.

As alluded to before, for the sake of the assistance they can give in herding stock or working about home the boys are taken away from school; thus encouraged to leave their studies and having little prospect of comfortably settling themselves the teachers have great difficulty to keep them when they attain a certain age. This inconvenience in the way of the proper training and civilization of the young Indians could be remedied by the establishment of of [sic] a small fund directed to the end of aiding the new families formed by the marriage of the boys and girls of the schools when of age. The prospect of this future aid might keep them longer at school.

I am very respectfully,
Your obedient servant,
Peter Ronan
U.S. Indian Agent.

October 28, 1889
LR 31,381/1889, RG 75, National Archives, Washington, D.C.

> See annotation for Ronan's of August 13, 1889, letter for more information about the need for a Flathead Reservation jail.

United States Indian Service,
Flathead Agency, M.T.
Oct. 28th, 1889.

The Hon. Commissioner of Indian Affairs,
Washington, D.C.

Sir:

Referring to Letter F – 23047 '89, 26236 – '89, 27114 '89, 27145 – '89, in regard to the repair of a jail erected by the missionaries, at a point on the reservation about twenty miles from the Agency head quarters, etc., advising to submit a detailed estimate for a moderately sized jail to be erected near the Agency, I would respectfully report that by furnishing forty thousand feet of logs delivered at the Agency mill at a cost of five dollars per thousand with the aid of the Agency employes and with such material as I have on hand in way of iron, glass, nails etc., I can erect a suitable jail for the necessities of this portion of the reservation, without any other cost than that paid for delivery of the logs at the mill.

In regard to your advice that you "do not consider the simple confinement of Indian prisoners in a jail to be productive of the best results which it is desired to be obtained with this class of Indians"; and that "they should be compelled to do labor of some Kind," the suggestion is quite right, and shall be acted upon to the best of my ability, to furnish guards, when there are prisoners to be looked after.

Under present circumstances I believe it to be for the best interests of the service to maintain a good jail at the point where the present one is erected as well as one at the Agency for the reason which I respectfully submit.

The Agency is at present situated at the extreme end of the Southern habitable portion of the reservation, a fact which will be readily admitted when it is known that not a single Indian farm is cultivated or inhabited between it and the southern boundary. It is also placed at the immediate foot of the mountains forming the Eastern line, thereby precluding any settlement in that direction. On the other hand to the North and West there are farms extending in the one case to a distance of forty and in the other to a distance of at least sixty miles.

Owing to this state of affairs it will be certain that the use of the mills and the service of the mechanics connected with the Agency cannot be utilized by the great majority of the Indians except at considerable cost and inconvenience as per consequence they have not the encouragement which it is the intention of the Government to afford them to follow civilized pursuits. This is especially apparant [sic] in connection with building and grain raising, two matters to which attention is most strongly urged by the Department, as well as by the Agent, since that the transportation by wagons of lumber and wheat exceeds the value of the article itself. For such reasons it was suggested several years ago to remove the Agency to a more central location. The Mission jail is near the center of population. However the removal of the Bitter Root Flatheads to the Jocko valley, renders the Agency mills and shops very available to this class of Indians, who are settling west and north of the Agency, but at convenient distance therefrom.

On the 27th day of April, 1887, a certain agreement was entered into by the Northwest Indian Commission on the part of the United States, and the Indians of the Confederated bands of this reservation, whereby it was provided that in consideration that said Indians allowed the removal of the Lower Kalispels to this reserve from Idaho, the Government would erect mills etc., for the use of said confederated tribes, in the vicinity of Crow Creek, about fifteen miles North of the Mission and thirty-five miles North of the Agency, which would be near the center of the reservation. If this agreement should be carried out, the Indians to the North and West of the Agency will be greatly benefitted.

With a population of some two thousand Indians and half-breeds, this reservation, surrounded as it is by white frontier settlements where they can procure all the whisky they can pay for, despite the law against such traffic, I trust the Hon. Commissioner will realize the fact that there are times when gangs of drunken half-breeds and Indians come from the towns, to the Agency and to the locality of the school, when it requires prompt measures from the Indian police to make arrests and to incarcerate the rioters and evil-doers. Such occasions do not often occur, but at times of horse-racing in the towns, the arrival of a circus, fourth of July and other celebrations, which draw the young Indians and half-breeds from the reservation, jails and prompt arrests are required.

General Henry B. Carrington, U.S.A., Special Agent, etc., is now at this Agency in performance of his duties and instructions from your office, to appraise, for sale, the lands and improvements attaching to 51 patents granted to Flathead Indians in the Bitter Root valley. Being upon the ground, and a gentleman of wide experience in dealing with the Indians, I have requested that he examine into this matter with view of reporting his views to you upon this subject.

I am,
Very respectfully,
Your obdt servt,
Peter Ronan
U.S. Indian Agent.

November 4, 1889
LR 32,188/1889, RG 75, National Archives, Washington, D.C.

United States Indian Service,
Flathead Agency,
November 4, 1889.

Hon. Commissioner Indian Affairs
Washington, D.C.
Sir:

At the close of the month I have the honor to report that October has been very eventful and busy in the discharge of my duties. As reported to you on the 16th of the month, I visited the Kootenai Indians, located on the Kootenai river in the Territory of Idaho. I also addressed a communication from that country, according to your instructions, under date of October 14th, 1889, to Joseph C. Straughan, U.S. Surveyor General for Idaho, giving him description of the country and other information which I thought might be deemed useful, in order that he might submit an estimate of the cost of the proposed survey to the Commissioner of the General Land Office. Although ample time has elapsed I am not yet in receipt of an acknowledgement of my report to him.

On the 17th of the month I held a conference with the commanding officer at Fort Missoula, in regard to the capture of the Indian murderers, and on the

19th of October reported results to you. I also reported to your office under date of October 22d, my correspondence held with the United States Attorney for Montana, relating to the Killing of the son of Chief Eneas of the Kootenai Indians at Demersville, in this Territory. These respective reports have shown some of the affairs which I have attended during the first portion of the month. Its closing days brought General Carrington to this Agency, under orders of the Interior Department and the Commissioner of Indian Affairs to appraise for sale, the lands and improvements attaching to fifty-one patents granted to the Flathead Indians in Bitter Root Valley. Under date of October 22d, the general addressed me a written request, asking advice and assistance as to their location, severally, within my knowledge; and also advice as to interpreter as well as guide who could render service in the direction indicated. I accompanied General Carrington to the Bitter Root Valley, and took with me my official interpreter Michel Revais, and Louison a Flathead Indian of influence, who is also one of the Judges of the Court of Indian Offences at this Agency. My return to the Agency was necessarially delayed until the morning of 3d of November. I am pleased to state that my mission to Bitter Root was very successful, as over half of the Indian owners of patents to lands have already signed an agreement to have their lands appraised and sold and to remove to this reservation. Business called me back to the Agency before interviewing all of the Indian land owners, but I feel confident that all will sign and consent to removal.

The various industries at the reserve have been carried out in a satisfactory manner during the month and peace and quiet prevail. I herewith have the honor to enclose sanitary report and report of funds and indebtedness for the month of October also report of farmer and have the honor to be

Very respectfully
Your obedient Servant
Peter Ronan,
United States Indian Agent.

November 11, 1889
LR 33,021/1889, RG 75, National Archives, Washington, D.C.

United States Indian Service,
Flathead Agency, Mont.
November 11th, 1889.

The Hon. Commissioner of Indian Affairs,
Washington, D.C.

Sir:

In reply to your communication "A" of 1st inst., I have the honor to state that there are no regular issues of beef made at this Agency, with the exception of a very small quantity issued to the Indian Police, and this is issued to them as such times as occasion demands; probably twice in a year. I assume, from your letter, that it refers to agencies where regular beef issues are included with the rations issued at stated intervals during the year, and therefor, does not apply to this agency, as such issues are not made here.

Very respectfully,
Your ob'd't serv't,
Peter Ronan
U.S. Indian Agent.

November 18, 1889
LR 33,819/1889, RG 75, National Archives, Washington, D.C.

United States Indian Service,
Flathead Agency,
November 18, 1889.

Hon. Commissioner Indian Affairs
Washington, D.C.

Sir:

Replying to circular (Land) dated November 1st, 1889, in which you are desirous of collecting the fullest possible information regarding the effects upon the Indians of the so-called "Wild-West" shows and similar exhibitions, with a view of suggesting such modifications in the policy of the Department as the facts may warrant.

In reply, I am pleased to report that no Indians belonging to the Confederated tribes of this reservation have ever been connected with these shows, and know but very little about them.

Occasionally a circus is advertised to visit a neighboring town, and the Indians are as fond of attending the performances as are their white neighbors, and as many as can avail themselves of the opportunity flock to the show. I have never heard an Indian express himself as desirous of following such a life although they enjoy the exhibitions. To my knowledge no inducements have been offered by any parties to Indians of this reserve to follow such a life, and if such inducements were offered I would oppose the acceptance of the same, from the fact that I believe the return of performers or exhibitors to the reservation, and their councils, especially with the young men of the tribes, would create discontent to a certain extent, and an inducement to leave the peaceful pursuits of agricultural and pastorial life for a gaudy display of paint, feathers and wreckless horsemanship to ap[p]lauding crowds.

I am very respectfully
Your obedient Servant
Peter Ronan
United States Indian Agent.

November 20, 1889
LR 33,895/1889, RG 75, National Archives, Washington, D.C.

> Defending and explaining Salish and Kootenai hunting rights under the 1855 Hellgate treaty were continuing necessities during the 1880s as conservation sentiment grew among Montana whites. See also Ronan's November 27, 1889, letter in *The Weekly Missoulian*. White complaints against Indian hunting reflected both an effort to preserve wildlife resources and an attempt to allow white sports hunters to monopolize game at the expense of subsistence and commercial hunters.[79]

United States Indian Service,
Flathead Agency,
November 20th, 1889.

Hon. Commissioner Indian Affairs
Washington, D.C.

Sir:

Circular from office of Indian Affairs, dated November 1st, 1889, calling attention of United States Indian Agents to the fact of frequent complaints being made to the Department that Indians are in the habit of leaving their reservations for the purpose of hunting; that they slaughter game in large quantities in violation of laws of the State or Territory in which they reside, and that in many instances large number[s] of wild animals are killed simply for their hides. I would report:

Some of the Indians of this reservation, after harvest season, are in the habit of leaving the reservation to hunt; their object is to obtain a winter supply of meat, which they dry and cure and pack home to the reservation for family use. The hides are dressed by the Indian women and sold at the Traders stores for cash or trade. I know of no instance where Indians of this reserve slaughter game for any other purpose than to supply food and to dress the hides for sale to supply their necessities. Under the 3d article of their agreement or treaty, made and concluded at Hell Gate, in the Bitter Root Valley, on the 16th day of July, 1855, the Indians claim the right to hunt off the reservation:

Article III:

The exclusive right of taking fish in all the streams running through or bordering said reservation is further secured
to said Indians, as also the right of taking fish at all usual
and accustomed places in common with citizens of the Territory, and of erecting temporary buildings for curing, together
with the privilege of hunting, gathering roots and berries, and
pasturing their horses and cattle upon open and unclaimed
land.

The Indians, I take it, have "exclusive" rights of fishing and hunting on the reservation, which not being under State control is not covered by the game laws of Montana. *Off* the reservation they have rights "in common with citizens of the Territory." Those laws [rights] are now defined and limited by law, and I believe apply to Indians just the same as citizens.

When Indians apply to me for written permission to hunt outside of the reservation, I discourage the idea, but find that with or without permission the hunters go. I believe it the proper policy to pursue here to do all in my power to break up their nomadic habits, but in the face of the third article of their treaty as above quoted, I see no other method than that of persuasion. Each year finds the followers of the chase from this reservation decreasing. As their agricultural and pastoral pursuits increase, the hunting parties decrease. The time is not distant when the hunters who go out from this reservation will go like their white neighbors: for a brief relaxation from their daily toil, and for the healthful exercise and excitement of the chase rather than for the profits which might accrue from indiscriminate slaughter of game.

I am very respectfully,
Your obedient servant,
Peter Ronan
U.S. Indian Agent.

November 27, 1889
The Weekly Missoulian, *November 27, 1889, page 1, col. 5.*

An Interesting Letter on the Hunting
Privileges of the Indians.

The following letter from Major Peter Ronan, will be of interest to the people of this section of the state and will satisfy those who are desirous of knowing what rights the Indians enjoy as to hunting:

Editor Missoulian:— Under date of November 13th, I noticed the following paragraph in your local columns:

"Sportsmen who have been in the Rock Creek country brings the information that the during the past few weeks Indians from the Flathead reservation have been slaying deer in that section in a manner that demands the attention of the authorities. They have been employing dogs in their hunts and have killed over 200 deer. This matter can certainly not be known to Major Ronan or he would be careful that the Indians under his charge would only pursue proper methods in hunting expeditions, and not slaughter game only in a legitimate manner. If Indians are allowed to shoot down deer as they have been doing this fall, within a few years deer will be as extinct as the buffalo."

As there are no hunting parties belonging to this reservation in the Rock Creek country, I presume the Indians complained of reside in the Bitter Root valley. But in order that your readers may understand the status of the Indians composing the confederated tribes of this reservation, I will state as I have heretofore stated, that whatever right is claimed for the Indians to hunt outside of the boundaries of their reservation is taken from the following paragraph in the third article of their treaty made and concluded at Hell Gate valley, in the Bitter Root valley, on the 16th day of July, 1855, which reads as follows:

"Article III. The exclusive right of taking fish in all the streams running through or bordering said reservation is further secured to said Indians; as also the right of taking fish at all usual and accustomed places in common with citizens of the territory, and of erecting temporary buildings for curing, together with the privileges of hunting, gathering roots and berries, and pasturing their horses and cattle upon open and unclaimed ground."

Some years ago a letter was directed to me from the Indian office, in Washington, in answer to inquiries and instructions asked for by me, in regard to the hunting privileges of these Indians, and I herewith quote a paragraph from it for public information.

"In reply I have to say that the privilege of hunting upon open and unclaimed land was granted to the Indians by the treaty of July 16th, 1855, Article III, Statu[t]e 12, page 976, and unless the conditions existing at that time have changed as to render the guaranties inoperative, I do not see how they can be denied the privileges which they still claim. * * *

The regulations of the department prohibits Indians from leaving their reservation without written permission from their agent. Even with such permission they incur risk by wandering from their reservation, and they should be discouraged as far as possible from going beyond their own borders. Every pretense for conflict with white settlers should be carefully avoided, and you will endeavor to encourage friendly feelings on both sides."

It will readily be seen that the reservation Indians have "exclusive" rights of fishing and hunting on the reservation which not being under state control is not covered by the game laws of Montana. Off the reservation, they have rights "in common with citizens of the territory." These rights are now defined and limited by law, and apply to the Indians just the same as to citizens. I see no reason therefore, why an Indian found breaking the game laws of the state of Montana, aside [sic] of the reservation, should not be arrested and tried the same as any other law breaker.

Respectfully Yours,
Peter Ronan,
U.S. Indian Agent.

November 29, 1889
LR 34,974/1889, RG 75, National Archives, Washington, D.C.

> See annotation for Ronan's September 9, 1889a, letter for more about the murder of Chief Eneas' son, Samuel.
> Captain David B. Wilson of Pennsylvania was a Civil War veteran. Promoted to captain in 1886, he retired as a lieutenant colonel in 1902.[80] Lieutenant Robert H. R. Loughborough was from Virginia. He was promoted to major in 1900.[81]

United States Indian Service,
Flathead Agency, Montana
November 29th, 1889.

The Hon. Commissioner of Indian Affairs
Washington, D.C.
Sir:
On the 11th of November I was visited by D. B. Wilson, Captain of the 25th Infantry, and R. H. R. Loughborough, 1st Lieut. 25th Inf., who informed me that the Commanding officer at Fort Missoula was in receipt of a telegram, dated at St. Paul, Nov. 9th, 1889, in which the Interior Department informed the Secretary of War of the request of the then Governor of Montana (White) asking that troops be speedily sent to the Flathead Lake Country, in said Territory, to protect the citizens against violence feared from Chief Eneas and his band of Kootenai Indians, arising from the bad feeling occasioned by the killing of the Chief's Son, and from previous trouble between whites and Indians. The above was communicated on the 9th of November by telegraph by the Division Commander, and the Department Commander directed that officers be sent to investigate the matter and report action and the result to Headquarters, at St. Paul, Minnesota.

To show that the affair was considered serious, on the 11th of November, referring to previous dispatches on the subject the Department Commander directed to continue dispatches from Division Headquarters after the word "Indians," as follows:

Also request that the commander of the military post nearest the vicinity referred to investigate the matter, and if he finds the same to be warranted by the fact, to use such military forces as may be necessary to secure the citizens against danger of harm from the Indians.

Under instructions from the Major General commanding the Army, the Division commander directs that he take the necessary steps to comply with request of Interior Department, reporting action in the premises by telegraph to head quarters.

The Department commander directed that the Commanding officer at Fort Missoula, send without delay, an officer accompanied, if necessary, by a detachment to investigate and report the condition of affairs in the Flathead Lake region, the present state of feeling between settlers and Indians. Whether any, and what unfriendly acts have recently been done by the latter or threats made or depredations committed.

Should it be found on report of the officer, or otherwise, that immediate action is necessary to protect settlers or prevent serious trouble, you will send without waiting further orders, a sufficient force to prevent harm. Acknowledge receipt and state any information of recent disturbance or cause for apprehension as you may have, also report by telegraph action taken hereon.

This was signed by command of General Ruger, commander of the District of Dakota and official copy furnished Captain D. B. Wilson, 25th Infantry, for his information and guidance.

In my interview with the Army officers I informed them that there was no necessity to take a military detachment with them; that there was no danger whatever to be apprehended by the citizens from the Kootenai Indians, under Chief Eneas, of this reservation; that although that Chief mourned the loss of a son killed at Demersville, at the head of the Flathead Lake, supposedly by whitemen, and that although two of his tribe were hung at the same place by a mob and without a trial, and other outrages committed, through the sale of whisky to Indians, that no fear might be apprehended by the whites from that kind-hearted Indian Chief, Eneas, who devotes his influence and his energies to keep his people from getting into trouble growing out of the sale of whisky by dissolute whitemen to his poverty stricken and unfortunate band.

Not having the time to spare to accompany the officers, I requested Mr. Lambert, head farmer at this Agency, to proceed with them, and to make report to me of his observations in regard to the apprehended trouble. I have the honor to enclose said report and, also, copy of official report of the Army officers sent to investigate the matter, addressed to the Post Adjutant at Fort Missoula.

I believe that attached reports clearly Show and bear out my views in all statements made by me to the Indian Office, in my communications in regard to affairs in the Flathead region.

I have the honor to be,
Very respectfully,
Your ob'dt Serv't,
Peter Ronan
U.S. Indian Agent.

First enclosure:

Copy

Fort Missoula, Mont.
November 20th, 1889

To the Post Adjutant,
Fort Missoula, Mont.

Sir:

We have the honor to report that, pursuant to Orders 126, Post, of November 11th, we left post same day enroute to Flathead Lake country, stopped one day at the Flathead Indian Reservation, interviewed Mr Peter Ronan, U.S. Indian Agent to learn from him the extent of the troubles, all the facts regarding the disturbances, their causes, &c. and the next day continued our journey to Demersville, ten miles north of the head of Flathead Lake, the centre of the country where the alleged troubles occurred; where we arrived on the 14th Inst.

We at once put ourselves in communication with the citizens, drove around through the villages and settlement, looked up and learned as far as possible the locality of all of the Indian camps, and interviewed as many of the leading citizens and settlers possible, from all parts of the country, probably from seventy to one hundred in all, and from the various opinions and statements attainable believe the following to be the facts and true condition of affairs, viz: —

Eneas, with his band of Kootenai Indians, who have their permanent home on Dayton Creek, is now camped with his tribe, (women and children) in various places in Pleasant Valley, Smiths Valley &c. hunting for the winter. His people, as a tribe, are peaceable and law abiding and are not disposed to create trouble or disturbances in any way.

In March 1888, two men of Eneas' band were seized by the citizens of the vicinity of Demersville, accused of having killed three white men, at or near Wolf Prairie, and after they were taken into custody by a Deputy Sheriff were again taken from him, by force, and hanged at or near that place.

Last August Eneas' son "Samuel," who was inclined to be wild and fond of liquor, became intoxicated, and when in that condition, tried to break into a house to get something to eat, as he said, and the occupants becoming alarmed, shot him.

In consequence of these troubles, although Eneas feels as though injustice was done and that it was not necessary to kill his son nor indeed the other Indians in 1888, until they had been properly tried and convicted by due process of law, has never threatened or even contemplated any violence in return. He only asks that due process of law be observed and justice be done. These troubles may have, however inculcated a spirit of revenge in some of his young and turbulent bucks, and in case of future trouble, his authority may be defied by some individuals of them.

A considerable number of renegade Kootenai, who acknowledge no tribal relations or authority, recruited probably by Stoney Indians of some character from across the British border, by troublesome bucks who, for various misdemeanors have been driven from the camps of all the peaceable indians in all the surrounding country, are reported to be encamped in various places in Tobacco plains, in Kootenai valley, and near or on the British line (and the murderers La La See and Pierre Paul, from near Ravalli, in the Flathead Reservation are said to have a refuge among them) are travelling to fro, gambling, would be isolated cases of marauding &c.

Thus far they are accused only of killing cattle (and no specific cases of these are named) and stealing food, tearing down fences and keeping the settlers, women and children, in a state of apprehension and terror.

A large part if not all the troubles existing between the indians and whites is clearly traceable to the use of liquor by the indians and the attending idleness and dissipation.

The liquor is purchased by tramps and vagabond whites at $1.00 per bottle and sold to the indians for $2.00 and thus they make an illicit living.

The Flathead country is now almost entirely settled up, nearly every claim being taken, and the whites exceed the indians living there, or that can come there in the ratio of ten to one or more and they can, ordinarily, if their peace officers will perform their duty, keep the indians in subjection, but in consequence of the community being scattered and the settlement new, unavoidable difficulties arise to enforcing the laws. The settlers are very much scattered, the men are employed about their farms, and in the woods at their labor, and their families are necessarily left alone a great portion of the time and are, of course, in a constant state of fear and trepidation.

The opinion among the settlers seems to be, with very few dissenting voices, that there will be no general outbreak of the indians, but that whatever trouble arises if any is contemplated, will be caused by these wandering and irresponsible vagabonds, strengthened by all the troublesome young braves of the various surrounding tribes who will defy the authority of their chiefs, and that there is no danger of them taking the war path or indulging in any violent acts now — that they are in winter camps and the snow on the ground until early spring, probably last of February or early in March, when the snow has partly or wholly disappeared and the grass is again available.

For the present the settlers appear quiet and until early spring arrives, they do not, we think, apprehend any danger.

The settlers, many of them old miners and frontiersmen who are accustomed to the trials and dangers of frontier life, are extremely anxious for the presence of troops, claiming that the very presence of an armed force will strengthen them and subdue these wild and ungovernable indians, and deter them from violence, and render them less saucy and arrogant.

Very respectfully,
Your obedient servant,
(Signed) D. B. Wilson,
Captain 25th Infantry.
(Signed) R. H. R. Loughborough,
1st Lieut, 25th Infantry.

★ ★ ★ ★ ★

1st Endorsement.

Fort Missoula, Montana.
November 21st 1889.

Respectfully forwarded to the Assistant Adjutant General Department of Dakota.

I would recommend that one company from this post filled to fifty men by details from other companies, be sent into the Flathead Country the first of March next to remain two or three months, or more, as circumstances may develop and I think good results would be attained if a strong troop of Cavalry could scout the country during the same time or even longer.

(Signed) Geo. L. Andrews,
Colonel 25th Infantry, Commanding.
Fort Missoula, Montana.
November 21st 1889.

Official copy respectfully furnished U.S. Indian Agent Peter Ronan.

By order of Colonel Andrews:
Geo. Andrews,
1st Lieut. & Adjt. 25th Infantry,
Post Adjutant.

Second enclosure:

United States Indian Service,
Flathead Agency, Montana
November 23d, 1889

Peter Ronan, Esq.,
U.S. Indian Agent,
Flathead Agency, Mont.

Sir:

In compliance with your order of 12th inst.; detailing me to accompany Capt. D. B. Wilson, 25th, U.S. Inf. to the head of Flathead Lake and assist in investigating the rumored disagreement between the Indians and the white Settlers of that section of the state, I have the honor to report to you the results of my observations:

Upon reaching Demersville, the head of navigation on the Flathead river, Capt. Wilson and myself proceeded to interview the representative citizens of that place and the farmers in the vicinity. After securing the views of these people and statements of such facts bearing upon the subject in hand as they could furnish, we went to the town of Ashley and met the leading Settlers of that portion of the valley. The Statements of the majority of the inhabitants of this place and the farms adjacent, were obtained.

After a thorough investigation of all rumors I am led to believe that whatever danger exists, is to be apprehended from renegade Indians from the British Kootenai, who reside at Tobacco Plaines, something more than a hundred miles Northwest of the reservation. These Indians are non-treaty Indians and claim allegiance to the British government, while residing on American soil; I understand some 15 lodges of this same band claim a residence at the head of Flathead Lake. There are about 12 lodges of these Indians now camped with some twenty-two lodges of British Stoney Indians, on Halfmoon Prairie, in the northern part of Flathead valley. There are, in addition to these foreign Indians, two or three lodges of Eneas' band of reservation Kootenais. These latter lodges are peopled by some young men who cannot be controlled by their Chief, and are gamblers and drunkards. This comprises the number of Indians now in the Flathead valley, so far as I could learn, and consists, as stated, of British Indians, with a very small proportion of reservation Kootenais.

My reason for thinking there might be outrages committed by these Indians when spring opens, lies in the fact that they can secure all the liquor they can pay for, as has been heretofore shown, the results of which have been demonstrated in the death of "Knock-i-o," a Kootenai, about May, last, and the recent killing of "Samuel," Son of Chief Eneas, both of which occurrences have, likely enough, engendered a spirit of revenge among the young Indians of the Kootenai tribes, — and the presence of Pierre Paul and La La See, the (Indian) outlaws and murderers, among the Kootenais at Tobacco Plains. The chief of the latter tribe has been reported to me as having said that if the whites attempted to arrest either of these renegades they would have to fight him and his tribe.

I am confident that Eneas, the Chief of the Kootenais belonging to this reservation, will do his utmost to prevent the members of his tribe from entering into conflict with the whites, and that whatever danger exists is from the British Kootenais from Tobacco Plaines and Possibly, a few renegades from Eneas tribe who may escape his control. I think, however, that all danger from the small number of Indians at the head of the Flathead Lake, could be prevented by the presence of a small body of troops during this winter and next summer, at, or near, the town of Demersville.

Very respectfully submitted,
Henry A. Lambert,
Agency Farmer.

December 2, 1889
LR 34,975/1889, RG 75, National Archives, Washington, D.C.

See the annotation to Ronan's October 22, 1889a, letter for more information about Carrington's negotiations with Charlo and the Bitterroot Salish.

The cases of selling liquor to Indians were against Conrad Fisher, the proprietor of the South Missoula Beer Garden, and his wife Lena Fisher.[82] Ronan wrote a detailed report about this case on March 15, 1889, but unfortunately that letter could not be located in the National Archives files. The Fishers were charged with serving liquor to Malta, Baptiste, Antoine, and another unidentified Indian during February and August of 1889.[83] In January 1890 Conrad Fisher was found not guilty in one case and the rest of the cases were dismissed.[84] See Ronan's February 1, 1890, letter about the outcome. The Fishers were prosecuted again for the same crime in June 1893.[85]

Jack Johnson was charged for a September 24, 1889, attempt to rape Mary Matte, who was less than fifteen years of age at the time. No details of the attack were located. Johnson was convicted by an all-white jury on Indian testimony and sentenced to one year in the Deer Lodge prison.[86]

United States Indian Service,
Flathead Agency, Montana
December 2d, 1889.

Hon. Commissioner Indian Affairs
Washington, D.C.
Sir:

The month of November closed with pleasant weather. Very little sign of snow appears except in the lofty mountain ranges, and the vallies look greener than they did during the fall and summer drought. Owing to failure of crops of last season a large number of Indian hunters absented themselves from the reservation with the hope of killing a supply of game for family use; but most of them have already returned, and Christmass [sic] week will find everyone at home with exception of the few lawless renegades.

The successful removal of Chief Charlot, and the remnant of his band, still making the Bitter Root Valley their home, is assured, as all except a few hunters who have been absent have signed the papers to that effect. I notified General Carrington, the Special Agent having this matter in charge, that the absantees [sic] have returned and are at the Agency ready to sign when he arrives here from the Bitter Root Valley, where he is now appraising value of Indian Lands.

I have made arrangements to put in place the matching and plaining machine furnished by the Indian Department, and shall forward estimates for shafting, pullies and belting in a few days.

All industries pertaining to the service here, in mill and shops have been attended to and I know of no special mention to make, save that the Grand Jury was in session last week, and I succeeded in having some indightments [sic] made against whitemen for selling liquor to Indians, and also had indightment brought against a whiteman for attempted rape upon a young Indian girl. The case of the Killing of the son of Chief Eneas, of the Kootenai tribe, will be under investigation this week. I have experienced much difficulty in bringinging [sic] in the Kootenai Chief and his witnesses, owing to the fact that they are hunting in the mountains. I trust to be able to get them in before an adjournment of the Grand Jury.

I herewith have the honor to enclose Sanitary report, and report of funds and indebtedness for the month of November, also report of farmer, and have the honor to be

Very respectfully
Your obedient servant,
Peter Ronan
United States Indian Agent.

December 23, 1889
LR 37,146/1889, RG 75, National Archives, Washington, D.C.

> See the annotation to Ronan's October 22, 1889a, letter for more information about Carrington's 1889 negotiations with Chief Charlo. The Salish expected to be moved during spring 1890, but due to bureaucratic delays the removal did not occur until the fall of 1891. The delay further depleted the resources of the Salish who were already suffering from the failure of their crops during the drought of 1889.

United States Indian Service,
Flathead Agency,
Montana, Dec. 23d, 1889.

Hon. Commissioner of Indian Affairs
Washington, D.C.
　　Sir:
　　At the close of the work of General Henry B. Carington, who was sent to this Agency to appraise for sale the lands of Chief Charlot's band of Bitter Root Flathead Indians, and as the consent of the Indians has been obtained to said appraisment and sale; and also their consent to remove to this reservation soon as practicable, General Carington requested me to report what I thought would be necessary for the comfortable settlement of the remnant of Chief Charlot's band upon their removal here.

In the first place it is my judgment that no time should be lost in closing up this business and that the sale of the land should not be delayed longer than the 1st day of March, 1890, if possible, as that date of sale would give purchasers an opportunity to plow and sow the land and harvest a crop within the year. It would also give the Indians, who sell their belongings, an opportunity to remove to this reservation in the early spring and at once set about making selections of land, fencing and plowing of the same, and seeding the ground and harvesting a crop next autumn. All this can be accomplished providing the necessary steps be taken at once and means provided to put the plan into execution. In replying to the mode of proceedure I would respectfully make the following statement:

Following instructions from Hon. Henry M. Teller, then Secretary of the Interior, on the 27th of March, 1884, I reported to the Indian office the result of a council which I held with Chief Charlot and his band, at Stevensville,

Montana. That Chief having refused to remove from the Bitter Root Valley in several conferences held with the Secretary of the Interior, in the winter of 1884, in Washington, at all of which I was present. Upon the return of the Chief and Indians to the Bitter Root Valley, I was instructed to look into their wants and necessities, and to offer such inducements as I thought reasonable to the heads of families who would remove to this reservation.

The final result was to induce twenty-one heads of families to sign an agreement to remove; and to them, following the views of the Hon. Secretary of the Interior, I promised to each head of family:

1st. A choice of 160 acres of land (unoccupied) on this reservation.

2d. Assistance in the erection of a substantial house.

3d. Assistance in fencing and breaking up of a field of at least ten acres.

4th. The following gifts:

Two Cows; a wagon and harness; a plow or two, with other necessary agricultural implements.

Seed for the first year and provisions until the first crop was harvested.

Seventeen families removed to the reservation under above promise and settled upon a large and beautiful plateau of land on the North side of the Jocko river.

Besides fulfilment of stated obligations, a good irrigation ditch was constructed for use in irrigating their gardens and farmes [sic]. Observing the thrifty and comfortable manner in which the first seventeen families were settled, other families followed to the number of fifteen. Although I asked for authority from the Indian office to submit estimates in detail for the necessary requirements for plowing of lands, fencing materials, house building, labor, cows, etc., for said fifteen families of Charlot's band that removed to this reservation with the reliance that they would be taken care of as in the case of the first seventeen families. They live up on this reservation and as yet are unprovided for, except by their own exertions and the small assistance I can give them from the scanty supplies and facilities at this Agency.

Should Chief Charlot and the remainder of his tribe remove here, as they have agreed to do, all, with exception of the first seventeen families, should be settled as in their case, and given an opportunity to cultivate the soil. Should some such plan be followed out as was inaugurated for the first removals, and provisions made to furnish the Indians with a good irrigation system, all of the Flathead tribe would soon be comfortably settled on this reservation, and in a short time become self-supporting.

Awaiting instructions which may be given to me in regard to this service,

I am very respectfully
Your obedient Servant,
Peter Ronan
United States Indian Agent.

Above: Michel Revais, interpreter, and Chief Charlo. Archives and Special
Collections, Mansfield Library, University of Montana, Missoula,
photograph number 82-84
Below: On the way to Ravalli to meet Bishop Brondel. Oregon Province
Archives, Gonzaga University, Spokane, Washington, negative 120.4.13.

1890

January 2, 1890a
LR 708/1890, RG 75, National Archives, Washington, D.C.

In this letter Ronan requested permission from the Commissioner of Indian Affairs to take a record keeping shortcut by delivering subsistence supplies for the Bitterroot Salish in bulk to Chief Charlo. Charlo would distribute the supplies to individual families. On January 13, 1890, the Commissioner rejected Ronan's request. The Commissioner decided Ronan would not have to make weekly distributions but would have to deliver the supplies to each family himself and get separate certified receipts from each family listing the supplies and signed by two disinterested witnesses and the interpreter.[1] Ronan's January 24, 1890, acknowledgment of these instructions used sarcasm to show his irritation. Ronan made a distribution of subsistence supplies to the Bitterroot Salish in the middle of January 1890.[2] The Bitterroot Salish especially needed assistance after the disastrous 1889 drought.

United States Indian Service,
Flathead Agency,
Jan. 2d, 1890.

Hon. Commissioner of Indian Affairs
Washington, D.C.
    Sir:
    Referring to letter 33726-89 Authority 21695, in which I am advised that Authority has been granted me to expend a sum not exceeding $500.00, in the open market purchase of bacon, beans, baking powder, coffee, flour, rice, sugar, soap, salt and tea; I would respectfully report that I shall make the purchases within a few days from date: In connection therewith I would respectfully ask that I be authorized to take receipt for goods from Chief Charlot, and give him Authority to make division of the same among the families of his tribe, now remaining in the Bitter [Root] Valley.
    I make this suggestion, because I think it the most economical mode of distribution, as my presence at each issue would involve travelling and hotel expenses: I can heartily vouch for a fair and honest distribution of the provisions by Chief Charlot to his people; and as a matter of economy recommend this mode of distribution among the families of Charlot's band in the Bitter Root Valley.

Very respectfully
Your obt Svt,
Peter Ronan
U.S. Indian Agent.

January 2, 1890b
LR 709/1890, RG 75, National Archives, Washington, D.C.

Philip John was a Nez Perce Indian who in August 1888 was traveling through the Bitterroot Valley with two other Nez Perce, Potlatch Fannie and Peter. They camped near a party of white men including John Rombaugh, a prospector. During the night, Peter shot and murdered Rombaugh. A Montana court convicted Philip John of the crime and sentenced him to hang in Missoula on February 7. Ronan assisted the defense in the case.[3]

Ronan, some other unnamed white people, and Philip John's lawyer appealed to Montana Governor Joseph Toole to pardon Philip John. Peter was killed during the attempt to arrest him and Potlatch Fannie feared to testify about the affair. After several reprieves by the Governor, Philip John's sentence was commuted to life in prison. See Ronan's monthly reports of February 1, March 2, April 1, and May 1, 1890, for the progression of the case.[4] The Montana governor between 1889 and 1893 was Joseph K. Toole, a Democrat. As Montana Territorial Delegate to Congress between 1885 and 1889 he had lobbied in Washington, D.C., on some Flathead Reservation matters. He was governor again between 1901 and 1908.[5]

United States Indian Service,
Flathead Agency,
January 2d, 1890.

Hon. Commissioner Indian Affairs
Washington, D.C.

    Sir:

    December closed in cold and stormy weather. The face of the country is covered by snow, and those who are not supplied with hay will suffer from loss of cattle and other stock unless more favorable weather sets in and the snow is melted from the ranges.

    As mentioned in my report for the month of November, owing to failure of crops last season, an unusually large number of Indians absented themselves from the reservation in the pursuit of game; with hope of securing supply of wild meat for family use. Before Christmas all of the hunters returned, and on that day, at mid-night Mass, at the Chapel of St. Ignatius, at least twelve hundred people were in attendance.

    Your advice of the 26th of December, giving authority to expend a sum not exceeding five hundred dollars in open market purchase of flour, bacon, beans, baking powder, coffee, rice, sugar, soap, salt and tea, all to be delivered at Stevensville, Montana, for issue to Charlots Band of Flathead Indians was received to-day. I shall make no unnecessary delay in purchasing the supplies and making proper issue of the same, as I am aware of necessities which require prompt attention.

    At the present term of Court in Missoula County, Philip, a young Nez Percie Indian was convicted of the murder of a prospector, near the Big Hole battle field, in the County of Missoula, Montana, and was sentenced to be hanged on the seventh day of February, in the jail yard in the town of Missoula.

    Several indightments were found by the Grand Jury against white men for the sale of intoxicating liquors to Indians, and the cases will be tried at the term of Court now in session at the County seat.

    All industries pertaining to the service have been promptly looked after. The Indians are contented, and the New Year opens upon peace, quiet and contentment on this reservation.

    I herewith have the honor to enclose sanitary report and report of funds and indebtedness, also report of farmer, and have the honor to be

Very respectfully
Your obedient servant,
Peter Ronan,
United States Indian Agent.

January 17, 1890
LR 2,094/1890, RG 75, National Archives, Washington, D.C.

On January 11, 1889, the Commissioner of Indian Affairs wrote Ronan about a case in the December 1889 sanitary or medical report of a white man treated for gonorrhea.[6] Ronan was ordered to discharge the infected employee. The gonorrhea patient was identified in Ronan's February 1, 1890, monthly report as Sherman Mallery, the agency miller. No further biographical information was located for Mallery.

United States Indian Service,
Flathead Agency, Mont.
January 17th, 1890.

The Hon. Commissioner of Indian Affairs
Washington, D.C.
Sir:
I have the honor to acknowledge receipt of your communication of 11th Jany. '90 "A" 712–90 — and to report that upon inquiry I ascertained from the Agency Physician, Doctor Dade, that the white man reported as having been treated by him for gonorrhoea was the Agency Miller who was employed on the first day of December, 1889. I have this day, in accordance with above information, discharged the man from the Indian Service at this Agency, and ordered him to remove from the reservation.

Very respectfully,
Your ob'd't. srv't.
Peter Ronan
U.S. Indian Agent.

January 21, 1890
LR 2,395/1890, RG 75, National Archives, Washington, D.C.

On February 1, 1890, the Commissioner of Indian Affairs informed Ronan that there were no funds available to provide subsistence supplies for the Bonners Ferry Kootenai.[7] See the annotation for Ronan's August 6, 1889, letter for information about making off-reservation allotments in the Kootenai River Valley to the Bonners Ferry Kootenai and the family of Richard Fry. See also Ronan's August 14, 1890a, letter and later letters relative to the conflict over allotments to the Fry family and the Bonners Ferry Kootenai.

United States Indian Service,
Flathead Agency,
January 21, 1890.

Hon. Commissioner Indian Affairs
Washington, D.C.
Sir:
Referring to "Law and Land — 12930, dated June 21st, 1889, enclosing copy of letter dated Ap[r]il 15, 1889, from United States Indian Agent R. D. Gwider [Gwydir], Colville Agency, Washington Territory, in relation to certain Kootenai Indians in Northern Idaho, "from which it appears that they are in a wretched condition."
In accordance with instructions contained in said letter I visited said Kootenai Indians and reported to your office under date of August 6th, 1889. Also

in accordance with instructions contained in your letter "Law and Land —
12930 — 1889 — 22436, 1889" dated August 28, 1889, I again visited the same
band and reported to you from this Agency, of date October 16th, 1889.

It is hardly necessary for me to enter into details regarding the necessities of this poverty stricken band. Their pressing necessities should at once be
relieved by an expenditure of at least six or seven hundred dollars to purchase
flour, sugar, Coffee, bacon and some clothing to cover their nakedness.

I have been so busy looking after the welfare of the Indians under my own
immediate supervision that I failed to make an appeal for this impoverished
and suffering band, until my attention was called by the receipt of letter herewith enclosed.

I am very respectfully
Your obedient servant,
Peter Ronan,
United States Indian Agent.

Enclosure:

Fry, Idaho, Jan. 14th, 18890 [sic]

Peter Ronan Indian Agent
Arlee P.O.

Dear Sir

by request of the Indians living in this Kootenai Country I will write you in
their behalf, they say that this is a severe winter with them and would be glad
to know if you could not help them with some provision and clothing. they say
there is more snow this winter than there has been for several years and they
can not Exist by hunting as they have done, as game is getting scarcer Every
year, they say if they could only get about $5— or 6— Dollars worth, in here,
and they would also like some agricultural Implements to try their hand farming this Spring. there are several of them who have some few head of Stock
but are dying now for the want of hay. they say about 1 Mower two Rakes.
they have one Mower which they bought themself, about 3 set of Harness and
several plows also about 5000 lbs of seed potatoes, some Turnips Cabbage and
Reudebages. there are about 220 Indians here now, they have nearly all taken
their allotments of land and they seem to be anxious to make improvements on
it. they are in poverty now and are compelled to live on stock that has perished
or died from starvation. some of those that are able to hunt have started out
through three feet of snow to try and get some furs so they can buy some flour
and Clothing for their famileys.

hoping that you may succeede in trying to do something for them

I am your obedient servant
R. Fry.
Respectfully submitted.
Peter Ronan
United States Indian Agent.

January 24, 1890
LR 2,735/1890, RG 75, National Archives, Washington, D.C.

> See Ronan's letter of January 2, 1890a, for his suggestion to simplify the paperwork involved
> in distribution of supplies to the Bitterroot Salish. The sarcasm Ronan expressed in this letter
> was rare in his official correspondence.

United States Indian Service,
Flathead Agency,
January 24th, 1890.

Hon. T. J. Morgan,
Commissioner of Indian Affairs
Washington, D.C.
Sir:
Referring to "A" — 708 — 90, dated at your office January 15, 1890. Allow me to thank you for the pains you have taken in giving me details in regard to the proper distribution of the five hundred dollars worth of subsistence which I was allowed to purchase for Charlot's Band of Flatheads, living in the Bitter Root valley; and the most economical mode of issue under my accountability. The accounting officers of the Treasury Department when they apply, which they invariable do, the full letter of the law in regard to such issues, make it very annoying to an Agent, whose ambition it is to have a clean record and to administer his affairs upon economy and common sense principles.

Thanking you again for your courtesy in giving in detail instructions in this matter.

I am respectfully
Your obedient Servant
Peter Ronan
United States Indian Agent.

February 1, 1890
LR 3,565/1890, RG 75, National Archives, Washington, D.C.

See Ronan's December 2, 1889, letter and annotation for more about the charges against Conrad Fisher and his wife for selling liquor to Indians. Nolle prosse meant the prosecutor decided to not proceed further with the case and it was dropped. Ronan's monthly report on March 2, 1890, has considerable information on Philip John's case. His May 1, 1890, report mentions Philip John's sentence was commuted to life in prison.

United States Indian Service,
Flathead Agency,
February 1st, 1890.

Hon. Commissioner Indian Affairs
Washington, D.C.
Sir:
January was a cold month on this reservation, and the snow was quite deep all over the country. The cattle suffered and some losses occurred to the Indians, but not so great as was apprehended. A chinook wind now prevails which is sweeping the snow from the ranges and the Indians feel confident that further losses to their herds will be small. Owing to a loss of crops last year the Indians are very poor. A large number of families that heretofore raised a surplus of grain crops, and vegetables on farms, and disposed of the same for cash with which to purchase supplies of sugar, coffee, tea, rice and other articles, are this winter in poor circumstances, and compelled to ask for relief at the Agency. The issues for the last quarter has therefore been unusually large. The utmost care will have to be exercised during the remainder of the fiscal year to make the supplies last through. During the month I made a trip

to Bitter Root Valley and purchased supplies in open market for the Indians, to the amount of five hundred dollars, under authority from your office. Chief Charlot was very much pleased and expressed his gratitude. The families were in pressing want and the relief was timely.

The Northern Pacific Railroad Company, this month, sent drafts to the amount of twelve hundred and fifty-eight dollars to pay individual claims of Indians for cattle Killed upon their track, passing through the reservation. The Company has dealt honorably with the Indians in regard to such claims in paying full valuation.

As mentioned in last months report, Philip a Nez Percie Indian was convicted of murdering a prospector in Missoula County, Montana, and was sentenced to be hung on the 7th day of February, 1890, in the jail yard in the County of Missoula. Although convicted and sentenced a doubt existed in the minds of many as to Philips connection in the crime, as another Indian and a squaw participated in the murder. In trying to make arrest of said Indian he was killed by a Deputy Marshal at Spokane Falls, State of Washington, and the Squaw has eluded arrest. After persistent effort by council who defended the Indian, citizens and myself, Governor Toole, on the 29th of January, granted a reprieve to Philip. His time was extended until March 7th, so that the case may be brought before the board of pardons, if the two Houses of Montana Legislature come together and prescribe the duties of the Board.

In the cases brought against parties before the present term of court in Missoula County, for selling whisky to Indians a *nolle prosse* was entered. The clipping enclosed from a Montana newspaper will probably throw some light upon the reason for such proceeding.

As the position of Agency miller, also includes that of sawyer and engineer, I forwarded a nomination to take the place of Sherman Mallery, discharged for cause — as such an employe is indispensible here.

I herewith have the honor to enclose sanitary report and report of funds and indebitedness; also report of farmer, and have the honor to be

Very respectfully
Your obedient servant,
Peter Ronan
United States Indian Agent.

Enclosed newspaper clipping from unidentified newspaper:

A Queer Jury.

Missoula county has a jury that takes the cake, if the reports concerning it be true. Some time ago a man named Fisher and his wife were arrested for selling liquor to Indians and three indictments found against them. In one case they were acquitted and in the other a nolle prosse was entered. It is stated that the reason for the nolle prosse was because the jury had intimated to the county attorney that even if they believed him guilty they would not convict and send a man to the penitentiary for such an offense; that in their opinion the punishment was too severe, and that if the state desired to secure convictions the offense must be changed from a felony to a misdemeanor. — Butte *Mining Journal.*

February 27, 1890
LR 7,092/1890, RG 75, National Archives, Washington, D.C.

The record breaking drought of 1889 was described by Ronan in his August 20, 1889, annual report. In his October 1, 1889, monthly report, Ronan estimated the 1889 crop on the reservation was less than two-thirds of normal.

On March 12, 1890, the Commissioner of Indian Affairs recommended that the Secretary of the Interior approve funds for 30,000 pounds of flour and 10,000 pounds of bacon for relief distribution on the Flathead Reservation until the 1890 crops were harvested.[8] On March 15, 1890, Ronan was informed by telegram that he had been authorized to purchase the flour and bacon on the open market in western Montana.[9]

> United States Indian Service,
> Flathead Agency, Mont.
> February 27th, 1890.

The Hon. Commissioner of Indian Affairs
Washington, D.C.

Sir:

Owing to failure of crops caused by the drought of last season, a great number of the Indian families of this reservation are in destitute circumstances, and if not relieved will suffer from hunger before another crop can be raised. I herewith attach letter to Rev. J. D'Aste, and trust that my action in the premises will be approved. I have some wheat on hand which I intend to grind into flour at the Agency Grist-mill, and issue to the hungry families. At least thirty thousand pounds of flour and ten thousand pounds of bacon should be furnished this Agency to bridge over the necessities of the Indians until the yield of another crop next fall. To add to other misfortunes, a cold storm prevailed during the month of February which killed a great number of Indian cattle. Even where good provisions were made for hay Indian cattle died from a prevailing disease called hollow horn.

> I am, very respectfully,
> Your obedient Servant
> Peter Ronan
> U.S. Indian Agent.

Enclosure:

> United States Indian Service,
> Flathead Agency,
> February 27th, 1890.

Rev'd J. D'Aste, S.J.

Dear Father:

I received your letter of the 24th, apprising me of the great necessities of Indian families near the Mission for supplies. I fully appreciate their great want in this year of drought and failure of crops, and every day I am besieged by applicants for assistance. The small amount of provisions which I have for issue to the Indians I am doling out as economically as I can, and in accordance with the regulations of the Department governing such issues. I can spare about 2000 lbs flour, and five hundred lbs of bacon, which I shall send for distribution among the families in want in your neighborhood. I shall appeal at once to the Indian department for assistance, and should my request be granted for a purchase of supplies, I shall loose no time in relieving the wants of the poor Indians who appealed to you to apprise me of their privations.

I am very truly yours,
Peter Ronan
U.S. Indian Agent.

February 28, 1890
LR 6,811/1890, RG 75, National Archives, Washington, D.C.

Ronan described a student celebration held at St. Ignatius Mission school to commemorate the signing of the Dawes Act into law which provided for individual allotments on Indian reservations and the sale of the remaining "surplus" land to white settlers. The white reformers thought the law would magically make American Indians into small agricultural land owners. Actually it turned out to be the vehicle for impoverishing Indian communities across the country through the forced sale of Indian land to whites at bargain rates.[10]

United States Indian Service,
Flathead Agency, Mont.
February 28th, 1890.

The Hon. Commissioner of Indian Affairs
Washington, D.C.
Sir:

The 8th of February, the day upon which the "Daw[e]s Bill," was signed by the President and became a law, was properly observed at the Indian School at St. Ignatius, on this reservation.

The teachers and Pupils entered into the spirit of the occasion with enthusiasm and the day was celebrated in Perfect accord with instructions from your office under date of January 24th, 1890. Enclosed Programme will give you an idea of the festivities of the happy occasion.

I am, very respectfully,
Your obedient servant,
Peter Ronan
U.S. Indian Agent.

Enclosure:

Franchise Day
at
St. Ignatius Mission School

At 7. A.M. Thanksgiving Service in the Mission Church with appropriate singing.

At 10 A. M. An address to the pupils "Privileges and Duties of American Citizenship." by the Superintendent of the School.

At 12. Banquet to the Pupils, Teachers and Employes [sic].

At 3 P.M. A game of BaseBall.

At 7 P.M. A concert in the Boys Exhibition Hall.

Programme

1. "Star Spangled Banner" by the Brass Band.
2. "Our Country" Song by the Girls' Choir.
3. "Tuba's Joy" March by the Brass Band.
4. Patriotic Recitations by the boys.
5. "Hail Columbia" by the Boys' Choir.
6. "Red, White and Blue" by the Brass Band.

3 cheers for "Our Country."

March 2, 1890

LR 7,135/1890, RG 75, National Archives, Washington, D.C.

See annotation to Ronan's January 2, 1890, letter for more information about Philip John's conviction for murdering John Rombaugh.

Inspector James H. Cisney filed complimentary inspection reports on the Flathead Agency and the St. Ignatius Mission schools on February 28, 1890.[11]

United States Indian Service,
Flathead Agency,
March 2d, 1890.

Hon. Commissioner Indian Affairs,
Washington, D.C.

Sir:

I have the honor to report affairs from this Agency for the month of February.

In the first week of the month a Chinook wind prevailed which swept the snow from the ranges, and the Indian stock owners felt confident that further losses to their herds would be small; but on the 23d the worst storm of the winter prevailed and its rigor has been kept up to present date. There was a driving wind and the average temperature was twelve below zero. The snow fall was heavy and as cattle were in poor condition to withstand a storm like that, I fear the result will be a great loss. In my experience the Indians of this reserve are in more pressing need of assistance for the necessaries of life and for seed for spring planting, as seeds of all kinds have been used for pressing necessity to sustain life. The failure of crops from drought last season is the cause of this state of affairs and cannot be attributed to the Indians who generally put forth greater efforts to seed their lands last year and looked forward to a bountiful yield.

I mentioned in my last month's report the case of Philip John a Nez Percie Indian who was sentenced to be hanged, at Missoula, Montana, on the 7th of last month, and who was reprieved for 30 days by persistent efforts. The expiration of the time allowed him to live will expire on the 7th of March. Meantime everything possible is being done to save him from the death penalty. In the month of February I forwarded a letter to the U.S. Indian Agent at Colville, State of Washington, enclosing an affidavit to be signed by "Potlatch Fannie" touching the case of Philip John. Agent Cole writes: "In this connection I have the honor to state that U.S. Indian Agent Warren D. Robbins, of Nez Percie Agency, Idaho, sent a messenger to me, arriving at this Agency on the evening of February 13th, and accompanied me to Nespilem the following morning, (a distance of about 75 miles) for the purpose of securing the desired affidavit. This however could not be had as "Potlatch Fannie" failed to put in an appearance, fearing that she would be arrested and taken away to be tried for the crime committed." Herewith I have the honor to enclose for your information the affidavit desired to be signed by the Indian woman. I believe that said affidavit is a true statement and it is unfortunate for the prisoner that the woman ran away and avoided signing, as I think it would have influence with the pardoning power of this State.

U.S. Indian Inspector J. M. Cisney, was at this Agency last week. He visited the School and made a thorough examination of all affairs pertaining to the service at this Agency.

Herewith I have the honor to enclose Sanitary report, and report of funds and indebtedness; also report of farmer, and have the honor to be

Very respectfully
Your obedient Servant
Peter Ronan,
U.S. Indian Agent.

Enclosed unsigned affidavit:
State of Montana: SS.
County of Missoula

Potlatch Fannie, an Indian, being first duly sworn, deposes and says that the name "Potlatch Fannie" is one by which she is generally known within the limits of the State of Montana, and that she has, at different times resided in said State of Montana, and particularly on the Flat Head Resrevation [sic] in the County of Missoula, Montana.

That in the month of August, 1888 she went, in company with one Phillip John and one Peter from the vicinity of the Town of Missoula, toward the head of the Bitter Root River and on or about said time camped with the said Indians Phillip John and Peter near some white men who were camped on the West fork of the Bitter Root River going toward the place called Mineral Hill.

That just prior to that time she had been married to the said Peter and on that night slept with him near the camp fire.

That Phillip John had rolled himself in his blanket and lain down near the fire.

That sometime during the night the said Indian Peter, got up, took a gun from the place where it was standing near a tree and fired a shot at the two white men who were sleeping in a bunk near the fire.

That one of the white men was awakened by the first shot and rolled over in his bunk, while the other white man raised himself up on his arm and asked Peter what he was doing, to which Peter made no reply, and then the white man ran away.

At the time Phillip John ran away from the fire and asked Peter what he was doing.

That this affiant saw Peter kill the white man, and that Phillip John had nothing to do with the killing of him, and remonstrated with Peter for his actions.

That after wards, the three Indians left the place where the killing was done, but before leaving the place Peter took what money the dead white man had in his pockets and also the white man's gun and carried the same with him to Idaho.

That afterwards the said Indian Peter was killed at or near Spokane Falls, Washington.

_____

Subscribed and sworn to before me this _____ day of _____ 1890.

March 17, 1890
LR 8,311/1890, telegram, RG 75, National Archives, Washington, D.C.

The Bitterroot Valley Salish had lost most of their crops in the 1889 drought and needed assistance to survive. On March 16, 1890, Ronan was authorized by telegram to issue 5,000 pounds of flour and 2,000 pounds of bacon to the Bitterroot Salish. These supplies were to come out of the flour and bacon Ronan had been instructed on March 15, 1890, to purchase for needy tribal members on the Flathead Reservation.[12] The telegraph operator in Washington, D.C., must have gotten the day wrong for this telegram, or Ronan may have sent the telegram a day earlier than was written on the copy in the National Archives. See Ronan's letter of April 9, 1890, for more about the problems facing the Bitterroot Salish as a result of the delayed move to the Flathead Reservation.

Mch 17th 1890
Arlee Mont

Commr Indian Affrs
Washn DC
 Shall I deliver five thousand pounds flour and two thousand pounds bacon from Authorized purchase to Bitter Root Indians who are now destitute of provisions.

Ronan Agent.

April 1, 1890
LR 10,506/1890, RG 75, National Archives, Washington, D.C.

The kindergarten for young Indian students started in 1890 at St. Ignatius Mission by the Ursuline Sisters was a determined effort to destroy tribal culture and indoctrinate the children into white American society. According to an Ursuline account, the parents willingly surrendered their children to the Sisters.[13] Ronan spelled out his support of the ideology behind the kindergarten in his August 14, 1890b, annual report.

 See the annotation to Ronan's August 21, 1887, letter for biographical information about Larry Finley and his legal troubles.[14]

United States Indian Service,
Flathead Agency,
April 1st, 1890.

Hon. Commissioner Indian Affairs
Washington, D.C.
 Sir:
 I have the honor to report affairs from this Agency for the month of March:
 The weather was cold and disagreeable and the frost so heavy at night that plowing to any great extent was not commenced until to-day. It is gratifying to witness the enthusiasm of the Indians in preparing their ground for planting. The wheat, oats, potatoes, thimoty and vegetable seeds furnished from the Department by your authority is a great blessing to them and highly appreciated. They are utalizing the advantage furnished and I regret that I have not double the quantity of seeds to issue as all called for would be planted. I have so many applicants that it is embarrassing to cut down the quantity to each individual who has his land plowed and prepared for seeding, or who is engaged in such preparation. Ground can be seeded in this locality until the 10th of May; could more seed be furnished before that date larger crops would be the result if a good season follows.
 The call for wagons, harness, plows and other agricultural implements for the past week has kept most of the employes engaged in assisting in making the issues.

The flour and bacon which I was authorized to purchase in open market, is a great assistance and is being issued according to the wants of Indians, which means nearly every family on the reserve.

Last week the missionaries and faculty at St. Ignatius School, established a Kindergarten, and started out with twelve little Indian children, and eight more were received since. Their ages range from three to six years. The Indians show great interest in this new institution. I shall make this matter the subject of a special report at an early date.

Under date of July 17th, 1889, I had occasion to report the pursuit and capture of a halfbreed outlaw and murderer of this reservation, named Lara Finley. This trial came up on March, and on the 22d of that month he was sentenced to ten years imprisonment in the State Penitentiary at hard labor.

The case of the Nez Percie Indian Philip John, also mentioned in my last report, who was sentenced to be hanged on the 7th day of February, and respited for thirty days, has again been respited until April 18th, by the governor, who commuted sentence to imprisonment for life, subject to the action of the board of pardons, which will meet on the 12th of April. Having been requested by the Attorney for the defense to appear before the board, I expect to go to Helena to do all in my power to avert the death sentence.

Herewith I have the honor to enclose sanitary report and report of funds and indebtedness; also report of farmer and quarterly school report, for quarter ending March 31st, 1890, and have the honor to be

Very respectfully,
Your obedient servant
Peter Ronan,
United States Indian Agent.

April 9, 1890
LR 11,409/1890, RG 75, National Archives, Washington, D.C.

> In 1889 Henry B. Carrington had led Charlo and the Bitterroot Salish to believe he would return early in the spring of 1890 to remove the band to the Flathead Reservation in time to allow them to plant crops during the 1890 growing season. Bureaucratic problems and lack of action in Congress delayed the final removal until the fall of 1891. The failure of their crops in the 1889 drought, combined with the lack of crops during 1890 and 1891, devastated the Bitterroot Salish economically, because they had to sell their possessions to survive during the interval. Ronan also pleaded for prompt action in his October 1, 1890, and December 6, 1890, letters.[15]

United States Indian Service,
Flathead Agency, Mont.
April 9th, 1890.

The Hon. Commissioner of Indian Affairs
Washington, D.C.
Sir:

The Flathead Indians of Charlot's band living in the Bitter Root valley, and whose land was appraised for sale by Special Agent, General Carrington, are sending inquiries to me as to whether they will make any attempt to put in crops this season on their farms. If so they desire seed wheat, oats and potatoes. As these Indians signed an agreement to remove to this Reservation, and as it was intimated that their land would be sold and provisions made to remove them before seeding time, they are very anxious for counsel and instruction. If seeds are not planted between this date and the 24th of May the Indians will be unprovided with food. In fact they will be destitute of provisions soon. Last month I issued to them five thousand pounds of flour and two thousand pounds of bacon from the open-market purchase made for the Indians of this reserve, such supply being their only food, flour and bacon is soon consumed.

I earnestly request instructions in regard to these Indians soon as possible, as the season is advancing and if they are not to be removed this year and provided for, their only recourse will be to put in crops or go into the mountains for game. The latter will be in violation of the game laws of the State and will result in arrest of the Indians.

Very respectfully,
Your ob'd't servt.
Peter Ronan
U.S. Indian Agent.

April 11, 1890
LR 11,564/1890, RG 75, National Archives, Washington, D.C.

> In 1889 U.S. Army troops were sent to the Upper Flathead Valley to help prevent conflict between Indians and white settlers in the area. The contest was complicated by cultural differences, alcohol, racism, and resource competition. In spring 1890 the U.S. Army sent troops to the area in a further effort to keep the peace.[16] The troops had a musical band that entertained the local whites at Demersville.[17] According to Ronan's telegram of July 21, 1890, and his August 1, 1890a, letter, the troops joined the white people from Demersville in surrounding the Kootenai village at Elmo and demanding at gun point that Chief Eneas produce several Kootenai charged with killing white people. The accused were not at the camp. Eneas complained that local white authorities were not interested in punishing white people who had killed Kootenai Indians, including his son. Eneas kept his temper, despite the provocations from the invading white posse and army troops, and he made sure the episode did not explode into violence.
>
> For biographical information on Captain D. B. Wilson see the annotation to Ronan's November 29, 1889, letter. For H. A. Lambert, Flathead Agency farmer, see the annotation to Ronan's September 7, 1889, letter.

United States Indian Service,
Flathead Agency, Mont.
April 11th, 1890.

The Hon. Commissioner of Indian Affairs
Washington, D.C.
Sir:

A detachment of troops consisting of fifty men, besides officers, under command of Captain D. B. Wilson, of the 25th Infantry, are now marching through this reservation, on their way to the Flathead Lake region, there to establish a camp for the Summer, near Demersville, the scene of so many complaints in the past few years, between the white settlers and the Indians, owing in a great measure to the sale of liquor to the latter. On the 29th of November, 1889, I had the honor to report to you the matters which led up to the ordering of troops to Demersville. Under that date I also enclosed copy of report of military officer, and the report of H. A. Lambert, farmer at this Agency.

The troops now on the reserve are colored men, and their march to Demersville will be through this reservation for a distance of about seventy miles. The Indians, and especially Chief Eneas, of the Kootenai tribe, have requested me to accompany the command on its march through the reservation, with an interpreter. Chief Eneas, also desires to hold a cou[n]cil with the officers in command when they reach his encampment at Dayton Creek, where he desires to make known his side of the controversy between the Lake country settlers and the Kootenai Indians. Captain Wilson has also requested me to accompany his command at least to Dayton Creek, which is the home of Chief Eneas and some sixty miles north of this Agency. In compliance, I shall leave with a special interpreter, this morning as the Agency interpreter cannot be spared at this time. The orders of Captain Wilson also embrace instructions to co-operate with the Agent in the arrest of Pierre Paul and La La See, the Indian outlaws and murderers, to be turned over to the civil authorities for trial if arrest is made. The outlaws are watchful and no doubt will take to the mountains upon learning of troops being on the reserve.

Trusting my action in the premises will be approved by the Hon. Commissioner of Indian Affairs.

I am, very respectfully,
Your obedient servant
Peter Ronan
U.S. Indian Agent.

April 23, 1890
LR 13,142/1890, RG 75, National Archives, Washington, D.C.

United States Indian Service,
Flathead Agency,
April 23d, 1890.

Hon. Commissioner Indian Affairs
Washington, D.C.
Sir:
Replying to "Education — 8069 — 1890," dated at your office April 9th, 1890, in reference to statement from the Superintendent of the Genoa Indian Industrial School, in regard to balls of rags which had been sewed to-gether and prepared for weaving into carpets, etc.

I would respectfully report that for the past ten years at least, to my knowledge, the Indian girls at the school on this reservation have been taught to utilize cloth and old stockings which otherwise would have been wasted, and are learning valuable lessons in the important art of making their rooms and houses attractive at trifling expense. During this time a loom has been in operation and I forward to your address for personal inspection one rug made of rags, one rug made of old stockings, and also one sample piece of woven carpet of rags, all collected, sewed into balls, made and woven by the Indian girls.

I would be pleased to have receipt of same acknowledged.

I am very respectfully,
Your obedient servant,

Peter Ronan
United States Indian Agent.

May 1, 1890
LR 13,987/1890, RG 75, National Archives, Washington, D.C.

United States Indian Service,
Flathead Agency, Mont.
May 1st, 1890.

The Hon. Commissioner of Indian Affairs
Washington, D.C.

Sir:

I have the honor to report the month of April was a very busy one for the Indians on this reserve. The weather was fine and the Indians in general went to work with a will to plow, plant and sow their fields and gardens. A large increase of acreage was fenced this year, and all the seed that could be obtained has been, or will be put into the ground by the 15th of May. I have devoted a good deal of attention to making provisions for the irrigation of crops, where it could be accomplished by labor of the Indian owners of farms. Small streams and rivulets where they might be turned upon farms in a manner to cover and irrigate the springing growth, insures a good crop, even if the season be a dry one. Inattention to irrigation by Indian cultivators at the proper time, where water facilities are already secured is very annoying, and a watchfulness to this matter is of great importance.

As cultivation is carried on to some extent in all of the agricultural districts of the of the [sic] reservation by Indians, long distances from the Agency headquarters cannot be well looked after in all details as there is only one farmer allowed to be employed at this Agency.

Sobriety and good conduct has been the rule of the Indians since my last report, and industry among the tillers of the soil is marked and encouraging.

The Nez Perce Indian, heretofore mentioned in my reports, as being confined in the County jail at Missoula, under sentence of death had his penalty commuted to the State Penetentiary for life and is now confined at that institution.

Although no trees were furnished by the department for planting on Arbor Day, Tuesday, April 15th, was observed for that purpose by the school, and also, in general by the Indian farmers. A quantity of fruit trees were procured by the latter at their own expense and planted. The children of the School succeeded in procuring trees which were also planted and will in time beautify Indian homes, cemeteries, highways, and school grounds. This custom of tree planting on Arbor Day, will be, in the future, appropriately and enthusiastically observed on this reservation, as the Indians entered into the spirit of the occasion with delight and appreciation of future results. In a special report I shall enter more fully into details of the pleasant introduction of Arbor Day among the Indians of the Flathead reservation.

Herewith I have the honor to enclose sanitary report and reports of funds and indebtedness, also, report of farmer, and have the honor to be,

Very respectfully,
Your obedient Servant
Peter Ronan
U.S. Indian Agent.

June 1, 1890
LR 17,464/1890, RG 75, National Archives, Washington, D.C.

> The mixed blood Indian arrested by Ronan at Arlee was Paul Harry who had been accused of murdering a woman and child on the Coeur d'Alene Reservation. He had been released from jail in Idaho because the witnesses to the crime had died. The Idaho authorities did not want him back. See Ronan's letters and enclosures of June 4, 1890, and July 1, 1890a, for more information on this case. According to one report, after Paul Harry was released from the Missoula jail he returned to Arlee, stole a horse, and then headed east off the reservation.[18] Later in July 1890 Paul Harry was convicted of stealing a horse from another Indian off the reservation and sentenced to the Deer Lodge penitentiary.[19]

United States Indian Service,
Flathead Agency,
June 1st, 1890.

Hon. Commissioner Indian Affairs
Washington, D.C.

Sir:

Thirteen years ago to-day I assumed charge of this Indian reservation. Short as the period is, in the march of time, a great change has marked the progress of the Indians. Instead of being roaming bands of vagrants and hunters, and at war with neighboring tribes, the great majority are now settled down to the peaceful practice of cultivation of the soil and pastoral pursuits.

Their children are being educated in church and school. Instead of the lodge, snug houses with well fenced fields, growing orchards, waving crops of grain, green meadows and vegetable gardens dot every valley on the reservation.

The drought of last year as very discouraging, as crops, generally were a failure and caused a great deal of distress, but the Indians went to work this year with confidence and planted all of the seed they could secure. Besides the grain and potatoes purchased for distribution for seed I issued all of the wheat on hand for that purpose, which in other years was turned into flour for issue to the Indians. The liberal amount of flour furnished by your office on account of the drought of last summer, gave me the opportunity to issue the wheat for seed. Although I could not fill all of the demands an increased acreage is being cultivated. The season so far has been good as we have had copious showers of rain, which, with the aid of irrigation has advanced the crops to a healthy growing state. I have no complaints against the Indians for the month, which is very refreshing as their every movement and indiscression is hearalded to the world through visionary correspondents of the press, and people who believe that the Indian have no right to breath the air outside of the limits of the reservation.

The enclosed paragraph from a Helena newspaper is a statement of an arrest I made, and the half breed mentioned is now in jail at Missoula, serving out a term for abuse and disturbance on the reservation, and also awaiting the action of the officials of Idaho Territory, to return him for trial for murder and brutal outrage committed there.

Herewith I have the honor to enclose sanitary report and report of funds and indebtedness; also report of farmer, and have the honor to be

Very respectfully
Your obedient servant
Peter Ronan,
United States Indian Agent.

Enclosed newspaper clipping from The Helena Journal *(daily), May 29, 1890, page 1, col. 4:*

Ronan Captures an Escaped Murderer.

Special Dispatch to The Journal.

Arlee, May 28. — Yesterday morning Indian Agent Ronan drove to this station for his mail. A strange half-breed was drunk and making it lively for the post trader and the station agent by threatening to kill them, etc. Major Ronan arrested the half-breed and sent him to Missoula in charge of Alex Dow.

Today Mr. Ronan will proceed to Missoula having learned that the man he placed under arrest is an escaped murderer from the jail in Rathdrum, Idaho. Something over a year ago a fine looking young half breed woman and her child were found in their cabin on the Cœur d'Alene reservation with their throats cut. The husband of the woman was away when the brutal crime of outrage and murder was committed. A half-breed by the name of Paul was suspected and he was sent to jail, but while awaiting trial he escaped. The Indians informed Mr. Ronan that the swaggering bully whom he put under arrest yesterday is none other than the escaped murderer.

June 2, 1890

LR 17,468/1890, RG 75, National Archives, Washington, D.C.

> See Ronan's letter of September 7, 1890, describing his trip to Butte to investigate these complaints from the manager of the Butte Butchering Company. The later report suggested that most of the Indian people camped around the slaughter house were Blackfeet or Idaho Shoshoni not Bitterroot Salish. No biographical information was located for Fred Brown, the manager of the Butte Butchering Company.

United States Indian Service,
Flathead Agency,
June 2d, 1890.

Hon. Commissioner Indian Affairs,
Washington, D.C.

Sir:

In my monthly report of yesterday's date will be found the following remarks:

"I have no complaints against the Indians for the month, which is very refreshing, as their every movement and indiscression is heralded to the world through visionary correspondents of the press, and people who believe that the Indian have no right to breath the air outside of the limits of a reservation!"

I am now in receipt of the following letter which I copy and which explains itself:

"Office of Butte Butchering Co.,
Fred Brown, Manager,
May 30, 1890.

Mr. Ronan, Agent.

Dear Sir:

Several lodges of your Indians are here and annoying us considerably as it is about impossible to keep them off of our property and slaughterhouse and unless they are removed from here I shall notify the authorities in Washington — hoping this will meet with your immediate attention.

Yours truly
Signed Fred Brown."

To which letter I replied:

Flathead Agency,
June 2d, 1890.

Fred Brown,
Manager Butte Butchering Co.,
Butte City, Montana.

Sir:

In answer to yours of the 30th of May, I would say that you are at perfect liberty to forward your threatened complaints to the authorities in Washington. Should the Indians you mention commit any unlawful act they are amenable to the law as well as yourself or any other person within the boundaries of the State of Montana. In the mean time I shall do my utmost to discharge my duties to the citizens as well as to the Indians, and also to the Department which I serve.

Yours etc.
Peter Ronan
U.S. Indian Agent.

Under date of April 9th, 1890, I addressed a letter to your office, in which I stated that the Flathead Indians of the Bitter Root Valley, whose land was appraised for sale by Special Agent Henry B. Carrington, were making certain inquiries etc., in regard to their future. The Indians asked for seed to plant if removal to this reserve was not at once contemplated by the Government. In March I issued to this band, by authority, five thousand pounds of flour and two thousand pounds of bacon. Such supply being the only food issued to them since that date as I have no further supplies, nor authority to purchase more. In my letter I also stated that the only resource this band had if not provided with food would be to go out into the mountains for game, and such resort would be in violation of the game laws of the State and might result in arrest of the Indians.

It is presumable that the Indians complained of are from the Bitter Root Valley, and belong to Charlot's Band. Some two or three families of their relatives from this reserve might have joined this party of scavangers who haunt the butcher yard and slaughterhouse of complainant.

I hardly know how to act in regard to the Flatheads of Bitter Root Valley, as the following will show:

"Head-quarters Fort Missoula, Montana.
Feb. 13th, 1880.

Official copy respectfully forwarded to Peter Ronan, Esqr., U.S. Indian Agent, Flathead Agency, Montana.

Signed Geo Gibson
Lieut Col. 3d Infantry
Commanding Post.

Head Quarters of the Army,
Adjutant Generals Office,
Washington, June 4, 1879.

To the Commanding General
Department of Dakota,
Thro' Headquarters of the Missouri:
Sir:

Referring to your endorsement of the 21st Ultimo, upon communication from the Commanding Officer, Fort Missoula, asking definate information as to the jurisdiction of the Military over 'peaceable' Indians 'non-treaty' and those off their reservation without written permission:

I have the honor to invite you[r] attention to the following views of the General of the Army, endorsed thereon, which are concurred in by the Secretary of War:

The Circular of December 23d 1878, is addressed to Indian Agents, and is not obligatory on Commanding Officers of Posts like Missoula, such passes, however, when given should be respected. The Flathead Indians in the Bitter Root Valley are domesticated Indians and be allowed to come and go as free as citizens subject to the laws of Montana.

* * * * *

I am sir, very respectfully

Your obedient Servant,
Signed E. D. Townsend,
Adjutant General."

Until sale is made of lands of the Bitter Root Valley Flathead Indians, and they are removed to this reservation, it appears to me that in accordance with above authority and views they *"should be allowed to come and go as free as citizens subject to the laws of Montana."*

No doubt one or two lodges of vagrants from this reserve visit some of the towns, occasionally, as white tramps and vagabonds visit this reserve. I try to do all in my power to discourage such action. Generally those camps are composed of old Squaws and old Indians, whose only offense is begging, and the picking up of the offall of slaughter houses.

I am very respectfully,
Your obedient servant,
Peter Ronan
United States Indian Agent.

June 4, 1890
LR 17,630/1890, RG 75, National Archives, Washington, D.C.

See the annotation to Ronan's June 1, 1890, monthly report for more information about Paul Harry's arrest by Ronan. Paul Harry had been accused of the murder of a woman and child on the Coeur d'Alene Reservation, but, according to this correspondence, the white

Idaho authorities did not want him back. See Ronan's July 1, 1890a, monthly report for the outcome of the case. T. J. McClung of the Missoula County Sheriff's Office, was active in local Republican politics and in 1891 resigned as undersheriff.[20]

United States Indian Service,
Flathead Agency,
June 4th, 1890.

Hon. Commissioner of Indian Affairs
Washington, D.C.
Sir:

In my report for the month of June, I inclosed a paragraph cut from a Montana newspaper, in regard to an arrest I made of a halfbreed, who was threatening the life and abusing the agent of the Northern Pacific Railroad Company at Arlee; on this reservation, and also the Indian trader at that place. It was reported to me, by the Indians, after the arrest, that the prisoner was the murderer of a halfbreed woman and child on the Couer D'Alene reservation and had escaped from Jail pending his trail [sic]. I requested the Sheriff of Missoula County, Montana, to address the Sheriff of Kootenai County, Idaho, in regard to the prisoner, and herewith attach correspondence.

The prisoner is now serving out a sentence of thirty days for the charges, upon which I put him under arrest. When discharged he will surely return to this reserve. He has made threats against my life for arresting him and also the lifes [sic] of others connected with the agency. Although evidence was not produced against him as explained in the sheriffs letter, the Indians claim that there is no doubt of his guilt, as the ravisher and murderer of Mrs. Pevy and her child, at the Couer D'Alene reserve. He belongs to that reservation; and I do not desire his return here. Will the Hon. Commissioner advise me what to do with the outlaw? I suggest, if no other course is advised, that I may be authorized to take him to his own reservation and turn him over to Chief Seltice, of the Couer D'Alene Indians or the Agent in charge. In any event this thief, gambler, outlaw and supposed murderer should not be allowed to return to this reservation.

Awaiting your orders.
I have the honor to be

Very respectfully
Your obt. svt.
Peter Ronan
U.S. Indian Agent.

First enclosure:

Wm. Martin,
Sheriff, Kootenai County,
Rathdrum, Idaho, May 30th, 1890

T. J. McChung [sic]
Dear Sir:

your letter of the 29 inst at hand, in regard to the Indian now in your Jail. I understand it is Paul Harry who Spent over two years in our County Jail charged with the murder of Mrs Pevey and Child. he was discharged in March, for want of evidence as the two main witnesse [sic] had died. I understand that he has been Stealing Horses this spring but have not been notified to arrest him. thanking you kindly for the information I remain yours

Respectfully
Wm. Martin.

Second enclosure:

Office of Missoula County Sheriff,
Missoula Mont. June 3d, 1890

Maj. Ronan
Flat-Head Agency
    Dear Sir
    Please find enclosed letter recd. from Sheriff Martin of Kootean Co. Wash.
which will explain itself.

Respectfully &c.
W. H. Houston
By T. J. McClung.

July 1, 1890a
LR 21,215/1890, RG 75, National Archives, Washington, D.C.

> The Cree Indians under Chief Wild Boy were considered British Indians and ineligible for most United States government support. The tribes on the Flathead Reservation refused to give them permission to settle on the reservation. Ronan was moved by their destitution to allow them to work on the reservation through the harvest, but he insisted they return to their homes east of the mountains after the work was completed. See also Ronan's letter of July 14, 1890, and the section of his August 14, 1890b, annual report about the British Cree.[21] In 1887 and 1888 the landless British Cree led by Pierre Busha had been refused permission to settle on the Flathead Reservation.[22] No further information was found about Cree Chief Wild Boy.
>
> See annotation to Ronan's June 1, 1890, monthly report for information about Paul Harry, the murderer from Idaho arrested by Ronan at Arlee. Andrew Seltice of the Coeur d'Alene tribe was chief from 1865 until his death in 1902. Seltice took part in the battles with the United States Army in the late 1850s, but later pursued a policy of peace to cope with the white invasion of the tribe's lands in northern Idaho. As game and wild food plants declined, Seltice guided the tribe in developing farming and cattle herds.[23]

United States Indian Service,
Flathead Agency, Mont.
July 1st, 1890.

The Hon. Commissioner of Indian Affairs
Washington, D.C.
    Sir:
    I have the honor to report condition of affairs from this Agency for the month of June. Everything pertaining to the welfare of the Indians is in good condition. The season has been unusually cool and moist, and rains prevailed during the month of June, which with the aid of irrigation assures an abundant harvest for all Indians who cultivated and seeded their farms. The haying season will commence next week and all who have stock to care for will begin their mowing.
    In regard to letter F15386/90, Authority 23318, granting permission to expend a sum not exceeding $147.60 in open-market purchase of material and

employment of labor, required to repair engine and boiler and saw-mill, and connect planer and shingle machine to same, I have to say that I was compelled to defer the work and purchases on account of other pressing labors. Soon as the haying season is over this matter will be given attention and the mill will be put in operation on the logs delivered by Indians at the mill to be put into lumber and shingles for their individual use.

On the 27th ultimo, Chief Wild Boy, son of Big Bear, the Cree chief who gave so much trouble during the Riell rebellion in the Northwest British Territory, now deceased, arrived at this Agency with eight lodges of Crees, consisting of thirty-four men, women and children. They came from the refugee Cree encampment on the American side of the line near Fort Assinaboine, where the encampment consists of 337 souls. Chief Wild Boy had letters of recommendation from Col. Otis of the 20th Infantry, Lieut. Ahern of the 25th Infantry, and other Army officers; also a letter expressive of good conduct for himself and people, from U.S. Indian Agent Fields. The chief stated to me that the Cree refugees were poverty stricken, and were it not for the kindness of Army Officers at Fort Assinaboine and other posts, who procured work for them, chopping wood for government, and other employment, they would suffer from starvation. His object in coming to this reservation, with eight lodges of his tribe, was to seek employment during the haying and harvesting season, from the Indian farmers of the Flathead reservation taking horses for their labor, as they have very little stock of any kind in the tribe.

Pierre Busha, second in command with Rielle, who was executed at Ragina, Northwest Territory, as leader of the half-breed uprising aided by Big Bear's band of Cree Indians, is here also, with several Cree half-breed families. The latter desire to settle upon this reservation, it is already nearly over run with half-breeds from Colville, Spokane and other Indian countries, I refused to allow them to take up any land or to settle upon this reservation.

I called a council of those Indians and half-breeds and stated to them, that while they had my personal sympathy as refugees upon American soil, they were still considered British Indians; that I would grant permission to them to work in the hay and harvest fields for the Indians of this reservation, who could afford to pay them for their labor in horses or other stock from their individual bands, if they refrained from dancing, drinking, gambling and observed the rules of morality and decency. That at the close of the season they should depart from this reservation and go back to their encampment on the Atlantic slope, unless orders of another character should be given to me from the Indian Department. As the Indian Office is doubtless fully informed of the status of this unfortunate people I shall not enter into any further details, and respectfully await suggestions and orders from your office.

On June 4th, 1890, I reported in regard to an arrest of a desparado at this Agency and his incarceration in Jail for a term of a few days. As intimated in report, he returned to this Agency, committed another crime, and is again loose on the community, as set forth in attached paragraph.

Herewith I have the honor to enclose sanitary report and reports of funds and indebtedness; also report of farmer and Quarterly school report for St. Ignatius School on this reservation, for quarter ending June 30th, 1890, and have the honor to be

Very respectfully,
Your obedient servant,

Peter Ronan
United States Indian Agent.

P.S. —

July 7/90

The enclosed report was held until this date awaiting arrival of Quarterly School Report from School at St. Ignatius. I have been advised that said report will arrive by next mail, when I will immediately forward it to your office.

Respectfully,
Peter Ronan
U.S. Indian Agent.

Enclosed clipping from Missoula Gazette *(daily), June 30, 1890, page 1, col. 3:*

A Very Bad Indian.

Chief Saltice of the Cœur d'Alene Indians is Now Advertising Him.

In June last a half-breed Indian was arrested by Agent Ronan at Arlee and sent to Missoula for using threatening language to the post-trader and railroad agent. He was sent to prison for a term. While in jail, it transpired that the prisoner was the person who was in jail at Rathdrum, Idaho, charged with the murder and outrage of a half-breed woman and her child on the Cœur d'Alene reservation some two years ago, but the witnesses died before the trial came on and he was discharged.

After serving his term in Missoula he went back to the agency, stole a horse from the section boys at Arlee and lit out. When last heard from, he was seen traveling with two white men near Big Blackfoot, above Missoula, who were driving horses belonging to Mr. Bandman which had strayed back to the Mission. Now, Chief Saltice of the Cœur d'Alene reserve, thus advertises him in the Farmington Register.

The notorious Paul Harry is, as usual, causing a great deal of trouble to the Cœur d'Alene Indians. His latest is to steal three horses and take them to some town near by, where he sells them for any amount he can get. During the past month six horses have disappeared, one of which belonged to Chief Saltice, branded S T on right hip and right ear slit. The following, of Paul, we are requested to publish for the protection of the whites who might purchase a horse from Paul Harry, not knowing him.

Do not purchase any horses of one Indian known as Paul Harry, who is about 5 feet 10, between 18 and 20 years old, rather light for an Indian, weight about 180, ears set well back on his head, and speaks the English language very well.

July 1, 1890b

The Helena Journal *(daily), July 10, 1890, page 7, col. 3-4.*

Ronan's travelogue of his summer 1890 trip up the Jocko Valley and into the Blackfoot River Valley included little information about life on the Flathead Reservation. The article did, however, illustrate tribal complaints about white hunting and fishing parties coming on the reservation at the same time authorities complained about Indian hunting off the reservation. Ronan did meet Robert "Bob" Irvine, a mixed blood tribal member, leading a prospecting party in the Blackfoot River Valley.

Ronan's traveling companion, Hugh McQuaid, was a longtime Helena newspaperman who came to Montana in 1864.[24] Eugene Humbert, who served as one of the cooks and packers on the trip, came to Montana in 1863. He worked as a miner and cattleman for many years in western Montana and had a business arrangement with Ronan to raise cattle on the reservation.[25] Alex Porrier, the mixed blood guide for the trip had a farm in the Jocko Valley. In 1885 he had 10 horses and 30 cattle, and raised 800 bushels of wheat and oats on 160 acres. Alex was half Chinook and his wife Susan De-w-su-mah was full blood Flathead according to the 1905 enrollment.[26] For biographical information about Robert Irvine, the mixed blood prospector Ronan's party encountered in the Blackfoot Valley, see the annotation to Ronan's October 31, 1890b, letter. Irvine was employed by Ronan as Kootenai farmer in Elmo. George Monture, the mixed blood interpreter murdered in the Blackfoot Valley in 1877, worked for the Hudson's Bay Company and, in the 1850s, for John Owen.[27]

Outing From Flathead

Major Ronan Describes a Trip from the Beautiful Jocko Reservation

Scores of Mirror Lakes, Valleys of Richness, Scenery Unsurpassed and Last a Mineral District Worth Seeing.

Flathead Agency, July 1. — One day last week, your correspondent and Mr. Hugh McQuaid, of your city, mounted our horses and followed our guides and packers outside of the Flathead agency enclosure. Charles des Jardain and Eugene Humbert acted as cooks and packers, while Alex Porrier and his wife were guid[e]s and general camp managers. Our trail on the first day followed fhe [sic] meanderings of the Jocko river and found a chain of three lakes which form the source of that stream. The clear water of the lakes literally swarmed with trout, and a cast into the bottomless blue water with either bare hook or a fly would bring hundreds of speckled beauties leaping to the surface. Here fishing became monotonous on account of the abundant capture. Our first day's ride brought us to the dividing waters of the Jocko and the Big Blackfoot, and we encamped for one night on the summit, where the waters took their course each way — one stream rushing to Missoula by the Big Blackfoot, the other formed the Jocko, emptying into the Pend d'Oreille river and out into that beautiful lake. In traveling around the Jocko lakes the trail ran up into what McQuaid termed "giddy heights," and piteously asked the guide when we would make our descent from the rim of the sky to the beautiful slopes below.

The second day's ride took us down a rippling brook, which formed one of the feeders of the Big Blackfoot river, and we encamped on the junction of the branches of the Clear Water. There our camp was visited by Bob Irvine, a half-bred son of Judge Caleb Irvine, of Butte, with two Indian companions. They had been out in search of the mythical Lost Cabin, which has attracted the attention of every mining precinct from Bret Hart's Roaring Camp on the Pacific Coast, to Alder Gulch, across the range in Montana, where the greasy Pike's Peakers and the tenderfeet from the States first made their advent upon the gold fields of the state. Bob had killed a grizzly bear and captured her two cubs. He tried to pack them back to the agency but the cubs fought so furiously they had to be put to death by a revolver, and their glossy pelts now grace the parlor of Mrs. Ronan as decoratives to rocking chairs. On the third day we left camp on the Clear Water and traveled along a wooded trail which led by several gleaming lake in the clear water of which could be seen trout in schools darting through its transparency, and leaping to the surface to capture flies and insects which dared to invade the surface of their element. After a few hours' travel we came out into the extensive valley which skirts the headwaters and lakes of the Big Blackfoot, and passed by several well fenced fields and meadows, with snug dwellings, grazing cattle and horses, all giving evidence of the seizure of the country by advancing civilization. In the afternoon Monture creek was crossed, a name which was interesting to the writer, as he had the satisfaction of arresting and turning over to the authorities of Montana territory the

Indian Murderer of George Monture,

the man after whom this stream is named. Chac-Tah was the name of the murderer, which means in English "Meat Broiler." He was tried for the murder of Monture eleven years ago, and sentenced to the penitentiary for life, at Deer Lodge, Montana. After three years of imprisonment he died. Strange, after the lapse of eleven years, the father of the boy who buried the murdered man was able to point out the spot where the dirt was heaped over his body, in the then wild lones [sic] of the Rocky mountains, to the person who brought the murderer to justice.

George Monture

was the brave halfbreed guide for Colonel [George] Wright when that officer avenged the defeat of Colonel [E. J.] Steptoe, by the capture of the Spokane Indians, who surrounded and defeated that officer's command at Hangman's creek, near the city of Spokane Falls, in the early days of our frontier history. After the capture of the Indians, their ponies were collected in a basin of the creek and all shot to death by order of Col. Wright. The Indians were put on foot and seventeen of their leaders were hanged.

General Morgan, who visited this country several years ago as inspector general of the army, and who, by the way, was the husband of the beautiful daughter of ex-Mayor Prince of St. Paul. She accompanied her husband to the scene of his youthful adventures, and by campfire the writer listened to his recital of the Spokane Indian hanging. General Morgan was a Catholic and of a very religious turn of mind. He was conscientiously opposed to capital punishment and in the officers' mess, while a young lieutenant, fresh from West Point, expressed his views against what he considered a barbarous practice. When Col. Wright ordered out the detail to hang the Spokane Indians Lieutenant Morgan was placed in command and

Ordered to Execute Them

to the number of seventeen, which duty he accomplished in a soldier-like manner, and strictly according to orders.

On the fourth day, on account of the drenching rain storm, we did not break camp until the afternoon, when we packed up ond [sic] journeyed on to the foot of the mountains. There we camped for the night, preparatory to making an ascent to the summit of the lofty and snow clad chain which towered high above our encampment.

On the fifth day we commenced winding up the trail, crossing two foaming cataracts which came leaping down the mountain, perhaps thousands of feet above the crossing. On we went up the steep, until we reached a level point to rest the panting riding and pack animals.

The View Prom [sic] This Lofty Point

was one of the grandest ever witnessed by myself or companion, although both of us had spent our days since the springtime of youth in the Rocky mountains. The valley of the Big Blackfoot lay green and smiling at our feet — flower-strewn and checkered with mirror-like lakes, while the clear river went winding on its way — a silver streak in a vale of green.

We tightened up our saddle girths, remounted and turned our gaze to the partially snow-clad summit we were toiling to gain. Our trail lay over immense drifts of snow, packed so hard that the horses' hoofs scarcely left an indenture. The air was cold and biting but the view was grand. "What a scene for an artist," I exclaimed. "Yes," replied McQuaid as he drew his coat around him and buttoned it tight to the chin, "Yes, I presume this scene would make a nice picture to hang in a warm room." We started at 8 and at 11 we reached the summit, and then commenced our descent into a dark canyon below. It took two hours and a half to descend the mountain and gain our camp in a pleasant little valley on the banks of the South Fork of the North Fork of the Big Blackfoot. Our animals were turned out to graze and we again went into camp.

In the morning we left our pack animals and horses and again began the ascent of a mountain, and after a few hours' toil gained the summit, where the mine was situated, which was one of the objects of our journey. A few hours spent in examination satisfied us for all the hardship of the trip, and we took our way back to camp.

McQuaid concluded that a return over the trail we had traveled would be monotonous, and he bargained with a halfbreed to guide us to the nearest station on the Northern Pacific railroad, and to take our horses back to the agency, while we could return on a palace car. The bargain was struck, and on ihe [sic] morning of our seventh day's outing, we started for Drummond, on the Northern Pacific railroad, and after a ride of sixty miles that day gained the station in the evening. Our horses were turned over to the man to take them over the trail to the agency. Mack arranged this matter of returning the horses, and as he was holding a conversation with the vcaquero [sic], I asked if he felt dissatisfied with the day's ride. "Oh! no," he replied. "I am merely discussing with this fellow the wild charge that he has made."

July 14, 1890

LR 22,233/1890, RG 75, National Archives, Washington, D.C.

See Ronan's July 1, 1890, monthly report and his August 14, 1890b, annual report for more information about Chief Wild Boy's Cree and their visit to the Flathead Reservation seeking seasonal employment. Lt. Col. James J. Van Horn, of the 25th Infantry, was in command of Ft. Shaw in central Montana in 1890. A Civil War veteran, he became a full colonel in 1891 and died in 1898.[28]

United States Indian Service,
Flathead Agency, Mont.
July 14th, 1890.

The Hon. Commissioner of Indian Affairs
Washington, D.C.

Sir:

I have the honor to enclose herewith, for information, correspondence from Lieut. Col. A. A. [J. J.] Van Horn, 25th U.S. Infantry, Commanding Fort Shaw, Montana.

I shall proceed to-day to gather into one encampment, the British Cree Indians and half-breeds, mentioned in the enclosed communication from the commanding officer at Fort Shaw, and order them to return, via Cadottes Pass, to their encampment on the Eastern slope of the Rocky Mountains. I anticipate no trouble, and expect with the assistance of the reservation police to quietly return this band of Indians to their original encampment in the vicinity of Lieut. Col. Van Horn's command. Should any trouble or resistance be made by the Crees, I shall at once wire for instructions.

Very respectfully,
Your ob'd't servant,
Peter Ronan
U.S. Indian Agent.

First enclosure:

Fort Shaw, Mont.
July 8th, 1890.

Major Peter Ronan
U.S. Indian Agent
Flathead Agency, Mont.

Dear Sir,

It having been reported to me on the 22nd ulto. that, about six or eight weeks since, a band of British Crees were enroute via Codot pass to visit the Flatheads, will you be kind enough to inform me if such is a fact, and if so, about the number, would like for your Indian police to make them return to this side of the mountains.

Very respectfully
Your obedient servant,
J. J. Van Horn
Lieut Col 25th Infantry
Commanding Post.

Second enclosure:

United States Indian Service,
Flathead Agency, Mont.
July 14th, 1890.

(Copy)
A. A. [J. J.] Van Horn
Lieut. Col. 25th Infantry,
Commanding Post,
Fort Shaw, Montana

Dear Sir:

I am in receipt of your letter of 8th inst stating that on the 22d ulto. it was reported to you that about 6 or eight weeks ago a band of British Crees were en route via Cadotte's Pass to visit the Flatheads. Your information is correct. A large party of Crees arrived at this Agency on the 27th ultimo, with Chief Wild Boy, son of Big Bear, who gave so much trouble during the Rielle rebellion in the Northwest British Territory, and now deceased. Chief Wild Boy had letters of recommendation from Col. Otis, of the 20th Infantry, Lieut. Ahern of the 25th Infantry and other Army officers. The chief claimed that he came here to secure work for his followers from the Indians of this reservation during the haying and harvesting season, and to obtain horses or any other stock for their labor. The Cree half-breed families desire to settle here, but the reserve is already nearly over run with halfbreeds from Colville, Spokane and other Indian Countries. The Crees are gamblers and dancers and their presence here is ruinous to the Indians. I shall proceed to round them up at once, and order them to recross the Mountains. If I cannot accomplish their ejection with the Indian police it will be necessary to call upon the troops. I cannot, at present, ascertain the number already here, but it has been reported to me that small bands are coming in almost daily and scattering over the reservation, I shall communicate with you soon as facts are ascertained.

> I am respectfully,
> Your obedient Servant
> Peter Ronan,
> U.S. Indian Agent.

July 21, 1890
LR 22,262/1890, telegram, RG 75, National Archives, Washington, D.C.

On July 22, 1890, the Commissioner of Indian Affairs instructed Ronan to make a full investigation of the Kootenai-white conflict in the Upper Flathead Valley.[29] Ronan's written report was dated August 1, 1890a.

> July 21, 189 [sic]
> Arlee, Mont.

Comr Indian affairs
W, DC

Rumors reached me through Indians that Kootenains of this reserve were surrounded by U.S. troops & Citizens & made demand on Chief Enas to deliver up an alleged murderer. agency farmer now taking Census writes under date eighteenth Inst from Stigmatius [St. Ignatius] Mission. I learn forty white men started from head of flathead lake on horse back for Kootenai Camp & about forty soldiers took steamer for same place surrounded Camp before daylight & surprised Indians. officer in Command demanded murderer. Chief pointed the Indiancy [sic] & said if you take him will fight. when you turn over the murderer of my son & Antoine who Killed finley I will give up to you every one of my Indians who have Killed any white men, otherwise I will not & if you attempt to take them I will fight. Officer told Enas he would give three days to deliver murderer otherwise would take him. Troops & Citizens then returned to head of Lake. I recd no notification of trouble from other citizens or soldiers but believe agency farmers Information substantially true. Kootenai Camp sixty miles from here. telegraph shall I proceed to Camp & Investigate. await instructions.

> Ronan
> Agt.

August 1, 1890a
LR 24,311/1890, RG 75, National Archives, Washington, D.C.

Ronan argued that much of the Kootenai-white conflict in the Upper Flathead Valley resulted from the sale of whiskey to Indians and the unwillingness of the white authorities
to prosecute white men who killed Indians. Cases of Indians killing white men, however,
were widely publicized and vigorously pursued.[30] As Ronan reported, in July 1890 a posse
of white men invaded the reservation, surrounded the Kootenai camp, and threatened Chief
Eneas. With remarkable restraint, Eneas pointed out that the accused murderers were not
in the camp, requested justice for Indians killed by white men, and avoided any reaction
that could escalate into violence.[31] See Ronan's August 14, 1890b, annual report where he
repeated his request for justice for the murder of Chief Eneas' son.

William Houston was elected Missoula County Sheriff in the fall of 1889 because he
promised to use aggressive tactics in the hunt for Indians accused of killing white people.[32]
Houston grew up in Indiana and worked on the railroad where he was involved in the pursuit and capture of several highway robbers. He also worked in the hotel business. After
his 1890-1892 term as sheriff, he was a railroad employee, developer, and businessman.
Houston served as police commissioner for the city of Missoula. In 1920 he was elected to
a second term as Missoula County Sheriff, but after eleven months he was removed from
office for incompetence and working with bootleggers.[33]

Captain Washington I. Sanborn of the 25th Infantry was born in Maine and joined the
army in 1862 from Washington Territory. During a long career across the American West, he
served mostly in the Pacific Northwest before retiring in 1898 as a major.[34]

United States Indian Service,
Flathead Agency, Mont.
August 1st, 1890.

The Hon. Commissioner of Indian Affairs
Washington, D.C.

Sir:

Referring to my telegram to you dated at Arlee, July 21st, 1890, which
called attention to rumored trouble between Kootenai Indians and settlers at
the head of Flathead Lake, and to your reply by wire, of July 22d directing me
to proceed to the Camp and investigate cause of trouble, and to use my best
efforts to prevent a conflict between whites and Indians, I now have the honor
to report as directed:

For a number of years my reports to your office have spoken of ill-feeling
prevailing between the settlers at the head of Flathead Lake and a band of
Kootenai Indians of the reserve that occupy land midway of the Lake and adjacent to the settlements of the whites. Whiskey has been sold to the Indians by
the whites and resulted in several rows in which some Indians were Killed by
the latter, and among them the son of Chief Eneas, of the Kootenais; two of the
Chief's Indians were also hung by a mob of settlers for alleged murder, without trial or recourse to law. Pending an investigation by the Missoula County
Grand Jury, into the Killing of the son of the Chief, it adjourned three days
before I was able to bring the Chief and his Indians witnesses into court. These
unfortunate circumstances have shaken faith in the mind of the Indians, as to
justice having been done them in the Courts, and murders and outrages have
been Committed by the Indians in retalliation [sic]. I trust this state of affairs

will be brought to a close by prompt arrest and speedy punishment of Indian, as well as white, law breakers.

The recent trouble which I was ordered to investigate may be stated as follows:

On last 4th of July, at a celebration at Eagan, some Indians got drunk and quarrelled among themselves. In the scuffle a gun went off in the hands of an Indian named Antoine, who was trying to arrest another Indian named Finlay. The slayer was arrested by the whites and taken to Demersville for trial. He became frightened, fearing that he would be lynched, and stated to a deputy sheriff who had him in charge, that he Knew he was going to be hung and had a confession to make. He stated that another Indian named Pascal, told him of the murder of a whiteman last spring, and pointed out to him where the body was concealed. Before a number of witnesses the Indian repeated his narrative. A party was then organized and taking the Indian with them proceeded to the spot where the body have been buried, and found the skeleton and clothes. Intense excitement was created among the white people at Demersville, when the crowd returned with the skeleton and clothing.

Antoine stated that the man was passing along the road on horseback and was met by a party of Indians. The Indians asked for whisky and the man gave them some out of a bottle. The bottle was returned to him and he started away, when Pascal shot him in the back, Killing him instantly. He also stated that the murder was committed in revenge for the previous Killing of the son of Eneas, the Kootenai Chief, by whitemen. A large sum of money, the Indian said, was found by the murderer in a money belt around the dead man's waist. A Coroner's jury was called and an inquest held over the remains and a verdict rendered that the unknown man came to his death by Pascal, according to the evidence of Antoine.

The citizens then organized to the number of about fifty determined to surround the Kootenai village and to capture Pascal and other Indian criminals that might be found there. It was arranged to start at seven o'clock, p.m. with a deputy sheriff and the citizens as a posse. A company of troops, under Command of Captain Sanborne of the 25th U.S. Infantry, who are encamped at Demersville, concluded to go to the reservation, with this party, as the Commanding officer has orders to arrest Pierre-Paul and La La See, two other reservation Indians accused of the murder of whitemen. On arrival of posse of citizens, the Indian Camp was surrounded and a demand made for the surrender of the murderers. Chief Eneas informed the leader that the Indians asked for were not there, and invited those who could identify them to search the camp. The posse then awaited arrival of the United States troops, who came about two hours after the arrival of the armed citizens. It being clearly ascertained that the Indians wanted were not in the camp, the troops and citizens returned to Demersville.

In accordance with your telegram of July 22d, I proceeded to the Foot of Flathead Lake by team, and from thence took steamboat. The high sheriff of Missoula County joined me on the steamer and we both proceeded to Demersville. On arrival there we found the town in wild commotion, and it was stated to the sheriff and myself, than an organization of two hundred men was formed, and that on Wednesday, the 30th of July, they would march to the Camp of the Kootenai Chief, on Dayton Creek, and capture the culprits even if it involved a fight with the chief and his band. If the Indians sought for were not found at the Kootenai camp then they would march to St. Ignatius Mission, where the Church and Indian schools are situated and where the annual feast of St. Ignatius would be celebrated on the 31st, and where a great gathering of Indians would be found. I informed some of the leaders that I was ordered on the ground to prevent a collision between the Indians and the whites; that a march of a mob of disorganized men would surely result in bloodshed, and would not accomplish the arrest of the outlaws, as it was evident as soon as warning came of the march the culprits would take to the mountains and escape while innocent parties would be made the victims, should a conflict occur.

The sheriff stated to the leaders that he would not take any responsibility for the action of the mob; nor would he authorize any of his deputies to do so. This settled their conclusion to give up the expedition for the present. But it was stated by the leader that a reasonable time would be given the authorities to capture the Indians accused of murder and their accomplices, or that the matter would again be taken in hand by them as they intended to hold the organization together and Compel arrest or a fight.

I sent a messenger to the Kootenai Camp and called Eneas, the Chief to meet me at St. Ignatius Mission, which he did. I demanded Pascal to be delivered up for trial for murder at Missoula, the County seat. After considerable discussion the chief said that, if Antoine, the accuser of Pascal for murder, would be brought to Missoula, as prosecuting witness, he would at once deliver Pascal to the authorities for trial. I readily acceed [sic] to this as sheriff Houston stated he would get Antoine for witness at once. I considered that by the arrest and trial of Pascal, the accused murderer of the traveller, that it would lead, in a short time, to the peacable arrest of every Indian for whom the Sheriff holds a warrant. I apprised the sheriff of the Chief's proposition, but did not yet learn if he acted upon it.

In order to settle the present difficulties between the white settlers at the Head of Flathead Lake and the Indians of this reservation, every Indian charged with crime should be arrested and tried and if guilt is proved, punished to the full extent of the law. The Indian Police are afraid to make the arrests as they claim the outlaws have a small number of followers who have given them warning that revenge on themselves and families will follow. The Chiefs are weak and afraid to act — in short the great majority of Indians who are peaceful and law abiding have been terrorized by a few gamblers and outlaws, who harbor and protect the criminals. It is my opinion, that those outlaws should be taken by the lawful authorities, no matter at what cost, or it will result in a conflict that will be ruinous to the civilized, the progressive and the inoffensive members of the confederation of Indians occupying this reservation and also, result in bloodshed of innocent white travellers and isolated settlers who will be made the victims of revenge, which is the Indian mode of warfare.

Very respectfully
Your obedient servant,
Peter Ronan
U.S. Indian Agent.

August 1, 1890b
LR 24,493/1890, RG 75, National Archives, Washington, D.C.

The printed program for the 1890 St. Ignatius Day celebration, a detailed newspaper account, and other material describing the events have been published in a recent collection of documents about St. Ignatius Mission in the early 1890s.[35]

United States Indian Service,
Flathead Agency, Mont.
August 1st, 1890.

The Hon. Commissioner of Indian Affairs
Washington, D.C.

Sir:

In reporting affairs from this agency for the month of July, I have the honor to state that in accordance with instructions wired to me from your office under date of July 22d, I proceeded to the head of Flathead Lake, and also held council with Chief Eneas of the Kootenai Indians, in regard to troubles between the white settlers in that locality and the Indians of this reservation. In a special report of this date I mailed to you a full report of investigation.

The annual celebration of the feast of St. Ignatius was celebrated at the Mission on Thursday, the 31st inst. by Church service, a school exhibition, music by the Indian band, etc. There was in the neighborhood of one thousand Indians at the celebration, and a great number of ladies and gentlemen from different towns in Montana, who are friends of Indian education, including the Governor of the State. Every portion of the programme was well carried out, and the visitors expressed delight at the agreeable conduct of the Indians and the success of the exhibition at the Indian school.

The Indians were employed during the month in cutting and stacking their hay and now the harvesting of grain has commenced in Some localities. The season was not so dry as last year, and the hay and grain yield very good crops.

The wild newspaper reports from this agency might lead to the belief that the Indians are attending to nothing but strife with their white neighbors. I am happy to report that such is not the case. There are a few murderous outlaws at liberty here and if they are caught and hanged or imprisoned, it would be a blessing to Indians as well as to whites, as the notoriety they get through those outlaws reflect upon all the Indian dwellers upon the reserve.

The band of British Crees mentioned in report for last month, are behaving well and the men are working in hay and harvest field for Indians and halfbreeds who can furnish them employment and pay for the same.

The blacksmith has been Kept very busy on repairs for mowing machines and implements of labor. The farmer has been away a good deal securing census for Indian Department as well as for the 11th Annual Census; and also collecting statistics. Other employes are making hay.

Herewith I have the honor to enclose Sanitary report and reports of funds and indebtedness; also, report of farmer, and his the honor to be,

Very respectfully,
Your ob't't servt.
Peter Ronan
U.S. Indian Agent.

August 14, 1890a

LR 25,423/1890, RG 75, National Archives, Washington, D.C.

> Conflict between white settlers and Kootenai Indians over land claims in the Bonners Ferry area festered during 1890.[36] In 1889 the Commissioner of Indian Affairs had requested that the General Land Office survey the land needed for allotments for the Bonners Ferry Kootenai. The request was denied. R. Fry, a member of a mixed blood family at Bonners Ferry, wrote to Ronan and directly to the Commissioner of Indian Affairs to plead for government action to survey the land and approve the Bonners Ferry Kootenai allotments. Several U.S. Army officers investigated the Kootenai-white land conflicts. On September 11, 1890, the Commissioner of Indian Affairs made a detailed report to the Secretary of the Interior, but the Secretary decided a separate congressional appropriation would be needed to cover the costs of surveying the Kootenai allotments.[37]

United States Indian Service,
Flathead Agency,
August 14, 1890.

Hon. Commissioner Indian Affairs
Washington, D.C.

Sir:

I have the honor to refer you to my special report, bearing date August 6th, 1889, in regard to instructions from your office of June 21st, 1889, office letter Law and Land 12930 – 1889. In connection with that correspondence, the letter herewith attached will explain itself. I Shall be ready to carry into execution any instructions which you may deem proper to give me in the matter.

I am very respectfully
Your obedient servant,
Peter Ronan
United States Indian Agent.

Enclosure:

Fry, Kootenai Co.
Idaho.
Aug. 7th 90

Peter Ronan, Esq.
Indian Agent
Arlee, Mont.

Dear Sir,

I beg to inform you that man named Wilson has staked off a claim 8 miles down from here on the west side of river on the Chiefs Son's ground. The Indians pulled the stakes up and threw them in the river. The Northern Pacific is surveying a line down Deep Creek where the Indians have got a good many locations round the mouth of said stream. The whites are trying to locate their land on the Indian ground. Something ought to be done. Either you ought to Come or send Some one or there is liable to be trouble.

Yours Respy
R. Fry.

August 14, 1890b

U.S. Commissioner of Indian Affairs, Annual Report of the Commissioner of Indian Affairs *(Washington, D.C.: U.S. Government Printing Office, 1890), pages 122-129.*

> In his 1890 annual report, Ronan summarized many situations confronting the reservation which were covered by earlier reports to the Commissioner of Indian Affairs. The band of Lower Kalispel Indians on the reservation, the Bitterroot Salish band, and the British Cree were all in limbo due to the failure of the United States government to follow through on agreements or make provision for them.
>
> The most interesting parts of the this report describe in detail the problems of unequal justice in nineteenth century Montana and the failure of the legal authorities to pursue those responsible for the murder of Chief Eneas' son in Demersville. Ronan's sections on schools and missionary work lay out his acceptance of nineteenth century views on the superiority of white American mores over traditional Indian culture.

Report of Flathead Agency.

Flathead Agency, Mont., *August* 14, 1890.

Sir: I have the honor to transmit my fourteenth annual report:

Agricultural.

Prospects for the year 1890 are very flattering. Unlike last year, we have had a good season of rain, and by the aid of irrigation a fair crop will be harvested. The season commenced early. Three self-binders, which were purchased by the Indians, were set at work on the 6th of August, while a few combined mowers and reapers were also started, but a large majority of the fields and small inclosures are being cut by grain cradles, which are handled very well by the Indian farmers. From careful estimate I expect the Indians to harvest about 45,000 bushels of oats and in the neighborhood of 40,000 bushels of wheat. The vegetable crop is also good; potatoes, turnips, cabbages, onions, etc., have done well and a good yield is expected from the small vegetable patches planted.

There are about 200 farms of from 8 acres to 160 acres inclosed and cultivated; making in the neighborhood of 900 acres under cultivation on the reservation. The Indians own about 10,000 head of cattle individually, and about 5,000 head of horses. They have over 1,200 head of swine and 5, 000 or 6,000 fowls. They live in comfortable houses, with out-buildings and sheds for the care of implements of labor. Some have good barns. They are doing fairly well and the prospects of a good harvest yield this year will encourage them to future exertions and to forget the disastrous drought of last year, which burned and destroyed their crops. When the grain is harvested the mill will be put into operation and the wheat required for family use ground into flour. The surplus grain and vegetables find a ready sale and good market. With ordinary energy the Indians on this reservation should soon not only become self-supporting but comfortable and independent.

The tribes or bands under my charge consist of the Pend d'Oreilles, the Flatheads, the Kootenais, Charlot's band of Bitter Root Flatheads, and Michel's band of Lower Kalispels. The following is the

Recapitulation:

Charlot's band:

Total number of Indians	176
Males above eighteen years	51

Females above fourteen years	55
Children between six and sixteen years	41
Confederated tribes:	
Males over eighteen years	463
Females over fourteen years	541
School children between six and sixteen years	339
Lower Kalispels:	
Number of Indians	57
Males over eighteen years	20
Females over fourteen years	33
Children between six and sixteen years	6

Chief Eneas' Band of Kootenai Indians.

When Governor Isaac I. Stevens made the treaty with the Indians now occupying the Flathead Reservation in Montana in 1855, and designated them as the confederated tribes of Flatheads, Pend d'Oreilles, and Kootenais, he found a detached band of the British tribe of Kootenai Indians occupying and camping upon the little valley of Dayton Creek, about midway on the west side of Flathead Lake. In designating the boundaries of the reserve the Kootenai encampment was included and the Indians made beneficiaries of the American Government, and, much to the disgust of the Flatheads and Pend d'Oreilles, included in the confederation of the tribes known as the Flathead Nation.

Generally the Kootenai Indians are a thriftless, lazy, and filthy tribe, addicted to gambling, drinking, and immorality. Some of them spend their time in wandering about, fishing and hunting, and lounging around white settlements where whisky can be found and a filthy living eked out. This class bring the whole band into disrepute, until they are all looked upon as vagrants. In fact, such is the case to a great extent, and unless the Government reaches out a helping hand they are doomed to destruction.

Their village is situated about 60 miles from the agency, where a field in common is fenced and cultivated. Agricultural implements are issued to those who try to cultivate the soil, but no resident farmer was ever assigned to direct their efforts and encourage them in agricultural and civilizing pursuits.

Chief Michel's Band of Lower Kalispels.

On the 27th of April, 1887, the Northwest Indian commission on the part of the United States and the chiefs and head men and other adult Indians of the confederated tribes of this agency entered into an agreement. At the council held at that date it was announced by the commission that it was the policy of the United States Government to remove to and settle upon Indian reservations scattered bands of non-reservation Indians, so as to bring them under the care and protection of the United States. Under certain promises of assistance the lower Pend d'Oreilles, or Kalispel Indians, then living in Northern Idaho entered into an agreement to remove to the Flathead Reservation. It was also agreed with the commission by the confederated tribes living here to allow the Kalispels to remove to and settle upon their lands in accordance with the agreement then entered into and signed. It seems up to the present date Congress has not confirmed or passed upon said agreement.

On the 25th of September of the same year I reported to the honorable Commissioner of Indian Affairs, that Michel, one of the chiefs of the wandering bands of Lower Kalispels, who met the Northwest Indian Commission at Sand Point, in Idaho Territory, and who signed the agreement to remove to this reservation with the families who acknowledged him as chief, was at the Flathead Agency; that he came to request transportation, by railroad or otherwise, for a number of families from Idaho to this reservation. The chief at the same time fully understood that the agreement with the Northwest Commission, which he signed, should be ratified by Congress before it could go into effect, and that there was no means at the disposal of the Indian Office to pay for transportation or to take care of those families until such provisions were made by Congress. Through my office he appealed to the honorable Secretary of the Interior and Commissioner of Indian Affairs to grant them the aid and facilities he desired to remove his band, as they were willing and anxious to come to the Flathead Reservation, where it was expected they would cultivate the soil, if aid was given them, and abandon their wandering and vagabond life. The Indian Office furnished means to bring the band to this reservation and provided means of support until the close of the fiscal year 1888. An allowance of provisions was furnished them on my requisition until the close of the fiscal year 1890.

With the little aid which could be expended from the agency, those poor people commenced farming in a small way and gave ample evidence that, with proper attention by the employment of a farmer to teach them and other assistance promised in the agreement with the Northwest Commission, they would soon become tillers of the soil and placed on the highway to civilization and self-support.

Several other families, parties to this agreement, came of their own accord from Idaho to settle on this reserve, but, finding no arrangements here for their assistance or to carry out the agreement, they returned to Idaho to wait results, as they claimed they could better support themselves in that Territory by fishing, hunting, and a general wandering career.

Chief Michel is on this reservation with about fifteen families, and I trust if the agreement mentioned should not be ratified I may be allowed means to place those families upon farms and to assist them with agricultural implements, food, and clothing until they can raise crops with which to keep them from starvation and nakedness.

Bitter Root Valley Flatheads.

The history of the dealings with Chief Charlot's band of Flathead Indians residing in the Bitter Root Valley has been so thoroughly discussed in public documents that I shall refrain from going into details. Suffice it to say that the last arrangement with this unfortunate band and the delay in its consummation has entirely discouraged the Indians. They are now helpless and poverty-stricken on their land in that valley, looking forward to the promise for the sale of lands patented to certain members of that band and to their removal to this reservation. The hope was given them, when their consent was secured for an appraisement and sale of their lands and improvements, that arrangements would be made to remove them to the Jocko reservation before the 1st of March, 1890, in order to give them an opportunity to select lands on the reserve and to put in crops to harvest this year. With that view, they could not be induced to plow or sow their land in the Bitter Root Valley. They are destitute of means or support and, if the contemplated appropriation to remove and support them until they can raise crops is not carried out this year, some means should be adopted to furnish them with provisions, or they will certainly suffer from starvation.

British Crees.

In a report to your office, bearing date July 14, 1890, I had the honor to inclose letter from Lieut. Col. A. A. Van Horn, Twenty-fifth United States Infantry, commanding, Fort Shaw, Montana, stating that it was reported to him that a band of British Crees were en route via Cadotte's Pass to visit the Flatheads, and if such was the fact would like to have my Indian police make them return to the eastern side of the mountains. About eighty Indian and Cree half-breeds are now on this reservation. I called the chief of the Cree Indians and some of the leading Cree half-breeds to the agency and stated the request of Lieutenant-Colonel Van Horn. A number of those people had gone to work in the hay and harvest fields of the Indians of this reservation, in order to earn horses and provisions for their labor. It was a pitiful sight to see strong men weep at the order or request for them to retrace their wearisome march back across the Rocky Mountains, through Cadotte's Pass, to the vicinity of Fort Shaw, without provisions to support their almost naked and famished wives and children. They appealed for time to earn something, and I granted them leave to remain until after the harvest, provided no dancing, drinking, or gambling would be indulged in and that they would work faithfully for those Indian farmers who could afford to employ them, to earn provisions and horses. The Crees have no right here and should be sent back, but I can not turn them into the mountains without provisions and mostly on foot and without arms to procure game. I shall insist that they leave the reserve at the close of harvest. The Indians here do not propose to allow them to settle upon their lands.

Crime.

In August of last year J. W. Noble, the Honorable Secretary of the Interior, communicated to the governor of Montana relative to the killing at Demersville, Mont., in that month, of the son of Eneas, chief of the Kootenai Indians of this reservation. With the communication was a report from the Hon. T. J. Morgan, Commissioner of Indian Affairs, of an investigation of the matter which embraced my report. As the killing of the chief's son has resulted in the murder of an unknown white man by a Kootenai Indian of Eneas' tribe, in revenge, and as there is now great excitement over the finding of the body of the murdered white man, and also as the affair may yet end in further bloodshed, I deem it important to give the facts here. The following is the Hon. Commissioner's report:

> It having been reported in newspaper dispatches dated Missoula. Mont., August 20, 1889, that Indians were menacing lives of whites at Demersville, Missoula County, Montana, and that they had broken into a house and one person was killed, this office under date of the 21st of August telegraphed the Indian agent at the Flathead Agency for information as to the truth of the report. The agent replied by telegram dated the 22d ultimo, reporting that one Indian was killed, and the trouble was caused by whisky, and that he would investigate the matter. I am now in receipt of a report on the subject from the agent, dated September 9, 1889, in which he states he will go to the county seat of said county and lay before the grand jury the following statement relative to the matter made by Eneas, Chief of the Kootenai Indians of the Jocko reservation and the father of the Indian who was killed, to wit:

The Chief's Story.

[Here Ronan quotes Eneas' testimony about the death of his son which was included in his September 9, 1889a, letter to the Commissioner of Indian Affairs reproduced above.]

To this the honorable Commissioner adds:

> If Chief Eneas's understanding of the matter is correct, it seems that the killing of his son was totally without justification as he was at the time being led away from the scene of trouble had with his slayer by Louie, the son-in-law of the chief, who was also threatened and had to leave immediately to escape danger. If the facts are correctly stated the failure to punish the person guilty of the murder would have a most demoralizing and unhappy, if not dangerous, effect upon the Indians, and at all events the matter should be thoroughly investigated with a view to a full understanding of the facts in the case and securing the prosecution of the guilty person if it should appear that the killing was unlawful.

> I would therefore respectfully recommend that the subject be submitted to the honorable Attorney-General, with the request that he will, if consistent with the rules and regulations of his Department, cause the United States attorney for Montana to make a thorough and immediate investigation of the matter, first notifying the agent at said agency thereof, and if it should appear therefrom that said killing was unlawful, that said attorney be instructed to take all the steps which may be legal and proper with a view to securing the prompt and adequate punishment, through the proper court, of the person guilty of the homicide.

> It is further recommended that a copy of this report (herewith inclosed) be forwarded to the governor of said Territory for his information, with request that he cause to be made an investigation of the facts in the case, and take such steps as may be necessary to bring the guilty party to justice.

This report was signed by Hon. John T. Morgan, Commissioner of Indian Affairs. The affair culminated by the presence of a sheriff's posse on the reservation in July, and the arrest was made, with assistance of the Indian police, of six Indians for whom the sheriff held warrants. At the next term of court the Indians will be held for trial for the several charges against them, from murder to house-breaking and horse-stealing. It is to be hoped that the same energy will be used by the officers of the law to bring forward for trial white men guilty of crime against the Indians.

Schools.

At the mission of St. Ignatius, about 20 miles north of the agency, the school of this reservation is situated. The school is conducted under contract with the Government by the missionaries of St. Ignatius and the Sisters of Providence, and provisions were made for the education of 300 boys and girls.

During the month of August there is a partial vacation, but it extends only to the suspension of certain studies, as it is the policy of the faculty to keep the children from going to their homes, where in a short time the former teaching is forgotten, and in many cases the parents encourage the children to remain away from school. The vacation is made attractive by camping out under charge of the teachers, while hunting, fishing, and outside sports are indulged in. The children are tractable and apply themselves as well, perhaps, as the youth of our own race.

As stated in my report of last year, I am still more forcibly impressed that educational and agricultural pursuits with a knowledge of such trades as are taught here, namely, carpentering, blacksmithing, shoemaking, harness-making, tinsmithing, printing, business, painting, sewing, milling, matching and planing, engineering, etc., are the great factors in civilizing the Indians, and the children should be compelled to attend school despite the wishes of some of the Indian parents who are opposed to the adoption of the methods of the white men. Indian education should be compulsory. As it is on a non-issue reservation the agent can use his influence and his persuasion, but is without power to enforce his demands that the children be sent to school. Soon as a boy attains an age when he can be useful in herding stock or doing other work to relieve the parents, he is taken away from school and placed under the demoralizing influence of Indian home surroundings.

If a fund could be appropriated to build a house, assist in fencing in a few acres of land, furnish a few implements of labor and seed to sow, to such couples as marry from the schools, the young people could be more easily induced to remain at school until they arrive at a proper age for marriage. By such assistance the young married couples would have an independent start in life and develop into thrifty domesticity.

The Indian school buildings at St. Ignatius, both for boys and girls, are not surpassed in the State of Montana for beauty of architecture, ventilation, modern improvements, accommodation of pupils, healthful surroundings, and attractiveness.

During the year a kindergarten was added to the school by the faculty. Having for some time past contemplated the establishment of such an institution, in connection with the Indian school for older children, the missionaries were unable, for want of proper buildings, to put the plan into execution until the spring of 1890. The result has proved most satisfactory. I am informed that the project of this enterprise was made known to Dr. Dorchester, superintendent of Indian schools, last year, and it not only met with his approval, but he very much encouraged the missionaries to make the trial.

Among others some of the following reasons might be urged for the encouragement of the work on the part of the Government: The children, if taken into school at the age of two or three or four years and kept there, only occasionally visited by their parents, will when grown up know nothing of Indian ways and habits. They will, with ease, be thoroughly, though imperceptibly formed to the ways of the whites in their habits, their thoughts, and their aspirations. They will not know, in fact be completely ignorant of, the Indian language; will know only English. One generation will accomplish what the past system will require generations to effect. The affection of the child being gained at its youngest age, it is likely to grow up with a love for the whites instead of the hatred, or at least diffidence, as is the case to a great extent at present. The training of the children in later years in the various departments of an industrial-school education will be much facilitated, its latent talents discovered and better cultivated, never having tasted of the roaming, free and easy-going, lazy life of the older Indian and not having been spoiled by the indulgence of parents or near relatives, which is generally the case with all grown children. This, love for a roaming, lazy life makes it at all times hard to get a boy or a girl of ordinary school age to resign himself or herself to the confinement of a boarding-school.

The mortality among the Indians rages principally among the younger children, because of want of proper care, of proper food, of proper clothing, and on account of exposure. Whilst actually at present many children are dying on the Flathead Reservation among the people at large, few deaths occur in the school, and none as yet in the kindergarten, where some fifty little ones are cared for. The older Indians seem well pleased with it, and contrary to expectations brought their children to it without scarcely any effort on the part of the missionaries and teachers. In view of the good undoubtedly to be derived from this institution I would recommend the Department to consider the kindergarten as part of the Ignatius Indian Boarding School, and change the age required from six years to two years of age.

Among those people, except the Kootenai tribe, who still lead a kind of nomadic life, and, for this reason being far from the influence of the missionaries and the agent, are opposed to the education of their children, both male and female, the other parents are more willing to send their daughters than their sons. The school for girls has always been more numerous than that of the boys. In school the girls are kept clean and nicely dressed, well fed, and well trained in the rules of politeness. They are taught to cut and sew their gowns, etc., and to trim and make their bonnets, knit stockings, weave carpets, make rugs and their own winter gloves and caps. They work at stated times in the garden, milk cows, make butter, learn baking, cooking, and pastry work. There is in this school a number of girls about fifteen years of age, and some who reached a score of years who are marriageable; but according to my knowledge of the Indians, among whom I have been for over thirteen years as agent, it will be a long time before women among them can have in the family that important and beneficial influence they have in general among white people.

The only hope and easiest way to attain this result is, in my judgment, that the new-formed families by the marriage of young Indians and girls educated in the school have a home of their own separated from the parents of either. By going back to their old people they find too many obstacles to overcome to live according to the principles and the ways they learned at school; and partly through fear and respect for their parents, partly because of their natural inclination to inactivity and carelessness, little by little they go back to the ways of the old people, whom it is almost impossible to persuade to do otherwise than their ancestors did.

To form these new families separate from the old people it takes material, means, and a good many of the children at school have not sufficient means for building a house and procuring the necessaries of life. As stated under another heading in this report, I believe that the Government would make great advancement in the civilization of the Indians by making a small appropriation as a fund to furnish the newly formed families with the necessary means to commence life. These families being then free and in great part independent from the baneful influence of the uneducated Indians could more easily and with better success live according to the principles and ways both the young girl and the young man have learned at school. Their example and prosperity would have a great effect on the other Indians and give them desire and courage to renounce their old Indian traditions and to follow the ways of civilized people.

Missionary Work.

The missionary labors are in the hands of the Jesuit fathers, and they devote their lives to the work of christianizing, civilizing, and educating the Indians. Owing to their devoted work the Indian inhabitants of this reservation are steadily gaining an advance over all other tribes in Montana in religion, civilization, farming, and pastoral pursuits. The sanctity of marriage is respected, with few exceptions, and unlawful cohabitation is punished by tribal laws. The degradation of the woman is no doubt great among the Indians as it has always been among pagan nations, though in the enjoyment of a higher degree of material and even intellectual civilization. But the teachings of religion among these Indians have considerably modified their ideas about women and raised her condition and position among them and they often set the example of Christian virtues.

I am happy to state that in the mission there are religious ladies who mingle among the Indian families and reach intellectually and morally numerous Indian girls and impart to them a practical knowledge of all the household work which a young woman should understand to fit her to keep a comfortable and well ordered house. Among these religious women there are some who understand medicine sufficiently to attend not only to the sick who call upon them for assistance, but also to the Indian women and the mothers of children. Through the numerous girls educated by them these self-sacrificing women exercise a great influence among the women of the reservation who are bound to come in contact with them when visiting their children at school and on this point training schools on a reservation among the Indians — witnesses to the constant and sensible progress in civilization of their children — according to my judgment, are more useful and more conducive to the civilization of the whole race than schools outside of the reservation, the Indians being deprived of the advantage of the good example set to them by the children at school and the encouragement they receive by witnessing the happiness of their children living according to the ways of the white people in contrast with the wretchedness of their fellow-children in the camp.

Court of Indian Offenses and Police.

As mentioned in my report of last year, this branch of the service has failed to give the satisfaction desired. The head chiefs are now reconciled to the authority of the judges and the police, but they have been forced to that conclusion by the arrest in August of the murderers and outlaws of the tribes by the sheriff of Missoula County and a posse of white men assisted by Indians of the reservation. Under the head of crime will be seen the unfortunate circumstances which led to the demoralization and inefficiency of the police force and the judges of the court of Indian offenses. This year as well as last year the Indian enemies of the police point out that while an Indian is held to the full penalty of the law and is being hunted down by armed white men, very little effort was made by the authorities to bring into court white offenders against Indians.

Upon assuming charge of this agency in 1877 I found a volunteer force of Indian police who made arrests of Indian law-breakers and punished them according to tribal usage. Some were fined a number of horses, some were imprisoned in the Indian jail, while others were sentenced to certain number of lashes with a whip. The crimes for which punishment was inflicted were horse stealing and other thefts, gambling, pagan dances, immorality, drunkenness, bringing whisky on the reservation, polygamy, and infidelity to the marriage ties. Until the passage of the railroad through the reservation this organization kept the Indians well in hand and they gave very little trouble.

Affairs changed, however, with the introduction of the railroad. The number and character of employés along the line, the swarms of tramps going east and west through the reservation, the whisky drinking and immorality of such people, naturally infected the Indians, and more stringent methods than the volunteer Indian police enforced were thought best to be adopted. On the 12th of February, 1885, I prepared and submitted a code of laws and rules to govern the reservation, which were incorporated in the rules already established, and they were adopted by the Indians, and also authorized for enforcement on this reserve by the Indian Department. Three Indians, supposed to be the most progressive and efficient, were then selected as judges, namely, Joseph, Baptiste, and Louison, with a captain and nine policemen. The police force was afterwards increased to fifteen including the captain, and Joseph Ka-too-lay-uch was added as judge. Those four judges continue to act until present date, though they have not been under pay for some time.

The circumstances detailed under head of crime leads to a demoralization of the judges as well as of the police. Joseph Ka-too-lay-uch was the only reliable man among the judges, and he was in favor of arresting every Indian outlaw for whom the sheriff held a warrant, but the other judges opposed him and lent their efforts to shielding the outlaws from arrest, and influenced a majority of the Indian police to do likewise. During the month of August, however, the judges and police changed their views (as I held them strictly responsible), and aided the sheriff of Missoula County in making arrests of Indians. The outlaws to the number of eight are now in jail at Missoula, only one having eluded arrest, and it is expected he will soon be captured by the Indians.

The judges, while they are progressive in the way of stock-raising, farming, etc., and also of good character, do not speak English. They wear citizens' dress and conform generally to the white man's ways, and encourage education of the children. With the exception, however, of Joseph Ka-too-lay-uch, they are vacillating and weak and afraid to face responsibilities or to oppose with sufficient energy and decision the lawless and non-progressive. The latter class, the old Indians and the chiefs, are not in favor of the allotment of lands in severalty.

About twenty individual members of the tribes were tried during the past fiscal year for offenses as mentioned before, such as horse stealing, theft from each other, drunkenness, gambling, bringing whisky on the reservation, dancing, polygamy, infidelity in regard to the marriage ties, etc., most of whom were found guilty, and penalties [imposed] of imprisonment for a certain number of days in the Indian jail and by fines.

The culprit is brought before one or more of the judges; prosecution witnesses are examined and also witness for the defense. The judges listen attentively to all of the evidence and render decisions accordingly, which has always been fair according to my knowledge of the cases tried. The rules give the right of appeal to the agent, and from him to the honorable Commissioner of Indian Affairs. No records of such trials have been kept owing to the fact that the judges live at a distance and in different localities from the agency, and a person competent to make record could not be procured except at great travel and inconvenience.

The influence of the court at present is not of any great importance on this reservation. I would recommend that the services of all the judges, with exception of Joseph Ka-too-lay-uch, be dispensed with, and that the latter be appointed chief of police and acting judge with instructions to report every offense directly to the agent, and when fine or imprisonment is imposed, to be carried out with the knowledge and consent of the agent, and a record of the same to be kept in the agent's office; that the police force be reorganized, and the inefficient, non-progressive, and malcontents be replaced by others; that the captain of police and acting judge be paid sufficient amount to give his whole time and attention to the duties of his office.

Very respectfully submitted.

Peter Ronan.
United States Indian Agent.

The Commissioner of Indian Affairs.

August 23, 1890

LR 26,002/1890, telegram, RG 75, National Archives, Washington, D.C.

August 23, 1890
Flathead Agency Via Arlee Mont

To Commr Indian Affairs
Washn, D.C.

Eight Indians now in Jail at Missoula including Pascal Lalaze and Piere Paul arrests made without trouble preliminary Examinations on twenty fifth report by mail after Examination no trouble apprehended.

Ronan Agent.

August 26, 1890

LR 26,991/1890, RG 75, National Archives, Washington, D.C.

See Ronan's March 4, 1889, letter and annotation about the killing of a Kootenai Indian by J. E. Clifford and a Dr. Cunningham in Demersville.

Ronan repeated here his argument for justice for Indians killed by white men as well as white men killed by Indians. White reports about the arrest of the accused Indian murderers say that Kootenai Chief Eneas and Pend d'Oreilles Chief Michelle were held hostage by Missoula Sheriff William Houston and Deputy Sheriff Ralph Ramsdell until the accused murderers were delivered by the Indian police.[38] See the annotation to Ronan's February 2, 1887, letter for more about the Ramsdell brothers and the annotation to his August 1, 1890a, letter for information about Sheriff William Houston. Both Eneas and Michelle worked to avoid a violent confrontation despite their treatment by the sheriff.

Most of the newspaper reports mentioned that the Indian police were involved but emphasized the role of the white authorities in the captures. In Ronan's version, the Indian police made the arrests, but the whites took the credit. Ronan does report that most of the reservation Indians were happy to see the outlaws detained. See also Ronan's September 1, 1890, monthly report. One of the suspects, Lalasee, surrendered to Duncan McDonald, who escorted him to Missoula.[39]

In 1895, when it came time to collect the reward for the capture of the four accused murderers, the bill in the legislature for the reward provided money for all the white people involved and Duncan McDonald but ignored the Indian police who had actually made the arrests.[40] Duncan declined his share of the reward and one of the Indian policemen, Pierre Cattullayeah, was included when the reward was finally paid in 1896.[41]

United States Indian Service,
Flathead Agency,
Auust [sic], 1890.

Hon. Commissioner Indian Affairs,
Washington, D.C.

Sir:

Replying to "L 24311 – 1890,["] bearing date August 11th, 1890, referring to my report dated August 1st, 1890, relative to the trouble between the Kootenai Indians and settlers at the head of Flathead Lake, and having directed me to report to your office all instances of murder having been committed within the past few years, by Indians against whites, and by whites against Indians, upon or near the reservation, and what steps have been taken to punish the guilty parties by the civil authorities, I now respectfully submit the following:

The commencement of all the trouble on this reservation between the Indians and the whites grew out of the killing of an Indian by a whiteman at Arlee, a report of which I furnished the Indian Office under date of December 17th, 1885, but as a matter of convenience I herewith furnish copy:

[Here Ronan quotes and summarizes his December 17, 1885, report to the Commissioner of Indian Affairs which is reproduced above.]

In the same year an Indian of this reservation named Ham-Ham, who was hunting west of the reservation, was killed by two white prospectors, in a dispute about a horse. The whitemen were never arrested to my knowledge.

Also, in the same year, an Indian by the name of Scoolm-l-Poo, who was a gambler, got into a game of cards with a white gambler, at Thompson Falls, about one hundred miles west of this Agency. The Indian won the whiteman's money, and the latter grabbed it from him. In the scuffle to regain the money, the white man shot and killed the Indian. The slayer was arrested by the citizens, but afterwards rescued by his friends and allowed to escape.

In my report dated April 2d, 1888, I stated that news was brought that the bodies of three white men were found where murdered by Indians, at the Head of Flathead Lake, North of the boundary line of the reservation; that one Indian was said to have confessed the crime and implicated two others. Warrants were issued and two Indians were arrested, the other having escaped. The arrested Indians were taken from the deputy Sheriff who had them in charge by a mob of white men and executed without trial. The alleged murderers belonged to Chief Eneas' band of Kootenais living on this reservation.

In my report under date of March 1st, 1889 [i.e., March 4, 1889], it is stated that one J. E. Clifford, who kept a store at the head of Flathead Lake, and North of the reserve, beat an Indian over the head with a pistol from the effects of which he died.

I had Clifford and another white man called Dr. Coningham [Cunningham], as accomplice in the Killing of the Indian arrested, but the Grand Jury of Missoula county failed to indight [sic] them, much to the anger of the Kootenai Chief Eneas, who believed the Indian who was killed was not altogether to blame.

Under date of June 1st, 1889, in submitting my report for the month of May, I spoke of having returned from a prolonged pursuit of a halfbreed outlaw and murderer, whom I was successful in capturing and placing in the Missoula County jail. On the 3d day of May, 1889, Finley killed a Kootenai Indian in a drunken row at the head of Flathead Lake. His arrest resulted in a sentance to the penitentiary for ten years. For particulars in regard to this noted criminal I respectfully refer to said report.

Previous to the arrest of Finley the body of a white man was found on the Jocko River bank, about twenty miles from the Agency. Finley confessed that he witnessed the murder of the man found, and also that of a companion, and stated that Lalla See and Piere Paul were the murderers and committed the crime in revenge of the Killing of the brother of Lalla-See at Arlee, by Coombs, and also of the killing of Ham-Ham in the Coeur 'd Alene mountains, (who was the uncle of Piere Paul) by whitemen as before related. Warrants were issued for arrest of the Indians at the time, and notwithstanding that a large reward was offered for their arrest, they eluded both the civil officials, the military and the Indian Police, until their recent capture and incarceration in the Missoula County Jail.

The killing of the son of Chief Eneas, of which full report and reference may be found in my annual report for 1890, furnished to your office this month, was another cause of ill feeling by the Indians against the citizens at the head of the Flathead Lake, which, at the time came very near involving trouble. In my report dated August 1st, 1890, I referred to the murder, as alleged, of a white man by an Indian named Pascal, and stated the particulars of a trip by a posse of citizens and a company of troops to the reserve for the purpose of arresting Pascal and Piere Paul and Lalla-See, all of whom were accused of the murder of white men.

I now have the honor to report that with the aid of the Indian Police, Piere Paul, Lalla See and Pascall were lodged in jail at Missoula the county seat of Missoula County, State of Montana, and after due process of law are held for trial at the October term of Court, for murder. Antoine and William Chacequel, two Kootenai Indians are also in Jail and will be tried at the same term of Court, as accessories to Pascal in the crime of murder. Marcale Scaltame and Antoine Guaema, two reservation Indians were also arrested and await trial for horse stealing. I also had arrested Paul Harry, an Indian from the Coeur 'd Alene Agency, for horse stealing, and Tom a Nez Percie, from the Nez Percie Agency for the same crime.

I only know of one bad Indian sought for by the Sheriffs posse and the Indian Police, who has thus far eluded pursuit, but I expect soon to have him under arrest.

As usual, where Indians are in the case, a great deal of unnecessary excitement was caused by exag[g]erated newspaper reports, and cheap notoriety sought for by ambitious officials.

In October of this year, when the next term of Court for this Judicial District will be in session, I trust to be able to present several cases of white ag[g]ressions against Indians. By doing so and having proper attention called to the cases by the Court it will have the effect of showing to the Indians that laws, courts and jails were instituted for the purpose of an effort for justice for all.

I am very truly,
Your obedient servant,
Peter Ronan,
United States Indian Agent.

September 1, 1890
LR 27,541/1890, RG 75, National Archives, Washington, D.C.

United States Indian Service,
Flathead Agency,
September 1st, 1890.

Hon. Commissioner Indian Affairs,
Washington, D.C.

Sir:

I have the honor to report matters from this Agency for the month of August, and it gives me pleasure to state that all of the supposed Indian outlaws and criminals, including Piere Paul, Lalla-See and Pascal, charged with murder, are in jail at Missoula, the County Seat, awaiting trial at the October term of Court. It is also a pleasure to state that in the serious matter of making arrests the Indian Police obeyed my orders and accomplished the arrest of every one of the Indians sought for by the Sheriff's posse, to whom they turned over the prisoners. The posse, however, took unto themselves all of the glory of the acchievement [sic] and sent forth to the public through the press, their bravery and perseverance in running down and capturing the Indians, but were careful not to give any sort of recognition to the Indians who were the real captors of the law breakers of their race, and who are now rejoicing over the fact that the reservation is rid of the Indian Criminals who have so long brought disrepute upon the different tribes occupying this reserve. It is now to be hoped that the County officials will give attention to the arrest and punishment of white ag[g]ressors against Indians, and those who sell them whisky, which is the real cause and foundation of all the trouble which exist between the Indians and the white settlers at the head of Flathead Lake.

A good harvest has been gathered and stacked by the Indians, and I now have the threshing machines at work. A casting on one of them broke, and I was compelled to send to the Manufacturer at St. Louis, Missouri, to have it duplicated.

Soon as the grain is delivered at the mill, I hope to have it in perfect running order, and shall commence at once on the repairs to the engine etc., authorized by you. The grist mill will then be set at work to grind into flour all of the Indian wheat delivered at the mill. The logs which have accumulated at the mill yard will be sawed into lumber for the Indians that hawled them; the matching and plaining machine will be put in place in the addition to the mill, which I shall erect soon as the wheat is ground and the Indian lumber cut.

Quiet and contentment rests with the Indians upon the reservation and all are engaged in their various pursuits, but the harvest fields and threshing machines claim their greater attention.

Herewith I have the honor to enclose sanitary report and reports of funds and indebtedness, and have the honor to be

Very respectfully,
Your obedient Servant,
Peter Ronan,
United States Indian Agent.

September 7, 1890

LR 28,356/1890, RG 75, National Archives, Washington, D.C.

Ronan's letter of June 2, 1890, had his earlier response to Fred Brown's complaints about Indians camped around his slaughter house in Butte. Apparently most of the Indians involved were from the Blackfeet Reservation or Idaho.

United States Indian Service,
Flathead Agency,
September 7th, 1890.

Hon. Commissioner Indian Affairs
Washington, D.C.

Sir:

Under date of June 3d, 1890, copy of letter from one Fred Brown of Butte City, Montana, was referred as follows:

"The Head of this Department is informed that there is about thirty lodges of Indians at this place, mostly from the Jocko reservation. Mr. Ronan is their Agent, in Missoula County, Montana. They have a number of ponies and are using our range; they came here on account of our slaughterhouse, and the property has to be guarded day and night. I have wrote to Mr. Ronan, and he has taken no notice of the communication. Indian named Ten-Doy from Lemhi Agency, with others is also here, and some from Ross Fork. Mr. Fisher is their Agent. I have ordered and even put them off our property but all to no purpose as they come in the night.

Hoping this communication will receive that attention that it requires at your hands,

I remain very respectfully
Signed Fred Brown["]

On this communication the following endorsement:

"Department of Interior
Office of Indian Affairs,
June 14th 1890

Respectfully referred to Peter Ronan, U.S. Indian Agent, Flathead Agency, Arlee, Montana, for investigation and report, and if the charges herein are found to be true, with direction to notify the Indians belonging to his Agency to immediately return to the reservation.

Signed T. J. Morgan,
Commissioner."

As I felt assured upon receipt of foregoing that there were no Indians from this reservation encamped at Butte City, or any where in the neighborhood of the Slaughterhouse of the complainant, as I had previously ordered two lodges, who were all from this place encamped there, to return, and they did so — I deferred making the investigation ordered until recently, as my time was occupied in affairs about the Agency, which required attention.

Upon arrival at Butte City, I visited the Slaughteryard, mentioned, and found that the Indians complained of had returned to their Agencies at Lemhi, and Fort Hall, in Idaho. I had an interview with Manager Brown, which bears his signature, and which I herewith attach:

Butte Butchering Co.
Butte City, Mont., August 30th, 1890.

Major Ronan
    Sir
    In my Former Letter to you Regarding the Indians at our place, I could not say where they all Belong. some were from Blackfoot some from Lemhi as I know Tendoy well and he told me himself that part of them were from the Jocko or Bitter Root. there was at one time Thirty two Lodges here. of Course for Years past they have been Coming here to our Slaughterhouse for the *Offalls* of the Cattle which I have no Objection to whatever, but I have a great objection to having a Lot of Drunken Indians around my place at all hours of the night. Whooping and making pandemonian in General it appears to me that the Indians come here to Gamble and get Whiskey and I tried to find out where they got it all to no purpose as the Indian Camp was at most times full of White Men of the Lowest Type. I am giving you these details for your enlightment sincerely hoping that if it lays in your power to keep the Indians away from here, as a Drunken Indian is no good, you will greatly oblidge and your Correspondant will for ever pray

Your Respectfully
Fred Brown.

It will be seen by this statement that the annoyance comes from Chief Ten-Doy's band from Fort Hall and Lemhi reservations, in Idaho. They are a great nuisance, and I trust means will be found to Keep them away from Butte City, and other towns in Montana. At this reservation there are some Indian gamblers, who are hard to be restrained from roaming. When they learn of an encampment of Indians from Fort Hall and Lemhi reservations, in Idaho, they naturally seek their camps to gamble and to spend their time in idleness. If the bands in question can be restrained from coming from the agencies named, there will be no cause of complaint in the future against the Indians of this reserve camping on the premises of Mr. Brown, as there would be no inducement for them to go to Butte City, if they could not meet the Snakes and Bannocks there.

In refutation of the complaint made to the Head of the Department by Mr. Brown, that I took no notice of his communication to me, I respectfully refer to my letter to your office, dated June 2d, 1890, which is also respectfully referred for information bearing on other points in regard to the complaint of Mr. Brown.

I am very truly,
Your obedient servant,
Peter Ronan,
United States Indian Agent.

September 11, 1890
LR 28,172/1890, telegram, RG 75, National Archives, Washington, D.C.

Rail shipments to Ravalli for transport to the Upper Flathead Valley were a valuable part of the business of Missoula merchants and the Northern Pacific Railroad. In 1890 construction of the Great Northern Railroad was in progress and the Northern Pacific Railroad and Missoula traders faced the loss of this business to commercial centers located on the Great Northern route. Western Montana capitalists incorporated the Missoula and Northern Railroad Company to construct a line north from Ravalli through the Flathead Reservation. When surveyors were sent on the reservation without the consent of the tribes, tribal members and Ronan objected. The Commissioner of Indian Affairs approved Ronan's actions forcing the surveyors off the reservation.[42] A congressional bill to give the railroad a right-of-way through the Flathead Reservation was amended to require the consent of the Indians to the construction.[43] In 1891, problems arose in selling stock in the Missoula and Northern Railroad and the Northern Pacific considered alternative routes to northern Montana.[44] The railroad north through the Flathead Reservation was not built until after the reservation was opened to white settlement in 1910. See also Ronan's October 1, 1890, monthly report.

Sept 11 1890
Arlee Mont

Commr Indian Affairs, Washn DC
Party of Surveyors for Northern Pacific railroad now on reservation making preliminary survey for branch route to head of flathead. Indians object to survey advised if I shall induce Indians to withdraw objections. Answer soon as possible.

Ronan, Agent.

September 15, 1890
LR 29,105/1890, SC 159, RG 75, National Archives, Washington, D.C.

See the annotation to Ronan's letter of August 6, 1888, about the Bitterroot Salish lands taken by the Northern Pacific Railroad branch line running through the Bitterroot Valley. Apparently the railroad never did pay for the lands.

United States Indian Service,
Flathead Agency,
September 15th, 1890.

Hon. Commissioner Indian Affairs
Washington, D.C.
Sir:
I am in receipt of a letter from E. H. McHenry, from the Office of the Principal Assistant Engineer of the Northern Pacific and Montana Railroad Company, dated at Helena, Montana, September 6th, 1890, from which I quote:
"Major Peter Ronan,
U.S. Indian Agent, Arlee, Montana
Dear Sir:
At the time our Missoula and Bitter Root Valley Railroad was built up the Bitter Root Valley, a number of strips of land belonging to Indians, who had filed Homestead Entries, were taken. These parties have been dispersed and scattered, and up to date we have not been able to find owners, in order to pay amounts due for the right of way taken.

The statement of the various ownerships and the amount due is as follows:

Indian D. S. No. 1; Widow Matte, Section 21, T. 9 N. R. 20 W. 6.36 acres, $76.32.

Indian D. S. No. 2; France Brooks widow, Sec. 15 T. 9 N. R. 20 W. 5.07 acres, 55.77.

Indian D. S. No. 3; Joseph Collyer, Sec. 10, T. 9 N. R. 20 W, 3.84 acres, 46.08.

Indian D. S. No. 4: Medicine Piere, Sec. 3 & 10 T. 9 N. R. 20 W. 6.47 acres, 58.23.

Indian D. S. No. 51; Baptiste Merengo, Sec. 34, T. 10 N. R. 20 W. 3.06 acres, 27.54.

Indian D. S. No. 45; Cecilia Parker, Sec. 33, T. 9 N. R. 20 W. 6.18 acres, 80.34.

Indian D. S. No. 41; Louie Vanderberg, Sec. 33, T. 9 N. R. 20 W. 6.18 acres, 74.16.

Indian D. S. No. 6; Narcisse Trochee, Sec. 8, T. 8 T. 8 N. R. 20 W. 6.10 acres, 74.30.

Indian D. S. No. 9; Peter Brown, Sec. 8, T. 8 N. R. 20 W. 6.09 acres, 66.79.

Indian D. S. Sanpelle James, Sec 19, T. 7 N. R. 20 W. 6.03 acres, 36. 18.

Ten tracts, amounting to $600.91.

I understand that all these Indians have since been removed to the Flathead Reservation, and are probably all under your charge, and jurisdiction, If you will be kind enough to indicate in what manner we can make the payments accordingly, I will have the deeds and papers prepared to make a final adjustment of the matter.

Signed E. H. McHenry
Principal Assistant Engineer."

The titles referred to are held by members of Charlot's band of Bitter Root Indians, and in accordance with the provisions of an act entitled "An act to provide for the sale of lands patented to certain members of the Flathead band of Indians in Montana Territory, and for other purposes," approved March 2d, 1890, Henry B. Carrington of Massachusetts was appointed a special Agent of the Indian Department to obtain the consent of the Indians to their removal to this reservation, and to appraise their lands as therein provided.

I presume the appraisals of Engineer McHenry are based upon the report of values place upon the Indian lands by Henry B. Carrington.

The report showing the work done under his instructions, 51st Congress — 1st Session — Senate — Ex. Doc. No. 70, will give information required by your office.

I would respectfully state that the long delay in consumating the sale of the Indian lands, after consent of Indians and appraisement by General Carrington, has wrought demoralization and poverty among these Indians, who refrained from planting crops on their lands in the Bitter Root Valley with expectation of sale of same and removal to this reserve, as faithfully promised, to give them time, in early spring, to put in crops on this reserve to be harvested this Season.

I trust that the Department will be able to allow the Indians mentioned in list furnished herewith to receive the payments for the railroad right of way through their land, which has already been appropriated by the company, in order that the sums allowed may be promptly paid to them, to relieve them, in a measure, of their very pressing and urgent necessities.

I am very respectfully
Your obedient servant
Peter Ronan
United States Indian Agent.

October 1, 1890
LR 31,237/1890, RG 75, National Archives, Washington, D.C.

United States Indian Service,
Flathead Agency,
October 1st, 1890.

Hon. Commissioner Indian Affairs,
Washington, D.C.
Sir:

In reporting from this Agency for the month of September, I have the honor to state that all matters pertaining to the Indian Service on this reservation is in good condition. A very fine crop of grain was harvested by the Indian farmers, and for the past twenty-five days the mill has been running steady grinding their wheat into flour. There is now wheat enough delivered to keep the mill running for the next thirty days, and more coming in each day. The abundance of this years wheat crop assures a plentiful supply of flour among the thrifty Indian farmers of the reserve and is a great encouragement for energetic toil in the way of farming next season.

During the month the presence of a party of surveyors on the reservation, in the employment of the Northern Pacific Railroad Company, who sought to survey and locate a branch line from the Jocko Station, on the reservation, running through the same for several miles, to the head of the Flathead Lake, caused some commotion among the Indians, and I forbade the the [sic] survey until made aware of the authority exercised by the Company. Your reply by wire under date of the 12th inst., to my telegram, informing me that the Northern Pacific Railroad surveyors had no authority to be on the reserve, and that my action in stopping them was approved, settled the matter, as the surveyors at once moved their camps from the reserve.

I trust that action may soon be taken for the sale of the lands of Charlot's band of Bitter Root Flatheads, and their speedy removal to this reservation. The promise that this matter would be settled last spring in time to give the Indians an opportunity to locate farms on the reserve and to put in crops for this year's harvest was unfortunate, as the Indians relying upon such promise, failed to farm their lands in the Bitter Root Valley, and sold off their implements of labor — stoves etc., and are now in the mountains depending solely upon the killing of game for a living.

I have no supplies on hand to relieve the Bitter Root Indians, nor to assist the aged and indigent of the tribes of the reserve. It is discouraging to the thrifty and the persevering Indians, who till the soil to share the fruits of their labor with the aged, the indigent and the improvident who are expected to look to the Agent to relieve their wants, but as no supplies are on hand or none reported in transit, I feel my helplessness.

Herewith I have the honor to to [sic] enclose sanitary report and report of funds and indebtedness, and have the honor to be

Very respectfully
Your obedient Servant
Peter Ronan,
U.S. Indian Agent.

October 31, 1890a
LR 34,244/1890, RG 75, National Archives, Washington, D.C.

The northern boundary of the reservation had been a point of conflict between the Flathead Reservation Kootenai and the white settlers for years. White cattlemen used the confusion as an excuse to trespass on reservation grass. The 1887 survey by E. P. Harrison that Ronan described excluded from the reservation land that the Kootenai had used for years for grazing and hay. In the twentieth century the U.S. Court of Claims agreed that the Harrison survey was too far south. See annotation to Ronan's August 20, 1883, letter for more information.

Clarence E. Proctor filed for a homestead on some of the land which had been used by the Kootenai and had been excluded from the reservation by the survey. Despite Ronan's pleas, the Commissioner of Indian Affairs accepted Harrison's survey as the northern boundary of the reservation. Ronan pointed out in his December 1, 1890, monthly report that Indian resentment about the northern boundary survey complicated government efforts to get tribal approval for the sale of a strip of land desired by the Northern Pacific Railroad to enlarge their station at Jocko or Dixon, Montana. In 1891 Ronan filed off-reservation allotments for the Kootenai ranchers and farmers who used the land just north of the Harrison boundary of the reservation. In the end, however, the United States government failed to protect the Kootenai allotments against encroachment by aggressive white homesteaders.[45]

Clarence E. Proctor came to the Flathead Valley in the late 1880s. He established a hotel, livery stable, and other businesses just north of the reservation boundary. In 1890 and 1891, he operated a real estate agency in Kalispell. Some of the available sources contradict each other about the dates of specific events in his life. He died in 1933.[46]

United States Indian Service,
Flathead Agency,
October 31st, 1890.

Hon. Commissioner Indian Affairs
Washington, D.C.

Sir:

Referring to "L. 1850 — 1890 — 17032 — 1890," I would respectfully state that until the month of October, a multiplicity of duties prevented my going upon the ground and making a proper investigation of the field notes and tracing of the map of the survey of that portion of the boundary of the Flathead Indian Reservation lying West of Flathead Lake and North of Clarks Fork of the Columbia river, executed by U.S. Deputy Surveyor E. P. Harrison, under his contract dated April 18th, 1887.

You also enclosed in the same connection, a copy of a letter from Clarence E. Proctor, Demersville, Montana, dated May 26, 1890, with reference to the Northern Boundary of the reservation and the claims of himself and other settlers, with instructions to investigate the location of these settlers in the light of this survey and report whether or not their claims are located within the reservation.

I found that Mr. Proctor's location is the only one made by any settler along this line, and in the "light of this survey" his location is not upon this reservation.

The Indians are somewhat excited about this survey; they called a council after they learned that I was instructed from the Indian office to report upon this boundary, and Chief Eneas of the Kootenai Indians was delegated to call upon me to give a detailed report to the Secretary of the Interior and to yourself of their dissatisfaction with the survey of U.S. Deputy Surveyor E. P. Harrison. I look upon the case as serious, and as I also believe that the Indians are correct in regard to their boundary, I shall try to make the views of the Indians as plain as possible in connection with this

Report:

On the 3d day of June, 1887, I had the honor of addressing a letter to your office from this Agency, in which I stated that the Indians of this reserve had a deep prejudice against the word "survey," as they claimed they have been robbed by a survey, and that it was a hard task to eradicate that idea. In the same letter I also stated:

[Here Ronan has an extended three page quote from his letter to the Commissioner of Indian Affairs on June 3, 1887, which is included in this collection under that date.]

As this still left the boundary in dispute, I recommended to the Department that a survey of such boundary should be made, and the dispute for ever settled between the settlers and the Indians. In due time I was notified from the Indian office that a contract for the survey of that portion of the boundary of the Flathead Indian reservation lying West of Flathead Lake and North of Clarks Fork of the Columbia river had been let by the Surveyor General of Montana.

I notified the Indians that when the U.S. Deputy Surveyor came upon the reservation to execute his orders, I would call them to-gether at the boundary and have the Indians point out the spot on the shore of the Flathead Lake where the surveyor would commence to run out his line, if such a point was agreeable to the Indian office. The Indians were satisfied, and I heard no more of the survey until the fall of 1887, when a gentleman drove up from the Arlee station to the Agency, and informed me that his name was Edmund P. H. Harrison; that he was a deputy U.S. surveyor; that he had completed his contract of the survey of that portion of the reserve lying West of the Flathead Lake and North of Clarke's Fork of the Columbia river; and asked me to look it over and accept the same. I asked if any of the Indians were aware that he made the survey. He stated that he had seen none nor had he consulted with any except a halfbreed whom he employed and to whom he referred me for information in regard to the line. As I was not consulted or in any way informed of the matter before the line was run, I concluded to have nothing whatever to do with it until so ordered by the Department.

In the following spring an Inspector of surveys accompanied the contractor to the reservation and I was again requested by the contractor to accompany them to his survey. I informed the contractor that his invitation to go upon the ground came too late, and that I would not go unless otherwise ordered by the Commissioner of Indian Affairs. In this way the matter has rested until your instructions which preface this report were received.

I went upon the ground in company with Mr. Proctor. I was upon the same ground years before looking up the old Thomas survey, and it struck me very forcibly that the Thomas line of former dispute was in very close proximity to the recent line run out by Mr. Harrison and now in dispute also.

I find that this boundary will run very close to Kootenai village or settlement on Dayton Creek. That it will take from the Indians land which they claimed on that creek ever since and before the Stevens treaty was made; that it will also cut in two a large meadow where the Indians cut their winters supply of hay for their stock, and which they have always claimed from the days of the Stevens treaty. I find that there are only about two sections of land that would be of any use to settlers if this line is adopted; one half a section would be public land, the other section and a half would come under the Northern Pacific Railroad Grant, and would belong to that Company. So ther[e] would really only be a half a section of public land left — just enough to bring a settler on the border to tantalize and fret the Indians, by cattle straying across the line, upon the reserve, which of course could not be prevented by that settler unless the Government saw fit to fence the reserve.

To prevent any discord or trouble upon the border I would suggest that the point designated by Governor Stevens to be "halfway in the center of the Flathead Lake," but afterwards found out by actual survey to be a couple of miles North of the center, be considered the Northern boundary, and another survey running from that point be ordered. That the Agent and the Indians be notified when such survey is to be made, and proper marks and bounds be set up. If this is ordered the Indian lands on Dayton Creek and all of the Indian meadow beyond, and claimed by Indians, will be placed inside of the boundaries of the reserve. A natural boundary of hills will keep the two races from encroaching upon each other, while the public domain will loose only about a half a section of agricultural land and the Northern Pacific Railroad Company will loose a section and a half of meadow and pasture land, all, prior to this survey, conceeded [sic] to belong to the Indians.

I am very respectfully
Your obedient servant,
Peter Ronan,
United States Indian Agent.

October 31, 1890b
LR 34,724/1890, RG 75, National Archives, Washington, D.C.

See the annotation to Ronan's October 31, 1890a, report on the survey of the northern boundary of the reservation for background on this problem.

On December 12, 1890, Ronan was authorized to employ a farmer for the Kootenai who would live near the Kootenai village and be paid $60 a month.[47] Ronan chose Robert H. Irvine, a mixed blood of white and Snake descent who spoke Kootenai and operated a cattle ranch on Crow Creek in the Mission Valley. Irvine had purchased $115 worth of fruit trees in 1887 and in 1891 sold his herd of 250 cattle to Alex Dow, a trader at Arlee.[48] Irvine also spoke Nez Perce and in 1877 served as interpreter during the Nez Perce War.[49]

Ronan reported that in 1891, with Irvine's help, the Kootenai had done well raising wheat at Elmo. He got drunk at a Fourth of July celebration in 1891, but promised Ronan he would abstain from alcohol in the future.[50] He died at Crow Creek on February 10, 1900.[51]

United States Indian Service,
Flathead Agency,
October 31st, 1890.

Hon. Commissioner Indian Affairs
Washington, D.C.
Sir:

Having lately returned from a trip to the Kootenai Indian village, at Dayton Creek, and West of the Flathead Lake, where I was ordered by you to investigate and report upon the boundary survey of Deputy U.S. Surveyor E. P. Harrison, a full report of which I forwarded to your office. Having had an opportunity to council and consult with Eneas, the Chief of this unfortunate band, who now realizes the deplorable condition of his people, and who expresses his willingness to enter into any arrangement looking to the bettering of their condition, I shall here outline the proposition I made to him, with your approval, and he fully agrees and seems delighted at a proposal which, I believe, in a short time will place himself and his band in comfortable independence.

Dayton Creek empties its waters into the Flathead Lake a few miles south of the center of that Lake, on the West side, and about sixty miles North of the Agency. Here a detached band of the British tribe of Kootenais made their homes long before the Stevens treaty was made, and here Governor Stevens found them when he entered into treaty with the Indians of this reserve, and included the band as a portion of the Confederation of Flatheads, Pend 'd Oreilles and Kootenais who were to occupy this reservation. The Kootenais are alines [sic] from the tribes of Flathead and Pend 'd Oreilles, and the latter tribes despise them for their filthy habits; their lack of thrift; their gambling and drinking proclivities; the beggarly and depraved lives both of men and women who hang around the saloons of the settlements outside of the reservation. Eneas, the Chief of this band, is a good meaning man, and if encouraged, will do all in his power to keep his Indians from wandering about, and to insist upon them turning their attention to farming and stock raising and other civilizing pursuits. I agreed to place a farmer in their settlement, there to permanently reside, whose duty it shall be to assist them next winter in getting out rails, and to fence individual farms for families who may desire to cultivate the land next Spring. To furnish seed and have the farmer teach them how to plant, cultivate and harvest. To furnish plows and other implements of labor, and if the crops warrant, to send a threshing machine to thresh their grain next season.

If the survey upon which I reported be not allowed to cut off the meadow and agricultural land claimed by the Kootenais from time immemorial, and if the Commissioner will permit me to employ a farmer, one whom the Chief has already recommended — a thrifty halfbreed farmer of this reserve, by the name of Robert H. Irvine, who was born among them — speaks the language, reads and writes English to a limited extent, and of good moral character. This man is willing to turn his own farm over to his brothers and take his family to the Kootenai village, and accept the position of farmer for them. I repeat, if I am ordered and assisted to carry out this plan, I shall have the Kootenai in an improved condition in a short time.

At the present term of court at Missoula, two of this tribe were sentenced to be hanged for murder. The chief and his band keenly feel their degredation, and if an energetic movement is made at once as above outlined, instead of scattering out in hunting and gambling parties, I can place these Indians at work fencing in farms and preparing for a season of labor.

On account of the large number of settlers who are now crouding into the country at the head of the Lake, it is necessary to have a reliable man at the Kootenai village, on the border of the reserve, to look after the interest of the Indians in other respects as well as to teach them to farm. The Northern portion of the reservation is one of the finest cattle ranges in the Northwest, and Chief Eneas complains that settlers at the head of the lake, drive great herds of cattle in the night to the boundary of the reserve and let them stray over and turn them loose on the reservation. This could be prevented by the farmer, who could take the Indians and round up and drive the cattle back across the border until trespassers would tire of having their bands herded and driven by Indians. Where cases have been brought against settlers having cattle on the reserves, notably at the Blackfeet reservation, the case was thrown out of court on the plea that stock could not be prevented from straying on the reserve unless the same was fenced.

Trusting this matter will receive your kind attention,

I am very respectfully,
Your obedient Servant,
Peter Ronan,
United States Indian Agent.

November 1, 1890
LR 34,725/1890, RG 75, National Archives, Washington, D.C.

> Ronan reported on the murder trials of Pascale, Antley, Pierre Paul, and La La See in this letter and one on November 13, 1890. In these reports and one on January 2, 1891, Ronan argued that the suspects were defended by good lawyers and convicted largely on Indian testimony. According to Ronan, the Indian police and chiefs cooperated in the arrests, and most tribal members felt the convictions were justified. According to newspaper reports, the defendants denied their guilt and claimed some of the witnesses lied.[52] The many conflicting accounts in the historical record make it almost impossible to determine whether the trials and convictions of the four Indians were fair.

United States Indian Service,
Flathead Agency,
November 1st, 1890.

Hon. Commissioner Indian Affairs
Washington, D.C.

Sir:

The month of October was very pleasant on this reservation. The weather was beautiful and the Indians succeeded in threshing one of the finest crops of grain ever raised on the reservation. The threshing machines are now housed and put away for next seasons work. The grist mill has run every day during the month of October, grinding Indian wheat, more of which is delivered fast as the flour is hauled away. The mill yard is also piled up with logs awaiting to be sawed, and as some of the Indians are clamerous [sic] for lumber to repair and build before winter, I shall probably shut down the grist mill for a short time during the month in order to get some lumber ahead.

At the present term of Court for this District, now in session at Missoula, Pascall and Antela, two Kootenai Indians belonging to the band of Chief Eneas, residing upon this reservation, were tried separately and found guilty of murder in the first degree. At 10 o'clock on the morning of October 27th, they were brought into Court for sentence. After reviewing the cases from the time of the arrests to the indictments by the grand jury, the trial and the conviction, Judge Marshall asked the two defendants whether they had any reason to offer why sentence of death should not be passed upon them according to law. Neither of them replied. The Judge then sentenced each of them to be hanged on Friday December 19th, between the hours of 10 o'clock in the forenoon and 2 o'clock in the afternoon. This is the longest time that the law allows in this State to be allotted to condemned murderers, it being eight weeks from the time of passing the sentence.

Pascall was found guilty by Indian evidence of having murdered a traveler to gain possession of his horse.

Antelay's crime for which he is to suffer the penalty of death, was complicity, as principal in the murder of three white prospectors, on Woolf Creek, in the fall of 1887. It was clearly proved, on Indian evidence, that a party of six Kootenai Indians, whose names were Jerome, John Annen, Koosta, Antoine, Domini, and Antelay, started from Pleasant valley to go to Tobacco Plains, where a band of British Kootenais camp, just at the International boundary line, to attend a sun dance which the British Indians were to give. While on their way they came upon a camp of three white prospectors on Woolf Creek. John proposed they kill the prospectors in retaliation for Indians killed by white men. Leaving their own camp the Indians crawled stealthily towards the prospector's camp. When within about twenty paces, John, who had the only gun in the party's possession, paused, raised his gun and fired. Two of the white men fell. The third started to run followed by the Indians. Soon as the first shot had been fired John dropped his own gun and seized on one belonging to the whites; Jerome seized another while Antelay grabbed the one John had discarded. All three started in pursuit of the fleeing man, firing as they ran. On the witness stand Antoine testified that Antelay fired the fatal shot. However that might have been, the third man fell mortally wounded, whereupon the Indians dragged his body to the camp, loaded it with the two others on their horses, conveyed them across the creek and there attempted to burn them.

Shortly afterwards John and Jerome were taken from the custody of a deputy sheriff, who had them under arrest, by a party of citizens, at the Head of Flathead Lake, and hanged them. The others escaped capture and it was not until the past summer that they were apprehended and brought to justice through the good office of Eneas, the Kootenai Chief, who arrested them and turned them over to the Sheriffs posse. There are two more Indians yet on trial, belonging to the Pend 'd Oreille tribe. Their names are Piere Paul and Lal-La-See, and are the desperados who terrorized this reserve for several years. At one time a reward of a thousand dollars was offered for their capture. Last summer I reported to your office that the Indians at last agreed to capture them which they did and turned them over to the Sheriff's posse. They were indicted for murder in the first degree and their trial is now proceeding in the District Court. The capture and conviction of those lawless Indians will have a good effect in awing and subduing the restless and savage spirit of some of the young would be braves. The Chiefs and the Indians generally are pleased that those outlaws have at last been brought to justice.

I have just received the news that Lal-La-See, was found guilty of murder in the first degree and will be sentenced on Wednesday the 5th of November. On that day the trial of Piere Paul, also indicted for complicity in murder with Lal-La-See, will be commenced.

Herewith I have the honor to enclose sanitary report and report of funds and indebtedness; also report of farmer and have the honor to be

Very respectfully
Your obedient servant
Peter Ronan
United States Indian Agent.

November 13, 1890
LR 35,861/1890, RG 75, National Archives, Washington, D.C.

United States Indian Service,
Flathead Agency,
November 13, 1890.

Hon. Commissioner Indian Affairs
Washington, D.C.
Sir:

Replying to your letter October 31st, 1890 – "L 26991 – 1890" relative to the arrest by the civil authorities of Missoula County, Montana, of Pascal, an Indian, for murder etc., I have to say that in my report for the month of October, I made reference to trial and conviction of Pascal, Antley and Lal-La-See and that the case of Piere Paul was on trial, all of whom are Indians belonging to this reservation. I may now report that by their verdict on Saturday afternoon, November 8th, 1890, in the case of the State vs. Piere Paul, a Pend 'd Oreille Indian, charged with murder in the first degree, have disposed of the last of the four Indians on trial for murder. They returned a verdict of guilty as charged in the indictment. On Tuesday, November 11th Judge Marshal sentenced Pere Paul to be hanged Friday, December 19th, the same day on which Lal-La-See, Antley, and Pascal are to be hanged.

Thus is ended the last of four trials which has continued to attract the attention and interest of the citizens of this State.

The prisoners were properly defended, as the best legal talent of the County and probably of the State, was assigned by Judge Marshall for their defence. The conviction rested upon the evidence of numerous witnesses of both races, and was of a convincing character.

The only hope that the condemned Indians now have left for their lives lies in the power of the Governor or supreme court to confer, and it is not probable, considering the nature of the crimes and the evidence against the defendants, that an appeal will be taken to the higher courts, or that the Governor of this State will commute the death sentence if applied to.

I am very respectfully,
Your obedient servant

Peter Ronan
United States Indian Agent.

November 22, 1890
LR 36,572/1890, RG 75, National Archives, Washington, D.C.

In 1890 large volumes of freight were delivered to Jocko Station on the Northern Pacific Railroad (now Dixon, Montana) to be shipped across the reservation for use in the construction of the Great Northern Railroad through the Upper Flathead Valley. On September 10, 1890, the Northern Pacific officially requested permission to purchase 22.76 acres of reservation land to build a roundhouse and enlarge the Jocko station. The Secretary of the Interior appointed Agent Ronan and Inspector Robert S. Gardner to negotiate the purchase of the strip of land from the tribes. Official instructions were issued and other preparations were made, but no records have been found to indicate that the negotiations or purchase were every carried out.[53] In Ronan's December 1, 1890, monthly report, he described how the problems with the survey of the northern boundary of the reservation would complicate the effort to purchase land to expand the Jocko (or Dixon) station.

United States Indian Service,
Flathead Agency,
November 22, 1890.

Hon. Commissioner Indian Affairs
Washington, D.C.
   Sir: —
   Acknowledging receipt of "L" – 34683 – 1890, dated Washington, November 10th, 1890; and also "L" – 34130 – 1890 – instructions etc., to R. S. Gardner, Esqr., U. S. Indian Inspector, and to myself, to confer and arrange, on the part of the United States, with the Indians on the Flathead Reservation for the extinguishment of their title to an additional strip of land desired by the Northern Pacific Railroad Company, for railway purposes, at a station designated as Jocko, on the said reservation.
   You state further that a copy of these instructions were forwarded by the Department to Inspector Gardner, on the 10th of November, and that he has been directed by wire to visit the Flathead Agency, soon as his work is completed at Blackfeet. I am directed to confer with him and arrange a date for the meeting of the Indian Council, and, in the meantime, I am also directed to prepare a list of all the male adult Indians occupying and residing upon the reservation.
   I am pleased to have been designated in conjunction with Colonel Gardner to attend to this business and will endeavor to discharge the duties enjoined upon me to the best of my ability, according to the instructions of the Department.
   I would respectfully report to you, as I shall to Inspector Gardner, that it is the custom among a number of the Indians, after harvesting and threshing their grain, and securing their crops, each fall, to absent themselves, for the purpose of hunting game in the mountains surrounding the reservation, not returning until Christmas week. It will therefore be almost a matter of impossibility to "prepare a list of all the male adult Indians occupying and residing upon this reservation," until after Christmas. As the Indians on this reserve do

not huddle together in villages, but are scattered over the vast extent of the reservation on farms and little belongings, where they live in log houses and numbers of them scarcely ever visit the Agency, but send their women to explain their wants or to ask for supplies. It will be seen that in furnishing such list time and travel will be involved, and it is my opinion that it will take until some time in January to make necessary arrangements, according to instructions.

Soon as the Indians return from their hunt I shall commence to prepare the list, and when that is accomplished, name a date for holding the Council and apprise the Department of the same. The United States Inspector could then be notified by the Department that all was in readiness for the Council and a procedure to business. Trusting that upon arrival at this Agency Col. Gardner may coincide with these views and that the Department will adopt the suggestions I have taken the liberty to make,

I am very respectfully,
Your obedient servant,
Peter Ronan,
United States Indian Agent.

November 29, 1890
LR 37,360/1890, special case 188, RG 75, National Archives, Washington, D.C.

In 1890 the Sioux Ghost Dance resulted in conflict in South Dakota and some newspaper reports expressed fear that the conviction and hanging of the four Indian murderers in Missoula at about the same time would result in violence on the Flathead Reservation.[54] Despite tribal unhappiness with the problem of bias in the white justice system, Ronan was confident no conflict would result from the hangings.

United States Indian Service,
Flathead Agency,
November 29, 1890.

Hon. Commissioner Indian Affairs,
Washington, D.C.
Sir:
Replying to "L," dated at your office, November 22d, 1890, I would respectfully report that I have kept myself as well informed as possible through press reports and private correspondence, in regard to the excitement among the Sioux of North and South Dakota, and other tribes connected with the "ghost dance!" I am pleased to state that the infection has not reached the Indians of this reservation and that they are pursuing the even tenor of their way, and are obedient to the regulations of the Department. It shall be the duty of all employes connected with this Agency, to keep a watchful eye upon all visiting or strange Indians who may come upon the reservation to prevent any spread of the Messiah theories or the "ghost dance," among the Indians under my charge.

Should anything occur creating a suspicion of an outbreak, or that the Indians have inaugurated any dances, etc., of the craze among Dakota Sioux, I shall at once communicate with your office.

I am very respectfully
Your obedient servant,
Peter Ronan,
United States Indian Agent.

December 1, 1890
LR 38,198/1890, RG 75, National Archives, Washington, D.C.

Ronan's monthly report for November 1890 noted that the hard feelings over the survey of the northern boundary of the reservation would complicate efforts to get the tribes to sell a strip of land at Jocko (or Dixon) station to the Northern Pacific Railroad. He also enclosed a newspaper article that the Ghost Dance craze had not reached Flathead. The article repeated tribal complaints that Indians who murdered white people were vigorously pursued while white people who killed Indians were not punished.

United States Indian Service,
Flathead Agency,
December 1st, 1890.

Hon. Commissioner Indian Affairs,
Washington, D.C.
Sir:

I have the honor to report that the month of November, like that of October, was mild and beautiful. On Saturday last we had the pleasure of grinding the last sack of Indian wheat delivered at the mill, which has been running continuously for nearly three months. The saw mill is now undergoing a renovation and general repair and when completed will be put in operation.

The Indians who have been out hunting in the mountains are returning from the chase. They report game unusually plentiful, and killed a large number of deer, elk, mountain goat, mountain sheep and bear.

There will be a large gathering of the tribes of the reservation at Christmas at the Mission. After New Years, I shall commence to make a list of the adult Indians in order to carry out your instructions to confer and arrange, on the part of the United States, with the Indians on this reservation for the extinguishment of their title to an additional piece of land, desired by the Northern Pacific Railroad Company for Railroad purposes, at a station designated as Jocko, on the said reservation.

I have not yet announced your decision to the Indians, communicated in letter "L" 34244, under date of November 10, 1890, in regard to the survey of a portion of the Northern boundary of this reservation. It is not my purpose to do so if it can be avoided until after arrangements have been made in regard to instructions above quoted, unless otherwise ordered, as the Indians believe they are honestly entitled by treaty to the land cut off the reserve by said survey and undoubtedly will evince an ugly feeling. I have no reason to believe that the line is not correctly located and marked on the ground except from statements made by Indians, and set forth in my report on this subject. When the time comes I shall explain to the Indians as fully as I can the whole matter and endeavor to convince them that the line is in the strictest accordance with the provisions of their treaty.

Conditions in regard to other tribes do not exist here, and as specially reported to you under date of November 29th, 1890, everything is harmonious. Enclosed please find newspaper clippings which truthfully state the case. Herewith I have the honor to enclose sanitary report, and report of funds and indebtedness, also report of farmer, and have the honor to be

Very respectfully
Your obedient servant,
Peter Ronan,
United States Indian Agent.

Enclosure. Ronan attached two newspaper clippings to his letter, only one of which is reproduced here. From The Helena Journal *(daily), November 30, 1890, page 2, col. 2:*

Nothing In It.
Missoula County Indians Ignorant of Any Messiah, Past or Present.
Special Correspondence of The Journal.

Missoula, Nov. 29. — Your correspondent has made extended inquiries among the Bitter Root and reservation Indians and has yet to find one who knows anything about the Messiah business. If anyone would know about it, Riley, a court interpreter for the Kootenais, would be the man, and when the pump was applied to him he was ignorant about the whole matter. There is more or less dissatisfaction among them over the coming execution, which is to take place at 10:30 o clock the morning of the 19th of December, but Michel, the blind interpreter, explains this. He says the Indians cannot understand why if an Indian kills a white man he should be hunted down for years, while if a white man kills an Indian that is the last of it. He says in his recollection thirty Indians have been killed on the reservation by white men, and not one of these was ever punished. But Eastern people and coming emigrants need not be alarmed at any reports sent out from here about "desperate fighting," etc. It does not exist except in the fevered imagination of some newspaper correspondent. . . .

[Second paragraph of article refers to an audit of Missoula city finances and was not included with Ronan's letter.]

December 6, 1890
LR 38,635/1890, RG 75, National Archives, Washington, D.C. Copy filed as 9374/1890, letters received, RG 48, Records of the Office of the Secretary of the Interior, National Archives, Washington, D.C.

> Congressional inaction on funding the removal of the Bitterroot Salish to the Flathead Reservation devastated the tribe economically. On December 26, 1890, the Commissioner of Indian Affairs renewed his request through the Secretary of the Interior for congressional action.[55] See also Ronan's letter of April 9, 1890.

United States Indian Service,
Flathead Agency,
December 6th, 1890.

Hon. Commissioner Indian Affairs
Washington, D.C.
   Sir:
   I have the honor to report that in November, 1890, General H. B. Carrington, of Massachusetts, as Special Agent of the Department obtained the

consent of the Indians to their removal to this reservation and to the appraise-
ment of their land for sale, in accordance with the provisions of an act entitled
"An Act to provide for the sale of lands patented to certain members of the
Flathead band of Indians in Montana and for other purposes."

If it was not solemnly promised, it was certainly understood by the Indians, that by complying with the wishes of the Government in this matter,
that arrangements would be made last winter to remove the families to this
reservation not later than March, 1890, in order to give them an opportunity to
select their new homes on this reserve, fence small fields, plow and cultivate
the same, to enable them to harvest small crops in the fall as a beginning towards self-support. Believing that this arrangement could not be carried out
so quickly, I went to Bitter Root Valley in early spring and advised the Indians
to cultivate their land that season, and even if the order came for the sale of
their land and their removal to the Jocko reservation, arrangements might be
made to allow them to harvest their crops and appropriate the same to their
benefit. Relying upon what they considered a promise that their removal was
assured in early spring, they neglected their fields until it was too late to plant
or sow. Having idled their time they are now entirely without anything upon
which to live. It has been reported to me that the wagons, harness, plows, and
other agricultural implements, and even their stoves which I issued to those
Indians in previous years are being bartered away to white settlers for provisions to feed their families and themselves. Owing to the fact that I have been
suffering a severe attack of rheumatism since my return from examination of
the Northern Boundary survey of the reservation, I was unable to personally
visit the Flatheads in the Bitter Root Valley and investigate this state of affairs. Chief Charlot, however sent a messenger to inform me that his people
are destitute of provisions and clothing and requested me to come to his relief.
From the small amount of supplies at this Agency, intended for the support of
the members of Charlot's band removed here, I shall ship by railroad to the
Bitter Root Valley, some flour, bacon, beans, tea, coffee, sugar, etc., to relieve
their immediate necessities and trust that the Hon. Commissioner will approve
my action.

There are about thirty-two families yet with Chief Charlot in the Bitter
Root Valley, awaiting the sale of their lands in this deplorable condition, and I
trust that I shall be authorized by the Honorable Commissioner to make requisition for provisions such as flour, bacon, coffee, tea, sugar, baking powders,
etc., for their support for at least four months from the first of January, 1891,
as it may be these Indians will not be removed from the Bitter Root Valley to
this reservation before the expiration of that time.

I am very respectfully,
Your obedient servant,
Peter Ronan,
United States Indian Agent.

December 19, 1890
LR 39,256/1890, telegram, RG 75, National Archives, Washington, D.C.

> Ronan gave more information about the hanging of the four Indians convicted of murdering
> white men in his January 2, 1891, monthly report. Much has been written about the hang-
> ing, but the most detailed description was published in the *Missoula Weekly Gazette*.[56]

Dec 19, 1890
Missoula Mont

Commissioner Indian Affairs
Washn, DC

Lalacee pierre paul pascal and antley pend oorille and Kootenai Indians of the Flat Head reservation will be hanged in the yard at Missoula tomorrow at ten thirty.

I shall take charge of bodies for burial in Mission Burying Ground on reservation. Have four head men and interpreter with me. No disturbances among the Indians need be apprehended as the better class realize that a fair trial was accorded and that the prisoners were guilty of murder; exciting rumors of Indian trouble I understand are going over wires but you can rely upon these facts.

Ronan Agt.

"Just Before the Drop," December 19, 1890.
Redrawn by Corky Clairmont from damaged original in
"Death's Decree: The Indian Quartette's Farewell to Earth,"
Missoula Weekly Gazette, *December 24, 1890, page 1, col. 2-5.*

St. Ignatius Mission Boys School Shops, 1890.
Oregon Province Archives, Gonzaga University, Spokane, Washington, negative 114.13.01a.

Excavation of new St. Ignatius Mission Church building. Note Indian cabins across road.
Jesuit Oregn Province Archives, Gonzaga University, Spokane, Washington, negative 114.3.02.

Alex Matt and view of irrigation canal built by him about 1890.
Photo ca. Sept. 1910.
Flathead Irrigation Project Papers, U.S. National Archives, Denver Region,
Denver, Colorado, 8NS-75-97-221, box 1, F15.

1891

January 2, 1891
LR 941/1891, RG 75, National Archives, Washington, D.C.

In his report for December 1890, Ronan described the hanging of four Kootenai and Pend d'Oreille Indians for murdering white men. They were hung in Missoula on December 19, 1890, after what Ronan felt were fair trials. According to Ronan, they were convicted on Indian as well as white testimony and most tribal members assented to their punishment.[1]

The sudden reappearance of traditional Indian dances and celebrations seemed to surprise Ronan. He attributed it to competition between Big Sam and Louison for influence. Ronan's control over law and order on the reservation had grown over the 1880s, and he moved vigorously to stop the dances. Apparently dances were held both in the Jocko Valley and at Crow Creek in the Mission Valley.[2] The rules of the reservation Court of Indian Offenses submitted by Ronan to the Commissioner of Indian Affairs on February 12, 1885b, and approved by the Secretary of the Interior, had outlawed participation in Indian dances and feasts. For a first offense rations were withheld but subsequent offenses could result in 30 days in the reservation jail. The Commissioner requested that the soldiers at Fort Missoula be authorized to back up Ronan, if needed.[3] Ronan also discussed the "dancing craze" in his letters of April 20, 1891, June 1, 1891, and July 1, 1891.

Ironically when the Ancient Order of United Workmen, a fraternal organization, was to have a national meeting in Missoula in June 1892, organizers included games and war dances by Flathead Reservation Indians on the program. In this case Ronan seemed to have approved of Indian dances for exhibition.[4]

Judge Charles S. Marshall worked as a lawyer for many years in Kentucky before moving to Missoula in 1888 where his eldest son had a prominent law practice. In 1889, Charles became a judge in the state court in Missoula.[5] Big Sam was a prominent leader among the Salish and would have been 56 years old in 1891. As a young man, he took part in horse stealing expeditions against the Blackfeet and the Crow. On one occasion his party captured Crow Indians who had stolen horses from white men, and they returned the horses to the whites. He farmed in the Bitterroot Valley before moving to the Jocko Valley where in 1885 he had 100 acres under fence and a crop of 200 bushels of wheat and oats. In 1885 he had 20 horses and 10 cattle. For a short time in the late 1880s he was an Indian policeman.[6] For Louison see the Biographical Sketches.

United States Indian Service,
Flathead Agency,
January 2d, 1891.

Hon. Commissioner Indian Affairs
Washington, D.C.
    Sir:
    I have the honor to report condition of affairs at this Agency for the month of December.
    On Friday the 19th day of the month, Piere Paul and Lallasee, members of the Pend 'd Oreille tribe, and Pascal and Antela, members of the Kootenai

tribe, belonging to this reservation, were executed in the jail yard, at Missoula Montana. All four were indited by the grand jury; tried in the circut court in Missoula County, found guilty by the jury and sentenced to be hanged by Judge Marshal, for the crime of murdering white men. The execution was not a public one, and a limited number were admitted. Attended by two Catholic priests the prisoners assended the scaffold with unfaltering steps, where prayers were said by the priests and repeated by the Indians. Their calm, quiet demenor neve[r] forsook them. The trap was sprung at a few minutes to eleven o'clock, A. M., launching them into eternity. As the last request of the doomed men, and also that of the Indians of the reservation, I took charge of the bodies and went to the reservation with them on a Northern Pacific train, where they were met on the night of the execution at Ravalli station by a large party of Indians, and conveyed to the mission. On the next day the remains were buried with the simple rites of the Catholic Church. No Indian demonstration followed, and after the graves were closed all quietly dispersed to their homes. In former reports I have given in detail the crimes committed which led to the execution of the Indians. They had a fair trail; were abely defended, were found guilty by a jury of good men and were hanged according to the law for their crimes. Outside of the immediate relatives and friends of the criminals, the Indians of the reservation feel that they were guilty and deserved their fate.

During the holidays much excitement prevails, caused principally by Indians obtaining whisky and bringing it to the reserve from surrounding towns; and also by gambling. I closed up the warehouse and announced to the Indians that no supplies, clothing or anything else would be issued until the Indian Judges, police, and head men announced to me that gambling and drinking was suppressed on the reserve.

A couple of rival politicians, Big Sam and Louison, who wish to obtain favor among the more wreckless and non-progressive young Indians I believe to be responsible for the present hilarious demonstrations. Each of them wish to be elected Chief instead of Arlee, deceased. Both are of the opinion that a vigorous denouncement of the Agent, and the tyrany of the Indian Department, in trying to induce them to follow the ways of the whiteman in civilizing pursuits, will capture this class. As each of those ambitious Indians have adopted the same tactics, which are demoralizing to the Indians, I feel confident that I shall defeat both of them in their ambitious aspirations.

On the 6th of December, 1890, I made special report of the condition of the remnant of Chief Charlots' Band, residing in the Bitter Root Valley, and later I forwarded to him a small quantity of supplies by rail from the Agency. I trust that my report of that date will received attention, and that I may have instructions as to whether I shall forward any mor[e] provisions from the limited amount on hand at the Agency.

The postal department established a post office at the Agency, called Jocko, and service commenced on the 1st inst. All communications should be addressed to Jocko, Flathead Agency.

Industries at the Agency are going forward as usual. The "ghost dance" has not reached us, and outside of the carousing before mentioned, order prevails on the reserve.

Herewith I have the honor to enclose sanitary report, and report of funds and indebtedness, and also report of farmer, and have the honor to be

Very respectfully
Your obedient servant,
Peter Ronan
United States Indian Agent.

January 3, 1891
LR 939/1891, RG 75, National Archives, Washington, D.C.

In 1891 Alex Dow, Jr., was the trader at Arlee station on the Flathead Reservation. Dow had purchased the Arlee store in 1889 from Alexander L. Demers.[7]

Flat Head Agency,
Arlee Montana
January 3rd, 1891

Major P. Ronan
U.S. Indian Agt.,
Montana
    Sir:
    Here in I beg leave to state that I have not sold or barter to Any Indians, Any Arms or Metalic Cartridges — What ever. Only about one half Dozen Small Cans of Powder and About Eight pounds of No. 4. Bird shot during the last Eight Months of the year 1890.

Very respt. yours
A. Dow
L. H. B.

Respectfully submitted.

Peter Ronan
U.S. Ind. Agt.

First enclosure:
    Copy

Department of the Interior
Office of Indian Affairs
Washington, D.C.
Dec. 5, 1890

Peter Ronan, U.S. Indian Agent
Flathead Agency, Montana
    Sir:
    Your special attention is invited at this time to paragraph 31 of "Laws and regulations relating to trade with Indian Tribes" which is as follows. Traders will not be allowed, under any circumstances, to sell to the Indians breech loading arms, pistols of any description fixed ammunition, or metallic cartridges (2136 R. S. Joint Res. Aug. 7, 1878). It is presumed that licenced traders among Indians will at all times strictly observe this regulation and that agents will see that they do so. But in view of the excited state of feeling at this time among some of the Indian tribes, the Office desires to receive specific information on this point. You will therefore obtain without delay, from each trader in your agency a written Statement as to whether he has or has not during the past six months sold to Indians any breech-loading arms pistols, fixed ammunition or metallic cartridges, and if he has done so exactly what quantities of each he has sold, and report the facts to this Office.

Respectfully
Signed T. J. Morgan
Commissioner.

Second enclosure:

United States Indian Service,
Flathead Agency,
Jan. 2d, 1891.

Alexander Dow,
Indian Trader,
Arlee, Montana
   Sir:
   Please return to me without delay, the written statement required by the Hon Commissioner of Indian Affairs, as requested in his letter, copy of which is herewith attached.

I am respectfully yours
Peter Ronan
United States Indian Agent.

January 7, 1891
LR 1,459/1891, RG 75, National Archives, Washington, D.C.

   In 1891 Alexander L. Demers operated the store at St. Ignatius. See Ronan's October 23, 1886, letter and annotation for more information.

Flathead Agency,
January 7th, 1891.
   Respectfully forwarded to the Honorable Commissioner of Indian Affairs Washington, D.C.

Peter Ronan
United States Ind. Agt.

Enclosure:

A. L. Demers,
St. Ignatius, M.T., Jan 3rd, 1891

Maj P. Ronan
U.S. Ind Agent
Flathead Agency
   Dear Sir:
   In answer to the copy of letter from the Hon. Commissioner of Indian Affairs I beg to say that I have not sold in the last six months any breech loading arms, pistols of any description, fixed amunition or metallic cartridges.

Very respectfully yours
A. L. Demers,
Trader.

January 31, 1891
LR 5,244/1891, RG 75, National Archives, Washington, D.C.

   On January 1, 1891, Isaac Conpae became captain of the tribal police in place of Antoine Still tell kan, who was demoted to private. Isaac Pelay and Joseph Touse were dismissed for incompetence; Charloaine resigned for health reasons; and Joseph Quin mah resigned with no reason given.[8]

Regarding the assignment of Ronan and Inspector Gardner to negotiate for an expansion of the railroad station at Jocko or Dixon, see Ronan's November 22, 1890, letter and annotation. For the continuing problems with the northern boundary survey see the annotations to Ronan's August 20, 1883, and October 31, 1890a, letters. See Ronan's August 25, 1891b, letter and annotation for the allotments Ronan issued to the reservation Kootenai for land they used just north of the boundary.

The emergency subsistence supplies for the Bitterroot Salish kept the Salish from starving during the two years it took the Washington bureaucracy to approve the 1889 agreement for the Salish to move to the Jocko Valley.[9]

United States Indian Service,
Flathead Agency,
January 31st, 1891.

Hon. Commissioner Indian Affairs,
Washington, D.C.

Sir:

I have the honor to submit my report for the month of January. In doing so it gives me pleasure to state that everything pertaining to the service on this reservation is in good order and that no disagreeable conditions prevail. Having reorganized the Indian Police and discharged from the force a few disturbing characters, the organization is now in harmony and is doing good service in preventing the introduction of intoxicants upon the reserve; insisting upon the sacredness of the marriage ties by punishing with imprisonment both sexes found guilty of adultry, or poligamy; inforcing good order and obeyance to rules and regulations governing the reservation.

I take liberty at this time to mention that in regard to "L" 34683 – 1890, dated at your office, November 10th, 1890; and also "L" 34130 – 1890, instructions, etc., to R. S. Gardner, Esqr., U.S. Indian Inspector, and to myself, to confer and arrange on the part of the United States, with the Indians on the Flathead reservation for the extinguishment of their title to an additional strip of land desired by the Northern Pacific Railroad Company for railway purposes, at a station designated as Jocko, on the said reservation. A copy of instructions was received by me and I have carried out my portion thereof in the matter by obtaining a list of all the male adult Indians occupying and residing upon this reservation, and I am now prepared to proceed to the consumation of the business required by said instructions whenever notified. In connection therewith I communicated with the chief assistant engineer of the Northern Pacific Railroad Company, and in his reply it was intimated that the company are in no hurry to acquire title and would notify when it was necessary for them to secure it for railway purposes.

I desire also to respectfully report that under my instructions, Robert H. Irvin, a halfbreed, who was appointed farmer for the Kootenai Indians of this reservation, on the 1st day of January, 1891, proceeded to their encampment or village and announced your decission to the Indians communicated in "L" 34244, under date of November 10, 1890. I deemed it best to announce this decission and to urge upon the Indians the necessity of securing their claim to the land by fencing and improving the same. The Indians believe that they are honestly entitled by treaty to the land cut off the reserve by United States deputy surveyor Harrison's line. I explained to the Indians as fully as I could the whole matter and endeavored to convince them that the line is in the strictest accordance with the provisions of their treaty. In obeyance to my request the farmer induced fourteen families of Kootenais to commence fencing the land they claim by occupancy outside of the boundary as designated by the Harrison survey, and I shall soon make a personal investigation in regard to such claims, and ask for instructions from your office with view of securing title to the Indian claimants.

In accordance with instructions by telegram, dated January 12th, 1891, confirmed by letter of the 4th of the same month — "Finance 38635 - '90, Telegram 673 - '91, authority 25479,["] I proceeded to the Bitter Root Valley and expended the sum of one thousand five hundred dollars in open market purchase, at the lowest obtainable rates of subsistence supplies and other necessities of life, for issue to Charlots' band of Bitter Root Indians. I found these Indians in the most abject poverty, with no provisions, or supplies of any kind. This timely expenditure was a boon and a blessing to the Indians. Chief Charlot expressed his gratitude warmly and stated himself and band were ready to obey any order to remove from the Bitter Root Valley to this reservation. I explained that the sale of their lands, etc., was in the hands of Congress and that at present I presumed the Indian office had no orders to give until necessary legislation was enacted.

The saw mill was employed during the month in cutting lumber for Indians from logs delivered by them.

The winter weather up to the last day of January was beautiful, and no snow fell until that date. Snow and cold weather now prevails.

Herewith I have the honor to enclose sanitary report and report of funds and indebtedness and also report of farmers and have the honor to be

Very respectfully
Your obedient servant
Peter Ronan
United States Indian Agent.

February 18, 1891
LR 6,948/1891, RG 75, National Archives, Washington, D.C.

> Inspector Robert S. Gardner's August 7, 1890, report on Flathead Agency recommended that a subagency be constructed nearer to the center of the reservation so that more tribal members could benefit from agency services.[10] On July 9, 1891b, Ronan reported on the amount needed to establish a subagency on Crow or Mud Creek. The topic of moving the agency had come up many times over the years but was always stopped by budget restrictions.[11] In this February 18, 1891, report, Ronan pointed out that the 1887 agreement made by the Northwest Indian Commission with the Flathead Reservation tribes would provide for building a subagency on the reservation if Congress ratified the agreement.[12]

United States Indian Service,
Flathead Agency,
February 18th, 1891.

Hon. Commissioner Indian Affairs,
Washington, D.C.
    Sir:

Referring to "L 28,763 – 1890," relative to Department reference for consideration and proper action of a report dated August 7th, 1890, from U.S. Inspector Gardner, stating that a large portion of the Indians of the Flathead reservation, Montana, live from fifty to sixty miles distant from the Flathead Agency; that the center of population is near Crow Creek, or Mud Creek; that at present they derive only a small benefit from the Agency grist and saw mill and carpenter and blacksmith shops; that the establishment of a sub-agency on that reservation, would in his judgment, be a decided advantage and for the best interest of the service; that the present Agency was located in one corner of the reservation for the convenience of the Agent and Agency employes, being near the town of Missoula, and not for or in the interest of the reservation Indians; that the time has now come when the Indians of that reservation should be more looked after and encouraged in civilization and Christianity; and that they are beginning to see and feel and know that they must depend upon themselves to make a living, and for this reason the aid which the government offers them should be easily accessible, not 35 or 40, 50, or 75 miles distant, causing them to travel these respective distances to get a machine, plow, wagon or harness repaired, or to obtain the services of the Agent or physician.

Inspector Gardner also states that it might be well to establish or locate an Agency on Crow Creek or Mud Creek, and retain the present Agency for the use of the Bitter Root Flatheads, and such other of the Confederated tribes as are now located and farming in the Jocko Valley; that Mud Creek would be preferable for an Agency or Sub-agency; that the valley there is from ten to twelve miles wide and from thirty to thirty five miles long, and is close to Pend 'd Oreilles, Little Bitter Root and Dayton Creeks; also to the Camas Prairie; that about two-thirds of the reservation Indians live in and near that vicinity; that the location suggested is about thirty to forty miles distant from the present Agency, and about twenty-four to twenty-five miles distant from Ravalli railway station, and eighteen or nineteen miles from St. Ignatius Mission, and twelve miles from the foot of the lake, and as they are industrious and peaceable the aid offered them should be within easy access.

In connection with this matter you direct that I shall investigate the matters and things referred to by Inspector Gardner, and to submit a full and complete report on the same, together with recommendations as to the necessity and practicability of establishing either an agency or a sub-agency at the place designated by that gentleman.

I would respectfully report that the views and statements of Inspector Gardner are eminently correct.

The Agency was originally located, and is at present situated at the extreme end of the Southern habitable portion of the reservation, a fact which will be readily admitted when it is known that only two Indian habitations are in existance between it and the Southern boundary. It is also placed at the immediate foot of the mountains forming the Eastern line, thereby precluding any settlement in that direction. On the other hand to the North and West there are Indian homes and farms extending in one direction a distance of forty and in the other a distance of at least sixty miles. Owing to this fact it will be evident that the use of the mills and the services of the mechanics connected with the Agency, cannot be utilized by the majority of the Indians, except at considerable cost and inconvenience in consequence of not having the encouragement the government intends affording them to follow civilizing pursuits. This is readily apparent in connection with building and grain raising — two matters to which attention is most strongly urged by the Indian Department — showing that the transportation by wagon of lumber, or wheat, for any considerable distance, exceeds the value of the article itself.

An argument in the favor of the removal is also furnished through the close relations in which the Agent and employes would be placed with those whom it is their duty to assist and direct. In opposition, no valid objection, with the sole exception of expense, can possible be raised to the removal.

A central site could be chosen which would not appreciatevely [sic] increase the present distance from a railway station and from a post office. As to the dwellers on the reservation who would then be more remote from Agency head-quarters, the majority consists of halfbreeds, who have had for years the benefits of contiguity and are proportionally well off, while the remainder are Indians in a like condition.

Having been brought in contact with the Indians of this reservation nearly fourteen years, with head-quarters at the present site, permit me to report that the benefits the government expect the Indians to gain from the appropriation of mills, agricultural implements, seeds, etc., cannot be fully directed in the present situation.

It is my impression that the Agency head-quarters should be removed to the center of population, as designated by Inspector Gardner, and that the grist and saw mill, blacksmith and Carpenter shops should be maintained at their present location, with a farmer in charge, for the benefit of Chief Charlots band of Bitter Root Flatheads, all of who will eventually settle in the Jocko valley, where those who formerly removed have made their homes. It would also be an injustice to the Indians and half-breeds, and particularly to the Bitter Root Flathead settlers to remove from their vicinity in the Jocko valley the mills and shops which have been in existence so long among them.

When the Northwest Indian Commission, in April, 1887, visited this reservation, on the part of the United States, they entered into an agreement with the Confederated tribes of this reservation, that as it was the policy of the government to remove and settle upon Indian reservations scattered bands of non-reservation Indians, so as to bring them under the care and protection of the United States; that in recompense for the consent of the Confederated tribes for the removal of such bands to this reservation, the United States would cause to be built for the benefit of the confederated Indians, Millshops etc., and maintain them, at or near Crow Creek. This agreement was signed by the Indians, and also by the Northwest Indian Commission, on the part of the United States. With this understanding Michels band of Lower Kalispels moved on to the reservation and took up farms on Camas Prairie. The remainder of the Lower Kalispels, under Chief Victor, notified me that they were ready to move from Northern Idaho, to this reserve, when arrangements are made to carry out the agreement to assist them to homes and civilizing pursuits. I understand that the agreement has not yet been ratified by Congress, while the Kalispels are wondering why houses were not built, and agricultural implements and other promised assistance have not been furnished to them as they carried out their part of the compact by removing from Idaho to this reserve. The Confederated tribes are also inquisitive why the mills and shops were not erected at or near Crow Creek as agreed upon, for giving the Kalispels the privilege to remove onto their reserve. Whether this agreement is ever to be consumated or not, the very best interest of the Indian service here, require either a sub-agency or Agency head-quarters established in the vicinity of that portion of the reservation described by Col. Gardner, United States Indian Inspector, as such, it would be a boon and a blessing to a great majority of the Indians of this reservation who are now struggling to the front as tillers of the soil, as it would give them a sustained assistance to self support, independence and comfortable homes.

I am very respectfully
Your obedient Servant
Peter Ronan,
United States Indian Agent.

February 21, 1891
LR 7,523 /1891, RG 75, National Archives, Washington, D.C.

The land claims of the Bonners Ferry Kootenai and conflicts with invading white settlers occupied much of Ronan's time during the last years of his life. See Ronan's August 6, 1889, letter and annotation for a brief outline of the situation. On December 14, 1891a, Ronan reported some of the Idaho Kootenai agreed to remove to the Flathead Reservation. On September 6, 1892, Ronan described filing claims for off-reservation allotments for those Kootenai who would not move to Flathead or Canada. The mixed blood members of the Fry family filed directly with the United States Land Office in Idaho for their own allotments. Unfortunately the government failed to protect the allotments from encroaching white settlers and by the late twentieth century the Bonners Ferry Kootenai were landless and poverty stricken.

In 1891 Congress failed to appropriate money to survey the Bonners Ferry lands and the Commissioner of Indian Affairs asked that in the meantime the entire tract of land be withdrawn from settlement by white people.[13] During the summer of 1891, the white settlers squatting in the Bonners Ferry area publicly agitated for military intervention and violence to keep the Kootenai Indians from asserting their land claims.[14]

On October 21, 1891, Ronan was authorized to negotiate with the Bonners Ferry Kootenai to get them to remove to the Flathead Reservation and was allocated $5,000 for removal expenses.[15] In December a delegation of some of the Bonners Ferry Kootenai visited the Flathead Reservation Kootenai and agreed to remove. Weather conditions caused the move to be delayed until spring 1892.[16]

For biographical information on Richard Fry and his family and Isaac, the second chief of the Bonners Ferry Kootenai, see Ronan's August 6, 1889, letter and annotation.

United States Indian Service,
Flathead Agency,
February 21, 1891.

Hon. Commissioner Indian Affairs,
Washington, D.C.
Sir:
Under the date of Washington, June 21st, 1889, I received, with reference, "Law and Land – 12930 – 1889,["] a letter from your office, enclosing copy of

a letter from U.S. Indian Agent, R. D. Guydir [Gwydir], Colville Agency, Washington, in relation to certain Kootenai Indians in Northern Idaho: "from which it appeared that they are in a wretched condition; that the land upon which they are located is not suitable for agriculture, and, that the whites appear to be overrunning the country and driving away the game which has thus far constituted the principal support of the Indians" etc.

In accordance with your desire expressed in said letter, to which I would most respectfully ask you to refer, I made as thorough investigation as the circumstances would admit and communicated my report under date of August 6th, 1889, to which report I also respectfully ask you to refer.

On receipt of said report, made pursuant to instructions of June 21st, 1889, I received your letter dated at Washington, August 28, 1889, – Law and Land 12930 – 1889 – 22436 – directing me to proceed to that country and obtain an accurate description of the same — etc., etc. In accordance with said instructions I had the honor to report to you under date October 16th, 1889, and also beg to call your attention to said report.

On January 21st, 1890, I made an appeal to the Department for the relief of this unfortunate and poverty stricken band, enclosing a letter dictated by the Indians, begging for their relief.

This band of Kootenai Indians are detached from any tribe, and I believe are not under the supervision of any Agent. Since my visits to their country, under your instructions, they look to me to forward their complaints and to ask for assistance.

Herewith I respectfully enclose a letter directed to me from the Kootenai band of that country, and respectfully ask if I have any duty to perform in regard to the wants, necessities and relief of this band of Indians.

I am respectfully
Your obedient servant,
Peter Ronan,
United States Indian Agent.

Enclosure:

Fry Idaho, Feb 15 – 91

To Peter Ronan of the U.S. Indian Service
Flathead Agency
Sir —

Isaac the Kootenai Chief is hard set to keep peace and order in his tribe and wished me to let the authorities know the nature of his trouble and as I in common with others here am considerably interested in these I consider it my duty to inform and not only inform but earnestly request that the most possible that can be done will be done to improve the condition of affairs with all speed.

In the first place there is a Saloon near, where the Indian not only has all the privilege of the white man but is even sought after and enticed to enter and gamble and drink and Scarcely ever fails to come away robbed and full of Firewater.

From that stage of the game I consider it only an idle waste of time to trace him further with the pen in writing to you because anyone with half the knowledge and experience, in Indian nature and Customs, under such circumstances, can far more easily imagine their Conduct than I can describe it.

All that is necessary to get whiskey is to have the money, and to raise that, many of them are offering their guns and such like for sale at from ½ to ¼ their value. Lives and property are endangered from time to time and trouble will certainly follow if the Gov't does not protect the Indians. Trouble that may cost thousands upon thousands besides the lives of many good citizens.

In the second place there is quite a large immigration to these parts which will increase in the spring Consequent upon the building of the Great Northern R. R. and the development of mining prospects, and numbers are beginning to [settle] upon the Indian Lands. Lands that they have set apart as their own according to your instructions when you were in here and even in some cases, lands that they and their fathers have owned and cultivated for years and in Consequence there is a great deal of annoyance and dissatisfaction among them. They are constantly coming to me with their complaints and I have put them off by assuring them that their rights will be given them soon, and in this way I have succeeded in keeping peace but cannot tell how long I will so Succeed.

What I would recommend is that a Special agent or Some Gov't official be appointed to assist the Chief as he acknowledges he is powerless under the existing conditions and that as soon as possible the Gov't take steps to have their land surveyed and allotted to them.

As you were sent in here upon two former occasions I thought I would apply to the Dept. through you and hope you will give the matter your serious attention. They have been completely neglected since you were over here.

Awaiting the result I am

Yours respectfully
Richard Fry.

March 2, 1891
LR 9,468 /1891, RG 75, National Archives, Washington, D.C.

United States Indian Service,
Flathead Agency,
March 2d, 1891.

Hon. Commissioner Indian Affairs,
Washington, D.C.

Sir:

Submitting my report for the month of February, I would respectfully state that snow commenced to fall for the first time during the winter about the 15th of the month, and at this date there is at least two feet of it on the level all over the reservation. As the weather was beautiful and no snow fell until the date mentioned, the Indian cattle and horses are in good condition to stand the present storm, especially as most of them are provided with hay and straw with which to feed until the snow disappears.

Taking advantage of the sleighing I have had most of the employes logging and succeeded in having hawled to the mill, about one hundred thousand feet of saw logs, to be cut into lumber for Agency purposes. Many of the Indians also took advantage of the easy hawling on sleds, and have delivered a large quantity of fine pine logs to be cut into lumber for their own use.

Owing to the cold weather and snow storm I have postponed the building of the addition to the mill, contemplated for the matching and plaining machine, the shingle machine and the cut-off saw, but expect to commence building when the weather is more favorable.

I have no especial matters to report save that there is no complaint of any moment among the Indians. Those who put in crops last year were rewarded with bountiful yields, and are in comparative comfort. Of course the thrift-less, the improvident and those who fail to take advantage of the tilling of the soil, and encouragements given in that respect, are in want and appeal for assistance at the Agency. The Indian, to a great extent, is a beggar, and the majority will ask for anything thought to be on hand at the Agency, whether in affluence or in abject want. A long acquaintance, however, with the dwellers on this reservation, enables me, to a great extent, to discriminate between them, and to relieve real necessity when occasion requires. The fact that they must earn their living as the white people are compelled to do is slowly but surely dawning upon them.

Herewith I have the honor to enclose Sanitary report and report of funds and indebtedness, and also report of farmers, and have the honor to be

Very respectfully
Your obedient servant
Peter Ronan,
United States Indian Agent.

March 10, 1891
LR 9,930 /1891, RG 75, National Archives, Washington, D.C.

Problems with the survey of the northern boundary of the reservation and general friction between Indians and whites in the Upper Flathead Valley had been simmering for years. The Commissioner of Indian Affairs declined to reexamine the northern boundary survey.[17] One example of the friction between the communities in August 1891 involved both alcohol and the cultural differences surrounding the proper treatment of guests who request food.[18]

The other boundary conflict involved the southwest corner of the reservation. The problem survey of the southwest corner of the Flathead Reservation cost the tribes at least 11,900 acres of land including some valuable agricultural land at the junction of the Clark Fork and Lower Flathead Rivers. In 1965, the United States Court of Claims ruled that the survey should have included the 11,900 acres on the reservation.[19] See also Ronan's October 20, 1891, telegram and annotation for more about the southwest boundary problem.

For more information about the proposed railroad north through the reservation, see the annotation to Ronan's September 11, 1890, letter. No biographical information was located on I. S. P. Weeks of the Northern Pacific Railroad, but see the reference to him in Ronan's December 4, 1885a, letter.

United States Indian Service,
Flathead Agency,
March 10th, 1891.

Hon. Commissioner Indian Affairs,
Washington, D.C.
Sir:
I am sorry to again trouble you in regard to the survey of that portion of the Flathead Indian Reservation, lying west of Flathead Lake and North of

Clarkes Fork of the Columbia, surveyed by Edmund P. H. Harrison, United States Deputy Surveyor; under his contract No. 208, dated April 18, 1887.

In connection therewith I respectfully call your attention to my special report on that subject dated at this Agency, October 31st 1891 [i.e. 1890]; and also to your reply to the same, dated at Washington, November 10th, 1890, "L 34244 – 1890."

It will be seen that my report referred altogether to the initial point, referred to in the field notes of the surveyor, determining that middle point of the Lake, which run the line very close to the Kootenai village, or settlement on Dayton Creek, and that it would take from the Indians land which they claimed on that Creek ever since the Stevens treaty was made; that it would also cut in two a large meadow where the Indians cut their winter's supply of hay for their stock, and which they have always claimed from the days of the Stevens treaty.

In my report of the month of January, 1891, it will be found that I took steps, according to my best judgment, to secure to the Indians the land they claimed on Dayton Creek, and that at a future time I would ask for instructions in securing their titles, etc.

Referring to the field notes on the eighty-first mile which ended the survey, the Deputy Surveyor states: "This corner is situated on the crest of the ridge, and is about 2500 feet above the Clarkes Fork of the Columbia river."

The treaty also defines: "Commencing at the source of the main branch of the Jocko river; thence along the divide separating the waters flowing into the Bitter Root river from those flowing into the Jocko, to a point on Clarkes Fork between the Camas and Horse Prairies; thence Northerly to, and along the divide bounding on the West, the Flathead river, to a point due West from the point half way in latitude between the Northern and Southern extremities of the Flathead Lake; thence on a due East course to the divide whence the Crow, the Prune the So-su-el-em and the Jocko rivers take their rise, and thence Southerly along said divide to the place of beginning."

As will be seen by annexed copy of letter from the Surveyor General of Montana, to a settler, the point of land formed by the junction of the Missoula and "Flathead" rivers, and between the two, and which has been occupied by Indians for years, in the firm belief that they were inside of the boundaries of the Flathead reservation, according to the points shown to them before the signing of the Stevens treaty, is now claimed to be on the public domain, according, I presume to the Harrison survey.

The river known as Flathead river flows from the North and empties its waters into the Flathead Lake at the head of that sheet of water. Demersville being situated at the head of navigation on said river.

The river flowing from the foot of the Flathead Lake, taking its rise within the boundaries of the reservation was always called Pend 'd Oreille river until it formed its junction with the Missoula river. From the point where the two rivers join, since the exploration of Lewis and Clarke, the river appears on the maps as Clarkes Fork of the Columbia, and known by travelers by that name.

The treaty distinctly states that a point on Clarkes Fork of the Columbia is the boundary; and the Indians cannot understand why this point of land between two rivers can be cut off their reservation when the point of their boundary is designated as being on Clarkes Fork of the Columbia, and must necessarily be below, or at the junction of the two rivers. This is the Indian understanding, and, in fact the old men of the tribes show the point as designated in the treaty.

Hon. Joseph Kay McCammon, Assistant Attorney General of the Interior Department, on behalf of the United States and the confederated tribes of Flathead, Kootenai and Upper Pend 'd Oreilles Indians, entered into an agreement for the sale of a portion of their reservation for the use of the Northern Pacific Railroad on September 2d, 1882. By reference to the published report of that gentleman, it will be seen that "by the terms of said agreement the said Confederated tribes surrendered and relinquished to the United States all their right, title and interest under the treaty of July 16, 1855, (12 Stat., 975) in and to a strip of land not exceeding 200 feet in width, that is to say 100 feet on each side of the track (or line) as laid down on the map of definite location (A) wherein said line runs through said reservation, entering the same at, or near Corriaccan Defile, passing by the valley of Finley Creek to the Jocko; along the Jocko to the Pend 'd Oreille river and down the valley of the Pend 'd Oreilles, passing out of the reservation at, or near the mouth of the Missoula river, said strip of land to be used by the Northern Pacific Railroad Company, its successors, or assigns as a right of way and roadbed and containing 1,300 acres."

Herewith, I enclose map of Western boundary of the Flathead Indian reservation, as established by myself and I. S. P. Weeks, Division Engineer of the Northern Pacific Railroad, from land marks pointed out by Indians in December, 1881.

I notice by press dispatches that a right of way was granted, at last session of Congress, for a branch railroad, commencing at a station on the Northern Pacific Railroad, on the Flathead reservation, and running through said reservation to the Head of the Flathead Lake. It is my impression that unless this disputed boundary line is settled and the Indians have a proper understanding of the location of the same, trouble will exist, and before the Indians consent will be given for the construction of said branch through the reservation they will insist upon a settlement of this disputed boundary.

The Indians at the disputed point on Clarkes Fork, who own farms there are also clamerous to know if they are right, or wrong in claiming that the disputed land is on the reservation.

Herewith, I enclose copy of the letter mentioned in the body of this report from the Surveyor General of Montana.

Trusting that enclosed map may be returned to me for reference, I have the honor to be

Very respectfully

Your obedient servant

Peter Ronan

United States Indian Agent.

The letter from the Surveyor General of Montana which Ronan referred to was not filed with this letter in the National Archives. The map he referred to is reproduced here:

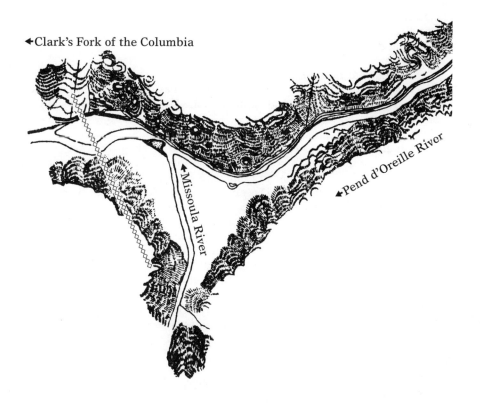

Clark's Fork of the Columbia

Missoula River

Pend d'Oreille River

Redrawn from "Plan Showing the Line of the Western Boundary of the Flathead Indian Reservation," enclosure with Peter Ronan to Commissioner of Indian Affairs, March 10, 1891, LR 9,930, RG 75, National Archives, Washington, D.C.

Line of white diamonds is western boundary of the Flathead Reservation. Caption on the negative copy in the National Archives is "Western Boundary of Flathead Indian Reservation As established by Maj. Peter Ronan and I. S. P. Weeks from Landmarks pointed out by Indians in Dec. 1881."

March 21, 1891
From Incoming Correspondence, reel 7, Indian Rights Association Records, 1864-
1968, Collection 1523, Historical Society of Pennsylvania, Philadelphia, Penna.

United States Indian Service,
Flathead Agency,
March 21st, 1891.

Hon. Herbert Welsh,
Indian Rights Association,
Philadelphia.

Dear Sir:

I received your favor of March 6th, 1891, and also copies of publications of Indian Rights Association, for which I am very thankful to you. With the exception of one I believe I am the oldest commissioned Agent in the service, having been appointed by President Hayes, in 1877, and on the 1st day of June next shall be fourteen years in continuous service as Agent.

The Indians of this reservation are in comparative prosperous condition.

Nearly all of them live in houses and are tillers of the soil and raise cattle and horses; they have well fenced fields and farms, and each year increases their acreage of cultivation. They receive no regular rations from the Government, and there is no issue of beef. Supplies are furnished each year on my requisition, which are issued to the old and the indigent. The Department also furnishes some clothing, etc., but the bulk of issues are wagons, plows, harness and all kinds of agricultural implements, and seeds. Last year the Indians had an abundant yield of grain and vegetables as the season was unusually good, and plenty of rain fell. The success of last year stimulated them to unusual efforts in cutting rails during the past winter and in fencing new fields and enlarging old ones. Although the winter was beautiful up to the first of February, an unusual amount of snow fell since that date. The Spring is backward and the country is still covered with snow; but I trust we will be able to commence to plow by the 1st of April.

Commissioner Morgan has given attention to the wants and necessities of these Indians whenever the matter was brought before him, and I know of no trouble or complaint among them.

I forward to your address a little book entitled "History of the Flatheads, their Wars and Hunts," etc., which I prepared for a newspaper and from its columns it was transferred into book form. The little work may be of interest to you and to your society. Trusting that I may hear from you again.

I am very respectfully yours
Peter Ronan,
United States Indian Agent.

March 23, 1891
LR 11,675 /1891, RG 75, National Archives, Washington, D.C.

Bureaucratic delays forced the Bitterroot Salish to wait in limbo for two years after the 1889 agreement to move to the Jocko Reservation. They lost the 1890 and 1891 growing seasons, which, compounded with the 1889 drought, plunged them into desperate poverty. The Commissioner of Indian Affairs finally wrote Ronan on April 29, 1891, that Congress had approved money for the removal. The draft of instructions to Henry B. Carrington was not submitted to the Secretary of the Interior until June 30, 1891.[20]

United States Indian Service,
Flathead Agency,
March 23d, 1891.

Hon. Commissioner Indian Affairs,
Washington, D.C.
   Sir:
   As reported on other occasions, I have the honor to state now, that in No-
vember, 1890 [i.e., 1889], General H. B. Carrington, of Massachusetts, as Special
Agent of the Indian Department, obtained the consent of Charlot's band of
Bitter Root Flathead Indians to their removal to this reservation, and to the ap-
praisement of their lands for sale, in accordance with the provisions of an "Act
to provide for the sale of lands patented to certain members of the Flathead
Indians in Montana, and for other purposes."
   The Indians profess to believe that a promise was made by the Special
Agent, that if they promptly complied with the wishes of the Department, by
agreeing to the sale of their lands, that arrangements would be made in the
winter of 1890, for the sale of the land and a removal of the families from the
Bitter Root valley to this reservation not later than March, 1890, in order to
give them an opportunity to select their new homes on the reserve — fence
small fields, plow and cultivate the same to enable them to harvest small crops
in the fall as a beginning towards self support on the reservation. Believing
that this arrangement would not be carried out as early as the Indians antici-
pated, I went to Bitter Root Valley in early spring of last year, and advised the
Indians to cultivate their land that season, and if the order came for the sale of
their land and their removal to the Jocko Reservation, arrangements would be
made to allow them to sell or harvest their growing crops for their own use and
benefit. Relying upon what they considered a promise from the Great Father
in Washington, that their removal was assured in early spring, they neglected
their fields until it was too late to plant. This left them entirely destitute. If it
were not for your timely instruction by telegram, dated January 12th, 1891,
confirmed by letter of the 14th of the same month — Finance 38635 – '90 –
Telegram 673 – '91 – Authority 25479, by which I was authorized to expend
the sum of one thousand five hundred dollars in open market purchase at the
lowest obtainable prices of subsistence supplies and other necessities of life
for issue to Charlot's band of Bitter Root Flathead Indians, they would have to
face hunger and nakedness. This timely expenditure was a boon and a blessing
to the Indians. Chief Charlot expressed his gratitude warmly and stated that
himself and band were ready to obey any order to remove from the Bitter Root
valley to this reservation. He has now sent an Indian to ask what orders I have
to give him, as the season for cultivating the soil is rappidly advancing. I sent
word to the Chief that I was not yet apprised if Congress had made any provision at its last session looking to the carrying out of the Carrington agreement
for the sale of their lands and the removal of the families to this reservation,
and that I would appeal to the Honorable Commissioner of Indian Affairs for
advice and instructions in regard to their movements this spring, and communicate his wishes to them.
   There are in the neighborhood of forty families yet with Chief Charlot
in the Bitter Root valley, and if they are not assisted and encouraged by an
issue of seed, and assistance in plowing their land they will be left entirely
for support to the charity of the Government, if not speedily removed to this

reservation or encouraged to cultivate their fields in the Bitter Root valley as stated.

I am very respectfully
Your obedient servant,
Peter Ronan
U.S. Indian Agent.

April 1, 1891

LR 12,808 /1891, RG 75, National Archives, Washington, D.C.

Ronan was particularly pleased to report the establishment of thirty new farms among the Kootenai Indians settled at Dayton Creek on the northern end of the reservation. After many requests, in 1890 the government had finally hired a farmer to work with the Kootenai. Robert Irvine, a mixed blood, was chosen. See Ronan's October 31, 1890b, letter and annotation for biographical information about Irvine.

United States Indian Service,
Flathead Agency,
April 1st, 1891.

Hon. Commissioner Indian Affairs,
Washington, D.C.
Sir:

In reporting from this Agency for the month of March, I have to state that the snow storms which commenced about the 15th of February, and covered the ground at this Agency, at the first of March, to a depth of nearly two feet, continued all through the month. The snow to-day, however, has disappeared from the valleys, but the ground is too wet to commence plowing. A couple of days of Chinook wind and sunshine will dry up the soil, and I look for plowing to commence in earnest next week. This is a late Spring, and the plowing and preparing of ground for planting must be commenced with energy soon as the soil will permit the turning of the sod.

The unusual spring moisture of the soil, produced by the late snow storms, is looked upon as a harbinger of bountiful crops and the Indians are preparing to put in a larger acreage than was ever before cultivated on the reservation. This may be particularly said of the Kootenai band on this reserve, who heretofore have been very hard to induce to give up their hunting and wandering proclivities for the cultivation of land, and attendant toil. The appointment of a farmer to reside at their village, which is about sixty miles from the Agency had a good effect, and he reports that over thirty new farms were commenced by the Kootenais, by splitting and hawling rails and enclosing the same since January 1st of this year. A continuation of their industry must be encouraged by assistance in plowing and sowing their fields. Thanks to the Indian Department for the liberal supply of seed for this year, which will enable me to furnish a fair start to those new beginners in agricultural pursuits.

A great number of the logs which were hawled to the saw mill by Agency employes, during the sleighing season of February and March, have been cut into lumber and shingles, and during the past two weeks, I have had erected entirely by Agency employes, and with aid of Indians working for supplies, an addition to the saw mill, which is forty-eight feet long, twenty feet wide, and two stories high. The lower floor is intended for the matching and plaining machine; the shingle machine, and also for a cut-off saw. The upper floor will be used for the storing of choice lumber for seasoning, and for lumber intended for finishing purposes.

Everything pertaining to the prosperity and advancement of the Indians on this reservation seem to be in prosperous condition. Outside of of [sic] jealousies and bickerings between the halfbreeds and the Indians, there is no cause for complaint or anxiety. The latter were not pleased with the superior evidence of comfort and prosperity surrounding the halfbreeds, who owe their thrift to superior knowledge and a more practical adaptibility to civilizing pursuits.

Herewith I have the honor to enclose sanitary report and report of funds and indebitness and also report of farmers and have the honor to be

Very respectfully
Your obedient servant
Peter Ronan
United States Indian Agent.

April 20, 1891
LR 15,179 /1891, RG 75, National Archives, Washington, D.C.

United States Indian Service,
Flathead Agency,
April 20th, 1891.

Hon. Commissioner Indian Affairs,
Washington, D.C.
Sir:

In my regular monthly report from this Agency, dated January 2d, 1891, I stated that during the holidays much excitement prevailed, etc.; that I closed up the warehouses and announced to the Indians that no supplies, clothing or anything else would be issued to them until the Indian Judges, Police, and head men announced to me that dancing, gambling and drinking was suppressed on the reservation, and I kept them so closed for several days until such announcement was made. I stated also that a couple of rival Indian politicians — Big Sam and Louison — who wished to obtain from among the more reckless and non-progressive young Indians, a following which would silence the quiet and progressive people into submission, I believed to be responsible for all the trouble, as each of them desired to take the place of Chief Arlee, deceased. Both were of the opinion that vigorous denouncement of the Agent and the tyrany of the Indian Department in trying to induce them to follow the ways of the whiteman in civilizing pursuits would capture this class to their support. As each of these ambitious Indians adopted the same tactics, they still continue their annoyance and try to outrival each other in encouraging the young men to neglect their work and to gather to-gether and indulge in dances which are prohibited by the laws governing the Indians on the reservation, and the rules of civilization and religion. They ride around and about the farms in paint and blankets jeeringly, and to the annoyance and demoralization of the young men, especially, of industrious habits. Both of the Indians named are well off and therefore have greater influence for good or evil. While they refrain from such action personally, Indians inform me that they are responsible for its continuance. It is demoralizing to the Indians of this reservation to have these dances go on, as the excitement draw young men from civilizing pursuits, who otherwise would devote themselves to the labor of cultivating their fields. This element has grown so strong in the Jocko valley, that they defy the efforts of fifteen policemen who are in service here, and they should be taught a lesson. I desire to say that I wish to enforce discipline and good order by suppressing this demoralizing dance. I would therefore ask that I may have authority to call upon the military at Fort Missoula, to back up the efforts of the Indian police, should it become necessary to enforce the breaking up of the dances and the arrest of the leaders who dare to incite the unrully class of Indians to disobedience of the rules of the Indian Department governing the reservation.

One of these would be Chiefs took it upon himself to warn some thrifty halfbreed cultivators of the soil to desist from plowing or attempting to cultivate their farms, as the full bloods intended to drive them from the reserve and to occupy their well improved farms. I assured these people that their rights would be protected, and I trust that the Honorable Commissioner will give me assurance that I will be upheld against this element who seek to undo all the good which has heretofore been accomplished among these Indians. This unruly element principally belong [to] the Bitter Root Flathead Indians, but is mostly confined to the young men abetted by the two old men named. They are averse to all police restraint, and the two older men in their councils claim when the Garfield agreement was made, under which they moved here, that they were promised by General Garfield that on the reservation they should be under no restriction but left free to indulge in their old Indian customs. It is needless to add that General Garfield never gave any such promise, but some old Indians are using this argument among the young men to break down the influence of the Agent and to cause bitter feelings against the police whose duty it is to prevent indulgance of the young men in this demoralizing dance, which leads to im[m]orality and idleness.

I am respectfully
Your obedient servant,
Peter Ronan
U.S. Indian Agent.

April 22, 1891
LR 15,585 /1891, enclosure of LR 36,238/1891, RG 75, National Archives, Washington, D.C. The tracing Ronan referred to was not filed with this letter in the National Archives but can be found in the version of the letter published in The Anaconda Standard *in 1892.[21]*

> This report on removing the obstructions for salmon from the Clark Fork River resulted from a March 24, 1891, inquiry by Senator W. F. Sanders to the Commissioner of Indian Affairs. On June 22, 1891, the Commissioner of Indian Affairs drafted instructions for Ronan to investigate the matter further, but the instructions were not approved by the Secretary of the Interior. On October 7, 1891, the Secretary directed the Commissioner of Indian Affairs to refer the matter to the United States Fish Commissioner.[22] In September 1892 the Fish Commissioner sent an engineer to inspect the rapids at the foot of Flathead Lake, Thompson Falls, and Sand Point, Idaho.[23]
>
> Wilbur Fisk Sanders was Senator from Montana from 1890 to 1893. He was a prominent lawyer and leader in the Montana Republican party.[24] The Kalispel chief Ronan referred

to in this letter was Chief Michel. See Ronan's September 25, 1887, letter and annotation for more information on him.

United States Indian Service,
Flathead Agency,
April 22d, 1891.

Hon. Commissioner Indian Affairs,
Washington, D.C.

Sir:

In reply to "Land 11171 – 1891," dated at Washington, April 2d, 1891, enclosing a copy of a letter, dated March 24, 1891, from Senator [W. F.] Sanders of Montana, in which he calls the attention of the Indian Office to the great desirability of clearing the obstructions in Clarkes Fork of the Columbia River, so as to allow the salmon free passage up the river and its tributaries to the Flathead Lake and Flathead reservation.

The clearing would result in a great benefit not only to the Confederated tribes of Indians occupying the Flathead reservation, but to the Indian dwellers around Pend 'd Oreille Lake, and down the Kalispel Valley to the Columbia river. Also, it would be a great source of supply to white settlers along Clarke's Fork of the Columbia river and its network of tributaries, and all of the streams and Lakes West of the Rocky Mountains, in the State of Montana.

From my Interpreter, and from the Chief of the Kalispels [Michel], who was born and reared near the falls on Clarke's fork of the Columbia river, I get the following statement: Below the Kalispel Valley, about 35 miles, on the continuation of Clarke's Fork of the Columbia river, which flows out from Pend 'd Oreille Lake, near Sand Point, in Idaho, is encountered the first fall or continuation of rapids; six miles below this is another fall or rapid; below this second fall is a swift rapid or rocky gorge some two hundred feet long — here is where the salmon are baffled on their way up the Clarke's Fork of the Columbia river, and all of the Lakes and rivers of Western Montana, which are tributary to the great Columbia river. On the left side of this rapid, going down, is a narrow outlet, from above the rapids, but it is walled up by a fall about twelve feet high. My informants have often been at this place and witnessed the salmon attempting to leep [sic] the fall, without success. The interpreter states that he has met whitemen at this place, who informed him that by clearing out this fall in the narrow outlet, that there would be no other impedement preventing the salmon from making the run up Clarke's Fork of the Columbia river, and as before stated, into the Pend 'd Oreille Lake, and on up to the Flathead Lake and to all of the rivers and lakes of Western Montana. This is the best information I can obtain, but it would require an examination of the river to verefy the statements. Herewith, I enclose an accurate tracing of all the rivers and creeks flowing into Clarkes Fork of the Columbia river in this direct vicinity, outlining also the reservation with its lakes and rivers, and names of same, wich [sic] cannot be found on any map that I have seen. The tracing is made from my own knowledge of the country, and assistance of my interpreter and the Kalispel Chief before mentioned.

You desire me to report to your office 1st, as to how far in my judgment the Indians of the Flathead reservation would be likely to be benefitted by the proposed clearing out of the river. This information is given in the body of this report and a glance at the enclosed tracing will show many of the numerous

Lakes and rivers on the reservation and tributary to it which would be at once stocked with salmon from the Columbia river were this obstruction removed.

2d. Whether it would be practicable for me to undertake to ascertain where the obstructions are, in that portion of the river indicated by Senator Sanders. To this question I would state that I have traveled over some of that country and it is familiar to me. I can also have the service of the Kalispel Chief and my interpreter to accompany me to the place.

3d. Whether I could make the necessary investigation without seriously interfering with my duties as Agent.

To this I would say that as the Month of July is proper time to witness the salmon making their efforts to ascend the falls, and as in that month the rush of directing the Indians in field and farms is over and there is a lull in their pursuits until harvest commences in August, the necessary investigation would not seriously interfere with my duties as Agent.

As to the 4th question in regard to the probable expense, I believe four hundred dollars would cover railroad fare, steamboat fare, hire of horses and row boats, and the expense of guide, interpreter, and any outside work I might be compelled to pay for.

You state that you would be pleased to have any proper suggestions in regard to the matter, and any information that would be of interest in regard to the present supply of salmon in the streams coursing the reservation etc., etc.

In reply to this matter I would respectfully state that the fall designated on the enclosed tracing, on the American side, and near the International boundary line, on Clarke's Fork of the Columbia river, prevent the salmon from coming up the river, and there they stop, as far as the American waters are concerned, drained by Clarke's Fork of the Columbia river. Just below the fall, it will be noticed on the tracing, that Salmon river empties its waters into Clarkes Fork of the Columbia river; but Salmon river heads up and runs through the British possessions. As it joins the river just below the fall it is well stocked with salmon.

All of the rivers and Lakes, as shown on the tracing, abound with trout, which run up from the lakes, where they winter, to spawn in the rivers and brooks and swarm into the mountain lakes at the head of the streams, particularly at the head of the Jocko, where they are caught from the month of May until October, as fast as a hook can be dropped into the water. In the Jocko and other mountain lakes, the trout do not seem to vary in size, being beautifully speckled and averaging not over a quarter of a pound each. These small trout remain in the lakes at the head of the streams in the winter season as well as in the summer.

There are three species of trout which run up those streams from the large lakes to spawn in the spring, that grow very large. It is common to catch them weighing from nine to fifteen pounds, and sometimes larger. They are calle[d] by some people "Land Locked Salmon!" — T[hey] have not the slightest appearance of salmon. One specie has a hook resembling the beak of a bird on the lower jaw — are thick and flat and have beautiful dark speckles like the small trout — fish white when cooked. Another of the large species is of the same appearance but longer and not so flat and thick — without hook in the jaw but darkley speckled like the first. The third is of a salmon tinge, with speckles a shade lighter. Has same color of salmon when cooked.

While no complaint can be made in regard to quality and quantity of trout in the streams coursing the reservation, it is lamentable that this obstruction is allowed to remain in Clarke's Fork of the Columbia river, to turn back the myriads of salmon, which otherwise would swarm the the [sic] American streams of Western Montana, into the waters of British Columbia.

Trusting that the Honorable Commissioner of Indian Affairs will have returned to me the enclosed tracing or copy of same.

I am very respectfully
Your obedient Servant
Peter Ronan
United States Indian Agent.

May 1, 1891
LR 17,249 /1891, RG 75, National Archives, Washington, D.C.

Joseph Barnaby, Jr., robbed Red Owl or Louison, a well-to-do tribal judge. Barnaby was born in 1860 which would have made him 31 years old in 1891. In October 1891 he was again in trouble with the authorities and was convicted of disturbing the peace. According to newspaper reports in May 1892, he was shot by another Indian in Horse Plains and needed an arm amputated, but Ronan reported in his June 1, 1892, letter that Barnaby refused the operation. In the 1890s he appeared in Missoula Justice Court for various alcohol related offenses. About 1899, he was operating a small store in the Jocko Valley. He related stories to Louisa McDermott, the teacher at the Jocko Agency school, about Indian medicine. Barnaby was killed in a railroad accident while returning from a trip to Missoula to buy supplies for his store.[25] For information on Louison, see the Biographical Sketches.

United States Indian Service,
Flathead Agency,
May 1st, 1891.

Hon. Commissioner Indian Affairs,
Washington, D.C.
Sir:

I have the honor to furnish my regular report for the month of April, and in doing so it gives me pleasure to state that never in the history of this reservation have the Indians shown so much industry in the cultivation of their lands. New farms have been commenced this spring in every agricultural valley on the reservation. Plentiful rain has fallen and the season bids fair to be good for crops of every description. The Kootenai Indians who are settled around Dayton Creek, some sixty miles from the Agency, heretofore have been, as a rule, thriftless vagarants [sic], are now, under the supervision of the Farmer, authorised to be appointed on the first of January last, doing excellent work in the way of cultivation of the soil. The Farmer reports twenty-two Indians of the Kootenais, who never farmed, induced to begin; the plowing and planting of eleven hundred and fifty acres, the building of 4,200 rods of fence and the erection of five houses. This I look upon as a good beginning this year for the future advancement and civilization of the Kootenai Indians of this reservation.

On the 10th of March, 1891, I had the honor of making special report to your office in regards to the survey of that portion of the Flathead reservation lying West of Flathead Lake and North of Clarkes Fork of the Columbia, surveyed by Edmund P. H. Harrison, United States Deputy Surveyor, under his contract No. 208, dated April 18, 1887. I beg that this matter may meet your speedy attention, as settlers are attempting to take up and improve the land while the Indians are determined that they shall not until it is definately settled where the point on Clarkes Fork of the Columbia, spoken of in the Stevens treaty, as being the boundary is situated. As will be noticed in said report, it is claimed by the Indians that said survey designates the boundary point on the Pend 'd Oreille river, which empties into Clarkes Fork of the Columbia, instead of the point designated in the Treaty as being on the latter river. If this matter is not soon attended I fear trouble between the Indians and settlers, and again ask for instruction.

On Tuesday night, April 28, the house of a well to do Indian, who slept with his family in an adjoining cabin, was broken into and cash to the amount of two hundred and seventy dollars, besides clothing were stolen. An attempt was made to fire the building in order to cover up the crime. When the affair was reported at the Agency, steps were at once taken to capture the criminal. Suspicion fell upon a halfbreed named Joe Barnaby, who disappeared from the Agency after the burgalary was committed. He was arrested in Missoula, and I have to day from the County Prosecuting Attorney the following:

"We tried Joe this morning and gave him ninety days in jail and one hundred dollars fine. This is the limit, unless we bound him over to the District Court, and I was afraid to do this because the question of jurisdiction to punish an Indian for an offense committed against another Indian on the Reservation would surely be raised. Joe is guilty and ought to be sent to the penitentiary, but under all circumstances this is the best we could do."

Herewith I have the honor to enclose sanitary report and report of funds and indebtedness, and also report of farmers, and have the honor to be

Very respectfully,
Your obedient servant,
Peter Ronan
United States Indian Agent.

May 15, 1891
Missoula Weekly Gazette, *May 20, 1891, page 12, col. 3.*
Caution to Stockmen.
A Bit of Correspondence That Will Prove of Interest to All Concerned.
The following correspondence between the government, Indian Agent Ronan and Kootenai Farmer Irvine is self-explanatory and should serve as a guide to all stockmen having cattle on the Flathead Indian reservation:

United States Indian Service,
Flathead Agency,
May 15, 1891.

To whom it may concern:

Robert H. Irvine, Farmer for the Kootenai Indians:

It is hereby ordered that all cattle illegally grazing upon this reserve be driven off by their owners on or before the 15th day of July, 1891. Should any owner of such stock not conform with this order, the cattle or other stock may be rounded up by the Indian police and driven beyond the boundaries of the reservation, and each owner may expect that a sufficient number of his herd will be taken by the Indians to pay for the trouble and expense incurred in such round-up and drive. The following are the orders from the Indian office relating directly to this matter:

"Peter Ronan, U.S. Indian Agent, Flathead Indian Agency, Montana:

As relates to cattle trespassing on your reservation, you will adopt the following plan: The brands and marks so herded to be ascertained and a list of the owners secured; the said owners to be given a certain time to round up their cattle and drive them off the reservation. If they fail to do so in the time allowed, the Indian agent to order the Indian police to make the round-up and drive the stock off the reservation and thereafter to exercise the utmost vigilance in seeing that all stock illegally grazing on the said reservation is driven beyond the limits of the same.

You are directed to put the same into operation."

The above is signed by the commissioner of Indian affairs.

As Indian Farmer, Robert N. Irvine is directed to put the order in operation.

Very Respectfully,
Peter Ronan,
U.S. Indian Agent.

June 1, 1891
LR 20,629 /1891, RG 75, National Archives, Washington, D.C.

For information on Baptiste Kakashee see Ronan's February 12, 1885b, letter and annotation. No information was located about Fish Hawk of the Umatilla Reservation.

United States Indian Service,
Flathead Agency,
June 1st, 1891.

Hon. Commissioner Indian Affairs,
Washington, D.C.
Sir:

At the close of the month of May, I have the honor to state that all industries connected with this Agency are in good condition and that the season so far has been very superior for growing crops. Rain has fallen plentifully and every indication gives hope for a bountiful harvest of every description. The Indian dancing that I reported has subsided since I called a Council of the Indians and informed them that unless it was suppressed by the Indian police, military force would be called upon and the leaders arrested. It may be commenced again, but as the Commanding officer at Fort Missoula has notified me of his readiness to assist in suppressing any insubordination, and as the dancing element is fully aware of the fact, I think they will scarcely attempt it again this summer.

Outside of this dancing craze which is confined to the young gamblers and roughs of the tribes, and not general, the conduct of the Indians is good. In connection with this subject I herewith attach a letter from a Nez Percie Indian to one of the chief men of this reservation, which would seem to indicate that this uncivilizing practice is spreading on other reservations.

The great rush of migration to the head of the Flathead Lake caused by the building of the Great Northern Railroad through that country, has brought immense amounts of freight to Ravalli, on the Northern Pacific Railroad. Ravalli is situated on this reservation, and with stage lines, freight trains and travelers the road is lined from that station to the foot of Flathead Lake, where freight and passengers are transferred to steamboats, which ply to Demersville, at the head of navigation. This constant travel and rush of business on this route, which runs through the reservation, is ever fraught with vexatious troubles, and the Indian Agent is called upon to settle the matters. It seems that no other route of travel is practicable to the Flathead country until the Great Northern Railroad will be completed across the range to the to the [sic] Western slope of the Rocky Mountains. I expect trouble and turmoils on this public road through this reservation during the summer, but shall try to promptly meet and check the disagreeable element that crowd to the frontier while a great railroad is in course of construction. The building of the Northern Pacific Railroad through this reservation has made me somewhat familiar with detail in regard to suppressing lawlessness upon the reservation from such an invasion.

The flour mill has been in operation since the 15th of May. A number of Indian farmers who have been successfully cultivating the soil, had a surplus of grain after their spring seeding, and they brought it to the mill to be ground into flour for family consumption until the new crops are harvested.

The farmer for the Kootenai Indians is now out on special orders from this office connected with reporting the number of cattle illegally grazing on the reservation and the names of the owners of the same. Upon his return I shall make special report to your office.

Herewith I have the honor to enclose Sanitary report and report of funds and indebtedness, and also report of Agency farmer, and have the honor to be

Very respectfully,
Your obedient servant,
Peter Ronan,
U.S. Indian Agent.

Enclosure:

United States Indian Service,
Umatilla Agency,
May 20, 1891.

Ka-Ka-sha
Arlee Montana
Dear Friend:
I have received a letter from the Warm Springs reservation the Indians are talking about the lines of the reservation it is now settled where the lines are now perhaps some of the warm spring indians will come here to spend the 4th. The Yakima Indians are also Coming over. Chief Joseph will be here in a day or two and also the Lapwai people are coming. I think they are coming from all the Reservations near. We will have horse races dances and elokeuy [sic] fun.

Liquor will not be permitted on the Reservation. Write soon.

Fish Hawk.

June 10, 1891

LR 21,659 /1891, RG 75, National Archives, Washington, D.C.

As Ronan described, the construction of the Great Northern Railroad during 1891 spawned a crush of freight and passengers from Ravalli to Polson. Duncan McDonald's hotel, store, restaurant, stables, and blacksmith shops at Ravalli stood to prosper handsomely from the business. McDonald did not appreciate the competition from a restaurant on the railroad right-of-way which offered cheaper meals. On June 26, 1891, the Commissioner of Indian Affairs decided the government could not protect McDonald from competition.[26] On July 14, 1891a, Ronan reported that the Missoula Superintendent of the Northern Pacific Railroad negotiated a truce between McDonald and the competing restaurant. The section house restaurant could continue to serve meals to the traveling public, but agreed to not use runners to advertise for business.

At the same time McDonald was running into competition, T. M. Adams opened a stage line between Ravalli and Polson to compete with the stage line run by Charles Allard. The competition between the two lines resulted in free transit from Ravalli to Polson. Allard finally absorbed the Adams line, ending the price war.[27] Presumably at the instigation of McDonald and Allard, Baptiste Kakashe and the tribal leaders in the Mission Valley demanded grazing fees from the freighters and possibly the competing stage line operation on the reservation.[28] For biographical information on Charles Allard see the annotation to Ronan's March 25, 1892b, letter; and for Duncan McDonald see the annotation to Ronan's February 4, 1878a, letter.

United States Indian Service,
Flathead Agency,
June 10th, 1891.

Hon. Commissioner Indian Affairs,
Washington, D.C.

Sir:

In my report for the month of May, I mentioned that the great rush of migration to the Head of Flathead Lake, caused by the building of the Great Northern Railroad through that country, has brought immense amounts of freight to Ravalli on the Northern Pacific Railroad. Ravalli is situated on this reservation, and with stage lines, freight trains, and travelers the road is lined from that station to the Foot of Flathead Lake where freights and passengers are transferred to steamboats that ply to Demersville, at the head of navigation. This constant travel and rush of business on this public route, which runs through the reservation, is ever frought with vexatious questions. Ravalli is naturally thronged with hungry travelers. Duncan McDonald, the licensed half breed trader at that point, in connection with his trading post, keeps a lodging house and restaurant, and it seems is agrevated [sic] because at the Section house that is owned by the Company, and situated on the Northern Pacific right of way, where meals are furnished to the Company work men, the keeper also furnishes meals to travelers who are not employes of the Railroad Company. McDonald claims sole right to this business, even though, it is stated, he charges more for entertainment than is charged at the Section house. The railroad Company complain that sufficient accomodations are not given by the trader and claim that if travelers desire to get meals at the section house maintained for the accomodation of railroad employes, at lower rates than given by the trader, their passengers and the men employed in hawling and handling freight from their depot have the right to eat their meals at their house on the right of way, if the keeper of the same desires to furnish accomodation.

Herewith I enclose the letter of McDonald, and trust that you will give me soon as practicable a decision in regard to the right of the trader and that of the railroad company and travelers in case cited.

I am very respectfully
Your obedient servant
Peter Ronan
U.S. Indian Agent.

Enclosure:

Ravalli, Montana, June 8th, 1891

Maj. P. Ronan
U.S. I. Agent
Flathead Agency
    Dear Sir
    Now I dont want you to think that I am putting some authority upon my shoulders regarding my business at Ravalli But Right is right and business is business if you dont check the white people here they will have a town of their own and some of these days we shall see a serious trouble between them & Indians. Section House & the Depot is already turned it to Hotels. When the Government Also the R. R. Co. agreed with the Indians not to permit any one to conflict with our business especially when we can do the work just as good as a white man. Now I have courteously written you these few lines to see if you can stop it. it is hard for me especially a member to furnish bonds & let the whites come before my nose & carry on business scatt free.

Yours Very truly
DMcDonald.

July 1, 1891
LR 24,117 /1891, RG 75, National Archives, Washington, D.C.

> For information on Col. George L. Andrews, of Fort Missoula, see the annotation to Ronan's July 1, 1889, letter.

United States Indian Service,
Flathead Agency,
July 1st, 1891.

Hon. Commissioner of Indian Affairs,
Washington, D.C.
    Sir:
    At the close of the month of June, I have the honor to report that the season so far bids fair to be prolific. The crops look well, and the continuous rains of June have advanced the growth and appearance of an abundant harvest.

The Indian cultivaters, at the first of the month, commenced to bring in their surplus wheat left over from sowing their fields, and it was ground into flour at the Agency mill, for family use.

On the 15th of the month the saw mill was started and has been running since that date, cutting into dimension lumber and shingles, the logs delivered by the Indians for their individual use.

All industries among the Indians have favorably progressed, and but for a few provoking causes, happiness, and progressiveness would mark their advance into civilization and comfort.

The first and chief cause I would mention, is the craze which now exists more than I have ever known heretofore, to engage in a demoralizing dance, which, when started, is the sure forerunner of gambling, debauchery, drinking, and breaking of family ties. Under the date of April 20th 1891, I made a special report in regard to this matter, and was honored by your reply dated May 1st 1891 — Land 15179 – 1889 [i.e., 1891]. I was also in receipt of the following letter.

> "Fort Missoula
> Montana
> May 18 1891
>
> Peter Ronan
> U.S. Indian Agent
> Flathead Agency, Montana
>   Sir:
>   I have the honor to inform you, I have this day received authority to comply with such request as you may make for aid to enable you to suppress the disturbing element reported by you to the Commissioner of Indian Affairs, under date of April 20, 1891.
>   I presume it is needless for me to say I shall do so most willingly.
>
> Very respectfully
> Your obedient serv't
> Geo. L. Andrews
> Col. 25th Inf'y, Commanding.["]

Armed with such authority I made [the] disturbing element clearly understand that the dance would no longer be tolerated, and that if the police could not suppress it, military aid would be called upon to assist the Indian police in arresting the leaders of insubordination. This had its effect, until present date, when, taking advantage of the preperation to celebrate the 4th of July in adjacent towns, I was informed by this questionable element of Indians, that it was their intention to celebrate also by a dance to last two days. My orders are, that the dance shall not proceed, under penalty of arrest of the leaders by the Indian police, and if they cannot accomplish such arrest, then I shall call upon the troops at Fort Missoula. I deem this necessary to preserve order and obedience, to the rules of the Department, and for the best interest of the Indians of this reservation — to preserve, also, the discipline which is necessary to controll the insubordinate young Indians, who scoff at labor and civilizating [sic] pursuits. The strong arm of the military may not be necessary to aid in suppression of the dance, but I shall call on such aid if I deem it advisable.

Herewith I have the honor to enclose sanitary report and report of funds and indebtedness, and also report of Farmer, and have the honor to be

Your obedient servant
Peter Ronan,
United States Indian Agent.

July 3, 1891
LR 24,358 /1891, special case 147, Nez Perce Allotments, RG 75, National Archives, Washington, D.C.

> This letter is Ronan's response to the Commissioner of Indian Affairs' June 3, 1891, letter requesting that any Nez Perce tribal members on the Flathead Reservation contact Alice Fletcher to get allotments on the Nez Perce Reservation.[29] Ronan had previously argued that tribal opposition to surveys and allotments would make it unwise to impose the allotment policy on the Flathead Reservation. The conflict and problems surrounding the allotment policy on the Nez Perce Reservation were explored in the published collection of letters written by E. Jane Gay, Fletcher's cook and camp companion at Nez Perce.[30]

United States Indian Service,
Flathead Agency,
July 3d, 1891.

Hon. Commissioner Indian Affairs,
Washington, D.C.
Sir:
Replying to "L. 19413 – 1891," dated at Washington, June 3d, 1891, stating your information that there are a number of Indians entitled by birth to take their allotments on the Nez Perce reservation, who spend considerable portion of the time among the Indians of this reservation.

In response to your order to inform any Nez Perce Indians, residing or visiting for any length of time upon this reservation, that they should apply to Special Agent [Alice] Fletcher, upon the Nez Perce reservation, in person, or by some friend, duly authorized, in writing, for an allotment of land there as soon as practicable. The Indians mentioned make their homes or visiting place around the foot of the Flathead Lake. I have sent the farmer for the Kootenai Indians, to notify the Nez Perces of your wishes, and they will, doubtless, soon report in person or through some authorized friend, to Miss Fletcher, for their allotments of land on the Nez Perce reservation.

I am very respectfully
Your obedient servant
Peter Ronan
United States Indian Agent.

July 6, 1891
LR 24,873 /1891, RG 75, National Archives, Washington, D.C.

> Lucy Finley filed for divorce from Peter Finley in Missoula on January 10, 1891. She charged Peter with abuse. Lucy claimed to be indigent and stated that Peter was worth $2,000. The Missoula court granted the divorce and entered a judgment against Peter for court costs and attorney fees of $138.80.[31] See Ronan's February 14, 1885, letter and annotation for biographical information on Peter Finley.
>
> On July 27, 1891, the Commissioner of Indian Affairs suggested that Ronan allow the state authorities to collect the cash judgement, and use moral suasion and the Court of Indian Offenses to combat the problem of divorce on the reservation.[32]

United States Indian Service,
Flathead Agency,
July 6th, 1891.

Hon. Commissioner Indian Affairs,
Washington, D.C.

Sir:

The Chiefs and head men of this reservation, in a talk held with me recently, deplored a practice which now seems to be spreading among the half breeds, especially, and wish by some means to be relieved from the disgrace and annoyance occasioned. Cases of divorce are now com[m]only brought before the State Court at Missoula, among this class of people occupying homes on this reservation, and it is generally among people of loose habits, who desire the bonds of marriage annulled, in order to marry again or cohabit with other parties on the reservation, and defy the rules governing the same, which strictly prohibit unlawful cohabitation.

I herewith enclose communication to the United States Attorney and also to the Sheriff of Missoula County, and shall try to explain as an illustration of the divorces which so far have been granted to halfbreeds claiming to live under the rules governing this reservation:

Peter Finley owns a good stock ranche on Crow Creek, on this reservation — is an expert in handling stock, and has been frequently engaged by stock purchasers from the East to take charge of transfers from Montana to St. Paul and other Eastern markets. On one of such trips his wife eloped, in his absence, with a halfbreed. Knowing that they could not return and live together on their reservation, they resorted to the State Court, and through a advertisement in one of the County papers, as service of process, divorce was procured, and the couple returned to the reserve to live together, after marriage by Justice of the Peace. The Chiefs and head men claim that such class should be ordered to leave the reservation and take up their residence under the laws which they invoked to procure divorce. The Indians assume that there should be no halfway government over the Indians who claim homes on the reservation, and this party as well as others who secured divorce in a similar manner should be requested to take up their habitation outside of the reservation. They claim that it is useless to try to enforce the sacredness of the mariage ties among Indians, while a halfbreed who is recognized as an Indian can elope with his neighbor's wife, secure a divorce, return to the reservation and settle down in lawful cohabitation, while the tribal laws punish and seperate the Indians guilty of such practice.

I desire, therefore, to be advised if I shall adopt the plan which the tribes suggest: that is not to allow such couples to remain on the reservation.

Herewith I have the honor to attach correspondence in the case of Peter Finley. Trusting that my duty in such cases may be clearly defined by the Honorable Commissioner of Indian Affairs,

I am very respectfully
Your obedient servant
Peter Ronan,
United States Indian Agt.

First enclosure:
        Copy

United States Indian Service,
Flathead Agency,
July 3d, 1891.

W. H. Houston,
Sheriff of Missoula County
Montana
        Dear Sir:
        It has been brought to my attention that you were about to proceed to the Flathead Reservation (Indian) to interfere with Indians under my charge as United States Indian Agent, arising under some process for indebtedness for fees in a divorce case against one Peter Finley. You will please take notice that under my authority as Agent of said Indians, I am required to prevent any such action on the part of any person, the said Peter Finley being an Indian belonging to the Confederated tribes of the Flathead reservation over which I have charge as Agent of the United States. I hope therefore, that you will refrain from taking any action that will make it necessary for me to resist as such Agent, under the laws of the United States.

I am very respectfully
Peter Ronan
United States Indian Agent.

Second enclosure:
        Copy

United States Indian Service,
Flathead Agency,
July 3d, 1891.

Hon. E. D. Weed,
United States Attorney for Montana
        Dear Sir:
        Herewith I enclose to you copy of letter I have this day mailed to W. H Houston, Sheriff of Missoula County, and desire to know if I am correct in the procedure which the letter explains. If the Sheriff insists upon seizing the property of the Indian, Peter Finley, who belongs to the Confederated tribes of this reservation, and whose property is on said reservation, is it not my duty to prevent such seizure, and to call upon you to defend my action? Please inform me at your earliest convenience.
        This divorce business is getting to be a questionable matter among the halfbreeds, especially, on this reservation which will soon be referred to the Commissioner of Indian Affairs, and Secretary of the Interior, but in the meantime I desire to protect an Indian under my charge from seizure of property by the Sheriff, for Court costs in a divorce suit of which he knew little about.

I am very respectfully
Peter Ronan
United States Indian Agent.

July 9, 1891a
LR 25,006 /1891, RG 75, National Archives, Washington, D.C.

United States Indian Service,
Flathead Agency,
July 9th, 1891.

Hon. Commissioner Indian Affairs,
Washington, D.C.
Sir:
Herewith I have the honor to forward for your consideration application of
Alex Dow, Indian Post trader at Arlee, to purchase from Indians enough lumber
for the erection of buildings to accomodate his trade.

I am very respectfully
Your obedient servt
Peter Ronan
United States Indian Agent.

Enclosure:

Alex Dow,
General Merchandise,
Arlee, Mont., July 6th 1891

Peter Ronan Esq.
U.S. Indian Agent
Flat Head Agency, Montana
Sir
As you Are Aware, I have been Conducting my trading Post Where it Was
originally built on the ground belonging to the Northern Pacific right of Way
but have concluded to remove the buildings out of the Rail-road Limit and
upon the land belonging to the Indians of the Confederated tribes[.] I Intend
to put up better and Larger Buildings for the accomodation of Indian Trade.
In doing so I Shall require about twenty five Thousand feet of lumber. And I
desire to know if I can purchase such lumber from Indians, who furnishes logs
at the Agency Mills[.] Such transaction will assist the Indians in making a little
money for their labor, in furnishing logs at the agency mill, and Will Also accomodate me both in reduction of price of material and the trouble and expences
of Shipping the same over the Northern Rail Road. I am under the impression that as Indian Trader I have the rights to procure from the reservation at
proper Compensation all material wich I may require for the construction of
my Trading post. I would thank you to Inform me if I may purchase such lumber as required from Indians who deliver saw logs at the Agency saw mill to be
converted into lumber.

I am Very respectfully
Yours
Alex Dow.

July 9, 1891b
LR 25,090 /1891, RG 75, National Archives, Washington, D.C.

United States Indian Service,
Flathead Agency,
July 9th, 1891.

Hon. Commissioner Indian Affairs,
Washington, D.C.

Sir:

Referring to "A" 6948 – 91, Under date of March 24, 1891, calling attention to receipt of my report of the 18th of February, in relation to the location of Flathead Agency, wherein I agreed with Inspector Gardner, that its present location is a very inconvenient one to a large portion of the Indians; that the benefits which should be derived from mills, shops &c., cannot be availed by those living at a distance of thirty, forty or fifty miles from the Agency, except at a great sacrifice of time, and in view of these facts, I recommended that a new Agency head quarters be established on Crow or Mud Creek, and that the present grist and saw mill, blacksmith and Carpenter shops should be maintained under charge of a Farmer for the benefit of Chief Charlots band of Bitter Root Flatheads. In your reply you stated that no funds were available during the remainder of last fiscal year for the removal or erection of buildings, and that the amount available for the present fiscal year is so limited that the question of expense becomes a vital one in the consideration of the recommendation.

In submitting statement showing the probable cost of the establishment of the proposed new Agency, in view of all the facts, I deem it better to advise the retainment of the present Agency as head-quarters, and to submit a statement showing the probable cost of a subAgency:

A saw mill with all necessary machinery, including engine and boiler, necessary to furnish power to run all required machinery, can be laid down at Ravalli, or any station designated, on this reservation, for two thousand five hundred dollars.

A matching and plaining machine and shingle machine for about six hundred dollars.

A cheap and complete flouring mill on a small scale, I am informed, can be procured from Straub Machinery Company, Cincinnati, Ohio. It consists of one run on wheat and one on corn, and as considerable corn is now raised on the reserve, with a slight added cost, this product might be further encouraged. The price complete, with full specifications, would be, on board, in the city of Cincinnati ($1,075) ten hundred and seventy five dollars — weight about five thousand lbs.

When the saw mill would be set up the cost of getting out lumber and shingles would be comparatively small for the erection of buildings. The grist mill would be the only building which would require immediate outlay, and would cost for a two story building, thirty by forty, about one thousand dollars.

The necessary tools to start a blacksmith and carpenter shop would cost in the neighborhood of two hundred dollars.

The erection of suitable buildings for shops and accomodation of employes, could be done from lumber furnished by the new saw mill and Agency labor. Sash, doors, glass, nails, locks etc., might be quoted at about two hundred dollars. Two teams, with harness and wagons would also be needed, at a cost of about one thousand dollars.

One Carpenter at eight hundred dollars per annum.

One blacksmith at eight hundred dollars per annum.

One farmer at eight hundred dollars per annum.

One miller who could run saw as well as grist mill, also shingle machine and matcher and plainer, and act as engineer, one thousand dollars per annum.

About a thousand dollars would be required for freighting expenses from railroad station; labor of various description and contingent expenses.

In connection with foregoing I would respectfully report that in company with Indians of good judgment, and with approbation of Chief of the Pen'd Oreilles, who resides in the neighborhood, I selected a place on Crow Creek — which is a bold mountain stream of never failing water — the land is unoccupied by any person. Excellent timber of white pine, tamerac and fir grow in the surrounding country and extends far back into the mountains in almost inexhaustable quantities, while good farming, grazing and hay land is also accessable.

I am very respectfully
Your obedient servant
Peter Ronan,
United States Indian Agent.

July 14, 1891a
LR 26,029 /1891, RG 75, National Archives, Washington, D.C.

See Ronan's June 10, 1891, letter and annotation relative to the conflict between Duncan McDonald and the restaurant at the railroad section house at Ravalli. S. G. Ramsey held various positions for the Northern Pacific Railroad between 1886 and 1892. Between 1890 and 1892, he was superintendent of the division of the Northern Pacific headquartered at Missoula. In 1892 he was elected to a term as Missoula County Sheriff.[33]

United States Indian Service,
Flathead Agency,
July 14, 1891.

Hon. Commissioner of Indian Affairs,
Washington, D.C.
Sir:

I have the honor to forward Copy of Communication to S. G. Ramsay, Supt. of the Northern Pacific railroad relative to stage route and other matters at Ravalli upon this reservation.

Very respectfully
Your obt svt,
Peter Ronan
U.S. Indian Agent.

Enclosure:

United States Indian Service,

S. G. Ramsey
Supt.
Northern Pacific Railroad
Missoula, Mont.
Dear sir:

I am in receipt of your letter of July 8th, in regard to your interview with Duncan McDonald, Indian Post Trader, at Ravalli, on this Reservation; Showing him at the time, copy of letter from the Hon. Commissioner of Indian Affairs, dated at Washington, June 25th, 1891; bearing upon the Subject.

I think your action in regard to instructions to boarding house keepers, in right of way at Ravalli not to Solicit or to Send runners to Solicit patronage, very conservative, and to my mind, should be satisfactory to McDonald, in the face of the letter from the Hon. Commissioner of Indian Affairs, Who writes:

"I appreciate the very natural desire of Mr. McDonald to controll this business himself. It can not be done for two reasons. The first is: It is not the practice of the office to grant anywhere an exclusive tradership, if the amount of trade is such, that competition will be of benefit to the Indians.

The Second is: That this office cannot exercise jurisdiction over any legitimate business carried on by a Railroad within its own Right of Way."

You State that McDonald also felt aggrieved about the people located on the Railroad right of way who are in the freighting business between Ravalli and Flathead Lake. Again quoting the same letter from the Hon. Com[m]issioner of Indian Affairs, he Says:

["]I trust that this influx of white people will not lead to any serious difficulty. This inroad of civilization, along established lines of travel is inevitable and the Indians must adjust themselves to the new conditions and the keener competition which it will necessarily involve, bearing in mind that, on the other hand, it gives to them increased value for all that they own and all they can produce."

In regard to your statement that your company has about completed negotiations with the Allard Stage Company, and the Flathead Transportation and Navigation Company, whereby you will ticket people from points on the Northern Pacific, to points on the Lake, and when this is done it practically gives your company a through line.

You ask if it would be good policy under these circumstances to request the people, to whom you have given permission to locate in your right of way, to remove and to extend this privilege to your connecting line only, which is the Allard and let the other parties make such arrangements as they can with them. In other words your connecting lines will act as gobetweens between outside parties and your company. You add that this suggestion is in the interest of harmony, and ask what I think of it.

My opinion is that such an arrangement will be beneficial to the traveling public as well as to the preservation of harmony at Ravalli.

The Allard Stage Company have had the mail contract from Ravalli to the head of the Lake for years, and I have heard of no complaint against them. The Starting of numerous modes of conveyance to connect your travel to the Lake with noisy & boisterous runners for each at the arrival of Trains at Ravalli is at least a nuisance and annoyance.

If any mode can be inaugerated by your company for conveyance of passengers to points on your line of travel from this reservation, which will aim to do justice to all, will receive my hearty co-operation.

In connection, I wish to state that complaints have reached me about people located on the right of way, ostensibly, in the forwarding & freighting business who take advantage of reduced rates which is intended presumably to furnish grain to their own freighters, to take advantage, and undersell the licensed trader on the right of way.

This should not be allowed.

They have no right to trade or sell on the right of way unless it is a legitimate business conducted or authorized by your company.

Very respectfully yours
Peter Ronan
U.S. Indian Agent.

July 14, 1891b
LR 26,030/1891, enclosure of authority 28,510/1891, RG 75, National Archives, Washington, D.C.

Lt. Letcher Hardeman from Fort Sherman in Idaho was from Missouri. He was an 1886 graduate of West Point. In 1901 he was a captain.[34]

United States Indian Service,
Flathead Agency,
July 14th, 1891.

Hon. Commissioner of Indian Affairs,
Washington, D.C.
Sir:

For special report, I desire to refer to Land 7523 – 1891, 16291 – 1891.

The same treats of my communication dated April 29th, 1891, enclosing a letter of April 25th, 1891, from one Richard Fry, relating to the destitute condition of Indians of the Kootnai Tribe in Northern Idaho. In the letter referred to, Mr. Fry states that there is a large migration into the Kootnai country occupied by these Indians, consequent upon the building of the Great Northern Railroad, and the development of mining prospects; that many whites are locating upon the land claimed by the Indians and used by them. Lands that they have selected for themselves and their families and which they and their fathers have owned and cultivated for years, that this encroaching on their lands, is causing much anxiety and dissatisfaction; that a saloon has been established in their midst by whites. To which they — the Indians not only have free access, but are even sought after and induced to enter the same to drink, and gamble, "coming away robbed and filled with fire water"; that the Indians are selling their guns and like articles for one half and even one fourth of their value in order to obtain money with which to buy whiskey; that lives and property are from time to time endangered; and that trouble will certainly follow if the Government does not protect the Indians in their holdings — trouble that may cost thousands of dollars besides the lives of many people. You state the fact that I called attention, by reference, to a former report to your office, dated August 16th 1889, that white settlers and adventurers are being drawn to that country; that but a short time will elapse ere the country will be settled up; that the Indians will be forced and driven from their camping grounds; and that therefore no time should be lost in giving them title to their lands and getting them to work for their sustance [sic]; that these Indians are like children; that they must have a guardian over them — a farmer in charge — or some other authority, other wise they will not do anything for themselves, and that I request in my letter of February 25th, 1891, to be advised of the steps taken by your office in the matter and whether I have any duty to perform in regard to the wants, necessities, and relief of this band of Indians.

In reply, you have to say that your office, on November 25th, 1891, made full and complete report of the matter to the Department, and recommended that the General Land Office be authorized to contract for the survey of the country occupied by these Indians, the cost of the same to be paid out of the appropriation for the survey of public land.

On December 13th, 1889, the Hon. Secretary of the Interior returned to your office the last named report, inviting attention to the report of December 10th, 1889, from General Land Office relative to the proposed survey of the land referred to for allotment under the fourth section of the the Act of Congress approved on February 8th, 1887 (24 Stats., 388)[.]

It was held in said General Land Office report that under the provisions of the appropriation Act of March 2d 1889 (25 Stats., 955) the expense of making desired extension of the requisite standard lines in order to reach the locality of the Kootnai Indians could not legally be made payable from the appropriation of the survey of public Lands for the fiscal year; and neither could the expense of extending the meander, township, and sectional lines of the township embracing the Indian localities, be properly chargeable to the said appropriation, for the reason that the Lands were not occupied in whole or in part by actual settlers, and the further reason that the Agricultural character of the Lands had not been demonstrated as superficially ~~demonstrated~~ required by the existing laws relating to public Land surveys. On April 8th 1890, your office reported to the Department, that in view of the facts in the case, the laws bearing thereon, and the decision of the Department, the Kootnai Indians were manifestly the actual settlers of the lands occupied by them with in the letter and spirit of the Act making appropriation for the survey of public land, and that the Agricultural character of the lands, the survey of which was asked for appeared to be satisfactorily demonstrated and repeated the recommendation of November 25, 1889.

Full statement was made in regard to the request of the Indian Office for a survey of certain lands in Northern Idaho, occupied by the Kootnai Indians. It was also set forth that congress failed to make the necessary appropriation for the survey of the Lands referred to that it was not propable that there would be any funds available during or at the end of the fiscal year for that purpose.

Your letter closed by stating that other steps had been taken for the protection of these Indians in their rights and when the matter is determined I will be advised.

In view of all the foregoing I deemed it necessary to make special report of the turn which affairs have taken among the Indians of the Kootnai tribe referred to, and to state their recent wishes and requests. Eneas, Chief of Kootnai Indians of this reservation, came to the Agency last week and reported that Isaac chief of the Kootnai Indians of Northern Idaho, sent a delegation to his camp at Dayton Creek to request permission that the Indians of the Kootnai tribe be allowed to remove to his vicinity, on this reservation as they concluded to abandon their lands in Northern Idaho, seeing that it was hopeless for them to retain said lands as they were already run over by white settlers, or land grabbers, who in some cases located on Indian claims by force of Arms, or at least an exhibition of that persuasion.

It is also represented to the Indians that the Northern Pacific Land Grant will extend to the Kootnai river, and that their claims to land there will be in endless & hopeless litigation.

Under such circumstances the Kootnai Indians of Northern Idaho, by delegation, beg to privilege to abandon their lands in that country and to take homes on this reservation with the consent of the tribes occupying the same and the permission of the Indian Department to which they appeal for reparation and assistance in their new homes for the Sacrifice they voluntarily make to leave the country they claim by inheritance and to seek new homes in this reservation.

I respectfully submit this matter for your consideration trusting that I may soon be able to give this unfortunate tribe a decisive answer in regard to the decision of the Indian office.

> I am, very respectfully,
> Your obedient servant,
> Peter Ronan
> U.S. Indian Agt.

First enclosure:

Fort Sherman, Idaho, July 22, 1891.

The Assistant Adjutant General
Headquarters Department of the Columbia,
Vancouver Barracks, Washington.

Sir:

I have the honor to report for the information of the Department Commander, that several citizens have represented to me that they have taken up land on or near the Kootenai River, and that the Indians object to their remaining on said land, and have warned them not to stay.

The land in question has never been surveyed, and I have reason to believe, though I may be misinformed, that the Indian title has never been extinguished. It is, I am told, hay land which both Indians and whites want. The whites are uneasy, but I don't think the Indians mean to use violence towards them. I have not deemed it necessary to send troops there yet, and therefore have not recommended it.

I have this moment received your telegram directing me to send troops. They will be started to-morrow. As a railroad is now being built through that region, thousands of white men of all nations are there on the road or coming to settle in the country. It is therefore urgently recommended that the proper authorities take steps at once to settle the land questions that have arisen, and will arise between the Indians and whites.

Whatever may happen, I don't believe the Indians will attack the whites, unless driven to it by rank brutality and injustice. But both whites and Indians should at once have their respective rights defined, and publicly known, in order to prevent future trouble.

> Very respectfully,
> Your obedient servant,
> William P. Carlin,
> Colonel 4th Infantry,
> Commanding.

Second enclosure:

Bonners Ferry, Idaho, July 29, 1891.

The Post Adjutant,
Fort Sherman, Idaho.

Sir:

I have the honor to report that I arrived here on the 27th and have gone into camp near the Indian camp, about two miles below the Ferry.

From what I have learned so far there have been two or three cabins and some fencing torn down by the Indians in the last two or three weeks. There has been some stock stolen in the last year.

There are settlers coming nearly every day to locate land.

The settlers have organized a company of rangers to protect any one, whether Indian or white man, who has legally located ranches. They say that if the Indians do not cease their depredations that some one will be killed.

The rangers promise to do nothing as long as I stay here.

The most reliable settlers are afraid that in some dispute over land some one may be killed, which will set the ball rolling, and this I think is the only way in which any serious trouble may arise.

It will take me a few days longer to complete my investigation.

The trouble will continue to exist until the Indians are permanently located in some way, so under the circumstances I do not know whether to remain or not.

Please advise me.

Very respectfully,

Your obdt servant,

Letcher Hardeman,

2d Lieut. 4th Cavy.

1 Endorsement.

Post of Fort Sherman, Idaho, July 31, 1891.

Respectfully forwarded to Headqrs. Dept. of the Columbia, recommending that Lt. Hardeman be instructed to return to this post after telling Indians not to distrust white people, to complain of any wrong to an Indian Agent.

William P. Carlin,

Colonel 4th Infantry

Commanding

* * * * *

2d Indorsement.

Headqrs. Dept. of the Columbia,

Vancouver Barracks, Wash., August 3, 1891.

Respectfully forwarded to the Adjutant General of the Army.

It is urgently recommended that the proper authorities have their attention called to the grave necessity of having the land in question surveyed at the earliest possible moment, that the Indians may be permanently located, their rights defined and publicly known.

It is generally believed that the Indian title has never been extinguished; the question should be settled at once. If this state of affairs is allowed to continue unchecked, serious trouble is apprehended.

Attention is respectfully invited to report on this matter made last year and forwarded to the Adjutant General of the Army (thro' Headqrs Div. of the Pacific) on June 20, 1890. Also copies of correspondence herewith leading to orders directing movement of troops to the Kootenai region.

Instructions are requested by telegraph.

Thomas Ward,

Assistant Adjutant General,

in absence Dept. Commander.

(1 inclo.)

August 1, 1891

LR 28,857/1891, RG 75, National Archives, Washington, D.C.

On July 23, 1891, Inspector James H. Cisney filed a positive inspection report on the Flathead Agency and concluded: "The Affairs of this Agency are well Managed."[35]

United States Indian Service,
Flathead Agency,
August 1, 1891.

Hon. Commissioner Indian Affairs,
Washington, D.C.

Sir:

During the month of July a great deal of rain fell, relieving the necessity of irrigating the growing crops. Haying season has commenced and the Indians are busy engaged in cutting and stacking their hay. The grain and vegetable crops look well and it is expected that the harvest will yield the largest ever gathered on the reservation.

Nothing occured to break the quiet which prevailed during the month, except some drunkeness among the Indians on the 4th of July.

The old Agency buildings need shingling and repairing, and I shall make requisition for logs delivered at the mill to convert into shingles and lumber for that purpose. A pair of good horses and a set of light harness is also required here, and are very necessary. The horses to take the place of the old ones condemned by an Inspector over a year ago.

During the month Inspector [James H.] Cisney visited the Agency and school, and seemed to be favorably impressed with administration of affairs here.

General Henry B. Carrington "Special and Disbursing Agent Removal of Flatheads" from Bitter Root valley to this agency is now in that country arranging for their removal. Having no instructions in this matter from the Hon. Commissioner of Indian Affairs, I await the result of the Special Agent's negotiations, and instructions from your office.

I have the honor to enclose here-with letter from one Richard Fry in regard to the trouble now pending between the Kootenai Indians of Northern Idaho, and the white jumpers of their lands. Fry is an old settler there — has a Kootinai Indian wife and is the father of a large half-breed family. I have brought this matter before the attention of your office on other occasions, and deem it not necessary to enter into any further details now.

All industries connected with the Agency are in good condition, and I have the honor herewith to enclose Sanitary report, and report of funds and indebtedness, and also report of farmers.

Very respectfully
Your obedient servant
Peter Ronan
United States Indian Agent.

Enclosure:

Fry Idaho July 24 91

Mr Ronan

Sir

My sons wife has located the land for two of her children and done about one hundred dollars worth of plowing on it and fenced it in[.] she has made application at the land office for the allotment according to law[.] this same land has been Jumped by a man (A. Southworth by name) who has driven off the men sent there to work, on one occation he knocked one man down with a club and forced him to leave the field with his team, only two days ago he stoped with a mob, a man who was cutting hay, he having cut about ten ton then placed himself on guard and swore he would shoot the first man who came onto the place to work, leaving the hay to spoil[.] there is yet about twenty or thirty ton to be cut but he swears it may not before it shall be cut by his men.

My sons wife has been putting these improvements on the land for the last two years and some of the improved land is seeded to timothy hay. A number of the Indians have made their applications in the land office but have no idea they can hold them against these mobs[.] Now what is to be done in this case. can you advise in the matter. You know about what justice these people can get in the local courts. Hoping to hear from you soon; I remain; Respectfully

R. Fry

(dictated).

August 25, 1891a
LR 31,597/1891, RG 75, National Archives, Washington, D.C.

The application for a traders license at Polson, or the Foot of Flathead Lake, had been submitted to the Commissioner of Indian Affairs by Phillips & McKenney, Washington, D.C., attorneys for Amos J. Thomas. Ronan described Thomas' efforts to trade on the reservation without a license. On March 3, 1892, the Commissioner denied Thomas' application.[36] According to Thomas' application for a traders license, he was born in 1829 in Philadelphia, Pennsylvania, and in 1891 had lived in Missoula County for five years. Statements attached to the application indicate he had been involved in the general merchandise business including selling sewing machines, organs, pianos, and jewelry.[37]

The mixed blood who was serving meals to travelers at Polson was Emily Brown Couture, the wife of Maxime or Mack Couture. She was the person who discovered the body of two murdered white men on the banks of the Jocko River in 1888. She testified at the 1890 murder trial of Lalasee and Pierre Paul, who were hung in Missoula for the crime. One account suggests that in 1891 Emily and Mack were working for Charles Allard and serving meals in Polson to passengers of Allard's stage coach line. In 1895 she married William Irvine, a prominent reservation cattleman, and they rode together in the 1908 roundup of the Pablo buffalo herd.[38]

United States Indian Service,
Flathead Agency,
August 25, 1891.

Hon. Commissioner Indian Affairs,
Washington, D.C.
   Sir:
   Referring to your letter "M" – 28469/'91, dated August 8, 1891, stating that your office is in receipt of application for the issuance of a license to trade at the South end or Foot of the Flathead Lake on the East side of the Flathead River (Pend 'd Oreille River) where it leaves said Lake. You ask if the licensing of an Indian Tradership at that place would be of advantage or disadvantage to the Indians.
   In reply I would state that the point designated is near the steamboat landing on the Flathead Lake, that the tradership would be of advantage there to the traveling public as well as to the Indian settlers in the vicinity, as the nearest trading post to the point is at St. Ignatius, some thirty miles distant.

An attempt was made by a person named Thomas, (who ran a peddling wagon around the reserve until notified to discontinue) to open a store there. When informed by a messenger from me that it was against the regulations of the Indian Department, to allow the sale of goods of any description on the Indian Reservation, without first obtaining license from the Hon. Commissioner of Indians Affairs, it was reported to me that he replied that he had "State and County license and would like to know what authority will prevent him from selling goods." Authority was shown and he desisted from selling goods. I afterwards refused to endorse his application for license to trade on this exhibition of "self reliance" and if he is the person who has made application and the license is granted, it will cary [sic] out his view of doing business against the orders of the Agent of the government who prevented his unlawful trade and show to the Indians and all others that a stand against an Agents authority can be overcome if persisted in.

A worthy halfbreed family are making a living there by furnishing meals to travelers. A request was recently made by the head of said family to recommend that a license be issued to trade and sell supplies as well as care for stock and furnish meals. I shall refrain from any recommendation for tradership at that place at present, or until you decide upon the application now before you.

I am very respectfully,
Your obedient Servant,
Peter Ronan,
United States Indian Agent.

August 25, 1891b
LR 31,598/1891, RG 75, National Archives, Washington, D.C.

The survey of the northern boundary of the reservation had caused problems for Ronan and the tribes and friction with neighboring whites for almost a decade. Much of the conflict had centered on grazing trespass by white owned cattle. In the twentieth century the United States Court of Claims agreed that the survey of the northern boundary of the reservation had been in error.[39] Since the Kootenai had traditionally used some of the land in question for hay and were starting grain farms on the land, Ronan requested permission to issue off-reservation allotments to the Kootenai. On September 7, 1891, the Commissioner of Indian Affairs instructed Ronan to make the allotments.[40] On October 30, 1891, Ronan reported making the allotments and filing the claims with the local land office. In October 1891, the Kootenai occupied the land, had built fences, and had planted grain.

In December 1891, however, armed white men from the head of the lake "jumped" the allotments and forced the Kootenai farmers off. Despite the provocations, Chief Eneas and the other Kootenai leaders were able to convince the younger men to pursue their claims through the white legal system rather than violence. The threats and aggression came just as a delegation of Bonners Ferry Kootenai were visiting Dayton Creek to consider removing from northern Idaho to the Flathead Reservation. The conflict attracted national attention, but a United States Marshal was able to remove most of the white squatters by the end of the year.[41]

The conflict over the Dayton Creek allotments occupied Ronan for the rest of his life. Two white men, Clarence E. Proctor and John Casey, were particularly diligent in finding legal arguments to advance their claims to homesteads in the contested area.[42] The whites dragged out the proceedings in the land office for years and harassed the Kootenai farmers until in 1904 and 1905 the government abandoned its promise and pressured the Kootenai into relinquishing their allotments.[43]

For information on Clarence E. Proctor see Ronan's October 31, 1890a, letter and annotation. The only additional information found about John Casey was that in 1890 he suffered an attack of rheumatism and went to a Yellowstone Valley hot springs for treatment.[44] Two sons of Chief Eneas were on the list of Kootenai allottees at Dayton Creek. Isaac became chief after Eneas' death in 1900 and Koostahtah became chief after Isaac's death in 1903.[45] In 1901, Isaac reinstated the use of the whip in punishment and had Father Augustine Dimier, S.J., bless his tribal police force. On April 3, 1901, Isaac chastened a visiting government delegation trying to buy part of the reservation: "My body is full of your people's lies." Isaac complained, "You told me I was poor and needed money, but I am not poor. What is valuable to a person is land, the earth, water, trees, &c., and all these belong to us. Don't think I am poor. . . . That is all I have to say, and you had better hunt some people who want money more than we do." In 1902, Isaac did consent to be formally enrolled, despite initial objections.[46] Koostahtah was able to protect his allotment from the aggressive white settlers north of the official boundary, but the other Kootenai allottees were driven off their land. Finally in 1904, Koostahtah, the only Kootenai farmer left in the area, was surrounded by hostile white neighbors. Given the unwillingness of the government to fulfill its promise to protect the rights of the Kootenai allottees, Koostahtah decided to relinquish his allotment and move south of the boundary line.[47]

United States Indian Service,
Flathead Agency,
August 25, 1891.

Hon. Commissioner Indian Affairs,
Washington, D.C.

Sir:

I respectfully desire to place special report before you relative to my late visit to the Kootenai Indians residing at Dayton Creek, on this Reservation.

At the urgent request of Chief Eneas and his head men, on the 12th of August, I started out to visit that tribe in order to report to your office, fully, upon their request in regard to certain lands which they honestly considered as rightfully belonging to them under treaty rights, and which they have always occupied.

In my report for the month of January, 1891, it will be found that under my instruction, Robert H. Irvine, a halfbreed, who was appointed farmer for the Kootenai Indians of this Reservation, on the 1st day of January, 1891, proceeded to their Camp or village, and announced your decision to the Indians, communicated in "L" 34244, under date of November 10th, 1890. At that time I stated that I deemed it best to announce your decision, and to urge upon the Indians the necessity of securing their claims to the land by fencing and improving the same. They believed that they were entitled by treaty to the land cut off the Reserve by United States Deputy Surveyor Harrison's line, of that portion of boundary of the Flathead Indian Reservation lying West of Flathead Lake and North of Clarkes Fork of the Columbia river, executed by that gentleman under his contract, dated April 18th, 1887. I explained to the Indians as fully as I could the whole matter and endeavored to convince them that the line is in the strictest accordance with the provisions of their treaty.

In obeyance to my request the following list of Indians, heads of families, and over twenty-one years of age, of the Kootenai tribe, were induced to commence farming and improving the land they claimed by occupancy, outside of the boundary as designated by the Harrison survey. My recent trip was to make personal investigation in regard to such claims and to ask for instructions from your office with view of securing title to the Indians through the local land office at Missoula in the County of Missoula, Montana:

1. Isaac, Son of Chief Eneas.
2. Malta Scoolchee.
3. Malta Cheetscum.
4. William Koomolsel.
5. Bazile Tetataskee.
6. Koostata, son of Chief Eneas.
7. John Eneas, son-in-law of Chief Eneas.
8. Abraham Sook-kuch-alakoo.
9. Patrick Kaska.
10. Matt Kowiltlum.
11. Philip Skoo.
12. Antice Kaowilkukatee.
13. Pell Kookewa.
14. Sipena JeanGrew.
15. Joseph JeanGrew.
16. Paul Chatchaluma.
17. George Kalkanew.

By General Land Office Circular of October 26, 1887, approved by the Department October 27th, 1887, Registers and Receivers everywhere "are enjoined and commanded to permit no entries upon lands in the possession, occupancy and use of Indian inhabitants, or covered by their homes and improvements," and "to exercise every care and precaution to prevent inadvertent allowance of such entries. It is presumed" the circular continues that you "know or can ascertain the localities of Indian possession and occupancy in your respective districts, and you will make it your duty to do so, and will avail yourself of all information furnished you by officers of the Indian service." They are further instructed that "when lands are unsurveyed no appropriation (of lands) will be allowed *within the region of Indian settlements* until the surveys have been made and the lands occupied by the Indians ascertained and defined."

I trust that the Honorable Commissioner of Indian Affairs will readily see the importance of at once giving me the necessary instructions as to proceedure in the local land office, or elsewhere, with blank applications for allotments and any other instructions needful.

The Indians whose names are herewith furnished, fenced in the land, sowed small crops of grain and are now busy harvesting the same. They are very anxious to cultivate their lands and I wish to encourage them by the assurance it will not be taken away from them either by the Government or by the whitemen who are now ready to pounce upon it. Trusting that this mat[t]er will receive your earliest convenience for attention, I am very respectfully,

Your obedient servant
Peter Ronan,
United States Indian Agent.

August 25, 1891c
LR 31,599/1891, RG 75, National Archives, Washington, D.C.

The claims of the heirs of Antoine Koo-koo-wee and Aquois-poo-ka-nee for the Bitterroot lands they improved and farmed were referred to in Henry B. Carrington's 1890 report to the Secretary of the Interior. According to Carrington, Aquois-poo-ka-nee had irrigated his farm and was living on it in 1889. Antoine Koo-koo-wee had lived on his farm for ten years in 1889 and had built a cabin and more than a mile of fence. Koo-koo-wee had raised wheat, potatoes, corn, and grass on his land.[48] No further information was found about Aquois-poo-ka-nee, but Antoine Koo-koo-wee had a large family and left many descendants on the Flathead Reservation. Some used Antoine for their family name and others Cocowee.[49]

Correcting this oversight in the 1872 Bitterroot allotments was never specifically authorized by an act of Congress and the matter dragged on for years.[50] Apparently Carrington accidentally switched the legal descriptions of the farms cultivated by these two men. Consequently, neither man could prove that he occupied the land he claimed as an allotment and the allotments were canceled and homesteads granted to white men in the 1890s.[51]

Anderson Buker, one of the two men Ronan mentioned as responsible for the 1872 allotments, had lost an eye in the Civil War. In 1869, he married a lady named Solitude Mary in Grass Valley, and between 1870 and 1871 was Missoula County Undersheriff. In 1871 he moved to the Bitterroot Valley and in the 1880s was a candidate for county surveyor and a justice of the peace.[52] Washington Hall came to the Bitterroot in 1867 and was Missoula County Surveyor in 1874.[53]

United States Indian Service,
Flathead Agency,
August 25, 1891.

Hon. Commissioner Indian Affairs,
Washington, D.C.
    Sir:
    In response to your letter "Land," dated at Washington, August 11th, 1891, enclosing copy of the printed report of Gen. Henry B. Carrington, upon the matter of appraisment &c., of the lands held by certain Indians of Charlot's band, under patent, in the Bitter Root valley, I proceeded to that place and made close and careful investigation of all the facts in the cases of the two Indians Aquios-poo-ka-nee and Antoine Koo-koo-we, of whom it was stated in Gen. Carrington's report, "have as good claims to the lands occupied by them as any in the valley," although, as verbally stated by the General, in your office, the patents failed to be issued to these two Indians on account of a clerical omission of the allotting Agent.
    I find that the land referred to in General Carrington's report as belonging to Aquois-poo-kanee, belonged to an Indian now deceased, called Lefthand Charley. Said Indian applied for patent on his land and it was surveyed and laid

off for him by the allotting Agent; and it further appeared by the statements of the surveyor of the land, Anderson Buker, who was assistant to Washington Hall, the allotting Agent, that the Indian claimant of the land, Lefthand Charley complied with all the provisions of Section 3 of the Act of Congress of June 5th, 1872, (17 Stats. 226,) which was quoted in your letter. Early white settlers of the valley and Indians concurred in this statement, and the title of the Indian, now deceased, to this land is not disputed although no patent was issued to him on account, as stated by General Carrington, of a clerical omission of the allotting Agent.

The widow and a blind sister of Lefthand Charley, reside in Bitter Root valley and are his proper heirs, and to them and not to Aquois-Poo-Kanee, should the land revert, and relief by given. The widow was absent at the time General Carrington held conference with the Indians, and it may transpire that Aquois Poo-kanee acted for her. General Carrington can question him when he returns to Bitter Root valley — he was absent on a hunt while I was there.

In the case of Antoine Koo-koo-wee: I would state that this Indian died last winter. He left a widow and three sons. All evidence and statements I could obtain, both from white settlers and Indians, and also from the surveyor of the Indian allotments, already mentioned, went to show that Antoine Koo-koo-wee, made proper application for his land to the allotting Agent; that it was surveyed and laid off by said Agent's assistant, Anderson Buker; that the Indian complied with all the provisions of the Act already quoted, and died in the full belief that he left an inheritance to his widow and children.

Anderson Buker, the surveyor, at a meeting of the Indians, when Gen. Carrington first came among them in an official capacity, stated in my presence, and was explicit in his statement, that he discharged his duty fully and that the negligance of Mr. Hall, the allotting agent, should not work to the prejudice of the claimants or their heirs; that he acted for them and that patents should have issued precisely the same as the other Patents issued. Each of them was the head of a family, or twenty-one years of age, and the actual occupant and cultivator of the land for which he claimed a patent, upon abandonment of his tribal relations and complied to his best intent and knowledge with the conditions of the Act of Congress applicable to the case. As a confirmatory proof, the public understand that both tracts are Indian lands and possession by them is not disputed.

I respectfully recommend that the heirs of Lefthand Charley and Antoine Koo-koo-wee, both of whom were entitled to Patent, obtain such relief that justice and fair dealing demand to remedy the hardship to which the heads of the families were subjected through no fault of theirs.

I am very respectfully your ob't. serv't.

Peter Ronan

United States Indian Agent.

August 27, 1891

LR 31,778/1891, RG 75, National Archives, Washington, D.C.

> Ronan made repeated appeals for funds over the years to assist the 15 Bitterroot Salish families who removed to the Flathead Reservation after Chief Arlee's group and before Charlo's removal in 1891. Even when funds were approved for 20 houses on September 14, 1891,

Ronan was told he could not use the money to build houses for any Bitterroot Salish families who removed before 1891.[54]

United States Indian Service,
Flathead Agency,
August 27th, 1891.

Hon. Commissioner Indian Affairs,
Washington, D.C.

Sir:

In reply to your letter "Finance" 28361 – '91 – 11675 – '91, dated August 10th, 1891, stating that you were in receipt of a letter from H. B. Carrington, Special Agent for the removal [of] Charlot's band of Flathead Indians to the Jocko reservation, wherein he states that I have not received instructions as to buildings or other preparations for the arrival of the Flatheads, and had no rations whatever on hand, and neither logs, lumber, nor other material for building purposes.

Reasons for not forwarding estimates not knowing how many families will be removed by Gen. Carrington, or when such removal will take place. I conferred with Mr. Carrington in regards to the buildings and as he was waiting instructions for the sale of said Indian lands he could not tell how many houses would be necessary or how many people to estimate provisions.

In connection with this I thought it best to give you a brief outline of the status of the members of Charlot's band who removed here under certain agreement with myself, which may assist in your conclusions in giving instructions in regard to the estimates I shall be ordered to make.

The visit of Charlot, accompanied by a party of his Indians and myself to Washington, in 1884, resulted in a failure to induce that Chief to abandon the Bitter Root Valley and remove with his band to this reservation. In compliance with verbal instructions from Hon. H. M. Teller, then Secretary of the Interior, (a full report of which may be found in the Indian office, under date of March 27, 1884,) I made certain propositions to individual families of Charlot's band to remove to this reservation and the result was that twenty-one heads of families agreed to move, and to them following the views of the Honorable Secretary of the Interior, as expressed to the Indians in Washington, I promised each head of a family:

1st. 160 acres of unoccupied land on the reservation.

2d. The erection of a suitable house.

3d. Assistance in fencing and breaking 10 acres of land for each family.

4th. The following gifts: 2 Cows, a wagon, set of harness, a plow, with other agricultural implements — seeds for the first year, and provisions until the first crop was harvested.

My action met with the approval of the Indian Office and I was enabled to carry out every promise made to the few families who first availed themselves of the offer. Ten families reported at the Agency and for them I erected ten houses, fenced their fields as agreed upon, and to-day they are harvesting excellent crops, with more extended enclosures. Three other families followed after I sent estimates for the first ten, and to them I assigned land; but had no appropriation to fence or build. This additional three families were provided with cows, however, and I assigned them to lands. Twelve more families followed the three mentioned, but I could do nothing for them but to assign them to land, as my requisition for houses &c., which was granted in the case of the first ten, was ignored, and they provided cabins for themselves with whatever aid I could give them. Those fifteen families claim, and I think justly, that they should have been provided with houses etc., as well as the first ten families that removed; or at least if houses are to be built for the members of Charlot's band who are to be removed by Gen. Carrington, they should also be treated in like manner. A number of those families left their patented land in the Bitter Root Valley and removed here, placing their faith in the Government to properly dispose of their lands in the Bitter Root Valley, and to give them the same treatment as the original ten removals, or those who are to follow under General Carrington's orders. The supplies which I am now commencing to receive for Charlot's band are not sufficient to supply those last mentioned families who removed here, and who are just beginning to cultivate their holdings.

It will therefore be necessary for General Carrington to give me the number of families who expect to move in order that I can properly estimate for houses and supplies to maintain them. Enclosed I furnish estimate for one house, like the houses for the ten families who moved here as stated, under the promises I made to the Indians, with the full consent and approbation of the then Secretary of the Interior, Hon. Henry M. Teller.

A matching and plaining machine, a shingle machine, and a cut-off saw, has been added to the saw mill at the Agency since the erection of the ten houses before estimated for, and everything, except the brick and lime, doors and sash and hardware can be manufactured here, which will enable me to put up a comfortable Indian house for the very low estimate herewith enclosed.

I am very respectfully your ob't. serv't.

Peter Ronan,

United States Indian Agent.

Enclosure:

"Estimate for Lumber for one house." Total lumber including for foundation, roof, flooring, shingles, finishing, and sheeting came to 4646 ft. per house.

Also "Estimate of Expense." Logging 4646 ft. $4.00 per m, $18.50; windows, $5.00; brick & Lime for flue, $5.00; nails, $10.00; Door, $4.00; hinges, $.50; Lock, $1.00; Sawing, $14.00; Hauling lumber, $12.00; cost of Erecting, $100.00; [total] $170.00.

August 30, 1891

LR 32,179/1891, RG 75, National Archives, Washington, D.C.

On September 14, 1891, the Commissioner of Indian Affairs approved spending $1,160 for materials and $2,240 for labor to erect 20 houses for Charlo's band removing to the Jocko Valley. That would allow $58 per house for materials and $112 per house for labor. The $170 per house corresponds to Ronan's estimate submitted on August 27, 1891, not Jos. R. McLaren's estimate submitted with this letter.[55] See also Ronan's November 27, 1891, letter about his efforts to use Indian labor to construct the houses.

Joseph R. McLaren was a carpenter and justice of the peace in Stevensville who had befriended Charlo and the Salish. According to Carrington, Charlo asked that Carrington and McLaren be the only white people to accompany the Salish on their move to the Jocko Valley in 1891. Carrington wrote that McLaren "had not only been a kind friend of the Flatheads, but was accounted by them as 'honest.'" McLaren was one of the witnesses to the 1889 agreement between Carrington and Charlo. In the late 1880s, McLaren operated a combined carpenter shop and justice of the peace court in Stevensville. In 1892, McLaren was appointed U.S. Circuit Court Commissioner in Stevensville, registering land claims and proofs.[56]

United States Indian Service,
Flathead Agency,
August 30th, 1891.

Hon. Commissioner Indian Affairs,
Washington, D.C.
      Sir:
      Under the date of August 27th, 1891, in reply to your letter "Finance" 28361 – '91 – 11675 – '91 dated August 10th, 1891, I enclosed estimate for one house similar to other houses erected for members of Charlot's band of Bitter Root Flatheads, who removed here under promises made by me from direction of Hon. Henry M Teller then Secretary of the Interior. The estimates therein enclosed showed that a comfortable house of square or sawed logs can now be erected by use of Agency mills and employes at a cost of about $170 each. Since the first houses were erected a matching and plaining machine, a shingle machine, and a cut-off saw has been added to the mill, which enables a house to be put up for that sum that formerly cost $300. A log house is warmer in winter and cooler in summer and much preferable to the Indians than a board house. However, it would be a great convenience if Mr. McLarne's [sic] estimate should be adopted, as lumber would be furnished from the outside, and the contractor would relieve the Agent of much trouble and responsibility. Gen. Carrington has not yet informed me how many houses will be required to be erected.

I am very respectfully,
Your obedient Servant
Peter Ronan
United States Indian Agent.

First enclosure:

United States Indian Service,
Flathead Removal Agency,
Stevensville, Montana, Aug. 25th, 1891.

Major Peter Ronan, U-S. Indian Agent,
Flathead Agency.
      Dear Sir.
      I enclose a careful estimate for one house of dimensions suggested. I was at Vandenburgs yesterday. His family is large, including children and grandchildren. I will go again on Thursday, and find out exactly what he needs.
      Charlot does not want the Arlee Place; but one, lower down, occupied by a woman with a French husband.
      I think the enclosed plan a good one; and, added some points for consideration of the Department.
      Shall be glad to get the Census List you spoke of. Will advise if this people come again for rations. The Removal Fund should not be used for their current support; but the Charlot Band supplies.

Yours Truly,
Henry B. Carrington
Special & Disbursing Agt. &c.

Second enclosure:

MEMORANDUM ESTIMATE of Jos. R. Mc Laren (Builder) for Flathead Houses, at JOCKO.

DIMENSIONS. Twenty-two (22) X- Sixteen (16) feet, Eight-foot Story, Shingle-roof (No 2 shingles) Floors and ceilings, common lumber, Brick Chimney.

ITEMS, PIECES. *[McLaren itemized the lumber pieces to be used in each house. The itemization has been omitted here.]*

3809.8" Feet of Lumber, @ $12.50 per M.	47.61
5 M. Shingles – @ $3.50	17.50
150 lbs-nails, @ 5 c.	7.50
75 lbs-spikes, @ 5 c.	3.75
2 Doors. (1-³⁄₈ths in. thick.[)]	6.00
4 Windows, Sash 1-¹⁄₈th in., 4 Lights, 12 in. X20 in. (S-glass)	10.00
2 Locks & 2 Hinges.	3.00
Brick. 336	5.04
Foundation	5.00
Hauling	5.00
Paper lining, throughout.	15.00
Nails (Shingle)	1.20
Lime.	1.50
Cost of materials	$127.10

Lumber can be delivered at Arlee station, at 11.25 to 12.50 ($) per M.
Estimate for labor; per Building;
if no Indian labor be employed

	$145.50
	$272.60

By use of mill at Reservation, some reduction can be made; but lumber will be green; and time will be lost.

This style of building has proven satisfactory at Stevensville.

It is not believed that Log buildings can be erected and weather-boarded, for any less sum; or as quickly.

Furnished U.S. Indian Agent Peter Ronan; for reference to Indian Department.

Mr Mc Laren would use his best mechanics; but employ any Indian labor at Jocko, that can be employed; and utilize the Mill wherever wise, to reduce expense.

Respectfully submitted,
Henry B. Carrington
Special Agent – IN RE, Removal of Charlot's Band, &c.

August 31, 1891
LR 32,182/1891, RG 75, National Archives, Washington, D.C.

> Henry B. Carrington worked hard to minimize the costs of the removal so there would be more money left to pay his personal expenses and compensation. He overspent his budget both in 1889, when he negotiated the relinquishments of the Salish allotments, and in 1891, when he supervised the removal.[57] The Commissioner of Indian Affairs did not approve Carrington's request to charge Bitterroot rations to Ronan's budget, and this letter was filed with no reply sent.

United States Indian Service,
Flathead Agency,
August 31st, 1891.

Hon. Commissioner Indian Affairs,
Washington, D.C.

Sir:

I am in receipt of a letter from Gen. Henry B. Carrington, Special Agent for the removal of Charlot's band of Bitter Root Flatheads from the Bitter Root Valley to this Reservation, in regard to furnishing supplies to those Indians, still living there, by shipment from this Agency. I cannot explain this matter better than to quote from my reply to Mr. Carrington, and to earnestly ask for early instructions as to how those Indians are to be fed and clothed and housed until they can produce crops from the land upon which they are to be assigned:

" In regard to rations — there are now twenty-eight families here of Charlot's band, exclusive of those who came under the Garfield agreement, with Chief Arlee. Ten of these families only were supplied with houses, fields, cows, etc., the ballance, except three families, who got two cows each, were left to take care of themselves in regard to houses, and other promises which were made to them, as my requisition in their behalf received no attention. A number of these families are the owners of the land you are about to sell. The supplies which are directed here for Charlot's band are not enough to supply them, in fact, the Flatheads who received the benefit of the Garfield agreement of fifty thousand dollars make the biggest effort to secure the lions share when such supplies arrive and claim to think they are robbed if not supplied. Here are my instructions: 'You are therefore directed to divide the above named supplies by the number of weeks (52) and issue only one fifty-second part of the same per week. Under no circumstances will you be allowed to issue any deficiency and you will be held responsible for the execution of this order.'

"You see by this that I cannot ship supplies by bulk to the Bitter Root Valley, unless this order is modified; then if I ship them Charlot's band who removed here will be left without supplies. I trust you will make this plain to the Indian office, and I shall also report and ask for instructions. It would be a pleasure to me and also a relief if I could turn over all the supplies to Charlot for issue to his Indians and take his receipt for the same."

I am very respectfully
Your obedient Servant
Peter Ronan
United States Ind. Ag't.

September 1, 1891a
LR 32,659/1891, RG 75, National Archives, Washington, D.C.

United States Indian Service,
Flathead Agency,
September 1st, 1891.

Hon. Commissioner Indian Affairs,
Washington, D.C.

Sir:

In reporting for August, I would respectfully state that it has been a very busy month on this reservation. The hay crop was good this year, and the grain crop is excellent. The latter part of July and the first week of August was employed in cutting and stacking hay, and since that time nearly all attention has been given to harvesting wheat and oats. A good deal of rain fell after the ground was seeded and with the aid of irrigation a fine crop of grain was raised on the reservation. The crops are now being harvested and consequently the Indians are steadily employed. The threshing machines will soon start up and then the grist mill be put in motion and grind into flour all Indian wheat delivered.

Considerable speculation exists in regard to the result of the survey of that portion of the boundary of this reservation lying West of Flathead Lake and North of Clarke's Fork of the Columbia river. In my letter of August 25th, 1891, I explained the situation as well as I could, and gave in detail an account of the efforts of the Indians to secure the land claimed by them which the survey of Deputy United States [Surveyor] Harrison, under his contract dated April 18th, 1887, cut off the reservation as claimed by the Indians. I earnestly request that definate steps be taken to settle this matter as white men who desire to select locations complain that they are prevented from putting notices or commencing any improvements upon the disputed ground by the Indians, until they (the Indians) are satisfied that they can hold their claims. I deem it of the utmost importance that an authoritative letter be sent to me to go over the line with the Chief and head men of the Kootenai Indians and indicate to them that the line has been accepted by the Government, and that no interference with the right of settlers outside of the established line of their reservation will be tolerated. It is desirable that the Indian claimants be assured of their titles to the land they claim outside of the boundary of the reserve, if such arrangement can be made; but it should be shown clearly to them that they must not interfere with the rights of settlers who do not attempt to infringe upon actual Indian locations. This matter must be settled at once in an amicable manner or an inconsiderate act on the part of the Indians or the seekers for homes on public lands may precipitate serious trouble which might end in bloodshed.

All industries pertaining to the Agency are attended and no event of particular importance transpired since my last report.

Herewith I have the honor to enclose sanitary report and report of funds and indebtedness, and also report of Agency farmers, and have the honor to be

Very respectfully
Your obedient servant,
Peter Ronan
United States Indian Agent.

September 1, 1891b

U.S. Commissioner of Indian Affairs, Annual Report of the Commissioner of Indian Affairs *(Washington, D.C.: U.S. Government Printing Office, 1891), pages 275-279.*

Ronan's 1891 annual report summarized a number of ongoing problems relating to the Flathead Reservation community which Ronan had discussed fully in other reports which are published in this collection. Many of the situations had festered for years and some would continue even after Ronan's death in 1893.

Report of Flathead Agency.

Flathead Agency, Mont., *September 1, 1891.*

Sir: In submitting my fifteenth annual report I have the honor to state that the Indians of this reservation are advancing in agricultural pursuits and in raising cattle. Their herds of horses are also being improved by their efforts in securing better breeds of stallions. The agricultural valleys of the reservation are now dotted by Indian homes with well-fenced farms of meadows, grain fields, vegetable gardens, and several thrifty orchards, where apples, plums, and small fruits grow abundantly when properly irrigated and cared for. With the rainfall and aid of irrigation, good crops will be harvested this season. The Indians are busy in their fields, and it is a hopeful sign to see them engaged cutting grain; a few with self-binders purchased with their own money, others with combined reapers and mowers, while in smaller inclosures the old fashioned grain-cradle is dexterously wielded. Agricultural pursuits can not be successfully carried on in this region without irrigation to supply all the land under cultivation.

This reservation is one of the best watered sections in the State of Montana, and its conditions warrant, physically and economically, the profitable expenditure of money in irrigation. On well-cared for and well-irrigated fields, crops of 40 to 60 bushels of wheat and 80 to 100 bushels of oats per acre are not uncommon, and where water was abundant even an exceptionally dry season had no effect in diminishing the crops. The comparison, in a dry season, of a sun-scorched field without means of irrigation with that of a neighboring field where irrigation is attainable, with its rich crop of grain, hay, and vegetables, which, perhaps, were never moistened by a shower of rain, teaches an object lesson of the value of irrigation.

After harvest the Indians deliver at the agency mill the wheat they wish ground into flour for home consumption, and their surplus grain and vegetables find ready sale and fair prices. As remarked in last year's report, with ordinary energy they should not only become self-supporting but comfortable and independent.

The tribes or bands under my charge consist of the Pend d'Oreilles, Flatheads, Kootenais, those of Charlot's band of Bitter Root Flatheads, removed since 1884, and Michel's band of Lower Kalispels. The following is the recapitulation from the census of this year, which accompanies this report:

Charlot's band:

Total number of Indians	176
Males above 18 years	55
Females above 14 years	56
Children between 6 and 16 years	39

Confederated tribes, total | 1,556

Males over 18 years	473
Females over 14 years	543
Children between 6 and 16 years	345

Kalispels, total | 56

Males over 18 years	24
Females over 14 years	21
Children between 6 and 16 years	5

Removal of agency, or establishment of subagency. — In a letter from the honorable Commissioner of Indian Affairs a report dated August 7, 1890, by United States Indian Inspector Gardner was forwarded to me. This report states that a large portion of the Indians of the Flathead Reservation live from 50 to 60 miles distant from the Flathead Agency; that the center of population is near Crow Creek, or Mud Creek; that at present they derive only small benefit from the agency grist and sawmill, carpenter and blacksmith shops; that the establishment of a subagency would, in his judgment, be a decided advantage and for the best interest of the service; that the present agency was located in one corner of the reservation for convenience of agent and agency employés — being near the town of Missoula — and not for or in the interest of the Indians; that the time has come when the Indians of the reservation should be more looked after and encouraged in civilization and Christianity, and that they are beginning to see and feel and know that they must depend upon themselves to make a living, and for this reason the aid which the Government offers them should be easily accessible, not 35, 40, 50, or 75 miles distant, causing them to travel these respective distances to get a machine, plow, wagon, or harness repaired, or to obtain the services of the agent or physician. Inspector Gardner also states that it might be well to establish or locate an agency at Crow Creek, or Mud Creek, and retain the present agency for the use of the Bitter Root Flatheads and such other of the confederated tribes as are now located and farming in the Jocko Valley; that Mud Creek would be preferable for an agency, or subagency; that the valley there is from 10 to 12 miles wide and from 30 to 35 miles long, and is close to Pend d'Oreille, Little Bitter Root, Dayton Creek, also to the Camas Prairie; that about two-thirds of the reservation Indians live in and near that vicinity; that the location suggested is about 30 to 40 miles distant from present agency and about 24 to 25 miles distant from Ravalli railroad station, 18 or 19 miles from St. Ignatius Mission, and 12 miles from foot of the lake, and as they are industrious and peaceable, the aid offered them should be within easy access.

In connection therewith the honorable Commissioner directed that I should investigate the matter referred to by Inspector Gardner, and submit a full and complete report on same, together with recommendation as to the necessity and practicability of establishing either an agency or subagency. I reported that I considered Inspector Gardner's views eminently correct.

The agency was originally located and is at present situated at the extreme end of the southern habitable portion of the reservation, a fact which will be admitted when it is known that only two Indian habitations are in existence between it and the southern boundary. It is at the immediate foot of the mountains forming the eastern line, thereby precluding settlement in that direction. To the north and west there are Indian homes and farms extending in one direction 40, and in the other a distance of at least 60 miles. Owing to this fact the use of the mills and services of mechanics connected with the agency can not be utilized by the majority of the Indians, except at considerable cost and inconvenience. Consequently the encouragement the Government intends affording the Indians can not be fully realized. This is apparent in connection with building and grain raising (two matters to which attention is most strongly urged by the Indian Office); for instance, transportation by wagon of lumber or wheat long distances exceeds the value of the article. An argument in favor of the removal is the closer relations in which the agent and employés would be placed with those whom it is their duty to direct and assist. In opposition, no valid objection can be made to removal, except expense.

Should the agency be removed, the grist and saw mills, blacksmith and carpenter shops should be maintained at their present location with a farmer in charge, for the benefit of Chief Charlot's band of Bitter Root Flatheads, all of whom will eventually settle in the Jocko Valley, where those who were formerly removed have made their homes. It would be an injustice to the Indian and half-breed settlers, particularly to the Bitter Root Flatheads, to remove from their vicinity in the Jocko Valley the mills and shops that have been in existence so many years.

When the Northwest Indian commission in April, 1887, visited this reservation on the part of the United States, they entered into an agreement with the confederated tribes of this reservation, that, as it was the policy of the Government to remove and settle upon Indian reservations scattered bands of nonreservation Indians, so as to bring them under the care and protection of the United States; that in recompense for the consent of the confederated tribes to the removal of such bands to this reservation, the United States would cause to be built for the benefit of the confederated tribes, mills, shops, etc., at or near Crow Creek. This agreement was signed by the Indians of that portion of the reservation described by United States Indian Inspector Gardner. The erection of shops and mills there would be a benefaction to a majority of the Indians of this reservation.

Chief Eneas's band of Kootenai Indians. — United States Deputy Surveyor Harrison, under contract dated April 18, 1887, surveyed a line of that portion of the boundary of the Flathead Indian Reservation lying west of Flathead Lake and north of Clark's Fork of the Columbia River. The Indians became excited over the result of that survey, and I reported their views in full to the honorable Commissioner of Indian Affairs. I found that according to that survey the boundary line ran close to the Kootenai Indian village or settlement on Dayton Creek; that it would take from the Indians land which they claimed on that creek ever since the Stevens treaty; also, that it would cut in two a large meadow, where the Indians cut winter's supply of hay for their stock, and which they had claimed since the time the Stevens treaty was made.

In order to prevent discord or trouble upon the border, I recommended in my report that the point designated by Governor Stevens, and understood by the Indians to be half-way in the center of the lake, but afterwards found by actual survey to be a few miles north of the center, be considered the northern boundary, and another survey running from that point be ordered. I stated that if this be ordered, the Indian lands on Dayton Creek and all of the Indians' meadow beyond and claimed by the Indians would be placed inside the boundaries of the reserve, and that a natural boundary of hills would keep the two races from encroaching upon each other.

The honorable Commissioner stated in reply that the treaty of July 16, 1855, which he quoted, described the boundaries, and added:

> However indefinitely a portion of the boundaries may be described there is at least one point in the description that can be determined beyond question, that is the point half-way in latitude between the northern and southern extremities of Flathead Lake. Whatever may have been the understanding of the Indians, and whatever mistake there may have been regarding the point where this description would follow, it is impossible to to accept other boundaries than those clearly

defined in the treaty. From Deputy Surveyor Harrison's plat there appears to be no question but that he carefully determined the point half-way in latitude between the northern and southern extremities of the lake, and that he ran the northern line due west therefrom. * * * It is of course a matter of great regret that the Indians should not have all the land to which they believe themselves entitled.

I was ordered to explain the matter to the Indians as fully as possible and endeavor to convince them that the line is run in the strictest accordance with the provisions of their treaty. This I did as well as I could, but they were steadfast in their claim to the land by all the laws of justice, and, as they understood it by treaty and occupancy by themselves and their ancestors. I compromised by requesting that Indian claimants proceed to fence in their claims, plow up the ground, and cultivate the soil, and I would do all in my power to secure title to them from the Government through the Land Office. This they did to the number of seventeen heads of families or men over 21 years of age. The Indians are now engaged in harvesting their little crops on said holdings.

I have made full report to the honorable Commissioner of Indian Affairs, hoping that he may see a way by which these Indians may get title to their land and not be disturbed in their efforts to commence cultivation of the soil instead of leading wandering and vagrant lives as heretofore.

Chief Charlot's band of Bitter Root Valley Flatheads. — The history of the negotiations which culminated in the division of the Flathead tribe, part of them on the Jocko Reservation and part still in Bitter Root Valley with Charlot, is, to say the least, remarkable. In report of the Commissioner of Indian Affairs for the year 1872, pages 109 to 117, will be found this history. In 1855 a treaty was made between the United States and Victor, chief of the Flatheads. By this treaty a large territory, extending near the forty-second parallel to the British line, and with an average breadth of nearly two degrees of latitude, was ceded to the Government. On ceding it the Indians insisted upon holding the Bitter Root Valley above the Lo Lo Fork as a special reservation for the Flathead people. On November 14, 1871, the President issued an order declaring that the Indians should be removed to this reservation and on June 5, 1872, Congress passed a bill appropriating $50,000 to pay the expense of this removal and to pay the Indians for the loss of their improvements in the Bitter Root Valley. This order the Indians refused to obey, and General Garfield was appointed as a special commissioner to visit the Flatheads and secure, if possible, their peaceful removal to the Jocko Reservation. This resulted in an agreement which was known as the Garfield agreement. A number of heads of families notified the superintendent that they had chosen to take up land under the first section of said agreement, which resulted in the issuance of a certain number of patents, while another party, under Chief Arlee removed to the Jocko and reaped the full benefit of the $50,000 appropriation, while those who adhered to Chief Charlot remained in the valley in poverty.

In 1884 Charlot, with some of his headmen, and accompanied by myself and interpreter, visited Washington at the request of the honorable Secretary of the Interior. The trip resulted in a failure to induce the chief to abandon the Bitter Root Valley and remove to the Jocko Reservation. In compliance with verbal instructions from the honorable Secretary of the Interior, on our return to Montana, I made certain propositions to individual families of Charlot's band to remove to this reservation, and the result was that twenty-one heads of families agreed to move, and to them I promised each head of a family—

First, 160 acres of unoccupied land on the reservation.

Second. The erection of a suitable house.

Third. Assistance in fencing and breaking 10 acres of land for each family.

Fourth. The following gifts: Two cows, one wagon, set of harness, a plow and other agricultural implements, seed for the first year, and provisions until the first year's crop was harvested. My action met with the approval of the Indian Office, and I was enabled to carry out every promise made to the few families that first availed themselves of the offer. Ten families reported at the agency, and for them I erected ten houses, fenced their fields as agreed upon, and to-day they are harvesting excellent crops with more extended inclosures. Three other families followed after I sent estimates for the first ten, and to them I assigned land, but had no appropriation to fence or build. However, the three families were provided with cows. Twelve families more followed the three mentioned, but I could not do anything for them, except assign them land, as my requisition for houses, etc. (which was granted in the case of the first ten), was ignored; they provided cabins for themselves with whatever aid I could give them. Those fifteen families claim, and I think justly, that they should have been provided with houses, etc., as well as the first ten families that removed.

Gen. Henry B. Carrington, of Massachusetts, was appointed special agent, under act of March 2, 1889, "To provide for the sale of the lands patented to certain members of the Flathead band of Indians in Montana, and for other purposes," to secure consent of the Indians thereto, and to appraise the lands and improvements thereof. Gen. Carrington is now in the field, and it is hoped that he may succeed in selling the land and removing the Indians to the reservation this fall, and thus settle this vexed question.

Chief Michell's Band of Lower Kalispels. — This band live at a remote place called Camas Prairie, on this reserve. The chief removed here with his following from northern Idaho, under an agreement made with them by the Northwest Indian Commission in 1887. The terms of the agreement were never ratified by Congress, and this poverty stricken band were cast here without shelter, clothing, or means to do anything for themselves. A limited amount of supplies has been issued to them, and they are doing the best they can to raise small crops of grain and vegetables. Of course they attribute the delay of assistance and the misery caused by poverty to the agent.

Crime. — On Friday, the 19th day of December, 1890, Piere Paul and Lalla-see, members of the Pend d'Oreille tribe, and Pascal and Antela, members of the Kootenai tribe, belonging to this reservation, were executed in the jail yard at Missoula, Mont. They were indicted by the grand jury, tried in the circuit court in Missoula, and sentenced to be hanged for the crime of murdering white men. The execution was not public, but a limited number were admitted. Attended by two Catholic priests, the prisoners ascended the scaffold with unfaltering steps; prayers were said by the priests and repeated by the Indians in their own language. Their calm, quiet demeanor never forsook them. The trap was sprung at a few moments to 11 a. m., launching them into eternity. As the last request of the doomed men, and also that of the Indians of the reservation, I took charge of the bodies and brought them to the reservation on a Northern

Pacific train. On the night of the execution the bodies were met at Ravalli station by a large party of Indians and conveyed to St. Ignatius Mission. The following day the remains were interred with the rites of the Catholic church. No Indian demonstration followed, and after the graves were closed all quietly dispersed to their homes.

It is unnecessary to give in detail the history of the murders committed and the manner in which these Indians terrorized the reservation. They had a fair trial, were ably defended, found guilty by a jury of good men, were sentenced and hanged according to the law. Outside of their immediate relatives, the Indians of the reserve feel that they were guilty and deserved their fate.

Court of Indian offenses and police. — Owing to jealousy and prejudices among the different bands and tribes of Indians and mixed bloods on this reservation, our court of Indian offenses and our police force are neither efficient nor worthy of any particular praise in discharging their duties. The Indians of Charlot's band of Bitter Root Flatheads removed here are the hardest to control. Raised among the whites in Bitter Root Valley, and, the young men with no restraint upon them, lounging around saloons in various villages of the valley, upon coming to the reservation they thought they could carouse and dance as they did there. Some of the leaders of this band openly avow that they are opposed to having a court of Indian offenses, or police to enforce the regulations governing the reserve, and that on an Indian reservation the Indians should be free from the white men's laws. If the Indian dances are permitted here, the consequence will be demoralization to a great extent. I have taken a determined stand against those dances and expect the Department to sustain my efforts.

Schools. — The school for this reservation is situated at St. Ignatius Mission, about 20 miles north of the agency, at the foot of the lofty Rocky Mountain spur known as the Mission range, and one of the most healthful and picturesque spots in the State of Montana. The school is conducted under contract with the Government by the missionaries of St. Ignatius and the Sisters of Providence. As it is the policy of the faculty to keep the children from going to their homes, where in a short time the former teaching is forgotten, and in many cases the parents encourage the children to remain away from school, only a partial vacation is granted in the month of August. It extends only to the suspension of certain studies. The vacation is made attractive by camping out under care of teachers, while hunting, fishing, and rude games born of the forest are indulged in.

A knowledge of such trades as carpentering, blacksmithing, shoemaking, harnessmaking, tinsmithing, printing business, painting, sawing, milling, matching and planing, engineering, and agricultural pursuits are added to their educational knowledge. I still adhere to my hitherto expressed views that Indian education should be compulsory. Soon as a boy can be useful in herding stock or doing other things to relieve his parents he is taken away from school. As this is a nonissue reservation, the agent can use his influence, but is without power to enforce demands, that the children be sent to school. Thus encouraged to leave studies, and having little prospect of comfortably settling themselves, the teachers have great difficulty in keeping them when they attain a certain age. I think the inconveniences in the way of the proper training and civilization of the young Indian could be remedied by the establishment of a small fund directed to the end of aiding the new families formed by the marriage of the boys and girls of the school when of age. The prospect of this future aid might keep them longer at school.

The girls under the care and training of the Sisters of Providence have improved remarkably in their studies. Indeed this is a model school and would reflect credit upon its managers and teachers in any country. Besides the ordinary education they are taught music, vocal and instrumental, drawing, needlework, and making of their own clothing.

New and commodious buildings have been erected for the pupils, with all of the modern appliances, of bathrooms and heating apparatus. The management of these schools is excellent, and the good work that is being done for the Indians by the Jesuit Fathers and the good Sisters of Providence can not be estimated.

The kindergarten, which was added to the school last year by the faculty, is a marked success, and the teachers now have more applications from Indian parents than they can accommodate. About 60 children, from 2 to 4 years of age, are now being cared for by the Ursuline nuns; and those self-sacrificing educated, and refined ladies are devoting their lives to the comfort and well bringing up of their poor little Indian charges.

Sanitary. — The health of the Indians has been very good, the cases of sickness being chiefly confined to the younger people and to children. At the school there was no sickness to speak of during the year.

Peter Ronan.

The Commissioner of Indian Affairs.

September 11, 1891

LR 34,139/1891, RG 75, National Archives, Washington, D.C.

> Ronan's recommendation for a joint lease for five acres of land at Polson for a steamboat landing site for the two companies operating on Flathead Lake was approved on October 1, 1891.[58] For information on James Kerr see Ronan's October 26, 1888, letter and annotation.

United States Indian Service,
Flathead Agency,
September 11, 1891.

Hon. Commissioner Indian Affairs,
Washington, D.C.

Sir:

Referring to "Land 26233 – 1891," stating that on February 19th, 1891, I enclosed the written request of William J. Cheney and John A. Houston to your office, to have the license of H. S. De Puy to occupy five acres of land at a place known as "Foot of the Lake," on the Flathead Reservation, Montana, revoked, and a similar license or authority, granted to them.

My recommendation in the premises was favorable because it was shown on what I considered satisfactory evidence, that H. S. De Puy sold his entire interest in the steam boat business to Cheney & Houston.

In accordance with your instructions, contained in above reference, I advised Messrs Cheney & Houston of the protest made by M[r]. De Puy, through his attorneys Messrs Halcombe & Johnston, of Washington, D.C., and of the affidavits filed in the case.

It was agreed by the parties interested that the papers received from your office should be submitted to the law firm of Woody, Webster & Wood, of Missoula, Montana, for advice as to settlement. I herewith attach copy of said attorneys advice and suggestions, and in connection would state that I proceeded to the office of the steamboat company of each party interested, at Flathead Lake, and submitted to them herewith annexed proposition, which was accepted as a basis of settlement as to right of steam boat landing at Foot of Flathead Lake on the Flathead reservation.

Having ascertained all the facts possible in the premises, and having interviewed both parties to the case, with their consent and knowledge, respectfully recommend that license or permission be granted jointly to W. J. Cheney, James Kerr and J. A. Houston, doing business as partners under the firm name and style of "The Flathead Transportation and Improvement Company," and H. S. De Puy, A. L. Lanneau and Frank Langford, doing business as partners under the firm name and style of "The Flathead Navigation Company." This will give them joint occupation and use of five acres of land at the foot of the Lake, on the Flathead Reservation, which should be ample to accomodate both parties with warehouses, wharfs, etc.

> I am very respectfully,
> your obedient servant
> Peter Ronan,
> United States Indian Agent.

Enclosure:

> Office of Woody, Webster & Wood, Attorneys at Law.
> Missoula, Montana, Aug. 26, 1891.

Major Peter Ronan,
U.S. Indian Agt.,
Flathead Agency, Mont.

Dear Sir:—

We have examined the two letters from the office of Indian Affairs, which you left with us the other day, and will say, that as the matter now is, we believe the best thing to be done will be to grant the license or permission jointly to the two Steamboat companies, or in other words, revoke the license of DePuy and make a joint grant.

The two companies at the present time have consolidated for the remainder of the year, and it is evident that the department will not grant permission to two different companies, and that being true, then the best thing for both of them will be to obtain joint permission. Then the license or permission should be granted jointly to W. J. Cheney James Keer [sic] and J. A. Houston, doing business as partners under the firm name and style of "The Flathead Transportation & Improvement Co.," and H. S. DePuy, A. L. Lanneau and Frank Langford, doing business as partners under the firm name and style of "The Flathead Navigation Co." This will give them joint occupation and use of five (5) acres of land at the foot of the lake, which should be ample to accomodate both parties, with ware-houses, wharfs, etc.

We have not had an opportunity to see or hear from either of the parties, but in our judgement this is the only correct solution of the difficulty. We feel however, that the department should, and we think will be willing to limit them, and not allow them to transfer their license or permission except from one of these parties to the other, which should be permitted, should one of the parties at any time purchase, the boats of the other. Enclosed please find the letters left with us.

Trusting that this will meet with your approval, and that you can endorse the same, and reccomend [sic] it to be granted as above stated, we are,

Very respectfully yours,
Woody, Webster & Wood.

Respectfully submitted
Peter Ronan
U.S. Indian Agent.

October 3, 1891

LR 36,493/1891, RG 75, National Archives, Washington, D.C.

Note that Ronan was making arrangements to use Indian labor to deliver pine logs to the agency sawmill to be made into lumber and shingles for the new Bitterroot Salish houses.

United States Indian Service,
Flathead Agency,
Mont. Oct. 3, 1891.

Hon. Commissioner Indian Affairs,
Washington, D.C.

Sir:

I have the honor to report from this Agency, for the month of September. The grain and vegetable crop raised by the Indians this season exceed in quality and quantity any crop ever before harvested by them on this reservation.

The unusual rain fall after the ground was seeded, aided by irrigation, resulted in production of excellent crops.

The threshing machines are at work, threshing Indian wheat, and oats, and the grist mill is in constant opperation [sic]. Under authority dated September 14, 1891, I let to some of the heads of Indian families contracts to furnish pine logs at the Agency sawmill in sufficient quantities to furnish lumber and shingles for the erection of twenty houses as specified in the estimate for one house, accompanying my letter of 27th of August — all required for use in the erection of said twenty houses in the Bitter Root valley, Montana, as may remove and settle upon this reservation, for the reasons fully set forth in the letter of Special Agent Henry B. Carrington, of July 29th 1891, and my letter above refered to. As yet I have not be[en] notified as to when the Indians are expected to remove here, where they desire to locate, or how many houses it will be necessary to erect before winter sets in. I deem it prudent, however to prepare necessary lumber and shingles and to purchase bricks, lime, doors, windows, &c. and be in readiness to erect houses when the Indians select farms.

From newspaper reports I understand that an attempt will be made to sell the Indian lands, referred to on the 5th of October, at the valuations made on the same by Special Agent Henry B. Carrington. After that date, if sales are made, I presume the Bitter Root Flatheads will remove, and ask that houses be built for them.

Have just returned from the Kootenai encampment, on Dayton Creek, on this reservation, where, under your instructions, I assigned unsurveyed lands, to 29 members, heads of families of that tribe, lying west of Flathead Lake and north of Clarkes Fork of the Columbia and out side of the boundary line of the Flathead reservation as surveyed under contract of E. P. Harrison. Soon as the work is completed, shall send full report to your office.

All matters pertaining to industries and welfare of the reservation have received attention, and no event of particular importance remains to be recorded.

Herewith I have the honor to enclose sanitary report and report of funds and indebtedness and also report of Agency farmers and have the honor to be

Very respectfully
your obedient Servant
Peter Ronan
U.S. Indian Agent.

October 16, 1891
LR 37,903/1891, RG 75, National Archives, Washington, D.C.

On October 3, 1891, the Commissioner of Indian Affairs complained to Ronan that the monthly Flathead Agency sanitary or physicians reports seemed to show almost no variation from month to month. (The sanitary reports to Washington, D.C., have been destroyed and were not preserved in the National Archives.) The Commissioner asked for a more detailed report from the agency physician. On November 5, 1891, the Commissioner complained that the report Ronan forwarded on October 16, 1891, was still not sufficient. On December 4, 1891, Thomas E. Adams, the agency clerk, forwarded a more detailed report to the Commissioner which was accepted.[59] At least according to the agency physician, the reservation population was remarkably healthy. See also the annotation to Ronan's December 2, 1891, letter and his February 18, 1892, letter about Dr. John Dade after Inspector B. H. Miller made a critical comment about Dade's age. For biographical information on Dr. Dade, see the annotation to Ronan's June 14, 1888, letter.

United States Indian Service,
Flathead Agency,
Oct. 16th, 1891.

Hon. Commissioner of Indian Affairs,
Washington, D.C.
Sir:

In compliance with office letter "A" 24497-27542 – 90; 31238-34726 – 90; 38201 –90; 943-5245 – 91; 9470-12810 – 91; 12750-20632 – 91; 24118 – 91 dated Washington, October 3d, 1891, I have the honor to forward herewith Report of Agency physician.

Very respectfully
Your obt. srvt.
Peter Ronan
U.S. Indian Agent.

Enclosure:

United States Indian Service,
Flathead Agency,

Maj. Peter Ronan
Agent Flathead Indians
Sir

In answer to the questions of the Hon. Commissioner of Indian Affairs would respectfully state that there have been a good many cases of Remittint and Intermittint fever among the Indians, Caused I suppose from the wet weather, the fevers have been of a mild form and easily relieved with tonics.

I would further state that the Indians are more generally confortably housed, and since they have given up their Medicine Men are learning to nurse and take Care of their sick.

I remain Your Obedient Servant
John Dade
Physician to Flathead Indians.

October 20, 1891
LR 37,743/1891, telegram, RG 75, National Archives, Washington, D.C.

> The survey of the southwest corner of the reservation was a long-term problem. On March 10, 1891, Ronan described the tribal claim to the bottom land at the junction of the Clark Fork and Lower Flathead Rivers. The Commissioner of Indian Affairs instructed Ronan, by telegram on October 22, 1891, to make allotments to the Pend d'Oreille Indians who had settled at the junction of the rivers believing they were on the reservation.[60] Ronan reported on specific land conflicts in the area on January 11, 1892, and March 24, 1892. The January 11, 1892, letter regarding a complaint by John H. Jackson of Plains could not be located at the National Archives, but the March 24, 1892, letter about the claim of Frank Foster of Plains, is reproduced here. On March 24, 1892, Ronan explained that he hesitated to allot the land along the river junction until the boundary survey was official because it was not certain that the final survey would place the land off the reservation. The surveyor working on the boundary, Samuel Bundock, was instructed to coordinate with Ronan, but as of October 24, 1892, he had not yet contacted Ronan.[61] The situation dragged on until after Ronan's death in 1893. On November 22, 1893, Agent Joseph Carter was instructed to allot the Indian farmers at the junction of the Clark Fork and Flathead Rivers, but no record has been found in the National Archives that the allotments were ever made.[62]
>
> In 1965 the United States Court of Claims agreed that the survey of the southwest corner of the reservation had been in error and awarded the Confederated Salish and Kootenai Tribes financial compensation for the land lost.

Oct. 20, 1891
Missoula, Mt

Comr Ind Affs
W D C

Completed allotments of land to Kootenai Indians on Dayton Creek under instructions sept seventh [penciled note added: LB 222 – 293] Surveyor now in the field to Complete survey where deputy surveyor harrison left off in eighteen hundred & eighty seven at Clarksfork of the Columbia river shall I allot lands at that place always Claimed by Pendorelle indians as being on the reservation according to instructions in Case of the Kootenai indians Conditions Precisely as in the Case of the Kootenai indians at dayton Creek.

Rolan [sic] Agt.

October 24, 1891
LR 39,445/1891, RG 75, National Archives, Washington, D.C.

The removal of Charlo and the remaining Bitterroot Salish Indians to the Flathead Reservation in October 1891 was a celebrated part of Montana history. There was some historical confusion about the role of the United States Army in the move, but there was no doubt that the move was traumatic and painful after the long struggle of the Salish to maintain their community in the Bitterroot Valley. Since the move was handled by Henry B. Carrington rather than Ronan, Ronan's reports do not convey a detailed account of the move.[63]

Ronan reported on November 27, 1891, that twenty houses were being built for the Bitterroot Salish. In his December 14, 1891b, letter he mentioned that the houses had been completed. Carrington had promised Charlo Arlee's farm in a written agreement signed on November 3, 1889.[64] In his December 14, 1891b, letter, Ronan described his efforts to accommodate Carrington's promises to give Charlo a larger house and Arlee's farm. Ronan felt it would be unfair to take Arlee's farm away from his heirs. Mrs. Catherine Finley Couture, the woman whose farm Charlo indicated he wanted, was the widow of Joseph Couture who had died in 1889.[65] In Ronan's March 10, 1892, letter, he reported that he had turned over the agency farm to Charlo in lieu of Arlee's farm.[66] The unfunded and unfulfilled promises Carrington made to Charlo and the Bitterroot Salish would bedevil Flathead Indian Agents for decades.[67]

October 24, 1891.

Hon. Commissioner Indian Affairs,
Washington, D.C.
Sir:

On Saturday the 17th day of October, 1891, General Henry B. Carrington, Special Agent for the removal of Charlot's Band of Bitter Root Flatheads, arrived upon the reservation, accompanied by that Chief and a number of families, consisting of about one hundred and sixty men women and children. In accordance with your telegram and the desire that everything possible should be done to render the removal of the Chief and his band from Bitter Root valley pleasant, I prepared a reception for them. I had slaughtered three head of cattle and also sent to their camp suplies to make a feast. The new comers were welcomed by delegations of Indians from all the tribes on the reservation. The Agency saw mill was running out lumber for the construction of the houses ordered to be built for their accomodation. The weather was beautiful, and all I desired from the Chief and his people was a choice of location when the houses would be pushed to completion, and the families to the extent of twenty, as authorized would be comfortably provided with homes.

Having given them ample time for rest and consideration I held an interview with Chief Charlot on the 22d of October, and informed him that I was prepared to commence the construction of houses upon any land that might be selected for homes to the extent of twenty. He informed or rather intimated that he came to the Jocko reservation to make homes for himself and his people; that he found some of the choice ranches under fence and cultivation by halfbreeds; that he had made up his mind to occupy a farm held by a certain halfbreed family, and seemed to expect that I should evict said family and place him in possession. I informed Charlot that I had been in charge of the Jocko reservation nearly fifteen years; that the family occupied the ranche before I cam[e] upon the reservation; that although the deceased father was a whiteman in former employment of the Hudson Bay Company, he married a woman of the tribes occupying this reservation; that the widow and her children were, in my belief, the rightful owners of the farm and could not be disturbed without payment for the improvements and proper consent of the family. The answer of the Chief was that a number of halfbreed families occupied choice lands and had good surroundings and that the Indians would like to take possession of the same; send the original occupants from their improved farms, take possession of the same and let the latter take farms on another portion of the reservation and commence life anew. I could not see the justice of such a movement and hence Charlot intimated that I was the friend of the halfbreeds to the detriment of the Indian interests. I have always understood from orders from my superiors that halfbreeds born to the soil have every recognition from the Government that is accorded to the full blooded Indian and shall adher[e] to that view unless informed differently.

One hundred and sixty Indians, or forty families, without any means of support, in addition to the impecunious Indians already here, have been removed to the reservation and it is absolutely necessary that they should be fed and clad. The supplies on hand for Charlot's band removed before this addition; for Chief Michels band of lower Kalispels, and also for the Confederated tribes occupying this reservation, is inadequate to meet the necessities, and I am compelled to mak[e] requisition for support for the Indians removed from the Bitter Root val[l]ey, until the close of the fiscal year.

I have the honor to enclose herewith said requisition, and am very respectfully,

Your obedient Servant,
Peter Ronan,
United States Indian Agent.

Enclosure:
"Estimate of Indian Supplies, &c." for 20,000 lbs. beef, 100 lbs. baking powder, 1,000 lbs. beans, 4,000 lbs. bacon, 1,000 lbs. coffee, 20,000 lbs. flour, 600 lbs. rice, 200 lbs. soap, and 300 lbs. tea, totaling $2811.50.

October 25, 1891
LR 38,302/1891, telegram, RG 75, National Archives, Washington, D.C.

Oct 25, 1891
Arlee Mont

Commissioner Indian Affairs, Washn DC
Moatenai [sic] Chief arrived with all wheat raised at Dayton Creek mill already crowded with Indian wheat and Sawing lumber for flathead houses. may I be authorized to Employ two additional hands for two months at Wages paid to regular employes to enable me to run mill night and day exigincies demand night and day work in mill to Commence at once.

Ronan Agent.

October 30, 1891
LR 39,947/1891, RG 75, National Archives, Washington, D.C.

For biographical information on Eugene Humbert, the deputy clerk of the Missoula court, see the annotation to Ronan's July 1, 1890b, letter. For Thomas E. Adams, the Flathead Agency Clerk, see the annotation to Ronan's August 21, 1887, letter.

United States Indian Service,
Flathead Agency,
October 30th, 1891.

Hon. Commissioner Indian Affairs
Washington, D.C.

Sir:

Referring to "Land 31598 — 1891," dated at Washington, September 7th, 1891, in which it was stated that my communication of the 25th of August, received your attention, wherein I reported that I visited, at the request of chief Eneas and his head men, the Kootenai Indians residing at Dayton Creek, on the Flathead reservation, in order to fully report to your office, upon their request, in regard to certain lands which they honestly considered as rightfully belonging to them under treaty stipulations and which they have always occupied.

You referred also to the fact that I stated that the decision of your office, rendered November 10th, 1890, relative to the boundary of the reservation was announced January, 1891; that it was fully explained to them that it was impossible to accept other boundaries than those clearly defined in the treaty of July 16, 1855; that I endeavored to convince them that the line as run by Deputy Surveyor Harrison, was in the strictest accordance with the provisions of the treaty; that I then urged upon the Indians the necessity of securing their claims to the lands occupied by them by fencing and improving the same; and that they believed they were entitled to the lands lying West of Flathead Lake and North of Clarkes Fork of the Columbia river, segregated from the reservation by the survey of the said Deputy Survey, under his contract dated April 18, 1887.

I further stated that in obedience to my request, seventeen heads of families, over 21 years of age, of the Kootenai tribe of Indians commenced fencing and improving the lands claimed and occupied by them outside of the reservation boundary as designated by the Harrison survey; that upon my recent visit to these Indians I made personal investigation in regard to such claims; that I found the Indians whose names I furnished had not only fenced to some extent the lands claimed, but had also, on some tracts, planted small crops of grain and were then engaged in harvesting the same; that they were anxious to be assured that their lands would not be taken from them by either the Government or the whites who are now ready to "pounce" upon them.

In accordance with my request to be advised as to the proper steps to take in order to save these Indians their homes and to assist them in acquiring title to the same you have to State:

"1st. That you will at once forward a description of the lands claimed by the said Indians to the local Land office of the District in which the lands are situated, and call attention of the local Land Officers to the General Land Office circular relative to lands in the possession of Indian occupants, issued October 27, 1887, whereby Registers and Receivers are every where instructed to peremtorily [sic] refuse all enteries [sic] and filings attempted to be made by other than Indian occupants upon lands in the possession of Indians who have made improvements of any value whatever thereon (copy furnished[)].

"2d. As the lands referred to are non-reservation lands, and as the Indians were residing thereon at the date of the approval of the General Allotment Act, February 8th, 1887, they should be allotted to the Indians under the 4th Section thereof, as amended by Act of February 28th, 1891 (26 Stats., 794.)

"You will therefore at your earliest convenience proceed to that locality for the purpose of assisting these Indians in making applications for allotments under the said Acts, (copies enclosed[)].

"I enclose also for your information and use in connection with this work, copy of circular issued September 17th, 1887, by the Department, showing what is necessary to be done, how to proceed, and the proof required under the Act first named, and copy of circular issued by the Department July 2d, 1891, setting forth the amendments to the General Allotment Act as made by Act of February 28, 1891.

"You will observe from the Act and circular last referred to that each Indian whether adult or minor, married or single, is allowed, if entitled to an allotment 80 acres each, and furnishing the proof required, if there is sufficient land subject to allotment in that vicinity. If there is not enough land for that purpose, you will first allot to heads of families, in tracts of eighty acres each, and next to worthy and industrious young men, then if there is still land left you will pro rata the same among the minor members of the families referred to in tracts of not less than forty acres each, and aid them in making application for allotment of the same.

"As above stated if the lands applied for or any legal subdivisions thereof are valuable only for grazing purposes, the same may be allotted in double quantities, and you will carry out this provision of the Allotment Acts, if it is ascertained there is enough land to do so.

"If the lands are unsurveyed, the applications should contain a description of the same by metes and bounds beginning with some natural object, or a permanent artificial monument or mound set for the purpose, or in such other manner as to admit of its being readily identified when the lines of the official survey come to be extended.

"When the applications shall have been made, you will deliver the same to the local land officers of the district wherein the lands are situated for certification by the Register, to the effect that there is no prior valid adverse claim to the lands applied for and described in each application, and to be forwarded by them to the General Land Office for Consideration and action."

In accordance with foregoing instructions, on the 18th day of September, 1891, I proceeded to the Kootenai village, on Dayton Creek, on this reservation, where I held council with Chief Eneas of the Kootenai Indians, and his band. After listening to the interpretation of my instructions from your office in regard to allotments of lands outside of the Northern boundary of their reservation, as surveyed by Deputy Surveyor Harrison, the Chief expressed for himself and his Indians, their gratitude to the Government and the Indian Office, for being allowed to get title, and to occupy the lands which they always believed to belong to them in accordance with the provisions of the treaty of 1855, but cut off on account of misunderstanding as to the exact point half way in latitude between the Northern and Southern extremities of the Flathead Lake. The Indians, always claiming the point, to be some six miles further North, until an actual survey decided the line as running very near to the Kootenai village, on Dayton Creek, and cutting off from them land which they and their fathers always claimed to be inside of the Northern Boundary of the Flathead reservation.

On the 23d of September, I commenced making the allotments, as designated by the Indians, to the following list of claimants, all being over twenty-one years of age and the head of a family.

No. 1. Antoine Dominic, 160 acres for Grazing purposes.

No. 2. Philip Kunikuka 80 acres for Farming purposes.

No. 3. Abraham Kanmekolla, 160 acres for Grazing purposes.

No. 4. Mat Kowiltawaam 160 acres for Grazing purposes.

No. 5. John Kallawat 160 acres for Grazing purposes.

No. 6. Patrick Kitcowholakoo, 80 acres for Agricultural purposes.

No. 7. William Kanklutepleta, 160 acres for Grazing purposes.

No. 8. Joseph Chuakenmum 80 acres for Agricultural purposes.

No. 9. Custa Smoketmalsukes 160 acres for Grazing purposes.

No. 10. Patrick Koskolt, 160 acres for Grazing purposes.

No. 11. George Kolkonee, 160 acres for Grazing purposes.

No. 12. Paul Chatchadoman 160 acres for Grazing purposes.

No. 13. Joseph Jean Jan Graw 160 acres for Grazing purposes.

No. 14. Bazile Tatscum 160 acres for Grazing purposes.

No. 15. Francis Nacksaw 160 acres for Grazing purposes.

No. 16. Malta Sechkolke 160 acres for Grazing purposes.

No. 17. Isaac Paul 160 acres for Grazing purposes.

No. 18. Lemo Wahomne, 160 acres for Grazing purposes.

No. 19. Jena Jan Graw, 160 acres for Grazing purposes.

This number of allotments to heads of families, being all the lands which Kootenai Indians claimed, or asked for, outside of the point half way in latitude between the Northern and Southern extremities of the Flathead Lake, as established by Deputy Surveyor Harrison, who ran the line due West therefrom. I trust, as the lands in question were unsurveyed at the time I made the allotments, that no prior valid adverse claim to the lands applied for and described in each application, will be made or substantiated. This allotment will have the effect to satisfy the Indians that no attempt has been made by the Government, in making the survey, to take from them any land that they have heretofore claimed or occupied in the honest belief that such land was inside of the boundary of the Flathead reservation.

Being advised that Non Mineral Affidavits required to be made before either the Rigister or Receiver of the Land District in which the land is situated, or before the Judge or Clerk of any Court of Record having a seal, I proceeded to Missoula, and applied to Judge Marshall, of the Circuit Court of Montana for the appointment of Eugene Humbert, as Deputy Clerk of said Court, with power to take Indian depositions, in order that the seal of the Court might be attached, without bringing the Indians, applying for allotments, either before the Register and Receiver of the local Land Office or a Clerk of a Court having a seal. This was done in the interest of economy as the Indians making applications, according to my information would be required to appear in person to make affidavit "either before the Register or Receiver of the Land District in which the land is situated, or before the Judge, or Clerk of any Court of record having a seal." Transportation would involve a distance by horseback or wagon, and by rail, of about one hundred miles, while subsistence etc., etc. for the Indian applicants would make the bill of expense a large one.

In the Second place the Chief especially requested that the Allotment papers be made legal without bringing the applicants to the town of Missoula, and thus avoid the annoyance which the temptations of the place and its surroundings might produce among the Indian applicants for title to their lands. The appointed Deputy Clerk of the Court accompanied me to the Indian village and witnessed their marks. I have the honor herewith to enclose receipt from the Register of the local Land Office for said applications and also vouchers covering expenses in the execution and completion of this work, and have the honor to be

Very respectfully
Your obedient Servant
Peter Ronan
United States Indian Agent.

First Enclosure:

Copy of notice

To whom it may concern

I claim this land as an Indian homestead, from this post or tree North one mile and east and west one Quarter of a mile. taken under instruction of the Commissioner of Indian Affairs to Peter Ronan, U.S. Indian Agent dated Sept 7th, 1891.

Antice Dominick
his X mark

witness
Peter Ronan, U S Indian Agent
Robert Irvine.

Second Enclosure. Clipping from The Anaconda Standard, *September 30, 1891, page 8, col. 3:*

Disappointed Indians
A Large Tract of Land That Does Not Belong to the Flatheads.
Result of a Late Survey
Thousands of Rich Acres Along the Flathead Lake Subject to Settlement by White men.

Special to the Standard.

Missoula, Sept. 29 — Major Ronan and his chief clerk, Thomas E. Adams, are in the city from the Flathead reservation. Surveys of the northern boundary of the reservation were recently made, and it was found that boundary line was six miles further south than where the Indians had always supposed it to be. A number of Indians had made homes on that six-mile strip, and when the boundary was determined white people commenced to file on the land, which is some of the best land in that district. Major Ronan wrote to the department of the interior about the matter and received instructions to make allotments to Indians who had homes there, and instruct the local land office not to accept filings upon the land so allotted. He accordingly parcelled out nearly 30,000 acres among 19 families, and came in to-day to arrange with the land office. At his request, Mr. Adams was appointed a deputy clerk of the district court to take steps necessary in connection with the taking up of this land by the Indians.

November 2, 1891
LR 40,207/1891, RG 75, National Archives, Washington, D.C.

> Ronan mentioned several important items in this monthly report. The new houses for Charlo's band of Bitterroot Salish Indians were being built mostly with tribal member labor.[68] Ronan was particularly pleased at the success of the Dayton Creek Kootenai in raising wheat to be ground into flour at the agency mill.

United States Indian Service,
Flathead Agency,
Nov. 2d, 1891.

Hon. Commissioner Indian Affairs,
Washington, D.C.

Sir:

I have the honor to report that every industry connected with this Agency, for the month of October, has been successfully carried on. Charlots band removed from Bitter Root valley during the month, and according to your telegraphic order, I have made them as comfortable as possible. The Indians have selected locations for their houses; lumber is being sawed and delivered as fast as possible from the Agency mill, and workmen have commenced the erection of houses, which will be pushed to completion fast as the weather will permit. Winter is advancing, but the Indians will be comfortable living in new lodges, as I purchased material for the women to manufacture them. They have always been used to living in lodges and will experience no hardship until the houses will be completed. The houses will be built mostly by Indian and Halfbreed labor, as many of them are competent to do the work, and eager to obtain employment. The saw mill is run in the day, while the grist mill is run at night. Thanks for authority which enabled me to make such arrangement.

Never, in the history of this reservation, have the Kootenai Indians before brought grain to the Agency mill to be ground into flour. Last week several teams arrived laden with wheat raised by the Kootenai Indians at Dayton Creek. The distance of the travel is over sixty miles, but the Indians made the trip with loaded teams in six days, crossing the Pend 'd Oreille river on a ferry boat. Chief Eneas was much elated at the acchievement [sic] of his Indians in raising and delivering wheat at the mill to be converted into flour. He accompanied the wagons to the Agency. I expect, with proper encouragement, that the Kootenai Indians hereafter will produce good crops of grain and vegetables. They feel encouraged and pleased that the question of a settlement of title to the land North of the boundary of the reservation has been undertaken by allotting it to them, a special report of which I have this day forwarded to your office.

In regard to your telegram and letter of instruction of October 21st to proceed to the Kootenai encampment in Northern Idaho, and try to induce that band to remove to the Flathead reservation. I thank you for the confidence you repose in me, and shall use every proper means and energy to make it a success. Chief Eneas is now here ready to accompany me soon as he recovers from an illness caused by a cold taken while coming to the Agency. I have already communicated with the Indians by sending a runner to their hunting ground to inform them that myself and Chief Eneas with an interpreter, desire them to collect and meet us at Bonners Ferry, on the Kootenai river, in Northern Idaho, soon as possible, where we will hold council with them. The delay of a few days here will not retard the business, as I should have, in all probability, to await for the Indians to come in from their hunt, at that place.

Upon my return from Idaho, shall proceed to allot land to the Pend 'd Oreille Indians, as suggested by my telegram of the 20th of October, and answered by you, by wire, on the 22d of the same month.

Herewith I have the honor to enclose sanitary report and report of funds and indebtedness; also report of farmer at Agency. The Kootenai farmer being absent at Dayton Creek, I am unable to forward his report at this time.

I am very respectfully,
Your obedient servant,
Peter Ronan,
United States Indian Agent.

November 7, 1891
The Spokane Review, *Nov. 7, 1891, page 3, col. 1-2.*

> This interview in *The Spokane Review* was a valuable source on Peter Ronan's life story. He also summarized the current status of the Bonners Ferry Kootenai removal, the Dayton Creek allotments just north of the reservation, and the removal of the Lower Pend d'Oreille or Kalispel Indians to the reservation.

A Montana Pioneer
Major Ronan, Who Holds an Office That Does Not Change With Administrations.

For Fifteen Years He Has Been Agent at the Flathead Indian Agency.

The Calispels and the Haughty Kootenais to Be Placed on the Reserve.

Amongst the visitors to Spokane during the past week were Major and Mrs. Peter Ronan of Jocko, Mont., who have been spending a few days in the city to see their boys, who are attending school at the Gonzaga college.

The worthy major has been the agent at the Flathead Indian reservation for the past 15 years and seems likely to continue there as long as he likes. He was one of the pioneers of Montana, having come to that state in '63 when all of Washington and Idaho were part of Oregon, and Montana was a part of Dakota. The story of his experiences in the northwest is an interesting and typical one, and a Review reporter in the course of a long conversation with him yesterday learnt much of it.

"I came to Colorado as a boy," said he, "and after living there several years went east to Leavenworth, Kan. I was there when the Florence excitement broke out, and along with hundreds of others got the gold fever. On the way I fell in with a lot of old Colorado men, and instead of going to Florence turned off to the camp at Bannock, which was the first capital of the territory of Montana. Here I met lots more Colorado boys, among whom were Sam McLean, the first delegate to congress from the territory, and Wash Stapleton, now one of the leading attorneys of Butte City. When Alder gulch was discovered I was one of the first stampeders, and saw the rise and ruin of Virginia City. The 6th of June, 1863, was a memorable day in that camp. We had the gulch pretty well staked out and on that day every man had to be on his own claim. I had one, and you bet I was there. Shortly afterward I started the Montana Democrat in Virginia City, with John P. Bruce as my partner. It was the second newspaper established in the territory, the Post being the first. When the Last Chance was discovered I started for Helena, and there started another paper, the Rocky Mountain Gazette. My partners in this enterprise were E. L. Wilkinson and Major McGinniss [Martin Maginnis], who was for 12 years delegate to congress from the territory, and is now state mineral land commissioner.

"At first the Gazette was only a weekly, but we soon changed it into a daily and had one of the very best newspaper offices in the west. Our building was a three-story granite block and we printed the paper on a steam power press. The whole office was lit by gas manufactured in our back yard. In '69 the whole thing went up in a blaze and broke us flatter than a pancake. We had the plant insured with a St. Louis company for $30,000, but it had bursted up some time before and did not have a dollar of assets. By hard rustling we resurrected the Gazette by forming a joint stock company — and this time we determined not to get the worst of it, so we put up a fire proof building. It stood just two years and then went up in smoke too. The fire proof building just melted right down when the fire reached it, leaving nothing but the interior brick walls standing. I had now had enough of journalism, or it had had enough of me; anyway, I went back to prospecting and mining again and had pretty good luck at Blackfoot city, in the famous Ophir gulch. The next thing I took hold of was in Helena again, where I was deputy sheriff. When the Indian agent at the Flathead reservation was suspended and ordered to Washington, Carl Schurz, who was at that time secretary of the interior, sent me orders to go there and take charge of the government property. Soon after that President Hayes sent my name to the senate for the agency, and I was confirmed and have held the office ever since.

"When I first took charge of the reservation all the Indians were hunters, game was very plentiful, and all used to cross the Rockies in summer time and spend several months in buffalo hunting. A great change has taken place since then. All of them are now good farmers. This year they have raised an enormous crop of grain, so large that the grist mill is kept running night and day, and so is the sawmill too, for that matter. The reason we are so busy in the sawmill just now is the Bitter Root Flatheads have just been removed to the reservation from their lands in the Bitter Root valley. They had patents from the government for all their lands there, but they agreed to sell their farms and move to the reservation. Over 140 families were moved in this way and have been given lands in severalty, and we are now putting up the first 20 houses for them. They have only been on the reservation a month, and last week I received orders from Washington to go as soon as possible to Bonner's Ferry and bring all the Kootenai Indians to the Flathead reservation too, if it could possibly be done. I have sent a runner in there to notify them that I would be there shortly. There are a number of Kootenai Indians on the reservation, and their chief, Incas [Eneas], is going with me to help arrange matters. He was taken sick just before I left but is recovering and will be able to go in a couple of weeks,

I think. All of the Kootenais there now reside on Dayton creek and there are altogether about 200 of them.

"I don't suppose you have any idea of the size of the reservation. It covers over 1,300,000 acres and is nearly all magnificent agricultural country. There are about 2,000 Indians on it now. The Great Northern railroad passes 50 miles to the north of it and the Northern Pacific traverses the southern part of it. About two years ago I was ordered to go to Bonner's Ferry and look up the Kootenais there, who were a kind of disorganized and neglected tribe, with no reservation or anything else. I made a proposition to them to move them all the Flathead, but they said they preferred to remain where they were provided they could get a title to their lands. They were allowed to take up lands in severalty, in fact encouraged to do it, but the advent of the Great Northern into that country brought no end of hard cases, and many of them were driven from their homes at the point of a shotgun. Their chief visited Flathead last July and told me all about their troubles and reported that his people were ready to move, but of course I could do nothing till I heard from Washington. Now, however, I hope to induce them all to come with me and that will settle all the difficulty.

"We came pretty near having some trouble with the Dayton creek Kootenais this summer. When they moved on to the reservation they made a treaty with Governor I. I. Stevens in 1855, who pointed out to them what would be their lands. The treaty read, 'south of the center line of latitude in Flathead lake.' Governor Stevens thought the middle of the lake would come about a certain point of rocks and pointed that out to them as the boundary line. When the engineer came to run the line this summer it was found to pass six miles south of it and 19 families had their holdings outside the reservation of their tribe. They were very indignant about it, but I told them they would have to give them up, but on reporting the whole matter to Washington I was instructed to give them their lands in severalty. They were very much overjoyed at the news and the 19 families were so much pleased that when I offered, as instructed, to give them a farm for each of their children north of this line, they refused, saying the government had given them all they were entitled to and that was all they wanted.

"I hope to be able soon to move another tribe from your neighborhood up there, too. You will remember when the northwest commission was out here a few years ago they made a treaty with the Calispels at Sand Point, which has never been carried out. I was ordered to go to Sand Point at that time and try to induce them to move to the Flathead reservation. I got the consent of the Flatheads to the proposition and then an agreement was entered into signed by a majority of the Calispels and by the commission which provided that if they would remove and settle the government would build them houses and furnish them with stock, provisions and means to commence farming. The treaty was never ratified by congress. About a year ago a chief called Michel came to see me and told me that he knew I could do nothing till congress acted, but that he wanted to move with fifteen families. I got the necessary authority from the secretary of the interior and settled them on farms, but could give them no assistance beyond a little clothing and the necessary provisions. Nothing more can be done without the authority of congress.

"Since that time Victor, the head chief, has died. He had refused very properly to move his people until the provisions of the treaty were carried out. His son Marcial is now in charge, and he has notified me that he is ready to move any time the agreement is ratified. There are only about 30 families of them altogether, and if congress would ratify the treaty and make an appropriation to carry out its terms the whole matter would be disposed of, the Indians collected on one reservation, where they will be made comfortable and can be looked after, and all their lands left free for white men to develop."

November 27, 1891
LR 42,825/1891, RG 75, National Archives, Washington, D.C.

On December 11, 1891, the Commissioner of Indian Affairs approved Ronan's proposal to use Indian labor to construct houses in the Jocko Valley for the Bitterroot Salish.[69] See also Ronan's August 30, 1891, letter and annotation on this subject.

United States Indian Service,
Flathead Agency,
November 27, 1891.

Hon. Commissioner Indian Affairs,
Washington, D.C.
Sir:
Referring to your letter September 14, 1891 — "Finance 11675 – '91 – 28361 – '91 – 28656 – '91 – 31178 – '91 – 32179 – '91. Authority 28042,["] advising that authority was granted to me to expend a sum not exceeding $1,160.00 in the open market purchase of bricks, lime, doors, windows &c., and a further sum, not exceeding $2,240.00, or so much thereof as might be necessary in the employment of labor at lowest obtainable rates, not however to exceed the rates and quantities specified in the estimate (for one house) accompanying my letter of the 27th ultimo, all required for use in the erection of twenty houses for such Indian patentees of lands in the Bitter Root Valley, Montana, as may remove and settle on the Jocko Reservation, Montana, for the reasons fully set forth in the letter of Special Agent H. B. Carrington, of July 29th, 1891, and my letter above referred to. Some of said houses are already built and occupied, while all will be completed within the next ten days, and I desire to make speedy settlement with employes and furnishers of material. The work of building the houses was entirely done by Indians and halfbreeds belonging to the reservation and to the band for which the houses were erected, under direction of the Agency carpenter; therefore, the entire amount of the appropriation was spent among the Indians, with exception of the purchase of bricks, lime, doors windows &c., After furnishing all material on the ground, I let to each Indian who desired to take the job the erection of the building, according to specifications, for the sum of one hundred dollars, as stated in my estimate as quoted. This hundred dollars I desire to pay over and take receipt from the builder, who pays from the same all bills for labor required in erection of house. I also desire in same way to pay log[g]ers, by measurement of number of feet of logs delivered at the mill at the rate of four dollars per thousand as estimated; and also, to pay for hawling and delivering of lumber and other material at the building site, according to estimated price. Those bills I desire authority to check for soon as the money becomes available. The open market purchases for bricks, lime doors, nails, locks, etc., will be submitted to your office for authority for payment in the usual way.

I trust the Hon. Commissioner will grant my request of settlement as the manner of employment I adopted for the erection of the houses was the most economical and expeditious, and allowed of the expenditure of the fund among deserving and progressive Indians who desired to work and earn. The work is being done as well as if executed by skilled white mechanics, and as Inspector [Benjamin H.] Miller, who is now here, has examined and inspected the buildings to his satisfaction, I trust the Hon. Commissioner of Indian Affairs will expedite matters by allowing me to settle the accounts in the manner indicated.

I am very respectfully,
Your obedient servant,
Peter Ronan,
United States Indian Agent.

November 30, 1891
LR 43,796/1891, RG 75, National Archives, Washington, D.C.

The last months of 1891 were to be yet another chapter in the long running conflict over land claims of the Bonners Ferry Kootenai.[70] In November Ronan escorted a delegation of Bonners Ferry Kootenai to the Flathead Reservation to examine the prospects of moving from northern Idaho to the reservation. Despite the concurrent aggression by local whites against the Dayton Creek allotments held by some reservation Kootenai, Ronan reported on December 11, 1891b, that part of the Bonners Ferry band agreed to move to the reservation.[71] Ronan reported on July 9, 1892, that some of the Bonners Ferry people had arrived on Flathead.

David McLoughlin was the mixed blood son of Dr. John McLoughlin who was head of the Columbia Department of the Hudson's Bay Company for two decades. Between 1864 and 1870, David operated a Hudson's Bay Company store on Kootenai Lake. According to Ronan, he married a Kootenai woman and they had a large number of children. In 1884, he wrote an extended essay on the Upper Kootenai Tribe and another on the Lower Kootenai for Rev. Father Pascal Tosi, S.J., a missionary stationed at Coeur d'Alene.[72] No further information was found about David, the son of the Bonners Ferry Kootenai chief in 1891.

United States Indian Service,
Flathead Agency,
Nov. 30th, 1891.

Hon. Commissioner Indian Affairs
Washington, D.C.
Sir:
Referring to your letter "Land" 26030 – 1891. Authority 28510, Dated October 21st, 1891, in reference to my letter of July 14th, 1891, reporting the status of the non-reservation Indians of Northern Idaho. You advise that the whole matter was submitted to the Secretary of the Interior for his consideration on the 27th of August last, and that the Secretary, under date of the 17th October, 1891, authorized you to instruct me to use every proper means to induce the said non-reservation Kootenai to remove to and settle on the Flathead Reservation. He also authorized the use of $5,000 of the funds for the relief of destitute Indians, for the purpose of supplying the non-reservation Kootenais

with food and the necessaries of life, provided they shall remove to and settle upon the Jocko or Flathead reservation in Montana. You also add that you are relying whol[l]y upon me to accomplish this business, and that you are not unmindful of other important duties which I have in hand — housing and caring for the Bitter Root Flathead Indians lately removed to the Flathead Reservation, etc., but that you are satisfied that I will so manage the business as to justify your belief that I will be able to accomplish the best results without the aid of any one not connected with the Agency.

First thanking you for the confidence reposed in me I shall proceed to report my action in this matter.

Learning that the Indians referred to were scattered in different hunting camps along the Kootenai river from the Montana boundary line at Tobacco Plains to 49th parallell on the Kootenai river, on the first of November I despatched a trustworthy runner well acquainted with the hunting grounds of the Kootenais, to advise them to meet me no later than the 15th of the same month at their village, some five miles below Bonner's Ferry, on the Kootenai river, in Northern Idaho.

On the 9th of November I left the Flathead Agency, and on the night of the 12th arrived at Eatonville, on Kootenai river. From that place I proceeded to Bonners Ferry, engaged an Interpreter and proceeded to the Indian encampment, where I learned that the Second Chief of the Kootenai had not arrived in camp; that they wished to wait for his council in the meeting, and that they also wished me to send for one David McLaughlin [McLoughlin], a mixed blood and the father of a large Kootenai family — an educated man and the son of Dr. McLaughlin [McLoughlin], who in the early history of Oregon, managed the Hudson Bay Fur Company. David McLaughlin, a mixed blood, as before stated, and considered a member of the Kootenai tribe, is an old man, born in 1821, and in accordance with the wishes of the Indians I sent a runner to his camp at the Boundary line, near the British Custom House, and invited him to the Council — a distance by canoe of sixty miles and overland thirty-five miles.

I found the Indians destitute of everything in the way of provisions and clothing, and in order to hold the camp together until all arrived and my business was fully understood by them, I was compelled to buy and distribute among them a sufficient quantity of provisions to support them while I remained near their camp.

At the first Council I fully stated to them the wishes of the Hon. Secretary of the Interior and Commissioner of Indian Affairs, that the Kootenai Indians should abandon the Kootenai river country and remove to the Jocko reservation, among their relations and brethren of the same tribe who resided on Dayton Creek, on Said reservation, and who were waiting for them with a warm welcome. That after removing to the reservation the Government would provide each family with land and necessary agricultural implements; with a house to live in; with seeds of all kinds to sow, and provisions and clothing; and to support each family until crops were raised by them and self sustainment secured.

The Indians were favorably impressed with the proposition, but I found an element among interested traders and squaw men, who encouraged the Indians to remain where they were and to secure title to the lands they occupied.

I pointed out that one by one the Indians were selling to white settlers their little improvements and rights to occupancy. That within a very short period the lands upon which their lodges stood would be occupied by the houses of white men, and but a short time remained until the lands would be fenced in all about them, and that they would have no place of refuge except their hunting grounds in the rocks and snow drifts of the mountains. The railroad called the Great Northern already swept through their valley; a townsite company were already booming the lands of the Indian village right where we stood in council; the miners had secured the surrounding mountains by staking them off for quartze claims mill sites etc., and the whites were gathering around them like the leaves of the forest.

The Council adjourned in the evening to meet next day, as the Indians expressed it "to talk and smoke and sleep over the words of the white Chief from the Flatheads!"

On the next day after hearing the speeches of the two head Chiefs, who are both very old men, it was decided that David, son of the head Chief — a man of some thirty years of age, who talks a little English, and is an uncom[m]only intelligent and moral Indian, with four of the most trusted head men of the band would accompany me back to the Jocko reservation, to examine the land and climate and to consult with Chief Eneas and the Kootenai Indians of the reservation.

We left Bonners Ferry on horseback and with pack animals, and after two days of most tedious travel through a dense forest and deep mud, caused by heavy rain storms, arrived at Kootenai, on the Northern Pacific Railroad. Here I purchased tickets of transportation for my ragged delegation, after remaining over one night, and took the Northern Pacific train for Arlee, where we arrived on November 23d.

Arriving at the Agency I found United States Inspector Miller, and learning that the Kootenai Indians of the reservation were out hunting and that their Chief Eneas lay sick at Dayton Creek, I sent word to the reservation Kootenais to gather at their village at Dayton Creek, and to let me know when they would be ready to meet the the [sic] delegation of their people from Northern Idaho. I expect in a few days from date to proceed to Dayton Creek, which will require wagon travel of over sixty miles. The Indian Delegation will go with me and it will probably be then and there decided as to their immediate removal to that locality on the reservation. The band or tribe I have to deal with consists of two hundred and twenty-seven people, who are in the most destitute circumstances — living in their cotton lodges, and with hardly clothing enough to cover their nakedness — without provisions except that which is purchased from the sale of skins and furs procured from their hunting excursions. Still, like all Indians I have had to deal with, they cling to home and their camping ground, and are loath to depart from the burying ground of their ancestors. However, the visit of their trusted young Chief and head men will have its influence. I have spared no pains to show the benefits conferred upon the reservation Indians by the Government, and I feel almost assured that I shall be able to remove the whole tribe within a reasonable time.

Herewith I transmit account of expenses incurred to date and trust that my actions may be approved and my accounts promptly authorized to be settled, as I paid the cash from my private funds and am in need of reimbursement.

I am very respectfully
Your obedient Servant
Peter Ronan
United States Indian Agent.

December 2, 1891
LR 43,723/1891, RG 75, National Archives, Washington, D.C.

Inspector Benjamin H. Miller filed a series of reports on Flathead Agency on December 15, 1891. The reports were generally favorable except for comments about Dr. John Dade, agency physician, and Robert Irvine, the Kootenai farmer.[73] Miller suggested that Dade was too old for the job and reported that Irvine was "a drinking man," See Ronan's defense of his two employes in his February 18, 1892, letter. The Commissioner of Indian Affairs had earlier questioned Dr. Dade's reports in October 1891.[74]

United States Indian Service,
Flathead Agency,
Dec. 2, 1891.

Hon. Commissioner Indian Affairs,
Washington, D.C.
Sir:

In forwarding my report for the month of November, I wish to state that it has been an unprecedented busy month at this Agency. The building of houses and caring for the Flathead Indians removed from the Bitter Root Valley; the necessity of running the mill night and day, sawing lumber and grinding wheat; the hauling of logs to the mill; the hauling of lumber from the mill to the building sites, wagons arriving laden with wheat, while others were being driven away with flour for distant Indian homes, lent a busy scene at this small Indian Agency. As will be seen by report forwarded yesterday [i.e., November 30], I made my trip to northern Idaho and returned with Chief David and four of the principal men of the tribe. We rested at the Agency while I sent word for Chief Eneas of the reservation Kootenais to meet us at Dayton Creek. I have made all arrangements to start, with the Indians, on Saturday. Will convey Indians, interpreter, and their lug[g]age by four horse ambulance, and I shall drive with an employe in a road-cart. Have procured a large tent, and Sibley stove, and will camp out during journey, and while at Dayton Creek. The weather is cold, but shall try to make it as comfortable as possible.

Flathead houses are completed with exception of two. When all are provided with stoves, they will have comfortable quarters.

Inspector Miller left the reservation for the Blackfeet on the 2nd inst.

Herewith I have the honor to enclose Sanitary report and report of funds and indebtedness; also report of farmers, and have the honor to be

Very respectfully,
Your obedient servant,
Peter Ronan,
United States Indian Agent.

December 4, 1891
LR 44,290/1891, RG 75, National Archives, Washington, D.C.

The transmittal letter for this medical report from the agency physician was signed by the Flathead Agency Clerk Thomas E. Adams in Ronan's absence from the reservation, but it is reproduced here because it has valuable information about the reservation and this letter is referred to in Ronan's letter of October 16, 1891, and annotation. This letter is marked "File," but see Ronan's February 18, 1892, letter defending Dr. Dade's work against charges made by Indian Inspector Benjamin J. Miller.

United States Indian Service,
Flathead Agency,
Dec. 4th, 1891.

Hon. Commissioner of Indian Affairs,
Washington, D.C.

Sir:

In the absence of the agent, on duty connected with removal of Kootenais Indians to reserve, I have the honor to forward communication from John Dade, Agency physician, the same, being a reply to office letter "A" 37903 – 91 dated November 5" 1891.

Very respectfully
Your obt. svt.
Thos E. Adams
Agency Clerk.

Enclosure:

United States Indian Service,
Flathead Agency,
Dec 4th, 1891.

Hon. Commissioner of Indian Affairs

In answer to your questions would respectfully state that the reservation is in a very healthy location and no causes surrounding it to produce sickness. I am satisfied that the great cause of sickness heretofore has been the Indians crowding themselves together in their tepees where the smoke and dirt caused the air to become very impure, they have now left their tepees and are living in good comfortable houses, they are using some industry in cultivating their farms and gardens raising good healthy vegetables they are learning to cook and prepare their food better. All these causes combined make them healthier.

I would also state that they are giving up some of their old customs, they have entirely given up their Medicine Men and very few Indians now use the sweathouse that was a great cause of sickness.

The fevers I have reported are of Mountain origin not Malarial the reason of my diagnosis was that the symptoms indicated a remission and I found Quinine relieved them readily.

I would further state that their better living and cleanliness has caused a great decrease in scrofula and lung diseases.

The Indians are now in fine health.

Your obedient
Servant
John Dade
Physician.

December 11, 1891a

LR 44,145/1891, telegram, RG 75, National Archives, Washington, D.C.

The aggressive actions of the Upper Flathead Valley whites in jumping the Dayton Creek allotments of Kootenai Indian farmers happened just as Ronan and the Office of Indian Affairs were trying to convince the Bonners Ferry Kootenai to move to the reservation. Ronan had just made the allotments in August 1891. See the annotation for Ronan's August 25, 1891b, letter for a summary of the conflict and the government's ineffectual efforts to protect the Kootenai farmers on Dayton Creek.

A Helena newspaper clipping dated December 22, 1891, relating to the Dayton Creek allotments and other Flathead Reservation affairs was filed with this telegram.[75] Ronan may have included the clipping in another letter to the Commissioner during late December 1891.

Dec. 11 1891
Arlee Mont

Commissioner Indian Affairs Washn DC

Party of twenty or thirty armed men came to Dayton Creek on day of my arrival and Commenced jumping land assigned to Indians under your instructions dated sept seventh eighteen hundred and ninety one. Indians proposed to meet them on equal terms with arms. My advice prevailed to remain quiet until your office was apprised of the pending trouble. Chief Eneas sick but controls his Indians; have Confidence he will prevent his band from being drawn into trouble with the land jumpers who are doing their utmost to aggravate Indians to hostility. Would advise that U S Marshall be ordered to scene at once with instructions to order whites from Indian land. If order not Complied with Send at least two Companies of troops, as land is north of boundarys. Jumpers Claim indians have no right to it and agents inter ference receives no attention from them as they claim the allotments of land to Indians was the Agents action and will not be sustained by Govt. Trouble Serious and will lead to blood shed unless immediate action is taken. Await instructions before proceeding to Idaho to remove the band who agreed to settle at Dayton Creek.

Ronan Agt.

December 11, 1891b

LR 44,146/1891, telegram, RG 75, National Archives, Washington, D.C.

See Ronan's August 6, 1889; February 21, 1891; and November 30, 1891, letters and annotations for more on the long running land conflict of the Bonners Ferry Kootenai.

Dec. 11 1891
Arlie Mont

Commr Indian Affairs Washn DC

Council at Dayton Creek successful; impediments throw[n] in way by whites but Indian delegation agreed to remove. They have Cattle and horses; if all Come will require fourteen Cars for transportation from Kootenia Idaho to Arlie Mont one hundred and fifty seven miles; from Kootenia river to Railroad City five miles; stock to be driven & families transported by wagons from agency to Dayton Creek Seventy miles; transportation by wagon and Drives stock; with authority granted to pay for transportation for all or as many Choose to Come at once? May I also Check in fund for transportation any expense already incurred and forward vouchers; no time should be lost in order to secure success will have to return to Idaho with delegation to arrange removal.

Ronan Agt.

December 14, 1891a
LR 45,207/1891, RG 75, National Archives, Washington, D.C.

United States Indian Service,
Flathead Agency,
December 14, 1891.

Hon. Commissioner Indian Affairs
Washington, D.C.

Sir:

Having learned from my messenger that Chief Eneas of the reservation Kootenai Indians at Dayton Creek, was very ill, and that pursuant to my call, most of the head-men and Indians had returned from their hunt and were ready to meet the delegation of Kootenai Indians that accompanied me from Northern Idaho, to look at the lands and advantages offered to them to remove to this reservation.

On the morning of the 3d of December, I left the Agency. A four horse ambulance, driven by Irvin, the Kootenai farmer, conveyed Chief David and his Indians, while I followed with an Agency empoye in a road wagon. The first night was spent at the trading post at St. Ignatius Mission, and in the morning I gave the Indians an opportunity to visit the industrial school for boys and girls. Never having seen an Indian school before they were delighted and astonished to see the boys in the work shops and school rooms, applying themselves to their trades and studies, and the girls in their classes and sewing rooms.

At Crow Creek, fifteen miles beyond the Mission, the tongue of our ambulance was broken in fording the stream which was lined on either side with ice; but but [sic] we procured a farm wagon from Sophie, an Indian woman and continued on that night to the Foot of Flathead Lake. On the 7th, through floating ice, we were ferried across the Lake, and by a hard drive over a rough and rocky road for twenty-two miles, reached the Kootenai village, at Dayton Creek.

On the morning of the 8th Council was held at the house of Chief Eneas, who lay ill upon his bed. I briefly recited the instructions which were sent to me from the Honorable Commissioner of Indian Affairs, of my trip to Idaho, with the hope of bringing the whole tribe back with me to the reservation; of the opposition which I met, already reported to your office; of the final conclusion of the Idaho Kootenais to send the delegation that now accompanied me to look at the country; council with Chief Eneas and his people, and, to finally decided whether they would leave their own country, or not and accept the generous offer of the Indian Department at Washington.

Chief Eneas gave them a warm reception from his sick bed, and advised them to listen carefully to what I had to say, vouching for my long tried fidelity to the Indians, and advising them to give up their hunting grounds, now over-run with white people, and betake themselves to raising stock and cultivating the land. It was only a short time since himself and his people had adopted this policy, but if he lived he would use all of his energy to induce his people to remain at home and cultivate the land. He aluded [sic] to the fact that at that hour there were twenty-five, or thirty armed men who arrived from the white settlements at the Head of the Lake, and announced their purpose to hold the land which was allotted to the Indians near their village, claiming that it was beyond the boundary of their reserve and that the Indians had no right to it. Although his young men demanded to go out on their allotments, on equal terms, with arms in their hands, he would listen to the Agent's advice, and restrain them from interfering with the trespassers, until the Great Father in Washington was apprised of their trouble and would take measures to protect the Indians in their rights. I purchased a beef for them and left them to welcome their guests, eat and talk. The Council lasted for two days and it was finally agreed that the Kootenai Indians of Northern Idaho would remove to Dayton Creek, and take up their homes among the reservation Kootenais, first having me to promise that they would be provided with provisions and clothing, houses, agricultural implements, wagons and harness, seed, and assistance in teaching them to farm. Some of the tribe own cattle to the amount of one hundred head, and about one hundred and fifty horses. They claimed, properly, that they could not march and drive their cattle such a long distance in winter time, on account of mountain ranges and deep snow, nor in early Spring, on account of high water in the numerous streams. They asked for transportation for all who had none from Kootenai river to Kootenai station, on the Northern Pacific railroad, thirty-five miles; then by rail to Arlee, near the Agency, 155 miles; and from the Agency to Dayton Creek seventy miles. When I meet the tribe in Northern Idaho, I shall try to induce those who own Stock to remain and winter them there, and offer provisions and clothing to those who remain there and take care of the stock and in the Spring, after the floods, to furnish provisions and assistance in making the march and drive to the reservation, in Montana. The presence of a mob of whitemen at Dayton Creek, jumping the allotments made by me to the members of Chief Eneas' band, on Dayton Creek, and North of the boundary, under instructions from the Hon. Commissioner of Indian Affairs, and the fact that one of the locators had commenced cutting a ditch about three miles above the Indian village, which would turn the water of the creek from its natural course and upon the land he located and completely cut off the supply which runs through the Indian village, was an ag[g]ravating piece of business to the young Indians of the village[, and it was a fortunate circumstance that I came there in time to prevent them from meeting the jumpers in open hostility.

This piece of business also had a chilling effect upon the Kootenai Indians from Northern Idaho, who had just left such scenes of land jumping by the whites from the Indians, to seek peaceful homes and an opportunity to be assisted in the support of themselves and their families on a reservation. My promise that the authorities in Washington, would settle the difficulty and do justice to the Indians as well as to the whites, and carry out every promise made to them, had the effect to assure them of protection and assistance. Soon as pressing business matters are adjusted at the Agency, I shall return to Northern Idaho with the delegation that accompanied me. A council will be held there and matters explained to the whole tribe by their representatives and myself, and I shall at once enter upon the work of removal. Herewith I enclose necessary expenses to date accompanied by vouchers.

I am very respectfully
Your obedient Servant
Peter Ronan
United States Indian Agent.

December 14, 1891b
LR 45,331/1891, RG 75, National Archives, Washington, D.C.

The problems Ronan encountered on fulfilling Henry Carrington's promises to Chief Charlo — especially regarding Chief Arlee's farm — are summarized in the annotation to Ronan's October 24, 1891, letter. On March 10, 1892, Ronan wrote that Charlo had received the agency farm in lieu of Chief Arlee's farm promised by Carrington.

United States Indian Service,
Flathead Agency,
December 14, 1891.

Hon. Commissioner Indian Affairs,
Washington, D.C.

Sir:

On the day of my second departure to consum[m]ate the removal of the Kootenai Indians from the vicinity of Bonners Ferry, Northern Idaho, I desire to make special report in regard to Charlots' band of Bitter Root Flathead Indians.

Their houses, to the number of twenty, are now completed and occupied by the Indian families. By issuing stoves from the supply on hand, to the exclusion of other deserving and needy applicants that occupy houses on the reservation, I was enabled to supply the new Flathead homes, each with a cooking stove and a heating stove, with exception of two families. Much jealousy exists among the Indians on the reservation on account of the new comers having a beef issue as well as a regular issue of supplies and comfortable new houses to live in while other families and patentees of land that removed before Charlot came with the small remainder of his band, are left to rely upon their own exertions. However, this is only one of the annoyances: Charlot claims that he was promised by special Agent Carrington, a more spacious house than those built for his people according to my specifications. A brick fireplace and chimney he states was also promised him, and the ownership of Chief Arlees ranche, (now deceased[)]. I have made arrangements to satisfy him in regard to a more spacious house by adding an addition sixteen feet square and to build for him a fire place and chimney which will make an additional cost for labor, lumber and other material of one hundred and fifty dollars. As to the occupancy of Chief Arlees ranch I believe this idea cannot be entertained as Arlee left the place to his grand daughter and her husband and the latter devoted himself this year to its cultivation and raised eight hundred bushels of wheat and oats, stacked forty tons of hay and has over one hundred head of cattle and horses, built by his own effort a new house, and is now a self supporting Indian. When I first assumed charge here, this Indian, Suasa, was one of the wildest and most uncontrollable young man of the reservation Indians. To thrust him forth from his wifes inheritance and the comforts of his own efforts would probably place him once more in his original role. Not gaining my consent to take this place, Charlot cast his eye upon or was advised to try to get the ownership of a farm belonging to the Indian widow of a whiteman, named Coture, who has a large family. I informed the Chief that improvements etc., could only be obtained by purchase and as it was one of the best improved farms on the Jocko valley, with good dwelling, barn, outhouses, milk house, orchard and timothy meadow, it could not be obtained for a less sum than five thousand dollars. The Agency farm also attracted his attention and in order to satisfy him — having made no promises outside of those I could fulfil through the Hon Commissioner of Indian Affairs, I would apply for the privilege to turn over the Government farm to him if he could get no other improved place, and make requisition for hay next year. Charlot desires to occupy the widows place in preference to any other farm and asked me to submit the matter to you. Unguarded promises should never be made by any person dealing with Indians. It is generally left to the Agent to fulfil them or to cope with the embittered feelings of the Indians who profess to to [sic] believe it is his fault if not carried out. I have no complaint to make against Chief Charlot — he is a just and agreeable man, but is a believer in the fulfilment of promises. He has always kept his word and expects the word of others to be kept. I made him no promise except such as I felt assured would be fulfilled and he seems to appreciate that fact.

> I am very respectfully
> Your obedient servant
> Peter Ronan
> United States Indian Agent.

December 14, 1891c
LR 45,156/1891, RG 75, National Archives, Washington, D.C.

> On November 18, 1891, Henry B. Carrington recommended to the Commissioner of Indian Affairs that a government school be established in Jocko for the Salish Indians who had just removed from the Bitterroot Valley. The Commissioner on November 27, 1891, asked Ronan for a report and cost estimates on establishing the school. Ronan's reply was filed and no further action was taken in the matter.[76]

> United States Indian Service
> Flathead Agency,
> Dec. 14th, 1891.

Hon. Commissioner Indian Affairs,
Washington, D.C.
Sir:
Referring to "Education 41846 — 1891," dated at Washington, November 27, 1891, stating that recommendation is made that a day school be established on the Flathead reservation near the Agency, to accomodate especially those children from the Bitter Root Valley, in the vicinity of the Agency. I would respectfully state that the missionaries having in charge the School at St. Ignatius Mission, have already established a day school as well as a night school in one of their own buildings near the Agency, and have in attendance at the day school an average number of twenty-nine, ranging in age from four to fifteen years. At the night school there is an average attendance of twenty-five young men, ranging from eighteen to thirty-five years of age. Great enthusiasm is displayed, especially by the young men who attend night school. Chief Charlot is a just man — but non progressive. In allowing the children to go to school, he warned the teachers that if the hair of the children was cut, he would at once withdraw them from the school. I trust this Indian prejudice will soon give away to reason. At present they must be humored to a certain extent. The faculty at the Mission are now preparing for the erection of suitable buildings to accomodate the School. It is my opinion that the establishment of any other school at present at the Agency, would create dissatisfaction among the Indians, and a clash which would be detrimental to the cause of education and civilization at this Agency. Howeve[r] if you so desire I shall submit estimate

for the erection of a school house for day school, and also that of an Industrial collage [sic] as there are no unoccupied buildings at this Agency.

I have the honor to be
Very respectfully
Your obedient Servant,
Peter Ronan,
United States Indian Agent.

December 31, 1891
LR 945/1892, filed with authority 29,484/1892, RG 75, National Archives, Washington, D.C.

For biographical information on Chief Isaac of the Bonners Ferry Kootenai, see the annotation to Ronan's August 6, 1889, letter. No further information was found on David, the son of the Bonners Ferry chief, or Moise, the second chief of the band in 1891.

United States Indian Service,
Flathead Agency,
December 31st, 1891.

Hon. Commissioner Indian Affairs
Washington, D.C.
Sir:

Following up your instructions of October 21st, 1891 — "Land 26030 — 1891, Authority 28510," on the 14th of December, 1891, accompanied by a trusted interpreter of the Kootenai language, and the five Indian delegates who accompanied me from Northern Idaho on my previous visit, sent by the Kootenai tribe of that locality to look at the Flathead reservation, consult with the Indians residing upon it, return to their people with me and report to them before fully deciding upon removal from the country they claimed as their own from time immemorial.

At Kootenai station, in Northern Idaho, where we arrived by the Northern Pacific railroad on the morning of the 15th, it was found that the stage carrying passengers and mail to Bonner's Ferry, on the Kootenai river, ceased running on account of condition of the road; rain storms having made the country almost a sea of mud. The mail being carried on horseback, I employed two saddle horses for self and interpreter, while the Indians accompanied us over the muddy road and through a dreary forest on foot. It occupied two days to make the trip to the Kootenai river, and arrived at Frys Post on the 16th. I proceeded from there to the Kootenai village on the day following. A fire was lit by the Indians in a little building erected by the Catholic Missionaries and occupied by them for religious purposes on the rare occasions of their visits to this much neglected and dissevered band from the Kootenai tribes of Indians. A Council was called and David, the head man of the delegation recited to the assembled Indians the pleasure of his visit and that of his companions to the Flathead reservation; and also explained the advantages of its soil, grazing, etc. — its schools, churches, workshops, mills and the Indian advancement in agricultural pursuits and the raising of stock by the Indians who lived there. Their homes and houses, cooking and heating stoves — their comfortable appearance, etc., and finally concluded by saying that it was his voice that the Kootenai Indians occupying the country of the Kootenai river valley at once signify to the Agent their willingness to remove to Dayton Creek, and settle among the reservation Kootenai now living with Chief Eneas.

The head Chief Isaac seconded the views of David, and was ready to advance the removal of such of the families of his people that were prepared to face the storm and remove to another country at this unfavorable season. As for himself he could not undertake the journey now he was an old man and had a mother who was a very old woman. He would remain until spring with his family and take care of his few head of cattle and ponies and then with the assistance of the young men who would travel with his camp to the Jocko reservation, over the Indian trail which ran North, up the Kootenai river, and thence South through Pleasant Valley, and on the Dayton Creek, on the Flathead reservation.

Noticing that Moise, the second Chief, was not present, and that some of the young men were absent, I inquired the cause and was informed that Moiese objected to the removal, stating that he belonged to the British Kootenais, and if pressed to move would go with his followers across the British line which was only some thirty miles distant from his camp. To this I replied and sent word to the Chief that I was glad of the information; that Moise and other British Indians would be at perfect liberty to depart from American soil, and take their belongings across the British line, while the American Indians would follow me to the reservation in Montana. I also sent word to Moise that British Indians could not acquire title to land on the American side of the boundary, and if he desired to separate from the band of Kootenais on the plea of belonging to the British portion of the tribe, that he must vacate the land, with all other Indians of the band holding the same views, and take up their homes on British soil, as I did not believe they could acquire title unless they became citizens of the United States.

Here I adjourned the Council until the following day and summoned Moise to come and explain himself in person.

On that day Moise and his brother agreed not to interfere with settlers in acquiring title to land, and that they would settle across the border when the head Chief and his followers would leave for the Flathead reservation.

Owing to the condition of the roads, transportation could not be procured to the Northern Pacific railroad unless an exorbitant price was paid. Three cents per pound for a hawl [sic] of thirty-two miles to Kootenai on the Northern Pacific Railroad was being offered at the time by traders in provisions and merchandise. The matter of expense of removing at that season, all of which would have to be paid from the fund placed to my credit for the relief of the Indians, provided they removed from Idaho, was fully discussed, and they agreed with me that it was better to remove in Spring, (and thereby save great expense) when I would accompany them and provide for them on their March over the old Indian trail to Dayton Creek on this reservation. The date fixed for all the Indians of the band to meet me at their village on the Kootenai river, and prepare for the march was fixed Easter Sunday, April 17th, 1892, when I shall keep my promise if health will permit.

Five of the Indians, and the wife of one of them, announced that they would accompany me back to the reservation when I should depart if I could provide for their journey. This I did, and sent them on to Dayton Creek, where I shall supply their necessities until joined by the tribe in the Spring.

I trust that the Honorable Commissioner will approve of my action and that he will strengthen my views in regard to insisting upon Indians who claim to be British subjects to remove across the line at the time I remove the American Indians, and to throw no impediment in the way of white settlers seeking to obtain homes upon public land. A letter to be read to such Indians at the next council will have the desired effect of taking all of the Indians from that locality and locating where they properly belong — the American Indians upon a reservation, and the British Indians on British soil.

Enclosed please find vouchers for necessary expenses incurred in carrying out this work so far.

I am very respectfully
Your obedient servant,
Peter Ronan,
United States Indian Agent.

First Communion at St. Ignatius Mission, June 21, 1891.
Oregon Province Archives, Gonzaga University, Spokane, Washington,
negative 120.2.03a.

1892

January 3, 1892
LR 1,154/1892, RG 75, National Archives, Washington, D.C.

In 1892 and 1893 the friction between the reservation Kootenai Indians and white settlers just north of the boundary continued to mushroom. Despite the fact that for years the Kootenai had harvested hay from the land and, at least by 1891, had built cabins, fences, and gardens on the land, hostile white settlers tried to jump the allotments Ronan made. See Ronan's August 25, 1891b, letter and annotation for more background information. See Ronan's July 25, 1892, telegram and later letters relative to the warrant for the arrest of Chief Eneas after the chief asked the white invaders to leave. See Ronan's March 24, 1892a, June 11, 1892, and July 9, 1892, letters for more about the government's fumbling efforts to protect the allottees.

> United States Indian Service,
> Flathead Agency,
> Jan. 3d, 1892.

Hon. Commissioner Indian Affairs
Washington, D.C.

Sir:

In forwarding my report for the month of December, I desire to say that the holidays have closed on this reservation in a most satisfactory manner. There was less drinking and carrousing among the Indians and mixed bloods during the festive season than was ever before noticed by me since taking charge of this Agency.

The close of the quarter is a busy one in the office, with paying off of regular employes, Indian Judges and policemen, and the additional settling of accounts with Indians for construction of Flathead Indian houses, hauling of saw logs, transportation of lumber from mill to building sites, etc. Etc. The Indians accomplished all of the work and are now receiving the reward of labor by payment for the work done. The Indians and mixed bloods are pleased that the money was expended among them for labor instead of paying it to white contractors from outside the reservation boundaries.

I spent several days of the month of December, in Northern Idaho, in obedience to your orders, special report of which has already been furnished to your office.

Affairs connected with the Agency are in good condition. Charlots band of Bitter Root Flatheads are comfortably settled in their houses, to the number of twenty families; all are agreeable and seem satisfied in their new homes.

The United States Marshall for Montana sent a deputy to order trespassers from Kootenai Indian land at Dayton Creek. Five of the trespassers refused to obey the Deputies instructions. In letter of recent date, the Marshall informs me that he will proceed to Dayton Creek in person, and attend to the enforcement of the law.

Herewith I have the honor to enclose sanitary report and report of funds and indebtedness, also reports of farmers, and quarterly School report, and have the honor to be

Very respectfully
Your obedient servant,
Peter Ronan
United States Indian Agent.

January 5, 1892
LR 1,412/1892, RG 75, National Archives, Washington, D.C.

In this letter Ronan gave valuable evidence about the state of the roads and transportation infrastructure on the reservation in 1892. Even if Ronan could get tribal members to work on the roads and bridges without compensation, he needed funds to pay for saw logs and spikes. On January 16, 1892, the Commissioner of Indian Affairs replied that there was no money available to pay for work done on reservation roads, but he suggested rules to require gratis road work from tribal members. No mention was made of the cost of materials. Ronan responded on February 3, 1892, with draft regulations requiring two days work per year from each able bodied male on the reservation. His proposed regulations exempted agency and St. Ignatius Mission employees and contractors working on the reservation, but did not explain why the white men working for the agency and mission should be excused. On March 3, 1892, the Commissioner of Indian Affairs approved the regulations.[1] Ronan included no discussion of road work in his August 26, 1892, annual report but did include the topic in his August 5, 1893, annual report.

United States Indian Service,
Flathead Agency,
January 5th, 1891 [sic].

Hon. Commissioner Indian Affairs
Washington, D.C.
    Sir:
    Referring to your letter "Land," dated at Washington, December 21st, 1891, permit me to state that I am very much impressed with the useful and practical sug[g]estions therein contained in regard to condition of roads on many Indian reservations which: "is a reproach to the Indian service."
    Last year there was raised by the Indians, on this reservation, at least eighty thousand bushels of wheat and oats; in some cases the Indians hauled their wheat from a distance of sixty-five miles to have it ground into flour at the Agency Mill, involving cost of ferrage across the Pend 'd Oreille river at the Foot of Flathead Lake, which by reference to some of my traveling expense vouchers, the Hon. Commissioner will at once notice is a very high bill of expense to Indians, travelers and freighters who are compelled to cross the river with teams. Yet the Ferry is maintained by an Indian at such expense that he must impose a good price upon travelers, who gladly pay for accomodation across a river that would be utterly impassable but for the present maintenance of the ferry boat.
    On the Jocko river over which the traveled road crosses to the Agency at three different places, and at certain seasons of the year is utterly impassable, except by bridges, I erected without any cost to the Government three bridges, two of which were swept away by high water. One of said Jocko bridges is about 350 feet long, and constructed with six solid piers embedded in the stream. The stringers and piers are in good condition, but it will be necessary to replank a

portion of it, and put up new railing. I constructed a new bridge in place of one swept away, but there remains another bridge to be built across the Jocko to replace one swept away as before mentioned.

At Ravalli Creek a bridge of some sixty feet in length should be constructed. Also one across Crow Creek 150 feet long, another across Post Creek, of a 100 feet in length and one across Mud Creek, of about one hundred feet in length.

As expressed in your letter: "the roads on the reservation are used mainly, if not almost wholly, for the benefit of the Indians, it is not unreasonable that they should be expected to perform the labor that is necessary to put the roads in proper condition for travel and to keep them in repair."

The labor of repairing of roads and assistance in building bridges across streams I have always insisted upon from the Indians, but means should be given me to supply material.

If the Hon. Commissioner will grant aid I shall proceed to make arrangements to build a bridge across the Pend 'd Oreille river at a point about seven miles below the ferry where the river narrows into a gorge and where a bridge can be thrown across at a comparative small expense, which I can hereafter approximate, and thus save to the dwellers on the West side of Flathead Lake, on this Indian reservation, the cost of ferrage when coming to the Agency or to the Northern Pacific railroad stations for supplies or freights — hauling wheat to the Agency mill to be ground into flour, or drawing lumber from the saw mill back to their camp for urgent and necessary use. The fact that I expect to remove, next April, the Kootenai band of Indians from Northern Idaho to Dayton Creek on this reservation should call attention at once to the utility of having free travel for the Indians over the reservation road to the Agency mills and shops, and to the different railroad stations on the reservation, even if a distance of sixty-five miles in some cases intervene.

As to building and repairing of bridges across the Jocko river, Ravalli Creek, Post Creek, Mud Creek etc., I can accomplish before spring planting and plowing commences, by aid of Indian and Agency labor if I may be allowed one hundred thousand feet of saw logs delivered at the Agency mill at a cost not exceeding four dollars per thousand feet, to be cut into three inch plank and four x four (4 x 4) lumber for railing. Timber for piers and abutments can be procured near the bridge sites. Six kegs of large spikes at five dollars per keg would be all the material required outside of saw logs as I have all necessary tools on hand.

I trust that the Hon. Commissioner will give this matter early attention as the winter season would be the proper time to accomplish the work before spring plowing and seed sowing commences.

As to the bridge across the Pend 'd Oreille river, it will require a great deal of work and expensive hauling of plank and rail material, but all of this work can be accomplished by the Indians, by a haul from Ravalli railroad station to the river, a distance of thirty miles, without expense to the Government, as all whom I talked with on the subject are in favor of building a bridge, across the Pend 'd Oreille river, and to contribute use of teams and labor to transport plank, etc., from the station at Ravalli. From Arlee to Ravalli, a distance of ten miles, the lumber should be sent by rail in order to save a bad wagon haul through a muddy canon. This bridge might receive after attention and consideration, but the Jocko, Ravalli Creek, Crow Creek, Post Creek and Mud

Creek bridges need prompt attention and will be promptly built and repared [sic] if I am allowed the saw logs and spikes estimated for in requisition herein enclosed.

It is readily apparent in connection with building and grain raising — two matters to which attention is most strongly and proper urged by the Indian Department that the transportation by wagon of lumber or wheat, for any considerable distance, exceeds the values of the article itself. Therefore if Indians must make such long hauls to the mills and shops at the Agency, no pains should be spared to give them good roads and bridges, especially where they are willing to contribute teams and labor to accomplish that desirable end.

I am very respectfully
Your obedient servant,
Peter Ronan,
United States Indian Agent.

Enclosed "Estimate of Indian Supplies, &c." for 40,000 feet of logs at $4.00 per thousand for $400 and 6 kegs of spikes at $5.00 each for $30.00.

January 23, 1892
LR 3,815/1892, RG 75, National Archives, Washington, D.C.

> See Ronan's October 24, 1891, and December 14, 1891b, letters and annotations for more information about fulfilling Carrington's promise to give Charlo Chief Arlee's farm. On March 10, 1892, Ronan reported that he had turned the agency farm over to Charlo in partial fulfillment of Carrington's promise.[2]

United States Indian Service,
Flathead Agency,
January 23d, 1892.

Hon. Commissioner Indian Affairs
Washington, D.C.
    Sir:
    Referring to "Land 45331 – 1891," acknowledging receipt of my letter of December 14th, 1891, making special report in regard to Chief Charlot's band of Bitter Root Flathead Indians and alluding to Charlot's claims in said report: that he was promised by Special Agent Carrington, the ownership of Chief Arlee's farm at Jocko reservation, in case of his removal from Bitter Root valley to that reservation, and my statement as to the reason the promise cannot be carried out. Also, as to the Chief not gaining my consent to occupy the Arlee farm, sought to get the ownership of a farm belonging to the Indian widow of a whiteman named Coture, which in all probability could not be obtained for a less sum than five thousand dollars, of which fact I informed him, and in order to satisfy him, I promised to make application for the privilege of turning over the Government farm &c. Your reply also states that your office can find no record "that Chief Arlee's farm on the Jocko reservation was promised Charlot, when he was at Washington, in consideration of his removal, with his band, from the Bitter Root valley to said reservation.["]
    I beg to say that no promise whatever made to Charlot, on his visit to Washington, was binding, as he refused to remove or to accept any proposition made to him. All promises that he now contends for he states were given to him in Bitter Root valley, Montana, by accredited officials of the Interior Department. In connection I respectfully refer to Senate Ex. Doc. No. 70 — 51st Congress,

1st session — page 4, where attention of Department is called to a certain "agreement" — see page 13 (report) entered into between General Carrington and Chief Charlot Victor, stipulating that the said Chief Charlot shall be located upon the old Arlee property upon the Jocko reservation, etc. etc.

Your letter also states that you feel "that all promises made by General Carrington, to Charlot should be carried out; it seems that it would be a great hardship on the heirs of Chief Arlee to take from them, even by purchase, the farm left them as an inheritance by their grandfather;" and you further state that you believe, "everything considered, that it is more desirable to placate Charlot by giving him some other farm than to attempt to get the heirs of Chief Arlee to abandon their farm in his behalf. The widows place of course could not be taken from her except by purchase."

You ask for further information as to the area of the Government farm, etc., and upon receipt your office will consider my recommendation in regard to giving it to Charlot:

The farm in question has a rail fence surrounding about 160 acres; with Agency labor and without other cost to Government this fence was built. In the same way I constructed an irrigation ditch to the farm; plowed considerable portion of the land and seeded it to hay. Not being enough meadow to supply hay for stock, each year I had land plowed and seeded to oats and wheat which was cut green and stacked for hay for supply for Agency stock. A potatoe patch and vegetable garden was also cultivated to supply Agency uses. The land was used for the best interests of the service, as it was not necessary, nor did I make an requisition to purchase hay for Government stock. I believe I can satisfy Chief Charlot by turning this farm over to him for cultivation. His son, who has a family, and his son-in-law also, can, with assistance and encouragement, cultivate good crops when the season opens, and in a very short period, earn their own support. Another convenient location can be procured for Agency farm by an outlay of $200 with which to purchase the improvements of a half breed Kootenai Indian, who desires to remove to another portion of the reservation, where he can have better stock growing facilities. I would suggest that this matter meet your consideration, and would recommend that Chief Charlot be made satisfied by letting him and his relatives have the Government farm, while, with an outlay of not more than two hundred dollars I can equip as good farm for the production of hay for Agency stock, and also for the production of roots and vegetables for Agency use. It seems to me that by adopting that plan the promise to Chief Charlot in regard to a farm can be cheaply and satisfactorily carried out.

On page 13, General Carrington's report, before cited, it will be seen that Chief Charlot's "main personal item desired was a new wagon and harness." Gen. Carrington adds: "he needs these and they were promised."

This promise I can readily fulfill as I have the farm wagon and harness on hand to issue to him.

"The requested cows should be supplied. This was promised."

"He desires a two seated covered spring wagon, to use in visiting his people and getting them settled at work. This was promised."

As those matters quoted seem to occupy the attention of Charlot at present, I desire to say that he should be provided soon as convenient with a set of harness and a two seated covered spring wagon; also that the Flathead families removed to this reservation, be given at least two cows to each family, and that in order to place them on the high road to civilization, self sustainment and independence at least ten acres of land should be fenced for each family, the same broken for seed sowing, and assistance given them to cultivate the soil by an irrigation system. If this opportunity is given them, the Flatheads removed from Bitter Root Valley, will, in a year or two, accomplish the desired end, viz: civilization and self support.

I trust that this report will receive consideration, and that I may be authorized at an early date to submit estimates in order that the coming Spring may witness the advancement of Indian culture and self support upon this reservation.

I am very respectfully,
Your obedient servant,
Peter Ronan,
United States Indian Agent.

February 2, 1892
LR 4,986/1892, RG 75, National Archives, Washington, D.C.
United States Indian Service,
Flathead Agency,
February 2d, 1892.

Hon. Commissioner Indian Affairs
Washington, D.C.
Sir:

At the close of the month of January, I have to report that a great deal of snow fell upon the reservation, but so far has not been followed by very cold weather. The Indian Stock have not suffered, owing in a great measure, that good care was taken of the straw, which was carefully stacked and fenced after threshing, and now, while the country is covered with snow, the cattle belonging to individual Indian families find feed at the stacks to sustain them without loss, to present date.

Nothing of particular mention transpired during the month, outside the regular business transactions of the Agency, and every thing pertaining to the service is in good order — no disagreeable conditions prevail, to my knowledge. The Indians are quiet and contented and seem in general to be taking unusual interest in their home surroundings.

Logging is pursued to considerable extent. Several thousand feet of lumber will be sawed at the Agency mill during the next few months for those who delivered logs.

All of the wheat delivered at the grist mill has been ground into flour, but I expect another delivery of grain soon from Indians who were not able to hawl to the mill all of their grain in the fall, but will now take advantage of the snow and the ice which bridges some of the rivers that heretofore were difficult to cross.

Herewith I have the honor to enclose sanitary report and report of funds and indebtedness, also report of farmers, and have the honor to be

Very respectfully,
Your obedient Servant,
Peter Ronan
United States Indian Agent.

February 3, 1892
LR 4,987/1892, RG 75, National Archives, Washington, D.C.

United States Indian Service,
Flathead Agency,
February 3d, 1892.

Hon. Commissioner Indian Affairs
Washington, D.C.
Sir:

I am in receipt of your letter of January 15th, 1892 — "Land 1412 – 1892," in reference to your office circular letter of December 21st, 1891, relative to condition of roads and bridges on Indian reservations, and requesting me to make it the subject of another communication to your office, submitting a draft of such rules and regulations as I may deem applicable, at least, to this reservation. The matter under consideration I deem of great importance and it shall have every attention that I can give to it, in carrying out your views and instructions. It is quite a task to attempt to arrouse Indians to the necessity of making better roads through the reservation; but it is one that should be continued and insisted upon until something is done. Roads are the channels of trade from the farm to the store, the railroads, the Agency mills and shops, and when they are out of repair and obstructed, expenses are increased in loss of time and breakage of wagons, while sometimes Indians and children are shut off for a time from church and schools. I have been doing what I can to show the Indians that the time given to road repair is work done for themselves and in making a good road they are increasing the durability of their teams and wagons, reducing the cost of getting their produce to market; their grain to the Agency mills, and lumber from the saw mill to their farms.

On this reservation as indicated in my letter of the 5th of January, the greatest necessity is the repair and construction of several bridges at different points on the reservation, which would subserve very materially the interests of the Indians. The roads are in fair order as I have always insisted upon work from the Indians to keep them in order.

I herewith submit a draft of such rules and regulations as deemed practicable on this reservation, as requested in your letter:

Rule 1. All able bodied men living on the reservation, except employes of the War and Interior Department, contractors, school employes and missionaries, will be required to perform two day's labor on the roads each year.

Rule 2d. As licensed traders at each place of business on the reservation are greatly benefited by good roads and bridges, each person holding a lisense [sic] will be required to perform two days labor each year, in their districts on the reservation.

Rule 3d. Where required by the Agency employe, having the work in charge, the Indians and other lawful dwellers on the reservation, amenable to requisition for work on roads and bridges, shall be required to use the wagons, teams, tools, etc., at their command in the road district in which they reside.

Rule 4th. At the proper season of the year required for work to be done on the roads and bridges through the reservation, the Agent shall designate one or more employes to take charge of the work, and it will be the duty of such employe to notify the required number of men and teams etc., to perform said work in their respective districts.

Rule 5th. Any person amenable to the rules who refuses or fails to perform the labor required, after having received due notice, will be reported to the Agent, who shall then take steps to enforce the rules, or provide for punishment by bringing the matter before the Court of Indian Offences for trial.

I believe an enforcement of such rules, as stated in your communication, "by the individual labor of the Indians themselves, will tend to educate them in habits of industry and obedience to laws, and prepare them for higher industrial pursuits, incident to civilized life."

I am very respectfully
Your obedient servant,
Peter Ronan,
United States Indian Agent.

February 18, 1892
LR 7,313/1892, RG 75, National Archives, Washington, D.C.

> This letter was Ronan's answer to a February 6, 1892, inquiry by the Commissioner of Indian Affairs based on a report on Flathead Agency by Inspector Benjamin H. Miller. Senator G. G. Vest of Missouri also wrote to the Commissioner to ask about any charges filed against Dr. John Dade, the Flathead Agency physician. The Commissioner accepted Ronan's defense of Dade; Robert Irvine, assistant farmer; and some of the Indian police and judges, and no further action was taken.[3] For biographical information on Dade see Ronan's June 14, 1888, letter and annotation. See also Ronan's October 16, 1891, letter relating to questions about Dade's monthly reports. For Irvine see Ronan's October 31, 1890b, letter and annotation.

United States Indian Service,
Flathead Agency,
February 18th, 1892.

Hon. Commissioner Indian Affairs,
Washington, D.C.

Sir:

Replying to "A" 45483 – '91, dated February 6, 1892, in which you state that you are in receipt of information in relation to certain matters at this Agency as follows:

"Agency Physician: Dr. John Dade is 64 years of age, and is scarcely equal, physically, to the performance of his duties as Agency Physician."

In reply to this I would state that Dr. John Dade was appointed to the place he now holds here originally from the Indian Office in 1886; that he has faithfully filled his position, and at the end of each fiscal year from that date, I have sent his renomination to your Department for consideration with record of his age which I suppose will be found on file in the Indian Office.

Doctor Dade is a man of excellent character — has the confidence of the Indians, and at no time to my knowledge, refused a call upon a patient, whatever the distance from his office to any point on the reserve. If his resignation is called for on account of his age I sincerely hope that a doctor may be appointed to this Agency who will be of equal moral character and as trustful to fulfilment of all duties connected with his profession when called upon by the Indians.

"Assistant Farmer: Robert Irvine, assistant, is reported as a drinking man. It is also stated that some months since he was drunk, and in consequence, became involved in a row."

Assistant Farmer Robert Irvine is a halfbreed, and upon my recommendation was appointed to assist the Kootenai Indians at Dayton Creek, which is 60 miles from this Agency, in commencing farming and other pursuits pertaining to the advancement of this much neglected tribe. How well he succeeded may be noticed from reports from this office showing that some twenty farmes were cultivated last year by this band who never before attempted to cultivate the soil, and that for the first time in the history of that tribe, after harvest last fall they hawled to the Agency a number of bushels of wheat to be ground into flour at the Agency mill, having hawled it by wagon over 60 miles. This advancement was done in a great measure through the efforts of Irvine, whom the Kootenai Chief especially requested nominated for the appointment because he talks the Indian language and the Chief reposes confidence in Irvines power to promote the interest of the Kootenai tribe in agricultural pursuits. The drinking affair was reported to me at the time, and Irvine was sent for. He acknowledged that on the 4th of July of last year he was in company with a number of white freighters and teamsters, and also halfbreed Indians; that on account of the celebration of the day, some one introduced intoxicants and he indulged; that a row commenced among the party, and that in trying to quell it he had to give one or two of the halfbreeds rough usage. They took advantage of the fact that he indulged with them and made complaint that he was intoxicated. I investigated the affair at the time and upon the agreement of Irvine to refrain from drinking in the future continued his employment with the express understanding that he would be discharged if a knowledge of such indulgence again came to my notice.

As to the Indian Judge reported I wish to state that the occurrance took place at the same time and place, and under the same circumstances as that of Irvine. The Judge reported the affair to me in person: Said that he was induced to drink liquor on that day — that he was sorry for it, and a like occurrance would never take place with him. His explanation was so comical that I related it to inspector Miller, at the Agency, after he had listened to the complaint against this particular Judge, from a halfbreed who is wealthy and always has a grievance if things are not conducted by the Indian Judges, police and others connected with the service to suit his particular views, which I have found in many cases to be selfish ones. The explanation of the Indian was: that he came among the party of freighters teamsters and halfbreeds. He was told it was the 4th of July — inducements were offered him to drink, which he did, and came personally to report the circumstances to me, and to state that he never would again be guilty of a like transgression. In his statement he said: "I have no fault to find with the white men who gave me the liquor — no complaint to make against the halfbreeds who induced me to drink it; the only complaint I have is against 4th of July, and when I hear of him hereafter I shall stay at home!"

The reason I did not discharge the men or report the case of the farmer and the Indian Judge was because of the circumstances under which the misdemenors occurred, and the solemn promises that occasion for complaint for such conduct would not happen again.

I am very respectfully
Your obedient servant
Peter Ronan,
U.S. Indian Agent.

February 27, 1892
LR 8,656/1892, RG 75, National Archives, Washington, D.C.

On March 11, 1892, the Commissioner denied the claim for Sabine Mary's medical care, because it was not an emergency.[4] For biographical information on Mary Sabine see Ronan's May 7, 1879, letter and annotation.

United States Indian Service,
Flathead Agency,
February 27th, 1892.

Hon. Commissioner Indian Affairs
Washington, D.C.
Sir:

Herewith I have the honor to enclose communication from the manager of St. Patricks Hospital, Missoula, Montana, which explains itself in regard to enclosed bill. The person treated, as explained in letter, is a woman of good character. Her husband who shot her while intoxicated, is now dead, while she lives upon a farm and with the assistance of her children make a living by cultivation of the soil. There is no hospital on this reservation and her home is about thirty miles from the Agency. She, therefore, placed herself in the care of the Sisters of Providence at Missoula, which is a private institution. The Sisters took care of her while at their hospital without charge, and as the attending physician presented his bill, relief was asked of me as U.S. Agent, in charge of the Indians where she belongs. I can only turn the matter over to the charitable consideration of the Indian Department, trusting that the case may be favorably acted upon, and that the physicians bill be paid.

I am very respectfully
Your obedient servant
Peter Ronan,
U.S. Indian Agent.

First enclosure:

St. Patrick's Hospital
Missoula, Feb 23rd 1892.

Peter Ronan Esq
Arlee, Montana
Dear Sir

Excuse me if I take the liberty of asking you a favor. Can the Government pay or help Sabine Mary, an indian, to pay the included bill. As you know, she is a woman worthy of a favor.

Thirteen years ago, Sabine Mary was shot by her husband in the shoulder, since that time it has discharged continually. Her arm was perfectly helpless, having no use of it whatever, and also caused her a great deal of pain. One of the physicians Dr. D. H. Billmeyer, inquired as closely as possible into the family history, and found woman with exceptionally good blood for an indian, as majority have blood contaminated with tuberculosis, scrofula etc. etc. His advice was sought for the case, and he advised an operation, which would not only relieve her of pain, but of the fetid discharge which flowed continuously from the several sinuses, he furthermore stated that by means of an operation he would not only restore a partially useful arm, but would indeed make a serviceable one. Case was at length given to Dr. Billmeyer and after a short preliminary treatment, performed first operation on the 3rd of December 1891.

The patient was apparently doing well, when from some unaccountable Source a severe attack of erysipelas followed and for many days temperature ranged from 105° to 103°, he finally succeeded in conquering the disease and when she was in condition performed second operation, removing in the two operations almost entire shoulder joint.

After the second operation she made a very rapid recovery, and was discharged finally on February 6th 1892, with a very useful member and one entirely free from pain.

The day before her dismissal from hospital, had a photograph taken of injured arm which accompany bill and statement.

Hoping to have a favorable answer soon,

I am,
Respectfully,
Sister Joseph.

Second enclosure: Bill from Dr. D. H. Billmeyer to Sabine Mary for two operations (December 3, 1891, and January 5, 1892) at $125 each and 67 visits for $200.
Third enclosure: Photograph of Mary Sabine wearing robe but showing shoulder with scars from operations.

March 4, 1892
LR 9,286/1892, RG 75, National Archives, Washington, D.C.

United States Indian Service,
Flathead Agency,
March 4, 1892.

Hon. Commissioner Indian Affairs
Washington, D.C.

Sir:

In submitting report from this Agency for the month of February, I have to state that the weather was notably pleasant and that the Indian farmers encouraged by their fine crops of last year, have already commenced preparations for larger acreage of grain and vegetables. The number of plows, wagons and harness on hand will fall short of the demand required for the use of the Indians who desire to cultivate the soil and who are making preparations for Spring sowing. The irrigation ditch carrying water over the West side of the of the [sic] Jocko Valley is being put in repair. Lumber has been cut and hawled on the ground for the repair of the flume, which has commenced to rot in places, and it will be repaired in time to turn water in for early irrigation.

Considerable annoyance and no small amount of trouble was caused during the month, involving travel and loss of time to me, in pursuit and capture of young Indian desperados and depredators not only from this reservation but from the Columbia and Spokane Country, account of which I shall give in Special report.

The saw mill is now in operation, cutting lumber for Indians who delivered logs at the mill by their own labor.

The amount of beef authorized for issue to Chief Charlots band of Bitter Root Flathead Indians is exhausted; bacon or dry salt pork is the only meat now issued to them. This band of Indians have no other resource of supply except that issued from the Agency stores, which are running low. No provisions have yet been made to assist the Flathead Indians to fence or plow their land although they all seem anxious to turn their attention to cultivation. However I shall do all in my power from Agency resources to assist as many of the families of Chief Charlot's band to commence farming this Spring as possible.

Herewith I have the honor to enclose sanitary report and report of funds and indebtedness, also report of farmer, and have the honor to be

Very respectfully
Your obedient servant,
Peter Ronan,
U.S. Indian Agent.

March 5, 1892
LR 9,648/1892, RG 75, National Archives, Washington, D.C.

On March 18, 1892, the Commissioner of Indian Affairs forwarded Jones' request to the War Department though official channels. The War Department reported on April 26, 1892, that Jones also had a wife on the Nez Perce Reservation whom he had failed to support and consequently the discharge request was denied.[5] No further information was found about William Jonas (Wistata), Nez Perce.

United States Indian Service,
Flathead Agency,
March 5th, 1892.

Hon. Commissioner Indian Affairs,
Washington, D.C.

Sir:

Herewith I have the honor to enclose copy of a document handed to me by William Jonas (Wistata) who was accompanied by Chief Charlot of the Bitter Root Flatheads. The Chief stated that the bearer, who is a Nez Percie Indian, married the daughter of Louis Vantelburg [Vanderburg], one of the Bitter Root Flatheads who removed with the Chief from that valley to this reservation under arrangements made with General Carrington; that the enlisted man has two children by said wife; that they make their home with Vantelburg, the Flathead Indian father of the Soldiers wife, who is too poor to maintain the family, and begs that the man be released from his enlistment in the army. Jonas (Winstata [sic]) requested me also to communicate with the Honorable Commissioner of Indian Affairs to interceed with the proper military authorities for his release as he ardently desires to live with his wife and children and use his best efforts to support them by the cultivation of land on this reservation.

I have the honor to be

Very respectfully
Your obe'dt Sev't,
Peter Ronan,
U.S. Indian Agent.

Enclosure:

To All Whom It May Concern,

The bearer hereof, William Jonas (Wistata), A Private of Troop "L." of the 4th Regiment of Cavalry, aged 26 years, 5 feet 7¼ inches high, Dark complexion, Black eyes, Black hair, and by profession a Soldier; born in the Nez Perce Res. of Idaho, and enlisted at Nez Perce Agency in the State of Idaho, on the 22 day of September 1891, to serve for the period of five years, is hereby permitted to go to Flathead Res. in the County of [blank space] State of Mont., — he having received a Furlough from the 1st day of March to the 20 day of March at which period he will rejoin his Troop or Regiment at Agency Nez Perce Res, or where ever it then may be, Or be Considered a Deserter.

Subsistence has been furnished to said _____ to the day of ____, and pay to the ____, day of ____, both inclusive.

Given under my hand, at Agency Nez Perce Res. this first day of March, 1892.

Sinned [sic],
Letcher Harduman [Hardeman],
2 Lieut 4th Cavly,
Commanding.

March 8, 1892
LR 9,583/1892, RG 75, National Archives, Washington, D.C.

> Ronan reported that tribal police were sent to Missoula in February 1892 to arrest tribal members camped near the town. The women in the camp were accused of living outside the bonds of matrimony. While the prisoners were being held in the Missoula jail, an unnamed Missoula resident hired an attorney to sue for their release under writ of habeas corpus. Ronan hired a Missoula attorney, Thomas C. Marshall, to defend the right of the Indian police to arrest tribal members off the reservation. Marshall won the case and the prisoners were later taken to the reservation jail. Marshall's fee of $50 was not allowed by the Commissioner of Indian Affairs in 1892, but in 1894 the account was twice submitted to Congress for a special appropriation. See Ronan's July 25, 1893a, letter for his resubmission of the bill.[6]
>
> The lawyer Ronan hired was Thomas C. Marshall, the lawyer for the Missoula Mercantile Company and other prominent Missoula businesses. The judge in the case was Thomas' father, Charles S. Marshall.[7] Isaac Conpae (married, 50 years old in 1891) was a private in the Flathead Agency police force in 1889 and appointed captain in January 1, 1891. In May 1889 he testified to Henry M. Marchant, Special Agent for the Department of Justice, that he publicly whipped offenders before Christmas 1888 when the Indian judges ordered the punishment. See also Ronan's May 1, 1889, letter and annotation.[8]

United States Indian Service,
Flathead Agency,
March 8th, 1892.

Hon. Commissioner Indian Affairs,
Washington, D.C.

Sir:

I have to report that occasionally young Indians of bad habits lure to the towns young squaws, and sometimes the wives of Indians of good character, where they establish camps, and use the women for immoral purposes to obtain whisky, or money upon which to gamble. The better class of Indians on the reservation feel the disgrace of such conduct, and the Indian police receive orders from the Indian Judges to arrest such class, bring them back to the reservation, give them a trial before the Court of Indian Offences and sentence them to fines, imprisonment, or hard labor for transgression of Indian laws governing the reservation. When the transgressor is a married woman who deserts her husband she and her paramour are held in jail and an effort is made by the judges to conciliate the husband and wife, who generally live together again.

On the 11th of February the captain of the Indian police, with fourteen of his men, proceeded to Missoula to arrest a number of women and men of the class described. I gave the police Captain a letter to the Sheriff of Missoula County, Montana, explaining the business and asking as a matter of courtesy and in the interest of the people of the town of Missoula, as well a com[m]on decency toward the Indians of the reservation, to give the police moral support in ridding the community of such a class. The Indian police succeeded in making the arrests and the County sheriff kindly allowed eight of the worst characters to be placed in the County jail for a few hours, or until the Western bound Northern Pacific railroad train arrived at the depot at Missoula, when the Indian prisoners would be transferred by the Indian police to the cars and brought to this reservation. I was notified that a citizen of Missoula employed an attorney and that a writ had been served upon the Sheriff requiring that the Indians be released from arrest. At the hour set for the hearing of the case before District Judge [Charles S.] Marshall, — deeming it for the best interest of the Indian service — with an employed Attorney, met the case. An afternoon was passed in court in the argument of legal points before the Judge. The Captain of the Indian police was made to testify and I was also called upon to testify before the Court in regard to the status of the Indian Court of offences. The Judge finally decided to place the prisoners in custody of the Indian police, and they were taken back to the reservation. There were four Indian women among the prisoners who were married and who had deserted their husbands to live a life of shame with the four Indian men who were arrested at the same time. The Indian Court of offence will hear the cases and all will be settled according to the regulations, sense of justice and regard for suppression of such disgraceful conduct. I herewith enclose bills that were necessary for me to make in order to enforce right and justice to the Indians in accordance with the law of the State and I trust my action will receive your endorsement and approval. I herewith enclose newspaper clippings regarding the affair.

I was compelled to employ council as the United States Attorney resides at Helena, the Capital of this State, and before he could be summoned in the case, the arrested Indians would probably be discharged under the writ of habeas corpus, a procedure that would have, in my opinion, a very bad effect upon the future effectiveness of the Indian police, when called upon to do duty outside of the boundary line of the reservation. Trusting that my action in the case will receive the approval of the Hon. Commissioner of Indian Affairs,

I have the honor to be

Very respectfully,
Your obedient Servant,
Peter Ronan,
U.S. Indian Agent.

Enclosed newspaper clipping from Missoula Gazette *(daily), February 12, 1892, page 4, col. 1:*

Those Bad Indians.
They Are Taken Back to the Reservation.

An Attempt to Release Them by Habeas Corpus Fails — They Are Runaway

Wives and Lovers.

Captain Isaac and his Indian police succeeded in rounding up eight of the renegade Indians they came after, and four of them were women. They were placed in the county jail and yesterday afternoon the sheriff was served with a writ of habeas corpus issued out of the district court ordering him to produce three of the prisoner, Peil Susue, Catherine and Rosalie and show why and by what authority he held them. These three are women.

H. C. Stiff appeared for the prisoners and T. C. Marshall for the sheriff. The law in the case simmered down to the question of whether the Indian police had authority to make arrests outside of the reservation boundaries or whether they had any particular authority for these particular arrests. Neither of the eminent counsel having had any time to investigate the regulations of the interior department concerning the government of Indian tribes and reservations, they made up what they lacked in information by length of argument until it finally appeared to the court, through an examination of Indian Agent Ronan that the police were acting under proper authority, when an order was made instructing the sheriff to turn the prisoners over to Capt. Isaac. During all of the argument two of the Indian women were in court. They did not seem to understand anything that was said and spent the time in attempting to flirt with the modest deputy sheriffs and other people about the court room. One of the squaws was rather pretty and quite young and dressed regardless of expense with brass rings and bracelets and gaudy handkerchiefs as though she was somebody's especial pet. Her Indian lover, who had lured her from her husbands tent, was not in court, so she devoted her attention to picking out possible substitutes from among the other people present. She could give points to her white sisters on Front street.

The prisoners were all taken back to the reservation last night and will be tried in the Indian courts there.

March 9, 1892
LR 9,649/1892, RG 75, National Archives, Washington, D.C.

Octave Finley was the tribal member accused of misplacing a railroad switch at Olive, near the western reservation boundary, which wrecked an engine and a caboose. He was arrested and held in the Missoula jail. The Indian witnesses in the case were held prisoners in the basement of a Missoula hotel. When the case came to trial, the witnesses declined to testify against Finley and the case was dismissed.[9] No further biographical information was located for Octave Finley.

The two teenagers accused of placing obstructions on the railroad tracks near Drummond were Thomas Lavatta and Pasqual Antay, of the Bitterroot Salish. They confessed and were sentenced to five years in the Montana State Prison. On October 22, 1892, Ronan asked the governor of Montana to pardon them, but the request was denied in June 1893. In March 1895, Chief Charlo and other tribal members persuaded the governor to pardon them and they were released.[10] See also Ronan's October 22, 1892, letter. Thomas Lavatta was the mixed blood son of Thomas Lavatta, Sr., a Mexican who settled near Deer Lodge in 1860, and Angelica, a Shoshoni woman.[11] No further biographical information was located about Pasqual Antay.

United States Indian Service,
Flathead Agency,
March 9th, 1892.

Hon. Commissioner Indian Affairs
Washington, D.C.

Sir:

On the night of the 10th of February, 1892, a switch lock was broken at a side track called Olive, near the West boundary of this reservation, on the Northern Pacific Railroad and a locomotive and tender were thrown over an embankment without, however, any injury to the crew or loss of life. It was suspected that the depredation was committed by Indians and I was notified to look into the affair. I made a careful investigation without being able to ascertain proof against any person. The attached letter marked No. 2 was sent to me after my efforts failed and in accordance with request therein contained, sent the Indian police out with Mr. Noble, who belonged to the Pinkerton Detective Agency.

While they were tracing up white tramps as well as Indians who were seen in the vicinity of the wreck, at the time it occurred, I learned of a young Indian having boasted that he did the mischief. I had him arrested by the Indian police and taken to Missoula, with a number of Indian witnesses, who will testify that he was seen at the place on the night of the occurance. The Indian boy waived examination and is now in jail in Missoula awaiting examination by the Grand jury. He denies having broken the lock and the evidence against him is purely circumstantial.

While engaged in looking up this affair letter No. 3, herewith attached, was received, and I went to Deer Lodge County to investigate the affair with the detective and my interpreter. I found two Indian boys under twenty years of age in the County jail. Both of them I recognized as outcasts and bad Indian boys, who belong to Chief Charlots band of Bitter Root Flatheads. They confessed that they were guilty of having placed the obstructions mentioned in the Superintendent's letter upon the track at a place called Drummond, in the county of Deer Lodge, Montana, but denied all knowledge of the breaking of the switch lock at Olive, on the reservation. They were held for trial in the District Court.

Chief Charlot expressed his pleasure when he learned from me that the boys were in jail, and as they confessed their guilt, trusted that their punishment by "whiteman's laws" would have a good effect upon other uncontrollable young Indians of this reservation. When the cases are disposed of I shall report the result to your office.

I am very respectfully
Your obedient servant,
Peter Ronan,
United States Indian Agent.

First enclosure:

Northern Pacific Railroad Company.
Office of Division Superintendent.
Missoula, Mont., Feb. 15th, 1892.

Major P. Ronan,
Arlee, Mont.

Dear Sir: —

This letter will be handed to you by Mr. A. F. Noble, who is out here for the purpose of investigating the wreck at Olive. He proposes to make open inquiries about this wreck to see if any information can be obtained that would justify further steps towards apprehending the guilty parties.

Please understand that in sending Mr. Noble to you it does not necessarily imply that the Indians are suspicious characters. In this connection I think, after you have talked the matter over with Mr. Noble, if you deem it expedient you might extend Mr. Noble the aid of your Indian police. I would be very thankful if you would, as it would be very gratifying to us to locate this matter where it belongs, and I presume it would be to you also in as much as it occurred on the Reservation.

Yours truly,
S. G. Ramsey
Supt.

Second enclosure:

Northern Pacific Railroad Company.
Office of Division Superintendent.
Feby 21st, 1892

Dear Major

Some rocks & fish plates were found piled on track about five miles East of Drummond this morning. Two Indians were found one hundred yards East of the point. our Train Crew are of the opinion the Indians placed the obstruction there. I have asked the Sheriff of Deer Lodge to arrest and hold them. Can you come over tomorrow. I would like you to see the Indians and perhaps we may be able to determine something about their character. If Noble is there please advise him.

Yours
S. G. Ramsey

You can Come over No 4 in the morning or if not convenient I will run you over later in the day.

SGR

Third enclosure, unidentified newspaper clipping:
Red Rascals.

Two young Indians were arrested here on Saturday evening by Deputy Sweeney on an order received from Col. Ramsey, Superintendent of the Rocky Mountain Division of the Northern Pacific, at Missoula. The cause of their arrest was not known until Monday, when a special car arrived bearing Major Ronan, officer Noble, Col. Ramsey and the interpreter. A short consultation was held with H. R. Whitehill, the attorney, and it was decided to have one of the "young bucks" brought before the gentlemen. It was then learned that the Indians had attempted to ditch a train last Thursday, four miles east of Drummond. The Indians denied the charge at first, but Major Ronan, in his unique way of handling these creatures, finally got a full confession out of him. The second prisoner was not brought out as the necessary information had been gained. County Attorney Shaw is now working on the case, and is confident that they will go to the penitentiary. Major Ronan spoke of them as being "very bad boys."

March 10, 1892
LR 9,857/1892, RG 75, National Archives, Washington, D.C.

United States Indian Service,
Flathead Agency,
March 10th, 1892.

Hon. Commissioner Indian Affairs
Washington, D.C.

Sir:

Replying to office letter of February 8th, "Land 385 – 1892" relating to the promised mad[e] to Chief Charlot, while in the Bitter Root val[l]ey, by General Carrington, and to the matter of turning over to him the Government farm in lieu of the old Arlee farm, and add: That I should be sure that Charlot feels satisfied with the change and accepts the Government farm in complete fulfilment of that part of Gen. Carringtons promise. According to your advice I made him feel and acknowledge in presence of the official Interpreter, and some Indians of his band, that the Government has substantially kept its promise in turning over to him for his use and occupancy the farm in question. He expressed his thankfulness, and stated that he was loosing his eyesight and could not do much, personally, in the cultivation of the land, but that his son and his son-in-law would commence work at once on the farm; that he would allow as many other families as the enclosure would accomodate to plow and cultivate for their own use and benefit the whole enclosure. I am now confident that this matter is settled in a manner satisfactory to him, and that it will be a great benefit to the tribe as several families will be enabled to raise grain and vegetables on the land turned over to him, which is better and more desirable land than the Arlee farm.

As you stated that there is no money at present available for the purpose of purchasing the improvements on the farm of the Kootenai, that it may be used for Agency purposes, I shall endeavor to make arrangements with him to plow and cultivate by Agency labor a portion of his place, and seed it down to oats and wheat to be cut green and stacked for the use of Agency stock, while a satisfactory portion of it will be left to ripen and be given to him to harvest for the use of his enclosure. I believe I can make this arrangement in a manner that will benefit the Indian as well as to make provision for hay for next winter or the Agency stock, without making requisition for funds to purchase it.

I am very respectfully
Your obedient Servant,
Peter Ronan
United States Indian Agent.

March 24, 1892a
LR 11,675/1892, RG 75, National Archives, Washington, D.C.

For more information on Elbert D. Weed, the United States Attorney, see the annotation to Ronan's October 22, 1889a, letter. For C. E. Proctor see October 31, 1890a, and for John Casey see August 25, 1891b. No biographical information was located about Wm. F. Furay, United States Marshall.

United States Indian Service,
Flathead Agency,
March 24, 1892.

Hon. Commissioner Indian Affairs
Washington, D.C.
　Sir:
　Herewith I have the honor to forward within attached letters which will give information in regard to the occupation of lands by whitemen, allotted by me to certain Kootenai Indians, at Dayton Creek, under orders from your office dated September 7th, 1891. If the trouble is not soon settled it will deter the Kootenai Indians of that place from putting in any crops this year, and perhaps may lead to trouble between the white people at the head of Flathead Lake and the Indians of this reservation.

I am very respectfully
Your obedient Servant
Peter Ronan,
U.S. Indian Agent.

First enclosure:

Office of the
United States Marshal
District of Montana
Helena, Montana, March 5, 1892.

Major Peter Ronan,
Arlee, Montana.
　Dear Sir:
　In conversation with Mr. Weed yesterday, prior to his departure for Washington, he expressed a belief that I had no legal authority in the Dayton Creek matter, until after having received notice in writing from both Attorney General Miller and Land Commissioner Carter, and such instructions should invest me with the power of ousting the trespassers, wherever found on Government lands, whether allotted or otherwise.
　After this consultation I have decided to remain quiet in the premises until I hear from Mr. Weed at Washington, which will be in a few days. I shall keep you fully advised in this matter and trust my instructions will soon be forthcoming.
　With kind regards to Mrs. Ronan and family, I am,

Your very truly,
Wm. F. Furay
U.S. Marshall.

Second enclosure. The handwriting was very hard to read and this is the editor's best interpretation:

Kalispell, Montana, Mar. 16, 1892

Magor Petter Ronan Esq Arle
　Dear Sir
　the Chiefs Eneas Son is making trouble at Dayton Creek he has threatened to Kill Dempsy in two days; and if there is not some thing done soon there is going to be trouble.
　We have done Every thing in our Power to favor and be friendly With the Indians but to hold our land and and [sic] Keep other White men off of it we will have to fence and Improve it. thare is a [*****] going Come down from Demersville that have tried to make all the Trouble boath for the Indians and White men they Could. there is No doubt but what there is two or three Indians that are intitled to land off of the Reservation. that is those that Settled

on land prior to February 8th, 1887. We make no Claim on those lands. the land We Claim is land that We Can Prove a Prior Write and Settlement to any Indian and We Intend to hold it untill Sutch time as the Land Department at Washington desides against us. I have it from Washington that all we Kneed is Proof Whitch We have that our first locations Was a head of any Indian and that thare was not any Indian living on the land at the time of the alotment Feb 8th, 1887 Whitch We Can also Prove.

of Corse those Indians that have Just Claims I am Willing to help them to Prove their rites. but it is unjust for you and them to hold out that all of that land is the Indians Simply because two of them have Probly been on this land long enough to hold it and it Will Caus troube for Boath Indians and us and Probably Blood Shed by the Way they are talking and Acting now.

I Wish you Would Consider and advise about What you Can do if any thing to make Peace if you Can not do any thing We Will have to look further for Protection.

Yours C. E. Proctor
John Casey.

Third enclosure:

Copy

United States Indian Service,
Flathead Agency,
March 22, 1892.

Messrs J. E. Proctor [i.e., C. E. Proctor] & John Casey:
Kalispel, Montana.

Gentleman:

I am in receipt of your letter of March 16th 1892, relative to the threats of the Son of Chief Enas, and also in connection with your occupancy of land claimed by the Kootenai Indians, Since and before the signing of the Stevens Treaty, believing that they were inside the boundary of the reservation. Under instructions from the Hon. Commissioner of Indian Affairs dated at Washington September 7th, 1891, "As the land refered to are non-reservation lands, and as the Indians were residing thereon at the date of approval of the General Allotment Act, February 8th 1887, they should be alloted to the Indians under the 4th Section thereof, as amended by Act of Feb. 28th. 1891 (26 Stats. 794)." As the land was unsurveyed I allotted to nineteen heads of families the land pointed out to me by each of said head of families, as that claimed by them, for either agricultural or grazing purposes.

On the 23 of September, 1891, I commenced making allotments, as designated by the Indians, to nineteen heads of families.

If any land was left I was instructed to allot it to unmarried men and among the minor members of Indian families. The Chief only desired land alloted to heads of families, who would point out their claims, and he asked for no furthur allotments, out side of the boundary as surveyed by Deputy Harrison. Having followed my instructions by forwarding a description of the land claimed by the Indians to the local Land Office of the district in which the lands are situated, and called attention of the local land Officers to the General Land Office circular relative to lands in possession of Indian occupants, issued Oct. 27, 1887, whereby Registers and receivers are every where instructed to peremptorily refuse all entries and filing attempted to be made by other than Indian occupants upon lands in the possession of Indians who have made improvements of *any value whatever, thereon.* I believe I have no further duty to perform, and that the matter now rests with the government as to who has proper title.

The cases of attempted occupancy of the land allotted by me to the Kootenai Indians, on Dayton Creek, have been reported by the Hon Commissioner of Indian Affairs to the Department of Justice, and I am not yet informed what steps will be taken, looking to the ajustment of conflicting claims. I trust however that good sense and love of justice to all will restrain the white claimants of these lands from any act that might lead to trouble with the Indians, until the title is settled by the proper authorities. I shall use every persuasion in my power with the Indians, to keep them from committing any act against the white claimants, and ask them to patiently await a decision from the government as to their right of occupancy.

I shall at once report you[r] commucation to the Hon. Commissioner of Indian Affairs.

Trusting that this question may meet a speedy and peaceful settlement.

I am very respectfully
Yours
Peter Ronan
U.S. Indian Agent.

March 24, 1892b
LR 11,798/1892, RG 75, National Archives, Washington, D.C. The February 11, 1892, letter Ronan referred to in this letter could not be located in the National Archives.

> That the final survey of the reservation boundary was in error on the southwest corner was acknowledged in the twentieth century by the U.S. Court of Claims. No final decision on issuing the allotments to the Indian farmers impacted by the error was made before Ronan's death in 1893, and, as far as can be determined, the proposed off-reservation allotments at the southwest corner were never made. See Ronan's March 10, 1891, and October 20, 1891, letters and annotations.
>
> Originally from California, Frank Foster came to Montana in 1882 and worked in mining until the early 1890s when he moved to the Paradise area of the Clark Fork River Valley. He farmed, prospected, and served in various county offices into the twentieth century.[12]

United States Indian Service,
Flathead Agency, Montana
March 24, 1892.

Hon. Commissioner Indian Affairs
Washington, D.C.

Sir:

I desire to call your attention to my report dated Jan. 11th, 1892, in regard to the survey of the Flathead Indian reservation, lying west of the Flathead Lake and North of Clarke's Fork of the Columbia river; surveyed by Edmund P. H. Harrison, U.S. Deputy surveyor under his contract, No. 208, dated April 18th, 1887; also, to my special report on the same subject dated March 19th, 1891 [i.e., March 10, 1891].

Having completed the work of allotment to the Kootenai Indians at Dayton Creek, as instructed, and having deposited the applications in the local land office, at Missoula, Montana, on the 10th, of October, 1891, I wired to your office in substance that the Pend d'Oreille Indians at the Western end of said boundary line at Clarkes Fork of the Columbia river, were in the same condition as to their land, as the Kootenia Indians at Dayton Creek, and asked for instructions; to which I received the following reply by telegraph:

Washington, D.C., Oct. 22, 1891.

Ronan Agent, Flathead Agency, Montana.

Replying to your telegram of the 20th, — allot land to Pend d'Oreilles same as Kootenai at Dayton Creek.

T. J. Morgan
Commissioner.

In my letter of Feb. 11th, 1892, I explained reasons of delay in making said allotments and now I beg to inform you why I hesitate to make allotments without further consulting you and asking information before I proceed to this duty. Referring to the field notes in the eighty-first mile which ended the survey, the Deputy Surveyor states: "This corner is situated in the crest of the ridge and is about 2500 feet above the Clarkes Fork of the Columbia river." The treaty also defines: "Commencing at the source of the main branch of the Jocko river; thence along the divide separating the waters flowing into Bitter Root valley from those flowing into the Jocko, to a point on Clarkes Fork between the Camas and Horse Plains prairies; thence Northerly to and along the divide bordering on the west the Flathead river to a point half way in latitude between the Northern and southern extremities of the Flathead Lake; thence and due East course to the divide where the crow, the Prune the Sonielem and the Jocko rivers, taking their rise, and thence Southerly along said divide to the peace [place] of beginning." According to the Harrison Survey, Settlers claim the point of land formed by the junction of the Missoula and Pend d'Oreille rivers, between the two rivers, which has always been claimed by the Indians, since the signing of the Stevens treaty. The Indians still contend that the Point designated in the treaty is below the junction of the Missoula river; and, as Clarkes Fork, to the best of my knowledge, takes its name from the junction of the rivers; the point designated in the treaty must be at, or, below the said junction, or it could not be on Clarkes Fork of the Columbia. If the ridge described by the Deputy Surveyor Harrison on the 81st. mile of the boundary survey is at, or, below the junction of the Missoula and Pend d'Oreille river, on Clarks Fork of Columbia, then the Indians are clearly in the right in claiming the land as being inside of the boundary of the reservation. If the ridge described by Harrison is on the Pend d'Oreille river above the junction of the two rivers, the Indians claim that the adoption of the survey will, take from them the land given them by treaty rights and the corner established by Harrison on the 81st. mile, will not be on Clarks Fork. This corner although claimed by the white settlers to be above the junction of the two rivers could not be found by the surveyor who had the contract last year for the survey of fifty one miles of the west and southern boundaries of the Flathead reservation.

This contract was approved and Mr. Samuel Bundock took the field last fall to commence his work where Mr Harrison left off and was ordered to notify me by letter of the time and place where he would commence said survey. Surveyor Bundock notified me that he could not find the point where Harrison left off, and that he had left the field, but expected to make the survey, this year.

As Deputy Surveyor Harrison made his survey without notifying either the Agent, or Indians, I do not know where to locate the 81st and last mile of Harrison's survey.

If it is at the junction of the Pend d' Oreille river and the Flathead river, the Indians will be satisfied; but if the ridge described is above the junction of the two rivers, the Indians will claim that the survey was made secretly in order to rob them of their lands. I herewith attach letter from a settler demanding that I go there and settle the question by giving two Indians their claims. As no other Indians have improvements there, the land left after allotting to the two Indian families will be immediately squatted upon by settlers and the Indians of the reserve will claim that they were cheated. It is my opinion that until the survey of fifty one miles of the West and Southern boundaries of the Flathead Indian reservation is made, Commencing where Mr. Harrison left off in 1887, according to the order of the Commissioner of the General Land Office; that the reservation boundary at Clarkes Fork should not be established, as it is not known: that the claimants of land there should be so notified, and that I make no allotments of land to Indians there until the line at Clarkes Fork of Columbia is fixed satisfactorily [sic].

If you desire that I allot the lands as directed in your telegram of Oct. 22nd, 1891, Please wire me and I shall at once proceed to do so.

> I am very respectfully
> Your obedient servant,
> Peter Ronan,
> U.S. Indian Agent.

Enclosure:

> Paradise Mch 12, 92.

Agt Ronan — Arlee Montana

Dr Sir —

Mr. Jackson of this place received notification some time since that the two indians, Bighead and Jo Cepes would receive allotments of land where they now live and that you were instructed to attend to it as soon as possible.

As there is some 400 or 500 acres of land here and the indians cannot hold all of it, the settlers would like the opportunity to farm their ranches which do not conflict with the indians rights.

I am putting in a crop on Mr. Edgar's ranch and the indians have allowed him only about thirty acres of land. As it is necessary to cultivate more land in order to live I shall do so and would much rather do it peaceably than other wise but shall do so at all hazards.

Mr. Burrill is not allowed to plow at all. I have been out three hours this morning hunting my horses which were driven off yesterday by the renegades at present laying around Jo Cepes.

If that trick is repeated I shall probably catch the indian in the act and there will be considerable like lihood of trouble.

If Mr Jackson's information was was [sic] correct (and it was signed T. J. Morgan Washington D.C. I believe) then it seems to us that it not only lays in your power but becomes your duty to adjust matters down here.

> Respy Yours
> Frank Foster
> Horse Plains
> Montana.

March 25, 1892a

LR 11,801/1892, RG 75, National Archives, Washington, D.C.

Ronan's attempts to resolve Bonners Ferry Kootenai land claims had continued for years. For background on the invasion of white settlers into the area, see Ronan's August 6, 1889, letter and annotation. On December 11, 1891b, Ronan reported that part of the tribe agreed to remove to the Flathead Reservation. Other tribal members were to move to Canada and still others were to get off-reservation allotments in the Kootenai River Valley. The mixed blood family of Catherine Fry had already filed in the Coeur d'Alene land office for off-reservation allotments. Unfortunately for Ronan, the Bonners Ferry Kootenai arrived on the Flathead Reservation just as the hostile Upper Flathead Valley white settlers were attempting to steal the Dayton Creek allotments from Chief Eneas' Kootenai band members. The failure of the government to protect the rights of the Dayton Creek Kootenai unfolded over 1892 and by October 8, 1892, Ronan reported that most of the Bonners Ferry Kootenai who had removed to Flathead had returned to Bonners Ferry.[13]

United States Indian Service,
Flathead Agency,
March 25, 1892.

Hon. Commissioner Indian Affairs,
Washington, D.C.

Sir:

Referring to "Land 945 – 1892," dated January 20th, 1892, approving my action in regard to the steps I have already taken in the proposed removal of the Kootenai Indians from Northern Idaho, to this reservation. I shall start from this Agency between the 10th and the 15th of April, in order to meet the Indians on the 17th of that month, as agreed upon. I shall not employ transportation by rail to remove the Indians except in cases of necessity. With the assistance of the young men of the tribe I expect to drive all of their cattle and ponies, and to remove their personal effects overland to the reservation, over the Indian trail running North up the Kootenai river, and thence South, through Pleasant Valley, and on to Dayton Creek, on the reservation, where the Indians have selected to settle. By this means, as you suggest, I will have a large balance of the fund set apart for their relief, at my command, and with which to supply their wants when removed to the reservation.

I shall require, however, to expend some money with which to furnish supplies on the trip, also lodges, some necessary clothing and shoes and stockings; and to provide for contingencies that may arise on the March. I desire, therefore authority to draw upon the fund for a sufficient sum to bear necessary expenses. After the removal is accomplished, I shall make requisition in the usual manner for their comfortable settlement in their new home. Lodges or tents will be required for the trip because Indian families of that tribe who have no cabbins live in lodges made of rushes woven together. In April, storms prevail in the mountain trail over which we shall pass, therefore lodges or tents should be furnished as well as a necessary supply of provisions and clothing.

I am very respectfully
Your obedient Servant,
Peter Ronan,
United States Indian Agent.

March 25, 1892b
LR 11,802/1892, RG 75, National Archives, Washington, D.C.

In this letter, Ronan repeated his claim in his August 16, 1888, annual report to have originated the idea of establishing a buffalo herd on the Flathead Reservation. His account was not backed up by other sources about the origins of the herd.

In 1892, Frank R. Miles, a Kalispell, Montana, promoter generated considerable publicity with his proposal to exhibit the buffalo along with a small number of Flathead Reservation Indians at the Columbia Exposition or Chicago World's Fair in 1893. On April 23, 1893, the Commissioner of Indian Affairs recommended to Ronan that Charles Allard and Michel Pablo exhibit the buffalo without Miles' assistance.[14] In a March 1893 interview, Miles discussed the serious problems he was having in arranging the exhibit on workable financial terms.[15] Miles' scheme for the exhibition in Chicago fell through at the last minute.[16] Allard exhibited the buffalo himself during October 1893 in various Montana cities, including Missoula.[17]

Frank R. Miles, who proposed the unsuccessful plan to exhibit the Flathead Reservation buffalo herd at the Chicago World's Fair, was born in New Brunswick, Canada, and moved to Montana in 1878. In 1896 he was promoting a buffalo and Indian exhibit for the 1900 Paris exhibition. In 1904, he led a group of investors who applied for permission to build a dam at the Foot of Flathead Lake.[18] Possibly Miles' most infamous scheme was to float saw logs down the Upper Flathead River, across Flathead Lake, and down the Lower Flathead River to the Northern Pacific Railroad at Dixon. Miles insisted that the idea was practical and the rapids at the Foot of Flathead Lake would be only a minor concern. During the summer of 1896 he made one shipment of logs which he was selling to the Union Pacific for railroad ties. Miles spawned much hype in the newspapers, but on September 25, 1896, he returned to Kalispell because his original crew quit when they saw the rapids at the foot of the lake. He finally hired a man with experience running logs in Michigan to get the logs stranded at the rapids. Newspaper accounts insisted that the enterprise was a success, but no record has been found that Miles or anyone else ever tried a second shipment.[19]

In the early 1880s, Samuel Walking Coyote sold a small herd of several dozen buffalo to Charles Allard and Michel Pablo, Flathead Reservation cattlemen and entrepreneurs. Pablo and Allard grazed the herd in the Lower Flathead Valley where it continued to multiply during the rest of the nineteenth century until the opening of the Flathead Reservation to white settlement forced the sale of the remaining buffalo to the Canadian government in 1906-1909.[20]

Charles Allard, Sr., was born in Oregon in the middle 1850s of mixed Indian-white parentage. Charles and his father moved to Montana in 1865 where they lived and worked in various mining camps. Charles; his wife, Emerence Brown; and their three children moved to the Flathead Reservation in 1880. In addition to the buffalo herd Allard owned with Pablo, Ronan's August 17, 1885, testimony listed Allard as having 30 horses and 700 cattle. In 1889, he opened a meat market at Ravalli. In 1896, his cattle herd was estimated at between 2500 and 3000 head. Allard died in July 1896 of complications from a knee injury he suffered the previous fall. The buffalo herd was divided on his death between Pablo and the Allard family.[21]

Michel Pablo was born in the 1840s, to a Mexican father and a Piegan mother, on the Montana plains. During the 1860s, he came to the Flathead Reservation and worked as the agency interpreter. In the middle of the decade, he was adopted into the Flathead Reservation tribes, started as a cattleman, and in 1866 married a tribal member, Agatte Finley. During the 1880s he became co-owner of the buffalo herd on the reservation. In 1892, he applied for permission to move to the Blackfeet Reservation, but was denied. By 1896, "by hard work and frugality [he] ... accumulated a large drove of cattle" and in 1903 he had 300 acres fenced and 5000 head of cattle. Also in 1903 he was formally added to the Flathead Reservation tribal rolls. After the reservation opened in 1910, he was so rich he "could lend money to all the white settlers about." In 1911 he and a partner opened a general store in Ronan, but the business was closed after a fire in 1912. He died in 1914.[22]

United States Indian Service,
Flathead Agency,
March 25, 1892.

Hon. Commissioner Indian Affairs
Washington, D.C.

Sir:

In my annual report to the Hon. Commissioner Indian Affairs for 1888, page 157, will be found the following in regard to Buffalo on this Reservation: "In 1878, one year after I took charge of the Flathead reservation believing that in the manner in which buffalo were being slaughtered by white hunters for their hides, and by travelers and would be sportsmen, who shot the animals down and left the carcasses to taint the atmosphere where they fell, I conceived the idea that this noble beast, which is now almost extinct on the American plains, might be saved from total annihilation by getting some of them on an Indian reservation where they could be bred, herded, and cared for by the Indians. There were no buffaloes west of the Rocky Mountains, and the nearest herd was on the eastern plains in the vicinity of Fort Shaw, in the territory of Montana. At my suggestion, Indians undertook and succeeded in driving two young buffalo cows and a bull from a wild herd near Fort Shaw, through Cadott's Pass and across the main divide of the Rocky Mountain range in to the Flathead Reservation, on the Pacific slope. The buffalo have increased from three to twenty-seven head. Besides several males were slaughtered by the Indians for their feasts, as it was deemed better for propagation not to have too many bulls running in the herd. The buffaloes are now owned by two individual halfbreed cattle owners owners [sic] of this reservation. Tempting offers have been made to them to sell the herd, but I advise a continuation of ownership. It seems to me that the Government should take steps to secure those buffalo, which are among the last remnants of the millions that roamed the great American plains in former days. They could be herded, cared for, and the number increased in proportion to that of similar herds of stock cattle."

It is four years since I wrote quoted report, and the buffaloes are owned by the same parties, Charles Allard and Michel Pabalo [sic], two men of mixed blood. The herd is now increased to sixty-five head, with about twenty spring calves. An offer has been made by a private party of fifteen thousand dollars to the owners for the use of the herd for six months during the World's Fair at Chicago, and another proposition is made to them by a person whose letter I herewith annex. Mr. Allard is a temperate, attentive business man, of excellent character, and more capable of handling his herd of buffaloes than any man perhaps in this country. His partner, Michel Pabalo, is a man of good morals and steady habits. With such qualifications they feel confident that they are able to handle their own business and the herd of buffaloes they raised and bred better than any outside party, provided they can get encouragement and assistance from the Indian Department to bring their case before the managers of the Fair, to exert an influence to give them ground and an opportunity to exhibit their buffaloes; also to conduct their own business under any rules the Indian Department might offer; and the regulations of the managers of the Fair.

In my opinion, if this matter will be carried out and receive your attention, it will successfully show to the world that men of Indian blood are not only capable of raising a herd of buffaloes but are as capable of handling them on the ground of the World's Fair as on their native plains. It will also show that they are as capable of their own business management as if under the management of the writer of the attached letter, or any other management. Trusting that I may be favored with your views on this subject at an early date.

I am very respectfully
Your obedient Servant,
Peter Ronan,
United States Indian Agent.

Enclosure:

Chicago, February 2, 1892.

Mr. Charlie Allard,
Ravalli, Montana.

Dear Sir: —

Acting upon your promise of the refusal of your Buffalo of exhibit at the World's Fair in this city, I have taken considerable pains to look the matter up the past few days, and now write you the result of my labors in that regard. I have visited the secretaries of the different committees in charge of the World's Columbian Exposition, and feel encouraged in the matter. I have visited the World's Fair ground and while it would seem that there was lots of land, yet they tell me that it will be difficult for me to procure five acres, although I have applied for ten. You will remember that I refer to lands within the Exposition grounds. Buffalo Jones, from Kansas, has been here; also Buffalo Bill's agent. I find that Jones has not very many buffalo and that Buffalo Bill's show is a Wild West show, comprised principally of ring performances; whereas ours is a straight, legitimate proposition of exhibiting the last of the original herd of buffalo from the plains of the Great Northwest, together with twelve lodges of Indians. I understand that the government have made some arrangement with Professor Putnam, Chief Department of Ethnology, to exhibit the different races of people that inhabit the North American Continent and in which of course the different tribes of Indians are included, but I am informed that under the circumstances, and from my statement, that it will be necessary for us to have these Indians, more to look after the buffalo, than as a feature of our exhibition, and I am inclined to think that we will be able to get them in.

I am going to Washington to see the head of the Indian Bureau in regard to the matter. I expect to meet Mr. Crawford, Secretary of Ways and Means, this afternoon again at five o'clock, to give him all information in my possession in regard to the exhibit.

I want you to write me fully your terms, together with all other information in regard to what you will require of me and my associates, for the use of these buffalo during a period of six months, or while this Exposition lasts. I will require your services in preparing this show, the training of the Indians, as well as to accompany the same to Chicago, and to remain here during the Exposition to look after said Indians, as well as the Buffalo. Write me immediately upon receipt of this letter fully, and enclose in enclosed envelope. I will call again here upon my return to Montana, which will be some time the last of this month, and learn further what has been done.

I will leave a representative here to look after the matter and keep me posted what action the different committees may take upon it.

Hoping to hear from you soon, I am

Yours very truly,

F. B. Miles.

April 2, 1892

LR 12,943/1892, RG 75, National Archives, Washington, D.C.

> For more information on the two cases of railroad vandalism see Ronan's March 9, 1892, letter and annotation.

United States Indian Service,

Flathead Agency,

April 2d, 1892.

Hon. Commissioner Indian Affairs
Washington, D.C.

Sir:

In reporting from this reservation for the month of March, it is my pleasing privilege to state that the Indians have commenced farming this year with more enthusiasm than ever before evinced by them. Plowing and seeding commenced early in the month and more than double the amount of land that was cultivated last year will be put under cultivation this year. The excellent crops raised by the Indians on this reservation last year has given encouragement to them, and if a good season prevails a large yield may be expected. As reported by letter from this Agency, dated March 10th, 1892, I turned over to Chief Charlot the Government farm and he now realizes that he has a better farm than the the [sic] old Arlee ranche which was promised to him by General Carrington, and is well satisfied. Four Flathead families, removed from Bitter Root Valley, besides his own, found room to farm inside of the enclosure and are now engaged in seeding the land. Every head of a family of Chief Charlots band removed here last fall from the Bitter Root Valley will be the cultivator of a field of wheat, oats and vegetables this year. My success in placing these people upon land to cultivate this year was beyond my expectation, as they had not an acre of their own under fence. The Indian farmers who allowed their brethren the privilege of cultivating and using their surplus land, under fence, deserve credit.

In a communication from this office dated March 8th, I informed you of two attempts at railroad wrecking. In both cases Indians were suspected and I had the parties under suspicion arrested. The two Indian boys mentioned in said communication, who confessed their guilt of placing obstruction on the Northern Pacific Railroad, near a station called Drummond, were tried in the

Court at Deer Lodge, Montana, and were each sentenced to the penitentiary for five years.

The case of the Pend 'd Oreille Indian, who was also reported in same letter to be under arrest on charge of breaking a switch lock at a station called Olive, on this reservation, which threw a locomotive and tender over a high embankment, on the same railroad, is set for trial on the 12th of April.

All industries connected with this reservation are receiving careful attention and the Agency employes are doing all in their power to assist the Indians in this busy season.

Herewith I have the honor to enclose sanitary report and report of funds and indebtedness, also report of farmers and have the honor to be

Very respectfully
Your obedient Servant,
Peter Ronan
United States Indian Agent.

April 26, 1892
LR 16,618/1892, RG 75, National Archives, Washington, D.C.

On June 15, 1892, the Commissioner of Indian Affairs denied Charlo's request for permission to visit Washington, D.C. The Commissioner recommended that Charlo communicate with the Indian Office in writing through Ronan.[23]

United States Indian Service,
Flathead Agency,
April 26th, 1892.

Hon. Commissioner Indian Affairs
Washington, D.C.
Sir:

I am requested by Charlot, Chief of the Bitter Root Flat Head Indians, removed to this reservation, to ask permission from you to visit Washington, in company with a delegation of his people, at as early a date as practicable. The Chief desires to consult the Department in regard to matters pertaining to the interests of his Indians. An early reply is respectfully solicited.

I am very respectfully
Your obedient servant
Peter Ronan
U.S. Indian Agent.

April 27, 1892
LR 16,619/1892, RG 75, National Archives, Washington, D.C.

For biographical information on Chief Isaac, of the Bonners Ferry Kootenai, see the annotation to Ronan's August 6, 1889, letter.

United States Indian Service,
Flathead Agency,
Mont, April 27, 1892.

Hon. Commissioner Indian Affairs
Washington, D.C.

Sir:

In obeyance to original instructions dated October 21st, 1891 — "Land 26030 – 1891. Authority 28510," I left this Agency for the Kootenai Indian Camp, on the Kootenai river, Northern Idaho, on the 13th day of April, 1892, to meet the Kootenai band of Indians, on the 17th day of that month according to agreement with them, as fully set forth in previous correspondence. At Sand Point Idaho, I found that connection from Northern Pacific R. R. to Great Northern R. R. over the Sand Point Spur was interrup[t]ed by a land slide that covered the track and could not be removed for several days. Other transportation could not be procured owing to the muddy and impassible condition of the wagon road and I was compelled to await the clearing out of the track over the Great Northern R. R. Spur. In the meantime I employed a runner who understood the Indian language to explain to Chief Isaac the cause of my delay. He undertook to make his way to the Indian encampment through the woods on foot. I reached the Indian village on the 19th of April.

A few Indians were at the encampment, who informed me that Chief Isaac, with the greater portion of the band had gone across the British line to visit the Mission of St. Joseph, situated at Wild Horse Prairie, British Columbia, a distance from their camp on the American side of the line, of one hundred and twenty miles, involving a march of two hundred and forty miles. Being informed by the Indians in camp that the Chief and his band would not get back from their visit in less time than ten days; and also having been informed by the Indians that they placed no reliance upon the halfbreed Interpreter I employed at Bonners Ferry, and requested that negotiations be conducted in regard to their removal through my former Interpreter, who lives at the Flathead Agency. To procure the service of Charles Finley as Interpreter, as requested by the Indians and also to transact necessary business.

I returned to the Agency and now have made all necessary arrangements to go back to the Kootenai country and arrange for removal of the band to this reservation as ordered.

I am very respectfully
Your obedient Servant
Peter Ronan
U.S. Indian Agent.

May 6, 1892
LR 16,836/1892, telegram, RG 75, National Archives, Washington, D.C.

On May 7, 1892, the Commissioner of Indian Affairs sent a telegram to Ronan at Bonners Ferry stating that those "Indian families who have made improvements, and desire to acquire title to their lands, should be encouraged to do so, especially when no conflict exists."[24]

May 6, 1892
Bonners ferry Ida

Commr Indian office
Washn DC

Indians divided one party will Cross british line other party will go to Reservation a few families desire title to land they occupy. Shalll [sic] I encourage latter to get title wire answer.

Roan Agt.

May 19, 1892
LR 19,442/1892, RG 75, National Archives, Washington, D.C.

In May 1892 some of the Bonners Ferry Kootenai relocated to Canada, but Canadian officials insisted they pay a twenty per cent duty on their cattle before they could enter. Apparently the disgusted Kootenai migrants paid the duty, but according to Ronan's September 6, 1892, letter, many had already returned to the Bonners Ferry area.[25] Chief Moise of the Bonners Ferry Kootenai, could not be further identified as several Upper Kootenai chiefs had the same Christian name. Ronan enclosed a clipping from the May 14, 1892, *Kootenai Herald* (Bonners Ferry, Idaho), "Treating with Indians," which is not reproduced here.

United States Indian Service,
Flathead Agency,
May 19th, 1892.

Hon. Commissioner Indian Affairs,
Washington, D.C.
    Sir:
    Under original instructions "Land 26030 — 1891 — Authority 28510," on the 27th day of April, 1892 I left the Flathead Agency, Montana, for the Kootenai Indian camp, in Northern Idaho, accompanied by a Kootenai interpreter whom the Kootenais requested me to bring from this Agency as they preferred to trust his interpretation of their views than to any English speaking Indian or mixed blood of their own country. At Sand Point, Idaho, transportation was obtained by wagon to Bonner's Ferry, on the Kootenai river, a distance of thirty two miles. Upon reaching destination, sent Interpreter out to gather the Indians at their usual camping ground near the Mission, for Council on Monday, May 2d, and upon that date, with my interpreter, met them at their camp. Only a portion of the band were present. The head Chief Isaac lay ill in his lodge, and spoke from his bed, intimating that his son Michel would talk for him. I briefly stated that I was at the camp according to promise, and in compliance with the orders of the Honorable Commissioner of Indian Affairs, to make arrangements for their removal to the Flathead Indian reservation. The Chief's son replied in substance that his father and grandmother were unable to leave their camp and could not possibly travel over the trail to the Flathead reservation; and that the family would not desert the old people, but would remain in camp until recovery or death from il[l]ness would relieve them from responsibility. The Chief's son also stated that the Second Chief Moise had revolted from the controll of the First Chief and had removed with the larger portion of the Kootenai Indians to the British Boundary with intention of crossing the border and settling in British Columbia. I concluded therefore to visit the camp of the revolting chief and on the evening of the 4th of May, left Bonners Ferry on the Steamer Alton for the British Customs office, on the Kootenai river. Upon arrival I found considerable excitement on account of the action of some of Chief Moies' [sic] Indians who undertook to and did run some of their cattle across the International Boundary, in defiance of the Customhouse officers who protested against the driving of cattle by Indians into British Columbia without the payment of duty, which was assessed at twenty per cent of the valuation of the cattle. I called a council on the American Border, at which the Indians agreed that they would drive the cattle back upon American soil, and hold them there until it was decided by the Superintendent of Indian Affairs

for British Columbia, if payment of duty on their domestic cattle would be insisted upon by the Government.

I wired to that officer as follows:

> "Bonners Ferry, Idaho, U.S.
> May 6th, 1892.
>
> A. W. Vowell,
> Superintendent Indian Affairs
> for British Columbia,
> Victoria.
>
> Indians who claim to be British subjects desire to know if they are required to pay full duty on their Cattle if driven across the line where they expect to make homes.
>
> Ronan,
> U.S. Indian Agent."

The Council at the British Boundary was attended by Second Chief Moise, three head men and twenty Indians. Having settled that the Indians would drive their cattle back upon the American side of the Boundary and make no further attempt to break the Canadian Customhouse laws by driving stock across the Boundary, I arranged to hold another Council at the Camp of the Head Chief, near the Mission, on Sunday, May 8th, and demanded that Chief Moise with his followers shoulded [sic] be present. Returned to Bonners Ferry, and upon the day designated met the Indians in Council at the appointed place. They were divided into three parties; the larger number under Chief Moise declared that they would abandon the place, cross the British Boundary and settle in British Columbia, while another party that claimed to be American Indians, agreed to remove to the Flathead Agency, and some of them would take their departure soon as supplied with provisions and other necessaries for the march; others would remain and try to dispose of their squatter right to public land to white settlers and follow soon as practicable. All of the American Indians agreed to abandon the Kootenai valley, and remove to the reservation with the exception of eight heads of families, who had cabins, small fenced fields and other evidence of improvements upon their holdings and upon which I was assured no conflict of title existed, asked that title might be obtained for them from the government. Under the circumstances, and by your instructions, I encouraged them to remain upon their places with the promise that I would ask the Honorable Commissioner to take steps to secure to them unquestionable title to allotments on their locations.

I informed the Indians who announced their determination to cross into the British Possessions that they were at prefect liberty to do so, and to depart from American soil; that if they desired to separate from the band that claimed to be American Kootenais, on the plea that they belonged to the British Kootenais, they must relinquish the land they occupied and in no way interfere with white American settlers in acquiring title to lands in that section of the Country, as no Indian who is the subject of a foreign country can secure a home upon the public domain. I informed Chief Moise also, that I felt authorized to say that the Canadian Government would not interfere with Indians who claimed to be British subjects and who wished to cross the Boundary, but would insist upon the payment of full custom duty on their cattle, and read to the Indians the following telegram:

"Victoria, British Columbia
Via Seattle, U.S.

To Indian Agent Ronan
Bonners Ferry, Idaho.
    Indians must pay full duty on cattle subject to nine days quarantee.

A. H. [i.e., A. W.]Vowel.
Superintendent."

The Indians fully agreed not to attempt to drive their cattle without paying duty, and stated that they would sell enough to cover the amount, and asked for a reasonable time to dispose of them, which I stated would be granted. The following families agreed to depart for this reservation on the next day, while others would follow soon as they could dispose of squatters rights they wished to sell to settlers:

Tepah 7 in family — driving ten head of Cattle.
Koostah 7 in family
Koostanna 3 in family
Francois Sackta 5 in family
Widow Cecile 2 in family
Antoine 5 in family
Joseph — no family
Agatha — no family.

Having purchased supplies for above families for their march over the trail of nearly two hundred miles, and having arranged for the delivery of a sufficient quantity of food to be issued to the families that will follow, I placed Antoine, the head of a Kootenai family in charge of the marching camp, and taking four Kootenai boys ranging from fourteen to six years of age, I left for the reservation where I placed the boys at school upon my arrival.

This practically settles the Northern Idaho Kootenai Indian question in regard to their future settlement, and in time will relieve that portion of the State of Idaho of the presence of the Kootenai Indians, with exception of the eight families mentioned, who will ask for title to their land. In connection therewith I desire to know if it is the desire of the Department for me to take steps to secure the same. If so I respectfully ask for instructions and the proper blanks. I have already sent the Agency Carpenter to Dayton Creek, where the Kootenai Indians will settle, to erect a warehouse in which to store their supplies, for which I shall submit requisition. The march from Northern Idaho, to Dayton Creek on this reservation will be a long one, as the Indians are slow in their movements, especially while traveling through a game and trout fishing country.

Herewith I have the honor to forward personal expenses incurred, supported by vouchers, and shall forward later vouchers for supplies purchased for the Indians for their march.

I am very respectfully
Your obedient servant,
Peter Ronan,
United States Indian Agent.

May 23, 1892
LR 19,162/1892, telegram, RG 75, National Archives, Washington, D.C.

On May 24, 1892, the Commissioner of Indian Affairs denied Ronan's request to employ a consulting physician unless Ronan furnished further information.[26] In his June 1, 1892, monthly report, Ronan identified the injured man as Joseph Barnaby, Jr. The agency physician decided Barnaby's arm needed to be amputated and a physician from Missoula offered to assist with the operation. Barnaby decided against the amputation and Ronan reported he was likely to die as a result, but Barnaby survived. See Ronan's May 1, 1891, letter and annotation for biographical information.

My 23 189
Flat Head Indian Agency Via Arlee Mont

Commissioner Indian Affairs
Washn, DC

Agent Ronan indian badly shot would ask consultation regard to amputation.

Dade Agency Physician

Shall I call aid of another Physician.

Ronan Agt.

June 1, 1892
LR 20,878/1892, RG 75, National Archives, Washington, D.C.

During the late nineteenth century tribal hunting rights were often in contention as government hunting regulations strove to protect the wild game from extermination. The regulations discriminated against subsistence and commercial hunters in favor of white sports hunters. See, for example, Ronan's November 20, 1889, and November 27, 1889, letters and annotations. In August and September of 1889, General Henry B. Carrington encouraged the Bitterroot Salish to hunt for subsistence and to keep the hunters busy during delays in the removal to the Jocko Valley. On August 25, 1891, Carrington wrote: "I keep most of the adult, able-bodied Indians out of town, and hunting their winter supply of meat."[27]

Adolph and Felix Barnaby, mixed blood tribal members, allegedly attacked Alexander Ashley with a knife and a stone at a dance held on the reservation by John Lumphry on February 19, 1892. They were charged with "assault with the intent to commit murder" and sent to Helena for trial in the United States Circuit Court. Adolph was convicted but there was a problem with the paperwork for Felix and he was released. Adolph's attorney then challenged the conviction and Judge Hiram Knowles concluded that the United States Code did not cover that particular crime and ordered Adolph freed. Bernard Leopold of Missoula was convicted of selling liquor to the Barnaby brothers and was fined $500 and sent to the penitentiary for two days.[28]

Adolph and Felix Barnaby were the sons of Joseph Barnaby, a mixed-blood Spokane Indian, and Lizette, a mixed-blood Kalispel Indian. Adolph was 30 or 31 years old in 1892 and married to a woman named Sophie. Their first child was born in 1890. Felix was twenty-five years old in 1892. He married in 1894.[29]

United States Indian Service,
Flathead Agency,
June 1st, 1892.

Hon. Commissioner Indian Affairs
Washington, D.C.

Sir:

I have the honor to report that I spent the greater portion of the month of May in Northern Idaho, under orders from your office. A full account of business attended in that locality has already been furnished you by special reports.

The weather in the first weeks of May was cold on the reservation, but the Indians succeeded in planting larger crops this year in every agricultural valley on the reservation than ever before and the weather is very favorable now to the growth and maturity of their harvest.

As before reported and in accordance with your instruction, I turned over to Chief Charlot the Agency farm in lieu of the old Arlee ranch which was promised to him by General Carrington, when he removed with his people from the Bitterroot Valley. Four families beside the Chief found room to plant crops on this farm. Every head of a family of Chief Charlot's band that removed to this reservation last fall from the Bitterroot valley is the cultivator of a small field of wheat, oats and vegetables. As before reported those Indians had no land under fence, but I was enabled to get them patches to cultivate inside the enclosures of other Indians who had more land under fence than they could cultivate. Charlots band, however, seem restless in their new homes, and in accordance with their usual custom, when their crops were planted, they left old people to look after irrigation, etc., and started to the mountains to hunt, and gave as an excuse that they were tired of living upon bacon, and desired to procure fresh meat. Only five hundred dollars was allowed me to furnish beef to this band of Indians since October, 1891, and at seven cents per pound furnished from the block, the beef issue was brief. I am constantly reminded by the Indians that one of the conditions of their removal from the Bitterroot valley, before their lands were sold was a promise from General Carrington that two beeves a week would be slaughtered at the Agency and issued to them. The Honorable Commissioner is well aware that this as well as other promises made to these Indians could not be carried out by the Agent as means to do so were not furnished.

A petition from the citizens of Bitterroot valley reached me on the 21st of May, asking that a hunting party composed of Chief Charlots Indians be immediately called back to the reservation. I returned the following reply to the petitioners, which I give herewith for information at your office.

"Flathead Agency, May 24, '92.

J. R. Faulds,
Editor Tribune
Stevensville, Montana.

Sir:

I am in receipt of enclosed petition from your citizens which will explain itself. On Sunday May 23d I called a council of the Flathead Indians at this Agency. Chief Charlot was present, and the petition herewith enclosed was interpreted to them with a statement from myself that the Indians mentioned by the petitioners were away from this reservation without permission, that I believed they were amenable to the game laws of the State when off the reservation and were liable to the penalty of law breakers precisely as in the case of any other person of the United States. The Chief expressed regret that his people might be brought into trouble by Killing game and said that they had no idea that they were law breakers because they had permission to hunt last year from General Carrington, and presumed that if they had that right last year they had the same right this year. I informed the Chief that the privilege of hunting out of season and in violation of the game law of the State could not be granted, and that any Indian who might kill game out of season, outside of the reservation, might expect punishment according to the law. The Chief asked as a favor that this statement should be given publicity, and requested that the Citizens of the Bitterroot valley who might come in contact with hunting parties from this reservation would inform them that they are away from the Agency without permission and that it is his desire as well as the Command of the Agent that they return to their homes on this reservation. In the meantime Chief Charlot states that he will do the best he can to gather the scattered hunters back to their homes.

> I am very respectfully
> *signed* Peter Ronan
> U.S. Indian Agent."

The grist mill has been in constant operation during the month of May, grinding the wheat of Indian farmers into flour that was left over from their seeding. Indians are now engaged in delivering saw logs at the mill to be cut into lumber for their use in buildings, etc.

During the month a halfbreed of this reservation named Adolph Barnaby, was convicted in the United States Court of an assault with intent to commit murder. The trouble grew out of whisky that one Bernard Leopold, a Merchant of Missoula, sold to two half breed brothers, Felix and Adolph Barnaby. These are the men whose testimony sent Leopold to the State penitentiary for two days and to pay a fine of five hundred dollars. The half breeds bought the whisky and went to a dance on the reservation. A row occurred which resulted in a half breed getting stabbed; the arrest of the party and conviction of one of the Barnaby brothers, and also the conviction of the Missoula dealer for selling whisky to Indians. This latter conviction will have a tendency to put a stop to the sale of whisky to Indians in Missoula. The Culprit was taken to the penitentiary to serve out his sentence. Before going he paid the fine of five hundred dollars. Another brother of the Barnabys, mentioned, named Joseph, was shot lately by a renegade Indian from the Columbia river, who accused Barnaby of being a spy on his horse thieving movements, in the interest of the Sheriff of Missoula County. The Indian who did the shooting escaped. The Agency physician concluded that the arm of the wounded man should be amputated, and another physician from Missoula volunteered his assistance. The wounded man refused to allow amputation and is likely to die of the wound.

I have the honor to enclose sanitary report and report of funds and indebtedness; also report of farmers and have the honor to be

Very respectfully
Your obedient servant
Peter Ronan
United States Indian Agent.

June 10, 1892
LR 22,582/1892, RG 75, National Archives, Washington, D.C.

On June 2, 1892, the Commissioner of Indian Affairs insisted the government would protect
the rights of the Kootenai Indian allottees. The Commissioner of Indian Affairs also endorsed
Ronan's and Joseph Catholuha's decision to drive white owned cattle off the reservation
without accepting any money which the white cattlemen could interpret as payment and
permission for further white grazing on the reservation.[30] See Ronan's July 25, 1892, telegram for the next escalation in the harassment of Chief Eneas and the Kootenai farmers by
white trespassers.

United States Indian Service,
Flathead Agency,
June 10th, 1892.

Hon. Commissioner Indian Affairs,
Washington, D.C.
Sir:
On the 3d day of this month I left the Agency for Kootenai Indian's Camp,
at Dayton Creek, in response to a message received by me from Chief Eneas of
that tribe, stating that he was not able to leave his bed on account of illness,
and that he was anxious to consult in regard to white settlers who took possession of lands that I allotted the Indians by your instruction, under dates 23d of
September to the 26th of the same month, 1891.

I reached the house of the Chief on the evening of the 5th inst., and held
consultation with him and his people. The Chief stated that the day after I left
his place, after making allotments to the Indians, a party of white people took
possession of a number of the allotments. (This portion of his statement was
fully reported to you at the time of occurance.)

The Chief continued his statement — that while some of the land jumpers were courteous and civil, they affirmed the belief that the Agent had no
authority to allot land to Indians that were outside of the boundary of the
reservation as surveyed by Deputy Surveyor Harrison, and expressed determination to hold their claims until disposessed by the land laws of the United
States.

Others of the jumpers were boisterous and uncivil to the Indians, and
seemed determined to agrivate a quarrel. I took your advice, he continued, and
held my people from getting into trouble with this class of people. It was hard
to do so when an Indian saw one of them run a fence around his little enclosure
and defy interference from the Indians with arms in hand.

You complained to-day, said the Chief, that the Indians did not improve
their farms as well as you expected this year. How could they do so? You will
find a party of white men yonder, digging a ditch from Dayton Creek, which
runs through our village that will shut off our only water supply. Some could

not build their fences without threats of violence. I am unable to leave my cabin but my people continue to obey me and keep quiet. I sent for you to come to ask you as our Agent, who made the allotments to my people, when can my children cultivate and improve their land without being insulted and ordered from the soil they believe belongs to them?

I could only reply that their allotment papers were in the hands of the Commissioner of the General Land Office and the Indians could only await for action there. In the mean time they must remain quiet and involve themselves in no trouble, but to place their reliance upon the justice of the law governing their case, and in due time the Great father in Washington would see that justice would be accorded them.

While at the Kootenai Indian Camp I was informed that one of the most insolent characters of the would be settlers was suspected of selling whisky to the Indians. I closely watched the matter and succeeded in getting Indian evidence against him that will secure his conviction. I have placed myself in communication with the United States Marshal and expect to have the man arrested in a few days.

A cattle roundup was in progress and the Indians were divided as how to deal with owners of stock illegally grazing upon the reservation. Previous to the commencement of the roundup I gave to the chief of Indian police to serve upon cattle owners the following order:

> "It is hereby ordered that all cattle illegally grazing upon this reservation be driven off by their owners on or before the 15th of July 1892. Should any such owner of stock of any description not conform to this order the cattle or other stock may by rounded up by the Indian police and driven beyond the boundary of the reserve; and each owner may expect that sufficient number from his herd will be taken by the Indians to pay for the trouble and expense incurred in such roundup and drive. This order is issued in accordance with instructions from the Honorable Commissioner of Indian Affairs now on file in this office.
>
> Peter Ronan
U.S. Indian Ag't."

One of the Judges of the Court of Indian Offences, charged that the Indians in former years who were intrusted with the carrying out of this order quietly appropriated any money they could collect from cattle owners and left the cattle to graze upon the reserve with intention of making a similar deal each succeeding year. The Indian Judge who makes this charge is determined to rid the reservation of the cattle as well as the imposition of the Indians who heretofore handled the case. With a party of Indian police he repaired to the roundup and demanded that no payments be taken from the cattle owners for grazing, but that all cattle be driven out, and owners warned that they must not attempt to drive them back. The other Indian faction opposed this as it would probably cut off their private revenue. I was sent for and repaired to the scene of the round up at Camas Prairie; where I held consultation with Joseph Catholuha — the Indian Judge — and his men. Catholuha contended that if money was accepted for grazing, the cattle owners would again take advantage and drive their cattle back with the expectation of settling with the Indians in in [sic] the usual way the next succeeding year. I felt that Cathoulah was right and that he was in earnest in his efforts to keep trespassing cattle owners from over running the Indian ranges with their herds. I advised him to take the field with his men and gave him the following letter:

> "In the Field
> Camas Prairie,
> June 7th, 1892

To Cattle owners:

    I was present at a Council of representative Indians last night, at which Joseph Cathoulaha Judge of the Court of Indian Offences was the principal speaker. It was decided by the council that Cattle illegally grazing upon this reservation should be rounded up by owners and driven off. As the regular Indian roundup is now in progress, all white owners of cattle are invited to be present, and are hereby notified to separate their cattle from the Indian herds and drive them away. No charges will be made by the Indians for grazing on their land in the past, but they demand that no more cattle belonging to white intruders be driven upon this reservation to feed upon the Indian ranges. White people who have stock on the reserve are notified that their cattle will be rounded up by Indians, the owner notified, and if not driven off, the Agent will be required by the Indians to take legal measures to prosecute such owners under the laws governing such cases. The Indians, under the lead of Joseph Cathoulaha will see that the decision of the council will be carried out.

> *Signed* Peter Ronan,
> U.S. Indian Agent."

I have the honor to submit my report for your consideration and approval and have the honor to be

> Very respectfully
> Your obedient Servant,
> Peter Ronan,
> United States Indian Agent.

July 4, 1892

LR 23,575/1892, telegram, RG 75, National Archives, Washington, D.C.

On July 9, 1892, the Commissioner of Indian Affairs authorized Ronan to spend $500 in the open market for subsistence supplies for Charlo's band.[31]

> July 4 1892
> Flathead Agency Via Arlee Mont

Commissioner Indian Affairs Washn

    Forty three families Chief C[h]arlots band bitter root flathead Indians depend upon weekly issue of supplies all provisions expended at Close of fiscal year how shall I feed them until annual requisition for food is received.

> Ronan agent.

July 9, 1892

LR 25,755/1892, RG 75, National Archives, Washington, D.C.

The Bonners Ferry Kootenai arrived at the Flathead Reservation just in time to witness the conflict between the reservation Kootenai and white trespassers who jumped the Dayton Creek allotments. In this letter Ronan says he was able to persuade the Idaho Kootenai to remain on the reservation, but by October 8, 1892, he reported most had returned to northern Idaho.

United States Indian Service,
Kootenai Indian Camp, Flathead Agency,
July 9th, 1892.

Hon. Commissioner Indian Affairs
Washington, D.C.

Sir:

On the 4th of July, information reached me that a disturbance might occur at the Northern Boundary of this reservation, near Dayton Creek, between the Kootenai Indians and white jumpers of some of the allotments that I made to the Dayton Creek Indians, North of the boundary, under instruction from your office: "Land 31578 – 1891" dated at Washington, September 7th 1891. I therefore proceeded by wagon to that place, which is about seventy miles north of the Agency. Matters were found quiet, although the Indians are restive and suspicious that the Government survey of the townships north of the line means that most of their allotments will be ignored and the land given to the white settlers.

I explained fully and clearly as I could the cause of the delay at the General Land Office, and that steps will be taken through the proper authorities to place each Indian allottee in possession of his lands, in order that he may enjoy full, free, peaceable and uninterrupted use and occupancy thereof. I advised patience and reliance upon the justice of the Government in dealing as to their claim to the lands. This matter is not only annoying, but a source of grievance to white settlers as well as to the Indians, and must be carefully watched in order to prevent trouble between the contending parties until title is settled.

Some of the Kootenai Indians of Northern Idaho, referred to in my letter of May 19th 1892, have arrived on the Flathead reservation and are encamped with the reservation Kootenai Indians at Dayton Creek. Others are following but their march is slow on account of high water in the rivers over which they have to cross. The new arrivals from Idaho felt much disappointed on learning of the trouble between white settlers and the Dayton Creek Kootenai Indians. It is fortunate that I got on the ground in time to prevent them from returning over the trail and disuading the others from coming upon the reservation. I issued to them a quantity of clothing and supplies of provisions from the purchase made "Finance 19666 – '92 — Authority 31024," and prevailed on the men to take pack animals and go back on the trail with a supply of provisions etc., for the comfort and convenience of their brethern. They gladly accepted the proposition and went out, the same day, to meet the marching camps and assist them with provisions etc., issued as stated.

It was stated to me that the Idaho Indians who choose to cross the British boundary, instead of coming to this reservation, have returned to Idaho, disappointed in regard to making their abode in the British possessions, and are awaiting my arrival at Bonner's Ferry. I expect to go there soon as business of this reservation will permit, to carry out your instructions under date of June 3d – "Land 19442 – 1892," and shall make full report. Trusting that my action in stated matters will receive your endorsement, I shall at once return to the Agency, and expect to arrive there on the 11th of July.

I am very respectfully
Your obedient servant
Peter Ronan
U.S. Indian Agent.

July 12, 1892
LR 25,596/1892, RG 75, National Archives, Washington, D.C.

On June 30, 1892, Ronan discharged Partee Kikishee, Louison Kul se me me, and Eneas Oostoo as Indian judges and replaced them with August Celo, Charles Moolman, and Antoine Moise. In 1892, Ronan also appointed new Indian policemen and made Pierre Cotullayuch captain.[32] For Kikishee see the annotation to Ronan's February 12, 1885b, letter. For Louison see the Biographical Sketches. According to Ronan's August 1885 annual report and his August 17, 1885, testimony, Charles Moolman had 160 acres under fence in the Mission Valley, 15 horses, and 25 cattle, and raised 300 bushels of wheat and oats. For Antoine Moise see the annotation to the excerpt from Ronan's book under January-February 1884.

United States Indian Service,
Flathead Agency,
July 12th, 1892.

Hon. Commissioner Indian Affairs,
Washington, D.C.
Sir:

As stated in my report from the Kootenai Indian village, at Dayton Creek, I arrived at the Agency, as expected, on the 11th of July, and my monthly report was consequently delayed until the present date.

I now have the honor to state that all matters pertaining to the service at this Agency, during the month of June have received careful attention. In some of the agricultural districts of the reservation the maturing crops give evidence of an average yield, particularly where the land was covered by irrigation ditches. As a rule where irrigation is not provided by ditches the crops are burned by drought and will be a failure. The haying season has arrived and many of the Indians are already engaged in mowing and stacking their hay. A large quantity of pine logs were delivered at the mill by Indians, and the saw is now running, cutting them into dimension for individual use, in building and improving their premises.

The police force and Court of Indian Offences have not given the satisfaction that I expected and I shall submit a revised list of Indian police and Judges for the service during this fiscal year, and ask for their confirmation, with the hope that the change may make an improvement.

During the month Mr. G. A. Lawrence came to the Agency to make measurements of Indians and to collect Ethnological material for the Department of Ethnology and Archeology of the Worlds Columbian Exposition. His success was good among the Indian inhabitants of the reservation except Chief Charlot's band of Bitter Root Flatheads. That Chief took exceptions to measurements of himself or his people and discouraged Indians from being measured. This Chief while a just and good man in various characteristics is a type of the Indian described by the Hon. Commissioner of Indian Affairs in his interesting speech at Woodstock, on the 4th of July, where he pictures some of the Indians of to-day as being "as distinct in their life, their manners, customs, traditions, hopes and aspirations as they were when the white man first set foot on American soil. x x x Standing aloof and cherishing toward us bitter hostility."

Charlot desires his followers to remain Indians in the full sense of the word, and is opposed to education and advancement; but his influence cannot hold long in the light of education and civilization in his new surroundings upon this reservation.

I have the honor to forward the quarterly School report, sanitary report and report of funds and indebtedness, also report of farmers, and am

Very respectfully, Your ob'dt Ser'vt,

Peter Ronan,

United States Indian Agent.

July 25, 1892
LR 26,671/1892, telegram, RG 75, National Archives, Washington, D.C.

In July 1892 Eugene McCarthy, a white settler, was attempting to jump Kootenai Indian allotments that had been used by the Indians for years and contained cultivated fields, stacks of hay, fencing, and houses. When Chief Eneas ordered him off the allotments, McCarthy filed charges against Eneas alleging the chief had threatened him. Chief Eneas was crippled with rheumatism, so Ronan traveled to Demersville to post a $500 bond for his appearance in court on the charges. Chief Eneas' restraint — despite language problems — in keeping the situation from erupting into violence was remarkable.[33] See also Ronan's August 1, 1892, and August 9, 1892, letters on the subject and his summary of the situation in his August 26, 1892, annual report. See Ronan's October 8, 1892, letter for the next step in the crisis.

Eugene McCarthy was employed in 1887 by the surveyors who laid out the northern boundary of the Flathead Reservation. The surveyors ran the line five or six miles south of where the Kootenai had understood it should have been. In the twentieth century the U.S. Court of Claims agreed that the line was too far south. McCarthy returned after 1887 to homestead on the land just north of the boundary, despite years of use by the Kootenai and off-reservation allotments filed by Ronan. McCarthy worked the land as a ranch until selling it in 1906. He worked at many different occupations such as hunting buffalo, constructing the Northern Pacific Railroad, surveying, and selling real estate over his years in Montana.[34]

July 25 1892

Missoula Mt

Commr Ind Affs

W DC

Information recd that Warrant issued for arrest of Chief Eneas for threatening Violence to Jumper of indian allotment at Dayton Creek. wired U.S. Marshall attempt no arrest until I arrive there to investigate arranged to start tomorrow morning.

Ronan Agt.

August 1, 1892
LR 28,687/1892, RG 75, National Archives, Washington, D.C.

United States Indian Service,
Flathead Agency,
August 1st, 1892.

Hon. Commissioner of Indian Affairs
Washington, D.C.
    Sir:
    I have the honor at the request of Agent Ronan, who is at the Kootenais camp, Dayton Creek, to forward copy of telegram Sent by the Agent to Hon. E. D. Weed, U.S. Attorney, Helena, Montana.

Very respectfully
Your obt. Servt.
Thos. E. Adams,
Agency Clerk.

Enclosure:

Dayton Creek
July 31st, 1892

E D Weed
U S Attorney
Helena Montana
    Trespassers on Indian allotments refuse to vacate unless arrested by united States authority; The best interests of the Indian service and Justice to settlers demand that a test case be made by arrest of one or two trespassers; Send Marshal Furey in person. I shall remain on the ground until he arrives no possie will be necessary; allotments were made to Indians according to law and department instructions an avoidance of bloodshed demand immediate action.

SgD Ronan
Agent.

August 8, 1892
LR 28,724/1892, telegram, RG 75, National Archives, Washington, D.C.

Airlee Mont

Indian Comr
Washn, DC
    Recd following from Northern Idaho
    Ronan Agt when will you be here whites are cutting the hay off of Indian locations they ask me to telegraph for you to Come protect their property answer R Fry
    answered go on the Tenth full report by mail

Ronan Agt.

August 9, 1892
LR 29,309/1892, RG 75, National Archives, Washington, D.C.

No further information was found about Charles Gardner, Flathead Agency employee, or Joseph Jean Jan Graw (Gingras) or Jean Jan Graw (Gingras), Kootenai Indian allottees.

United States Indian Service,
Flathead Agency,
August 9th, 1892.

Hon. Commissioner Indian Affairs
Washington, D.C.
 Sir:
On the 25th day of July I received the following letter:

> "Demersville, Montana,
> July 22d, 1892.

> Ronan, U.S. Indian Agent:
> Sir: Charles Gardner, one of your Agency employes, re-
> quests that I inform you that there is a warrant sworn out for
> the arrest of Chief Eneas, at Dayton Creek by one Eugene Mc-
> Carthy, he claiming that the Chief ordered him off *his ranche*;
> that in case he did not vacate would Kill him. You are asked to
> come at once to the the [sic] scene of the difficulty.

> Yours very respectfully,
> *Signed* James Kerr,
> Captain Steamer,
> 'State of Montana.'"

Upon receipt of quoted letter I wired to the United States Marshal:

> "Information received that warrant issued for the arrest
> of Kootenai Chief Eneas, for threatening violence to jumper
> of Indian allotment at Dayton Creek. Wire your deputies to at-
> tempt no arrest until I arrive there and make investigation.

> Ronan, Agent."

Received the following reply:

> "Your telegram just received: Instruct all my deputies to
> make no arrest unless you direct.

> Furay,
> U.S. Marshal."

I also wired:

> "Arlee, July 25th, 1892,

> Commissioner Indian Affairs
> Washington, D.C.
> Information received that warrants issued for the arrest
> of Chief Eneas for threatening violence to jumpers of Indian
> allotments at Dayton Creek. I wired U.S. Marshal to attempt
> no arrest until I arrived there to investigate. Arranged to start
> to-morrow morning. If instructions necessary wire to Arlee,
> to-day.

> Ronan, Agent."

Accordingly I left the Agency on the morning of the 26th of July, and arrived at Dayton Creek on the evening of the 27th.
 Chief Eneas informed me that allotment No. 19, to Jean Jan Graw, under
date of September 26th, 1891, and that of Joseph Jean Jan Graw No. 13, allotted on the 25th of the same month and year were occupied by whitemen who
were cutting hay on each of said allotments despite the fact that on allotment
19, the Indian or halfbreed occupant had a house, barn, enclosed and cultivated field, and also a stack of hay cut from last year, of at least fifty tons. The
hay on this allotment, the Indian family claim, has been cut and stacked by
them for the past twelve years. Allotment No. 13, also jumped by whites, has
a log cabin, a small enclosure for a garden, and the hay has been cut by the

Indian family on the same for years. The Chief being unable to walk on account of rheumatism, was carried to a wagon and driven to allotment 19; not having an interpreter, he claims that he informed the men working in the hayfield, as best he could make them understand, that the land belonged to his people by years of occupancy as well as by allotment by the Government, and desired them to vacate; the whites did so, but swore out a warrant against the Chief, in the town of Demersville, before a Justice of the Peace, who sent a constable on the reservation to make the arrest. The Chief resisted the arrest by stating that he was too ill to leave his house. The Chief then sent a messenger to the Agency to apprise me of the circumstances. The trip from the Agency to Dayton Creek involves a distance of about seventy miles. The day after my arrival at that place, the Constable from Demersville again made his appearance and demanded the arrest of the Chief, stating that if he refused to accompany him, a possie of citizens were likely to march to the reserve and make arrest by force of arms. I sent for the Chief who was hawled to my camp by the Indians in a wagon. He was willing to go before the Court, but felt in his condition the trip would be death to him. Therefore, in order to preserve peace and to prevent the coming of an armed possie of excited people to the Kootenai Indian village to arrest their Chief, I volunteered to accompany the constable to Demersville, where I went before the justice of the peace who issued the warrant and signed a bond in the sum of five hundred dollars to bring Chief Eneas before his court on the 2d day of October, 1892, to answer the charge preferred against him if he were alive and able to accompany me. I returned to camp and sent the Farmer to notify trespassers on allotments 19 and 13 to appear before me at my Camp where I would try to explain to their satisfaction that they were trespassing upon Indian allotments, and that time, trouble, and expense might be saved if my advice would be listened to. A curt reply was sent that they intended to cut the hay and hold the ground unless arrested by lawful authority, and if Indians attempted to cut the hay they would have them arrested by State authority. Before appearing before the Justice of the peace at Demersville, I sent the Indian farmer out to the nearest telegraph office and wired the following:

"E. D. Weed, United States Attorney,
Helena, Montana.

Trespassers on Indian allotments refuse to vacate unless arrested by U.S. Authority. The best interest of the service and justice to the settlers demand that a test case be made by arrest of one or two trespassers. Send U.S. Marshall Furay in person. I shall remain on the ground until he arrives. No possie will be necessary. Allotments were made to Indians according to law and Department instructions. An avoidance of bloodshed demand immediate action."

Received the following reply:

"Helena, Montana
August 2, 1892.

Peter Ronan,
U.S. Indian Agent
Kootenai Camp via Arlee,
Montana.

Dear Sir:

Your telegram of the 1st inst., relating to trespassers on Indian allotments etc., with the request that U.S. Marshal Furay be requested to proceed immediately to the scene of the difficulty has been received. I endeavored to bring the matter at once to the attention of the Marshal but he seems to be out of town and his office is locked up. I am unable to find any of his deputies here. I do not know where he is. As soon as I can ascertain his whereabouts I will repeat your telegram to him and request him to comply with your suggestion.

> Very respectfully
> E. D. Weed,
> U.S. Attorney.["]

Upon receipt of above I ordered the Indians upon the ground and set them at work cutting their hay. I asked the Justice of the Peace at Demersville to notify the trespassers not to come again upon allotments 19 and 13 under penalty of arrest. Having put the Indians in possession without the aid of the United States Marshal, whose presense I did not expect for an indefinite period, according to the letter received from the U.S. Attorney, I returned to my camp, only to receive the following dispatch, from the Kootenai Indians at Bonners Ferry in Northern Idaho:

> "Bonner's Ferry, Idaho,
> August 6, 1892.

Ronan, U.S. Indian Agent,
Flathead, Montana,

When will you be here? Whites are cutting the hay off of Indian locations. They ask me to telegraph for you to come and protect their property. Please answer.

> R. Fry."

I wired that I shall leave the Agency for Northern Idaho on the 10th day of August, to carry out your instruction in regard to certain allotments of lands to Indians in that country: "Land 23602 — Authority 31323," under date Washington, July 7, 1892.

I expect to find locations and lands of Indians occupied by white men who will persist in cutting hay and otherwise trespassing. I therefore desire that full instructions be forwarded to me at Bonner's Ferry, Idaho, upon receipt of this letter, as to what authority I shall call upon, and what steps I shall take to give Indians that occupy their lands in Idaho, full, free and uninterupted occupancy of the same, and the right to cut their hay without molestation. Unless I have some authoritive instructions to act or to call upon State or United States authority to aid in this work my presense there will be a useless failure, and I trust that I shall be sustained by the Indian Office in doing justice to the best of my ability to the Indians as well as to the white occupants of public land, in my humble capacity of Indian Agent, acting under orders from the Honorable Commissioner of Indian Affairs.

> I have the honor to be
> Very respectfully
> Your obedient Servant,
> Peter Ronan,
> United States Indian Agent.

August 12, 1892
LR 29,984/1892, RG 75, National Archives, Washington, D.C.

This is a report on the case of Robert Philips, who was charged with the murder in northern Idaho of Felix Burns, a Flathead Reservation tribal member. The case was brought on the complaint of tribal members and largely based on Indian testimony. Ronan mentioned in his letter of September 6, 1892, that the trial had been postponed, but no information was found on the outcome of the case.[35]

No further information was found about Robert Philips, the accused murderer, or Felix Burns, the victim. For biographical information on Joseph Cathoulihou, the Indian judge, see the annotation to Ronan's March 15, 1888, letter. For Duncan McDonald see the annotation to Ronan' February 4, 1878a, letter.

United States Indian Service,
Sand Point, Idaho.
August 12, 1892.

Hon. Commissioner Indian Affairs
Washington, D.C.
Sir:

On the 9th of August I left the Flathead Agency, for Bonner's Ferry, Idaho in response to an urgent telegram from the Indians of that locality, which I quoted in my last report from the Agency. On arrival at Sand Point, found a telegram urging my presense at Hope, Idaho, to investigate the suspected murder and robbery of an Indian from the Flathead reservation by a whiteman by the name of Philips, who was then under arrest, and to assist in prosecuting the case. Deeming it best for the service to act in this matter before proceeding to the Kootenai Indian Camp, I returned to Hope. Here I found encamped Joseph Cathoulihou, one of the Judges of the Agency Court of Indian Offences, Duncan McDonald, a halfbreed, some of the Indian Police, the wife and sister of the Indian whose body was found, and several Indians from the Kalispel Country. At the Indian Camp it was stated to me that a well to do Indian of the Flathead reservation, called Felix Burns, left his home some time previous to the 4th of July, having on his person about two hundred dollars. On the evening of the 3d of July, Alto and his brother Alexander, Indians also of the Flathead reservation, arrived at Sand Point, in Idaho. While at the depot Robert Philips a whiteman, called by the Indians "Buckskin Shirt," approached them and told them that there was an Indian at his cabin and asked them to go there and see him. The Indians accompanied Philips to the cabin where they found the Indian Felix Burns. Philips had a large flask of whisky and the Indians and the whiteman commenced drinking. Philips went out at different times and bought whisky — three bottles were drank. In the morning when they recovered from their carrousal, Alto noticed Felix giving Philips money; after he went out Felix informed Alto that he had given the white man ten dollars to buy whisky. Philips came back with keg and a sack of provisions. They then gathered up the empty bottles and filled them from the keg with whisky. Philips then went after a boat, and returned with it. Their blankets, whisky and sack of provisions were put in the boat. Philips, Felix and Alto got into the boat the other Indian refusing to go. They landed at different times to drink, etc. At the last landing Philips held a conversation with Felix and the latter got into the boat alone, and was pushed off from the bank. Alto and Philips then started towards the Great Northern Railroad track, when Alto became so drunk by the whisky plied to him by Philips that he remembered no more, and finely [sic] made his way back to the reservation. The Friends of Felix Burns became anxious at his long absence and as Alto was the last seen with him Joseph Catholueluhu, the Indian Judge, McDonald, some of the Indian Police and the sister of Felix took Alto to Idaho to search for him. The body of Felix Burns was found by the Indians on the shore of the river running out of the Pend 'd Oreille Lake towards the Kalispel valley, below where he was shoved off alone in the boat by Philips. The Indians instituted a search for the latter, and warrant was sworn out for his arrest. His trial was set for three o'clock of the 10th, but I had it postponed in order to procure an interpreter from the Agency. At ten o'clock of the 11th the trial commenced, and the evidence given sustained the details in this report. The defence asked for a continuence until Wednesday the 17th of August. I demanded that the prisoner be placed under a heavy bond for his appearance on that day. The bond was placed at one thousand dollars. The Indians and Indian witnesses went into camp near Hope, Idaho, to await the trial. On the morning of the 12th I left again for Sand Point, on my way to Bonners Ferry over the Great Northern Railroad, from that place.

The case is a serious one, and if the man Philips is allowed to escape, or is not severely punished by the law for furnishing whisky which led to the death of the Indian Felix Burnes, it will cause great discontent among the Indians, particularly as they feel assured that Philips is guilty of the murder of the Indian. I informed the Indians that if they suspected justice would not be done to their side of the case to send a messenger to me at Bonner's Ferry, and I would leave my business there long enough to give attention to the prosecution of this outlaw Philips, who has made a business of the selling of whisky to Indians for years without punishment, although arrested and tried several times for the crime. A suspicion also of the murder and robbery of Felix Burns, demand that the case be sharply looked after, and give Indians confidence in the enforcement of the Laws of the whiteman.

Trusting that my action in this matter may meet the approval of the Hon. Commissioner of Indian Affairs.

I am very respectfully
Your obedient Servant
Peter Ronan,
United States Ind. Ag't.

August 15, 1892
LR 29,642/1892, telegram, RG 75, National Archives, Washington, D.C.

> In this telegram and his September 6, 1892, letter, Ronan reported that he had made off-reservation allotments to the Bonners Ferry Kootenai still in the Kootenai Valley and had filed them at the Coeur d'Alene land office. These allotments were in addition to the allotments to the Catherine Fry family which she had filed previously. The Office of Indian Affairs insisted the rights of the Kootenai would be protected. However, the local whites continued to trespass on the allotments and hired attorneys to drag out the proceedings. The sources are not clear, but most of the conflict seems to have involved the Fry family allotments.[36] Despite the government efforts to protect the allottees, the trespassing and harassment

in Idaho continued. As mentioned in the annotation to Ronan's August 6, 1889, letter, the
Idaho Kootenai allotments were eventually lost.

Aug 15 1892
Bonners Ferry Ida

Indian Commr
Washn, DC

Allotments to ten indian applicants at this place receipted for by register
local land office July twentieth eighteen hundred & ninety one at Coeur De
alene Idaho interfered with by white trespassers who are Cutting hay & prevent indian allottees from Cutting hay from land occupied by indians prior to
allotment what legal steps if any shall I take to protect the indian owners from
trespass.

Ronan Agt.

August 26, 1892
U.S. Commissioner of Indian Affairs, Annual Report of the Commissioner of
Indian Affairs *(Washington, D.C.: U.S. Government Printing Office, 1892), pages
291-295.*

In his 1892 annual report, Ronan summarized the status of several continuing problems
which were also covered in other Ronan letters to Washington, D.C. These included the
settlement of the Bitterroot Salish in the Jocko Valley, Kootenai claims to land just north of
the reservation boundary, settling the land claims of the Bonners Ferry Kootenai, and the
unratified agreement with Michel's band of Lower Kalispel Indians. Ronan also relayed tribal
opposition to allotment on the reservation.

Report of Flathead Agency.

Flathead Agency, *August 26, 1892.*

Sir: In accordance with instructions, I herewith submit my sixteenth annual report, with census and accompanying statistics:

Census. — The confederated tribes of this reservation consist of the Pend
d'Oreilles, the Flatheads and Kootenais, Charlot's band of Bitter Root Valley
Flatheads, and Michel's band of Lower Kalispels.

Charlot's band:	
Total number	174
Males above 18	54
School children between 6 and 16	48
Females above 14	56
Confederated tribes:	
Total number	1,569
Males above 18	469
Females above 14	550
School children between 6 and 16	349
Kalispel:	
Total number	58
Males above 18	24
Females above 14	25
School children between 6 and 16	8

Making a full total of 1,801 Indians.

Advancement. — During the years that have marked my service among the confederated tribes of this reservation many great changes must naturally have taken place that belong to Indian history more than to a synopsis of affairs for the past years. In the first years of my administration little attention was given by the Indians to agricultural or civilizing pursuits. As the buffalo and other large game were plentiful, the Indians resorted to the chase on their ancient hunting grounds for sustenance rather than to the toil of a settled life. The dwelling house and barn now take the place of the lodge, and well-fenced fields of meadow, grain, and garden dot the valleys; but this is rather an enforced condition among many of them, caused by the disappearance of game and the necessity of gaining a living by the cultivation of the soil and the adoption of the pursuits of advancing civilization that now surround them.

Among older Indians of the tribes are still found that type described by the Commissioner of Indian Affairs, in his speech at Woodstock on the 4th of July, 1892, where he pictured some of the Indians of to-day as being as distinct in their life, their manners, customs, traditions, hopes, and aspirations as they were when the white man first set foot on American soil — standing aloof and cherishing towards us bitter hostility. The rising generation educated at this reservation school show a different disposition, especially where the intermarriage of the boys and girls that have been educated occurs at the time of graduation, just as they leave school. The experience of teachers attests that this works admirably. There is no transition from the school to their wild homes, but from school they start to keep house for themselves on the plan they have been taught, as attested by teachers and observers. They thus at once continue the routine of work they have been accustomed to, and the balance of their tribe, with whom they now come in more frequent contact, are improved by their industrious example and general good behavior. The new educated couples give certain tone to their nation, and the effect is beneficial and elevating.

Crops. — Last year the crops were excellent and produced an unusually large yield of wheat and oats that commanded good prices. This encouraged the Indians to make greater efforts to produce crops; therefore the acreage put under cultivation this year was nearly doubled. A cold season followed the planting, and when warm weather came it was intensely hot, with drying winds that stunted the growth, and will probably cause limited crops this year. However, where irrigation was obtainable drought and hot, drying winds had but little effect, and in such districts full crops will be harvested, thus carrying out views before expressed that irrigation is absolutely necessary for an abundant field at harvest time. Different conditions prevail upon different Indian reservations.

Factions. — The inhabitants of this reserve are of such mixed character that it is one of the most trying and difficult tasks to keep them in order and to overcome their jealousies and prejudices against each other. Here we have the original confederated bands of Pend d'Oreilles, Flatheads, and Kootenais, that signed the Stevens treaty of 1855. To those are added Lower Kalispels of the Columbia River, the Kootenais of northern Idaho, the half-breeds of Canadian and Scotch extraction from nearly all other Indian reservations, and Chief Charlot's band of Bitter Root Flatheads. The latter are the most incorrigible of all the bands and factions on this reserve, owing mostly to the fact that the young Indians were raised without the restraint of reservation rules in the

Bitter Root Valley, where the saloons and gambling houses were open to them when they had money to spend.

Chief Charlot's Band. — Chief Charlot is an Indian with a grievance, who is always complaining of broken promises from the Government. On his visit to Washington in 1884 he refused to remove with his people from the Bitter Root Valley to this reservation or to accept any proposition made to him the honorable Secretary of the Interior. All unfulfilled promises that he now complains of, he states were made to him in the Bitter Root Valley, Montana, by an accredited official of the Indian Department. In connection I respectfully refer to Senate Ex. Doc. No. 70, Fifty-first Congress, first session, with which was transmitted the report of Gen. Henry B. Carrington upon the matter of the surrender and appraisment of lands (and improvements thereon) in the Bitter Root Valley, in Montana, which are covered by patents issued to certain Flathead Indians under, the act of Congress approved June 5, 1872 (17 Stats., 226). Gen. Carrington was successful in removing Chief Charlot and his band to this reservation. That chief is a nonprogressive Indian; opposed to education and advancement; opposed to the Indian court of offenses and Indian police paid by the Government; opposed to civilized dress, and threatened to take the Indian children of his band from school if their hair was cut. I believe his influence can not hold long in the light of education and civilization in his new surroundings upon this reservation. Up to the present date the register of receipts issued by the receivers of public money at Missoula, Mont., for lands sold from October 6, 1891, belonging to the Bitter Root Indians under act of March 2, 1889, foots up $14,674.53 from sale of seventeen pieces of land. Among other things, the chief claims that money from the sale of each piece of land was promised to be sent at once for distribution to the owners or heirs of the same.

Chief Eneas' Band of Kootenai Indians. — In my last annual report I gave an outline of the trouble caused by the survey of that portion of the boundary of the Flathead Indian Reservation lying west of Flathead Lake and north of Clarke's Fork of the Columbia River. I recommended in special report that the Kootenai Indians at Dayton Creek should get title to the land they always considered belonging to them under the terms of the Stevens treaty of 1855, which was cut off from the reservation by the Harrison survey, under contract dated April 18, 1887. I received instructions from the Honorable Commissioner of Indian Affairs to forward a description of the land claimed by the Indians to the local land office of the district in which the lands are situated; also to call the attention of the local land officers to the General Land Office circular relative to the lands in possession of Indian occupants, issued October 27, 1887, whereby registers and receivers are everywhere instructed to peremptorily refuse all entries and filings attempted by others than Indian occupants upon lands in possession of Indians who have made improvements of any value whatever thereon.

On the 23d of September, 1891, I commenced making the allotments as designated by the Indians to nineteen claimants, all being over 21 years of age and each the head of a family, this number of allotments being all the lands that the Kootenai Indians claimed or asked for outside of the point half-way in latitude between the northern and southern extremities of the Flathead Lake as established by Deputy United States Surveyor Harrison, who ran the line due west therefrom. As the land in question was unsurveyed at the time

I made the allotments, I believe that no prior valid adverse claim to the land applied for can be sustained. This allotment will have the effect of satisfying the Indians that no attempt has been made by the Government, in making the survey, to take from them any land that they have heretofore claimed or occupied in the honest belief that such land was inside of the boundary of the reservation. In September, 1891, I inclosed to your office receipt from the register and receiver of local land office for said applications, numbered from 1 to 19. In special report to the Indian Office it has been fully set forth that white men came upon several of the allotments made to the Kootenai Indians, and that Chief Eneas made bitter complaint of such encroachments. As instructed from the office of the Commissioner of Indian Affairs, under date July 2, 1892, I informed Chief Eneas of the following clause in that letter:

As soon as the Indian allotment applications belonging to members of his band shall have been transmitted to the Indian Office by the General Land Office for consideration, and action, and the lands covered thereby shall have been allotted to the respective Indian applicants upon satisfactory proof of their being entitled thereto under existing laws, steps will be taken through the proper authorities to place each allottee in possession of his lands in order that he may enjoy the full, free, peaceable, and uninterrupted use and occupancy thereof.

The jumping of land by white men discouraged the Dayton Creek Indians from making much effort to cultivate the soil this year, and consequently very little will be raised by the Indians at that place.

The nonreservation Indians of northern Idaho. — Under date of October 21, 1891, the honorable Commissioner of Indian Affairs wrote:

Referring to your letter of July 14, 1891, reporting that the nonreservation Kootenai Indians of Northern Idaho requested permission to be allowed to remove to and settle upon the Flathead Reservation, seeing that it was, as they said, hopeless for them to retain the lands where they now reside, and reporting also that the Indians of the Flathead Reservation had given them a cordial invitation to share their reservation with them, I have to advise you that the whole matter was submitted to the Secretary of the Interior for his consideration on the 27th of August last, and, as indicated in my telegram to you of this date, the Secretary authorized me to instruct you to use every proper means to induce the said nonreservation Kootenais to remove to and settle on the Flathead Reservation. We also authorize the use of $5,000 of the funds for the relief of destitute Indians for the purpose of supplying the nonreservation Kootenais with food and other necessaries of life, providing they shall remove and settle upon the Jocko or Flathead Reservation.

Upon my first visit to the Kootenais in northern Idaho a delegation of five of their headmen was sent to the Flathead Reservation to look at the country, consult with the tribes, and report back whether it would be advisable to remove. After remaining some time on the reserve they returned to Idaho and advised the removal of the tribe to settle among the reservation Kootenais at Dayton Creek. Isaac, the head chief, fully indorsed the removal, but Moise, the second chief, objected, stating that he preferred to live with the British Kootenais, and if pressed to remove would go with his followers across the British line to reside among their relatives. It was found that there were three factions. One party would go to this reservation, some families take allotments in Idaho, while Moise, and his followers would cross the boundary into British possessions. The close of this year will find this matter disposed of, as I have been authorized by the Indian Commissioner to make allotments to the families who desired to remain, while some families have already arrived on the reserve and others are following.

Chief Michel's band of Lower Kalispels. — Under an agreement made with the Northwest Indian commission, in 1887 this band of Indians removed to this reservation. As reported last year, the terms of the agreement have not yet been ratified by Congress, and, as usual in such cases, the agent is held responsible by the Indians for inducing them to leave their homes in the Kalispel country, in Idaho, under promises which are not yet fulfilled. They have built log cabins, fenced in fields, and with the aid of a small amount of supplies issued them at the agency they make out to live.

Police and court of Indian Offences. — This branch of the service continues to be a source of annoyance, mainly on account of the opposition of Chief Charlot and his band of recent removals to this reserve. That chief is disposed to be jealous of the judges, and professes to believe that their appointment is an innovation upon the power and influence of the chief, and advocates a volunteer force of police, named by himself and to act under his control. Learning that some of the police and judges were inclined to cater to his views, at the close of the fiscal year I reorganized the force and forwarded to the Commissioner of Indian Affairs a new list for confirmation. The gradual breaking up of tribal relations and consequent waning power of the chiefs is the cause of the opposition to the court of Indian offenses and to the police. The sooner tribal relations are broken the better for all classes of Indians, particularly for the rising generation of educated youth.

Crime. — Outside of gambling and drinking, occasional horse-stealing, and elopements, no serious crime in the way of murder or outlawry has come under my notice during the year.

Sanitary. — Sickness prevailed during cold and damp weather of spring, and a great many deaths occurred, principally among the children in Indian homes. At school the health of the children was exceedingly good.

The industries pursued at this reservation consist of stock-raising, tilling the soil, and raising crops of various kinds.

A few of the young Indians have acquired a knowledge of blacksmithing, carpentry, shoemaking, painting, and saddle and harness making, and work at the trades wherever employment can be secured. A herd of buffalo, consisting of about seventy head, has been raised on the reservation by men of Indian blood. Negotiations are being carried on to have them exhibited at the Columbian Exposition.

Allotments in severalty. — The chiefs bitterly opposed the allotments of land in severalty, and are upheld in their prejudices by most of the full-blooded Indians of the reservation. No allotment has yet been made to any Indian within boundary. Great prejudice prevails against a survey of any kind, and the chiefs and Indians constantly state that a "measurement" of land means a robbery of the Indians. There are some of the young and more enlightened Indians who desire allotments and titles to their lands, but it is unpopular to discuss it, and they are silent on the subject. Nearly every head of a family on this reservation occupies definite, separate, though unallotted tracts, and their fences or boundary marks are generally respected. They also live in houses, and a majority of their homes present a thrifty, farm-like appearance.

Education. — It is hardly necessary to state that the industrial school at St. Ignatius Mission, on this reservation, is classed by officials of the Indian Department, as well as those who are interested in the education of Indian youths, as one of the most perfect institutions of its kind on any Indian reservation in the United States. The total number of pupils enrolled during the fiscal year 1891-'92 amounts to 423; 75 of this number are cared for by the Ursuline nuns in the kindergarten, an institution which, though in operation but two years, proves to be the most beneficial one both for the moral and physical training of the little ones. The Indian mothers and fathers already appreciate this fact and willingly give their little ones to the care of the nuns.

All the buildings for boys, girls, and babies are kept in excellent condition. They are well-finished frame buildings, furnished with all-modern improvements. Three of the boys of the school were married to school girls in the course of the year. The missionaries built dwelling houses for these couples, the sisters fitted them out with furniture, cooking utensils, etc., and they were provided with agricultural implements from the agency. The children who remained at the school during vacation, about 200 in number, lived during a month under large tents, pitched on the loveliest and healthiest spots of the reservation, near mountain lakes and streams where there is plenty of fishing, gunning, boat-riding, bathing, and athletic sports of all kinds. As to trades, produce, and expenses, information is carefully given in the school statistics.

St. Ignatius Mission school erected near the agency during this fiscal year a commodious school building for the children of Charlot's band, lately removed to this reservation from the Bitter Root Valley. The fathers have already spent over $4,000 on this school. It is managed and maintained on the same solid principles of the main school, of which it is a branch and preparatory department. All of the Indian-school buildings on this reservation erected under the auspices of the missionaries of St. Ignatius Mission, both for boys and girls, are not surpassed in the State of Montana for beauty of architecture, ventilation, modern improvements, accommodation of pupils, healthful surroundings, and attractiveness. In my report for 1890 I stated that a kindergarten was added to the school by the faculty. The result has been most satisfactory.

Missionary work. — The missionary labors are in the hands of the Jesuit fathers, who, as yearly reported, devote their lives to the work of Christianizing, civilizing, and educating the Indians. Owing to their devoted work the Indian inhabitants of this reservation are steadily gaining an advance over all other tribes in Montana in religion, civilization, farming, and other pursuits. The sanctity of marriage is generally respected, and unlawful cohabitation is punished by tribal laws.

I am, very respectfully, your obedient servant,

Peter Ronan,
U.S. Indian Agent.

The Commissioner of Indian Affairs.

September 6, 1892
LR 33,599/1892, RG 75, National Archives, Washington, D.C.

For information on Catherine B. or Justine Fry, see Ronan's August 6, 1889, letter and annotation.

United States Indian Service,
Flathead Agency,
Montana, Sept. 6th, 1892.

Hon. Commissioner Indian Affairs
Washington, D.C.
Sir:

On the 12th of August I had the honor to report to you from Sand Point, Idaho, in regard to arrest of a whiteman, at that place for the sale of whisky to an Indian, whose body was afterwards found, and the circumstances pointed to the same individual, as being guilty of the murder of the Indian to whom he sold the whisky. The case having been postponed until Wednesday the 17th of August, I proceeded to Bonners Ferry in response to an urgent telegram from some of the Indian owners of land, complaining that whitemen commenced cutting hay on the land they always occupied and which they held under the 4th Section of the General Allotment Act, as amended by the act of February 28, 1891. (26 Stats. 794) It was also my business there under your instruction to allot land to certain Kootenai Indian families, and to assist them to make applications for allotments under said act and amendment, as instructed in "Land 1942 — 1892 dated June 3rd, 1892"; also "Land 23602 — 1892 — Authority 31323.["] On the morning of 15th of August, I made inquiries into the trouble in regard to Whites cutting hay on Indian Land, and found that Catherine B. Fry, as the head of a Kootenai family, on the 20th of July, 1891, availed herself of the privilege of the 4th Section of the General Allotment Act, as amended by Act of February 28, 1891, (26 Stats 794) proceeded under the law to have allotted to herself and children and decendants certain tracts of land to the number of ten, from 40 to 80 acres in each tract, for which the following receipt was issued.

United States Land Office
Coeur 'd Alene, Idaho,
July 20, 1891.

We hereby certify that the foregoing is a full, true and correct abstract of all Indian Allotment Applications, under Section 4 Act of February 8, 1887, made at this office.

Signed James E. Russell,
Register.

A majority of the Allottees are minors but some of them are the owners of cattle — given them by relatives. Until lately the head of the family and the children held peaceful possession of the land and each year put up the hay to feed their own cattle during winter. This season new seekers after locations have taken possession of some of this Indian land, and commenced cutting and stacking the hay, and defy the Indians to come on the premises. Although appealed to, as the Agent of the Interior Department (who advised the Indians under instructions to make application for allotments under said law) to protect their interests, I could not see how it was in my power to do so without stepts [sic] were taken by the proper authorities to put them in full and peaceful possession of the land they claim as lawfully belonging to them. The land was enclosed by barbed wire fences at the expense of the guardian or head of the said Indian family, but broken down by the jumppers [sic] in order to drive their teams on the land to take possession of the same. The administration of justice is in a crude state in this portion of the State of Idaho and the distance from Bonners Ferry to the local land Office is in the neighborhood of nintyfive miles.

I know of no other way to turn for assistance or advice than to the Hon. Commissioner of Indian Affairs, and I therefore wired the following

Bonners Ferry, Idaho.
August 15, 1892.

Indian Commissioner,
Washington.

Allotments to ten Indian applicants at this place, receipted for by Register local land Office July 20th 1891. at Coeur 'd Alene, Idaho, interfered with by white trespassers, who are cutting hay ect. and prevent Indians from cutting hay from land occupied by the Indians prior to Allotment. What legal steps if any shall I take to protect the Indian owners from tresspass?

Ronan, Agent.

On the 15th of August I called a Council of the Kootenai Indians at the old Mission Church, and stated to them that I was there according to the instructions of the Hon. Commissioner of Indian Affairs to make allotments to certain Indian families, who chose to occupy the land they lived upon rather than remove to the Jocko or any other reservation. I then explained that the Children of the families were entitled to Allotments as well.

The Chief stated that several Indians who chose to cross the British line, rather than go upon the Reservation had returned to their homes in Idaho, and were anxious to settle upon and cultivate their land, if alloted them. I informed the Indians that if no authenticated dispute arose in regard to the rightful ownership of the land between Indians and whitemen, and if proof was furnished that they were born in the United States, I would allot to American Indians the land they claimed and occupied. The Chief expressed his thankfulness and announced that only the heads of families, except in one case, would ask for Allotments, and if made they and their Children would occupy and cultivate the soil and ask no further assistance from the Government. Other families and young men would go to the reservation and avail themselves of the liberality of the Government in their new home. Time he said must be allowed to some in order to dispose of the rights they might at present hold to land and small improvements, by right of occupancy, but would be abandoned to settlers upon payment from them for improvements before their removal to the Flathead reservation.

Some families had already moved to the reservation while others would follow, but would hunt and fish enroute and did not expect to report at Dayton Creek until driven in by cold weather. As before reported the prosecution of a whiteman for the sale of liquor to Indians as well as suspicion that the prisoner was guilty of the murder and robbery of an Indian would call me to Hope, Idaho, on the 17th of August, it was arranged that I would commence allotting on the 19th, and requested that the Indian be on their land on that date, and as aggreed [sic] upon, the work commenced on that day. I was compelled to engage the assistance of an interpreter and a man to assist in raising mounds and stakes, and measuring off land in order to give proper description, on the blanks furnished, to the General Land Office through the local land Office at Coeur 'd Alene, Idaho. As the allotments were situated along the bank of the Kootenai river, a boat and rowers had to be procured, to land at different locations. Although the description of the land Allotted represented the farthest distance from the town of Bonners Ferry across the country, some 24 miles, the real distance following the meandering of the river by boat is over sixty miles.

On some of the Indian lands where they had houses and improvements in the way of cultivated vegetable gardens ect. I found whitemen running mowing machines and stacking hay, where the Indians heretofore cut hay for their cattle and lived upon the land.

The procedure is a palfable [sic] outrage and not at all encouraged by the bona fida citizens and settlers there, who state that the hay is only being cut by speculative parties for sale to cattlemen, next winter.

Some steps should be taken to protect Indian allottes from such outrage, as several of the Indians have cattle to feed in the winter, and two of such families are provided with mowing machines, which they purchased from their own resources. On those two farms in particular the Indians were running their mowing machines, while right along side of them the whites were running mowing machines on the Indian claims, and it seemed to be a race between them to see which would cut the most hay. The Indians are very quiet and peaceful under such aggravating circumstances, and are hopeful that they soon will be freed from the presence of such aggressive intruders, by full and free title to their land from the Government.

Having completed the Allotments to the number of twenty two, eighty acre tracts to Indian heads of families, I proceeded to the local Land Office at Coeur 'd Alene City, Idaho, which is distant from the town of Bonners Ferry about ninty five miles, and delivered to the Register and Receiver, descriptions of the same, made on proper blanks furnished from your office, and took receipt for same, to be forwarded to the General Land Office at Washington. It is my belief that the Indian question, as to the Kootenai tribe, is now permanently settled. Those that have asked for their land in severalty in that country claim that they will, when they have the full possession of the same, be able to support themselves without any aid from the Government. I would recommend, however, that an issue of proper agricultural impliments be made to them, and that seed be furnished next spring, and a farmer appointed for one year to direct their efforts. If this plan be adopted a colouny [sic] of industrious and peaceful Indians will be put on the highway to self support and self respect. The Indians that chose to come to the reservation are a wandering band, who support themselves and their families by hunting and fishing.

It will take time and patience to make them permannent [sic] settlers on the reservation and to induce them to give up such life in the mountains and their ancient hunting grounds. But after the permanent settlement of a few industrious families, that have already selected land on the reservation, gradually the nomandic [sic] members of the tribe may be induced to give up their wandering lives for permanent homes, as they realize that game is fast disappearing and subsistence must be made, by cultivation of the soil & civilizing pursuits. Herewith I have the honor to enclose bills and vouchers covering expense while in the discharge of my duties in Northern Idaho, and have the honor to be

Very respectfully
Your Obedient Servant
Peter Ronan,
United States Indian Agent.

September 7, 1892
LR 33,744/1892, RG 75, National Archives, Washington, D.C.

> The mixed blood accused was Sam Pablo who was tried before the United States Commissioner in Missoula and later released on the basis of self defense. According to Father Jerome D'Aste, S.J., the Indian murdered on September 2, 1892, was Cree and gambling was the cause of the altercation.[37]

United States Indian Service,
Flathead Agency,
September 7th, 1892.

Hon. Commissioner Indian Affairs,
Washington, D.C.
   Sir:
   Owing to a multiplicity of duties: Allotting lands in Northern Idaho, to the Kootenai Indians; prosecuting Robert Philips, in the same State, for sale of liquor to Indians from this reservation; arresting and turning over to the United States authorities a halfbreed of this reserve for the killing of a Chipawa Indian from Minnesota; collecting statistics and making census for Annual Report, etc., is my excuse for the delay of my regular monthly report from this Agency for the month of August.
   A very dry season with extremely hot weather having set in after a cold and backward spring, the crops of this year on the reservation will fall short and will not yield half the amount of grain to the acre as the yield of last year. Harvesting is now over and the threshing machines are in operation keeping the Indians busy threshing and storing their grain.
   The saw mill and shingle machine have also been in operation, cutting lumber for the Indians who furnished saw logs at the mill. Some fifty thousand feet was cut into dimensions for Indian use, and also thirty thousand shingles were manufactured for them during the month.
   Turning over the Government farm to Chief Charlott, of the Bitter Root Flatheads, made it necessary to bargain with Indians who were in possession of hay land for the privilege to cut hay for the use of the Agency stock. Enough hay is now provided to feed them through the winter. Hay will be a scarce article here if deep snow should fall in the winter. The drought has burned up the grass on the ranges, and fall rain will not now do much good.
   On Friday, the 2d of September a young halfbreed Indian of this reservation became involved in a quarrel with three Chipawa Indians from Minnesota, who recently camped on the reserve near the Agency. The quarrel resulted in the death of one of the Minnesota Indians who had his skull broken by a stone or or [sic] some other weapon in the hand of the Agency mixedblood. I had him placed under arrest and turned him over to the United States authorities at Missoula for trial.

This week the new and handsome school house erected by the Mission school at St. Ignatius, at this Agency, will be open to the children of Chief Charlot's band of Bitter Root Flatheads as well as to other Indian children residing in the Jocko valley. Teachers have already taken possession of the building, and it is to be hoped that parents will appreciate the benefit of an education and fill the school to its capacity with Indian children.

I have the honor to enclose sanatory [sic] report and report of funds and indebtedness, also report of farmers, and have the honor to be

Very respectfully
Your obedient Servant,
Peter Ronan,
United States Indian Agent.

September 12, 1892
LR 33,334/1892, telegram, RG 75, National Archives, Washington, D.C.

Sept 12 1892
Arlee Mont

Commr Indian Affairs
Washn, DC

No land was allotted by me except to Indian occupants. Fry is the father of a half breed indian family and made application through the local land office himself in eighteen hundred and ninety one for allotment to his children under the general allotment act. Trespassers are now occupying some of the land of the Fry applicants cutting hay and building houses. S. E. Henry is attorney for trespasser.

Ronan U S Indian Agt.

October 5, 1892
LR 36,987/1892, RG 75, National Archives, Washington, D.C.

For more information on the proposal to remove obstructions that kept salmon out of the Flathead River Basin, see Ronan's April 22, 1891, letter and annotation.

United States Indian Service,
Flathead Agency,
October 5th, 1892.

Hon. Commissioner Indian Affairs
Washington, D.C.

Sir:

I now have the honor to submit my report from this Agency for the month of September.

The weather has been hot and dry and the valleys and cattle ranges present a crisp appearance that will make it difficult for range cattle to winter. I look for heavy losses in stock if an unusual cold winter sets in.

Threshing of grain is now Completed on the reservation, but the backward, cold spring, followed by unusual hot, dry weather prevented the full maturing of crops as in other seasons. I believe that hardly one fourth of the usual yield of grain to the acre was harvested this season. Encouraged by the fine yield of last year the Indians exerted energy in increasing their acreage, and more than double the amount of grain was seeded this year than in any previous year in the history of this reservation. Notwithstanding the partial failure of the grain crop, the Agency flour mill is taxed beyond its capacity at present in grinding wheat for the Indian producers.

At this season, Indian families take themselves to the mountains to hunt until Christmas, when they return to their homes on the reservation. They want wheat ground before departure; I therefore put on two crews this week from regular employes and run the grist mill on double time in order to grind into flour the surplus wheat now on hand at the mill.

The saw mill was also in operation cutting lumber for the Indians, but was closed down in order to set the flour mill in operation.

I accompanied Dr. C. E. Gorham, Engineer of the Fish Commission to the rapids where the Pend 'd Oreille river or main branch of the Clarkes Fork of the Columbia river flows out of the Flathead Lake. The Doctor was accompanied by Professor Woolman. After examination there they proceeded to Thompson Falls, in Montana, and from thence to Sand Point, Idaho, where they took the Great Northern railroad to examine the principal falls or rapids further down the river and near where it empties into the Columbia river.

I continued on to Dayton Creek to settle some trouble about land there, and was successful in making arrangements between the Indians and a settler to await the action of the General Land Office in regard to the rightful ownership and occupancy of a certain piece of land allotted by me to an Indian. This business and other matters connected with Kootenai Indians at Dayton Creek will be the subject for a special report to your office soon as time will permit.

The Indians of the Jocko valley express their appreciation of the efforts now being made to bring in a supply of water for irrigation purposes and otherwise, and are especially pleased to be informed that if the work is ordered they will have an opportunity to earn wages in excavation, hawling logs to the mill, etc., etc.

All industries in connection with the Agency are in good condition and peaceful and neighborly feelings prevail within the boundaries of the reservation.

I have the honor to forward quarterly school reports sanitary report and report of funds and indebtedness, also report of farmers and have the honor to be

Very respectfully
Your obedient Servant
Peter Ronan
United States Indian Agent.

October 8, 1892
LR 37,894/1892, RG 75, National Archives, Washington, D.C.

While the government made promises to protect the Dayton Creek Kootenai allottees, officials found legal technicalities to hold up enforcement and hostile white settlers continued to invade improved Indian farms. Clarence Proctor was so aggressive that he built a fence to surround an Indian farm. Apparently the federal government's response was to argue that the state courts did not have jurisdiction in the matter. The contests stood in limbo until the summer of 1893 when they flared up again. See Ronan's June 1, 1893b, letter.

United States Indian Service,
Flathead Agency,
October 8th, 1892.

Hon. Commissioner Indian Affairs,
Washington, D.C.

Sir:

I now desire to draw your attention to affairs at Dayton Creek, the home of the Kootenai Indians on this reservation, and, as preliminary, respectfully refer you to my report on that business dated August 9th, 1892, which will give particulars in regard to matters that lead to the following report:

It will be seen by report referred to that Eneas, Chief of Kootenai Indians, at Dayton Creek, on this reservation, was placed under arrest by a constable upon warrant issued by a Justice of the Peace, at Demersville, Head of Flathead Lake, Missoula County, Montana. I was upon the ground when the Constable made the second arrest of the Chief, (the first was claimed to have been resisted.[)] The Constable Stated that if he (the Chief) refused to accompany him, a posse of citizens were likely to move on the reservation and make arrest by force of arms. As stated in report, in order to prevent the coming of an armed posse of excited people to the Kootenai village to arrest their Chief, I volunteered to accompany the constable to Demersville, where I went before the Justice of the Peace who issued the warrant and signed a bond in the sum of five hundred dollars to bring Chief Eneas before him on the 2d day of October, 1892, to answer any charges that might be preferred against him.

In the meantime I returned to the Agency, and by letter, laid the matter before Elbert D. Weed, United States Attorney at Helena, for the District of Montana.

While this matter was under consideration, as wired to your office, I was notified to Come to Dayton Creek again, as Chief Eneas was involved in more trouble over land allotted by me to members of his tribe. Upon arriving there I found that one Clarence Proctor, who made location near Dayton Creek, was in conflict with a certain Kootenai Indian, of Chief Eneas band. Mr. Proctor claimed that he located the land before any Indian made attempt to occupy it; while the Indian claimed that he selected the place some nine years before Proctor, for a home, and before the Harrison boundary survey was made and accepted by the Interior Department, and when it was supposed to be inside of the boundaries of the reservation set aside for the Flathead Indians and Confederated tribes. Upon such representation made to me by the Indian, at the time I was ordered to allot lands to this band, I made the allotment to said Indian. Chief Eneas undertook to prevent the employes of Proctor from building fence and otherwise improving, and as before stated, I was sent for. I explained to the Chief "that as soon as the Indian Allotment applications of his Indians shall have been transmitted to the Indian office, by the General Land Office for consideration and action, and the lands covered thereby shall have been allotted to the respective Indian applicants, upon satisfactory proof of there [sic] being entitled thereto, under existing law, steps will be taken through the proper authorities to place each allottee in possession of his lands in order that he may enjoy the full, free, peaceable and uninterrupted use and occupancy thereof."

It was thereupon agreed between Proctor and the Chief, that the former might go on with his improvements until final decision was arrived at in the proper Department. Proctor having run a fence around the Indian enclosure, it was agreed that the Indian should have free access to his field through the gate of Proctor, until the question of ownership was decided. In the meantime the Indians would not interfere with fencing and improvement by Mr. Proctor. Thus I closed the matter until title is decided in the usual way.

Most of the Kootenai Indians were out in the mountains hunting, but before going the building in which supplies were stored for the Bonner Ferry Kootenai Indians was broken into and robbed of a large quantity of supplies and articles of clothing and blankets. It was evidently done by Indians. I informed Kootenai Chief Eneas that no more supplies would again be stored at Dayton Creek, and that the Indians should have to come to the Agency hereafter to have their wants relieved.

Owing to failure of Crops this year the Kootenai Indians are without means of support at Dayton Creek, and all are now out hunting with exception of the Chief, who is suffering from rheumatism, and a few families of old people and children. The Kootenai Indians who came from Bonners Ferry, Idaho, this fall, were discouraged and few remained. They found the crops at Dayton Creek a failure; Chief Eneas under arrest for trying to prevent white trespassers from cutting hay upon land always occupied by Indians under the belief that it was inside the boundaries of the reservation, and when learned, by actual survey, to be outside of said boundary, was allotted to the Indian occupants by the Agent under a proper instruction from the Hon. Commissioner of Indian Affairs. Under such disadvantageous circumstances the Kootenai Indians of Northern Idaho that intended to settle are restless. Untill the Dayton Creek Indian allotments are finally settled, they will continue wandering between the two localities.

As the pressing necessities of Chief Eneas and his Camp required immediate relief, I made an issue to them of supplies from the warehouse at Dayton Creek.

By attached correspondence, the Hon. Commissioner of Indian Affairs will learn of the present disposition of the case of the arrest of Eneas, the Chief of Kootenai Indians of this reservation by procedure of rural Justice of the Peace.

> I am very respectfully,
> Your obedient Servant,
> Peter Ronan,
> United States Indian Agent.

First enclosure:

> Department of Justice.
> Office of United States Attorney,
> District of Montana,
> Helena, Montana.
> Helena, Montana, Sept. 29, 1892.

Peter Ronan, Esq.
U.S. Indian Agent,
Arlee, Montana.

My Dear Sir: –

Your telegram concerning the arrest of the chief of the Kootenai tribe has been received. Any crime, whatsoever committed by an Indian, upon an indian reservation, is in the exclusive jurisdiction of the Federal Courts. I wired Mr. [Seth] McFarr[e]n at Demersville advising him that the U.S. had jurisdiction of the matter in all probability and to defer action until further advised[.] It seems to be immaterial what the facts may be so long as the gravamen of the charge would locate it upon reservation.

I will advise you by wire or by letter of any thing further occurring in the matter referred to.

Yours respectfully,
John M. McDonald
Assistant U.S. Attorney.

Second enclosure:

Department of Justice.
Office of United States Attorney,
District of Montana,
Helena, Montana.
Oct. 3, 1892.

Peter Ronan, Esq.
U.S. Indian Agent,
Flat Head Agency,
Jocko, Mont.

Dear Sir: –

Your communication of Sept. 30th now lies before me. I have read the matter enclosed concerning your report to the Honorable Commissioner of Indian Affairs. It was determined in a case recently tried before Judge Knowles — U.S. vs. Casey, for murder, that wherever the crime was committed, either upon the Reservation, or upon an allotment made in pursuance to regulations or treaties, that the Federal Courts had exclusive jurisdiction. There were other jurisdictional questions raised and urged in that case, but were all determined in favor of the Federal Courts retaining the jurisdiction alleged. Our opinion, in the matter now before you, wherein Chief Æneas of Kootenai tribe, is arrested by Judge McFarren, is that the case is one of Federal jurisdiction and not lodged at all in that Court. I have to-day so telegraphed to Mr. McFarren, to discharge Æneas.

Yours very respectfully,
John M. McDonald,
Asst. U.S. Dist. Atty.

October 22, 1892
LR 38,910/1892, RG 75, National Archives, Washington, D.C.

For more information on the case of the two teenagers convicted of vandalizing the railroad near Drummond, see Ronan's March 9, 1892, letter and annotation. Prison records give their names as Pasqual Antay and Thomas Lavatta, but Ronan identified one of them as Antoine in this letter. Ronan's October 1892 request for pardons for the boys was unsuccessful, but they were pardoned in March 1895. For biographical information on Montana Governor Joseph K. Toole, see the annotation to Ronan's January 2, 1890b, letter.

United States Indian Service,
Flathead Agency,
October 22d, 1892.

Hon. Commissioner Indian Affairs
Washington, D.C.

Sir:

Herewith I have the honor to enclose to you copy of a letter I addressed to Hon Joseph K. Toole, Governor of Montana, which will explain itself.

I am very respectfully,

Your obedient servant,

Peter Ronan,

United States Indian Agent.

Enclosure:

United States Indian Service,

Flathead Agency,

October 22nd, 1892.

To the Hon Joseph K Toole

Governor of Montana

Sir

A few days ago I had the honor to consult with you in regard to the case of two Indian boys Antoine [i.e., Thomas Lavatta] and Pascall [Antay] by name of the Flathead Indian tribe of this reservation, now serving a sentence of five years in the State Penitentiary, at Deer Lodge, for placing obstructions on the track of the Northern Pacific railroad, at or near Drummond in Deer Lodge County, Montana. I appealed for pardon, as I believed the boys have already served a term commiserate with the crime for which they [were] tried and sentenced. You were kind enough to ask me to give you the particulars in writing for consideration and action, and herewith I respectfully submit the history of the case as reported at the time.

In February 1892, I received a letter from the Superintendent of the Rocky mountain Division of the Northern Pacific Railroad, stating that obstructions had been placed upon the track near Drummond, in Deer Lodge County, and that two Indians were in custody under suspicion of being the guilty parties. I went to Deer Lodge with my interpreter, and was joined by Mr Noble, a Pinkerton Detective, and the Superintendent of the Division.

I found two Indian boys under twenty years of Age in the County jail, and recognized them as belonging to Chief Charlots band of Bitter Root Indians. They confessed to me (in presence of the railroad Attorney the prosecuting Attorney, the detective and the Railroad Superintendent[)] that they put a fish plate in the space where the rails are joined, "just to see the engine jump." It is my information that such obstruction could not cause the wreck of a train, I looked upon the matter as a boyish, mischievious piece of folly, more than an attempt to cause the wreck of a train or the loss of life. I met Mr Noble (the detective, who was present when the boys confessed the matter to me a few days ago, and he fully agrees with me in my view of the case and is willing to sign a petition for the release of the Indian boys whom he thinks have already served enough time in the Penitentiary to serve the cause of Justice, and to teach them a lesson that will prevent them from attempting such an act of folly, or crime, as interpreted by the law. Trusting that you will Kindly give this matter attention in the cause of Mercy.

I am very respectfully

Your obedient Servant

Peter Ronan,

United States Indian Agent.

October 24, 1892

LR 38,911/1892, RG 75, National Archives, Washington, D.C.

See Ronan's March 10, 1891; October 20, 1891; and March 24, 1892b, letters and annotations on the problems with the survey of the southwest boundary of the reservation. The Commissioner of Indian Affairs did not reply to this letter.

United States Indian Service,
Flathead Agency,
October 24, 1892.

Hon. Commissioner Indian Affairs,
Washington, D.C.

Sir:

I would respectfully call your attention to my letter of March 24th, 1892, and your reply "Land 11798 – 1892, – 17865 – 1892," dated May 18, 1892, in reference to allotting certain land to Pend 'd Oreille Indians. I stated in said letter that I hesitated to to [sic] proceed to assist the Pend 'd Oreille Indians to make applications for allotments of lands under the 4th Section of the General Allotment Act, as Amended by Act approved February 28, 1891, for the reason that I was unable to determine whether the said Indians were outside the boundary line of the Flathead Indian reservation, etc., etc.

Mr. Samuel Bundock, alluded to in said letter, who entered into contract last year — which contract was duly approved by the General Land Office, for the survey of 51 miles of the Western and Southern boundaries of the Flathead reservation; that the surveyor under contract referred to, took the field last fall to commence his work where Deputy Surveyor Harrison left off; that he was unable to establish the last corner of the 81st mile as made by Mr. Harrison; that he notified me that he abandoned the field for the reason above stated; but that he would return there some time this year for the purpose of making the survey of said boundary line.

I stated in my letter that on account of the strained relations existing between the Indians referred to and the white settlers in that vicinity that the boundary line should be determined at as early a date as possible and that allotments should be made to the Indians according to instructions heretofore given me in relation to the matter in order to prevent further and serious trouble.

I now desire to report that Deputy Surveyor Samuel Bundock, up to present date, failed to notify me that he has taken the field to complete the said survey, as stated in your letter he was directed to do. The season is now too far advanced for the survey to be made in the mountainous region called for under the contract.

The Indians living at the place indicated on the Pend 'd Oreille river now notify me that white settlers have taken possession of land they occupied for over twenty years and always considered their occupancy within the boundary of the Flathead Indian reservation. Whether on or off the reservation, it is my opinion that the Indians are the rightful occupants of the land.

I shall therefore proceed, at my earliest opportunity ~~to allot~~ to allot the land to the Indians under instructions wired to me as follows:

"Washington, D.C.
October 22d, 1891.

Ronan Agent,
Flathead Agency, Montana
    Replying to your telegram of the 29th, allot land to Pend
'd Orellies same as Kootenais at Dayton Creek.

Signed T. J. Morgan,
Commissioner."

As it is my belief that the survey will not be made this year, I would respectfully state that it might be better for the settlers, as well as the Indians, to make the allotments, as I believe the latter are justly entitled to the land for which they now ask title. Awaiting your suggestions and orders in the matter.

I am very respectfully,
Your obedient Servant
Peter Ronan,
United States Indian Agent.

November 12, 1892
LR 41,640/1892, RG 75, National Archives, Washington, D.C.

> The diphtheria outbreak on the reservation resulted in alarming reports in the local press. Father Jerome D'Aste, S.J., referred to students at St. Ignatius Mission with sore throat and croup between October 4 and November 1, 1892.[38] Ronan did not comment on the irony of an Indian school celebrating Columbus Day.

United States Indian Service,
Flathead Agency,
Nov. 12th, 1892.

Hon. Commissioner Indian Affairs
Washington, D.C.
    Sir:
    The cause of delay in my report for the month of October, has been sickness of myself and four members of my family. For two weeks I have been confined to bed with rheumatism and now four of my children are down with scarlet fever. This has been an unhealthy season, on this reservation, diphtheria prevailed at one time to an alarming extent among the Indian children. At the kindergarten, there were thirty-seven cases of diphtheria, but as soon as the disease became known to the faculty at St. Ignatius school two of the best physicians of Missoula, were summoned to consult with Dr. Dade, the Agency physician.
    The little ones stricken with the disease were separated from the school, and placed in quarters, where no communication with the other children was permitted. Only three cases proved fatal at the school. The doctors were unanimous in attributing this small fatality among the children, to the careful nursing and watchful tenderness of the Ursuline nuns who have charge of the school.
    There were a number of deaths of children in the Indian camps, caused by the same disease. The Agency physician promptly attended to every case when notified and generally succeeded in the recovery of the patients, but there were a number of deaths of children in camps where Indian ignorance or superstition prevented them from calling for medical aid from the Agency physician. The disease has entirely disappeared from the school and no other cases have lately been reported from any portion of the reservation.

October 21st 1892, the celebration of "Columbus Day" was appropriately carried out, and the following programme was the order of the day:

The pupils assembled at half past nine o'clock in the church to express their gratitude to Divine Providence for the devout faith of the discoverer and for the Divine care and guidance which has directed our history and so abundantly blessed our people.

At 11 o'clock the national flag was raised amidst the cheers of teachers and pupils assembled in the yard. Meanwhile national and patriotic airs were rendered by the St. Ignatius brass band.

Afternoon Observances.

3.00 P.M. Great Base-ball Game.

4.00 P.M. Lunch, specially prepared to make the day of memorable festivity.

7.30 P.M. Entertainment given by the pupils of St. Ignatius Mission School.

Programme

1. Reading of the President's Proclamation.
2. Song of Columbus Day.
3. Responsive Exercise — Questions and answers about the meaning of the Day's Celebration and the Four Centuries.
4. Patriotic Song.
5. Recitation — The Morning of the Discovery.
6. Dialogue — 1492–1892 in historical costumes.
7. Song — Four Hundred Years Ago To-day.
8. Recitation — Columbia, the Gem of the Ocean.
9. Song — America.
10. Ode — Columbus.
11. Exercise — The Claims of the Nations in historical costumes.
12. Address — delivered by the Superintendent.
13. Song — Echoing Adown the Ages.

I have several Indians at work delivering saw logs at the mill to be cut into dimensions for the enlargement of the old flume of the irrigation ditch, as authorized by you. The survey of the new ditch will commence on Monday the 14th inst. and if the ground does not freeze I expect to have it completed before New Years, as the Indians are anxious to get to work on it to earn wages.

The flour mill has been constantly employed during October and to present date, grinding Indian wheat. Every industry connected with the Agency has received usual attention and the Indians are attending to their civilizing pursuits and occupations in a quiet and orderly manner.

Herewith I have the honor to forward sanitary report and report of funds and indebtedness, also report of farmers and have the honor to be

Very respectfully,
Your obedient servant
Peter Ronan
United States Indian Agent.

November 16, 1892

LR 41,864/1892, RG 75, National Archives, Washington, D.C. See Ronan's June 3, 1887, letter. The map Ronan enclosed was not filed with this letter in the National Archives.

Despite personally believing in the allotment policy, Ronan had recommended on June 3, 1887, against implementing the policy on the Flathead Reservation. In 1892 both of Montana's senators, Wilbur F. Sanders and Thomas C. Power, lobbied for allotment on the Flathead Reservation. In this letter and his August 26, 1892, annual report, Ronan opposed forcing allotment on the tribes. Allotment was delayed for twelve years which helped protect some of the tribal land base.[39]

> United States Indian Service,
> Flathead Agency,
> November 16th, 1892.

Hon. Commissioner Indian Affairs,
Washington, D.C.

Sir:

Referring to "Land 21161 – 1892," dated Washington, October 15, 1892; also "Land 38739 – 1892," dated November 2d, 1892 transmitting map of Montana, on which I am directed to indicate the townships which should be surveyed and subdivided in order to make allotments on the Jocko reservation, as directed in office letter of August 15th, 1892, which did not reach me, and a copy of which was furnished me October 15, 1892.

"It has been suggested to this Office that allotments in severalty should be made to the Indians on the Jocko reservation. In order that the matter may be considered intelligently, you will, without delay, give me your opinion as to whether allotments ought to be made to these Indians, and the facts upon which my [sic] opinion is based."

In reply, I believe the language I used in my report for 1892, will show how the Indians of this reservation feel in regard to allotments in severalty: "The Chiefs bitterly oppose the allotment of land in severalty, and are upheld in their prejudices by most of the full blooded Indians of the reservation. No allotment has yet been made to any Indian within its boundary. Great prejudice prevail against a survey of any kind, and the Chiefs and Indians constantly state that a "measurement" of land means a robbery of the Indians. There are some of the younger and more enlightened Indians who desire allotments and title to their lands, but it is unpopular to discuss it, and they are silent on the question. Nearly every head of a family on this reservation occupy, definite, separate, though unallotted tracts, and their fences or boundary marks are generally respected. They also live in houses and a majority of their homes present a thrifty, farmlike appearance."

For the reason stated I do not believe it would be wise to negotiate with them for the cession of any surplus lands, or to attempt at present to have the lands surveyed and allotted. In their present views the Indians will not listen to any negotiation looking either to allotments in severalty or to negotiations for the cession of any surplus lands within the boundaries of their reservation. As you request I have indicated the townships on the map that should be surveyed and subdivided in order to make the allotments.

As stated before it is my opinion the Indians will not listen to any proposition on the subject at present.

> I am very respectfully
> Your obedient servant,
> Peter Ronan,
> United States Indian Agent.

November 29, 1892a
LR 43,386/1892, RG 75, National Archives, Washington, D.C.

On October 15, 1892, the Commissioner of Indian Affairs approved $5,870 for the construction of an irrigation ditch to serve the Bitterroot Salish who had settled in the Jocko Valley. As Ronan mentioned in this letter, tribal members delivered saw logs to the agency sawmill for the project, worked on the sawmill crew, and did the excavation work. In his July 1, 1893, monthly report, Ronan mentioned that the irrigation ditch was completed.[40]

United States Indian Service,
Flathead Agency,
November 29, 1892.

Hon. Commissioner Indian Affairs
Washington, D.C.
Sir:
Referring to "Land 35549 – 1892 – Authority," dated at Washington, October 15, 1892, advising me that under the date of October 11, 1892, the Department granted authority to me to expend not exceeding $5,870 in enlarging the present irrigation canal and in constructing a new canal on the Flathead reservation, payable from the appropriation for irrigation on Indian reservations in Araizona [sic], Nevada and Montana.

I woul[d] respectfully report that the work is already in progress, and that the completion is being pushed forward fast as possible. The survey of the new canal has been made and contracts by the rod let to Indians, all along the line, who are enthusiastic in pushing their jobs to completion in order to receive their pay. Indians are filling the contract for the delivery of logs at the mill, and the saw mill is also running, cutting the logs into dimensions for the enlargement of the flume on the present irrigation canal, with an Indian crew assisting the sawyer and engineer. The Indians will expect their pay soon as their jobs are completed. I would therefore respectfully request that the amount to be expended in the work be placed to my credit at your earliest convenience.

I am very respectfully,
Your obedient servant,
Peter Ronan
United States Indian Agent.

November 29, 1892b
LR 43,385/1892, RG 75, National Archives, Washington, D.C.

One specific contest over a Bonners Ferry allotment involved Nicola Jerome and Joseph Parent, a white man. Jerome reportedly was willing to relinquish the allotment which was also claimed by Parent to avoid conflict and wanted to select an alternate allotment. On May 18, 1893, the Commissioner of Indian Affairs suggested to the Secretary of the Interior that Nicola Jerome's allotment application be held up until the case could be investigated further. When Ronan died in August 1893, the case was still in limbo. See also Ronan's January 17, 1893, and April 18, 1893, letters on the subject.[41] No further information was located for Nicola Jerome, Bonners Ferry Kootenai, or Joseph Parent, the white man who claimed Jerome's allotment. Two additional affidavits by white men repeating Parent's claims filed with this letter are not reproduced here.

United States Indian Service,
Flathead Agency,
November 29th, 1892.

Hon. Commissioner Indian Affairs
Washington, D.C.

Sir:

Upon receipt of the enclosed letter marked "A," I wrote to Joseph Parent, at Fry, Idaho, in substance, that in allotting land in severalty to Indians at Bonner's Ferry, Idaho; in August, 1892, I followed my instructions from the Indian Office, and allotted lands to certain heads of Indian families that was pointed out to me by said Indians as belonging to and occupied by them. Among these was allotment No. 3, assigned to Jerome Nicala. No person appeared upon the ground to make protest — against said allotment No. 3, and on August 19th, 1892, said allotment was made by posting the following, etc.:

> "Notice is hereby given that I the the [sic] undersigned being the head of a family of the Kootenai Indian tribe claim 80 acres of this land, under allotment Act of February 8th, 1887, as amended by Act of February 28, 1891, (26 Stat., p. 794,) beginning at a post and mound set up on the right bank of the Kootenai river, and at the West end of the allotment of Louie Temia, thence running down the bank of the Kootenai river one quarter of a mile; thence running at right angles one half a mile from the river; thence on quarter of a mile at right angle in an Easterly direction; thence one half a mile to place of beginning, containing 80 acres of land for agricultural purposes, being about four miles west of the town of Bonner's Ferry, in the State of Idaho, Kootenai County.
>
> Nicala Jerome his X mark

Witness

Richard Fry["]

Several of the Kootenai Indians at Bonner's Ferry, stated in Council, that they would remove to the Flathead reservation when they could dispose of their little holdings to white settlers, while others proposed to remain on their land and make application for the same under the allotment Act of February 8, 1887, as amended by Act of February 28, 1891 (26 Stat. 794.)

I was informed that several Indians instead of applying for allotments of land disposed of their claims to settlers as above. I advised the complainant to produce affidavits vouching for statements made in his letter herein enclosed and that I would forward same to the Hon. Commissioner of Indian Affairs for examination, with view of canceling said allottment No. 3, if in his judgment the settlers claim was valid. In this connection I would state that in my opinion there are Indians who would not hesitate to take a price for their claims from settlers and then have it allotted to them by the Agent by false representations.

I herewith enclose all papers in the case for consideration, and have the honor to be

Very respectfully
Your obedient servant,
Peter Ronan,
United States Indian Agent.

First enclosure:

Bonners Ferry, Sept. 28th 1892

Peter Ronan Esq.
Agt. Jocko, Montana
　　　Dear Sir,

　　　When you were here allotting Land to the Indians a short time ago; you allotted my claim to Indian Nicola Jerome. You were not probable aware that I was occupying the place as my House is on the River bank and can not be seen from the medow. I have been in peaceable possession for about one year and Paid $25.00 to the Indian who laid claim to the place. Chiefs Isaac & David were parties to the transaction and I went in to possession peaceably and with the consent of the Indians; I must say I was Considerably Surprised to find on my return Home from Haying down the River that you had allotted my Land to the Indians; I was advised to write you in regard to the matter as your well Known reputation for Square dealing leads me to believe their has been a mistake made in the matter. Hoping to hear from you in regard to this matter I will not intrude further. my claim adjoins Chief Isaac's south line 1 1/2 miles down the River from the mission.

Yours Respectfully
Joseph Parent,
Fry Idaho.

Second enclosure:

Bonners Ferry, Nov. 15th 1892

Peter Ronan Esq.
Kocko [Jocko], Montana.
　　　Dear Sir

　　　Herewith I hand to you affidavits in regard to the allotment made to Indian Nicola Jerome. (no. 3). I hope you will give this matter your earnest consideration. I was a witness to the purchase of said Land and can assure you that Mr. Parent went into the possession of said Land in good faith and did not try, to wrong any Indian of his rights. Mr Parent is an industrious and deserving man and I can assure you that when you come this way again and make a personal investigation in to the matter you will be convinced that the proper thing to do is to with draw the allottment made to Indian Nicola Jerome. Mr. P. has never been molested in his possession by any of the indans he is the only settler on that side of the River that has not been interfered with by the Indians. The first Location he made was claimed by Nicola Jerome he promptly moved off when advised that he had located on Jeromes place and bought the place he now hold from David and I Know of my personall Knowledge that he inquired and notified all the indians at the mission that he was about to buy the place from David and if any other Indians, laid claim to the place to let him Know before he paid for it or made any improvements on the place. Mr. Parent has been waiting for Nicola Jerome to get back from a hunt before taking any action in the matter. Nicola came back a few days ago. I was present at the interview had with him he said he did not want Mr. Parents Claim and never did claim or occupy the place now held by Mr. Parent. I hope you will give Mr. Parent Justice in this matter and I Know you will find on your next visit here that every thing has been in good faith on his Part. I have aquainted Mr. Fry of the action take by Mr. Parent in this matter.

Respectfully
John Hoban,
Justice of the Peace
Bonners Ferry Idaho

To Major Peter Ronan
Indian Agt. Flathead.
Third enclosure:
County of Kootenai
State of Idaho

Jos. C. Parent, being first duly sworn deposes as follows. My name is Jos. C. Parent an a resident of Bonners Ferry Precint Kootenai Co Idaho, and a citizen of the United States. On the 20th day of March 1892 I located 160 acres of Land 1/2 mile west of the Indian mission — School Said Mission School being about 3 miles west of Bonners Ferry. after I had been living about 4 days on said Land an Indian Known as "Nicola Jerome" came to me and told me that I was on his Land and notified me to leave, he also told me that Indian — David had a Ranch to Sell. I met David shortly afterwards and he took me to a piece of Land about 1 mile west of the Mission School and informed me that the Land was his and he would sell it to me for $25.00. I paid him $5.00 and took possision of the Land; the said Land was wholly unoccupied and unimproved. I notified Chief Isaac and several other Indians that I had bought the place and if their was any other indian that laid any claim to said Land to come forward and Speak before I made final payment for the Same. I have been residing continuously on said Land since the Seventh day of April 1892, and have had no trouble of any Kind with the Indians they all were satisfied that I should hold the Land, and Nicola Jerome sayes that he does not claim the Land that I occupy and that he never did occupy said Land. during the month of August I was employed haying for one of my neighbors and while absent from my Claim, the said claim was allotted to "Indian Nicola Jerome" by allotting agent Major Peter Ronan.

I have made valuable improvements on the said Land described as follows to wit. 1 Log building. 1 story high 14 x 20 — cleared one acre of heavily timbered Land. have also broke up and plowed one acre. all of said improvements were made before the Land was allotted to said Nicola Jerome.

Joseph C Parent

Subscribed and sworn to before me this 15th day of April (Nov.?) 1892.

Samuel E. Henry
Notary Public.

November 30, 1892a
LR 43,536/1892, RG 75, National Archives, Washington, D.C.

The government was collecting money from the sale of Bitterroot Salish allotments but seemed in no hurry to get the proceeds to the allottees. Bureaucratic procedures delayed the first payments to the Salish owners until March 1894 — twenty-nine months after the removal. The Salish were also unhappy to find that the government deducted General Henry B. Carrington's 1889 and 1891 expenses from the proceeds. That meant tribal members paid for Carrington's compensation and expenses.[42]

United States Indian Service,
Flathead Agency,
November 30, 1892.

Hon. Commissioner Indian Affairs,
Washington, D.C.

Sir:

I desire to report that Chief Charlot and his band of Flathead Indians, removed from the Bitter Root valley, Montana, to this reservation, in accordance with the provisions of "An Act entitled An Act to provide for the sale of lands patented to certain members of the Flathead band of Indians in Montana Territory, and for other purposes," have asked me to report their views and wishes in regard to the disposition of payments already made for some of said tracts of land.

Henry B. Carrington of Massachusetts was appointed special agent of the Indian Department, to obtain the consent of the Indians to remove to this reservation, and to appraise their lands for sale as therein provided. It has been ascertained that some seventeen tracts of the land appraised has been sold, and as the Indians to whom the money belongs are in very poor circumstances — unable to fence or improve the farms they selected on the reservation — Chief Charlot earnestly begs of the Hon Commissioner of Indian Affairs to look into this matter and to have the money paid over to the Indians that were owners of the land thus sold. Chief Charlot claims that one of the principal inducements to the Indians to abandon their land in the Bitter Root valley for sale, and to remove to this reservation was the promise given them by General Carrington that soon as land was disposed of the money would be sent to the rightful owners or heirs to assist them in making comfortable homes on the reservation.

I take this opportunity of respectfully urging the suggestion that the amounts already paid for sale of said lands in the Bitter Root valley be paid to the Indians in cash soon as practicable so that they may have ocular [sic] and positive proof that they are being justly dealt with according to the promise of General Carrington. My experience prove the desirability and necessity of not allowing any chance of a misunderstanding by Indians of any of the bearings of a case in which they are interested. The Indians in question are perfectly competent to take care of and expend advantageously any money that may come into their possession. I trust their prayer may be granted — that the money may be paid over to the Indians to whom it belongs.

I am very respectfully,
Your obedient servant.
Peter Ronan,
United States Indian Agent.

November 30, 1892b

LR 43,537/1892, RG 75, National Archives, Washington, D.C.

On January 12, 1893, the Commissioner of Indian Affairs approved Ronan's suggestion that the Cree refugees be allowed to remain on the Flathead Reservation until June 1893. See Ronan's December 3, 1892, letter relative to diphtheria and the Cree around Missoula. See Ronan's August 6, 1887; December 18, 1888; and July 1, 1890a, letters and annotations for other examples of Cree Indians seeking to settle on the Flathead Reservation.[43]

United States Indian Service,
Flathead Agency,
Nov. 30, 1892.

Hon. Commissioner of Indian Affairs
Washington, D.C.

Sir:

For several years this reservation has been infested by wandering bands of Cree Indians and half breeds, most of them being refugees from across the British boundary who took part in the uprising in Northwest Territory, and which led to the hanging of [Louis] Riel, their leader, at Regina in British Territory, a few years ago. The Indians of this reservation object to their camping or living among them, claiming that they have enough renegades and gamblers of their own tribes to take care of without being troubled and annoyed by foreign Indians and half breeds. Among these people there are good men and women with families, who are industrious and law abiding, and who are only seeking to better their condition by working at the Mission or for thrifty half breeds or Indians of the reservation. It is hard to expel such people of Indian blood from the reserve, but the Indians here claim that it is owing to the presence of the better class of Crees that the rougher and idle ones follow, and they seem determined to rid the reservation of all the Crees now here and to prevent them from again returning.

A council was held recently by the Indians and it was their unanimous conclusion to expel these people from their country. I believe it is a right accorded to the reservation Indians to prevent any other tribe or band from removing or settling upon their reservation without the consent of the Indians that occupy the same, even though such tribe or band be native American Indians.

At this advanced season their expulsion would cause suffering among women and children as well as among hardy and strong men who are willing to work for the support of their wives and children. I believe the reservation Indians are determined to expel the Crees and in doing so, trouble may arise between them, which I desire to prevent if possible.

If in the opinion of the Hon. Commissioner of Indian Affairs, it is advisable to encourage the reservation Indians to carry out the unanimous resolution of the Council, to gather up the Cree families and force them from their camps and dwellings at this inclement season, however distasteful it may be, I shall consider it my duty to enforce their departure. I believe it would be advisable to get the consent of the Indians to allow such of these people who have families and who are earning a living by working as before stated to remain, say, until the 15th of June, 1893 and then to take their departure, if they have no right here, not again to return to the reservation. An advisory letter from the Hon. Commissioner as to what procedure to take and to be read to the Indians in council, called for that purpose, I believe will be adopted by them and whatever council you may give them in this case will be followed. An early reply is earnestly requested.

I am very respectfully
Your obedient servant
Peter Ronan
United States Indian Agent.

December 2, 1892
LR 44,386/1892, RG 75, National Archives, Washington, D.C.

United States Indian Service,
Flathead Agency,
Dec. 2nd, 1892.

Hon. Commissioner of Indian Affairs
Washington, D.C.
Sir:

I have the honor to report from this Agency for the month of October [sic]. It is gratifying to state that all industries pertaining to the Agency and reservation are in progressive condition. In the immediate vicinity of the Agency Indian industry presents a busy scene. The building of enlargements of flume on the old irrigation canal furnishes employment to Indians delivering saw logs at the mill; the sawing of lumber into dimensions for the flume gives employment to an Indian crew to assist sawyer and engineer. The excavation of new irrigation ditch has also commenced, and a large number of Indians are employed in the work. They take contacts by the rod, and so eager are they to finish job and Collect wages, they work long hours and utilize all the labor they can furnish from their families and dependent relatives. If the ground does not freeze hard within the next month, I expect to complete excavation of new ditch and have it ready to turn in water for irrigation, early as required in the Spring. The same may be said of enlargements of old flume and canal, that furnishes water from Jocko river, for the irrigation of the Indian farms along the line of excavation. The Indians here are willing and eager to work if employment can be obtained. I trust the Hon. Commissioner will give my estimate dated Oct. 1st 1892 for ditch and water works, described in said letter favorable consideration, as such improvement is an absolute necessity and the amount expended will give employment to Indians, which is the best civilizing method that can be adopted. The earning of wages gives the Indians a sense of self reliance and independence never to be obtained by gratuitously furnishing them supplies etc. The chief and head men of the tribes express appreciation for the opportunity the present work affords Indians to earn wages at home, and thereby keep a number of them from the vagrant life led by the strong healthy Indians in neighboring towns, often, because no employment can be obtained by them on the reservation. I have the honor to forward sanitary report and reports of funds and indebtedness; also reports of farmers and have the honor to be

Very respectfully
Your obedient Servant
Peter Ronan,
U.S. Indian Agent.

December 3, 1892
Morning Missoulian, *December 6, 1892, page 1, col. 3.*

This letter was Ronan's response to a December 3, 1892, article in *The Anaconda Standard* blaming the Flathead Reservation Indians for diphtheria in the Missoula area.[44]

Major Ronan Replies.
No Diphtheria at the Agency — Crees are the Nomads Around Missoula.

Flaehead [sic] Agency, Dec. 3. — To the Editor of the Missoulian: In your issue of the 2d inst. I find the following:

The board of health has instructed Major Peter Ronan of the Flathead agency not to allow any of the Indians to leave the reservation until further notice. There are several cases of diphtheria among the red men and it was thought best to take precautionary measures to prevent a spread of the disease.

I would respectfully state that no case of diphtheria is known to the agency physician on this reservation at present, and from careful inquiry I fail to learn of any case of that dread disease at present date either at the schools or camps. Some of the Indians of this reservation have passed through Missoula lately, returning from their hunt, but I do not know of one lodge of agency Indians encamped in the vicinity of Missoula. The Anaconda Standard of the same date as your paper rightly states: "The great trouble has been with the roving bands of Cree Indians who have infested the city for the past two months. They can be seen any day on the streets, whole families of them, from a papoose strapped to the mother's back, to a full grown buck." The Indians of the reservation claim that the Crees brought dip[h]theria and scarlet fever among their people, and as an order has been issued for those wandering people from across the British border to leave this reservation, it may possibly become the duty, however hard at this inclement season, for the citizens of Missoula to request those unfortunates who arrive from the reservation to "move on." Respectfully yours,

Peter Ronan,
U.S. Indian Agent.

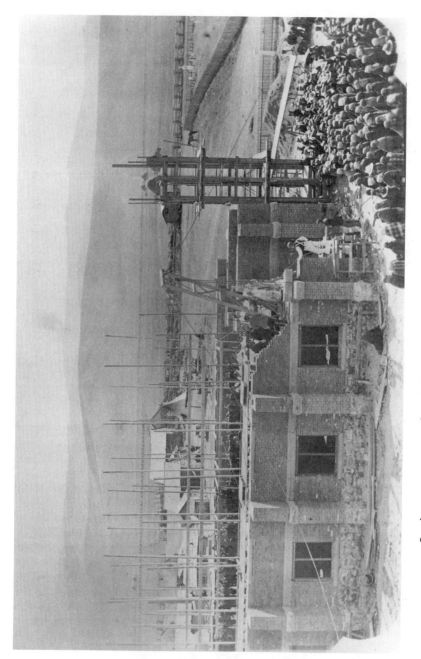

Laying cornerstone of new St. Ignatius Mission Church, April 19, 1892.
Jesuit Oregon Province Archives, Gonzaga University, Spokane, Washington, negative 114.5.08a.

Bishop Brondel laying cornerstone of new St. Ignatius Mission Church, April 19, 1892.
Jesuit Oregon Province Archives, Gonzaga University, Spokane, Washington, negative 114.5.9a.

1893

January 4, 1893
LR 1,837/1893, RG 75, National Archives, Washington, D.C.

Newspaper reports described drunken violence at Arlee involving some of the recently paid workers digging the irrigation ditch. The newspapers suggested Sacalee Clarke was passed out on the railroad tracks, but Ronan suspected he died while trying to get off the train while it was moving.[1] The 1882 negotiations for a railroad right-of-way through the reservation had included a verbal promise of free rides on the railroad for Indians, but this promise had not been included in the written agreement.[2] Clarke's death could have happened because the train crew was not willing to stop to let off a nonpaying Indian passenger.

According to tribal sources, Captain William Clark left a son from a liaison with a Salish woman during his brief stay with the tribe in 1805. A slightly garbled newspaper account in 1886 described Captain Clark's reputed grandson, Sacalee Clarke, as a determined independent who objected to settling down to a life of farming. Palmer Henderson, a visiting journalist, described Sacalee Clarke and his three year old son attending the Jocko church in 1890.[3]

United States Indian Service,
Flathead Agency,
January 4th, 1893.

Hon. Commissioner Indian Affairs,
Washington, D.C.
    Sir:
    At the beginning of the New Year, it is my pleasant duty to report for the month of December, every industry at this Agency in good and progressive condition. The excavation of the new water ditch was continued during the month of December, by the Indians. The Christmas and New Years holidays interfered somewhat with their labors, as the Indians of this reservation are enthusiasts in the celebration of those days. At this date the weather is pleasant and the frost does not interfere with the excavation, they have gone to work again with a will. As a rule the Indians made good use of their earnings, but a few of the young men were enabled to procure whisky and convey it to the reservation on the railroad trains concealed in their blankets. I instructed officers at Missoula to search suspected Indians before boarding the train. This resulted in finding several bottles of of [sic] whisky concealed by a squaw in her blanket. The Indians who accompanied her as well as herself were put in jail until they informed the officer from whom they purchased the whisky. This information obtained they were released and the white man who sold the whisky was arrested and placed in jail to await trial. The importation of whisky from Missoula on the Northern Pacific trains in this manner stopped, for the present.
    A young Indian called Sacalee Clarke, the reputed grandson of Captain Clarke, the explorer, was killed at Arlee station, on the reservation, on the night of December 27th, by attempting, it is supposed, to get off the train while in motion.
    The saw mill was kept running during a portion of the month, cutting into dimensions the saw logs delivered by the Indians for the construction of of [sic]

the new flume on the old irrigation ditch. A large number of logs belonging to individual Indians have been delivered during the month and will be sawed for their use soon as convenient.

Herewith I have the honor to forward sanitary report and report of funds and indebtedness, also reports of farmers, and have the honor to be

Very respectfully
Your obedient servant
Peter Ronan
United States Indian Agent.

January 11, 1893
LR 2,127/1893, RG 75, National Archives, Washington, D.C.

> General Henry B. Carrington made a number of promises to Charlo and the Bitterroot Salish that the government did not fund or funded only reluctantly. See, for example, Ronan's October 24, 1891, letter and annotation. In this case, on March 1, 1893, Ronan was authorized to spend $2,172.50 for open market purchases of subsistence supplies for the various bands that had been recently removed to the Flathead Reservation.[4]

United States Indian Service,
Flathead Agency,
January 11th, 1893.

Hon. Commissioner Indian Affairs
Washington, D.C.

Sir:

On the 17th day of October, 1891, General Henry B. Carrington, Special Agent for the removal of the Flathead Indians of the Bitter Root Valley, and also for the valuation and sale of their lands, placed forty families of those people at this Agency, where rations have been issued to them since that date. One hundred and fifty-seven people of this band live in the immediate vicinity of the Agency, and while they are provided with houses to live in and meager supplies of rations, they complain that the promises of Carrington have not been complied with in furnishing them with a plentiful supply of beef as well as bacon and other articles that furnish a living; also his promise to assist them in fencing land; plowing fields for cultivation; furnishing each family with two cows, etc., and numerous articles (not necessary) to mention, is unfulfilled. These Indians without means of support, and without energy enough to commence the cultivation of the soil unless fields are plowed and fenced for them, will always require the issue of rations, as the most of them refuse to help themselves, relying totally upon promises given that fields would be fenced and plowed, etc., for their use. The Agent is always confronted with this excuse when he urges self reliance by the cultivation of the soil, and he is also reminded that the sale of their land in the Bitter Root Valley is retarded because the Special Agent placed so high a valuation upon it, that purchasers cannot be found who would pay the prices set upon most of the farms. Under date of November 30th, 1892, I had the honor to make special report of the views of Chief Charlot and his band in regard to the disposition of the money realized by the sale of some seventeen tracts of the land appraised by General Carrington. The Indians to whom the money belong, as stated in said letter, desire to have it paid to them in order that they may be enabled to improve and cultivate their farms on the reservation, as no assistance has been given to them to fence and plow as promised by General Carrington. No reply has yet been received to the letter mentioned. I now desire to state that there are very many destitute Indians on this reservation. Among the Kalispels who were induced to remove here from their homes in Idaho, over five years ago, by an agreement entered into by the Northwest Indian Commission and this unfortunate band. Said Agreement has not yet been confirmed by Congress; among Chief Eneas' band of Kootenais, at Dayton creek; and among the band of Kootenais that removed last summer from the vicinity of Bonner's Ferry, in Idaho. There are also the old, the infirm and paupers among the Confederated tribes of Indians on the reservation, and all look to the Agent to supply their necessities. Each band of new Indians settlers is jealous of the other, and all make it a point to be on hand to make demands for provisions and articles for issue. With the most economic distribution of provisions by the Clerk, Mr. Adams, and myself, I find that the supply now on hand will not cover the time intervening between this date and the close of the fiscal year, and that there will be an exigency which will call for the shipment of more supplies of provisions to this Agency, or an open market purchase. I trust this communication will receive prompt attention that I may be advised if provisions will be made for the necessities of dependent Indians for the last quarter of this fiscal year, especially for Charlots band.

I am very respectfully,
Your obedient servant,
Peter Ronan,
United Sates Indian Agent.

January 16, 1893
LR 2,718/1893, enclosure in 5,717/1893, RG 75, National Archives, Washington, D.C.

On February 13, 1893, the Secretary of the Interior informed the Commissioner of Indian Affairs that new legislation would have to be passed by Congress to allow the sale of the Bitterroot allotments for less than the appraised price set by Carrington in 1889.[5]

Francois Eneas or Lamoose was part Iroquois and baptized in St. Louis in 1835 at the age of ten years. During the 1850s, he worked as an interpreter and fellow traveler for trader and agent John Owen. In the 1880s he ate frequently at the Stevensville Hotel and on one occasion insisted on paying more for his meal when he thought he had been undercharged. In 1883 about $600 of his money in the safe at the Eddy, Hammond & Company's Stevensville store was stolen by three white men. The robbers were soon captured and the money returned. In 1889 Francois was living in the Jocko Valley and worked as interpreter for Henry B. Carrington to relocate the remaining Bitterroot Salish Indians to the Flathead Reservation. Carrington described Francois as one of his "tireless and trustworthy advisers and companions" in the negotiations. In 1890 journalist Palmer Henderson visited his "well cultivated farm" in the Jocko Valley. Peter Francois, Francois Eneas' son, was born in 1844 on a buffalo hunt. Peter's Bitterroot allotment had no improvements in 1889, so this request made no sense relative to the sale of his land.[6]

United States Indian Service,
Flathead Agency,
Jan. 16th, 1893.

Hon. Commissioner Indian Affairs,
Washington, D.C.

Sir:

I earnestly desire to call your attention to the request of Eaneas Francois, owner of land — patent No. 31 — N. ½ S.E. ¼ Sec. 15, T 9, R. 20 — 80 acres. Ex. Doc. No. 70 — 51st Congress — 1st Session, page 16, described by Henry B. Carrington, U.S. Army, Special Agent, as follows:

"This is fair land used mostly for pasture; was tilled by owner before he removed to Jocko Reservation: three cabins, corrall [sic] and fences are valued at $660. It extends to the river. The portion near the river although sometimes overflowed is good for grass. It is appraised at $10 per acre. No 32 patent of Peter Francois, son of Eneas Francois — described: N. ½ S.W. ¼ sec. 14 T 9, R. 20; 80 acres — East of 31; somewhat more gravelly; no improvements. Appraised at $9 per acre.["]

The petitioner Eneas Francois is an English speaking Indian, and the man of all others who assisted General Carrington in his business transactions with the Bitter Root Flathead Indians, that resulted in the appraisal for sale of the lands of these Indians, and their removal to this reservation. He now claims that the appraisal on his log cabins, corrall and fence were too high as they were built years ago, and are now unfit for use. This fact prevents the sale of this land and that of his son, and as both have removed in good faith to the Jocko Reservation, and desire means to improve their holdings here, they earnestly ask from the Hon. Secretary of the Interior, permission to sell lots 31 and 32, at the appraised value of the land, without consideration for improvements, which are now valuless to a purchaser on account of decay of material and will always prevent the sale of said land.

I would earnestly ask the Hon Secretary of the Interior and Commissioner of Indian Affairs, to grant the request of Eneas Francis [sic], and would also add that if General Carrington was consulted in this matter, I believe he would join in the request that the prayer of this worthy Indian and his son might be granted.

I am very respectfully
Your obedient servant
Peter Ronan
U.S. Indian Agent.

January 17, 1893
LR 3,010/1893, RG 75, National Archives, Washington, D.C. An enclosed copy of the public notice of the allotment, describing the land claimed, is not reproduced here.

See annotation to Ronan's November 29, 1892b, letter for more information on the conflicting land claims of Nicola Jerome and Joseph Parent in northern Idaho.

United States Indian Service,
Flathead Agency,
January 17th, 1893.

Hon. Commissioner Indian Affairs
Washington, D.C.

Sir:

Replying to "Land 43385 – 1892" in regard to the receipt of my letter dated November 29, 1892, enclosing therewith one dated September 28, 1892, from Joseph Parent, Bonners Ferry, pertaining to the application of an Indian named Nicola Jerome for certain Lands in Kootenai County, Idaho, under the provisions of the 4th Section of the General Allotment Act, as amended by Act of February 28, 1891, (26 Stats. 794), together with certain other affidavits pertaining to the same matter.

The application was made by the Indian named for the land described but as certified to in enclosed papers he now desires to abandon said tract and asks that another tract be allotted to him in lieu of the same.

I am very respectfully
Your obedient servant
Peter Ronan
U.S. Indian Agent.

Enclosure:

State of Idaho
County of Kootenai

I, Nicola Jerome do solemnly swear that I am an Indian of the Kootenai Tribe and the head of a family. That I have abandoned my tract of land, allotment No. 3 [13 added], and would ask for the allotment of another tract in lieu of the same.

Nicola his X mark Jerome

Witness to mark
Richard Fry
George Fry

Subscribed and sworn to before me this 13th day of January 1893;

Thos J. Jones
Notary Public

[*Notes added to bottom of page:* Seal out of date. No certificate of court for notary.]

February 1, 1893

LR 5,182/1893, RG 75, National Archives, Washington, D.C.

United States Indian Service,
Flathead Agency,
February 1st, 1893.

Hon. Commissioner Indian Affairs,
Washington, D.C.

Sir:

I have the honor to forward my report for the month of January. For the past week the weather has been very stormy. Strong winds drifted the snow into banks, in places, Eight feet high. The weather is very cold. Cattle owned by the Indians require to be fed, and as the hay crop was light last year, on account of drought and lack of irrigation facilities, if the cold, drifting snow storms continue a loss of stock must follow.

Up to the cold weather work on excavation of the irrigation ditch by Indians was continued, but at present nothing can be done by them. In the carpenter shop the work of framing, tenoning, mortising etc., of timber for construction of flume is being done. Some Indians are taking advantage of the snow and are delivering logs at the mill for lumber for their own use, which will be sawed soon as the weather permits.

Charlots' band of Indians removed from the Bitter Root Valley are a trifling set as a rule, especially the young men. Many of them cannot be induced to make any exertion towards splitting rails or fencing their land to cultivate crops, relying upon the weekly issue of rations — a demoralizing piece of business to other tribes of Indians on this reservation who exert themselves for self support. They are willing to work, if paid cash for doing anything for their own benefit, and rely upon promises they claim to have been made by General Carrington that they would be plentifully supplied with food, clothing and other articles of diverse description suitable to their fancy for an indefinate [sic] period, or at least until all of the money accruing from the sale of their land in the Bitter Root Valley was paid over to them by the Government, without any deduction of any part of the money for any expenses whatever.

All industries pertaining to the Agency are being pushed forward as well as the weather will permit.

Herewith I have the honor to forward sanitary report and report of funds and indebtedness; also report of farmers, and have the honor to be

Very respectfully
Your obedient servant,
Peter Ronan,
United States Indian Agent.

February 27, 1893
LR 8,310/1893, RG 75, National Archives, Washington, D.C.

> The proposal to either move the Flathead Agency to a central location on the reservation or establish a subagency in the Lower Flathead Valley had been discussed for years. With the new funds from the 1893-1894 Indian Appropriation Act, the project finally moved forward, but was not completed until after Ronan's death in August 1893. Despite the plans for a government sawmill on Crow Creek, on March 25, 1893, the Commissioner of Indian Affairs granted Charles Allard permission to erect a sawmill near that location. Allard was to keep his charges fair and reasonable and not market lumber off the reservation. The Commissioner did not consider how Allard could compete with a government mill that would be almost free for tribal members.[7]

United States Indian Service,
Flathead Agency,
Feb. 27th, 1893.

Hon. Commissioner Indian Affairs,
Washington, D.C.
Sir:
I beg to call attention to my letter to your office, under date of February 18th, 1891, Referring to "L 28,763 – 1890" relative to Department reference for consideration and proper action of a report dated August 7th 1890, from U.S. Inspector Gardner, stating that a large portion of the Indians of Flathead reservation, Montana, live from fifty to sixty miles distant from the Flathead

Agency; that the center of population is near Crow Creek or Mud Creek, that at present they derive only a small benefit from the Agency grist and saw mill and carpenter and blacksmith shops; that the establishment of a Sub Agency on that reservation would, in his judgment, be a decided advantage and for the best interest of the service; that the present Agency was located in one corner of the reservation for the convenience of the Agent and Agency employes, being near the town of Missoula, and not for, or in, the interest of the reservation Indians; that the time has now come when the Indians of that reservation should be more looked after and encouraged in civilization and Christianity; and that they are beginning to see and feel and know that they must depend upon themselves to make a living, and for this reason the aid which the government offers them should be easily accessible, not thirty five, forty, fifty, or seventy-five miles distant, causing them to travel these respective distances to get a machine, plow, wagon, or harness repaired, or to obtain the service of the Agency physician etc. etc. * * * * * *

In said reply I reported that the views and statements of Inspector Gardner were eminently correct.

I now also, in same connection, respectfully call your attention to my letter to you dated July 9th 1891, referring to A. 6948 – '91, under date of March 24, 1891, calling attention to receipt of my report of the 18th of February in relation to the location of the Flathead Agency, giving detailed statement as required by you.

In the Act (Public — No. 119) for fulfilling treaty stipulations with various Indian tribes for the fiscal year ending June 30th, 1893, and for other purposes, page 19 — miscellaneous — the following paragraph is published:

"Substation and mills, Flathead Agency, Montana: Establishment of Substation, purchase of saw and flour mills, construction of necessary buildings for same; purchase of animals and pay of employes at Flathead Agency, Montana, ten thousand dollars."

From above I take it that appropriation has been made to carry out the views for a substation etc., at Crow Creek or Mud Creek, and would thank you to let me know if it is the intention of the Indian Department to order said improvements during this fiscal year. Herewith I attach copy of a letter from Charles Allard, a mixed blood, and one of the owners of the herd of one hundred buffalo that range near Mud and Crow Creek, in the vicinity of which a site was selected for the substation.

Also my reply to him. I have the honor to be,

Very respectively yours,
Peter Ronan
United States Indian Agent.

First enclosure:

Charles A. Stillinger,
Flathead Stage and Express Line
Ravalli, Mont., Feb 22 1893

Maj Peter Ronan

I had to take a saw mill on a debt[.] could I have a permit to saw lumber around my place providing I did not sell any out of Reservation

I need a lot of lumber & so does Pablo and there is quite a few around mud creek that would like to have me bring that mill there as I suppose you are aware we are buying outside of the Reservation every year and it, the first cost & R. R. charges & then hauling it so far. when we could haul it ourselves and save all this trouble

I have no cattle sheds of any kind and if you could do this for me I could build in good shape with very little expence.

the cheapest I can lay down lumber at home, that is the Roughest lumber is about $22.00 a thousand

and the very best at about $45.00 a thousand

you know we cant afford to build cattle sheds for large herds at these figures, every body are looseing cattle more or less and if they had s[h]eds for their cattle if they would not loose as much

I hope you will do what you can in your power in regard to this matter and Oblige

Yours truly
Chas Allard

Second enclosure:

United States Indian Service,
Flathead Agency,
Feb. 23d, 1893.

Charles Allard,
Flathead Reservation.

Sir:

I am in receipt of your letter in regard to your expected purchase of a saw mill to be erected someplace on mud Creek for the purpose of sawing lumber for yourself and for any of your neighbors willing to pay a price for lumber that would cover expenses, and not to be sold outside of the limits of the reservation. I know that a great deal of lumber is necessary for the use of the dwellers on that portion of the reservation; and I also know that the distance from the Saw Mill at the Agency, is too great to utilize the Government mill, as the hauling alone would exceed the price of the lumber. The permission you ask for however cannot be granted by me, but must come through the Kind office of the Hon. Commissioner of Indian Affairs. I shall immediately communicate with Col. T. J. Morgan, the Commissioner of Indian Affairs, and state the matter to him. If the communication should reach that kind officer before his resignation takes place on the 4th of March, I feel that he will give your request a careful examination, and grant any favor that he thinks will be of assistance to the progressive Indians and mixed bloods of your locality.

I am yours respectfully
Peter Ronan
U.S. Indian Agent.

March 1, 1893

LR 8,842/1893, RG 75, National Archives, Washington, D.C.

> Ronan published a news article about the accident at the Sisters' school in *The Anaconda Standard* which was almost identical to his description here, except in the newspaper article Ronan mentioned that Marcus Daly and the Anaconda Company had furnished the pump for the student fire brigade. See the bracketed portion of the fourth paragraph in this letter.[8]

United States Indian Service,
Flathead Agency,
Mar. 1st, 1893.

Hon. Commissioner Indian Affairs,
Washington, D.C.

Sir:

At the close of last month I had to report deep snow and stormy weather, and am sorry to state that the same continued all through the month of February. Cattle owned by the Indians had to be fed, and as the hay crop of last year was light, owing to drought and lack of irrigating facilities, few were prepared to feed for such a long and stormy spell of deep snow and drifting storms, seldom known to this reservation. A heavy loss of cattle has already been sustained by Indian herders, and if a change does not soon occur in the weather, I fear the loss will be very great to the Indian dwellers on this reservation.

The work of framing, tenoning, mortising, etc. of the timber for construction of the large irrigation flume is nearly completed, and the hauling of the same upon the ground will be commenced next week.

On Saturday February 5th about one o'clock P.M., the water-tank recently erected by the Sisters of Providence in their school yard at St. Ignatius Mission, on a 60 foot trestle, fell down without a moment's warning, destroying completely the new addition, which in the second story contained a steam laundry just completed and furnished with all the modern improvements; and below it the boiler room, with two boilers and everything necessary for heating all the buildings of the Indian girls' school and those occupied by the Sisters' community, and supply them with water. It was only three days after the whole system was completed. The conductors of the school after so many weeks of annoyance began to feel a little comfortable with their new improvements. The mess and destruction is hardly conceivable.

When the accident happened there were four men in the boiler room, only two were injured. The fire which broke out of the furnace for a while endangered the group of fine buildings belonging to the school, but was soon gotten under control by the fine water supply at once furnished from the water-tower and the steam pump of the Indian boys' school at St. Ignatius Mission, just across the street from the girls' school. The larger boys of the Indian school have been thoroughly drilled as a fire brigade, to act promptly if such an occasion required their energy. When the steam whistle of the Indian college announced the alarm of fire, the Indian boys at once ran out their hose cart, and almost as quickly as it takes to write, had a stream of water upon the fire, forced by a magnificent pump [presented to the Indian school by Marcus Daly, with the compliments of the Anaconda company, several years ago]. In fact, the Indians, the employes, and everyone at the scene, lent a helping hand, to save the property of the Sisters, that was edifying to look upon.

The Monday previous to the accident was the first time the Indian girls of the school used the new laundry, and if the accident happened then, or upon the following Monday, it is hard to say how many of the Indian school girls and their preceptors, the good Sisters of Providence, would have been buried in the ruins; as the large tank filled for the first time with water, fell with its immense weight, right on the roof, smashing the two-story building into thousands of splinters, down to the bottom of the boiler-room in the basement.

The Sister Superior of this now celebrated school for the education of Indian girls, deserves the sympathy of every friend of education and advancement of Indian civilization and female advancement in particular among the Indian tribes of our state and country. For five months she used her energies and her limited means to put up all these improvements, and seeing them destroyed in less than a minute is sickening and disheartening. The loss will probably exceed three thousand dollars, not counting the great discomfort that must be endured at this season and during the extreme cold weather while the country is covered with snow. The Fathers at St. Ignatius mission, of course, will do all in their power to give relief to the sisters of the Holy Family school, who have more than one hundred fifty Indian girls to make comfortable in this their trying hour, and as they cannot call upon the government for relief, their case appeals to all who are conversant with their great work.

All industries pertaining to the Agency are being pushed forward as well as the weather will permit. Herewith I have the honor to forward sanitary report and report of funds and indebtedness; also report of farmers and have the honor to be

Very respectfully,
Your obedient servant,
Peter Ronan
United States Indian Agent.

March 20, 1893
LR 10,922/1893, RG 75, National Archives, Washington, D.C.

> In answer to this request the Commissioner of Indian Affairs placed a large order for garden seeds with a Detroit company with instructions to deliver them to Flathead and also approved the distribution to Flathead Reservation farmers of 45,000 pounds of seed which was on hand.[9]

United States Indian Service,
Flathead Agency,
Mar. 20th, 1893.

Hon. Commissioner of Indian Affairs
Washington, D.C.
Sir:

I have the honor to acknowledge receipt of office letter "F" 7720-93 – Authority 34348 authorizing the expenditure of two hundred and fifty, $250.00, dollars in the open market purchase of field and Garden Seeds; and in connection therewith would say, that, owing to failure of crops last season, as reported, also the unprecedented Severity of the present season upon cattle, horses and other stock, the Indians of this reservation are totally destitute of Seeds of Any Kind. At the present ruling prices of Garden Seeds — also of Seed oats and potatoes, it will be almost impossible for me to fullfil [sic] the wants of the Indians, in this direction for the Sum of two hundred and fifty dollars. The field Seeds can be purchased for the above amount, if the Department Could Kindly furnish the garden seeds. I have on hand at this Agency forty five thousand (45,000) pounds of wheat, which can be used for seed, Should the Hon. Commissioner of Indian Affairs so authorize. Seed potatoes and oats are however essential, in order, that the Indians should have an opportunity to plant Crops, and reap the benefit thereof.

I have the honor to be

Very respectfully
Your obt. svt.
Peter Ronan
U.S. Indian Agent.

April 1, 1893
LR 12,829/1893, RG 75, National Archives, Washington, D.C.
United States Indian Service,
Flathead Agency,
April 1st, 1893.

Hon. Commissioner of Indian Affairs,
Washington, D.C.

Sir:

At the close of March in my regular monthly report, I have to state that the past winter has been the most severe known to the occupants of this reservation. The partial failure of the crops of last year, owing to drought, was followed by early snow storms and cold weather that continued through the entire winter and up to the present date. Indian owners of cattle and horses were not prepared for the deep snow that covered the cattle ranges of the reservation for such a long period. When their hay was exhausted those who had credit or money were compelled to purchase hay and transport it by railroads from distant parts of the state at a cost of twenty dollars a ton. Others who could not feed lost most of their cattle by cold and starvation. The loss of cattle and horses to the Indians of this reservation is very discouraging. But in future it will teach them not to rely so much on the fine winter climate which heretofore was the rule in this portion of Montana. At this date last year the Indian farmers had their crops planted or nearly so; but inclement weather, snow, and frost have, as yet, prevented even the commencement of plowing. It will require energetic movements to get Indian fields plowed and sowed in seasonable time. In the hope of keeping their cattle alive a great many Indians used their reserved seed for feed, consequently, unless liberally helped in field, as well as garden seeds, their planting will not be as extensive as usual, and will cause suffering and want among the Indians next winter. I trust that my estimate for seed, or as much thereof as can be spared to those Indians, will be granted. They are easily discouraged but the announcement that they will be fully supplied with seed will encourage plowing and preparation for planting. After the present rainstorm ceases, I expect the frost will leave the ground and warm spring weather will closely follow, necessitating energetic efforts on the part of the Indians in order to plow, sow, and otherwise cultivate their fields.

Industries pertaining to the welfare of the Indians and their gradual effort toward self support have all the encouragement this Agency affords.

Herewith I have the honor to forward sanitary report and report of funds and indebtedness, also report of farmers and have the honor to be,

Respectfully,
Your obedient Servant,
Peter Ronan,
United States Indian Agent.

April 18, 1893
LR 14,575/1893, RG 75, National Archives, Washington, D.C.

See annotation to Ronan's November 29, 1892b, letter for more information on the conflicting land claims of Nicola Jerome and Joseph Parent in northern Idaho.

United States Indian Service,
Flathead Agency,
April 18th, 1893.

Hon. Commissioner Indian Affairs,
Washington, D.C.
Sir:

Replying to "Land 43385 – 1892 – 3010 – 1893,["] dated at Washington,
March 31, 1893, replying to my letter of January 17, 1893, in reply to office
letter dated December 16, 1892, the latter being in regard to the rights of
Nicala Jerome, an Indian, to the lands applied for by him in Indian Allotment
Application No. 13, Coeur'd Alene, Idaho Land Office, upon which one Joseph
Parent has settled and which he is cultivating, and claiming that the Indian is
not entitled to the land and does not lay claim to it. I was directed to report
whether Nicala Jerome or any other Indian now claims the land in question,
and to recommend whether in view of all the facts and circumstances in the
case the allotment application of the Indian should be rejected, and the Indian
permitted to make application for another tract.

In reply I enclosed in my letter of January 17th a statement by the said Nicala Jerome, in the form of an affidavit, dated January 13th, 1893, to the effect
that he has abandoned the land allotted to him, and asks for another allotment
in lieu of the same.

In relation to this matter you have to say that in order to enable the Indian
allottee to relinquish his right to lands allotted to him, authority to relinquish
must first be obtained from the Secretary of the Interior. You also state in this
case no reason whatever is given by the Indian for surrendering the lands allotted to him, and in the absence of good and sufficient reason for such step your
office cannot present the matter to the Secretary for his consideration and action. Adding that the affidavit of the Indian above mentioned is of no force or
effect and his right to the land in question remains in tact.

According to your instruction I notified the parties in interest to that effect, and also that the allotment of the Indian, with others, will shortly be
transmitted to the Secretary of the Interior for approval.

I desire to state that the information contained in the affidavit of the Indian above mentioned and the statement of the settler, Parent, to the effect
that he bought the Indian Claim and paid for the same before the allotment
was made, is all of the information I can obtain without again visiting the locality in Northern Idaho. It is claimed now by Nicala Jerome that his reason
for abandoning the claim and asking that he be allowed another allotment
in place of No. 13, is because another Indian by the name of David, sold his
claim to Parent, a white settler, without his knowledge, and he wishes to avoid
trouble with the whiteman who bought the Indian title and made settlement
on Government land in good faith for a homestead.

In view of statements and affidavits of whites as well as of the Indian
claimant now on file in your office, and the willingness of the latter to abandon
the said Allotment and to take another in its place, for the sake of harmony be-

tween the Indians and the white settlers, I believe the following to be the most advisable course: to reject the application of the Indian for Allotment No. 13, and permit him to make another application for an indisputable tract of land.

I am very respectfully
Your obedient servant
Peter Ronan,
United States Indian Agent.

May 1, 1893

LR 17,093/1893, RG 75, National Archives, Washington, D.C.

United States Indian Service,
Flathead Agency,
May 1st, 1893.

Hon. Commissioner Indian Affairs,
Washington, D.C.
Sir:

At the [end] of March, in my report for that month, I stated that the past winter was the most severe known to the Indians on this reservation. Following a partial failure of crops last year — owing to drought — early snow storms and cold weather set in and continued throughout the entire winter. Although Indian cattle owners supplied themselves with the usual amount of hay for horsse [sic] feed relying upon the ranges the feed the hardy cattle and horses that were turned out, the unusual depth of snow and continuance of the same until late in Spring has caused a heavy loss, and one from which it will take years of industry by some of the most thrifty Indian families to recover. Rain and snow up to present date prevent the usual amount of planting; but it is to be hoped that the coming month may give opportunity to get an average acreage under cultivation.

Work on the flume and irrigation ditch is being pushed forward with all the energy that the cold, wet weather will allow. Completion will be made in time for irrigation season.

The work of plowing land by the Indians is being done as fast [as] weather will permit. Indian horses are in poor condition to work, and their grain was used in trying to keep some of them alive throughouth [sic] the winter. Seed oats, wheat and potatoes reserved from last years crop were used by the Indians for that purpose, and if it were not for the liberal supply allowed to me by the Hon. Commissioner of Indian Affairs, for distribution, very little farming could be done on this reservation this year.

Industries at this Agency pertaining to the welfare of the Indians has careful attention, and matters are progressing in the usual quiet and agreeable manner. Herewith I have the honor to forward sanitary report and report of funds and indebtedness; also report of farmer and have the honor to be

Very Respectfully
Your obedient Servant
Peter Ronan
United States Indian Agent.

June 1, 1893a

LR 21,138/1893, RG 75, National Archives, Washington, D.C.

United States Indian Service,
Flathead Agency,
June 1st, 1893.

Hon. Commissioner Indian Affairs,
Washington, D.C.

Sir:

In my report for May, I may state that cold, rainy and gloomy weather prevailed throught [sic] the entire month, and the spring is backward in vegetation. The Indians of the reservation were persevering in plowing and seeding their land, and more than an average crop was planted despite the cold and wet weather. The unusual rain storms of the spring are looked upon as a blessing, however, by those who planted crops, as it will not necessitate irrigation late on, and a good harvest is confidentially [sic] looked for.

The irrigation ditch and flume, under course of construction, will be completed at the close of June, and will afford a good supply of water for irrigation, which is of the greatest importance, and without which, good crops could not be raised in dry seasons.

All industries pertaining to the welfare of the Indians have been carefully looked after. Peace and quiet prevail, with exception of some trouble at the Kootenai Indian village on Dayton Creek, where allotments were made to Indians, but are now being interfered with by white settlers. A special report in regard to this matter will follow this regular report.

Herewith I have the honor to forward sanitary report and report of funds and indebtedness; also report of farmers, and have the honor to be

Very respectfully
Your obedient servant
Peter Ronan,
United States Indian Agent.

June 1, 1893b
LR 21,139/18923 RG 75, National Archives, Washington, D.C.

The government promised to protect the Kootenai allotments on Dayton Creek, but in May 1893 white trespassers returned to the area. Chief Eneas complained to Ronan and worked to keep the peace. The complaint was even reported in *The Washington Post*.[10] See Ronan's August 25, 1891b, letter and annotation for background on this controversy.

In this letter, and his letter of June 30, 1893, Ronan again asked the federal government to protect the allottees. The enclosed letter from Judge Hiram Knowles, Ronan, and U.S. Attorney Elbert Weed suggested that the Interior Department needed to formally approve the allotments and adjust them to the recently completed land survey so the Indians could be secure in their rights. The General Land Office held up opening the affected lands to white homesteading until the Kootenai allotments were finalized, and the Justice Department authorized the Montana U.S. Attorney to enforce the Kootenai claims.[11] This is where the situation stood on August 20, 1893, when Ronan died. After Ronan's death, no one seemed to have continued the effort to remove white trespassers who jumped the Dayton Creek allotments.

Despite the many promises to protect the rights of the Kootenai farmers, the white trespassers were able to drag out the legal proceedings until the early twentieth century, when the Kootenai were pressured to relinquish their allotments to the trespassers in exchange for small payments.

For biographical information on Judge Hiram Knowles see the annotation to Ronan's December 28, 1878, letter. For Elbert D. Weed, U.S. Attorney, see the annotation to Ronan's October 22, 1889a, letter.

United States Indian Service,
Flathead Agency,
June 1st, 1893.

Hon. Commissioner Indian Affairs
Washington, D.C.

Sir:

I desire to call attention to my report from this Agency, under date of October 30th, 1891, referring to "Land 31598 — 1891," dated at Washington, September 7th, 1891, and respectfully ask that it receive attention at this time, as I am called upon to take action in regard to persistant trespassers who refuse to vacate the allotments made by me to the Indians, as stated in report to which attention is called, under orders from the Interior Department, in 1891, to make such allotments to the Indians under the 4th section of the General Allotment Act as amended by the Act of February 28th, 1891.

Last year the Indians were deterred from making improvements, or any efforts to cultivate their allotments on account of the settlement of white people upon some of the land allotted to them.

The Indians complained bitterly against such trespass. Under date of July 2d, 1892 — "Land 23582, 1892," the Hon. Commissioner wrote: "That as soon as the Indian allotment applications of the Indians referred to shall have been transmitted to this office, by the General Land office, for consideration and action and the lands covered thereby shall have been allotted to the respective Indian applicants, upon satisfactory proof of their being entitled thereto, under existing law, steps will be taken through the proper authorities to place such allottees in possession of his lands in order that he may enjoy the full, free, peaceable and uninterrupted use and occupancy thereof and you will so notify Chief Eneas."

At the time of the receipt of quoted communication it required much tact and energetic movements to prevent the young Indians from forceably removing the trespassers from the allotments. Such action on the part of the Indians would probably involve them in a fight with the settlers that might lead to bloodshed and an expensive Indian trouble. Last year after consultation with the United States Attorney for Montana, I proceeded to Dayton Creek, the home of the Kootenais, and most of the trespassers left the Indian allotments, and quiet prevailed until the opening of Spring of this year, when they returned and again took possession of Indian allotments. Exictement [sic] again prevailed among the Indians. Chief Eneas of the Kootenai tribe came to the Agency and demanded of me the peaceful possession of the allotments made to nineteen Indians of his tribe, all being heads of families and over twenty-one years of age. Fortified by the following letter from Hon. Elbert D. Weed, U.S. Attorney for Montana, dated May 11th, 1893, I left for the Indian settlement at Dayton Creek, where I arrived on the evening of the 21st of May, 1893:

"You state that these patents have not yet issued, but that the selections of land by the Indians have been duly certified according to law to the Department of the Interior. In the routine of business of that great Department, the mechanical work of preparing and issuing the patents for said lands to these Indians has not yet been attended to. Under the law, the title of these Indians to the land in question was absolute from the time the selections were made and officially certified to the proper department. The equitable title to the land has been perfect in the Indians since that time. The legal title since then has been held by the United States in trust for them, and said land and no part thereof is in any sense whatever public land of the United States. These Indians have as perfect and absolute a right to the lands in question selected by them as allotments, as whitemen would have to the lands filed upon by them under the homestead laws of the United States. Trespassers upon these allotments, be they Indians or whites, have no legal or equitable rights whatever as to said lands. I believe it to be the duty of the Great Government of the United States to protect these Indians in their rights: to guarantee to them the quiet, peaceable and unmolested possession of the lands which they have lawfully selected as their own individual property. As the duly authorized agent and representative of the government of the United States in charge of these Indians, I am of the opinion that it is your duty to see that they are protected in said rights, and that they are saved from the molestation of trespassers upon their lands. Doubtless these trespassers are men of good but mistaken intentions, and your statement of the law and rights of the Indians on the premises to them will doubtless be sufficient to cause them to cease further unlawful interferance with the rights of the Indians. In case this should not be sufficient, it would clearly be the duty of the United States Marshal to lend you such assistance as might be necessary in causing their removal and enforcement of the law."

A written notification from me to the trespassers, accompanied by a copy of the letter above quoted from the United States Attorney, brought back the verbal reply that they (the trespassers) ignored the authority of a United States Indian Agent, and would not vacate the land unless compelled by the laws of the United States. The suggestion to take the Indian police and compell them to leave the allotments did not meet with my approval for the reason that resistance upon the part of settlers might cause bloodshed in the present excited state of the Indians, and I therefore consulted the United States Attorney in person as to the advisability of ejecting the trespassers by aid of the United States Marshal, or to at once have them arrested as trespassers, and bring the matter before the Court. Having returned to the Agency by the quickest conveyance, I wired as follows:

"Arlee, May 27, 1893

To E. D. Weed, U.S. Attorney, Helena, Montana.

Can I meet you on arrival of East bound train at Helena, on the twenty-ninth. I desire to take action against trespassers on Indian lands.

Peter Ronan
U.S. Indian Agent."

In accordance with the following reply, on the morning of May 29th I took train for Helena.:

"Helena, Montana
May 27,

Will meet you as requested.

Weed
U.S. Attorney."

Upon consultation with the United States Attorney, and also with the United States District Judge, Hon. Hiram Knowl[e]s, at Helena, Montana, it was determined to lay the case before the Honorable Secretary of the Interior, for consideration and action.

Herewith I have the honor to transmit through the Hon. Commissioner of Indian Affairs, said letter addressed to the Hon. Secretary of the Interior, with the hope that it may receive prompt attention.

I am very respectfully,
Your obedient Servant,
Peter Ronan,
United States Indian Agent.

Enclosure:

Office of United States Attorney,
District of Montana,
Helena, Montana.
May 30, 1893.

To The Honorable Secretary of the Interior,
Washington, D.C.

Dear Sir: —

In 1855, Governor I. I. Stevens of Washington Territory made a treaty with the Confederate Tribes of Indians, known as the Flathead, Pend' Oreille and Kootnai Indians, residing within what is now the State of Montana, and in that treaty a Reservation for said Indians was agreed upon. The lines of that reservation were not then surveyed. In 1887, a contract was made by the United States with one Harrison, a Deputy U.S. Surveyor, to survey the North boundary line thereof, and said boundary was established by him during that year. As has been explained by Peter Ronan, Agent for said Indians, in a communication to the Hon. Commissioner of Indian Affairs, Oct. 30, 1890 [i.e., 1891], the said line thus established fell some six miles farther South than expected by said Indians. In fact they claimed that the true North line of said reservation ran across the Flathead Lake some six miles farther North. With this understanding, all of the Kootnai Indians included in said treaty had made their village North of the said line as established, and South of the line as claimed by them. Small patches of this land, they had improved and cultivated. Under these conditions, the said Agent, Peter Ronan was authorized by the Commissioner of Indian Affairs to allot these lands occupied by said Kootnai Indians in severalty under the provisions of Section 4 of the Act to Provide for the Allotment of Land in Severalty to Indians, &c. Supplement to Revised Statutes of U.S., 898. In pursuance of this order, said Ronan between Sept. 23, 1891 and Sept. 26, of same year, allotted certain lands to said Indians as will be found in his report of Oct. 30, 1891, to the Hon. Commissioner of Indian Affairs. Under rules prescribed by the Secretary of the Interior, proper applications were made for these allotments, and proper affidavits of non-mineral character of the land also filed in the office of the Register and Receiver of the U.S. Land Office, District of Montana, and were transmitted to the General Land Office at Washington. By virtue of Sec. 5 of Act of February 28, 1891, Supplement to Revised Statutes of the United States, 898, these allotments may be finally approved by the Secretary of the Interior. No notice has been received by the

Agent for those Indians that this had been done. During the time that this matter has been in abeyance, a number of whites have settled upon a portion of these lands so allotted. The Indians are much disturbed on this account, and ask that something be done to insure them these lands. Upon an examination of the law we have been unable to find any authority for these Indians to whom allotments have been made, to bring suit for the possession of these lands. They have not the legal title to the same. They never had the actual possession of all the land allotted to them, only portions of each allotment perhaps. Then they would be considered as severed from the mass of public lands and not subject to settlement, and suit could be brought by the United States to eject these white settlers. If the patents were issued making the United States a trustee of the legal title for the benefit of these Indians, then the way to protect them in their rights would be open and clear. Under these circumstances, we, the undersigned, would urge some action on your part in this matter to the end that trouble may be avoided. Restless whites under ill informed and incompetent advisers, will insist upon going upon some of these lands until the matter is settled. The Indians feeling that they have been promised these lands, suspect bad faith on the part of their Agent and the United States, as long as the matter remains in abeyance and whites insist on going upon their allotments.

Hoping that you will see a way to help us out of the difficulties presented,

We subscribe ourselves,
Your Obedient Servants,
Hiram Knowles, U. S. District Judge.
Peter Ronan, U.S. Indian Agent, Flathead Agency, Montana.
Elbert D. Weed, U.S. District Attorney.

June 30, 1893
LR 24,849/1893, RG 75, National Archives, Washington, D.C.

United States Indian Service,
Flathead, Agency,
June 30th, 1893.

Hon. Commissioner Indian Affairs
Washington, D.C.
Sir:

I desire to call attention to my letter to your office dated June 1st 1893, and also your reply dated at Washington, June 17th 1893, relative to trespasses committed by whites upon the lands allotted to certain Indians at Dayton Creek, Montana.

In relation thereto I now desire to state that on September 23th, 24th and 25th, 1891, nineteen applications were filed in the United States Local Land Office by me, under certain instructions from the Indian Office at Washington, to make such allotments. The land applied for being unsurveyed and lying North of the Flathead Indian Reservation, said applications were transmitted, I am informed by the local land office at Missoula, to the General Land Office, October 23d, 1891.

The locations were made by metes and bounds, and since that time this land has been surveyed. Plat of said land was received at the local land office in Missoula, Montana on June 15th, 1893. On and after July 19th, 1893, filings will be received at that office on the township in which these Indian claims are located. All of said claims when adjusted, will be in Township 25 North, Range 21 West.

As it is certain that on that day, — (July 19th 1893), parties will apply to file on part of said land, now covered by said Indian locations, I believe it will be necessary that the officers of the local land office at Missoula be instructed by the General Land office as to the course to pursue in order to avoid conflict with entry-men and these Indian allottees.

I would therefor respectfully recommend that action be taken at once to the effect that an adjustment to the survey of these Indian locations should be made before any filings are placed on record in said Township 25 North, Range 21 West.

I would respectfully suggest — the time being so short — that immediate action be taken and the Register and Receiver in the Land Office at Missoula, Montana be notified by telegraph of such orders as may be given in the matter.

I am respectfully
Your Obedient servant
Peter Ronan
U.S. Indian Agent.

July 1, 1893

LR 25,736/1893, RG 75, National Archives, Washington, D.C.

For more information on the just completed irrigation ditch Ronan referred to in this letter, see Ronan's November 29, 1892a, letter and annotation. Ronan's trip to the Chicago World's Fair was noted in the Missoula newspaper.[12]

United States Indian Service,
Flathead Agency,
July 1st, 1893.

Hon. Commissioner Indian Affairs
Washington, D.C.

Sir:

The close of the fiscal year at this Agency, find matters pertaining to the Agency and to the service in a condition that is gratifying to those immediately concerned in the administration of its affairs, as well as creditable to the Indians.

Unusual cold weather with heavy rain storms prevailed during the month of June. The growing grain crops are looking well, but gardens and vegetables were seriously retarded by the cold rains. Unless warm weather prevail during July and August, the grain will be retarded from maturing and ripening. A largely increased acreage of grain was sowed this year by the Indian farmers. It would have a discouraging effect should the crops fail to any material extent.

The irrigation ditches estimated for in October, 1892, were completed at the end of June. Water was turned in on both of the ditches, and an abundant supply now flows through them, at a fall of one fourth of an inch to the rod, which gives it a gentle flow, and covers a vast area of land that hereafter can be cultivated without fear of failure of crops from dry seasons. All of the excavation was done by Indian labor, while the flume work was done by skilled white labor.

Shingling and repairing of the Agency buildings and fences has been nearly completed.

A large number of logs were delivered at the Agency saw mill during the winter months by Indians for their individual use. A mill crew of Indians have been assisting the sawyer and engineer in cutting the logs into required dimensions for building purposes, and within the next week the yard will be cleared of saw logs, and the lumber hawled away by the Indian owners to build houses, barns and sheds. The haying season will follow, and thus this reservation always presents quite a busy scene for an Indian community.

I took advantage of the leave of absence granted me by the Department and returned from Chicago within fourteen days from time of departure. During my absence all industries of the Agency were conducted in a satisfactory manner.

Herewith I have the honor to enclose monthly statement of funds and indebtedness; also sanitary report and report of farmers. The School Report for the quarter ending June 30th, will follow soon as submitted.

I am very respectfully
Your obedient Servant,
Peter Ronan,
United States Indian Agent.

July 21, 1893
The Anaconda Standard, *July 24, 1893, page 6, col. 1.*

> More information on the 1893 St. Ignatius Day celebration and the dedication of the new church building can be found in the personal diary of Father Jerome D'Aste, S.J., and the St. Ignatius Mission House Diary.[13] Rev. James J. Rebmann, S.J., was a German who served as President of Gonzaga College in the 1880s and during the 1890s was superior of different Montana Indian missions including St. Ignatius in 1893.[14] For biographical information on Rev. Leopold Van Gorp, S.J., see the annotation to Ronan's June 23, 1877, letter.

For Indian Children
Surprising Extent of the Work at St. Ignatius' Mission.
A New Church Erected
It Will Be Dedicated This Month —
The Jesuit School at the Mission and Its Pupils.

Flathead Agency, July 21. — On Monday July 31, 1893, the feast of St. Ignatius will be appropriately observed at St. Ignatius mission. On that day, the magnificent church which has been under course of construction for the past two years will be dedicated by Bishop [John B.] Brondel with all the beautiful ceremony of the Catholic church. This church, erected by the Jesuit fathers of St. Ignatius mission, on the Flathead Indian reservation, and at their entire expense, when fully completed, will be the finest church edifice in the state of Montana. It is 128 feet by 54, built in the gothic style. The basement is of stone, the upper church, of brick.

Since the missionaries of this great mission have asked for no contributions, the generous gift which they make to the Indians, by building for them such a beautiful edifice for divine worship should be appreciated by all classes of the people throughout the state of Montana, as well as by the poor Indians for whom it was raised.

The Indian school at St. Ignatius mission is composed of over 300 Indian children and is a boarding school, comprised of three departments: The boys' department, conducted by the fathers; the girls' department, in charge of the Sisters of Providence; and St. Joseph's kindergarten, composed of over 60 Indian babies under 6 years old, in charge of the Ursuline nuns. The superior of St. Ignatius mission, Rev. J. Rebmann, S.J., is superintendent of the three departments, and is assisted by 20 male and 23 female teachers and employes. The various departments have their quarters in 10 large and extensive frame buildings, equipped with all the modern improvements — steam heating, hot and cold water, bath rooms and plunge bath, cheerful infirmaries, ample recreation room, large and well ventilated dormitories. Large play grounds afford ample facilities for healthy out door amusement. The garden with flowers, bowers, lawns, shade and fruit trees give the entire institution a very pleasing appearance.

A school exhibition will be given by the children and the St. Ignatius brass band, composed of 16 Indian boys, will discourse music. At the church service, confirmation will be conferred on Indian children by the bishop. It is expected that a large number of clergymen from distant dioceses will be present, including Rev. Father [Leopold] Van Gorp, S.J., formerly superior at St. Ignatius, but recently appointed in Rome as the superior general of all the Rocky Mountain Jesuit schools and missions, extending to the interior of Alaska.

P. R.

July 25, 1893a
LR 28,244/1893, RG 75, National Archives, Washington, D.C.

See Ronan's March 8, 1892, letter and annotation for more information about the circumstances surrounding Ronan's employment of outside legal counsel in February 1892.

United States Indian Service,
Flathead Agency,
July 25th, 1893.

Hon. Commissioner Indian Affairs,
Washington, D.C.

Sir:

Herewith please find attached letter from the law firm of Marshall Francis and Corbett of Missoula Montana, and in connection therewith beg to call your attention to my report of the case, in which Mr. Marshall was called upon to defend the right of the Indian Police of this Reservation in arresting certain Indian men and women and bring them back to the reserve from the town of Missoula where they were leading disgraceful lives. Said report is dated March 8th 1892, and shows that I was compelled for the best interests of the Indian service to employ counsel, as the United States Attorney was a resident of Helena Montana, a distance of one hundred and fifty miles from the town of Missoula and before he could appear in court, the arrested Indian outlaws would be discharged under writ of habeas corpus, taken from the custody of the Indian Police, and their authority made a mockery of, a proceedure that would have a very bad effect upon the future effectiveness of the Indian Police when called upon to do duty outside the boundary of the reservation. Mr. Marshall was successful in the case, and well earned his fee of fifty dollars. Attention was called to the matter in proper time, but as shown by the letter no payment was made, or authorized to be made. Trusting this matter will receive you[r] favorable consideration, I am

Your obedient servant
Peter Ronan
U.S. Indian Agent.

Enclosure:

Marshall, Francis & Corbett,
Attorneys at Law,
Missoula, Montana, July 19, 1893.

Maj. Peter Ronan,
Arlee, Mont.

My dear Major: –

Sometime ago, at your request, I defended a writ of habeas corpus of certain indians who were then detained under authority of the indian police, and it was agreed that you would report the charge to the Indian Department and have it allowed, since which time we have not heard what disposition was made of it. Kindly advise us at your early convenience the status of the same, and, if in condition, would be greatly obliged to receive the amount.

Faithfully yours,
Thos. C. Marshall.

July 25, 1893b
LR 28,345/1893, case 147, Nez Perce allotments, RG 75, National Archives, Washington, D.C.

On July 14, 1893, the Commissioner of Indian Affairs wrote to Ronan asking if the Angus McDonald family wanted to remain on the Flathead Reservation and decline allotments on the Nez Perce Reservation.[15] No biographical information was located about Annie Wilson, Nez Perce.

United States Indian Service,
Flathead Agency,
July 25th, 1893.

Hon. Commissioner of Indian Affairs,
Washington, D.C.

Sir:

In reply to your letter of July 14, 1893, "Land 17733 – 1893,["] in relation to certain relatives of one Annie Wilson, a Nez Perce allotte, who lives on the Flathead Reservation, have made application to your office for allotments upon the Nez Perce Reservation in Idaho.

Duncan McDonald, the head of the family, is now absent, but will shortly return, to the reservation. Before making report in regard to the status of the family, I desire to confer with him. Upon his return I shall at once communicate a full report in the matter.

I am very truly,
Your obedient Servant,
Peter Ronan,
United States Indian Agent.

August 1, 1893

LR 30,050/1893, RG 75, National Archives, Washington, D.C.

United States Indian Service,
Flathead Agency,
August 1st, 1893.

Hon. Commissioner Indian Affairs,
Washington, D.C.

Sir:

In submitting my report for the month of July, I have to state that the weather during the month was very warm and greatly helped the growing crops which were looking bad from the cold weather and cold rain storms that prevailed in June. From present appearance an abundant crop of wheat and oats will be harvested by the Indian farmers. The haying season has commenced and all are busy in the hay field. Little else will receive attention, until harvest time, when the gathering of grain will commence.

Nothing of sufficient importance to mention has taken place on the reservation except the annual gathering of the Indians and half breeds at the Mission to assist in the annual celebration of St. Ignatius day, July 31st. A new church erected by the Missionaries at St. Ignatius Mission, was dedicated by the bishop of Montana. It is built of brick and stone in Gothic style and is the largest church edifice in the state of Montana. Confirmation was also given by the Bishop to several Indian children and a school exhibition followed in the afternoon.

Herewith I have the honor to enclose monthly statement of funds and indebtedness; also sanitary report and report of farmers, and have the honor to be,

Very respectfully
Your obedient servant
Peter Ronan
United States Indian Agent.

Postscript added to letter:
Sanitary report enclosed with quarterly papers by mistake.

August 5, 1893

U.S. Commissioner of Indian Affairs, Annual Report of the Commissioner of Indian Affairs (Washington, D.C.: U.S. Government Printing Office, 1893), pages 182-187.

Ronan's 1893 annual report — dated a few weeks before his death — summarized problems Ronan had worked on for many years. The Bitterroot Salish Indians had moved to the Jocko Valley but still waited for the money from the sale of their Bitterroot allotments.[16] A General Land Office decision to sell the land in 80 acres units under appraisals based on the value of the full 160 acre allotments meant that some units were sold at bargain prices.[17] Tribal sentiment on the Flathead Reservation opposed allotment and the sale of "surplus" lands to whites, but families occupied separate farms.

White people were still trespassing on the Dayton Creek Kootenai allotments just north of the reservation boundary. The government had failed to finalize the Bonners Ferry Kootenai allotments and deliver titles to the allottees. Consequently the Idaho Kootenai could not legally defend their ownership of the land. Northern Idaho whites continued their legal and physical attacks on the Indian claims after Ronan's death and were eventually successful.[18]

In 1893 a new irrigation ditch had been built in the Jocko Valley with Indian labor. Competition continued between Ronan and the chiefs for control of the Indian court and Indian police on the reservation. The only case of murder on the reservation for 1892-1893 was tried in a Montana state court and the killer was acquitted on self-defense. Money was finally appropriated for a subagency on Crow Creek in the Mission Valley.

Report of Flathead Agency.

Flathead Agency, Mont., *August 5, 1893.*

Sir: In accordance with instruction from your office, I herewith submit my seventeenth annual report, with census and accompanying statistics.

The tribes and bands of this reservation consist of the Pend d'Oreilles, the Flatheads, and Kootenais, Chief Charlot's band of Bitter Root Valley Flatheads, and Chief Michel's band of Lower Kalispels, divided by tribal organization as follows:

Charlot's band:	
Total number	172
Males above 18	49
School children between 6 and 16	48
Females above 14	53
Confederated tribes:	
Total number	1,626
Males above 18	471
School children between 6 and 16	344
Females above 14	529
Lower Kalispels:	
Total number	58
Males above 18	24
School children between 6 and 16	7
Females above 14	21
Kootenais (removed from Idaho):	
Total number	58
Males above 18	16
School children between 6 and 16	17
Females above 14	15

Making a full total of 1,914.

Confederate Tribes.

The original Indian tribes who signed the treaty of 1855, promulgated by Gen. I. I. Stevens, are designated as the confederated tribes of Flatheads, Pend d'Oreilles, and Kootenais. They are generally quiet and peaceable Indians, and are advancing in education and civilizing pursuits. Other bands have removed and settled among them, notably Michael's band of Columbia River Kalispels and some Kootenai Indians from northern Idaho. A number of families of mixed blood from other reservations, who claim kinship with the confederated tribes of this reserve, with their consent, have removed here, and now occupy part of the choice lands of the reservation.

They are all advancing in the agricultural pursuits and the raising of stock, live in houses, and a majority have fields of grain, vegetable gardens, and some have small orchards of bearing apple trees, plums, and cherries. The lodge is almost abandoned except for hunting purposes and for visiting. The families instead of being huddled together in lodges near the Agency, waiting to draw supplies, as is the case at agencies where the ration system prevails, are scattered out through the agricultural valleys, tilling their inclosures, taking care of their stock, and struggling to increase their holdings as well as their scanty means will allow.

Issue of rations. — A regular issue of rations of supplies to Indians is a detriment to industry, advancement to independence, and self-support. Chief Charlot's band of Bitter Root Flatheads were promised regular issues of supplies by the agent who negotiated their removal to this Agency and the sale of their lands in the valley of the Bitter Root.

This agency heretofore was a nonration agency and the Indians were contented with agricultural implements, supplies of seed, and assistance in articles of clothing, blankets, and an irregular issue of provisions to indigent and nonself-supporting Indian families. This regular issue to Chief Charlot's band causes jealousies among the Indians of other tribes and bands, who think they have as much right to be regularly fed by the Government.

The sooner the Bitter Root Indians are paid for their lands now being sold by the Government and the regular ration system abolished the better for them and all the Indians on the reserve. The money received for the Bitter Root lands will furnish the Bitter Root Indians with means to open new farms, procure a start in stock, and thus commence a life of self-reliance, and self-support. The old, the infirm, and those making a beginning on a new farm are the only people to whom food should be given.

Flathead lands in the Bitter Root Valley. — Chief Charlot and his band of Flathead Indians removed from Bitter Root Valley, Montana, to this reservation in accordance with the provisions of an act entitled "An act to provide for the sale of lands patented to certain members of the Flathead band of Indians in Montana and for other purposes." These Indians are very anxious in regard to the payment to them of the money already paid to the Government from sale of certain tracts of said lands, claiming that it was promised to be sent without delay for distribution to the owners or heirs of the same, in order to enable them to improve and cultivate their new farms on their reservation.

It is my opinion that a serious mistake was made in regard to the sale of the land in question when the following order was issued:

Department of the Interior,
Washington, January 2, 1891.

The Commissioner of the General land Office:

Sir: I transmit herewith copy of Department telegram of October 20, 1891, to Gen. H. B. Carrington, special agent in the removal of the Flathead Indian act, and of his reply to the same.

You will please instruct the local officers to sell in 80-acre tracts when appraisement offered, and to do all possible to carry into effect the sale at appraisement value. Express to them the fact that the President will expect these sales to be accomplished, and that all should be informed that no reduction of prices need be expected.

I inclose herewith 100 copies of the report of Gen. Carrington (Senate Ex. Doc. 70, Fifty-first Congress, first session) for use of local office.

Very respectfully,

John W. Noble,
Secretary.

It is now claimed by the Indians that persons desiring to purchase Indian land under said act make a choice selection of 80 acres from 160 acres, at appraisement value, leaving the worst portion of the land in such shape that it can not command appraisement value, and therefore will remain forever unsold under the present act.

Allotments in severalty. — In varied correspondence with the Department in regard to the allotment of lands to the Indians in severalty, I have stated that the chiefs bitterly oppose the measure, and are upheld in their opposition by nearly all the full-blooded Indians of the reservation; therefore no allotment under the severalty act has been made or asked for by any dwellers within the boundary of this reserve. The Indians evince a prejudice against a survey of any kind upon the reserve, and state that a "measurement" of land by a white surveyor means a robbery of the Indians. Some of the younger and educated Indians desire allotments and title to their lands, but it is unpopular to advocate it and they remain silent on the question.

Nearly every head of a family on this reservation occupies definite, separate, though unallotted tracts, and their fences and boundary marks are generally respected. They live in houses, and a majority of their homes present a thrifty, farm like appearance. At present I deem it unwise to negotiate with them for the cession of any surplus land, or to attempt to have the lands surveyed and allotted. With their present opinions it would be difficult to induce them to listen to argument tending to the consummation of such policy.

The survey of the boundary of that portion of the Flathead Indian Reservation lying west of Flathead Lake and north of Clark's Fork of the Columbia River, surveyed by Edmund P. N. Harrison, United States deputy surveyor, under his contract No. 208, dated April 18, 1887, gave great dissatisfaction to the Indians, as they claimed that the initial monument on the first mile set by the surveyor on the west shore of the Flathead Lake, running thence due west to a point on Clark's Fork of the Columbia River, should have been 6 miles farther up the lake to a point where the Indians claimed it was pointed out as being the northern boundary and half way, or in the center of the lake, as defined by the treaty of July 16, 1855, and signed by the confederated tribes of Flatheads, Pend d'Oreilles, and Kootenais. A decision was rendered November 10, 1890, by the Indian Office, accepting the line as surveyed. In January, 1891, according to instructions, I explained to the Indians that it was impossible to accept other boundaries than those clearly defined in the treaty, and endeavored to convince them that the line was in strict accordance with its published provisions. I urged upon the Indians the necessity of securing their claims to the lands segregated from the reserve by the survey by fencing and improving the same.

In accordance with request to be advised as to the proper steps to be taken in order to save these Indians the land they claimed as homes, and to which they believed they were entitled, under the Stevens treaty of 1855, I was instructed by the Hon. Commissioner of Indian Affairs to allot the land to them in severalty under provisions of the general allotment act, February 8, 1887, and under the fourth section thereof as amended by act of February 28, 1891, (28 Stats., 794). On September 23, 24, and 26, 1891, nineteen applications were filed by me in the local United States land office in Missoula, Mont., and were transmitted by that office on the 28th of October, 1891.

White settlers took possession of several of those Indian locations, and are still trespassing upon them notwithstanding my appeals for relief to the proper department of justice. The action of the whites in trying to dispossess the Indians of their allotments has had a baneful effect upon the Indians of the Kootenai tribe, who were the applicants. It has almost totally discouraged them from making any effort to cultivate their land, as I advised them to avoid trouble with the whites by remaining peaceable towards the trespassers until their titles to the lands were secured. The delay has been so long that the Indians begin to believe that the Government has not acted in good faith with them, and their only resort is to dispossess the whites by force. I trust to be able to preserve peace among the Indians until their allotments are adjusted to the survey of the township, and they are put in peaceful possession of the lands they properly and lawfully applied for.

The same condition prevails among the Indians at Bonner's Ferry, northern Idaho, where I made allotments to nonreservation Kootenai Indians, under instruction from the honorable Commissioner of Indian Affairs, dated, August 28, 1889. Their titles, have not been received, and the result is that their allotments are being trespassed upon, and the unfortunate Indians, who have no aid of any kind from the Government, are deterred from attempting to improve or cultivate some of the land they always occupied and to which they are entitled by allotment under the laws of the United States, as before quoted.

Irrigation ditches in Jocko Valley. — In 1884 several families removed to the Jocko Valley, in the vicinity of the agency, from Bitter Root Valley, and settled upon an extensive and fertile plateau on the north side of the Jocko River. Irrigation was necessary for the production of crops, and I was authorized to construct a waterway to cover the land. With Indian labor a canal was excavated for a distance of about 6 miles. It covers a fertile body of land, and the Indians, with the aid of irrigation, raise excellent grain and vegetable crops on their small inclosures.

The old ditch was 2 feet deep, 3 feet wide in the bottom, and 4 feet wide on top. In order to bring the water to the head of the plateau, the ditch had to be constructed through a rough and rocky canyon for about 2 miles and most of the distance had to be flumed, requiring nearly 100,000 feet of lumber. The logs were delivered by Indian labor at the agency mill and cut into proper dimensions. The flume was constructed 3 feet wide in the bottom — of 3-inch plank, 2 feet high of 1½-inch plank — bottom sills 4 by 6; side pieces 4 by 4; cap pieces 2 by 6, all mortised and tenoned. Like the ditch it has a fall of one-quarter of an inch to the rod. This waterway was completed in a surprisingly short time, as the Indians desired employment and also wished to have their land irrigated. It was an entire success and the work was praised by all who examined it. The fall is sufficient to give it a rippling current from the head to the foot of the ditch.

The irrigating facilities caused a number of Indians to settle upon the land, and last year it was found that the water capacity was not sufficient to accommodate all of the Indian farmers. Authority was given last October to enlarge the ditch and flume to double the former capacity. With Indian labor and the assistance of some skilled mechanics this work was accomplished during the winter months, and water was turned into the ditch in June in time to irrigate the land.

Chief Charlot and his band, who recently removed to this agency from the Bitter Root Valley, made their homes on the south side of the Jocko Valley. Without irrigation it would be a hopeless task for them to undertake to cultivate the land. Authority was given in October, 1892, to construct a waterway to their settlement, and the work was accomplished by Indian labor during the winter months. The waterway is fed by a natural reservoir or mountain lake and covers several thousand acres of land.

These Indians have no excuse now to offer against making an effort to fence and cultivate their land, as it is furnished with good means of irrigation that secures a sure crop in any season. They are a trifling class of Indians, however, and will always, when urged to work for themselves, refer to the promises they claim to have been made, that fields would be fenced and plowed for them at the expense of the Government, and other promises of subsistence, cattle, etc., until the money from the sale of their lands in the Bitter Root Valley is turned over to them.

Stock-raising. — As well as being a fine agricultural country, this reservation offers the best of facilities for stock-raising, and quite a number of the Indians and mixed bloods are taking advantage of the situation, and are increasing their herds. In fact, a few half-breed cattle owners on this reservation may now be ranked as comparatively wealthy, and the full-blooded Indians are profiting by their example. Twice a year a regular round-up is inaugurated, and all Indian owners of stock join the force on horseback. The stock is gathered into bands and each owner selects his cattle, brands the calves, and then allows his band liberty to roam the common range until another round-up is arranged.

Roads and bridges. — It is a task to attempt to arouse Indians to the necessity of making better roads through the reservation, but it is one that has been insisted upon in the past and will receive attention in the future. Roads are the channels of trade from the farm to the store, the railroad, the agency mills and shops, and should be kept in repair.

On this reservation the great necessity is the repair and construction of bridges. Unusually high water in all the mountain streams prevailed this year and some of the bridges were wrecked or swept away entirely. They will be replaced and repaired, after the haying and harvest season is over, by Indian labor, and according to the rules and regulations deemed practicable on this reservation. Copy submitted to the Indian Office February 3, 1892.

Indian police and judges. — This branch of the service has not always given the satisfaction it should. The dwellers on the reservation are made up of so many different bands and factions, and so many jealousies exist among them, that it is difficult to adjust the troubles that sometimes arise when a policeman of one faction attempts to make arrest of a member of another faction. The old chiefs of the tribes are also opposed to the police and judges of the court of Indian offenses, as in bygone days they exercised the full power to punish their people and enforce their regulations, generally with the whip. However, the best class of Indians, the stock-raisers and the tillers of the soil, are in favor of the police system, as protection is given them against molestation from the lawless young men of the tribes, who are now arrested and punished by incarceration in the jail for any criminal offense they may commit.

On the reservation during the past year only one case of killing among the Indians occurred, and that case was brought before the State court and the Indian was acquitted under the plea of self-defense. Outside of occasional horse-stealing, elopement of Indian married men and women, introduction of whisky on the reservation by Indians and half-breeds, occasional sprees in some of the camps on holidays, such as the Fourth of July, Christmas, and New Years, gambling, and other similar offenses, the police force and judges have little else to look after.

Subagency. — United States Indian Inspector R. S. Gardner, after a visit to this agency, reported to the Interior Department that a large portion of the Indians of this reservation live from 50 to 60 miles distant from the agency; that the center of population is near Crow or Mud Creek; that at present they derive only a small benefit from the agency grist and sawmill and carpenter and blacksmith shops; that the establishment of a subagency on the reservation would be a decided advantage and for the best interest of the service; that the present agency was located in early days in one corner of the reservation for convenience of the agent and agency employés, being near the town of Missoula, and not for or in the interest of the reservation Indians; that the time has now come when the Indians of that reservation should be more looked after and encouraged in civilization, and that they are beginning to see and feel and know that they must depend upon themselves to make a living, and for this the aid which the Government offers them should be easily accessible — not 30, 40, 50, or 75 miles distant, causing them to travel these respective distances to get a machine, plow, wagon, or harness repaired or to obtain the service of the agency physician.

It was also represented that it might be well to establish or locate an agency on Crow Creek or Mud Creek and retain the present agency for the use of the Bitter Root Flatheads and such other of the confederated tribes as are now located and farming in the Jocko Valley. In the locality of Mud or Crow Creek it would be preferable for the agency or subagency to be established. The valley there is from 10 to 12 miles wide and 35 miles long, and is close to Pend d'Oreille River, Little Bitter Root Valley, Dayton Creek, and the Indian settlements around the Flathead Lake. About two-thirds of the reservation Indians live in and near that vicinity. The location suggested is about 30 miles distant from Ravalli, a station on the Northern Pacific Railroad, or 18 miles north of St. Ignatius Mission. As the Indians are industrious, peaceable, and anxious to become self-supporting and independent, the aid offered them should be in easy access.

I was directed to fully report upon the feasibility and necessity of establishing a subagency in the country suggested, which I did under date of February 18, 1891. It seems the matter was favorably considered, as in the act (Public, No. 119), for fulfilling treaty stipulations with various Indian tribes for the fiscal year ending June 30, 1893, and for other purposes, p. 19, miscellaneous, the following paragraph is published:

> Substation and mills Flathead Agency, Montana: Establishment of sub-station purchase of saw and flour mills, construction of necessary buildings for same, purchase of animals, and pay of employés at Flathead Agency, Montana, ten thousand dollars.

The act of Congress making appropriations for the ensuing fiscal year (1893-'94) also made provision for substation and mills at this agency, granting $3,500. As directed on the 24th of April, 1893, I submitted a detailed and separate estimates for substation, purchase of saw and flour mill, etc., mentioned in said act of Congress, with recommendations in the premises. I have not been notified if the matter has yet been acted upon.

Education. — There is one school existing on this reservation. It is located at St. Ignatius Mission, about 15 miles northwest of the agency, and is a boarding school comprised of three departments: Boys' department, conducted by Jesuit fathers; girls' department, in care of Sisters of Providence, and St. Joseph's Kindergarten, under the control of Ursuline nuns. The Superior of St. Ignatius Mission is superintendent of the three departments; he is assisted by 20 male and 23 female teachers and employés.

The various departments have their quarters in ten large and expensive frame buildings, equipped with all the modern improvements, as steam heating, hot and cold water plant, bath rooms and plunge bath, cheerful infirmaries, ample recreation rooms, large and well-ventilated dormitories. The class rooms are bright, furnished with folding desks and large blackboards. The pupils receive three regular meals and an afternoon lunch. Large playgrounds afford ample facilities for healthy outdoor amusements. The gardens with flowers, bowers, lawns, shade, and fruit trees, give the entire institution a very pleasant appearance.

As an industrial school it has shops, in which the pupils receive, by competent teachers, instruction in baking, blacksmithing, carpentry, saddlery, harness and shoemaking. Girls are taught cooking, laundering, plain and fancy needlework, knitting, dairywork, and other useful industries. By means of the saw and grist mill, the matching and planing machine, the shingle machine, the engine rooms, stables, threshing and mowing machines, combined reapers and binders, on the extensive farm the pupils become acquainted with manual labor such as they will probably have to do after leaving school. All the work is so arranged as not to be irksome and discouraging. It seems to be the endeavor of the institution to render every pupil skillful in some special line, but at the same time their work is varied enough to give them an acquaintance with other branches.

As to school work, as far as practicable, the course of study which was two years ago especially designated for reservation boarding schools by the honorable Commissioner of Indian Affairs is followed.

New Year's Day, Washington's Birthday, Arbor Day, Fourth of July, Thanksgiving Day, and Christmas were appropriately observed as holidays by civil and religious exercises, hoisting the American flag, entertainments, in which St. Ignatius Indian brass band, composed of 16 boys, always takes a prominent part, also during the vacation evenings, especially in the summer.

Since Chief Charlot's band was removed from the Bitter Root Valley to the Flathead Agency, a school for the children was opened at the agency by the faculty of St. Ignatius Mission School and given into the care of the Ursuline Nuns. The reason the fathers went to the expense of erecting a separate branch school at a cost of $4,500, while there is ample room for all the children of the reservation at St. Ignatius Mission, was the opposition of Chief Charlot and his followers to separate from their children. They insisted upon seeing them educated under their own eyes or not at all.

The school is doing fairly well considering the many obstacles petty Indian prejudice throws in the way of getting the younger generation civilized. To quote some of their expressed prejudices will suffice: "In the school the hair of our children shall not be cut. We do not wish to see our children with short hair; only the white man was created by God to wear short hair. The Indian was made by Him with long hair * * * In school our children learn English; when they know English they can buy whisky from white men; the white man would not understand them if they spoke Indian and asked for whisky. When our girls leave school, where they dressed well and lived in nice houses, they do not like to stay with their poor parents; they love the whites better than their Indian relatives, etc."

Missionary work. — Ever since the advent of Father De Smet into the Indian country this reservation has been under the fostering guidance of the Catholic Jesuit Indian missionaries. Here was established St. Ignatius Mission, now the largest institution of the kind in the United States. The improvements in church and school buildings, furniture, shops, tools, agricultural imple-ments, outhouses, machinery, etc., can not fall short of the estimated value of $180,000. These improvements belong to the Missionary Society and are mostly the result of the toil and frugal habits of the founders of the mission and school and of their successors, who have continued the work. The Indian dwellers on the reservation all claim to be Catholics. Polygamy is prohibited by the laws of their religion and the Indian tribal laws severely punish the perpetrators of the crime. The fathers of the Society of Jesus devote themselves with great zeal and hard labor toward the Christianizing, educating, and civilizing the Indians, both at St. Ignatius Mission and the agency. Several times during the year the fathers visit the Kootenai tribe under Chief Eneas, also the Lower Kalispels, who removed from Idaho to this reservation, headed by Chief Michael. These visits always have a good effect on the Indians, restraining them from gam-bling, superstitions, dances, unlawful cohabitation, and exhorting them to the practice of Christian virtues, the education of their children in the school, and the peaceful pursuit of civilizing industries.

A new church is now being built by the Jesuit fathers at St. Ignatius Mis-sion, and at their entire expense, which when completed will be the finest church edifice in the State of Montana. It is 128 by 54 feet, built in the Gothic style; the basement of stone, the upper church of brick. Since the missionaries asked no contributions from the Indians, the generous gift which they make by building for them such a beautiful edifice of divine worship should be appreci-ated by all classes of people throughout the State of Montana as well as by the poor Indians, for whom the edifice was raised.

I am, very respectfully, your obedient servant,

Peter Ronan,
United States Indian Agent.

The Commissioner of Indian Affairs.

August 15, 1893
Seattle Post-Intelligencer, *August 15, 1893, page 2.*

> After returning from the Chicago World's Fair, Ronan was diagnosed with a serious heart ail-ment. The physician recommended Ronan move to a lower altitude, and Ronan and one of

his sons traveled to Seattle and Victoria, British Columbia. He returned to the Jocko Valley on August 20 1893, seemingly in better health, but he died unexpectedly that evening.[19]

Maj. Peter Ronan in Town.
A Talk With the Famous Montana Pioneer and Indian Agent.

Maj. Peter Ronan, Indian agent at the Flathead agency in Montana, accompanied by his son, who is attending college in Spokane, is a guest at the Occidental. He has been ill for some time and he is taking a trip for his health, his physicians having recommended that he come to the Coast. Maj. Ronan is one of the best known men in Montana, of which state he is a pioneer.

"Yes, I have been with the Flatheads a long while. It has been seventeen years since I was first appointed agent over there," said he to a **Post-Intelligencer** reporter last night.

"They have developed under my eye from warlike tribes of savages into educated, thrifty, industrious, moral and law-abiding communities. There are three different tribes consolidated at my agency, the Pend d'Oreilles, the Kootenays and the Flatheads. When I first knew these Indians they were nomadic hunters. Their habitat was chiefly in the region they now live in, west of the mountains, but twice a year they used to make excursions across the mountains to hunt buffaloes. When they had killed their season's meat they would return to their homes, plant small crops and thus they spent their lives, except when at war.

As the buffalo ranges were not overwell stocked, the incursions of these mountain Indians upon the plains were resented by the Crows, Sioux and other plains Indians, and bitter wars resulted, which kept their tribes from increasing. Since they have quit fighting they have increased in numbers, and are now a strong, sturdy and healthy race. Why the Flathead tribe was ever given that name I cannot conceive, because their heads are not flat, nor have they ever adopted such a barbarous custom. I have often talked with their aged men about the matter, and they never even heard of such a thing. There are now about 2,000 Indians on the reservation, which is one of the most valuable large tracts of land in the Rocky Mountain region. The Indians all live in comfortable houses built by themselves. They are good farmers and stockraisers and are prosperous, contented and happy, and some of them are quite well off.

We have the largest Indian mission school in the country, with 300 pupils, and the only Indian kindergarten, which is taught by the Catholic sisters. nearly all of the Indians are Catholics, and to the Jesuits belong the credit of their transformation into civilized citizens. These priests have been among them for the last fifty years and have labored incessantly to teach them the arts of peace. While they are all good Indians, I think the full-blooded are better than the half-breeds. There are some of the latter, though, who are on the high road to fortune through a piece of enterprise they have been patiently following for the last ten years.

About that long ago during a buffalo hunt on the plains we drove a buffalo bull and two heifers through a pass in the mountains on to the reservation. Shortly afterwards Charles Allard and Michel Pabalo [sic] bought them and have since carefully herded their offsprings, until now they have a herd of 100 head. They are quite well off now, but this herd of buffalo will make them wealthy. There was only one other herd in the country, which was owned by a man called Buffalo Jones in Kansas. But times got hard in Kansas and these two half-breeds went down and bought up these 50 buffaloes, so that now they have the only herd in this country. They are getting orders all the time for animals to be sent to the different zoological gardens in this country and Europe, and they sell them for $500 and upwards apiece.

As time goes on the rarity of the animal will make them increase in value. These men lost $20,000 recently by trusting in the word of a World's Fair speculator. He offered them $20,000 for the privilege of exhibiting the herd at the fair, and they reluctantly consented. But when it was too late for them to secure accomodations at the fair themselves the speculator went back on his promise."

August 21, 1893a

LR 31,235/1893, telegram, RG 75, National Archives, Washington, D.C.

Aug 21 189

Missoula Mont

Hon Comm Ind Afrs W DC

peter Rolan [sic] US. Indian Agt flathead Agency Mont. died evening Aug twentieth please telegraph instructions at Arlee Montana

Joseph L Carter

Agency Clerk.

August 21, 1893b

The Evening Missoulian, *August 21, 1893, page 1, col. 5-6. The death notice reproduced in this article was followed by a biographical sketch of Ronan which duplicated information elsewhere in this collection and is not reproduced below.*

Passed Peacefully Away.
A Good and True Man Gives Up His Life Without a Struggle.

The startling news reached Missoula last evening that Major Peter Ronan, agent of the Flathead agency, had died suddenly at his home at Jocko. The report was soon verified and particulars are to the effect that the major passed quietly and peacefully away in the presence of his wife shortly after 9 o'clock last evening. Deceased was just retiring for bed and simply remarked that he did not feel very well. Before his wife could inquire into his ailment, he gently careened over onto the pillow and with a few expiring gasps, died without a struggle. The major's demise, while painful to hear, was not unexpected by his relatives and immediate friends, nor by himself for that matter, as the gentleman hastily and unexpectedly returned on Friday last from Seattle where he had gone in the hope of improving his physical condition. He returned home unannounced and several weeks before his time for arrival, telling his wife that he had a premonition that he could not long survive and preferred being at home should dissolution occur. Heart failure, superinduced by a killing attack of rheumatism contracted last winter, was the immediate cause of his death.

Major Ronan will be missed; his family will miss him; the government will miss him; thousands of Indians who have learned to love and obey him will miss him and mourn the loss of a leader; his friends, who number legions will miss him. Ronan was, indeed a singular spirit; charitable to a degree, generous to a fault, he was one of God's noblest men. No one, whether in distress or sorrow, turned away from him disappointed, and his reigning principle appeared to be the desire to make all happy. Ever of a cheerful disposition he thus always greeted his friends and it is doubtful if ever a secret sorrow pervaded his breast. A model husband, a man among men, scrupulously honest and upright — so did he live, so did he die. He leaves an amiable wife and most estimable family of sons and daughters and thousands throughout the state to mourn his departure. The funeral will occur from the Catholic church tomorrow morning at 9 o'clock at which all friends and acquaintances are invited. . . .

August 22, 1893

The Evening Missoulian, *August 22, 1893, page 1, col. 6.*[20]

Earth to Earth.

Major Peter Ronan Laid to Rest in the Catholic Cemetery.

The remains of the late Major Peter Ronan were laid to rest in the Catholic cemetery today. Last evening a number of friends of the family went to the agency, among whom were Mrs. A. B. Hammond, Mrs. F. L. Worden, Mr. and Mrs. W. C. Murphy, Mr. and Mrs. H. A. Lambert, of Missoula; General Curtis and wife, Mrs. Ross Deegan and Hugh McQuaid, of Helena, and John Caplice, of Butte. Early this morning the casket containing the body was taken from the agency to Arlee, a large escort of Indians following, sincere mourners for their friend, and placed aboard the train for Missoula. Arriving here at 6 o'clock this morning, the remains were taken to the Catholic church where they, were allowed to remain in state until 9 o'clock, when services for the dead were held, Father Palermo officiating, assisted by Father Guidi and the venerable Father D'Aste, who is 77 years old and who came here from the mission to pay respect to the memory of his old friend. The singing was led by the well known soprano, Mr. Adolph La Salle, of Helena, who was ably assisted by a superb choir. The funeral sermon was by Father Guidi, who touchingly alluded to the virtues of the deceased and the merit of his life work among the Indians. The floral offerings were numerous and beautiful, many being arranged by Mrs. Lillian M. Higgins, Miss Grace Lambert and Mesdames Hammond and Worden. When the casket was opened by Undertaker Flynn most of those in the church went forward to take a last look at the familiar features soon to be shut from sight forever.

The pall-bearers, all old friends of the deceased, were: T. J. McNamara, Wm. Kennedy, Sr., G. A. Wolf, Michael Flynn, William C. Murphy and H. A. Lambert. The funeral cortege was one of the largest ever in Missoula.

Mrs. Ronan and daughter Mary were not present owing to the illness of Mrs. Ronan which confines her at home and her daughter is by her side. All of the major's sons, however, were present at the obsequies.

A singular incident in connection with the major's death is the fact that Mrs. Ronan was taken seriously ill on Sunday night and the major went to the station at Arlee to telegraph to Missoula for a physician. When he returned home he complained of feeling ill, lay down upon his bed, and within a few minutes afterwards expired.

Among those out of town at the church, besides those mentioned, were noted Major McKibben and other officers of Fort Missoula, Alex. Dow of Arlee, Alex. Demers of St. Ignatius mission, J. T. Hundley of Arlee, Constable Geo. Good of Thompson Falls and Agency Clerk Carter of Jocko.

Afterword

Ronan's unexpected death from a heart attack at the age of fifty-five left his widow, Mary, without financial resources to support herself and her young children.[21] As discussed in Peter Ronan's biographical sketch, the Missoula County probate records show that Peter's debts in 1893 roughly equaled his assets.[22] Joseph T. Carter, Ronan's agency clerk, succeeded Ronan as agent with the understanding that Carter would employ Peter's son, Vincent Ronan, as agency clerk.[23] In 1895, Carter married Peter's daughter, Mary, and the Ronan family was able to live at the agency until 1898 when Carter's term as agent concluded.

In the months between Ronan's death and Carter's appointment, Thomas P. Smith, a Special Indian Agent, had charge of the Flathead Agency.[24] Ironically, in September 1893, some western Montana residents tried to get Duncan McDonald, Ronan's frequent critic, appointed agent.[25] In October 1893, Carter took charge of the Flathead Agency.[26] In 1898, at the end of his term, Carter moved to Butte and Mary Ronan, Peter's widow, and the four youngest Ronan children moved to Missoula.[27]

Carter was succeeded as agent by W. H. Smead, a Missoula businessman and politician, who had recently led an effort in the Montana Legislature to get the Flathead Reservation allotted and open to white settlement. Neither Carter nor Smead showed Ronan's diplomatic skill working with tribal leaders.

Peter Ronan's 1877 to 1893 term as Flathead Indian Agent left an important legacy that dramatically impacted the Flathead Reservation. In 1877, he cooperated with the tribal leaders to keep the Montana tribes out of what could have been a disaster in the Nez Perce War. For much of the 1880s and early 1890s, he worked with Kootenai Chief Eneas to try to avoid open conflict with hostile and openly aggressive white settlers in the Upper Flathead Valley. Many of Ronan's efforts to protect Kootenai rights and property were ultimately unsuccessful, but Ronan and Eneas were able to avoid the deaths that would have resulted from war. Ronan and the tribal leaders also worked together to move the reservation economy from hunting and gathering supplemented by small farms and cattle herds, to one based on ranching and farming supplemented by hunting and gathering activities. During the entire time, the Flathead Reservation tribes received some government assistance but were always basically self-supporting even after the loss of the buffalo and other traditional resources. In law and order on the reservation, Ronan worked with the chiefs to keep the peace but also opposed the chiefs to slowly build up the power of the government paid Indian police and Indian court. Ironically, Ronan also delayed the disastrous allotment policy on Flathead for twenty years. Peter Ronan's tenure as agent was not without controversy, but it had many positive impacts on the reservation and tribal community.

Historical Writings

Peter Ronan, Historical Sketch of the Flathead Indian Nation from the Year 1813 to 1890 *(Helena, Mont.: Journal Publishing Co., 1890), pages 72-78.*

> Ronan contributed historical articles about the Flathead Reservation tribes to a number of Montana newspapers. Some of the articles repeat information in his letters which are published here. A series from the *Helena Journal* was reprinted in 1890 as a small book titled, *Historical Sketch of the Flathead Indian Nation*. The portions of the book which Ronan drew from his personal experience included the description of the 1884 Salish delegation to Washington, D.C., which is reproduced above. He also included biographical sketches of Big Canoe, the Pend d'Orellle chief, and two Bitterroot Salish chiefs, Adolph and Arlee. These biographical sketches are only a small glimpse of what Ronan might have left us if he had lived to write his memoirs.
>
> No biographical information was found about Joseph, the Pend d'Oreille chief before 1848, or Big Smoke, the Pend d'Oreille war chief. Alexander was Pend d'Oreille chief between 1848 and 1868. He was known for his personal bravery and his support for the missionaries and peace with the whites.[28] See the annotations for Ronan's May 1, 1878, letter for Big Canoe and his January 10, 1878, letter for Adolph. Arlee is included in the Biographical Sketches.

Sketches of Big Canoe, Adolph and Arlee, of Montana Indian Fame.

Big Canoe, who was war chief of the Pend d'Oreilles, died in 1882, at the Flathead agency, and was buried in the Indian burying ground at Fort [St.] Ignatius Mission. He was 83 years of age at the time of his death, and was considered by the Indians to be one of the greatest war chiefs the tribe of the Pend d'Oreilles ever had. The stories of battles led by him against Indian foes would fill a volume. As this aged warrior was well known to the old settlers of Missoula county, I feel tempted to give one of his stories, which was related to the writer in front of a blazing camp fire some years before his death, and which was noted down almost word for word as repeated from his lips by the interpreter.

Story of Big Canoe.

Many snows ago, when I was a boy, and while Joseph or "Celp-Stop" (Crazy Country) was head chief of the Pend d'Oreilles, I was one of a large hunting and war party who left the place where the white men call Missoula, for the purpose of killing buffalo and stealing horses in our enemies' country. We (the Flathead and Pen d'Oreilles) were at war with the Blackfeet, the Crows the Sioux, the Snakes and the Gros Ventres. The Nez Percies were our allies and friends and assisted us to fight those tribes.

While encamped in the Crow country Big Smoke, one of the bravest war chiefs of the Pen d'Oreilles, discovered Crow signs, and taking a party of his braves with him, followed upon the trail. The Crow camp was soon discovered, and, as Big Smoke started out more to get horses than to secure scalps, informed his warriors that he did not intend to attack the small party of Crows, who were now at his mercy, as the Pen d'Oreilles and Flatheads had crept upon their camp undiscovered, and the Crows were resting in fancied security, their horses grazing upon the pleasant slopes unguarded, while the old warriors lolled about the camp smoking their pipes, and the young men were engaged in the wild sports and rude game practiced among the tribe.

The announcement that we were not to have a fight was received with great marks of disfavor by our braves, and, as I was a young man and had not as yet taken my first scalp, I could not restrain myself, but cried like a woman. Big Smoke was known to be the bravest man in the tribe and no one of us dared impute his action to cowardise, and we therefore acquiesced in his plans, and when night came silently and cautiously we ran off the whole band of Crow horses and left our enemies on foot. We soon found our main encampment and the horses were divided up. One particular fine black horse was given to our head chief. The day after our return the chief announced to us that our powder and lead was nearly exhausted, and as there was no way of procuring any without going to the Crow trading post, asked if there was any of his warriors brave enough to undertake the feat.

Alexander, or Tem-Keth-tasme, which means No Horse, who afterwards succeeded Joseph as chief, and who was then a young warrior and burning to distinguish himself, immediately volunteered, and disguising himself as a Crow, after darkness came on, set out on his perilous journey. Arriving at the Crow stockade, he was immediately admitted by the trader, and was at once discovered to be a Pend d'Oreille by a Crow who was lounging about the post. Word was sent to the Crow camp that an enemy was in the stockade, and soon a loud demand was heard at the gate for admittance. The gate was opened and a single Indian was admitted. He was a tall, noble-looking fellow, dressed in the full war costume of a Crow brave. Halting immediately in front of Alexander, he reached out his hand and cordially grasped the hand of the Pend d'Oreille. "Canoe man you are brave. You have come among your enemies to purchase powder and lead. You are dead but still you live. I am Red Owl. Your warriors stole into my camp, they took my horses; they were strong, but stole upon us while we were unaware and spared the lives of my band. Canoe-man on that night I lost my war horse — a black horse with two holes bored in his ears. He was my fathers gift to me. Is there such a horse in your camp?["] Alexander replied that such a horse was given to his chief by Big Smoke after the capture. "Red Owl will go back with you into his enemies camp," and striding out of the stockade he harangued, and then picking out twenty of his braves desired them to accompany him. Alexander was then allowed to make his purchase and on the next morning accompanied by Red Owl and twenty of his warriors set out for the Pend d'Oreille camp.

When arriving there the Indians were astonished to behold their trusted brave, Alexander, leading the Crow warriors armed to the teeth, up to the lodge of their chief, who was soon surrounded by his brave Pend d'Oreilles in such overwhelming numbers that there was no escape or even hope to escape for the Crows. Red Owl dismounted and asked Alexander which was his chief. The person being pointed out Red Owl addressed him: "Chief of the Canoe Indians, your braves captured a band of horses from my people. Among them was my war [horse], and I love him for he was the gift of my father. I desire the horse and have brought you as good to replace him." Our chief, who did not like to part with the horse, and who perfectly knew the advantage he possessed, bent his head in silence. Red Owl repeated his speech, but our chief gave no reply but stood in stolid silence. "Chief of the Pend d'Oreilles," exclaimed Red Owl, "twice have I spoken to you, and you gave me no answer. I repeat it again for the third time!" We were listesing [sic] to the conversation, continued Big Canoe, and as young as I was; I could not but admire the brave Crow; surrounded as he was with his followers by implacable enemies, only awaiting the signal to begin the slaughter. But the brave bearing of the Crow, and his indifferent manner won the respect of us all, and we could not help but admire him; and to such an extent did this feeling prevail that a murmur of applause went around when the Crow concluded his last sentence. Straightening himself up to his full height, the Crow continued turning to us: "Pen d'Oreilles, you have heard me address your chief; he gave me no answer; he buried his head low; he changed his color; this the subterfuge of a woman, Pend d'Oreilles, your chief is a woman; I give him my horse!" And mounting at the head of his band he rode from our camp and not one movement was made to stay his progress. So overwhelmed was our chief with confusion that he gave no orders, and Red Owl, with his followers, returned safe to his camp.

Adolph,

first war chief of the Flatheads, died at the agency in 1887, at the age of 78 years. He marshalled and led the young warriors when the council was held at the agency, represented on the part of the United States by Hon. Jos. K. McCammon, assistant attorney general of the interior department. The Northern Pacific Railroad company was represented, as attorney, by Hon. W. F. Sanders, now senator from Montana, while the Indian leaders and speakers in the council were Michel, chief of the Pend d'Oreilles; Eneas, chief of the Kootenais, and Arlee, chief of the reservation Flatheads. The council was held to negotiate with the Indians for the right of way for the Northern Pacific Railroad company. On occasions the scenes were wild and stormy, but the level headed McCommon [sic] carried out the views of the government to a wise, generous and honorable settlement, and the memory of Mr. McCammon is cherished by the old chiefs of the tribes who still survive.

Adolph was considered a great warrior and led the Flatheads as war chief against their enemies, which constituted all of the tribes who hunted buffalo on the Atlantic slope, except the Nez Perces, who were the friends and allies of the Flatheads.

A battle with the Gros Ventres was fought about fifty years ago, about one mile west of O'Keefe's ranch, at the mouth of the canyon where the Northern Pacific crosses the great Marant tressle and sweeps from the east into the Jocko mountains. Chief Factor Kitson [William Kittson], of the Hudson Bay Fur company, who had his headquarters at Thompson Falls on the Pend d'Oreille river, came with a pack train of supplies from that post to trade with the Flathead Indians, who were encamped near the site of the present city of Missoula. Having made his trade and secured the furs Mr. Kitson started his pack train up the canyon to unload at the company's warehouse at Thompson Falls. Two South Sea Islanders in the employ of Chief Factor Kitson went ahead with the train, but as they gained the entrance to the canon were fired upon by an ambushed party of Gros Ventres, consisting of about 100 Indians. The two packers were slain, Mr. Kitson and others of his party were about a mile in the rear of the advance party or he and his companions would have shared the same fate. Kitson turned back and informed the Flathead camp of the attack and the chiefs at once sounded the alarm. The warriors mounted their horses and headed by Adoph and Arlee made an advance on the camp of the hostiles. The

Gros Ventres retreated across the hills and up Savallie creek, which is about seven miles west of Missoula. The Flatheads killed and scalped about one half of their number before they made their escape. The canon [sic] leading from O'Keefe's ranch to the reservation was called Coviaca Defile, after one of the unfortunate South Sea islanders who was killed by the Gros Ventres.

Arlee.

On Thursday, August 8, [1889] at 4:30 p.m., Arlee, the last war chief of the Flatheads, and of the confederated tribes, died at his ranch, near the Flathead agency, and the Northern Pacific railroad station, called after him. His death-bed was surrounded by his Indian relatives, head men of the tribes and friends. Major Ronan, United States Indian agent, Mrs. Ronan, Dr. Dade, the agency physician, and others connected with the agency staff were present. The Sunday before he died he was visited by Bishop Brondel, of Helena, and Rev. J. D'Aste, S.J., superior of St. Ignatius mission, and from the latter received the last sacraments of the Catholic church. Arlee was baptized in his youth in the Bitter Root valley by Father De Smet. He accepted the terms of General Garfield and removed to the Jocko reservation, and was made head chief of the reservation Flatheads by Mr. Garfield. Chief Charles never recognized Arlee afterwards; never spoke to him nor visited him up to the day of his death. Arlee was buried near the little church at the agency. He has gone to the happy hunting ground....

Conclusion of Blessing Ceremony, St. Ignatius Mission Church, July 31, 1893. Archives and Special Collections, Mansfield Library, University of Montana, Missoula, photograph 78-34.

Biographical Sketches

Most biographical information on the people mentioned in the Peter Ronan letters is included in the annotations preceding each letter, except for a few cases which needed extended treatment. This section has biographical sketches of five Salish and Kootenai chiefs who played major roles in Flathead Reservation history between 1877 and 1893 and in the letters included in this collection. Those chiefs are Arlee (Salish/Nez Perce), Charlo (Salish), Eneas (Kootenai), Louison (Salish/Nez Perce), and Michelle (Pend d'Oreille).

Chief Arlee
Salish/ Nez Perce
(ca. 1815–1889)

As a young man Arlee was an exceptionally brave warrior, and he became second chief of the Salish at the death of Chief Ambrose in 1871. He was part Nez Perce, but lived all his life with the Salish. After moving from the Bitter-root Valley to the Flathead Reservation in 1873, he was a frequent critic of the operation of the Flathead Agency and the St. Ignatius Mission. Despite his unhappiness, he cooperated with Flathead Agent Peter Ronan in keeping peace on the reservation and was a prominent speaker at church celebrations. Almost all we know about his views were recorded by his opponents, but he was obviously a capable, opinionated person who would not agree to let white men run tribal affairs.[1]

Arlee became well known as a warrior, but only a few examples of his bravery were recorded. In 1835 Arlee had a horse shot out from under him while leading the attack on a retreating party of Blackfeet who had just killed three

Hawaiian Hudson's Bay Company employees at Evaro. According to Duncan McDonald, Arlee was "in many big battles which took place between the various western tribes."[2]

In addition to his war exploits, Arlee was a successful farmer and rancher in the Bitterroot Valley. In 1860 or 1861, Arlee traded 3¾ bushels of wheat to Thomas W. Harris, a white man living in the Bitterroot Valley, in exchange for $18.00 in merchandise at the local store. On February 20, 1864, Arlee sold Harris a two year old steer.[3]

Arlee was elected second chief of the Bitterroot Salish in 1871. According to Duncan McDonald, the younger Salish were worried that, since Charlo did not drink or gamble, they needed a second chief who would be less severe: "So the young gamblers elected Arlee as second Chief. But Arelee [sic] fooled the gamblers & wets. & reformed. change to a good sober temperate man he was more severe one than Charlo."[4]

Angus McDonald described the twenty year old Arlee as "a bold, well proportioned youth," but in later years Arlee was corpulent. In 1877 Bishop James O'Connor described Arlee: "He wore a white Kossuth hat and a blue blanket, and an eagle's wing hung at his girdle. Obesity had taken all grace from his figure, but I thought I had never seen a finer head or face than his. I could hardly take my eyes off him." Peter Ronan's wife, Mary, described Arlee as "a fat and pompous monarch." In 1887 he was five feet four inches tall and weighed over two hundred pounds.[5]

In 1872, when Congressman James Garfield came to the Bitterroot Valley to negotiate with the Salish, Arlee and Adolph agreed to leave, but Charlo refused. Arlee worried that the government would take the Jocko Valley from the Salish just as they had the Bitterroot Valley, but he finally signed.[6] Arlee and five related families moved from the Bitterroot Valley to the Jocko Valley on the Flathead Indian Reservation in 1873. Later that year, Flathead Agent Daniel Shanahan had the federal government recognize Arlee as head chief of all the Salish.[7] With the support of Agent Charles Medary, Arlee organized a police force among the Salish in 1875 which was under Arlee's control.[8]

Between 1875 and 1877, Arlee was involved in a bitter fight with Flathead Indian Agent Charles S. Medary. Arlee's opposition to Medary had some support from Chief Michelle of the Pend d'Oreilles, and considerable financial and legal support from T. J. Demers, a white Frenchtown merchant who had married into the tribes. Arlee's complaints about Flathead Agency management under Medary were aired in Montana Territory newspapers and a federal grand jury. Arlee made so much trouble for Medary that the Commissioner of Indian Affairs asked for Medary's resignation. Basically Arlee and his allies were able to run the agent out of town.[9]

Arlee frequently criticized the Jesuit missionaries at St. Ignatius Mission, but also took a leading role in church festivals. In 1875, missionary Philip Rappagliosi, S.J., visited Arlee in the Jocko Valley and tried to mollify Arlee's anger at the mission. Rappagliosi never really explained Arlee's complaints and believed Arlee was motivated only by an irrational pique. Whatever the basis of Arlee's feelings, Rappagliosi claimed he won Arlee "back completely," and Arlee came to St. Ignatius for the next Easter feast.[10] In July 1883, Arlee complained to U.S. Indian Inspector S. S. Benedict about the management of the St. Ignatius Mission school and said "he wants his people to be taught something besides how to pray." Ronan argued in two letters, November 24,

1883, and December 26, 1883, that Arlee was just a general complainer motivated by greed.[11]

That fall, Arlee repeated his complaints about the mission school to Senator G. G. Vest and his party who were visiting Flathead Agency. Vest concluded Arlee was upset because his son had been put to work on the harvest while a student at the school. Ronan made the same argument in his letter of November 24, 1883.[12] In 1887, Arlee wrote the "Supretenant of indian Afares" complaining about the Flathead Agency and St. Ignatius Mission: "we have a Cotholic Skool here 23 years and none of my children Can reade or write yet. we want a skoole here. we dont want any Priests they are no good."[13]

But, even as Arlee complained about the missionaries, he was an active speaker and participant in church celebrations. According to an oral tradition, on Christmas Day 1876 Arlee was on the buffalo plains and led a Christian religious service to celebrate the occasion.[14] A Helena newspaper story about the 1882 St. Ignatius Day celebration reported that after the school program was completed, Arlee spoke to the assembled crowd in Salish. He welcomed Archbishop Charles Seghers to the mission, condemned the young Indians for drinking and fighting, and led the crowd in the rosary. Arlee also spoke at the 1884 St. Ignatius Day celebration, but then his speech was that the school exhibition was "all very good but that he was very hungry, and that it was time to go and eat."[15]

Arlee's relations with Agent Peter Ronan could also be contradictory: including both support and complaints about how Ronan ran the agency. On July 11, 1877, Ronan reported that Arlee swore that he and his people would defend the white people against the hostile Nez Perces. During the fall of 1881, Arlee was said to have told General John Gibbon that his opinion of Ronan was positive: "As the agent of the government we respect him; as a friend, an advisor and a neighbor, we love him, and I trust I may never live to see the appointment of his successor."[16] In 1882 a Col. Warrington visited the Flathead Reservation and Arlee's house. Warrington recollected that Arlee had a log cabin with a fenced yard which also enclosed a tepee and estimated that Arlee was worth some twenty thousand dollars. The cabin contained "a rusty stove, with an old tin coffee-pot on it, a deal table, a chair, a pile of blankets down in one corner, for a bed" and a picture of President James Garfield on the wall.[17]

Arlee could be very diplomatic in his personal relations. On one occasion he informed Ronan's young daughter, Mary, that she had been given the Indian name of "Red Hair," but little Mary objected. Arlee then declared that the girl's Indian name would be "Pretty Hair," which met with the her approval.[18]

In August 1882 Arlee played a prominent role in the negotiations between the Flathead Reservation tribes and Joseph McCammon for the sale of the right-of-way for the Northern Pacific Railroad through the reservation. Arlee wanted the railroad to head down the Clark's Fork River and by-pass the reservation, but McCammon said he was not able to change the route. Arlee countered by asking for a million dollars for the right-of-way. A shocked McCammon argued that the whole reservation was not worth that much. McCammon finally conceded that the reservation might be worth a million dollars to the tribes, but refused to offer more than $16,000 plus reimbursement for the timber used by the railroad. The chiefs got McCammon to promise to use his influence to get the Upper Flathead Valley added to the reservation. With this concession, the chiefs finally agreed to let the railroad have use of the land

— but not to outright sell the right-of-way land — and they signed the agreement. The written agreement, however, had language transferring full title to the right-of-way land to the railroad. McCammon did submit a request to the Department of Interior to enlarge the reservation, but by 1883 the tribes decided they could not risk any boundary changes and dropped the idea.[19]

On June 21, 1882, Koonsa Finley murdered Frank Marengo on the reservation during a drinking party. After sobering up, Koonsa went to Chief Michelle and confessed. Arlee and Michelle took Koonsa's horses and put him in the tribal jail as punishment for the murder. To Ronan's disgust, the U.S. District Court dismissed federal murder charges against Koonsa, because he had already been tried for the crime under tribal law and prosecution in federal court would be double jeopardy which was prohibited under the U.S. Constitution.[20]

This case was the opening volley in a long running battle between Arlee and Ronan over control of law and order on the reservation. Arlee's testimony in the federal case against Koonsa in late 1882 was published in a local newspaper. Arlee defended traditional Indian justice dispensed by the chiefs which did not allow for long terms in the territorial prison in Deer Lodge or hanging. Arlee also claimed that the white men who sold the liquor shared responsibility for the murder: "When an Indian is drunk and kills another Indian we don't consider that he did anything. The Indian never had whiskey before the white man came here, and we blame the white people who gave him the liquor."[21]

Ronan and Arlee cooperated to arrange a series of foot and horse races by tribal members during the summer of 1883 to entertain a group of Northern Pacific Railroad officials who were visiting the Jocko Valley. The white visitors paid for the prizes for the winners.[22]

On December 4, 1883, Inspector C. H. Howard reported to the Secretary of Interior about complaints by Indians on the Flathead Reservation. Most of the complaints seem to have come from Arlee. Arlee's criticisms indicated Agent Ronan had stolen agency cattle and ran his personal cattle with the stock of white men trespassing on the reservation. But when Howard questioned Peter Finley, who Arlee claimed originally made the allegations, Finley denied the charges.[23] According to Ronan's January 15, 1884b, letter, Arlee later recanted and claimed the charges against Ronan were based on hearsay. Tribal members Louison and Thomas McDonald supported Ronan's rebuttal to the charges.

In December 1885, Arlee joined other tribal leaders and Agent Ronan to defuse a hazardous situation that developed from the killing of an intoxicated Indian by the white trader and the white postmaster at Arlee station. The crisis brought the Missoula County Sheriff and an armed white posse on the reservation. The sheriff wanted to arrest the surviving Indian involved in the altercation, Big Jim, and take him to Missoula. Some tribal members wanted to keep Big Jim on the reservation to try him under tribal law. Arlee supported allowing the sheriff to take Big Jim to Missoula to avoid conflict with the whites. The final decision by the assembled tribal members was to let the sheriff take Big Jim to be tried by the white justice system. In the end, the two white men were released by the court on the basis of self-defense and Big Jim was released for lack of evidence.[24]

In the final years of his life, Arlee opposed the Flathead Agency sponsored courts and police established in 1885, which undermined the authority of the traditional chiefs on the reservation. In an April 29, 1887, speech on the reservation before the Northwest Indian Commission, Arlee said, "We don't want any judges or policemen. We want the chiefs to rule the people." Arlee charged that the judges had a sick man and a pregnant woman whipped and the woman had a miscarriage.[25]

Ronan wrote on January 1, 1887, about his efforts to arrest a member of Arlee's household who had been accused of adultery. Arlee's refusal to acknowledge the authority of the agency court and police led to an impasse where Ronan would no longer deal with Arlee on tribal business. Ronan also charged that Arlee had received money from the government and grown personally rich and greedy. The characterization of Arlee as personally greedy was also made by Agent Medary during their battles in the middle 1870s. Unfortunately we do not have Chief Arlee's side of the argument to balance the charges against him.

Arlee did become well-to-do on the reservation. On March 19, 1878, Ronan reported that Arlee, his son, and his daughter together owned 2 hogs, 100 cattle, and 100 horses. In his August 1885 annual report, Ronan credited Arlee as having 160 acres under fence and an 1884 crop of 800 bushels of wheat and oats. In his August 17, 1885, testimony, Ronan listed Arlee as having 100 horses and 150 cattle.

In early 1889, the conflict between Arlee and the agency sanctioned tribal court flared up again. Arlee made two trips to the offices of *The Weekly Missoulian* to complain about "merciless" whippings administered by the tribal judges to both men and women: "Recently, it is claimed, men and women have been beaten cruelly and out of all reason." During his second visit, Arlee's "right hand man" claimed "an Indian who had broke jail was hung up by his hands and kept there for forty-eight hours. An Indian woman who is supposed to have deserted her husband was given 120 lashes and is now lying in a precarious condition and her recovery is extremely doubtful." Arlee wanted offenders to be punished "just as white people are punished; no more and no less."[26] In letters to the Commissioner of Indian Affairs on May 1, 1889, and June 17, 1889, and a May 14, 1889, article in *The Helena Independent*, Ronan argued that Arlee's only supporters were murderers and rapists, particularly Larra Finley, who made "sensational and lying complains against the cruelty of the Indian police."[27]

On August 8, 1889, Arlee died at his house in the Jocko Valley of dropsy at about 74 years of age. On his death bed Arlee was surrounded by his relatives, tribal leaders, and Agent Ronan and other agency employees. He had recently been visited by Bishop John Brondel and Father Jerome D'Aste, S.J., who gave him the last rites of the Roman Catholic Church. According to Mary Ronan, his funeral was "a grand occasion and Indians gathered from far and wide to attend." His funeral was at the Jocko Church and his burial in the Jocko Cemetery. One account said over a half a dozen fat steers were roasted for the funeral feast.[28]

Much of the surviving evidence about Chief Arlee's life is contradictory and incomplete. He was a dynamic but enigmatic figure in Flathead Reservation history.

Chief Charlo

(Little-Claw-of-a-Grizzly-Bear)

Salish

(1830-1910)

Charlo succeeded his father, Victor, as chief of the Bitterroot Salish tribe in 1870. He continued Victor's policies of allying with the white men against the Blackfeet, Sioux, and other Plains tribes, and protecting the tribe's right to their homeland in the Bitterroot Valley. As the buffalo declined, he worked hard to expand the tribe's farms and stock herds to maintain its economic independence.

In his July 11, 1877, letter, Flathead Indian Agent Peter Ronan reported that Charlo refused to join the Nez Perce in fighting the white settlers. Charlo said he and his tribe would protect the Bitterroot whites if needed, but otherwise would not attack the Nez Perce. Charlo wanted peace with the white people, but insisted that a correct interpretation of the 1855 Hellgate Treaty entitled the Salish to a reservation in the Bitterroot Valley.[29]

Father Lawrence Palladino, S.J., characterized Charlo as

a man of a quiet yet firm disposition, a true representative of his race and a thorough Indian. . . . His conduct during the Nez Percés outbreak gained him the admiration of all, and proved once more the loyal friendship for the whites on the part of the Flat Heads. . . . But while friendly toward the whites, he surely is not in love with their ways. . . .Charlot is a sincere and practical Christian.[30]

Between 1877, when Ronan began his term, and 1889, Charlo worked to develop his farm and encouraged other tribal members to do the same. In 1877 a newspaper reporter described his farm:

Charlos, the Flathead chief, has a home in their [the Bitterroot Flathead settlement's] midst. His dwelling is a two-story log house with four rooms, and his farm which covers over a pretty little park before his house, encloses seven or eight acres, upon which there is a good growing crop of wheat.[31]

In 1889, the Bitterroot Salish and their white neighbors suffered through a record drought and the resulting poverty forced Charlo and the Salish to agree to remove to the Jocko Valley.

Between January and March 1884, Charlo, four other Bitterroot Salish leaders, interpreter Michel Revais, and Ronan visited Washington, D.C. The government tried to induce the Salish to move to the Flathead Reservation, but Charlo insisted he only wanted to secure the tribe's right to remain in the Bitterroot Valley. Their time in Washington was well documented in Ronan's surviving writings and correspondence. While in Washington, Charlo had a successful operation to remove cataracts from his eyes.

In the Bitterroot Valley during the 1880s, Charlo and the other Salish maintained a delicate balance trying to protect their rights while also maintaining peace with their white neighbors. Ronan's November 1, 1881, letter described Charlo's efforts to get justice for the murder of Cayuse Pierre in a drunken brawl with two white men in Stevensville.

Ronan's letters gave only brief glimpses of the 1889 negotiations between Henry B. Carrington and the Salish, where drought and poverty finally forced Charlo and the Salish to agree to leave the Bitterroot Valley. The letters do detail the further impoverishment of the Salish between 1889 and 1891 resulting from the delay in the removal which Carrington promised would happen in the spring of 1890.

After the removal in 1891, Ronan had trouble getting the government to fund the promises Carrington had made to Charlo and the other Salish. In his March 10, 1892, letter Ronan described turning the agency farm over to Charlo in lieu of the late Chief Arlee's farm which Carrington had promised. Ronan's November 30, 1892a, letter related the difficulties the Salish had in getting the government to pay them for the Bitterroot allotments as they were sold.

On the reservation, Charlo worked hard to preserve the tribal culture and ways and was worried about the negative impact schooling would have on Salish youth. An Ursuline Nun working at the Jocko Agency school during the early 1890s described dealing with Charlo:

> The chief was an Indian to the core. Although he had always been on good terms with the whites, he detested their ways. "Our children," he objected, "will learn English in school. When they know English, they will go to the white towns and buy whiskey. The white man would not understand them if they spoke in Indian. In the school the hair of our children will be cut. We do not wish to see them with short hair. Only the white man was made by God to wear his hair short. God made the Indian with long hair. Our children will become like whites in other ways in school and, when they grow up they will fly away like birds and leave their parents.". . . . The chief protested up to the very day we opened [the Jocko school]. Nevertheless, he sent his own son, little Victor.[32]

Charlo joined the other tribal leaders on the reservation in fighting to protect the reservation land base from white encroachment. During the early twentieth century he fought vigorously to prevent the reservation from being allotted and "surplus" land sold to white settlers. He died in the Jocko in 1910 just as the government was completing the forced allotment and opening of the reservation without tribal consent.[33]

Chief Eneas Big Knife

Kootenai

(1828-1900)

Eneas, the chief of the Dayton Creek or Ksanka Kootenai for thirty-five years was born in 1828 to an Iroquois father, Big Knife, and a Kootenai mother, Suzette or Ahn-Akah.[34] The historical evidence suggested he was a remarkable man, and Flathead Indian Agent Peter Ronan obviously came to respect him highly over their years working together. During the 1880s and early 1890s, the reservation Kootenai faced white aggression in the Upper Flathead Valley, but somehow the Kootenai under Eneas' leadership were able to avoid war and continue the struggle to protect their interests and rights. The government often failed to fulfill its promises to protect Kootenai property and rights, but the small band avoided the destruction and death that could have resulted from open warfare.

As a young man, Eneas was a leading warrior and a war chief. He took part in repeated battles with the Blackfeet, Cree, and other tribes.[35] At six feet four inches tall, Eneas was an imposing figure.[36] According to Flathead Agent Charles Hutchins, Eneas became head chief on January 1, 1865, after his predecessor, Battiste, was killed by the Blackfeet while returning from the buffalo country. Eneas was only 37 years old then. In 1866, Flathead Agent Augustus Chapman requested funds to build a house for Eneas and his family.[37]

In his first annual report on August 13, 1877, Flathead Indian Agent Peter Ronan wrote that Eneas was "better respected and has more influence among his people than any other chief on the reservation." Ronan was especially impressed that Eneas used his salary as chief to purchase a mowing and reaping machine and a set of blacksmith's tools for the use of his tribe. Eneas was "a good man, kind and generous, and spends all the money he receives from Government in relieving the wants of his poor and struggling people." In his August 12, 1879, report, Ronan commended Eneas for working to induce the Kootenai to turn to farming to replace the declining game and gathering resources in western Montana. By 1879, the Kootenai had enclosed several farms.

By August 1885, Eneas and the Kootenai had 200 acres fenced and "about 1,000 bushels of wheat [were] raised in common, besides potatoes, turnips, cabbage, onions, carrots, parsnips, peas, &c." But farming in common offended Ronan's Euro-American cultural values, and in August 15, 1886, Ronan proposed that a farmer be employed to show the Kootenai how to set up individual family farms like white people had.

In 1883 when Joseph McCammon came to Montana to negotiate for the sale of the right-of-way for the Northern Pacific Railroad to cross the reservation, Eneas emphasized the importance of the reservation to the tribes. Eneas questioned selling part of the reservation because: "It is a small country; it is valuable to us; we support ourselves by it; there is no end to these lands supporting us; they will do it for generations."[38]

Due to their location on the northern boundary of the reservation, the Kootenai were particularly affected by problems with the survey of the reservation boundary. Eneas and the Kootenai thought the northern line followed a ridge of hills which provided a well defined natural boundary. The official survey placed the line several miles south of the natural boundary. In the twentieth century the U.S. Court of Claims decided the official boundary had been in error but still placed the line south of the boundary preferred by the Kootenai. This change in the northern boundary made it harder to keep white owned cattle off the reservation and also cut off hay and pasture land used for years by the Kootenai. Some of the white cattle owners paid Eneas for grazing, but trespassing cattle and loss of land caused problems for Eneas and his tribe for the rest of the nineteenth century.

During the late 1880s and early 1890s, the Kootenai continued to exercise their right to seasonally hunt, fish, and gather plants in the Upper Flathead Valley. Most of the Kootenai-white interactions were peaceful but some were complicated by language and cultural differences, alcohol, and white aggression. In 1888, two reservation Kootenai were lynched for murdering two white men at the head of Flathead Lake in 1887. After the lynching, an armed mob of white men invaded the reservation and confronted Eneas and the Kootenai. Eneas kept calm and was able to defuse the crisis and no further violence broke out. Eneas did not object to the punishment of Kootenai murderers, but he felt they should at least receive a fair trial.[39]

In 1889, Eneas kept up his efforts to get justice while avoiding open warfare. Two white men killed a Kootenai Indian in an altercation that probably involved alcohol. Eneas threatened to kill the two guilty whites but made clear that other white people would not be harmed.[40]

In a June 8, 1889, council with Ronan and a special agent of the U.S. Justice Department about the whiskey problem, Eneas emphasized his work to punish Kootenai guilty of violence resulting from alcohol use. Traditional Kootenai practice had the chief use the whip to punish lawbreakers, but white officials opposed whipping because it offended nineteenth century white sensibilities. Eneas complained that without the whip, he could not control tribal members who got drunk and committed adultery or other crimes. He pointed out that the Kootenai did not have good jails, so he had no alternative punishment available. One account quotes Delima Demers Clifford, a tribal member, as seeing Eneas drinking alcohol on New Years Eve 1887. But, even if Eneas was not a teetotaler, he vigorously opposed the violence and other crimes that sometimes resulted from drinking.[41]

Eneas' struggle to get justice for the Kootenai while keeping the peace struck a personal note in August 1889 when his son, Samuel, was murdered by white people in Demersville. Eneas traveled to Demersville to find out what happened. The white people fed the Kootenai but refused to help bring the murderer to justice. The Demersville whites fumed and ranted that Eneas' visit had been an invasion. Ronan put Eneas' side of the story in writing, sent it to Washington, D.C., and had it published in a Helena newspaper and the Commissioner of Indian Affairs' annual report.[42] In December, Ronan tried to get the case before a grand jury, but the jury adjourned before he was able to get Eneas and the Indian witnesses to the courthouse. No one was ever punished for the murder.[43]

In July 1890, U.S. Army troops and a posse of white men surrounded the Kootenai camp and demanded that Eneas surrender Kootenai Indians accused of murdering white men. Eneas offered to cooperate, but he asked why white men who killed Kootenai were not also punished. According to newspaper reports, Missoula County Sheriff William Houston held Eneas hostage until the accused Indian murderers were surrendered, but Ronan's letters suggested Eneas decided himself to help the sheriff. Ronan wrote that Eneas did not object to Indians murderers being punished but wanted equal justice for white people who murdered Indians.[44] Father Jerome D'Aste, S.J., recorded the hostage version of Eneas' role in his diary.[45] One newspaper account noted that "it is largely due to his [Eneas'] aid that Pascale and other Indian criminals have been apprehended."[46] Two Kootenai Indians were convicted in a Montana court of murder and hung in Missoula in December 1890.

In January 1891, Robert H. Irvine, a mixed blood tribal member chosen by Eneas, was finally appointed as Kootenai farmer and moved to Dayton Creek to begin work. That October Eneas and the Kootenai brought several wagonloads of wheat to the agency to be ground into flour. The trip of 60 miles to the agency took six days and a ferry crossing the Flathead River at the Foot of Flathead Lake. According to Ronan, Eneas was "much elated at the acchievement [sic]."[47] That summer Eneas and the reservation Kootenai extended an invitation to the Bonners Ferry Kootenai to settle with them at Dayton Creek.[48]

In August 1891 Ronan traveled to the Kootenai camp and laid out off-reservation allotments for land just north of the official reservation boundary. The land had been used by the Kootenai for years believing it was on the reservation. Unfortunately, by December of that year, white homesteaders were already jumping the Kootenai allotments. Ronan was able to get the government to remove the first white trespassers, but others persisted in harassing the Kootenai farmers.[49]

In one particularly egregious example of white belligerence, Clarence Proctor actually built a fence around the improvements of a Kootenai farmer and claimed the right to the land in the enclosure, including the Kootenai farm.[50] In another case, Eugene McCarthy, a white settler who had worked on the erroneous boundary survey, claimed the land of a Kootenai farmer, Jean Jan Graw (Gingras), which contained a house, barn, and enclosed field that the Kootenai had occupied for twelve years. Eneas was crippled by rheumatism and hindered by language problems, but he tried to explain to McCarthy that the land belonged to the Kootenai farmer as a result of years of occupancy and a government allotment. McCarthy then proceeded to Demersville and filed charges against Eneas claiming that Eneas had personally threatened him. Ronan put up a bond for Eneas to appear in court on the charge since Eneas was too sick to travel just then. Apparently the charges were later dropped as the case dragged on in the courts.[51] The restraint shown by Eneas and the aggrieved Kootenai farmers was remarkable. No open conflict flared, but white trespassers continued over the years to encroach on the Kootenai claims, and, after Ronan died in 1893, no one else seemed to pressure the government to act. Finally in the early twentieth century the Kootenai had lost possession of almost all of the allotments and the government pressured the Kootenai allottees to relinquish their claims in return for small payments from the white trespassers.

On February 1, 1894, Eneas, most reservation tribal leaders, and many tribal members signed a petition asking for a resurvey of the northern boundary of the reservation, but then agent Joseph Carter panned it as a "matter worthy of little attention." The Commissioner of Indian Affairs refused to consider a resurvey.[52] In 1895 Eneas returned Goosta, a Kootenai Indian accused of horse stealing, to jail after he escaped.[53] Eneas was again called upon to defend the tribe in 1898 when Missoula County tried to tax most of the mixed bloods and adopted tribal members on the reservation. When Eneas claimed jurisdiction over the reservation and tribal members, the Missoula Deputy County Treasurer replied: "What I want to tell that old Indian is that he may go to h---. . . . Tell him that this is not his country, but that it belongs to the government at Washington." Fortunately, despite the racist hostility of the county officials the government won most of the court cases against the taxes.[54]

In much of the late 1890s, Eneas was confined to his bed and not able to exercise his authority as chief. Father Augustine Dimier, S.J., complained that Eneas' disability permitted gambling and other sins to re-infect Kootenai life.[55] Eneas died in 1900.[56]

Louison

Kulkul-Snine

(Red Owl)

Salish/Nez Perce

(1836-1912)

In the 1880s, Louison was a wealthy rancher, farmer, and tribal judge living in the Jocko Valley. He was on the first Flathead Reservation Court of Indian Offenses and supported Ronan's efforts to expand the agricultural economy on the reservation. He also backed the tribal judges in their competition with the chiefs to control law and order. But he either did not agree with the government efforts to repress traditional dances and social gatherings or changed his mind in the 1890s. The surviving historical record is incomplete, but Louison was an influential leader of strong opinions and character.

He was half Nez Perce and half Salish. His father was Red Owl, an important Nez Perce leader during the Nez Perce War.[57] According to Ronan's account, in January 1884 Louison defended Ronan against Chief Arlee's charge that Ronan had allowed a white man to steal Indian cattle. Louison thought Arlee had grown senile.[58]

Louison had 100 acres under fence in the Jocko Valley in 1885 and in 1884 had produced 300 bushels of grain. Ronan reported that in 1885 Louison had 200 horses and 160 cattle.[59] An 1891 report by Special Agent Horatio L. Steward stated Louison had a big herd of cattle and horses and was worth $15,000 or $20,000.[60]

On February 14, 1885, Ronan nominated Louison as one of the first judges in the Court of Indian Offenses. Ronan described the new judges as "among the most influential best behaved and reliable of the Indians of this reserve."[61] On January 1, 1887, Ronan described Louison and the other judges as "the most intelligent, honest and industrious Indians on the reserve" who "appreciate largely the new order of things and the necessity for self support by honest industry."[62]

Mary Ronan, the agent's wife, described Louison as

> a self-important individual who elaborated his beaded and fringed Indian costume with a tall beaver hat of the kind modish for evening wear for gentlemen of fashion in the late seventies and eighties. His superiority complex was owing to his marriage with a wealthy [woman] . . . . Sunday after Sunday, after church services he would assemble the Indian congregation around him and deliver a long harangue, harping always on the same theme and bewailing, "Oh, the times. Oh, the manners. Oh, the customs."[63]

Mary attributed much of Louison's economic success to the business acumen of his wife, Christine.[64]

General Henry B. Carrington described Louison's appearance on the occasion of the Bitterroot Salish arrival at Jocko in 1891. Louison was "a man rich in cattle and horses, and on this occasion brilliantly combining rare Indian ornaments with the military blouse, brass buttons, stove-pipe hat and other emblems of his judicial, military and police dignity."[65]

By 1890, however, Ronan was becoming disappointed with most of the tribal judges, including Louison. During 1889 and 1891, the soldiers from Fort Missoula, the Missoula County Sheriff, and a posse of neighboring white men invaded the reservation seeking to arrest Indians accused of murdering white men. Tribal members, however, were unhappy because white men who had killed Indians were not also being pursued. In his August 14, 1890, annual report, Ronan described the judges, including Louison, as "progressive in the way of stock-raising, farming, etc., and also of good character," but, "With the exception, however, of Joseph Ka-too-lay-uch, they are vacillating and weak and afraid to face responsibilities or to oppose with sufficient energy and decision the lawless and non-progressive."[66] Unfortunately we do not have Louison's side of the story.

During the winter of 1890-1891, Ronan accused Louison of encouraging a "dancing craze" among the non-progressive Indians as Louison and Big Sam competed to replace the recently deceased Arlee as chief. According to Ronan, the dancing craze subsided after he threatened to call army troops from Fort Missoula.[67] Finally in 1892, Ronan dismissed Louison as judge.[68] Louison may have supported Ronan in expanding agriculture and stock raising on the reservation, while at the same time he opposed government efforts to criminalize traditional dances and ceremonies. It was also possible Louison changed his views over the years.

Louison may not have always agreed with Ronan, but his disagreements with Joseph Carter, the next Flathead Agent, led to open conflict in 1895. The surviving accounts are one-sided and confusing, but apparently Carter had Louison arrested and put in the agency jail for encouraging a traditional dance. A group of tribal members led by Swasah, Nicolla and Louis Coull-Coullee tried to break Louison out of the agency jail, but were overpowered, sent to Missoula, and placed in the county jail. The would-be rescuers were freed on a writ of habeas corpus secured by an attorney hired by Duncan McDonald. The charges against the rescuers were re-filed and the case proceeded to federal court in Helena. Presumably Louison received a short sentence in the agency jail and was released soon after. Duncan McDonald argued that the episode that led to Louison's arrest was the result of poor translation and misunderstanding.[69]

Carter and Louison must have reconciled, as Carter reappointed Louison as a tribal judge in 1897. Louison continued to serve as judge until at least 1909.[70] In 1898, Louison traveled to Omaha, Nebraska, as part of the Flathead Reservation delegation to the Indian Congress at the Trans-Mississippi Exposition.[71] Louison died in 1912 at about the age of 75 years.[72]

Chief Michelle
Pend d'Oreille
(1805-1897)

Chief Michelle of the Upper Pend d'Oreille Indians actively worked to maintain peace with the white settlers and supported the missionaries at St. Ignatius Mission. Most accounts suggest he was less active and influential in tribal affairs than his predecessor Alexander. He was spokesman for decisions reached by the tribal community, often after long hours of collective deliberation.[73]

According to information that probably came from Michelle Revais, the Pend d'Oreille Flathead Agency Interpreter, Michelle was elected Pend d'Oreille chief in 1868. Michelle had previously been only a minor chief, but two more senior sub-chiefs, Andre and Pierre, declined the office. Little has been recorded about his life before 1868.[74]

The one event before 1868 that has been documented was the 1864 lynching of Michelle's son by white miners at Hell Gate, near present day Missoula. A white miner named Ward had been killed near Hell Gate by an Indian in the fall of 1863. Michelle's son was accused of the murder but maintained his innocence. According to an account given by Michelle in the early 1880s, Michelle asked his son to "sacrifice his life for the good of his people" and "go bravely to death" to avoid war with the whites. His son was lynched and later evidence indicted the murder had been committed by an Indian from another tribe.[75]

Michelle was known for his Christian piety and loyalty to the missionaries. In 1882 he delivered a speech at the St. Ignatius Day celebrations, but the topic was not recorded. According to Duncan McDonald, Michelle "punishes severely to this day any member of his tribe who refuses to believe in his creed." McDonald also reported that sometime around 1870, Chief Michelle used traditional Indian medicine to attract buffalo to a Pend d'Oreille hunting camp on the Plains. He may have valued the power of both Christianity and traditional Pend d'Oreille religious beliefs.[76]

Michelle suffered a tragic accident in late April 1872 when he was thrown from his horse and dislocated his hip. The agency doctor and Father Anthony Ravalli were not able to reset the joint, and Michelle was crippled for the rest of his life.[77]

In December 1873, Michelle recounted the recent history of conflict between the Pend d'Oreille and the Crow Indians. The Crows had killed four Pend d'Oreille during the summer of 1873, including Michelle's father-in-law Cow-ackan. During spring 1873, the Crows killed two more Pend d'Oreille and wounded three women and a boy. One of the women was not expected to survive. The Crows stole 31 Pend d'Oreille horses and a mule from a hunting camp in the Little Blackfoot in the fall of 1872. Ten years before, in 1863, the Crows stole 80 Pend d'Oreille horses and blamed it on the Snakes, igniting a war between the Pend d'Oreille and the Snakes. Michelle complained: "When we go to the Crow country we always go in peace but the Crows always attack us first."[78]

Michelle swore out a statement on May 2, 1874, before a justice of the peace complaining about Flathead Agent Daniel Shanahan. The statement was forwarded to Washington, D.C., by T. J. Demers, a white Frenchtown merchant who had married into the tribes. Michelle accused Shanahan of stealing tribal annuities and of trying to force off the reservation five white men who had tribal member wives and had mixed blood children. Michelle also complained that Shanahan had stopped the treaty payments to the St. Ignatius Mission schools. Other treaty promises of services to the tribes had never been fulfilled. Michelle wanted Shanahan removed as agent and asked that "the choice of an agent for them [the Flathead Reservation tribes] be left to the Indians themselves and that they by Election or otherwise with the approval of the reverend fathers of the mission — shall name who shall be agent for them."[79]

During 1874, Chiefs Michelle and Arlee demanded that the agency employees cut their hay and grain. Agent Peter Whaley asked the Commissioner of

Indian Affairs for instructions because while Michelle was poor and crippled, Arlee was well-to-do and, according to Whaley, did not need the help.[80] In his September 12, 1874, annual report, Whaley reported that, while on the annual buffalo hunt, the Pend d'Oreille stole horses from other tribes and refused to return them. Since Michelle was crippled, he could no longer accompany the buffalo hunters and was unable to stop the raids. Michelle was "powerless to exact obedience to his commands." Whaley wanted the government to promote the second chief, Andre, to head the Pend d'Oreille, because Andre "appears to have the confidence of his people and to influence them according to his will."[81]

Michelle's dealings with Flathead Agent Charles S. Medary between 1875 and 1877 were also stormy. Michelle supported Chief Arlee's complaints against Medary about the operation of the agency. In December, Michelle, Arlee, and Duncan McDonald, a mixed blood trader on the reservation, traveled to Deer Lodge to present their complaints to the United States grand jury. Most of the indictments referred to the failure of the government to fulfill promises made in the 1855 Hellgate Treaty and 1872 agreement between Congressman James Garfield and the Bitterroot Salish. During the 1870s, Michelle lived on a farm near the agency in the Jocko Valley while most of the Pend d'Oreille lived near the St. Ignatius Mission in the Lower Flathead Valley. Since Michelle did not live among his tribe and could not accompany them on the buffalo hunts, in 1875 Medary wrote that Andre was "chief in all but drawing a salary from the Government." Medary did claim in September 1876 that he had convinced Michelle to give up the practice of whipping women who were guilty of adultery.[82]

Michelle's relations with Flathead Agent Peter Ronan, 1877-1893, were much more cordial. In his July 11, 1877, letter during the Nez Perce War crisis, Ronan wrote that Michelle joined the other reservation chiefs in promising to maintain peace with the whites. Michelle personally assured the Ronan family of protection during the scare and offered to guard the agency.[83]

In his August 13, 1877, annual report, Ronan wrote that Michelle had lost influence among the Pend d'Oreille because he lived at the agency, some twenty miles from most of the tribe, and could no longer travel on the buffalo hunts. Ronan concluded that Michelle "has in a great measure lost control, a fact which he is well aware of himself, as he came to consult in regard to removing from the agency and going back among his people, with a view of regaining his lost influence." On March 19, 1878, Michelle lived in the Jocko Valley and had 26 cattle and 19 horses.

Ronan forwarded a report to the Commissioner of Indian Affairs on July 29, 1878, about a July 14, 1878, council with Chief Michelle about recent violence committed by some Nez Perce refugees returning from exile in Canada. Michelle informed Ronan of a message he had received from Sitting Bull threatening the Pend d'Oreille if they did not join the fight against the whites. Michelle replied that the Pend d'Oreille were friends of the whites and traditional enemies of the Sioux. He assured Sitting Bull that: "We are not well armed, and have nearly forgotten the modes of war; but a mouse though small, if trodden upon will turn and bite. Tell your chief if he comes we will give him battle, and die by our homes." When asked to provide scouts to watch for possible war parties coming west across the mountains, Michelle agreed, but only if the scouts were given supplies, arms, and pay and were under his and Ronan's control.[84]

In November 1878, Michelle demonstrated his personal diplomatic skills when he bestowed his Indian name, Plenty Grizzly Bear, on the Ronans' newborn son. Michelle then had no Indian name until the Lower Kalispel granted him permission to take the Indian name of their recently deceased chief, Man Who Regrets His Country. The name transfers were formally announced at the 1878 Christmas celebrations at St. Ignatius Mission.[85]

Koonsa Finley committed murder on June 21, 1882, but, after sobering up, he went to Chief Michelle and confessed. Michelle and Arlee took Finley's horses and put him in the tribal jail for a short term. When Ronan came to arrest Finley and transport him to Missoula, Michelle argued that he was chief and had already decided the case. Ronan countered that Finley had committed an offense against the United States government and so fell under the jurisdiction of the agent and the federal courts. Finley was tried for murder in the United States court in Deer Lodge but was released because he had already been tried and punished under tribal law. This frustrated Ronan's efforts to try Finley in a white court where he could have been sentenced to the penitentiary at Deer Lodge or hung.[86]

During the September 1882 negotiations between Joseph McCammon of the U.S. Interior Department and the Flathead Reservation tribes for the Northern Pacific Railroad right-of-way, Michelle supported selling the right-of-way. When McCammon replied to Chief Arlee's request for $1,000,000 for the right-of-way by stating that the whole reservation was not worth that much, Michelle was offended: "Now I do not agree with you." McCammon explained that he did not mean the reservation was not worth a million dollars to the Indians. Michelle countered that the government's offer of $15,000 was too low, as after the railroad was completed, it would make that much in a day. Michelle offered to exchange the right-of-way for an extension of the reservation boundary to include the Upper Flathead Valley. During the negotiations Michelle emphasized that the tribes were not selling the land, just the use of the right-of-way:

> Michelle. . . . it is borrowing this strip of land.
>
> Commissioner. It is the use of it.
>
> Michelle. I don't want you, after you get away, to let the white people suppose you have bought the reservation, and let the white people squat on it. That is the way I think. It is like the railroad borrowing the strip of land.
>
> Commissioner. It is just buying the use of the strip of land.

The written agreement, however, said the tribes "do hereby surrender and relinquish to the United States, all the right, title, and interest which they now have" to the right-of-way land.[87]

When Senator G. G. Vest of Missouri and Montana Delegate Martin Maginnis visited the reservation in September 1883, tribal members met for two days ahead of time to discuss the issues and select Michelle to be their spokesman for the collective decisions. Tribal members decided they did not want to run the risk of being cheated in moving the boundary of the reservation north to the Canadian border, so they opposed any boundary changes. The Bitterroot

Salish were welcome to move to the reservation, but the tribes categorically rejected allotment:

> Senator Vest. Don't you think it would be better to have more money and cattle and less land?
>
> Michelle. If I had good and plenty land and few cattle and a little money I would be glad. The reverse would not please me, because my children are cultivating the land more and so get money.

When asked if the St. Ignatius school children were happy, Michelle replied: "Yes; because their fathers send the children to learn, and therefore they will be happy if they are taught to read and write." Michelle also wanted the white people to stop selling liquor and playing cards to the Indians.[88]

The Northwest Indian Commission negotiated with the Flathead Reservation tribes in April 1887, and Michelle declared that the Lower Pend d'Oreille or Kalispel Indians and Spokane Indians would be welcome on the reservation. The proposed agreement also "set apart" two sections of land for the use of the Jesuits and Sisters at the St. Ignatius schools "for educational and religious purposes, as long as they are used for said purposes and no longer." Michelle made sure during the negotiations that the land was being lent and not sold to the the missionaries.[89]

By the middle of the 1880s, Michelle had moved to a ranch on Mud Creek, 16 miles north of the Mission. In 1885 he had 160 acres under fence and in 1884 he raised 250 bushels of wheat and oats. In 1885 he had 20 horses and 15 cattle. In 1887 he purchased $31.00 worth of fruit trees for his ranch.[90]

Some time during the summer or autumn of 1888 Chief Michelle's nephew and family were murdered while hunting in the Sun River area. Evidence found at the scene suggested that the murderers were either white men or Cree mixed bloods. Despite Ronan's efforts to publicize the case and get the local white authorities to investigate, no one was ever charged with the crime.[91]

The white Montana justice authorities showed much more interest in pursuing Indian people who were accused of murdering white people. During August 1890, Missoula County Sheriff William Houston arrested Chief Eneas of the Kootenai and Chief Michelle and held them hostage until local Indian people and the Indian police delivered up tribal members wanted for murdering white men. Baptiste Kakashe and a party of armed Pend d'Oreille tried to force the white posse to release Michelle, but, in order to avoid conflict, Michelle refused to go. Michelle was released after Pierre Paul was captured by the Indian police and a white posse. Ronan gave most of the credit to the Indian police, but the Montana newspapers played up the role of the sheriff and posse.[92]

On May 11, 1897, Chief Michelle died at his home on Mud Creek at the age of 92. He was buried at St. Ignatius Mission.[93]

Photograph credits for Biographical Sketches.

Chief Arlee: Peter Ronan, *Historical Sketch of the Flathead-Indians from the Year 1813 to 1890* (Helena, Mont.: Journal Publishing Co., 1890), page 78.

Chief Charlo: Photograph by John K. Hillers, Bureau of American Ethnology, Washington, D.C., Montana Historical Society Archives, Helena, Mont. (detail from native number 954-526).

Chief Eneas: Archives and Special Collections, Mansfield Library, University of Montana, Missoula, Mont. (photograph number 81-284).

Louison: Photograph by F. A. Rinehart, National Anthropological Archives, Smithsonian Institution, Washington, D.C. (negative number 03545500).

Chief Michelle: Drawing by Gustavus Sohon, National Anthropological Archives, Smithsonian Institution, Washington, D.C. (negative number 08501400).

Footnotes

Abbreviations Used in Footnotes

ARCIA — *Annual Report of the Commissioner of Indian Affairs*

AS — *The Anaconda Standard*

Bigart, *Getting Crops* — Robert J. Bigart, *Getting Good Crops: Economic and Diplomatic Survival Strategies of the Montana Bitterroot Salish Indians, 1870-1891* (Norman: University of Oklahoma Press, 2010)

Bigart, *St. Mary's Mission* — Robert J. Bigart, ed., *Life and Death at St. Mary's Mission, Montana: Births, Marriages, Deaths, and Survival among the Bitterroot Salish Indians, 1866-1891* (Pablo, Mont.: Salish Kootenai College Press, 2005)

Bigart, *Zealous* — Robert J. Bigart, ed., *Zealous in All Virtues: Documents of Worship and Culture Change, St. Ignatius Mission, Montana, 1890-1894* (Pablo: Salish Kootenai College Press, 2007)

CIA — Commissioner of Indian Affairs

DM — *The Daily Missoulian*

Heitman — Francis B. Heitman, *Historical Register and Dictionary of the United States Army* (Washington, D.C.: U.S. Government Printing Office, 1903)

HI — *The Helena Independent* (daily)

HJ — *The Helena Journal*

IL — *The Inter Lake* (Demersville and Kalispell, Mont.)

Mary Ronan, *Girl From the Gulches* — Mary Ronan, *Girl from the Gulches: The Story of Mary Ronan*, ed. Ellen Baumler (Helena: Montana Historical Society Press, 2003)

Miller, *Illustrated History* — Joaquin Miller, *An Illustrated History of the State of Montana* (Chicago: The Lewis Publishing Co., 1894)

MCT — *Missoula County Times* (Missoula, Mont.)

MG — *Missoula Gazette*

MGD — *Missoula Gazette* (daily)

MGW — *Missoula Gazette* (weekly)

MM — *Morning Missoulian*

MWG — *Missoula Weekly Gazette*

NA — National Archives, Washington, D.C.

NA CIA LR — Letters Received, Records of the Commissioner of Indian Affairs, RG 75, National Archives, Washington, D.C.

NA CIA LS — Letters Sent, Records of the Commissioner of Indian Affairs, RG 75, National Archives, Washington, D.C.

NAmf — National Archives Microfilm Publication

NAmf M234 — U.S. Office of Indian Affairs, "Letters Received by the Office of Indian Affairs, 1824-1880," National Archives Microfilm Publication M234

NAmf M1070 — U.S. Department of the Interior, "Reports of Inspection of the Field Jurisdictions of the Office of Indian Affairs, 1873-1900," National Archives Microfilm Publication M1070, reel 11, Flathead Agency

Sanders, *History of Montana* — Helen Fitzgerald Sanders, *A History of Montana* (Chicago: The Lewis Publishing Company, 1913)

Whealdon, *Meat for My Salish* — Bon I. Whealdon, et. al., *"I Will Be Meat for My Salish": The Buffalo and the Montana Writers Project Interviews on the Flathead Indian Reservation* (Pablo and Helena, Mont.: Salish Kootenai College Press and Montana Historical Society Press, 2001)

WM — *The Weekly Missoulian*

1888

1. CIA to Ronan, Feb. 24, 1888, letterbook 170, p. 380, land, NA CIA LS.

2. CIA to Ronan, July 3, 1888, letterbook 175, pp. 250-51, land, NA CIA LS.

3. Kenneth F. Ross, "Memoirs of a Pioneer: Kenneth F. Ross," *The Missoulian*, Feb. 23, 1964, p. 7-A.

4. CIA to Ronan, Jan. 25, 1888, letterbook 135, part 2, p. 40, finance, NA CIA LS.

5. Bigart, *Getting Crops*, pp. 195-96.

6. Secretary of Interior to CIA, May 19, 1888, 13,358/1888, NA CIA LR.

7. Rosters of Agency Employees, Flathead Agency, vol. 18-23 (1888-1894), entry 978, RG 75, NA; Joseph T. Carter to CIA, Aug. 20, 1894, ARCIA (1894), p. 175.

8. See annotation to Ronan's Feb. 2, 1887, letter for biographical information on Ralph and William Ramsdell.

9. "Horrible Massacre," WM, Mar. 21, 1888, p. 3, col. 3. Two other white interpretations of these events were "A Speck of War," *Helena Daily Independent*, Mar. 31, 1888, p. 4, col. 5; and "Hi Yu Skookum!," *Bozeman Weekly Chronicle*, Apr. 11, 1888, p. 1, col. 6.

10. CIA to Ronan, July 2, 1888, letterbook 175, p. 231, land, NA CIA LS.

11. "The Noll Habeas Corpus Case," WM, Jan. 25, 1893, p. 2, col. 4.

12. Paul C. Phillips, *Medicine in the Making of Montana* (Missoula: Montana Medical Association and Montana State University Press, 1962), p. 277; Missoula Publishing Company, *Flathead Facts: Descriptive of the Resources of Missoula County* (Missoula, Mont.: Missoula Publishing Company, 1890), p. 18; "Death of Dr. Dade," *Daily Democrat-Messenger* (Missoula, Mont.), Aug. 12, 1898, p. 1, col. 6; "Death of Dr. Dade," DM, Aug. 12, 1898, p. 8, col. 2-3.

13. CIA to Ronan, Apr. 6, 1888, letterbook 172, pp. 73-74, land, NA CIA LS.

14. MGW, June 23, 1888, p. 2, col. 1.

15. CIA to Ronan, Aug. 14, 1888, letterbook 139, part 2, p. 212, finance, NA CIA LS.

16. CIA to Ronan, Aug. 10, 1888, letterbook 176, p. 330, land; CIA to Ronan Oct. 31, 1888, letterbook 178, p. 229, land, NA CIA LS; "A Crazy Indian," MGD, Oct. 27, 1888, p. 4, col. 3.

17. Bigart, *St. Mary's Mission*, pp. 298-99.

18. See Ronan's Mar. 15, 1888, letter; Rosters of Agency Employees, vol. 18 (1888-1889), p. 24, entry 978, Records of the Commissioner of Indian Affairs, RG 75, NA.

19. See, for example, Chief Arlee's speech from 1887 which was quoted in "A Smart Indian," MCT, Feb. 1, 1888, p. 3, col. 4.

20. CIA to Secretary of Interior, Oct. 22, 1888, letterbook 178, pp. 84-88, land, NA CIA LS; Secretary of Interior to CIA, Nov. 22, 1888, 28,902/1888, NA CIA LR; CIA to Secretary of Interior, Dec. 29, 1890, letterbook 209, pp. 148-56, land, NA CIA LS.

21. W. H. Smead to CIA, July 27, 1901, 41,495/1901, NA CIA LR; CIA to W. H. Smead, Aug. 6, 1901, letterbook 495, pp. 320-26, land, NA CIA LS.

22. Samuel Bellew to CIA, May 15, 1905, 38,398/1905, NA CIA LR.

23. Miller, *Illustrated History*, pp. 410-11; *Progressive Men of the State of Montana* (Chicago: A. W. Bowen & Co., ca. 1900), pp. 306-307.

24. CIA to Ronan, Aug. 17, 1888, letterbook 139, part 2, p. 300, finance, NA CIA LS.

25. "Removal of the Indians," MCT, Jan. 18, 1888, p. 2, col. 3.

26. See Whealdon, *Meat for My Salish*.

27. CIA to Ronan, Nov. 24, 1888, letterbook 179, p. 46, land, NA CIA LS.

28. General Land Office to CIA, Jan. 2, 1889, 192/1889, NA CIA LR.

29. *North West Tribune* (Stevensville, Mont.), Apr. 5, 1889, p. 1, col. 6; R. L. Polk & Co., *Minnesota, North and South Dakota, and Montana Gazetteer and Business Directory, 1894-95* (St. Paul, Minn.: R. L. Polk & Co., 1894), p. 1835.

30. U.S. Census Bureau, "10th Census, 1880," NAmf T9, reel 742, Montana, Missoula County, Bitter Root Valley, p. 442A, number 4; "Stevensville News," MG, Apr. 3, 1889, p. 1, col. 8; "Stevensville Items," MG, Dec. 18, 1890, p. 4, col. 2.

31. CIA to Ronan, Sept. 3, 1888, letterbook 177, pp. 57-58, land, NA CIA LS.

32. CIA to Ronan, Nov. 9, 1888, letterbook 178, pp. 343-44, land, NA CIA LS.

33. WM, Oct. 1, 1886, p. 3, col. 2; MG, Aug. 14, 1891, p. 2, col. 3-4.

34. "Stage Line Change," MGD, Jan. 5, 1892, p. 1, col. 6; "Around the Town," DM, Feb. 28, 1923, p. 2, col. 3; Tom Stout, *Montana: Its Story and Biography* (Chicago: The American Historical Society, 1921), vol. 3, p. 1277.

35. "Democratic Candidates," WM, Sept. 10, 1886, p. 2, col. 1-4; Miller, *Illustrated History*, p. 555; Paul C. Phillips, *Medicine in the Making of Montana* (Missoula: The Montana Medical Association and Montana State University Press, 1962), p. 281.

1889

1. "Sawmill To Be Removed," *The Missoula Pioneer*, Feb. 16, 1871, p. 3, col. 2; "Frank Decker," *The Pioneer* (Missoula, Mont.), Aug. 3, 1872, p. 3, col. 3; "Lynch & Decker," WM, Jan. 8, 1874, p. 4, col. 7.

2. "Married," WM, Apr. 9, 1874, p. 3, col. 4.

3. "On the Reservation," WM, Nov. 8, 1878, p. 3, col. 2-3.

4. "She Fell Off a Bridge," AS, Apr. 10, 1894, p. 6, col. 1; "Was It Murder?," WM, Apr. 11, 1894, p. 5, col. 3.

5. Carle F. O'Neil, *Two Men of Demersville* (n.p., 1990), pp. 59-100.

6. "Unwarranted Excitement," WM, Feb. 20, 1889, p. 3, col. 4; "The Sum Total," MGW, Mar. 6, 1889, p. 3, col. 3; "Flatheads Are Arming," *The New-York Times*, Feb. 21, 1889, p. 1, col. 4; "Kootenais, Not Flatheads," *The Washington Post*, Feb. 23, 1889, p. 1, col. 4.

7. "Discharged," WM, Mar. 13, 1889, p. 3, col. 5.

8. WM, Apr. 3, 1889, p. 3, col. 1.

9. CIA to Ronan, June 18, 1889, letterbook 186, pp. 93-94, land, NA CIA LS.

10. "Arlee Objects," WM, Jan. 9, 1889, p. 3, col. 3; "Frightful Atrocities," WM, May 1, 1889, p. 3, col. 3.

11. Department of Justice to Department of Interior, June 24, 1889, 16,830/1889, NA CIA LR.

12. "Finley Caught," *Great Falls Tribune*, May 23, 1889, p. 1, col. 3; "Behind the Bars," MGW, May 29, 1889, p. 3, col. 4.

13. See copy of statement in Ronan to Thos. H. Ruger, June 27, 1889, enclosure in Ronan's July 1, 1889, letter to the CIA.

14. Whealdon, *Meat for My Salish*, p. 263; Sloan to CIA, Nov. 10, 1903, 76,959/1903, NA CIA LR; "United States v. Heyfron, County Treasurer," Apr. 24, 1905, *The Federal Reporter*, vol. 138 (July-Sept. 1905), pp. 968-69; Velma R. Kvale and Margaret Sterling Brooke, *Where the Buffalo Roamed* (St. Ignatius, Mont.: Mission Valley News, 1976), pp. 46-49.

15. "Flathead Fears," HJ (daily), Apr. 27, 1889, p. 1, col. 8; "A Word in Return," HJ (daily), May 12, 1889, p. 1, col. 8.

16. "The Kootenai Indians," MGW, Mar. 13, 1889, p. 1, col. 7-8.

17. Rebecca Timmons, et. al., "The History and Archaeology of Sophie Morigeau," *Archaeology in Montana*, vol. 42, no. 1 (2001), pp. 1-53.

18. CIA to Secretary of Interior, May 3, 1889, letterbook 183, pp. 490-91, land; CIA to Ronan, July 8, 1889, letterbook 186, pp. 456-57, land, NA CIA LS.

19. U.S. Bureau of Indian Affairs, "Indian Census Rolls, 1885-1940," NAmf M595, reel 107, fr. 172-253.

20. "Help for Heyfron," WM, June 26, 1889, p. 2, col. 2-3; "Still In War Paint," *Butte Semi-Weekly Miner*, June 29, 1889, p. 1, col. 3; "The Posse Returns," WM, June 26, 1889, p. 2, col. 3, and p. 3, col. 4-5; "Flatheads Resist the Law," *The Washington Post*, June 26, 1889, p. 1, col. 5; "To Arrest Indian Murderers," *The New-York Times*, June 26, 1889, p. 2, col. 3; "Flatheads Bent Upon War," *The Washington Post*, June 28, 1889, p. 1, col. 6; *The New-York Times*, July 1, 1889, p. 4, col. 2.

21. "Liber Defunctorum," 1874-1898, St. Ignatius Mission, St. Ignatius, Mont., p. 59.

22. Thos. H. Ruger, "Report of Brigadier-General Ruger," *Annual Report of the Secretary of War* (1889), p. 162.

23. CIA to Secretary of Interior, June 28, 1889, letterbook 186, pp. 295-96, land, NA CIA LS; "Quiet on the Reservation," MGW, July 3, 1889, p. 3, col. 2.

24. "Many Matters From Missoula," HJ, Sept. 12, 1889, p. 1, col. 6; WM, Sept. 18, 1889, p. 4, col. 3.

25. "Democratic Candidates," WM, Sept. 10, 1886, p. 2, col. 1-4; Miller, *Illustrated History*, pp. 680-81; Robert Raffety and John C. Moe, *Sheriffs of Missoula County, Montana, and Their Times, 1860-1978* (n.p., 1988?), pp. 105-111.

26. L. R. Hamersly, *Records of Living Officers of the United States Army* (Philadelphia: L. R. Hamersly & Co., 1884), p. 347; Heitman, vol. 1, p. 166.

27. U.S. Bureau of Indian Affairs, "Indian Census Rolls, 1885-1940," NAmf M595, reel 107, fr. 268-319.

28. "What Duncan Said," MWG, Aug. 27, 1890, p. 5, col. 2-3.

29. MGW, July 10, 1889, p. 3, col. 1; "Court House Cullings," WM, July 17, 1889, p. 4, col. 5.

30. "Work of White Barbarians," *The Washington Post*, July 31, 1889, p. 1, col. 2; "Indians Killed and Robbed," *The New-York Times*, July 31, 1889, p. 2, col. 3.

31. CIA to Secretary of Interior, Aug. 19, 1889, letterbook 188, pp. 278-81, land; CIA to Ronan, Aug. 19, 1889, letterbook 188, pp. 275-77, land, NA CIA LS.

32. "Flatheads in Council," AS, February 19, 1893, p. 9, col. 5-6.

33. See Bigart, *Getting Crops*, pp. 190-92, for more information.

34. Robert J. Bigart, editor, *A Pretty Village: Documents of Worship and Culture Change, St. Ignatius Mission, Montana, 1880-1889* (Pablo, Mont.: Salish Kootenai College Press, 2007), pp. 298-99.

35. Ronan's Sept. 6, 1892, letter.

36. Elders of the Kootenai Nation, *Century of Survival: A Brief History of the Kootenai Tribe of Idaho* (Bonner's Ferry, Id.: Kootenai Tribe of Idaho, 1990), pp. 7-15.

37. CIA to Ronan, June 21, 1889, letterbook 186, pp. 179-80, land, NA CIA LS.

38. CIA to Ronan, Aug. 28, 1889, letterbook 188, pp. 426-29, land, NA CIA LS.

39. CIA to Secretary of Interior, Nov. 25, 1889, letterbook 191, pp. 501-505, land, NA CIA LS.

40. Boundary County Historical Society, *History of Boundary County Idaho* (Bonners Ferry, Id.: Boundary County Historical Society, 1987), pp. 290-93; Rosa Causton and White Otter (Simon Francis), "History and Folklore of the 'Kootenais,'" Holland Library Archives, Washington State University, Pullman, Wash., manuscript 386, chapter 13.

41. CIA to Ronan, Aug. 28, 1889, vol. 147, pt. 1, pp. 13-14, finance; CIA to Ronan, Oct. 15, 1889, vol. 147, pt. 2, pp. 329-30, finance, NA CIA LS.

42. See Ronan's Sept. 17, 1889, letter.

43. See Ronan's Sept. 21, 1889a, letter.

44. Ronan's Apr. 12, 1878, letter.

45. Ronan's June 12, 1889, letter.

46. Wm. W. Junkin to Secretary of Interior, Sept. 11, 1889, NAmf M1070, 5552/1889.

47. Department of Justice to CIA, June 24, 1889, 16,830/1889, NA CIA LR.

48. Ronan to CIA, July 10, 1889, 20,449/1889; Ronan to CIA, July 10, 1889, 20,450/1889, NA CIA LR.

49. See annotation to Ronan's Feb. 2, 1887, letter.

50. "Indians in War Paint," HJ, Aug. 20, 1889, p. 1, col. 1; "An Indian Outbreak Feared," *The New-York Times*, Aug. 21, 1889, p. 2, col. 1.

51. CIA to Ronan, Aug. 21, 1889, telegram, letterbook 188, p. 329, land, NA CIA LS.

52. Missoula Publishing Company, *Flathead Facts: Descriptive of the Resources of Missoula County* (Missoula, Mont.: Missoula Publishing Co., 1890), pp. 18-19; WM, Nov. 24, 1882, p. 3, col. 2-3; "The Flathead Country," WM, Oct. 10, 1884, p. 2, col. 1-3.

53. "The Facts in the Case," WM, Aug. 28, 1889, p. 4, col. 5; "The Kootenai Indians Again," IL, Aug. 30, 1889, p. 4, col. 3.

54. "The Red Man's Story," HJ (daily), Oct. 25, 1889, p. 5, col. 1-2; Ronan's Aug. 14, 1890b, annual report.

55. CIA to Secretary of Interior, Sept. 28, 1889, letterbook 189, pp. 391-95, land, NA CIA LS.

56. CIA to Ronan, Oct. 14, 1889, letterbook 190, pp. 209-210, land, NA CIA LS.

57. CIA to Secretary of Interior, Nov. 2, 1889, letterbook 191, pp. 46-48, land, NA CIA LS.

58. WM, Nov. 27, 1889, p. 3, col. 2; "News From the Lake Country," WM, Nov. 27, 1889, p. 3, col. 5; "Criminal Cases in Missoula," AS, Nov. 28, 1889, p. 4, col. 2; Ronan's Dec. 2, 1889, letter.

59. "Old Timer Tells Tale of Demersville Scare," *The Daily Inter Lake* (Kalispell, Mont.), Mar. 12, 1950, p. 11, col. 1-3.

60. "A Squaw Shot," AS, Mar. 2, 1896, p. 10, col. 3; *Flathead Herald-Journal* (Kalispell, Mont.), Mar. 5, 1896, p. 8, col. 2.

61. Robert H. (Bob) Gatiss, *Memories of One Lifetime* (n.p., 1993), pp. 139-42.

62. Harry Holbert Turney-High, *Ethnography of the Kutenai*, Memoir of the American Anthropological Association No. 56 (1941), pp. 135-39.

63. "The Beautiful Lake Country," MG, May 26, 1888, p. 4, col. 1-2; *Missoula Daily Gazette*, Feb. 22, 1890, p. 8, col. 2; "Jangled Bells," *Missoula Daily Gazette*, Feb. 26, 1890, p. 4, col. 2.

64. Robert Bigart and Clarence Woodcock, editors, "St. Ignatius Mission, Montana: Reports from Two Jesuit Missionaries, 1885 & 1900-1901 (Part I)," *Arizona and the West*, vol. 23, no. 2 (Summer 1981), pp. 163-64; Andrew W. Swaney, "Statement of Andrew W. Swaney," Henry Elwood Papers, MC 309, box 4, folder 26, Montana Historical Society Archives, Helena, pp. 4-5.

65. "To Frenchtown," WM, Nov. 10, 1875, p. 3, col. 2; WM, Oct. 18, 1878, p. 3, col. 2.

66. "Heavy Taxpayers," WM, Dec. 10, 1886, p. 2, col. 1.

67. "The Oldest Old Timer," *The Kalispell Bee*, Oct. 8, 1907, p. 3, col. 3-5; "An Old Timer Gone," IL, Oct. 11, 1907, p. 5, col. 4.

68. IL, Aug. 30, 1889, p. 1, col. 2.

69. CIA to Ronan; Supt. Indian Warehouse, New York City; and Elias Story, Bozeman, Sept. 27, 1889, vol. 147, pt. 2, pp. 21, 22, 30, finance, NA CIA LS.

70. William W. Junkin, to Secretary of Interior, Sept. 14, 1889, NAmf M1070, 5657/1889.

71. CIA to Secretary of Interior, Sept. 16, 1889, letterbook 189, pp. 184-85, land; CIA to Ronan, Oct. 3, 1889, letterbook 190, p. 24, land, NA CIA LS.

72. Territory vs. Larra Finley, Nov. 27, 1889, case 1295, criminal, District Court Records, Missoula County Courthouse, Missoula, Mont., territorial, reel 17, fr. 1248-75; Territory vs. Lala See, Nov. 27, 1889, case 1296, criminal, District Court Records, Missoula County Courthouse, Missoula, Mont., territorial, reel 17, fr. 1276-1313; Territory vs. Pierre Paul, Nov. 27, 1889, case 1297, criminal, District Court Records, Missoula County Courthouse, Missoula, Mont., territorial, reel 17, fr. 1314-36.

73. Bigart, *Getting Crops*, pp. 190-92.

74. Francis P. Prucha, *American Indian Policy in Crisis: Christian Reformers and the Indian, 1865-1900* (Norman: University of Oklahoma Press, 1976), pp. 220, 305-309.

75. Bigart, *Zealous*, pp. 73, 167-69.

76. Miller, *Illustrated History*, pp. 118-19.

77. AS, Nov. 1, 1889, p. 8, col. 2; "The Indian Lands," WM, Dec. 4, 1889, p. 3, col. 3; Bigart, *Getting Crops*, pp. 194-217; *Dictionary of American Biography*, vol. 3, pp. 520-21; Catherine McKeen, "Henry Beebee Carrington: A Soldier's Tale," unpublished PhD dissertation, State University of New York at Stoney Brook, 1998, DAI 9912592.

78. Robert J. Bigart, editor, *A Pretty Village: Documents of Worship and Culture Change, St. Ignatius Mission, Montana, 1880-1889* (Pablo, Mont.: Salish Kootenai College Press, 2007), pp. 275-328.

79. "It Should Not Be Allowed," WM, Nov. 13, 1889, p. 3, col. 3.

80. William H. Powell, *Powell's Records of Living Officers of the United States Army* (Philadelphia: L. R. Hamserly & Co., 1890), pp. 650-51; Heitman, vol. 1, p. 1045.

81. Heitman, vol. 1, p. 643.

82. *Wright & Woodward's Missoula City Directory, 1890* (n.p., 1890), p. 6.

83. Territory vs. Conrad Fisher, Mar. 13, 1889, cases 1178-1181 (4 cases), criminal, District Court Records, Missoula County Courthouse, Missoula, Montana, territorial, reel 15, fr. 1903-1931; Territory vs. Lena Fisher, Sept. 21, 1889, case 1282, criminal, District Court Records, Missoula County Courthouse, Missoula, Montana, territorial, reel 17, fr. 915-21.

84. "Notes from Missoula," AS, Jan. 9, 1890, p. 4, col. 3.

85. "They Arbitrated," AS, June 22, 1893, p. 1, col. 6; "Discharged," AS, June 23, 1893, p. 8, col. 1; WM, June 28, 1893, p. 8, col. 4.

86. Territory vs. Jack Johnson, Nov. 27, 1889, case 1292, criminal, District Court Records, Missoula County Courthouse, Missoula, Mont., territorial, reel 17, fr. 1187-1202.

1890

1. CIA to Ronan, Jan. 13, 1890, letterpress vol. 108, pt. 1, pp. 265-67, accounts, NA CIA LS.

2. WM, Jan. 15, 1890, p. 4, col. 3.

3. "To Hang in February," AS, Dec. 19, 1889, p. 4, col. 2; "Will Philip Hang?," HJ, Dec. 14, 1889, p. 1, col. 4.

4. "His Story of the Crime," AS, Jan. 5, 1890, p. 5, col. 3; "Philip John," *Missoula Daily Gazette*, Feb. 14, 1890, p. 1, col. 4-5; "Philip's Life Saved," MGD, Apr. 14, 1890, p. 4, col. 3.

5. *Dictionary of American Biography*, vol. 18, pp. 589-90.

6. CIA to Ronan, Jan. 11, 1890, letterpress vol. 108, pt. 1, p. 256, accounts, NA CIA LS.

7. CIA to Ronan, Feb. 1, 1890, vol. 149, pt. 2, p. 367, finance, NA CIA LS.

8. CIA to Secretary of Interior, Mar. 12, 1890, vol. 150, pt. 2, pp. 304-305, finance, NA CIA LS.

9. CIA to Ronan, Mar. 15, 1890, telegram, vol. 150, pt. 2, p. 391, finance; CIA to Ronan, Mar. 19, 1890, vol. 151, pt. 1, pp. 55-56, finance, NA CIA LS.

10. Leonard A. Carlson, *Indian Bureaucrats and Land: The Dawes Act and the Decline of Indian Farming* (Westport, Conn.: Greenwood Press, 1981).

11. James H. Cisney to Secretary of Interior, Feb. 28, 1890, NAmf M1070, 1501/1890 and 1502/1890.

12. CIA to Ronan, Mar. 16, 1890, telegram, vol. 151, pt. 1, p. 7, finance, NA CIA LS.

13. [Mother Angela Lincoln], *Life of the Rev. Mother Amadeus of the Heart of Jesus: Foundress of the Ursuline Missions of Montana and Alaska* (New York: The Paulist Press, 1920), pp. 117-18.

14. "He Gets Ten Years," *Missoula Daily Gazette*, Mar. 19, 1890, p. 4, col. 2.

15. CIA to Ronan, May 13, 1890, letterbook 198, p. 389, land, NA CIA LS.

16. War Department to Secretary of Interior, Apr. 12, 1890, 11,433/1890, NA CIA LR; Thos. H. Ruger, "Report of Brigadier-General Ruger," *Annual Report of the Secretary of War* (1890), pp. 188-89 and 191-92.

17. "A Musical Treat," IL, Apr. 25, 1890, p. 1, col. 4.

18. In addition to the newspaper clipping Ronan enclosed in his letter see "Said to Be a Murderer," MGD, May 28, 1890, p. 1, col. 1.

19. "A Very Bad Indian," MGD, July 25, 1890, p. 1, col. 2.

20. "The Primaries," MG, Sept. 1, 1890, p. 1, col. 5; MG, July 14, 1891, p. 8, col. 1.

21. AS, June 9, 1890, p. 3, col. 1; MGD, Aug. 8, 1890, p. 8, col. 2.

22. Ronan's Aug. 6, 1887, and Dec. 18, 1888, letters and annotations.

23. Kimberly R. Brown, "Overview of Coeur d'Alene History," in Joseph Seltice, *Saga of the Coeur d'Alene Indians* (Fairfield, Wash.: Ye Galleon Press, 1990), pp. 305-336.

24. James H. Mills, "Reminiscences of an Editor," *Contributions to the Historical Society of Montana*, vol. 5 (1904), pp. 273-78.

25. James U. Sanders, ed., *Society of Montana Pioneers, vol. 1* (1899), p. 209; "Another Pioneer Is Called Across the Last Divide," DM, July 13, 1915, p. 8, col. 2; Estate of Peter

Ronan, Probate File 339 (1893), Clerk of District Court, Missoula County Courthouse, Missoula, Mont., items 40, 43, and 47.

26. Ronan's Aug. 1885 annual report and Aug. 17, 1885, testimony; U.S. Bureau of Indian Affairs, "Selected Records of the Bureau of Indian Affairs Relating to the Enrollment of Indians on the Flathead Reservation, 1903-08," NAmf M1350, reel 1, fr. 1, numbers 33 and 34.

27. George F. Weisel, ed., *Men and Trade on the Northwest Frontier as Shown by the Fort Owen Ledger* (Missoula, Mont.: Montana State University Press, 1955), pp. 171-72; Charles W. Frush, "A Trip From the Dalles of the Columbia, Oregon, to Fort Owen, Bitter Root Valley, Montana, in the Spring of 1858," *Contributions to the Historical Society of Montana*, vol. 2 (1896), pp. 337-42.

28. William H. Powell, *Powell's Records of Living Officers of the United States Army* (Philadelphia, Penna.: L. R. Hamersly & Co., 1890), p. 610; Heitman, vol. 1, p. 982.

29. CIA to Ronan, July 22, 1890, telegram, letterbook 201, p. 464, land, NA CIA LS.

30. "A Horrible Discovery," IL, July 11, 1890, p. 3, col. 4; "Dead Men's Bones," MGD, July 14, 1890, p. 1, col. 5; "Killed for Money," MGD, July 15, 1890, p. 1, col. 5; "Turned Him Loose,"IL, July 18, 1890, p. 3, col. 4.

31. "A Midnight Ride," IL, July 18, 1890, p. 3, col. 3.

32. WM, Oct. 2, 1889, p. 3, col. 3; G. M. Houtz, "Old-Time Flathead Tales: Some Modern Instances," DM, Oct. 10, 1937, p. 4, col. 2-3.

33. Bob Raffety and John C. Moe, *Sheriffs of Missoula County, Montana, and Their Times, 1860-1978* (n.p., 1988?), pp. 115-18, 169-72; Will Cave, "Bill Houston's Story," DM, May 2, 1937, ed. sec., p. 7, col. 1-8, and May 9, 1937, ed. sec., p. 7, col. 1-8.

34. William H. Powell, *Powell's Records of Living Officers of the United States Army* (Philadelphia, Penna.: L. R. Hamersly & Co., 1890), p. 519; Heitman, vol. 1, p. 858.

35. Bigart, *Zealous*, pp. 48-53.

36. Annotation to Ronan's Aug. 6, 1889, letter.

37. CIA to Secretary of Interior, Sept. 11, 1890, letterbook 204, pp. 43-53, land; CIA to Secretary of Interior, Dec. 6, 1890, letterbook 208, pp. 122-25, land; CIA to R. Fry, Dec. 22, 1890, letterbook 209, pp. 29-30, land, NA CIA LS.

38. "Cleverly Caught," MGD, Aug. 5, 1890, p. 1, col. 3-4; "After the Redskins," AS, Aug. 7, 1890, p. 1, col. 6; "One of Them Caught," MGD, Aug. 7, 1890, p. 1, col. 5; "A Big Catch," IL Aug. 8, 1890, p. 3, col. 3.

39. "Will Give Himself Up," WM, Aug. 20, 1890, p. 3, col. 2; "Were Hot on His Trail," HJ (daily), Aug. 21, 1890, p. 1, col. 6.

40. "It's a Very Funny Bill," AS, Feb. 23, 1895, p. 6, col. 1; "A Bit of History," *The Kalispell Graphic*, Feb. 27, 1895, p. 2, col. 1-3; "Jim Conley's Side of It," AS, Mar. 8, 1895, p. 3, col. 1.

41. DM, May 16, 1896, p. 2, col. 2.

42. "The Tie That Binds," MWG, July 30, 1890, p. 1, col. 5; CIA to Ronan, Sept. 12, 1890, telegram, letterbook 204, p. 88, land, NA CIA LS; "Work Delayed," WM, Sept. 17, 1890, p. 3, col. 4; "Indians Object," HJ (daily), Sept. 25, 1890, p. 5, col. 1; "Missoula and Northern Railroad Company," U.S. House of Representatives Report No. 3317, 51st Cong., 2d Sess. (1890), serial 2885; "North From Missoula," AS, Apr. 21, 1891, p. 1, col. 4-5.

43. CIA to Secretary of Interior, Jan. 9, 1891, letterbook 209, pp. 385-86, land; CIA to Secretary of Interior, Mar. 3, 1891, letterbook 212, pp. 153-55, land, NA CIA LS.

44. "May Not Be Built," AS, July 11, 1891, p. 8, col. 1-2.

45. CIA to Ronan, July 10, 1890, letterbook 201, p. 266, land; CIA to Thomas H. Carter, July 19, 1890, letterbook 201, pp. 428-29, land; CIA to Clarence E. Proctor, July 19, 1890, letterbook 201, p. 430, land; CIA to Ronan, Nov. 10, 1890, letterbook 206, pp. 473-76, land, NA CIA LS.

46. Chief Cliff Homemakers, *Chief Cliff Country* (Dayton?, Mont.: Chief Cliff Homemakers, 1990), pp. 61-64; "C. E. Proctor & Co.," MG, Dec. 31, 1890, p. 5, col. 6; "An Embryo City," MG, Sept. 3, 1891, p. 1, col. 5-6; "Funerals," *The Daily Inter Lake* (Kalispell, Mont.), July 15, 1933, p. 3, col. 4.

47. CIA to Secretary of Interior, Dec. 6, 1890, letterbook 233, pp. 300-301, accounts; CIA to Ronan, Dec. 12, 1890, letterbook 233, p. 483, accounts, NA CIA LS.

48. Ronan's Aug. 27, 1887, annual report; MGD, May 5, 1891, p. 8, col. 2.

49. "Startling If True," HI, Aug. 5, 1877, p. 3, col. 2; "The Indian Situation," HI, Aug. 7, 1877, p. 3, col. 2.

50. B. H. Miller to Secretary of Interior, Dec. 15, 1891, 45,483/1891, NA CIA LR; Ronan's Feb. 18, 1892, letter.

51. "Burial Register, 1898-1963," St. Ignatius Mission, St. Ignatius, Montana, p. 2.

52. "Pierre Paul Talks," MWG, Nov. 12, 1890, p. 5, col. 1; "Deny Their Guilt," MGD, Dec. 18, 1890, p. 1, col. 5.

53. T. F. Oakes to CIA, Sept. 10, 1890, 28,476/1890, NA CIA LR; CIA to Secretary of Interior, Oct. 28, 1890, letterbook 206, pp. 179-83, land, NA CIA LS; Secretary of Interior to CIA, Nov. 4, 1890, 34,130/1890, NA CIA LR; CIA to Secretary of Interior, Nov. 8, 1890, letterbook 206, p. 448, land, NA CIA LS; CIA to Indian Inspector and Ronan, Nov. 8, 1890, letterbook 206, pp. 449-55, land, NA CIA LS; Secretary of Interior to CIA, Nov. 10, 1890, 34,683/1890, NA CIA LR; CIA to Ronan, Nov. 10, 1890, letterbook 207, pp. 5-6, land, NA CIA LS.

54. WM, Dec. 3, 1890, p. 3, col. 1; "St. Ignatius Items," MWG, Dec. 17, 1890, p. 12, col. 6.

55. CIA to Secretary of Interior, Dec. 26, 1890, letterbook 209, pp. 96-98, land, NA CIA LS.

56. "Death's Decree," MWG, Dec. 24, 1890, pp. 1-3, 5.

1891

1. See Ronan's Nov. 1, 1890, letter and annotation for more about the trials.

2. "Items from St. Ignatius," MGD, Jan. 9, 1891, p. 5, col. 2.

3. CIA to Secretary of Interior, May 1, 1891, letterbook 216, pp. 30-31, land; CIA to Ronan, May 1, 1891, letterbook 216, p. 32, land, NA CIA LS.

4. "For the A. O. U. W.," MGD, May 27, 1892, p. 1, col. 1-2; "Workmen's Meeting," AS, May 27, 1892, p. 6, col. 2; "The Indians Win," MGD, May 28, 1892, p. 1, col. 4.

5. Miller, *Illustrated History*, pp. 657-59.

6. U.S. Bureau of Indian Affairs, "Selected Records of the Bureau of Indian Affairs Relating to the Enrollment of Indians on the Flathead Reservation, 1903-08," NAmf M1350, reel 1, fr. 5, nos. 162-63; Arthur L. Stone, *Following Old Trails* (Missoula, Mont.: Morton J. Elrod, 1913), pp. 151-52; James Wright to CIA, Mar. 28, 1873, NAmf M234, reel 496, fr. 427-31; Ronan's Aug. 17, 1885, testimony; Ronan's Aug. 1885 annual report; Rosters of Indian Police, vol. 7 (1886-1887), p. 10, entry 982, RG 75, NA.

7. Miller, *Illustrated History*, pp. 317-18.

8. Rosters of Indian Police, vol. 9 (1890-1891), p. 10, entry 982, RG 75, NA.

9. "The Bitter Root Indians," MGD, Jan. 16, 1891, p. 1, col. 5.

10. Robert S. Gardner to Secretary of Interior, Aug. 7, 1890, NAmf M1070, 5223/1890.

11. CIA to Ronan, Mar. 24, 1891, letterbook 238, pp. 408-409, accounts; CIA to Ronan, July 20, 1891, letterbook 245, pp. 223-24, accounts, NA CIA LS.

12. See Ronan's Aug. 27, 1887, annual report and annotation.

13. CIA to Ronan, May 9, 1891, letterbook 216, pp. 299-303, land; CIA to Secretary of Interior, June 4, 1891, letterbook 218, pp. 68-75, land, NA CIA LS.

14. "Have Built a Fort," *The Spokane Review*, July 16, 1891, p. 5, col. 3; "Sarcastic Settlers," *The Spokane Review*, July 23, 1891, p. 2, col. 5; "That Indian Scare," *The Spokane Review*, July 25, 1891, p. 7, col. 1; "The Indian Scare," *The Spokane Review*, Sept. 20, 1891, p. 5, col. 2.

15. CIA to Ronan, Oct. 21, 1891, telegram, letterbook 224, pp. 261-62, land; CIA to Ronan, Oct. 21, 1891, letterbook 224, pp. 265-67, land, NA CIA LS.

16. "As to the Indians," WM, Dec. 2, 1891, p. 4, col. 3; "Missoula Notes," AS, Dec. 2, 1891, p. 3, col. 2; "Missoula Matters," *Butte Weekly Miner*, Dec. 31, 1891, p. 4, col. 6-7.

17. CIA to C. E. Proctor, Demersville, Mont., Mar. 23, 1891, letterbook 213, pp. 267-69, land; CIA to Secretary of Interior, June 27, 1891, letterbook 219, pp. 148-50, land, NA CIA LS.

18. "The Political Pot," MGD, Sept. 3, 1891, p. 1, col. 7.

19. Confederated Salish and Kootenai Tribes vs. United States, docket 50233, decision Nov. 12, 1965, U.S. Court of Claims, vol. 173, p. 398.

20. CIA to Ronan, Apr. 29, 1891, letterbook 215, p. 450, land; CIA to Gen. Henry B. Carrington, June 30, 1891, letterbook 219, pp. 234-37, land, NA CIA LS.

21. "Let the Salmon Come," AS, Feb. 21, 1892, p. 12, col. 1-3.

22. CIA to Ronan, June 22, 1891, letterbook 219, pp. 27-33, land, NA CIA LS; Secretary of Interior to CIA, Oct. 7, 1891, 36,238/1891, NA CIA LR; CIA to U.S. Fish Commissioner, Oct. 12, 1891, letterbook 224, pp. 69-70, land, NA CIA LS; "Salmon for the Flathead," HI, Nov. 25, 1891, p. 1, col. 3.

23. Ronan's Oct. 5, 1892, letter; "Fish for Flathead," MM, Sept. 23, 1892, p. 1, col. 2.

24. *Dictionary of American Biography*, vol. 16, pp. 336-37; Tom Stout, *Montana: Its Story and Biography* (Chicago: The American Historical Society, 1921), vol. 3, pp. 956-57.

25. WM, Apr. 29, 1891, p. 3, col. 3; WM, Apr. 29, 1891, p. 4, col. 3; MWG, May 6, 1891, p. 3, col. 3; Bigart, *St. Mary's Mission*, pp. 241-42; Register of Prisoners Confined in County Jail, 1882-1893, MS 310, series II, vol. 110, Missoula County Records, Toole Archives, University of Montana Library, Missoula, p. 119 (no. 230) and p. 133 (no. 388); WM, May 18, 1892, p. 4, col. 1; MGD, May 27, 1892, p. 8, col. 1; Justice Court Dockets, 1888-1900, MS 310, series II, Missoula County Records, Toole Archives, University of Montana Library, Missoula, vol. 135 (p. 168), vol. 136 (p. 210), vol. 152 (p. 270), vol. 52 (p. 271); Louisa McDermott, "Ethnology and Folklore: Selish Proper," unpublished masters thesis, University of California, Berkeley, 1904, pp. 29-31.

26. "Foot of the Lake," WM, May 27, 1891, p. 4, col. 1; "Ravalli and Arlee," MGD, Aug. 12, 1891, p. 4, col. 1; CIA to Ronan, June 26, 1891, letterpress, vol. 6, part 1, pp. 336-37, miscellaneous, NA CIA LS.

27. MWG, June 10, 1891, p. 3, col. 2; "A Fierce War," WM, July 15, 1891, p. 4, col. 1; WM, Aug. 12, 1891, p. 4, col. 2; "Tales of Montana's Early Days: The Allard Stage Line," AS, Nov. 26, 1899, p. 19, col. 1-7.

28. "Indians and Freighters," MGD, July 16, 1891, p. 1, col. 5; "News From Missoula," AS, July 17, 1891, p. 8, col. 1; "The Freighters' Troubles," AS, Aug. 9, 1891, p. 1, col. 2.

29. CIA to Ronan, June 3, 1891, letterbook, 218, p. 41, land, NA CIA LS.

30. E. Jane Gray, *With the Nez Perces: Alice Fletcher in the Field, 1889-92* (Lincoln: University of Nebraska Press, 1981). See also Elizabeth Jean James, "Forging an Indigenous Future: The Nez Perces, 1893-1934," unpublished PhD dissertation, Arizona State University, Tempe, 2002, DAI AAT 3069811.

31. Lucy Finley vs. Peter Finley, divorce, Jan. 10, 1891, case 236, District Court Records, Missoula County Courthouse, Missoula.

32. CIA to Ronan, July 27, 1891, letterbook 220, pp. 367-70, land, NA CIA LS.

33. Miller, *Illustrated History*, pp. 537-38.

34. William H. Powell, *Powell's Records of Living Officers of the United States Army* (Philadelphia, Penna.: L. R. Hamersley & Co., 1890), p. 264; Heitman, vol. 1, p. 499.

35. James H. Cisney to Secretary of Interior, July 23, 1891, NAmf M1070, 5803/1891.

36. CIA to Ronan, Oct. 8, 1891, vol. 6, part 2, p. 137, miscellaneous; CIA to Phillips & McKenney, Mar. 3, 1892, vol. 7, part 1, p. 124, miscellaneous, NA CIA LS.

37. Phillips & McKenney to CIA, Aug. 4, 1891, 28,469/1891, NA CIA LR.

38. Whealdon, *Meat for My Salish*, p. 253; "Polson Woman Tells of State's Infancy," DM, May 10, 1930, p. 3, col. 1; June Allard Green and Joe Green, *Joseph Allard, 1876-1964: Pioneer, Cowboy, Stagecoach Driver, Rancher* (n.p., 1986), pp. 157, 233.

39. See Ronan's Aug. 20, 1883, letter and annotation.

40. CIA to Ronan, Sept. 7, 1891, letterbook 222, pp. 293-97, land, NA CIA LS; "Outside the Line," MGD, Oct. 2, 1891, p. 4, col. 1.

41. Ronan's Dec. 14, 1891a, letter; CIA to Ronan, Dec. 12, 1891, telegram, letterbook 227, p. 140, land; CIA to Secretary of Interior, Dec. 12, 1891, letterbook 227, pp. 131-36, land, NA CIA LS; "Drove the Indians Off," HI, Dec. 13, 1891, p. 1, col. 7; AS, Dec. 14, 1891, p. 2, col. 1; "Flathead Indians Indignant," *The New-York Times*, Dec. 15, 1891, p. 3, col. 5; IL, Dec. 18, 1891, p. 2, col. 1; "The Flathead Trouble," HI, Dec. 22, 1891, p. 1, col. 6; "Troublesome White Men," AS, Dec. 22, 1891, p. 1, col. 6; "From Helena," *Butte Weekly Miner*, Dec. 24, 1891, p. 8, col. 1.

42. CIA to C. E. Proctor, Kalispell, Mont., Nov. 6, 1891, letterbook 225, pp. 108-112, land, NA CIA LS.

43. CIA to Secretary of Interior, Jan. 27, 1904, letterbook 649, pp. 183-93, land; CIA to W. H. Smead, June 9, 1904, letterbook 681, pp. 351-56, land; CIA to Samuel Bellew, Oct. 22, 1904, letterbook 711, pp. 16-27, land; CIA to Bellew, Mar. 20, 1905, letterbook 743, p. 422, land, NA CIA LS.

44. Sam E. Johns, "The Pioneers," typescript, Flathead County Library, Kalispell, Mont., vol. 4, p. 176.

45. "Kootenai Chiefs Memorial Draws Hundreds," *Char-Koosta* (Dixon, Mont.), vol. 2, no. 14 [Nov. 15, 1972], pp. 11-12.

46. Robert Bigart and Clarence Woodcock, eds., "St. Ignatius Mission, Montana: Reports from Two Jesuit Missionaries, 1885 & 1900-1901 (Part II)," *Arizona and the West*, vol. 23, no. 3 (Autumn 1981), pp. 273, 276; Crow &c. Commission to CIA, Apr. 18, 1901, 22,670/1901, NA CIA LR; Chas. S. McNichols to CIA, Dec. 31, 1902, 822/1903, NA CIA LR.

47. W. H. Smead to CIA, Oct. 23, 1902, 64,431/1902; Smead to CIA, May 30, 1904, 36,739/1904, NA CIA LR.

48. U.S. President, "Message from the President of the United States, Transmitting a Report Relative to the Compensation of Henry B. Carrington, a Special Agent for the Sale of Certain Indian Lands," Senate Executive Document 70, 51st Congress, 1st Session (1890), serial 2686, pp. 8, 12, 17, 19-20.

49. Bigart, *St. Mary's Mission*, pp. 236-37.

50. CIA to Secretary of Interior, June 30, 1891, letterbook 219, pp. 230-33, land; CIA to Ronan, Aug. 11, 1891, letterbook 221, pp. 253-55, land; CIA to Secretary of Interior, Dec. 2, 1891, [i.e, Dec. 23, 1891], letterbook 228, pp. 2-11, land, NA CIA LS.

51. Joseph Carter to CIA, Mar. 27, 1896, 13,456/1896, NA CIA LR.

52. WM, June 4, 1880, p. 3, col. 2; Robert J. Bigart, ed., *Crossroad of Cultures: Sacramental Records at St. John the Baptist Catholic Church, Frenchtown, Montana, 1866-1899* (Pablo, Mont.: Salish Kootenai College Press, 2009), p. 25, no. A72; "Appointments by the Sheriff," *Missoula and Cedar Creek Pioneer*, Oct. 6, 1870, p. 3, col. 2; "The Right Man in the Right Place," *The Missoula Pioneer*, May 18, 1871, p. 3, col. 2; *The Missoula Pioneer*, Sept. 28, 1871, p. 3, col. 2; "Democratic Ticket," WM, Sept. 15, 1882, p. 2, col. 1; "Proceedings of County Board," WM, Dec. 14, 1883, p. 1, col. 4-5.

53. John Owen, *The Journals and Letters of Major John Owen, 1850-1871*, ed. Seymour Dunbar and Paul C. Phillips (New York: Edward Eberstadt, 1927), vol. 2, p. 69; "Missoula County Officers," WM, Jan. 8, 1874, p. 3, col. 1.

54. CIA to Ronan, Sept. 14, 1891, vol. 172, part 2, pp. 364-65, finance, NA CIA LS.

55. CIA to Ronan, Sept. 14, 1891, vol. 172, part 2, pp. 364-65, finance, NA CIA LS; MWG, Oct. 7, 1891, p. 12, col. 6.

56. Henry B. Carrington, "The Exodus of the Flatheads," manuscript, Carrington Family Papers, Sterling Library, Yale University, New Haven, Conn., chapter 10, p. 12; *The Western News* (Stevensville, Mont.), Oct. 13, 1891, p. 3, col. 2; "Arrived Safe," *The Western News*, Oct. 20, 1891, p. 2, col. 1; U.S. President, "Message from the President of the United States, Transmitting a Report Relative to the Compensation of Henry B. Carrington, a Special Agent for the Sale of Certain Indian Lands," Senate Executive Document No. 70, 51st Congress, 1st Session (1890), serial 2686, pp. 12-13; "Stevensville," WM, Feb. 6, 1885, p. 3, col. 3; "Election Returns," WM, Nov. 12, 1886, p. 2, col. 1; "Stevensville," MCT, Dec. 22, 1886, p. 4, col. 2; *The Western News* (Stevensville, Mont.), Jan. 12, 1892, p. 3, col. 2.

57. Bigart, *Getting Crops*, pp. 203-204, 212-13.

58. CIA to Secretary of Interior, Sept. 23, 1891, letterbook 223, pp. 121-25, land; CIA to Ronan, Oct. 1, 1891, letterbook 223, pp. 308-309, land, NA CIA LS.

59. CIA to Ronan, Oct. 3, 1891, letterbook 249, pp. 213-14, accounts; CIA to Ronan, Nov. 5, 1891, letterbook 250, pp. 399-400, accounts, NA CIA LS; Ronan's [i.e., Thomas E. Adams'], Dec. 4, 1891, letter.

60. CIA to Ronan, Oct. 22, 1891, telegram, letterbook 224, p. 281, land, NA CIA LS.

61. CIA to Ronan, May 18, 1892, letterbook 237, pp. 388-90, land, NA CIA LS; Ronan's Oct. 24, 1892, letter.

62. Thomas P. Smith to CIA, Sept. 23, 1893, 36,376/1893, NA CIA LR; CIA to Joseph Carter, Nov. 22, 1893, letterbook 269, pp. 17-21, land, NA CIA LS.

63. "He Dreams a Dream," MGD, Oct. 12, 1891, p. 1, col. 7; "Arrived Safe," *The Western News* (Stevensville, Mont.), Oct. 20, 1891, p. 2, col. 1; "Removal of Charlos," *The Spokane Review*, Nov. 29, 1891, p. 3, col. 5 6; U.S Secretary of Interior, *Annual Report of the Secretary of Interior* (1891), pp. xlv-xlvii; Bigart, *Getting Crops*, pp. 205-212.

64. U.S. President, "Message from the President of the United States, Transmitting a Report Relative to the Compensation of Henry B. Carrington, a Special Agent for the Sale of Certain Indian Lands," Senate Executive Document 70, 51st Congress, 1st Session (1890), serial 2686, pp. 12-13.

65. Whealdon, *Meat for My Salish*, p. 245.

66. Ronan's Jan. 23, 1892, and Mar. 10, 1892, letters; CIA to Ronan, Jan. 6, 1892, letterbook 228, pp. 210-12, land; CIA to Ronan, Feb. 8, 1892, letterbook 230, pp. 328-30, land, NA CIA LS; "Flathead Indian Crops," MGD, Apr. 5, 1892, p. 4, col. 3.

67. Bigart, *Getting Crops*, pp. 212-17.

68. See Ronan's Nov. 27, 1891, letter.

69. CIA to Ronan, Dec. 11, 1891, letterbook 252, pp. 194-95, accounts, NA CIA LS.

70. See Ronan's Aug. 6, 1889, and Feb. 21, 1891, letters and annotations.

71. "As to the Indians," WM, Dec. 2, 1891, p. 4, col. 3; "Missoula Notes," AS, Dec. 2, 1891, p. 3, col. 2; "Missoula Gossip," *Butte Weekly Miner*, Dec. 3, 1891, p. 1, col. 1.

72. Bruce McIntyre Watson, *Lives Lived West of the Divide: A Biographical Dictionary of Fur Traders Working West of the Rockies, 1793-1858* (Kelowna, B.C.: The University of British Columbia, Okanagan, 2010), vol. 2, pp. 672-73; "Son of a Pioneer," *The Spokesman-Review* (Spokane, Wash.), July 28, 1901, p. 23, col. 6-7; David McLoughlin, "A Short History of the Lower Kootenai Indians" and "The Upper Kootenai Tribe of Indians. . . .," vertical file, MONAC Collection, Eastern Washington State Historical Society, Spokane, Wash.

73. Benjamin H. Miller to Secretary of Interior, Dec. 15, 1891, NAmf M1070, 9325/1891; Miller to Secretary of Interior, Dec. 15, 1891, 45,483/1891, NA CIA LR.

74. See Ronan's Oct. 16, 1891, letter and annotation.

75. "The Flathead Trouble," HI, Dec. 22, 1891, p. 1, col. 6.

76. Carrington to CIA, Nov. 18, 1891, 41,846/1891, NA CIA LR; CIA to Ronan, Nov. 27, 1891, letterbook 174, pp. 34-35, education, NA CIA LS.

1892

1. CIA to Ronan, Jan. 16, 1892, letterbook 229, pp. 46-48, land; CIA to Ronan, Mar. 3, 1892, letterbook 232, p. 164, land, NA CIA LS.

2. "Flathead Indian Crops," MGD, Apr. 5, 1892, p. 4, col. 3.

3. CIA to Ronan, Feb. 6, 1892, vol. 128, part 1, pp. 89-90, accounts; CIA to Sen. G . G. Vest, Feb. 6, 1892, letterbook 255, pp. 81-82, accounts, NA CIA LS.

4. CIA to Ronan, Mar. 11, 1892, letterpress, vol. 180, part 1, pp. 205-206, finance, NA CIA LS.

5. CIA to Secretary of Interior, Mar. 18, 1892, letterbook 233, pp. 225-26, land; CIA to Ronan, Mar. 22, 1892, letterbook 233, p. 331, land; CIA to Ronan, Apr. 29, 1892, letterbook 236, pp. 292-93, land, NA CIA LS.

6. WM, Feb. 17, 1892, p. 4, col. 1; "The Bad Women," WM, Feb. 17, 1892, p. 3, col. 3; "The Indian Racket," WM, Feb. 17, 1892, p. 3, col. 4; CIA to Ronan, Mar. 31, 1892, vol. 181, part 1, pp. 195-96, finance; CIA to Secretary of Interior, Sept. 8, 1893, letterbook 264, pp. 389-91, land, NA CIA LS; U.S. Secretary of Treasury, "Accounts of J. J. Hitt et al.," House of Representatives Executive Document No. 92, 53d Congress, 2d Session (1894), serial 3223, pp. 11-12; U.S. Acting Secretary of the Treasury, "J. G. McCoy," House of Representatives Executive Document No. 182, 53d Congress, 2d Session (1894), serial 3226, pp. 15-17.

7. Miller, *Illustrated History*, pp. 410-11.

8. Rosters of Indian Police, vol. 9 (1890-1891), p. 10; vol. 10 (1892-1893), p. 12, entry 982, RG 75, NA; Department of Justice to Secretary of Interior, June 24, 1889, 16,830/1889, NA CIA LR.

9. "A Bad Indian," AS, Feb. 28, 1892, p. 1, col. 2; MGD, Feb. 29, 1892, p. 4, col. 2; "Missoula Notes," AS, Mar. 2, 1892, p. 6, col. 2; WM, Feb. 24, 1892, [i.e., Mar. 2, 1892], p. 4, col. 2 (2 items); MGD, Apr. 12, 1892, p. 3, col. 2.

10. "On the Move," AS, Feb. 23, 1892, p. 1, col. 5; MGD, Feb. 23, 1892, p. 4, col. 3; untitled record of prisoners, 1891-1892, Montana State Prison Records, State Microfilm 36, Montana Historical Society, Helena, reel 5, p. 40; "Here Is News" WM, June 7, 1893, p. 8, col. 2; "Seeking a Pardon," AS, Mar. 6, 1895, p. 6, col. 1-2; DM, Mar. 8, 1895, p. 4, col. 2; "Probably Will Be Pardoned," DM, Mar. 15, 1895, p. 1, col. 4-5; *The Daily Democrat* (Missoula, Mont.), Mar. 20, 1895, p. 4, col. 1.

11. F. W. Lander, "Report of F. W. Lander, Superintendent, &c., to the Commissioner of Indian Affairs," in U.S. President, "Message of the President of the United States, Communicating, In Compliance with a Resolution of the Senate, Information in Relation to the Massacre at Mountain Meadows, and Other Massacres in Utah Territory," Senate Executive Document No. 42, 36th Congress, 1st Session (1860), serial 1033, p. 138; Louis R. Maillet, "Historical Sketch of Louis R. Maillet," *Contributions to the Historical Society of Montana*, vol. 3 (1903), p. 218.

12. Helen Fitzgerald Sanders, *A History of Montana* (Chicago: The Lewis Publishing Company, 1913), vol. 2, p. 1222.

13. "All Harmonious," WM, Jan. 20, 1892, p. 3, col. 5; CIA to Ronan, Jan. 20, 1892, letterbook 229, pp. 136-38, land; CIA to Ronan, Apr. 6, 1892, vol. 181, part 2, pp. 42-43, finance; Ronan's May 6, 1892, telegram; CIA to Ronan, May 7, 1892, telegram, letterbook, 237, p. 53, land, NA CIA LS; MGD, May 14, 1892, p. 8, col. 1.

14. CIA to Frank R. Miles, Washington, D.C., Mar. 1, 1892, letterpress vol. 7, part 1, pp. 86-87, miscellaneous; CIA to Ronan, Apr. 23, 1892, letterpress vol. 7, part 1, pp. 379-81, miscellaneous, NA CIA LS; H. J. Mock, "A Frontier Exhibit," *The Daily Inter Ocean* (Chicago, Ill.), June 7, 1892, p. 10, col. 1.

15. "Not Declared Off," IL, Mar. 3, 1893, p. 1, col. 6-7.

16. See Ronan's Aug. 15, 1893, interview.

17. *Western Democrat* (weekly) (Missoula, Mont.), Oct. 22, 1893, p. 4, col. 3; *Western Democrat* (weekly) (Missoula, Mont.), Oct. 22, 1893, p. 4, col. 2; "A New Buffalo," AS, Nov. 1, 1893, p. 6, col. 3.

18. [M. A. Leeson], *History of Montana, 1739-1885* (Chicago: Warner, Beers & Company, 1885), p. 1346; "Miles' New Scheme," AS, May 21, 1896, p. 10, col. 3; CIA to J. M. Dixon, Oct. 15, 1904, letterbook 709, pp. 140-41, land, NA CIA LS.

19. "Down the Flathead," IL, Jan. 10, 1896, p. 8, col. 4; "That Tie Contract," IL, Jan. 24, 1896, p. 8, col. 3-4; "Miles' Proposition," *The Call* (Kalispell, Mont.), July 9, 1896, p. 4, col. 3; IL, Sept. 25, 1896, p. 4, col. 2; IL, Oct. 2, 1896, p. 4, col. 2; *Flathead Herald-Journal* (Kalispell, Mont.), Nov. 5, 1896, p. 2, col. 1.

20. J. B. Monroe, "Montana's Buffalo: The Pablo-Allard Herd," *Forest & Stream*, vol. 59, no. 2 (July 12, 1902), pp. 24-26; Ken Zontek, "Sacred Symbiosis: The Native American Effort to Restore the Buffalo Nation," unpublished PhD dissertation, University of Idaho, Moscow, 2003, DAI 3085730, pp. 108-119; Whealdon, *Meat for My Salish*, pp. 87-98.

21. Robert J. Bigart, ed., *Crossroad of Cultures: Sacramental Records at St. John the Baptist Catholic Church, Frenchtown, Montana, 1866-1899* (Pablo, Mont.: Salish Kootenai College Press, 2009), pp. 188-89; WM, Oct. 30, 1889, p. 4, col. 3; John Lane to CIA, Feb. 8, 1896, 6,433/1896, NA CIA LR; "Severe Wind Storm," AS, July 22, 1896, p. 10, col. 3; "Charles Allard Dead," DM, July 22, 1896, p. 1, col. 5-6.

22. "United States v. Heyfron, County Treasurer (Circuit Court, D. Montana. Apr. 24, 1905.)," *The Federal Reporter*, vol. 138 (July-Sept. 1905), pp. 964-68; U.S. Bureau of Indian Affairs, "Selected Records of the Bureau of Indian Affairs Relating to the Enrollment of Indians on the Flathead Indian Reservation, 1903-08," NAmf M1350, reel 1, fr. 17, numbers 605-611; Jack Holterman, *Pablo of the Buffalo* (West Glacier, Mont.: Glacier Natural History Association, 1991); Geo. Steell, Blackfeet Agency, to CIA, Sept. 20, 1892, 35,088/1892, NA CIA LR; CIA to Steell, Sept. 29, 1892, letterbook 245, pp. 206-207, land, NA CIA LS; John Lane to CIA, Feb. 8, 1896, 6,433/1896; Charles S. McNichols, Jocko, Mont., to CIA, Jan. 5, 1903, 1,789/1903; Charles S. McNichols to CIA, Feb. 6, 1903, 9,822/1903, NA CIA LR; [Mother Angela Lincoln], *Life of the Rev. Mother Amadeus of the Heart of Jesus: Foundress of the Ursuline Missions of Montana and Alaska* (New York: The Paulist Press, 1923), p. 114; "Pablo & Potvin," *The Ronan Pioneer*, July 7, 1911, p. 3, col. 5-6; "Will Quit Business on January First," *The Ronan Pioneer*, Dec. 27, 1912, p. 1, col. 5-6; "Michel Pablo Dies Suddenly at Ronan," DM, July 12, 1914, p. 1, col. 5-6; "Funeral of Pablo Is Attended by Hundreds," DM, July 15, 1914, p. 1, col. 4; "Michel Pablo Dies Suddenly," *The Ronan Pioneer*, July 17, 1914, p. 1, col. 3.

23. CIA to Ronan, June 15, 1892, letterbook 239, p. 181, land, NA CIA LS.

24. CIA to Ronan, Bonners Ferry, Id., May 7, 1892, telegram, letterbook 237, p. 53, land, NA CIA LS.

25. "The Indians Will Move," MGD, May 18, 1892, p. 8, col. 1; "Disgusted Chiefs," *Butte Weekly Miner*, May 19, 1892, p. 1, col. 3.

26. CIA to Ronan, May 24, 1892, telegram, letterbook 261, p. 201, accounts, NA CIA LS.

27. H. B. Carrington to CIA, Aug. 25, 1891, 31,713/1891; Carrington to CIA, Sept. 8, 1891, 34,086/1891, NA CIA LR.

28. MGD, Feb. 25, 1892, p. 1, col. 7; MGD, Feb. 26, 1892, p. 4, col. 3; WM, Feb. 24, 1892, [i.e., Mar. 2, 1892], p. 4, col. 2; AS, Mar. 8, 1892, p. 6, col. 2; WM, Apr. 27, 1892, p. 4, col. 2; "More Indictments," WM, May 4, 1892, p. 3, col. 4-5; "Drunken Dance," HJ (daily), May 19, 1892, p. 5, col. 3; "Missoula Culprits," WM, May 25, 1892, p. 2, col. 6; "United States v. Barnaby (Circuit Court, D. Montana. June 7, 1892.)," *The Federal Reporter*, vol. 51, (Aug.-Nov. 1892), pp. 20-24.

29. Bigart, *St. Mary's Mission*, pp. 241-42.

30. CIA to Ronan, July 2, 1892, letterbook 240, pp. 182-85, land, NA CIA LS.

31. CIA to Ronan, July 9, 1892, letterpress vol. 185, part 1, p. 494, finance; CIA to Ronan, July 18, 1892, telegram, letterpress, vol. 185, part 2, p. 345, finance, NA CIA LS.

32. Rosters of Agency Employees, vol. 21 (1891-1892), p. 20, entry 978, RG 75, NA; Rosters of Indian Police, vol. 9 (1890-1891), p. 10, and vol. 10 (1892-1893), p. 12, entry 982, NA.

33. "Will Investigate," MGD July 26, 1892, p. 1, col. 6; "The Old Chief Arrested," WM, Aug. 3, 1892, p. 4, col. 4; "The Indian Trouble," MWG, Aug. 10, 1892, p. 1, col. 1-2; WM, Aug. 10, 1892, p. 4, col. 1; *The Kalispell Graphic*, Oct. 5, 1892, p. 3, col. 4 (2 items).

34. Tom Stout, *Montana: Its Story and Biography* (Chicago: The American Historical Society, 1921), vol. 3, pp. 996-97.

35. "An Indian Murdered," MGD, Aug. 9, 1892, p. 1, col. 2; CIA to Ronan, Aug. 24, 1892, letterbook 243, p. 150, land, NA CIA LS.

36. CIA to Ronan, June 3, 1892, letterbook 238, pp. 319-22, land; CIA to Secretary of Interior, Aug. 17, 1892, letterbook 242, pp. 456-60, land, NA CIA LS; WM, Aug. 17, 1892, p. 3, col. 2; CIA to Ronan, Aug. 24, 1892, letterbook 243, pp. 186-87, land, NA CIA LS; MM, Sept. 2, 1892, p. 8, col. 1; CIA to Ronan, Sept. 12, 1892, telegram, letterbook 244, p. 266, land, NA CIA LS; Ronan's Sept. 12, 1892, telegram; CIA to Ronan, Sept. 12,

1892, letterbook 244, p. 302, land; CIA to S. E. Henry, Bonners Ferry, Id., Sept. 13, 1892, letterbook 244, pp. 330-31, land; CIA to Ronan, Sept. 14, 1892, letterbook 244, p. 376, land; CIA to W. D. & S. M. Murphy, et. al., Bonner's Ferry, Id., Sept. 21, 1892, letterbook 245, pp. 1-3, land; CIA to Ronan, Sept. 21, 1892, letterbook 245, p. 4, land, NA CIA LS; "After Indian Lands," MM, Sept. 24, 1892, p. 1, col. 2; CIA to Ronan, Oct. 15, 1892, letterbook 246, pp. 199-201, land; CIA to Messrs. Keat & Fogg, Bonner's Ferry, Id., Oct. 22, 1892, letterbook 246, pp. 379-84, land, NA CIA LS.

37. "An Indian Killing," MM, Sept. 6, 1892, p. 1, c. 6; MM, Oct. 23, 1892, p. 1, c. 2; Bigart, Zealous, p. 159.

38. "They Have Diphtheria," AS, Oct. 23, 1892, p. 1, col. 5; "On the Reservation," AS, Oct. 24, 1892, p. 1, col. 2; "Sick Flathead Indians," AS, Nov. 23, 1892, p. 1, col. 5; Bigart, Zealous, pp. 161-63.

39. CIA to Secretary of Interior, Aug. 15, 1892, letterbook 242, pp. 401-403, land; CIA to Ronan, Aug. 15, 1892, letterbook 242, pp. 406-407, land; CIA to Ronan, Oct. 15, 1892, letterbook 246, pp. 186-87, land; CIA to Thomas C. Power, Dec. 7, 1892, letterbook 248, pp. 405-406, land; CIA to Wilbur F. Sanders, Dec. 7, 1892, letterbook 248, pp. 403-404, land; CIA to Shoshone Commission, Dec. 4, 1892, letterbook 249, pp. 393-98, land, NA CIA LS.

40. CIA to Secretary of Interior, Oct. 10, 1892, letterbook 245, pp. 448-51, land; CIA to Ronan, Oct. 15, 1892, letterbook 246, p. 181, land, NA CIA LS; "How the Indians Work," AS, Dec. 12, 1892, p. 8, col. 1-2; MM, Dec. 21, 1892, p. 4, col. 2.

41. CIA to Ronan, Dec. 16, 1892, letterbook 249, pp. 183-85, land; CIA to Ronan, Mar. 31, 1893, letterbook 255, pp. 284-85, land; CIA to Secretary of Interior, May 18, 1893, letterbook 259, pp. 30-35, land, NA CIA LS.

42. CIA to General Land Office, Dec. 21, 1892, letterbook 249, pp. 332-33, land; CIA to Secretary of Interior, Jan. 14, 1893, letterbook 250, pp. 393-97, land; CIA to Ronan, Jan. 21, 1893, letterbook 251, pp. 53-54, land, NA CIA LS; Bigart, Getting Crops, pp. 215-16.

43. CIA to Ronan, Jan. 12, 1893, letterbook 250, pp. 262-63, land, NA CIA LS; "Crees on the Flathead Reservation," AS, Feb. 12, 1893, p. 9, col. 5-6.

44. "Keep 'Em on the Reserve," AS, Dec. 2, 1892, p. 1, col. 5.

1893

1. "Drunk and Dead," WM, Dec. 28, 1892, p. 7, col. 2; MM, Dec. 29, 1892, p. 1, col. 6; "Afraid of Houston," MM, Dec. 30, 1892, p. 1, col. 5.

2. U.S. President, "Message from the President of the United States Transmitting a Letter from the Secretary of the Interior Respecting the Ratification of an Agreement with the Confederated Tribes of Flathead, Kootenay, and Upper Pend d'Oreilles Indians, for the Sale of a Portion of their Reservation in Montana Territory," Senate Executive Document No. 44, 47th Congress, 2d Session (1883), serial 2076, pp. 16, 18-20.

3. "Captain Clarke's Grandson," MCT, Aug. 11, 1886, p. 3, col. 5; Palmer Henderson, "The Flathead Indians," The Northwest Illustrated Monthly Magazine, vol. 8, no. 8 (Aug. 1890), pp. 1-3.

4. CIA to Ronan, Jan. 26, 1893, vol. 194, part 2, p. 381, finance; CIA to Ronan, Mar. 1, 1893, vol. 196, part 1, pp. 359-60, finance, NA CIA LS.

5. Secretary of Interior to CIA, Feb. 13, 1893, 5,717/1893, NA CIA LR; CIA to Secretary of Interior, Jan. 25, 1893, letterbook 251, pp. 164-67, land; CIA to Ronan, Feb. 23, 1893, letterbook 253, pp. 1-3, land, NA CIA LS.

6. Bigart, St. Mary's Mission, pp. 287-88; George F. Weisel, Men and Trade on the Northwest Frontier as Shown by the Fort Owen Ledger (Missoula: Montana State University Press, 1955), pp. 63-65; Belle C. Hershey, "John B. Catlin," Montana Pioneers Collection, MC 64, folder 3, Montana Historical Society Archives, Helena; "Stevensville," MCT, Dec. 19, 1883, p. 2, col. 4-5; U.S. President, "Message from the President of the United States Transmitting a Report Relative to the Compensation of Henry B. Carrington, a Special Agent for the Sale of Certain Indian Lands," Senate Executive Document No. 70, 51st Congress, 1st Session (1890), serial 2686, pp. 12, 16, 24-25; Henry B. Carrington, "The Exodus of the Flatheads," unpublished manuscript, Carrington Family Papers, Sterling

Library Archive, Yale University, New Haven, Conn., chapter 12, p. 7; Palmer Henderson, "The Flathead Indians," *The Northwest Illustrated Monthly Magazine*, vol. 8, no. 8 (Aug. 1890), pp. 1-3.

7. CIA to Ronan, May 8, 1893, vol. 199, part 1, pp. 401-404, finance; CIA to Ronan, Mar. 25, 1893, letterbook 255, pp. 107-110, land, NA CIA LS.

8. "An Accident at St. Ignatius," AS, Feb. 11, 1893, p. 6, col. 2.

9. CIA to Ronan, Apr. 1, 1893, vol. 138, no. 276, p. 181, accounts; CIA to Ronan, Apr. 1, 1893, vol. 197, p. 228, finance; CIA to D. M. Ferry & Co., Apr. 3, 1893, vol. 197, pp. 271-72, finance, NA CIA LS.

10. "Get Thee Gone," *The Evening Missoulian*, May 16, 1893, p. 1, col. 6-7; "Flathead Indians Angered," *The Washington Post*, May 27, 1893, p. 1, col. 5.

11. CIA to Secretary of Interior, June 16, 1893, letterbook 260, pp. 351-56, land; CIA to Ronan, June 17, 1893, letterbook 260, p. 375, land; CIA to Ronan, July 17, 1893, letterbook 262, p. 98, land, NA CIA LS; "Indian Lands," AS, July 14, 1893, p. 1, col. 3; WM, July 19, 1893, p. 8, col. 2; "Still Unsettled," IL, July 21, 1893, p. 3, col. 3; *Flathead Herald-Journal* (Kalispell, Mont.), July 21, 1893, p. 8, col. 3; CIA to Ronan, July 29, 1893, letterbook 262, pp. 424-27, land, NA CIA LS; "Will Be Bounced," *Western Democrat* (weekly) (Missoula, Mont.), Aug. 6, 1893, p. 2, col. 4.

12. WM, June 14, 1893, p. 6, col. 4.

13. Bigart, *Zealous*, pp. 207-210.

14. William N. Bischoff, S.J., *The Jesuits in Old Oregon* (Caldwell, Id.: The Caxton Printers Ltd., 1945), p. 231.

15. CIA to Ronan, July 14, 1893, letterbook 262, pp. 26-27, land, NA CIA LS.

16. CIA to Thomas Smith, Flathead Agency, Sept. 21, 1893, letterbook 265, pp. 296-99, land, NA CIA LS.

17. "An Important Decision," WM, Jan. 20, 1892, p. 4, col. 2.

18. IL, Aug. 4, 1893, p. 2, col. 3.

19. *The Montana Populist* (Missoula, Mont.), July 27, 1893, p. 4, col. 2; Mary Ronan, *Girl from the Gulches*, pp. 219-20.

20. See also a laudatory editorial about Ronan, "Peter Ronan," *The Evening Missoulian*, Aug. 22, 1893, p. 2, col. 1; and another obituary, "Death of Peter Ronan," *Western Democrat* (weekly) (Missoula, Mont.), Aug. 27, 1893, p. 3, col. 2-3.

21. Mary Ronan, *Girl from the Gulches*, pp. xvii-xviii, 219-20.

22. Estate of Peter Ronan, Probate file 339 (1893), Clerk of District Court, Missoula County Courthouse, Missoula, Mont.

23. "Major Ronan's Successor," AS, Aug. 25, 1893, p. 5, col. 2.

24. *Western Democrat* (weekly) (Missoula, Mont.), Aug. 27, 1893, p. 4, col. 1.

25. *The Evening Missoulian*, Sept. 16, 1893, p. 4, col. 1-2.

26. "At the Flathead Agency," AS, Oct. 13, 1893, p. 1, col. 4; *Western Democrat* (weekly) (Missoula, Mont.), Oct. 15, 1893, p. 4, col. 1.

27. *The Butte Inter Mountain*, June 20, 1902, evening, p.3, c. 3.

28. John C. Ewers, *Gustavus Sohon's Portraits of Flathead and Pend d'Oreille Indians, 1854*, Smithsonian Miscellaneous Collections, vol. 110, no. 7 (1948), pp. 47-50.

Biographical Sketches

1. Bigart, *St. Mary's Mission*, pp. 238-40; *Challenge to Survive: History of the Salish Tribes of the Flathead Indian Reservation: Unit IV: Charlo and Michel Period, 1870-1910* (Pablo, Mont.: Salish Kootenai College Tribal History Project, 2011), pp. 64-69.

2. "Historical," WM, Feb. 3, 1882, p. 3, col. 4; "When the Indians Owned the Land," AS, Mar. 25, 1906, p. 13, col. 3-4; Bigart, *St. Mary's Mission*, pp. 322-23.

3. Thomas W. Harris Diaries, SC 231, Montana Historical Society Archives, Helena, folders 2 and 3.

4. Duncan McDonald to L. V. McWhorter, May 30, 1930, Lucullus Virgil McWhorter Manuscripts, Archives and Special Collections, Holland Library, Washington State University, Pullman, file 184.

5. "Historical," WM, Feb. 3, 1882, p. 3, col. 4; Rev. James O'Connor, "The Flathead Indians," *Records of the American Catholic Historical Society of Philadelphia*, vol. 3 (1888-1891), p. 104; Mary Ronan, *Girl from the Gulches*, p. 182; "Missoula Mentionings," *Butte Semi-Weekly Miner*, Jan. 15, 1887, p. 1, col. 8.

6. James A. Garfield, "Conference of Hon. James A. Garfield, Special Commissioner, with the Indians of the Bitter Root Valley, Montana," *Fourth Annual Report of the Board of Indian Commissioners* (1872), pp. 171-74; J. U. Sanders, "When Garfield Visited Montana," AS, May 24, 1908, part 2, p. 7, col. 1-4.

7. Peter Whaley to CIA, Sept. 12, 1874, ARCIA (1874), p. 263; Daniel Shanahan to CIA, Dec. 12, 1873, NAmf M234, reel 496, fr. 153.

8. Chas. S. Medary to CIA, Sept. 13, 1875, ARCIA (1875), p. 306.

9. Robert Bigart, "The Travails of Flathead Indian Agent Charles S. Medary, 1875-1877," *Montana: The Magazine of Western History*, vol. 62, no. 3 (Autumn 2012), pp. 27-41.

10. Philip Rappagliosi, *Letters from the Rocky Mountain Indian Missions*, ed. Robert Bigart (Lincoln: University of Nebraska Press, 2003), pp. 55-58.

11. S. S. Benedict to Secretary of Interior, July 10, 1883, NAmf M1070, 3093/1883.

12. G. G. Vest and Martin Maginnis, "Report of the Subcommittee of the Special Committee of the United States Senate, Appointed to Visit the Indian Tribes in Northern Montana," Senate Report No. 283, 48th Congress, 1st Session (1884), serial 2174, p. xiv; Peter Ronan to CIA, Nov. 24, 1883, 22,106/1883, NA CIA LR.

13. Arlee Antwine Skulep Squalshey to Supretenant of indian Afares, Feb. 17, 1887, 5,858/1887, NA CIA LR.

14. "Indians in State Celebrate Yule Fifty-First Time," DM, Dec. 23, 1937, p. 1, col. 5; p. 6, col. 3.

15. Robert J. Bigart, ed., *A Pretty Village: Documents of Worship and Culture Change, St. Ignatius Mission, Montana, 1880-1889* (Pablo, Mont.: Salish Kootenai College Press, 2007), pp. 76-82, 148-53.

16. WM, Jan. 27, 1882, p. 3, col. 2.

17. Lucy S. White, "Garfield!: An Incident," *The Christian Union* (New York), vol. 32, no. 21 (Nov. 19, 1885), pp. 10-11.

18. Mary Ronan, *Girl from the Gulches*, p. 155.

19. U.S. President, "Message from the President of the United States, Transmitting a Letter from the Secretary of the Interior Respecting the Ratification of an Agreement with the Confederated Tribes of Flathead, Kootenay, and Upper Pend d'Oreilles Indians, for the Sale of a Portion of Their Reservation in Montana Territory," Senate Executive Document No. 44, 47th Congress, 2d Session (1883), serial 2076, pp. 8-18.

20. Annotation and Ronan's Dec. 1, 1882, letter; E. D. Bannister to Secretary of Interior, Oct. 20, 1888, NAmf M1070, 5,261/1888.

21. "The Kuntza-Marengo Murder Trial," NNW, Jan. 12, 1883, p. 3, col. 4.

22. "His Mystery," WM, Mar. 27, 1885, p. 1, col. 5-7; R. M. Rylett, *Surveying the Canadian Pacific: Memoir of a Railroad Pioneer* (Salt Lake City: University of Utah Press, 1991), p. 235.

23. C. H. Howard to Secretary of Interior, Dec. 4, 1883, NAmf M1070, 5,061/1883, pp. 27-29.

24. Mary Ronan, *Girl from the Gulches*, pp. 205-207; annotation and Ronan's Dec. 17, 1885, letter.

25. "Reduction of Indian Reservations," House of Representatives Executive Document No. 63, 50th Congress, 1st Session (1888), serial 2557, p. 71.

26. "Arlee Objects," WM, Jan. 9, 1889, p. 3, col. 3; "Frightful Atrocities," WM, May 1, 1889, p. 3, col. 3.

27. "A Red Desperado," HI, May 14, 1889, p. 1, col. 7.

28. "To the Happy Hunting Grounds," HJ, Aug. 13, 1889, p. 1, col. 5; "Death of an Indian Brave," *Butte Semi-Weekly Miner*, Aug. 21, 1889, p. 3, col. 2; Mary Ronan, *Girl from the Gulches*, p. 212; Missoula Publishing Company, *Flathead Facts: Descriptive of the Resources of Missoula County* (Missoula, Mont.: Missoula Publishing Company, 1890), p.

15; Hubert A. Post, S.J., "Sweet Revenge," *The Indian Sentinel*, vol. 2, no. 1 (Jan. 1920), pp. 15-16.

29. See Ronan's May 10, 1880, letter.

30. L. B. Palladino, S.J., *Indian and White in the Northwest: A History of Catholicity in Montana, 1831 to 1891*, 2nd ed. (Lancaster, Penna.: Wickersham Publishing Company, 1922), pp. 85-86.

31. Will Sutherlin, "West Side of the Bitter Root — Sweat House Farmers," *Rocky Mountain Husbandman* (Diamond City, Mont.), Aug. 16, 1877, p. 2, col. 2-3.

32. Gabriel M. Menager, S.J., "Reminiscences of a Missionary Sister," *The Indian Sentinel*, vol. 22, no. 4 (Apr. 1942), pp. 59-61.

33. Bigart, *St. Mary's Mission*, pp. 252-54; Bigart, *Getting Crops*; *Challenge to Survive: History of the Salish Tribes of the Flathead Indian Reservation: Unit IV: Charlo and Michel Period, 1870-1910* (Pablo, Mont.: Salish Kootenai College Tribal History Project, 2011), pp. 12-15, 61-64, 82-86; Philip Rappagliosi, *Letters from the Rocky Mountain Indian Missions*, ed. Robert Bigart (Lincoln: University of Nebraska Press, 2003), pp. 108-109

34. "Kootenai Chiefs Memorial Draws Hundreds," *Char-Koosta* (Dixon, Mont.), vol. 2, no. 14 [Nov. 15, 1972], pp. 11-12; Chas. Hutchins to Montana Superintendent of Indian Affairs, June 30, 1865, ARCIA (1865), p. 246; Harry Holbert Turney-High, *Ethnography of the Kutenai*, Memoir of the American Anthropological Association, No. 56 (1941), pp. 134-39; Carling Malouf and Thain White, "Kutenai Calendar Records," *Montana: Magazine of History*, vol. 3, no. 2 (Spring 1953), pp. 34-39.

35. Ronan's June 12, 1889, letter; Mary Ronan, *Frontier Woman: The Story of Mary Ronan as Told to Margaret Ronan*, ed. H. G. Merriam (Missoula: University of Montana Publications in History, 1973), pp. 124-25.

36. Rev. James O'Connor, "The Flathead Indians," *Records of the American Catholic Historical Society of Philadelphia*, vol. 3 (1888-1891), p. 104.

37. Chas. Hutchins to Montana Superintendent of Indian Affairs, June 30, 1865, ARCIA (1865), p. 246; Augustus Chapman to CIA, Apr. 20,1866, NAmf M234, reel 488, fr. 178.

38. U.S. President, "Message from the President of the United States Transmitting a Letter from the Secretary of the Interior Respecting the Ratification of an Agreement with the Confederated Tribes of Flathead, Kootenay, and Upper Pend d'Oreilles Indians, for the Sale of a Portion of Their Reservation in Montana Territory," Senate Executive Document No. 44, 47th Congress, 2d Session (1883), serial 2076, p. 11.

39. Ronan's Apr. 17, 1888, letter.

40. Ronan's Mar. 4, 1889, telegram.

41. Ronan's June 12, 1889, letter; E. D. Bannister to Secretary of Interior, Oct. 20, 1888, NAmf M1070, 5261/1888, p. 6.

42. "The Red Man's Story," HJ (daily), Oct. 25, 1889, p. 5, col. 1-2; Ronan's Aug. 14, 1890b, annual report.

43. Ronan's Sept. 1, 1889; Sept. 9, 1889a; Dec. 2, 1889, and Aug. 1, 1890a, letters.

44. Ronan's July 21, 1890; Aug. 1, 1890a; Aug. 26, 1890; and Nov. 1, 1890, letters; and newspaper reports in the footnotes to these letters.

45. Bigart, *Zealous*, p. 54.

46. "Four of a Kind," MWG, Nov. 12, 1890, p. 3, col. 1-3.

47. Ronan's Jan. 31, 1891; and Nov. 2, 1891, letters.

48. Ronan's July 14, 1891b, letter.

49. Ronan's Aug. 25, 1891b, and Dec. 11, 1891a, letters.

50. Ronan's Oct. 8, 1892, letter.

51. Ronan's July 25, 1892; Aug. 9, 1892; and Oct. 8, 1892, letters.

52. Joseph Carter to CIA, Feb. 6, 1894, 6,591/1894, NA CIA LR; CIA to Carter, Feb. 21, 1894, land, letterbook 274, pp. 394-96, NA CIA LS.

53. "Very Near a Good Indian," *The Kalispell Graphic*, Mar. 13, 1895, p. 3, col. 1.

54. "All Same M'Kinley," AS, Aug. 24, 1898, p. 10, col. 2.

55. Augustine Dimier to Rev. Father Provincial, Apr. 1901, Robert Bigart and Clarence Woodcock, eds., "St. Ignatius Mission, Montana: Reports from Two Jesuit Missionaries, 1885 & 1900-1901 (Part II)," *Arizona and the West*, vol. 23, no. 3 (Autumn 1981), pp. 275-76.

56. "Noted Chief Dead," *The Kalispell Bee*, July 27, 1900, p. 1, col. 5.

57. Ronan July 11, 1877, letter.

58. Ronan Jan. 15, 1884b, letter.

59. Ronan Aug. 1885, annual report; Ronan Aug. 17, 1885, testimony.

60. U.S. Census Office, *Report of Indians Taxed and Indians Not Taxed* (Washington, D.C.: U.S. Government Printing Office, 1894), p. 363.

61. Ronan Feb. 14, 1885, letter.

62. Ronan Jan. 1, 1887, letter.

63. Mary Ronan, *Frontier Woman: The Story of Mary Ronan as Told to Margaret Ronan*, ed. H. G. Merriam (Missoula: University of Montana Publications in History, 1973), p. 125.

64. "Chief Louison Is Dead," DM, May 17, 1912, p. 8, col. 2-3.

65. Henry B. Carrington, "The Exodus of the Flatheads," ms., Carrington Family Papers, Yale University Archives, Sterling Library, New Haven, Conn., chapter 12, p. 7.

66. Ronan Aug. 14, 1890b, annual report.

67. Ronan Jan. 2, Apr. 20, June 1, July 1, and Aug. 1, 1891, letters.

68. Rosters of Agency Employees, vol. 21 (1891-1892), p. 20, entry 978, RG 75, NA.

69. Carter to CIA, Mar. 4, 1895, 10,563/1895; Carter to CIA, May 7, 1895, 20,518/1895; and Senator T. H. Carter to CIA, Mar. 9, 1896, 9,381/1896, NA CIA LR; "A Flathead Fracas," *The Daily Democrat* (Missoula, Mont.), Mar. 5, 1895, p. 1, col. 8; "Went on the War Path," AS, Mar. 6, 1895, p. 6, col. 3; "Their Hearts Are Bad," AS, Mar. 8, 1895, p. 6, col. 3.

70. Rosters of Agency Employees, vols. 27-38 (1897-1909), entry 978, RG 75, NA.

71. Robert Bigart and Clarence Woodcock, "The Trans-Mississippi Exposition and the Flathead Delegation," *Montana: The Magazine of Western History*, vol. 29, no. 4 (Autumn 1979), pp. 14-23; Robert Bigart and Clarence Woodcock, "The Rinehart Photographs: A Portfolio," *Montana: The Magazine of Western History*, vol. 29, no. 4 (Autumn 1979), pp. 24-37.

72. "Chief Louison Is Dead," DM, May 17, 1912, p. 8, col. 2-3.

73. John C. Ewers, *Gustavus Sohon's Portraits of Flathead and Pend d'Oreille Indians, 1854*, Smithsonian Miscellaneous Collections, vol. 110, no. 7 (1948), pp. 50-52.

74. James A. Teit, "The Salishan Tribes of the Western Plateaus," ed. Franz Boas, *Forty-fifth Annual Report of the Bureau of American Ethnology* (1927-1928) (Washington, D.C.: U.S. Government Printing Office, 1930), p. 377.

75. W. P. Clark, *The Indian Sign Language* (Philadelphia: L. R. Hamersly, 1885), p. 301; Frank H. Woody, "Historical Sketch of Missoula County," WM, July 19, 1876, p. 2, col. 3-7 and p. 3, col. 1-4; Arthur L. Stone, *Following Old Trails* (Missoula, Mont.: Morton John Elrod, 1913), p. 134.

76. Robert J. Bigart, ed., *A Pretty Village: Documents of Worship and Culture Change, St. Ignatius Mission, Montana, 1880-1889* (Pablo: Salish Kootenai College Press, 2007), p. 78; Duncan McDonald, "More About Indian 'Medicine,'" NNW, Feb. 21, 1879, p. 3, col. 3.

77. "Accident," *The Pioneer* (Missoula, Mont.), May 4, 1872, p. 3, col. 1.

78. Daniel Shanahan to CIA, Jan. 21, 1874, NAmf M234, reel 500, fr. 262.

79. T. J. Demers to Martin Maginnis, May 2, 1874, Martin Maginnis Papers, MC 50, Montana Historical Society Archives, Helena, box 1, folder 22.

80. Peter Whaley to CIA, Aug. 14, 1874, NAmf M234, reel 500, fr. 1124; President to Secretary of Interior, Nov. 18, 1874, NAmf M234, reel 500, fr. 190.

81. Peter Whaley to CIA, Sept. 12, 1874, ARCIA (1874), pp. 262-63.

82. Attorney General to Secretary of Interior, Jan. 8, 1876 [1877], NAmf M234, reel 508, fr. 382; Chas. S. Medary to CIA, Sept. 13, 1875, ARCIA (1875), p. 304; Chas. S. Medary to CIA, Sept. 1, 1876, ARCIA (1876), p. 493.

83. Mary Ronan, *Girl from the Gulches*, pp. 158-59.

84. Ronan's July 28, 1878, letter; "Indian Matters," HI, July 21, 1878, p. 3, col. 3.

85. Mary Ronan, *Girl from the Gulches*, pp. 184-86; "Wayside Notes," HI, Nov. 22, 1878, p. 3, col. 3.

86. Ronan's Dec. 1, 1882, letter and annotation; WM, June 30, 1882, p. 3, col. 3.

87. U.S. President, "Message from the President of the United States, Transmitting a Letter from the Secretary of the Interior Respecting the Ratification of an Agreement with the Confederated Tribes of Flathead, Kootenay, and Upper Pend d'Oreilles Indians, for the Sale of a Portion of Their Reservation in Montana Territory," Senate Executive Document No. 44, 47th Congress, 2d Session (1883), serial 2076, pp. 11-19.

88. G. G. Vest and Martin Maginnis, "Report of the Subcommittee of the Special Committee of the United States Senate, Appointed to Visit the Indian Tribes in Northern Montana," Senate Report No. 283, 48th Congress, 1st Session (1884), serial 2174, pp. xxv-xxvii.

89. Reduction of Indian Reservations," House of Representatives Executive Document No. 63, 50th Congress, 1st Session (1888), serial 2557, pp. 58-60, 69-72.

90. Ronan's Aug. 1885 annual report; Aug. 17, 1885, testimony; and Aug. 27, 1887, annual report.

91. Ronan's July 31, 1889, letter and annotation and Aug. 20, 1889, annual report.

92. "Cleverly Caught," MGD, Aug. 5, 1890, p. 1, col. 3-4; "One of Them Caught," MGD, Aug. 7, 1890, p. 1, col. 5; Bigart, *Zealous*, p. 54.

93. "Old Cheif [sic] Michel," DM, May 14, 1897, p. 1, col. 3; "Chief Michael Dead," AS, May 14, 1897, p. 10, col. 2.

Index

Since there was no standard spelling for Indian names in the nineteenth century, most of the full blood Indian people in this index were entered under their Christian names, except in cases where the Indian name later became a family name. As a consequence some individuals appear under both their family and their Christian names. Since more than one person had the same Christian name, it was not possible to tell who was referred to in some of the letters. Mixed bloods usually used family names and they are entered in the index in the tradtional way. Despite these shortcoming, the editor hopes this index will help the reader locate information about individuals and topics of interest.